**W9-CCC-965**

# BARCELONA
## 2nd Edition

by George Semler

---

Where to Stay and Eat
for All Budgets

---

Must-See Sights
and Local Secrets

---

Ratings You Can Trust

---

Fodor's Travel Publications   New York, Toronto, London, Sydney, Auckland
**www.fodors.com**

**FODOR'S BARCELONA**

**Editor:** Maria Teresa Burwell

**Editorial Production:** Tom Holton
**Editorial Contributors:** George Semler, Nina Callaway, Christopher Culwell, Erica Ducey
**Maps & Illustrations:** David Lindroth, *cartographer*; William Wu, Bob Blake, and Rebecca Baer, *map editors*
**Design:** Fabrizio LaRocca, *creative director*; Guido Caroti, Siobhan O'Hare, *art directors*; Tina Malaney, Chie Ushio, Ann McBride, *designers*; Melanie Marin, *senior picture editor*; Moon Sun Kim, *cover designer*
**Cover Photo:** (Parc Güell by Antoni Gaudi): Steve Vidler/SuperStock
**Production/Manufacturing:** Matthew Struble

2nd Edition

ISBN 978–1–4000–1903–8

ISSN 1554–5865

**SPECIAL SALES**

This book is available at special discounts for bulk purchases for sales promotions or premiums. Special editions, including personalized covers, excerpts of existing books, and corporate imprints, can be created in large quantities for special needs. For more information, write to Special Markets/Premium Sales, 1745 Broadway, MD 6-2, New York, New York 10019, or e-mail specialmarkets@randomhouse.com.

**AN IMPORTANT TIP & AN INVITATION**

Although all prices, opening times, and other details in this book are based on information supplied to us at press time, changes occur all the time in the travel world, and Fodor's cannot accept responsibility for facts that become outdated or for inadvertent errors or omissions. So **always confirm information when it matters,** especially if you're making a detour to visit a specific place. Your experiences—positive and negative—matter to us. If we have missed or misstated something, **please write to us.** We follow up on all suggestions. Contact the Barcelona editor at editors@fodors.com or c/o Fodor's at 1745 Broadway, New York, NY 10019.

PRINTED IN THE UNITED STATES OF AMERICA
10 9 8 7 6 5 4 3 2 1

# Be a Fodor's Correspondent

Your opinion matters. It matters to us. It matters to your fellow Fodor's travelers, too. And we'd like to hear it. In fact, we need to hear it.

When you share your experiences and opinions, you become an active member of the Fodor's community. That means we'll not only use your feedback to make our books better, but we'll publish your names and comments whenever possible. Throughout our guides, look for "Word of Mouth," excerpts of your unvarnished feedback.

Here's how you can help improve Fodor's for all of us.

Tell us when we're right. We rely on local writers to give you an insider's perspective. But our writers and staff editors—who are the best in the business—depend on you. Your positive feedback is a vote to renew our recommendations for the next edition.

Tell us when we're wrong. We're proud that we update most of our guides every year. But we're not perfect. Things change. Hotels cut services. Museums change hours. Charming cafés lose charm. If our writer didn't quite capture the essence of a place, tell us how you'd do it differently. If any of our descriptions are inaccurate or inadequate, we'll incorporate your changes in the next edition and will correct factual errors at fodors.com immediately.

Tell us what to include. You probably have had fantastic travel experiences that aren't yet in Fodor's. Why not share them with a community of like-minded travelers? Maybe you chanced upon a beach or bistro or B&B that you don't want to keep to yourself. Tell us why we should include it. And share your discoveries and experiences with everyone directly at fodors.com. Your input may lead us to add a new listing or highlight a place we cover with a "Highly Recommended" star or with our highest rating, "Fodor's Choice."

Give us your opinion instantly at our feedback center at www.fodors.com/feedback. You may also e-mail editors@fodors.com with the subject line "Barcelona Editor." Or send your nominations, comments, and complaints by mail to Barcelona Editor, Fodor's, 1745 Broadway, New York, NY 10019.

You and travelers like you are the heart of the Fodor's community. Make our community richer by sharing your experiences. Be a Fodor's correspondent.

¡Buen viaje!

Tim Jarrell, Publisher

# CONTENTS

## CLOSE UPS

## MAPS

## BARCELONA IN FOCUS

### EXPLORING BARCELONA

### WHERE TO EAT

# ABOUT THIS BOOK

## Our Ratings

Sometimes you find terrific travel experiences and sometimes they just find you. But usually the burden is on you to select the right combination of experiences. That's where our ratings come in.

As travelers we've all discovered a place so wonderful that its worthiness is obvious. And sometimes that place is so unique that superlatives don't do it justice: you just have to be there to know. These sights, properties, and experiences get our highest rating, **Fodor's Choice** indicated by orange stars throughout this book.

Black stars highlight sights and properties we deem **Highly Recommended** places that our writers, editors, and readers praise again and again for consistency and excellence.

By default, there's another category: any place we include in this book is by definition worth your time, unless we say otherwise. And we will.

Disagree with any of our choices? Care to nominate a place or suggest that we rate one more highly? Visit our feedback center at www.fodors.com/feedback.

## Budget Well

Hotel and restaurant price categories from ¢ to $$$$ are defined in the opening pages of their respective chapters. For attractions, we always give standard adult admission fees; reductions are usually available for children, students, and senior citizens. Want to pay with plastic? **AE, D, DC, MC, V** following restaurant and hotel listings indicate whether American Express, Discover, Diners Club, MasterCard, and Visa are accepted.

## Restaurants

Unless we state otherwise, restaurants are open for lunch and dinner daily. We mention dress only when there's a specific requirement and reservations only when they're essential or not accepted—it's always best to book ahead.

## Hotels

Hotels have private bath, phone, TV, and air-conditioning and operate on the European Plan (aka EP, meaning without meals), unless we specify that they use the Continental Plan (CP, with a Continental breakfast), Breakfast Plan (BP, with a full breakfast), or Modified American Plan (MAP, with breakfast and dinner) or are all-inclusive (AI, including all meals and most activities). We always list facilities but not whether you'll be charged an extra fee to use them, so when pricing accommodations, find out what's included.

| Many Listings | |
|---|---|
| ★ | Fodor's Choice |
| ★ | Highly recommended |
| ⊠ | Physical address |
| ✛ | Directions |
| ⌂ | Mailing address |
| ☎ | Telephone |
| 🖷 | Fax |
| ⊕ | On the Web |
| ✉ | E-mail |
| 🖾 | Admission fee |
| ☉ | Open/closed times |
| Ⓜ | Metro stations |
| ▭ | Credit cards |

| Hotels & Restaurants | |
|---|---|
| 🏨 | Hotel |
| ⌁ | Number of rooms |
| ☖ | Facilities |
| ❑ | Meal plans |
| ✕ | Restaurant |
| ⌁ | Reservations |
| ↘ | Smoking |
| ⌸ | BYOB |
| ✕🏨 | Hotel with restaurant that warrants a visit |

| Other | |
|---|---|
| ☾ | Family-friendly |
| ⇨ | See also |
| ⊠ | Branch address |
| ☞ | Take note |

# Experience Barcelona

**WORD OF MOUTH**

"Parts of Barcelona remind me of Paris, specifically the 7th [arrondissement] on the left bank. It's a friendly, outgoing city—and bright, even on a rainy day."

—Robert2533

"We LOVED Barcelona and are going back in April. For me a real positive is all the Gaudí architecture that is so amazing. Don't miss Parc Güell [or] the view at sunset from the Miró museum!"

—artlover

# BARCELONA PLANNER

## When to Go

For optimal weather, fewer tourists, and a sense of local life as it is, the best times to visit Barcelona, Catalonia, and Bilbao are April–June and mid-September–mid-December. Catalans and Basques themselves vacation in August, causing epic traffic jams at both ends of the month. Major cities are relaxed and, except for tourists, empty in August, though Gràcia's Festa Major in Barcelona and Semana Grande in Bilbao keep these two cities very much alive during the festivities. Small shops and some restaurants shut down for the entire month, musical venues are silent, but museums remain open.

Summers in Barcelona, though occasionally very hot, are usually not too steamy for comfort. Temperatures rarely surpass 100°F (38°C), and air-conditioning is becoming more widespread. In any case, dining alfresco on a warm summer night is one of northern Spain's finest pleasures. Bilbao's legendary *siri-miri* (drizzle) keeps the city cool in summer, though winters can be irritatingly wet. All in all, spring and fall offer the best weather and temperatures at both ends of the Pyrenees. Barcelona winters are chilly enough for overcoats, but never freezing: ideal for walking, fireside dining, and hearty winter cuisine.

## Getting Around

The best way to get around Barcelona is on foot, though a combination of subways, taxis, tramways, and walking will be required for covering the entire city. The central FGC (Ferrocarril de la Generalitat de Catalunya) train that runs between Plaça Catalunya and Sarrià is comfortable, air-conditioned, and leaves you within a 20- to 30-minute walk of nearly everything. (The metro and the FGC close at 11:45 weekdays and Sunday and run all night Friday and Saturday.) The main attractions requiring taxis or the metro are Montjuïc (Miró Foundation, MNAC, Mies van der Rohe Pavillion, Caixaforum, and Poble Espanyol), most easily accessed from Plaça Espanya; Parc Güell above Plaça Lesseps; and the Auditori at Plaça de les Glories. Gaudí's Sagrada Familia is served by two metro lines (2 and 5), but the walk from the FGC's Provença stop is an enjoyable half-hour jaunt that passes three major Moderniste buildings: Palau Baró de Quadras, Casa Terrades (les Punxes), and Casa Macaia.

Sarrià and Pedralbes are easily explored on foot, though (depending on hiking ambition and footwear choice) the Torre Bellesguard or the Colegio de les Teresianas might require taxi hops. Walking from Sarrià down through the Jardins de la Vil.la Cecilia and Vil.la Amèlia to the Cátedra Gaudí is a pleasant stroll, while from there to the Futbol Club Barcelona you can cut through the Jardins del Palau Reial de Pedralbes and the university campus or catch a two-minute taxi.

All of Ciutat Vella (Barri Gòtic, Rambla, Raval, Ribera-Born, and Barceloneta) is best explored on foot, though an after-dinner taxi from Barceloneta to your hotel (usually not more than €10) is best called from your restaurant by radio taxi.

The city bus system is also a viable option, allowing a better look at the city as you travel, but the metro is faster and more comfortable. The tramway is a verdant and quiet ride down grassy tracks if you're headed from Plaça Francesc Macià out the Diagonal to the Futbol Club Barcelona, or from behind the Ciutadella park out to Glòries and the Fòrum at the east end of the Diagonal.

## Leave Barcelona with Everything You Brought—or Bought

Although muggings are practically unheard of in Barcelona, petty thievery is common. Handbags, backpacks, camera cases, and wallets are favorite targets, so tuck those away. Coat pockets with zippers work well for indispensable gear, while cash and a few credit cards wedged into a front trouser pocket are almost unassailable. Handbags hooked over chairs, on the floor or sidewalk under your feet, or dangling from hooks under bars are easy prey. Even a loosely carried bag is tempting for bag-snatchers. Should you carry a purse, use one with a short strap that tucks tightly under your arm without room for fleet hands to unzip. A plastic shopping bag for your essentials will attract even less attention.

## Catalan for Beginners

Anyone who questions how different Catalan and Spanish are need only have a look at the nonsensical Catalan tongue twister *"Setze jutges d'un jutjat menjen fetge d'un penjat"* (Sixteen judges from a courthouse eat the liver of a hanged man) in Spanish: *"Dieciseis jueces de un juzgado comen el higado de un ahorcado."* Catalan is derived from Latin and Provençal French, whereas Spanish has a heavy payload of Arabic vocabulary and phonetics. For language exchange *(intercambios)*, check the bulletin board at the Central University Philosophy and Letters Faculty on Gran Via or any English bookstore for free half-hour language exchanges of English for Catalan (or Spanish). It's a great way to get free private lessons, meet locals, and, with the right chemistry, even begin a cross-cultural fling. Who said the language of love is French?

## Top Festivals & Events

**Carnaval** dances through Barcelona in February just before Lent, most flamboyantly in Sitges, though Barcelona's Carnestoltes are also wild and colorful.

**Semana Santa** (Holy Week), the week before Easter, is Spain's most important celebration everywhere but Barcelona, where the city empties.

**La Diada de Sant Jordi** is Barcelona's Valentine's Day, fused with International Book Day, celebrated on April 23 to honor the 1616 deaths of Miguel de Cervantes and William Shakespeare.

**La Fira de Sant Ponç** brings farmers to town with produce and natural remedies on May 11.

**La Verbena de Sant Joan** celebrates the summer solstice and Midsummer's Eve with fireworks and all-night beach parties on the night of the June 23–24.

**La Festa Major de Gràcia** Barcelona's village-turned-neighborhood, Gràcia celebrates its fiesta in honor of Santa Maria with street dances and concerts in mid-August.

**Festes de La Mercé** celebrates Barcelona's patron saint, Nostra Senyora de la Mercé (Our Lady of Mercy) for a wild week beginning September 24.

# TOP BARCELONA ATTRACTIONS

### Gaudí's Sagrada Família

**(A)** The city's premier icon, Gaudí's gargantuan unfinished Temple Expiatori de la Sagrada Família (Expiatory Temple of the Holy Family) is entering its 125th year of construction. The peculiar pointed spires, with organic shapes that resemble a honeycombed confection, give the whole place a sort of fairy-tale quality that would suit a Harry Potter film.

### Museu Picasso

**(B)** Pablo Picasso's connection to Barcelona, where he spent key formative years and first showed his work in 1900, eventually bore fruit when his manager Jaume Sabartés donated his collection to the city in 1962. Nearly as stunning as the 3,500 Picasso works on display are the five Renaissance palaces that have been renovated and redesigned as an elegant and naturally lighted exhibit space.

### The Boqueria Market

**(C)** The oldest mid-city, open-air market of its kind in Europe, the Boqueria market, a jumble of color and aromas just off the Rambla, is the heart, as well as the stomach, of the city. As Barcelona's culinary fortunes soar, the Boqueria is increasingly assuming its pivotal role as the prime supplier of the fish, foul, meats, wild mushrooms, fruits, and vegetables.

### Santa Maria del Mar Basilica

**(D)** For peace, symmetry, and Mediterranean Gothic at its classical best, Santa Maria del Mar is the Sagrada Família's polar opposite. Burned back to its original bare-bones structure by a fire at the start of the Spanish Civil War in 1936, post-Bauhaus architects charged with the church's restoration saw the purity of stonemason Berenguer de Montagut's original 1329 design and maintained the elegant and economical lines of the seafarer's waterfront basilica.

## Palau de la Música Catalana

**(E)** Often described as the flagship of Barcelona's Modernisme, this dizzyingly ornate tour de force designed by Lluís Domènech i Montaner is a catalog of Art Nouveau crafts and recourses including ceramics, sculpture, stained glass, paintings, and a plethora of decorative techniques. Much criticized during the aesthetically somber 1939–75 Franco regime, the city's long-time prime concert venue is an exciting place to hear music.

## Casa Batlló & the Manzana de la Discòrdia

**(F)** The Manzana de la Discòrdia (Apple of Discord) on Passeig de Gràcia is so called for its row of eye-knocking buildings by the three most famous Moderniste architects—Domènech i Montaner, Puig i Cadafalch, and Gaudí. Of the three, Gaudí's Casa Batlló, with its undulating dragon-backed roof, multicolor facade, skull-and-bones balconies, and underwa-

ter interior, is the most remarkable and the only one open to the public.

## Parc Güell

**(G)** Gaudí's light and playful park in the uppermost reaches of the village of Gràcia was originally developed as a garden community for Count Eusebi Güell and his closest friends. The flower-choked hillside contains a series of Moderniste gems ranging from the undulating ceramic bench around the central square to the gingerbread gatehouses.

## Museu Nacional d'Art de Catalunya (MNAC)

**(H)** Barcelona's answer to Madrid's Prado hulks grandly atop the stairway leading up from Plaça Espanya. MNAC houses nearly all of Catalonia's art, from Romanesque altarpieces to Art Nouveau masters like Casas.

# GREAT ITINERARIES

### Ciutat Vella, Quintessential Barcelona

Stroll the Rambla and see the colorful Boqueria market before cutting over to the Catedral de la Seu in the city's hushed and resonant Gothic Quarter. Detour through stately Plaça Sant Jaume where the Palau de la Generalitat, Catalonia's seat of government, faces the town hall. The Gothic Plaça del Rei and the neoclassical Plaça Reial (not to be confused) are short walks from Plaça Sant Jaume. The Museu Picasso is five minutes from the loveliest example of Catalan Gothic architecture, the basilica of Santa Maria del Mar. An evening concert at the Palau de la Música Catalana after a few tapas and before a late dinner is an unsurpassable way to end an epic day in Barcelona.

The Raval, behind the Boqueria, holds the Museu d'Art Contemporani de Barcelona, the medieval Antic Hospital de la Santa Creu, the Sant Pau del Camp church, and the medieval shipyards at Drassanes Reiales. Palau Güell, just off the lower Rambla, is a key Gaudí visit. A short hike away, the waterfront Barceloneta neighborhood is one of Barcelona's most characteristic and picturesque districts, as well as a prime place for a paella on the beach.

### The post-1860 Checkerboard Eixample

A morning touring the Eixample begins at Gaudí's still-in-progress magnum opus, the Temple Expiatori de la Sagrada Família. On the way back to the Eixample's vertebral Passeig de Gràcia, swing past Moderniste architect Puig i Cadafalch's Casa Terrades as well as his Palau Baró de Quadras. Spend the afternoon in the Eixample touring the undulating facades and stunning interiors of Casa Milà and Casa Batlló. Other Eixample architecture includes Gaudí's Casa Calvet not far from Plaça Catalunya, the Fundació Tàpies, and more far-flung Moderniste gems such as Casa Golferichs, or Casa de la Papallona out toward Plaça Espanya. Rambla Catalunya's leafy tunnel is a cool and shaded promenade lined with shops and sidewalk cafés.

### Upper Barcelona: Gràcia and Sarrià

For a more rustic and restful urban excursion, try the formerly outlying towns of Gràcia and Sarrià. Gràcia is home to Gaudí's first house, Casa Vicens, and his playful Parc Güell above Plaça Lesseps, while the tree-lined lower reaches of this intimate neighborhood are filled with houses by Gaudí's right-hand man, Francesc Berenguer. Sarrià is a village stranded in the ever-expanding metropolis, with diminutive streets, shops and restaurants, and the Monestir de Pedralbes, a venerable monastery with a superb Gothic cloister. Also in Sarrià are Gaudí's Torre Bellesguard and the Colegio de les Teresianas.

### Art in Montjuïc

Montjuïc offers various art collections at the Museu Nacional d'Art de Catalunya, while the nearby Fundació Miró features Catalan artist Joan Miró's colorful paintings and a stellar Calder mobile. Down the stairs toward Plaça Espanya are the Mies van der Rohe Barcelona Pavilion and the restored Casaramona textile mill, now the Caixaforum cultural center and gallery.

### Peripheral Barcelona

The new Diagonal Mar complex at the eastern end of Avinguda Diagonal, built for Barcelona's 2004 Forum de Universal

les Cultures, is filled with interesting new architecture. Plaça de les Glòries is the site of Jean Nouvel's Torre Agbar as well as Rafael Moneo's inside-of-a-guitar-like music venue, L'Auditori, and Ricardo Bofill's contemporary-classical Teatre Nacional de Catalunya. A stroll through the Collserola hills above and behind the urban sprawl takes you by Norman Foster's giant communications tower.

## Out & About in Catalonia

Side trips within Catalonia, including a possible overnight or two, could lead you inland to the mountains and vineyards, north and south along sandy beaches and rocky coasts, or into the fruited farmlands of the Empordà. To the south are the beaches of Sitges and the provincial city and onetime Roman capital of Tarragona; to the west are Montserrat and the monasteries of Poblet and Santes Creus, while to the north lie the highlands of Montseny, the towns of Girona, Figueres, and Cadaqués, and the inlets and headlands of the Costa Brava.

## The Best of Bilbao

If you take the overnight train or the one-hour plane to Bilbao, start at Frank Gehry's shimmering Guggenheim Bilbao before walking up the river over Santiago Calatrava's Puente de Zubi-Zuri to the Mercado de la Ribera. Then dive into the old town, or Casco Viejo. Other don't-miss sights in Bilbao are the Museo Vasco—the Museum of Basque Archaeology, Ethnology, and History, in an austerely elegant 16th-century convent in the Casco Viejo—and the Museo de Bellas Artes near the Guggenheim, one of Spain's finest permanent collections.

# WHAT'S WHERE

**1 La Rambla.** Running just over a mile, the Rambla is the city's most emblematic promenade. A stroll on the Rambla—pickpockets, buskers, scammers, street theater and all—passes the Boqueria market, the Liceu opera house, and, at the port end, Drassanes, the medieval shipyards. Just off the Rambla is Plaça Reial, a neoclassical square, while off the other side is Gaudí's masterful Palau Güell.

**2 The Barri Gòtic.** The medieval Gothic Quarter, on the high ground the Romans settled in the 1st century BC, includes the medieval Jewish quarter, antiquers' row along Carrer de la Palla and Carrer Banys Nous, Plaça Sant Jaume, and the seats of government, Plaça del Rei.

**3 The Raval.** Once a rough-and-tumble slum, this area has brightened considerably, thanks partly to the Barcelona Museum of Contemporary Art. Behind the Boqueria market is the stunning Antic Hospital de la Santa Creu, with its high-vaulted Gothic Biblioteca de Catalunya reading room. Sant Pau del Camp, Barcelona's earliest church, is at the far corner of the Raval.

**4 Sant Pere, La Ribera & El Born.** Northeast of the Rambla, Sant Pere is the city's old textile neighborhood. La Ribera and the Born-Ribera neighborhood is filled with shops, restaurants, tiny medieval streets, and the Picasso Museum. Passeig del Born, once the medieval jousting ground, draws crowds to its shops by day and to its saloons by night.

**5 Barceloneta.** Barceloneta was open water until the mid-18th century when it was landfilled. Laundry-festooned streets and the city's best seafood restaurants make Barceloneta a city favorite for Sunday-afternoon paella gatherings.

**6 The Eixample.** Uphill from Ciutat Vella, the Eixample contains most of Barcelona's Moderniste (Art Nouveau) architecture, including Gaudí's Sagrada Família church. Passeig de Gràcia, the city's premier shopping street, also offers more Gaudí at Casa Batlló, Casa Milà (La Pedrera), and Casa Calvet.

C. de Viladomat
C. del Comte Borrell
C. del Comte d'Urgell
C. de Villarroel
C. de Casanova
C. d'Aragó
C. de la Diputació
Gran Vía de les Corts Catalanes
C. de Sepulveda
C. de Floridablanca
C. de Tamarit
C. de Manso
RAVAL
Joaquín Costa
C. de Hospital
Rda. de Sant Pau
Carretes
C. de Sant Pau
Sant Pau del Camp ◆
C. de Blai
C. Nou de la Rambla
Avda. del Paral·lel
Pg. de Montjuïc
Moll de Sant Bertrán
TORRE DE JAUME I

0  450 yards
0  450 meters

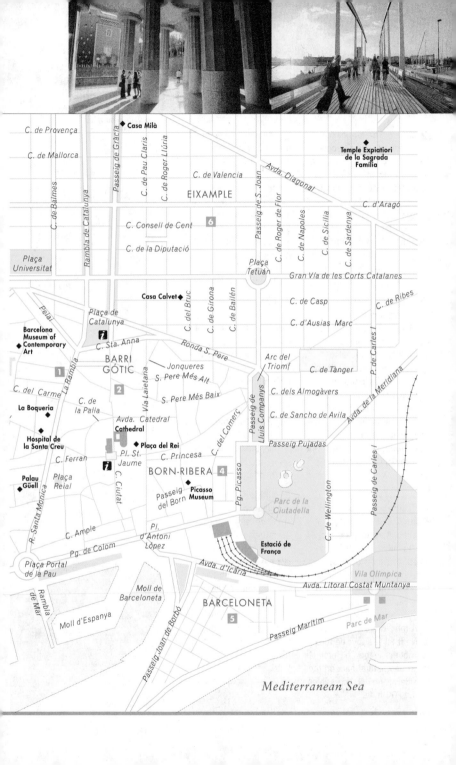

C. de Provença

Casa Milà

C. de Mallorca

Temple Expiatiori
de la Sagrada
Família

Passeig de Gràcia

C. de Pau Claris

C. de Roger Llúria

C. de Valencia

Avda. Diagonal

EIXAMPLE

C. d'Aragó

C. de Balmes

Rambla de Catalunya

Passeig de S. Joan

C. de Roger de Flor

C. de Napoles

C. de Sicilia

C. de Sardenya

6

C. Consell de Cent

C. de la Diputació

Plaça
Tetuán

Plaça
Universitat

Gran Vía de les Corts Catalanes

Casa Calvet

C. del Bruc

C. de Girona

C. de Bailén

C. de Casp

C. de Ribes

Plaça de
Catalunya

C. d'Ausias Marc

P. de Carles I

Pelai

Barcelona
Museum of
Contemporary
Art

C. Sta. Anna

Ronda S. Pere

Arc del
Triomf

C. de Tànger

BARRI
GÓTIC

Jonqueres

C. dels Almogàvers

Avda. de la Meridiana

La Rambla

1

2

Via Laietana

S. Pere Més Alt

S. Pere Més Baix

C. de Sancho de Avila

C. del Carme

C. de
la Palla

La Boqueria

Avda. Catedral

Cathedral

Passeig de Lluis Companys

Passeig Pujadas

Passeig de Carles I

Hospital de
la Santa Creu

Plaça del Rei

C. Ferran

Pl. St.
Jaume

C. Princesa

BORN-RIBERA

4

C. del Comerç

Pg. Picasso

Parc de la
Ciutadella

C. de Wellington

Palau
Güell

Plaça
Reial

C. Ciutat

Passeig
del Born

Picasso
Museum

R. Santa Mónica

C. Ample

Pg. de Colôm

Pl.
d'Antoni
Lòpez

Estació de
França

Plaça Portal
de la Pau

Avda. d'Icària

Vila Olímpica

Avda. Litoral Costat Muntanya

Rambla
de Mar

Moll de
Barceloneta

Passeig Joan de Borbó

BARCELONETA

Parc de Mar

Moll d'Espanya

5

Passeig Marítim

Mediterranean Sea

# WHAT'S WHERE

**7 Gràcia.** The former outlying village of Gràcia begins at Gaudí's playful Parc Güell and continues down past his first house, Casa Vicens, through two markets and various pretty squares such as Plaça de Rius i Taulet and Plaça del Sol. Carrer Gran de Gràcia is lined with buildings designed by Gaudí's assistant Francesc Berenguer.

**8 Sarrià & Pedralbes.** Sarrià is a country hamlet within the burgeoning metropolis. Wandering through these peaceful streets reveals several interesting buildings, antiques shops, boutiques, and a handful of fine dining opportunities. Nearby is the Monestir de Pedralbes, a 14th-century architectural gem with a rare triple-tiered cloister; not far away are Gaudí's Colegio de les Teresianas and his Torre Bellesguard.

**9 Tibidabo, Vallvidrera & the Collserola Hills.** Tibidabo, Barcelona's perch, is generally a place to avoid unless you're seduced by amusement park kitsch. The square at the funicular however, has restaurants with terrific views over the city, and the Gran Hotel la Florida up above it all is a tour de force. Even better is the Collserola forest and natural park on the far side of the hill, accessible by the FGC train.

**10 Montjuïc.** Compared to the electric street scene in the rest of Barcelona, Montjuïc may seem dull, but the Museu Nacional d'Arte de Catalunya (MNAC) in the Palau Nacional holds great art, as does the Joan Miró Foundation. That plus its many architectural sites makes this neighborhood a worthy detour.

**11 Catalonia: The Costa Brava to Tarragona.** The famed Costa Brava stretches north from Blanes (60 km, or 37 mi, north of Barcelona) to Cadaqués and the French border. It's long been colonized by sleek hotels, sun worshippers, and celebrated artists, most notably Salvador Dalí. Closer to Barcelona, the legendary Montserrat and Montseny, to the north, offer easy escapes.

**12 Bilbao.** Centered on the gleaming titanium structure Museo Guggenheim Bilbao, the Basque Country's formerly industrial city has been completely transformed. With two good art museums, numerous culinary standouts, and an Old Quarter that's getting better every day, Bilbao is now a booming cultural destination.

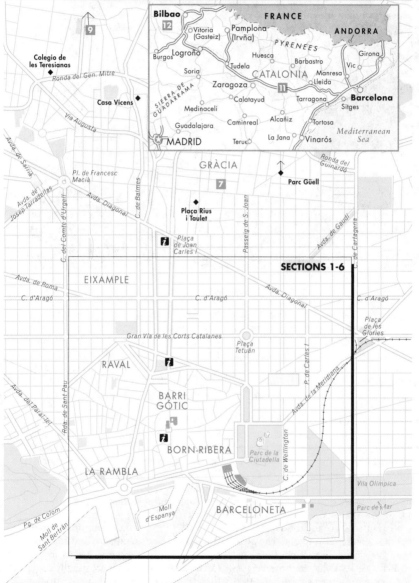

**9**

**Colegio de
les Teresianas**

Ronda del Gen. Mitre

**Casa Vicens** ◆

Via Augusta

Avda. de Sarrià

Avda. de
Josep Tarradellas

C. del Comte d'Urgell

Pl. de Francesc
Macià

Avda. Diagonal

C. de Balmes

**GRÀCIA**

**7**

Passeig de S. Joan

**Parc Güell** ◆

Ronda del
Guinardó

**Plaça Rius
i Taulet** ◆

Plaça
de Joan
Carles I

Avda. de Gaudí

D. de Cartagena

Avda. de Roma

**EIXAMPLE**

Avda. Diagonal

C. d'Aragó

C. d'Aragó

C. d'Aragó

Plaça
de les
Glòries

Gran Via de les Corts Catalanes

Plaça
Tetuán

**SECTIONS 1-6**

**RAVAL**

**BARRI
GÓTIC**

P. de Carles I

Avda. de la Meridiana

Rda. de Sant Pau

Avda. del Paral·lel

**BORN-RIBERA**

Parc de la
Ciutadella

C. de Wellington

**LA RAMBLA**

Pg. de Colom

Moll de
Sant Bertran

Moll
d'Espanya

**BARCELONETA**

Vila Olímpica

Parc de Mar

**INSET MAP:**

**Bilbao** **12**

**FRANCE**

Vitoria
(Gasteiz)

Pamplona
(Irvña)

**ANDORRA**

Burgos

Logroño

**PYRENEES**

Huesca

Barbastro

Girona

Vic

Soria

Tudela

**CATALONIA**

Manresa

SIERRA DE
GUADARRAMA

Zaragoza

Lleida

**11**

Calatayud

Tarragona

**Barcelona**

Medinaceli

Alcañiz

Sitges

Guadalajara

Caminreal

Tortosa

**MADRID**

Teruel

La Jana

Vinarós

*Mediterranean
Sea*

# QUINTESSENTIAL BARCELONA

### Grazing: Tapas & Wine Bars

Few pastimes in Barcelona are more satisfying and exciting than spontaneous wandering, tippling, and tapas-hunting. Whether during the day or after dark, meandering semi-aimlessly through the Gothic Quarter, Gràcia, Barceloneta, or the Born-Ribera district offers an endless selection of taverns, cafés, bars, and restaurants where wines, beers, *cava* (Catalan sparkling wine), or *txakolí* (a fresh young Basque white wine served in the increasingly popular Basque taverns) accompany little morsels of fish, sausage, cheese, peppers, wild mushrooms, or tortilla (potato omelet). If you find yourself stuck on Passeig de Gràcia or the Rambla in bars that serve microwaved tapas, know this: you're missing out. The areas around Passeig del Born, Santa Maria del Mar, Plaça de les Olles, and the Picasso Museum are the prime *tapeo* (tapa-tasting) and *txikiteo* (tippling) grounds.

### Openings, Presentations, Lectures & Musical Events.

Check listings in the *Guía del Ocio* or in the daily newspapers *El País* or *La Vanguardia* to find announcements for art gallery openings, book presentations, and free public concerts. Often serving cava and canapés, these little gatherings nearly always welcome visitors (if it's announced in the papers, you're invited). Famous authors from Vikram Seth to Martin Amis or local stars such as Javier Marías or Carlos Ruiz Zafón (author of *The Shadow of the Wind*) may be presenting new books at the British Institute or at bookstores such as La Central. Laie Libreria holds jazz performances in its café, while the travel bookstore Altair has frequent book signings and talks by prominent travel authors. Events in the town hall's Saló de Cent are usually open to the public, providing a glimpse into the city's cultural life.

If you want to get a sense of local Barcelona culture and indulge in some of its pleasures, start by familiarizing yourself with the rituals of daily life. These are a few highlights—things you can take part in with relative ease.

### Sunday Sardanas, Puppets & Castellers

The Sunday-morning papers carry announcements for local neighborhood celebrations, flea markets and produce fairs, puppet shows, storytelling sessions for children, sardana dancing, bell-ringing concerts, and, best of all, *castellers*. The castellers, complex human pyramids sometimes reaching as high as 10 stories, are a quintessentially Catalan phenomenon that originated in the Penedés region west of Barcelona and are performed regularly at neighborhood fiestas or key holidays. Most Sunday-morning events are over by two o'clock, when lunchtime officially reigns supreme, so an early start is recommended. The Barcelona town hall in Plaça Sant Jaume is a frequent castellers and sardanas venue, as is Plaça de la Catedral. The Fundació Miró regularly holds Sunday-morning puppet shows and children's events.

### Soccer: FC Barcelona

As FC Barcelona's soccer fortunes soar, sports bars proliferate throughout the city. Though the pubs showing soccer near the Rambla are usually heavily populated by foreign tourists, the taverns and cafés in Barceloneta, El Raval, Gràcia, and Sarrià are generally local *penyas* (fan clubs), where passions run high. To see what *fútbol* really means to rank-and-file Barcelona fans, these little bars are the places to check out. Notoriously intolerant toward supporters of FC Barcelona adversaries, especially Real Madrid, locals will be unhappy if a visitor cheers for anything but a home victory. For the real thing, of course, there is the Camp Nou stadium and the FC Barcelona museum; strangely, the stadium, though beautiful, often seems soporific compared to the taverns and bars where 90% of Barcelona's soccer fans get their weekly hit of "the opium of the masses."

# IF YOU LIKE

## Music & Music Festivals

If, as St. Augustine wrote, music and architecture are twin arts, it should be no surprise that Barcelona's musical offering rivals its architectural patrimony. With the Liceu opera house, Rafael Moneo's sleek modern, acoustically impeccable Auditori, and the Palau de la Música Catalana completing the city's triumvirate of gorgeous music venues, Barcelona has impressive music offerings that have become one of the city's greatest resources. In addition, extraordinary churches such as Santa Maria del Mar, Santa Maria del Pi, Sant Pau del Camp, Sant Felip Neri, and others present outstanding choral events, especially prior to Christmas and Easter. Caixaforum and historic monuments such as the medieval shipyards at Drassanes or the lovely, triple-tiered Monestir de Pedralbes also schedule exquisite concerts. The Early Music Festival in April and May fills the Gothic Quarter's prettiest squares with gorgeous music, from medieval harp to viola de gamba and choral soloists. With a tapa before and a light dinner or an onion soup afterward, musical events—especially combined with memorable architectural settings—make a nearly perfect Barcelona evening. Jazz and popular music are also in good supply here. Rare is a Barcelona month without a music festival: the fall jazz festival, the winter guitar festival, the spring early-music festival, and the summer *Grec* performing arts festival round out the calendar.

## Markets: Urban Horns of Plenty

"Collecting" markets is a rewarding passion—many veteran travelers consider it the best way, in fact, to get to know people and places. So, if you want to dive into Barcelona headfirst, there's no better way to start than with a visit to the Boqueria market on the Rambla—the oldest and last still-functioning market of its kind in Europe, a colorful chaos of produce ranging from lychee nuts and kumquats to partridges, chanterelles, scallops, bonito, and sea snails. As if wandering through this exciting display of raw materials weren't enough, excellent dining opportunities are stacked in there, from Pinotxo—a famous counter (a dozen bar stools) serving the best jumbo shrimp and scrambled eggs with wild mushrooms in town—to Quim de la Boqueria, with more places to sit and excellent fare as well. Other produce markets are scattered throughout the city. The markets of Gràcia, Barceloneta, and Sarrià, to name just a few, will make you feel like part of the neighborhood. The Mercat de Sant Antoni—a food, book, and clothes market—rages on weekends; Els Encants, Barcelona's flea market, near the Sagrada Família at Plaça de les Glòries, is a colorful collection of odds and ends; the Thursday antiques market in front of the cathedral is a good browse; Plaça de Sarrià holds a cheese, bread, pâté, and sausage market every second Thursday; the cheese, honey, and herb market open alternate Saturdays in Plaça del Pi is an oasis of farm-fresh fragrance downtown.

## Museums

The Museu Picasso is probably Barcelona's best-known museum, but the city has far superior collections of art, the finest of which are the stellar collections of the Museu Nacional d'Art de Catalunya on Montjuïc, which includes outstanding Romanesque murals, late-19th-century and early-20th-century impressionists and Modernistes, and the Thyssen-Bornemisza Collection of old masters. Caixaforum, just above Plaça Espanya, has excellent temporary exhibits. Gaudí's famous Pedrera (Casa Milà), on the Passeig de Gràcia, has a superb permanent exhibit on the architect's life and work in the Gaudí-designed attic, as well as a model apartment and rotating exhibitions on the main floor. The Museu d'Art Contemporani de Barcelona (MACBA), in the Raval west of the Rambla, has an excellent and well-guided collection of contemporary art featuring works by Calder, Tàpies, Oteiza, Rauschenberg, and Brossa. The Centre de Cultura Contemporània de Barcelona offers shows, lectures, concerts, and events of all kinds. Other museums with excellent displays are the Museu d'Història de la Ciutat in the Plaça del Rei, the Museu d'Història de Catalunya in the Port Vell's Palau de Mar, and the CosmoCaixa-Museu de la Ciencia in upper Barcelona. For a secret museum in a superb building, look for the Reial Acadèmia de les Belles Arts de Sant Jordi in La Llotja, near Santa Maria del Mar.

## Art Nouveau Architecture & Design

More than any other city in the world, Barcelona is filled with buildings and other works of the late-19th-century artistic and architectural movement known as Art Nouveau. The curved line replaced the straight line; flowers, fruits, and wild mushrooms were sculpted into facades. The pragmatic gave way to ornamental profusion. Barcelona's Palau de la Música Catalana by Lluís Domènech i Montaner, considered by many the most anthological representative of the movement, is a stunning compendium of Art Nouveau resources and techniques ranging from acid-etched glass to stained glass, polychrome ceramic ornamentation, carved wooden arches, and dozens of sculptures on the facade and inside the music hall itself. Antoni Gaudí has become, of course, the most famous of the Moderniste architects, but his personal style, as evidenced in the intensely naturalistic treatments of La Pedrera and the Sagrada Família, his last two buildings, took off in a direction all his own. Modernisme is everywhere in Barcelona, not only because it tapped into the playfulness of the Catalan artistic impulse (as evidenced in the works of Picasso, Miró, Dalí, and others) but because it coincided with Barcelona's late-19th-century industrial prosperity and an upsurge of nationalistic sentiment. Though the Eixample is a living Art Nouveau architecture museum, Moderniste buildings and facades are found throughout the city: Gràcia is the home of Gaudí's first house as well as a dozen works by his assistant Francesc Berenguer; Sarrià has several notable Moderniste houses, as well as Gaudí's Bellesguard, Colegio de les Teresianas, and the Pavellons Güell.

# BARCELONA TODAY

Capital of an ever-more-autonomous Catalonia, Barcelona continues to thrive as a bilingual (Catalan and Spanish) city in love with everything avant-garde.

## A Tale of Two Cities

Having languished for centuries in official "second-city" status compared to Madrid, Barcelona's drive to excel, create, innovate, and improvise is largely a result of its ongoing obsession with eclipsing its eternal rival. Even within Barcelona, a healthy sense of national identity goads designers, architects, merchants, and industrialists to ever higher levels of originality and effectiveness. Ever since 1990, when the International Olympic Committee announced that the 1992 Olympic Games were to be held in the Catalan capital, Barcelona has been booming with pride and confidence in its ever brighter future as (finally!) a bona fide European capital on its own.

## Art, Design, Architecture, Fashion & Style

Now that the city's haute couture status is increasingly recognized as biting at the heels of more-established runway stars such as Paris and Milan, present-day Barcelona more and more resembles a carousel of postmodern visual surprises from "cool hunter" Bread & Butter fashions to Jean Nouvel's Torre Agbar gherkin, or Norman Foster's giant erector-set communications tower on the Collserola skyline.

## Haute Cuisine Hotbed

Ever since Ferran Adrià and El Bulli became an infamous reference for La Nueva Cocina (aka molecular gastronomy) in Northern Catalonia's Roses, the spin-off success, especially in Barcelona, has exponentially expanded. With more than a dozen superstar restaurants winning international awards and more on the way, keeping abreast of the city's culinary rock stars can be a dizzying pursuit. Direct Adrià disciples such as Sergi Arola at the Hotel Arts and Carles Abellán at Comerç 24 join Adrià precursors such as Jean Louis Neichel or old pals like Fermin Puig at the Hotel Majestic's Drolma, along with relative newcomers such as Jordi Artal of Cinc Sentits or Jordi Herrera of Manairó in a glittering galaxy of gastronomical creativity. Meanwhile, carpetbaggers like the Roca brothers from Girona or Martin Berasategui from even farther afield in San Sebastián have opened award-winning hotel restaurants in, respectively, the Omm (Moo) and the Condes de Barcelona (Lasarte) even as younger and smaller restaurants such as Saüc, Ot, and Tram-Tram are producing creative and streamlined cuisine at less than bank-breaking prices.

## Political Progress

The approval of Catalonia's controversial new Autonomy Statute in 2006 has ushered in a wave of change in Catalonia. Bitterly opposed by the right-wing Partido Popular, the new autonomy agreement gives Catalonia a larger slice of local taxes and more control of its own infrastructure such as ports, airports, and the high-speed AVE train. Perhaps more importantly, the new statute reinforces the use of the Catalan language and formally establishes Catalonia as one of the most progressive pockets in Europe, with special provisions safeguarding human rights on same-sex marriage, euthanasia, and abortion that would win scant support in other more-traditional regions of Spain.

# Exploring
# Barcelona

**WORD OF MOUTH**

"The Sagrada Família is spectacular; even if you've seen pictures you won't believe it in real life. I would describe it as surreal. I loved the use of color and mosaics, and found it very unusual and uplifting...If you do go up and you are at all afraid of heights I would recommend taking the elevator back down rather than the narrow winding staircase—I'm not at all afraid of heights but the open center of the spiral had me scared going down!"

—kireland

By George
Semler

**THE THRONGING RAMBLA, THE REVERBERATION** of a flute in the medieval Gothic Quarter, bright ceramic colors splashed across Art Nouveau facades, glass and steel design over Roman stone: one way or another, Barcelona will find a way to get your full attention. The Catalonian capital has barnstormed into the new millennium in the throes of a cultural and industrial rebirth comparable only to the late-19th-century *Renaixença* that filled the city with its flamboyant Moderniste (aka Art Nouveau) architecture. Today, new architecture and design—including some of Europe's hottest new fashions in hip boutiques—provide the city with an exciting effervescent edge. Wedged along the Mediterranean coast between the forested Collserola hills and Europe's busiest seaport, Barcelona has catapulted to the rank of Spain's most-visited city, a 2,000-year-old master of the art of perpetual novelty.

The city's palette is vivid and varied: the glow of stained glass in the penumbra of the Barri Gòtic; Gaudí's mosaic-encrusted, undulating facades; the chromatic mayhem at the Palau de la Música Catalana; Miró's now universal blue and crimson shooting stars. Then, of course, there is the physical setting of the city, crouched catlike between the promontories of Montjuïc and Tibidabo, between the Collserola woodlands and the 4,000-acre port. Obsessed with playful and radical interpretations of everything from painting to theater to urban design and development, Barcelona consistently surprises.

Barcelona is wired with a vitality that somehow stops short of being intimidating. Just about the time you might begin to drop into a food- and wine-induced slumber at two in the morning, *barcelonins* are just heading out, when the city's night scene begins to kick in for real. Irrepressibly alive, creative, acquisitive, and playful in about equal doses, the city never stops. Regardless of outside governmental regimes that once tried to hold the reins, Catalans just kept on working, scheming, playing, and building. Now, with its recent past as a provincial outpost well behind, the city is charging into the future with more creativity and raw energy than ever.

Barcelona's present boom began on October 17, 1987, when Juan Antonio Samaranch, president of the International Olympic Committee, announced that his native city had been chosen to host the 1992 Olympics. This single masterstroke allowed Spain's so-called "second city" to throw off the shadow of Madrid and the 40-year "internal exile" of the Franco regime and resume its rightful place as one of Europe's most dynamic destinations. Not only did the Catalan administration lavish untold millions in subsidies from the Spanish government for the Olympics, they then used the games as a platform to broadcast the news about Catalonia's cultural and national identity from one end of the planet to the other. Madrid who? Calling Barcelona a second city of anyplace is playing with fire; modern Spain has always had two urban focal points, even though official figures dubiously counted Madrid's suburbs, but not Barcelona's, to feed the illusion that the Catalan capital was a provincial port.

More Mediterranean than Spanish, historically closer and more akin to Marseille or Milan than to Madrid, Barcelona has always been ambitious, decidedly modern (even in the 2nd century), and quick to accept the most recent innovations. Its democratic form of government is rooted in the so-called Usatges Laws instituted by Ramon Berenguer I in the 11th century, which

**2**

| TOP 5 |
| --- |
| ■ The Boqueria market |
| ■ Santa Maria del Mar |
| ■ Gaudí's Sagrada Família |
| ■ Parc Güell |
| ■ Palau de la Música Catalana |

amounted to a constitution. This code of privileges represented one of the earliest known examples of democratic rule, while Barcelona's Consell de Cent (Council of 100), constituted in 1274, was Europe's first parliament and is the true cradle of Western democracy. More recently, the city's electric light system, public gas system, and telephone exchange were among the first in the world. The center of an important seafaring commercial empire with colonies spread around the Mediterranean as far away as Athens when Madrid was still a Moorish outpost marooned on the arid Castilian steppe, Barcelona traditionally absorbed new ideas and styles first. Whether it was the Moors who brought navigational tools, philosophers and revolutionaries from nearby France spreading the ideals of the French Revolution, or artists like Picasso and Dalí who bloomed in the city's air of freedom and individualism, Barcelona has always been a law unto itself.

In the end, Barcelona is a banquet for all the senses, though perhaps mainly for sight. Not far behind are the pleasures of the palate. The air temperature is almost always about right, more and more streets are pedestrianized, and tavern after tavern burrows elegantly into medieval walls. Every now and then the fragrance of the sea in the port or in Barceloneta reminds you that this is, after all, a giant seaport and beach city with an ancient Mediterranean tradition that is, at the outset of its third millennium, flourishing—and bewitching visitors as it has for centuries.

### GETTING YOUR BEARINGS

Barcelona's main subdivisions include the Ciutat Vella (Old City) between Plaça de Catalunya and the port; the Eixample, the grid square of city blocks built after 1860 when Barcelona was allowed to tear down the city walls that were asphyxiating the city; and the outlying districts, formerly separate towns, of Gràcia, Sarrià, Horta, and Sants. Within the Ciutat Vella, with the Rambla as its center promenade, are the Barri Gòtic (Gothic Quarter), around the old Roman city; the Barri de la Ribera (the now-trendy waterfront neighborhood also known as Born-Ribera), farther northeast, and formerly at the edge of the port; and El Raval (the slum or suburb), to the southwest, once the rough district outside the second set of city walls. Barceloneta, originally open ocean, then a marshy wetland, later a mid-18th-century landfill housing project, is the beachfront and old fishermen's district. The Port Olímpic lies north of Barceloneta. Above the Ciutat Vella, the Eixample

(Expansion) contains most of Barcelona's Moderniste architecture. The promontories of Montjuïc and Tibidabo stand on either side of the city, while the Collserola hills rise sharply and verdantly up behind Barcelona to the north. At the northeastern end of Avinguda Diagonal is the new Diagonal Mar commercial, office, and residential development.

To avoid noise and air pollution, pedestrians should avoid walking main crosstown traffic arteries such as the Diagonal and the main up-and-down streets such as Balmes, Muntaner, Aribau, and Comtes d'Urgell. It's harder to avoid Passeig de Gràcia because of its dense endowment of Moderniste architecture, but you can also walk the charming and leafy Rambla de Catalunya, the upper extension of the Rambla between Plaça de Catalunya and the Diagonal.

The main bus and subway hub is Plaça de Catalunya, with the principal entrance at the top of the Rambla in front of the Café Zurich. Become familiar (especially) with the air-conditioned and comfortable Ferrocarril de la Generalitat de Catalunya (FGC), a separate train or subway line run by the Generalitat (Government of Catalonia), connecting Plaça de Catalunya with Sarrià and, beyond the Collserola hills behind the city, the suburban towns of San Cugat, Terrassa, and Sabadell. Between the FGC trains and the regular subway system, the odd taxi (a longish trip across town rarely exceeds the equivalent of $15 on the meter), and your own two feet, Barcelona is easy to navigate.

If you don't object to being bused around town with a few dozen (other) tourists, the Barcelona Bus Turístic operates daily in double-decker buses that leave from Plaça Catalunya and the Olympic Port. The red- and blue-line tours leave from Plaça Catalunya and take in, respectively, upper Barcelona and lower Barcelona. The green-line tour originates in the Olympic Port and takes in the eastern waterfront and the Fòrum complex. Tickets cost €19 for one day, €23 for two consecutive days. The ticket also gives you a card with discounts (worth up to €90) at most of Barcelona's museums and attractions. But for independent operators, Barcelona's a breeze on foot, with a taxi now and then, and the Sarrià train as your main up and downtown connection. Since Barcelona's street signs are printed in Catalan, note the most prevalent signage: *carrer* (street); *plaça* (square); *passeig* (boulevard); *rambla* (avenue or promenade); *avinguda* (avenue); and *passatge* (passage).

# THE RAMBLA: THE HEART OF BARCELONA

The central pedestrian artery and people-watching event in the city, La Rambla is Barcelona's best-known and most historic promenade. Lined with a succession of newspaper and magazine kiosks, bird merchants, and outdoor florist stands, festooned with colorful signs and lurid paraphernalia of every description, the Rambla is a rainbow of a street roaring just over 1 km (½ mi) through the heart of the Ciutat Vella—the Old City—from Plaça de Catalunya past the Boqueria market and the Liceu opera house to the Christopher Columbus monument at Portal de la Pau at the edge of the Barcelona port. Although the city has prettier places and other areas have far better cafés at which to linger, a walk here, among the spectacle of humanity, remains a quintessential Barcelona experience.

Centuries ago, the avenue was a (usually dry) watercourse, a sandy arroyo called *rmel* (Arabic for "sand"), from which the word Rambla evolved. Today, medieval seasonal hydraulics have been replaced by a constant flood of humanity. No wonder Federico García Lorca famously called this street the only one in the world he wished would never end: the show is always raging here with street performers of every stripe, from painted human statues to mimes, acrobats, jugglers, musicians, puppeteers, portraitists, break-dancers, rappers, and rockers, all hard at work beneath the canopy of giant plane trees. The Rambla is a thoroughfare where an endless deluge of locals and travelers tumbling down its central pedestrian island between two traffic lanes.

The crowd seethes and dawdles, at once busy and nonchalant. Couples sit at tiny café tables no bigger than tea trays while the never-ending parade files by. Nimble-footed waiters dodge traffic, bringing trays of coffee from kitchens to the tables' patrons. Peddlers, kiosk owners, parrots, and parakeets along the stretch called the Rambla dels Ocells (Rambla of the Birds) all contribute to a polyphony of birdsong and catcalls that clamors over the din of taxis and motorbikes, each note adding to the greater urban symphony. Here, in busy, frantic Barcelona, the Rambla is perennially plugged with squads of laughing, walking revelers, usually more animated at 3 AM than at 3 PM.

The Rambla's original sandy expanse followed the course of an old riverbed flowing down from the Collserola hills along the edge of the pre-13th-century ramparts that encircled the Gothic Quarter and the Barri de la Ribera. When, in the late 13th century, walls enclosing the Raval were erected along what are now the Rondas de Sant Antoni and Sant Pau, the open space outside the second set of walls was left as a mid-city promenade and forum. For more than a thousand years the Rambla has been a meeting place for peddlers, workers in search of jobs, farmers selling produce or livestock, and, especially these days, fleets of brazen thieves and pickpockets (note: watch your belongings).

Collectively known as La Rambla, each section has its own title and personality: Rambla Santa Monica at the southeastern, or port, end was named for an early convent; Rambla de les Flors in the middle is named for its traditional flower merchants; and Rambla dels Estudis at the top leading down from Plaça de Catalunya is so called for the Barcelona university located there until the early 18th century. From the universal rendezvous point at the head of the Rambla at Café Zurich to the Boqueria produce market, the Liceu opera house, or the Rambla's lower reaches with their variegated denizens of the night, there is something for everyone at any hour along this vertebral column of Barcelona street life.

An even more comprehensive macro-Rambla trek could begin at the Diagonal (at the bizarre reclining bronze giraffe) and continue down leafy Rambla de Catalunya through the Rambla proper, between Plaça

## Catalan First, Spanish Second

Throughout a topsy-turvy history of political ups and downs, prosperity rarely abandoned Barcelona, as the city continued to generate energy and creativity no matter who imposed authority from afar: Romans, Visigoths, Franks, Moors, Aragonese, French, or Castilians. Catalonia's early history hinges on five key dates: the 801 Frankish conquest by Charlemagne that wrested Catalonia away from the encroaching Moors; the 988 independence from the Franks; the 1137 alliance through marriage with Aragón; the 1474 unification (through the marriage of Fernando of Aragón and Isabella of Castile) of Aragón with the Castilian realms of León and Castile; and the 1714 defeat by Felipe V, who abolished Catalan rights and privileges.

The Roman Empire annexed the city built by the Iberian tribe known as the Laietans and established, in 133 BC, a colony called Colonia Favencia Julia Augusta Paterna Barcino ("Favored Colony Barcino of Father Julius Augustus"). After Rome's 4th-century decline, Barcelona enjoyed an early golden age as the Visigothic capital under the rule of Ataulf and the Roman empress of the West, Galla Placidia (388–450), daughter of Theodosius I and one of the most influential and fascinating women of early European history. Ataulf, assassinated in Barcelona in 415, was succeeded by Visigothic rulers who moved their capital to Toledo, leaving Barcelona to a secondary role through the 6th and 7th centuries. The Moors invaded in the 8th century; and in 801, in what was to be a decisive moment in Catalonia's history, the Franks under Charlemagne captured the city and made it a buffer zone at the edge of Al-Andalus, the Moors'

empire on the Iberian Peninsula. Moorish rule extended to the Garraf Massif just south of Barcelona, while Catalonia became the Marca Hispánica (Spanish March or, really, "edge") of the Frankish empire.

Over the next two centuries the Catalonian counties, ruled by counts appointed by the Franks, gained increasing autonomy. In 985 the Franks failed to reinforce their allies against a Moorish attack, and, as of 988, Catalonia declared itself an independent federation of counties with Barcelona as its capital. The marriage, in 1137, of Sovereign Count Ramon Berenguer IV to Petronella, daughter of King Ramiro II of Aragón, united Catalonia with Aragón. The crown of Aragón, with Barcelona as its commercial and naval center, controlled the Mediterranean until the 15th century. The 1474 marriage of Ferdinand II of Aragón and Isabella of Castile and León brought Aragón and Catalonia into a united Spain. As the main city of Aragón's Mediterranean empire, Barcelona had grown in importance between the 12th and the 14th centuries, and only began to falter when maritime emphasis shifted to the Atlantic after 1492.

Despite the establishment of Madrid as the seat of Spain's royal court in 1562, Catalonia continued to enjoy autonomous rights and privileges until 1714, when, in reprisal for having backed the Austrian Habsburg pretender to the Spanish throne during the War of the Spanish Succession (1700–14), all institutions and expressions of Catalan identity were suppressed by the triumphant Felipe V of the French Bourbon dynasty. Not until the mid-19th century would Barcelona's industrial growth bringabout a *Renaixença* (renaissance) of nationalism and a cultural flowering that recalled Catalonia's former opulence.

Barcelona's power and prosperity continued to grow in the early 20th century. After the abdication of Alfonso XIII and the establishment of the Second Spanish Republic in 1931, Catalonia enjoyed a high degree of autonomy and cultural freedom. Once again backing a losing cause, Barcelona was a Republican stronghold during the Spanish civil war. When the war ended, Catalan language and identity were once again brutally suppressed by such means as book burning, the renaming of streets and towns, and the banning of the Catalan language in schools and in the media. This repression or "internal exile" lasted until Franco's death in 1975, when it became evident that the Catalans had once again, more stubbornly than ever, managed to keep their language and culture alive. Catalonian home rule was granted after Franco's death in 1975, and Catalonia's parliament, the ancient Generalitat, was reinstated in 1980. Catalan is now Barcelona's co-official language, along with Castilian Spanish. Street names are signposted in Catalan, and newspapers, radio stations, and a TV channel publish and broadcast in Catalan. The culmination of this rebirth was the staging of the Olympics in 1992—ring roads were constructed, new harborside promenades were created, and Catalonia announced its existence and national identity to the world. The urban renewal for the Olympics under Mayor Pasqual Maragall (later president of the Generalitat) was just the beginning. Mayor Joan Clos, with the 2004 Fòrum Universal de les Cultures, engineered the new Diagonal-Mar development, stretching from Plaça de les Glòries to the mouth of the Besòs River and populated with Jean Nouvel, Oscar Tusquets, and Herzog & de Meuron buildings that keep architecture students on a perennial field trip.

Catalonia's controversial new Autonomy Statute, approved in 2006 under the Socialist government of José Luis Rodríguez Zapatero, placed still more power in local hands. Although there are now varying degrees of Catalonian nationalism in play ranging from radical pro-independence militants to conservative Spain-firsters, most Catalans today think of themselves as Catalans first and Spanish citizens second.

■TIP→ **Learning a few Catalan phrases will give you a much warmer reception than the usual Spanish. A friendly "bon dia" (good day) goes a long ways.**

de Catalunya and the Columbus monument at Portal de la Pau and across the port on the Rambla de Mar boardwalk to the Maremagnum and the Port Vell (Old Port). In the end, you might come to know Barcelona quite well without ever even straying far from the Rambla.

*Numbers in the text correspond to numbers in the margin and on the Rambla map.*

## A GOOD WALK

Start at one of the landmarks of the **Plaça de Catalunya** ❶, a standard meeting point astride the city's central metro and bus stops: the **Café Zurich** ❷, at the head of the Rambla. Just down the Rambla on the right is the **Font de Canaletes** ❸, a fountain with a plaque explaining that if you drink the water, you will fall under the spell of Barcelona and always return. This section of the Rambla is the Rambla dels Estudis, so named for the early university located here until Felipe V banished the unruly students to Cervera, some 100 km (62 mi) west of Barcelona. Next is the Rambla dels Ocells (Rambla of the Birds), where all manner of fowl from parrots to partridges are sold, a practice carried down from the days when markets and conglomerations of peasants looking for work clustered outside the city walls, making the sandy arroyo into the popular meeting point it has remained. At Carrer Portaferrissa, check out the baroque-era landmarks of **Església de Betlem** ❹, the church on the right, and the **Palau Moja** ❺ on the left, along with the **Portaferrissa fountain** ❻ on the right, with its ceramic-tile representation of what the Rambla looked like in the 14th century, as you turn left into Carrer Portaferrissa.

The Rambla de les Flors is aromatically unmistakable, famous among 19th-century Catalan impressionists as a source of beautiful flower vendors who frequently became their models and, often, their wives. After a look through the historic **Palau de la Virreina** ❼—now an exhibition center—stroll through the spectacular **Boqueria** ❽ food market. Back on the Rambla, note the colorful Joan Miró mosaic underfoot at Pla de la Boqueria and the bizarre Art Nouveau–neo-Egyptian **Casa Bruno Quadros** ❾ house. From Pla de la Boqueria, cut in to the Plaça del Pi and the church of **Santa Maria del Pi** ❿, with its celebrated rose window. Explore this area, especially **Carrer Petritxol** ⓫; stop in for a break at one of this historic street's *xocolaterías* (hot-chocolate shops) before returning to the Rambla. Just across Pla de la Boqueria on Carrer Hospital, take a look at the leafy square and unusual church of **Sant Agustí** ⓬ before continuing left on Carrer de l'Arc de Sant Agustí past the torn-away lateral facade of the church to the Art Nouveau **Hotel España** ⓭ on Carrer de Sant Pau. Heading back out to the Rambla, you pass the back entrance to the **Gran Teatre del Liceu** ⓮, Barcelona's famous opera house. As you head south, off to the left of the Rambla is **Plaça Reial** ⓯, an elegantly neoclassical square that's been an address to the rich and famous as well as a ragtag contingent of street people.

Gaudí's spectacular **Palau Güell** ⓰, west of the Rambla on Carrer Nou de la Rambla, is the next stop and a stunning introduction to the work of Barcelona's most iconic architectural genius. **Carrer Escudellers** ⓱—

lined with interesting sights, from an Art Nouveau saloon to Barcelona's best ceramics store, Art Escudellers—goes left at Pla del Teatre. Continue down the Rambla toward the port to the towering column honoring Christopher Columbus, the **Monument a Colom** ⓲, and the **Port** ⓳, accessed by the Rambla de Mar (from here consider making a brief probe into the modern Port Vell complex, with its shopping center, IMAX theater, and aquarium). Back at the Columbus monument, investigate the medieval **Drassanes Reials** shipyards and the **Museu Marítim** ⓴, with exhibits devoted to Barcelona's maritime history. For a fitting finale, retire to a Rambla café to watch the passing parade before dinnertime.

TIMING    Allow three to four hours, including stops, for this walk of about 5 km (3 mi). The best times to find things open and the Rambla rollicking are 9 AM–2 PM and 4 PM–8 PM, although this populous runway has a life of its own 24 hours a day. Some museums remain open through the lunch hour but others close—check hours. Most church hours are 9 AM–1:30 PM and 4:30 PM–8 PM; there is usually a midday closing.

HOW TO GET THERE    The Plaça Catalunya metro stop will put you at the head of the Rambla in front of Café Zurich, Barcelona's most famous rendezvous point. From here, it's just a few steps down to the Canaletes fountain on the right side of the Rambla.

### WHAT TO SEE: MAIN ATTRACTIONS

**⑧ Boqueria.** Barcelona's most spectacular food market, also known as the

Fodor'sChoice ★   Mercat de Sant Josep, is an explosion of life and color sprinkled with delicious little bar-restaurants. A solid polychrome wall of fruits, herbs, wild mushrooms, vegetables, nuts, candied fruits, cheeses, hams, fish, poultry, and provender of every imaginable genus and strain greets you as you turn in from La Rambla, the air alive with the aromas of fresh produce and reverberating with the din of commerce. Within this steel hangar, the market occupies a neoclassical square built in 1840 by architect Francesc Daniel Molina. The Doric columns visible around the edges of the market were part of the mid-19th-century neoclassical square constructed here after the Sant Josep convent was torn down. The columns were uncovered in 2001 after more than a century of being buried in the busy market. Highlights include the sunny greengrocer's market outside (to the right if you've come in from the Rambla), along with **Pinotxo**—*(Pinocchio)*, just inside to the right—which has won international acclaim as a food sanctuary. Owner Juanito Bayén and his family serve some of the best food in Barcelona. (The secret? "Fresh, fast, hot, salty, and garlicky.") Pinotxo—marked with a ceramic portrait of the wooden-nosed prevaricator himself—is typically overbooked. But take heart; the **Kiosko Universal** over toward the port side of the market, or **Quim de la Boqueria**, offer a delicious alternative. Don't miss herb and wild-mushroom expert Llorenç Petràs at the back of the Boqueria (ask anyone for the location), with his display of wild mushrooms, herbs, nuts, and berries ("Fruits del Bosc"—Fruits of the Forest). ✉ *Rambla 91, Rambla* ⊕ *www.boqueria.info* ☉ *Mon.–Sat. 8–8* Ⓜ *Liceu*.

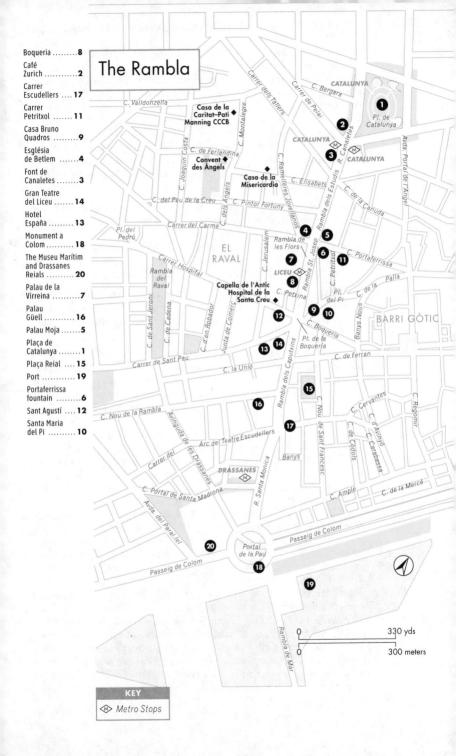

# The Rambla

KEY

◈ Metro Stops

★ ⑭ **Gran Teatre del Liceu.** Barcelona's opera house has long been considered one of the most beautiful in Europe, in the same category as Milan's La Scala. First built in 1848, this cherished cultural landmark was torched in 1861, then later bombed by anarchists in 1893, and once again gutted by a blaze of mysterious origins in early 1994. During that most recent fire, Barcelona's soprano Montserrat Caballé stood on the Rambla in tears as her beloved venue was consumed. Five years later, a restored Liceu, equipped for modern productions, opened anew. Even if you don't see an opera, don't miss a tour of the building; some of the Liceu's most spectacular halls and rooms (including the glittering lobby foyer known as the Saló dels Miralls, or Room of Mirrors) were untouched by the fire of 1994, as were those of Spain's oldest social club, El Círculo del Liceu. The Espai Liceu downstairs provides the city with daily cultural and commercial operatic interaction. With a cafeteria; a shop specializing in opera-related gifts, books, and recordings; a small, 50-person-capacity theater running videos of opera fragments and the history of the opera house; and a Mediateca featuring recordings and filmings of past opera productions, Espai Liceu is the final step in the Barcelona opera's Phoenix-like resurrection. ⊠ *La Rambla 51–59, Rambla* ☎ *93/485–9913* ⊕ *www.liceubarcelona.com* ✉ *Guided tours €8.50* ⊙ *Tours daily at 10* AM *in English (the 75-min visit includes El Círculo del Liceu, with the extraordinary Ramon Casas collection of paintings). Unguided express tours at 11* AM, *noon, 12:30, and 1* PM *are shorter (20 mins) and lesscomprehensive; cost is €4* Ⓜ *Liceu.*

> ## EUROPE'S PROTO-DEMOCRACY
>
> Barcelona's Consell de Cent (Council of 100) was Europe's earliest democratic assembly, established in 1249 and composed of 100 leaders from different trades and professional guilds as well as nobility, clergy, and army. The council elected the three *consellers* (councillors) who presided over municipal affairs, named Pere de Aragón count-king of Barcelona in 1474, and defended the city against the 1714 Bourbon siege.

⊙ ⑳ **Museu Marítim.** The superb Maritime Museum is housed in the 13th-century **Drassanes Reials** (Royal Shipyards), at the foot of the Rambla adjacent to the harbor front. This vast covered complex begun in 1378 built and launched the ships of Catalonia's powerful Mediterranean fleet directly from its yards into the port (the water once reached the level of the eastern facade of the building). Today, these are the world's largest and best-preserved medieval shipyards; centuries ago, at a time (1377–88) when Greece was a province of the House of Aragón, they were of crucial importance to the sea power of Catalonia (then the heavyweight in an alliance with Aragón). On the Avinguda del Paral.lel side of Drassanes is a completely intact section of the 14th- to 15th-century walls—Barcelona's third and final ramparts—that encircled the Raval along the Paral.lel and the Rondas de Sant Pau, Sant Antoni, and Universitat. (*Ronda* was originally used to specify streets or circumvolutions running around the outside of the city walls.) The earliest part of Drassanes is the section farthest from the sea along Carrer de

Fodor's Choice
★

Portal de Santa Madrona. Subsequent naves were added in the 17th and 18th centuries.

Though the shipyards seem more like a cathedral than a naval construction site, the Maritime Museum is filled with vessels, including a spectacular collection of ship models. The life-size reconstruction of the galley of Juan de Austria, commander of the Spanish fleet in the Battle of Lepanto, is perhaps the most impressive display in the museum. Figureheads, nautical gear, early navigational charts, and medieval nautical lore enhance the experience, and headphones and infrared pointers provide a first-rate self-guided tour. Concerts, often featuring early-music master and viola de gamba virtuoso Jordi Savall, are occasionally held in this acoustical gem. The cafeteria is Barcelona's hands-down winner for dining in the midst of medieval elegance. Don't miss the small bronze reproduction of a sailing ship, commemorating the 1571 Battle of Lepanto, out on the Rambla corner nearest the port. ⊠*Av. de les Drassanes s/n, Rambla* ☎*93/342-9920* ⊕*www.museu-maritimbarcelona.org* ⛟*€6.50; free 1st Sat. of month 3–7* ☽*Daily 10–7* Ⓜ*Drassanes.*

★ ⑯ **Palau Güell.** Disneyesque chimneys, a flying-bat weather vane, parabolic arches, neo-Byzantine salons, and post-Mudejar ornament all accent this imposing mansion—one of the first and greatest masterpieces built by that genius of Barcelonan Modernisme, Antoni Gaudí, and one of the few private Gaudí houses usually open to public view. At the time of this writing, it had closed for repairs and was scheduled to reopen by 2008. Gaudí built this mansion in 1886–89 for textile baron Count Eusebi de Güell Bacigalupi, his main patron and promoter. Gaudí's principal obsession in this project was to find a way to illuminate this seven-story house tightly surrounded by other buildings in the cramped quarters of the Raval. The prominent *quatre barras* (four bars) of the Catalan *senyera* (banner) on the facade between the parabolic (looping) entrance arches attest to the nationalist fervor that Gaudí shared with Güell. The dark facade is a dramatic foil for the treasure housed inside, where spear-shape Art Nouveau columns frame the windows and prop up a series of detailed and elaborately carved wood ceilings.

If you're visiting when the house reopens, begin downstairs in the stables with the "fungiform" (fungus- or mushroom-like) columns supporting the whole building. Note Gaudí's signature parabolic arches between the columns and the way the arches meet overhead, forming an oasis-like canopy of palm fronds, probably little consolation for political prisoners (such as Andreu Nin, who was never seen again) held there during the 1936–39 Spanish civil war when the space was used as a *cheka* (the Russian word used for Republican secret-police dungeons). The patio where the horses were groomed receives light through a skylight, one of many Gaudí devices and tricks used to create, or seem to create, more light: mirrors, skylights, even frosted-glass windows over artificial lighting, giving the impression of exterior light. Don't miss the faithful hounds in the grooming room with rings for hitching horses, or the wooden bricks used as cobblestones in the upstairs entryway and on the ramp down to the basement grooming area to deaden the sound of horses' hooves. The chutes on the Carrer Nou de la Rambla side of the basement were for loading feed straight in from street level overhead, while the catwalk and spiral staircase were for the servants to walk back up into the main entry.

Upstairs are three successive receiving rooms, the wooden ceilings progressing from merely spectacular to complex to byzantine in their richly molded floral and leaf motifs. The third receiving room, the one farthest in with the most elaborate ceiling ornamentation, has a jalousie in the balcony over the room, a double grate through which Güell was able to inspect and, almost literally, eavesdrop on his arriving guests. The main hall, with the three-story-tall tower reaching up above the roof, was the room for parties, dances, and receptions. Musicians played from the balcony, and the overhead balcony window was for the main vocalist. A chapel of hammered copper with retractable kneeling pads and a small bench for two built into the right side of the altar is enclosed behind a double door. Around the corner is a small organ, the flutes in rectangular tubes climbing the mansion's central shaft.

The dining room is dominated by a beautiful mahogany banquet table seating 10, an Art Nouveau fireplace in the shape of a deeply curving horseshoe arch, and walls with floral and animal motifs. Note the Star of David in the woodwork over the window and the Asian religious themes in the vases on the mantelpiece. From the outside rear terrace, the polished Garraf marble of the main part of the house is exposed and visible, while the brick servants' quarters rise up on the left. The passageway built toward the Rambla was all that came of a plan to buy an intervening property and connect three houses into a major structure, a scheme that never materialized.

Gaudí is most himself on the roof, where his playful, polychrome ceramic chimneys seem right at home with later works such as Parc Güell and La Pedrera. Look for the flying-bat weather vane over the main chimney, symbol of Jaume I el Conqueridor (James I, the Conqueror), who brought the house of Aragón to its 13th-century imperial apogee in the Mediterranean. Jaume I's affinity for bats is said to have stemmed from his Majorca campaign when, according to one version, he was awakened by the fluttering *rat penat* (literally, "condemned mouse") in time to stave off a Moorish night attack. Another version attributes the presence of the bat in Jaume I's coat of arms to his gratitude to the Sufi sect that helped him successfully invade Majorca,

## STALINIST CHEKAS IN BARCELONA

The Stalinist purge carried out against Trotskyist elements in the Republican left early in the Spanish civil war came very close to claiming the life of George Orwell, who had joined a Trotsky-affiliated militia unit when he volunteered to fight against the forces of fascism in Spain in 1936. The basement of Palau Güell was used as a *cheka* (the Russian word for prison or detention center) by the Stalinist faction and it was into this dungeon that Andreu Nin, secretary-general of Barcelona's Trotsky forces, disappeared in 1937, never to be seen again.

using the bat as a signal indicating when and where to attack. See if you can find the hologram of COBI, Javier Mariscal's 1992 Olympic mascot, on a restored ceramic chimney (hint: the all-white one at the Rambla end of the roof terrace). ⊠ *Nou de la Rambla 3–5, Rambla* ☎ *93/317–3974* 🖃 *€7.50* ⊙ *Daily 9–8* Ⓜ *Drassanes, Liceu.*

⓯ **Plaça Reial.** Nobel Prize–winning novelist Gabriel García Marquez, architect and urban planner Oriol Bohigas, and Pasqual Maragall, president of the Catalonian Generalitat, are among the many famous people known to have acquired apartments overlooking this potentially elegant square, a chiaroscuro masterpiece in which neoclassical symmetry clashes with big-city street squalor. Plaça Reial is bordered by stately ocher facades with balconies overlooking the wrought-iron **Fountain of the Three Graces** and treelike, snake-infested lampposts designed by Gaudí in 1879. Third-rate cafés and restaurants line the square, but the buskers, thieves, and homeless who occupy the benches on sunny days make hanging out here uncomfortable. Plaça Reial is most colorful on Sunday morning, when crowds gather to trade stamps and coins; after dark it's a center of downtown nightlife for the jazz-minded, the young, and the adventurous (it's best to be street-wise touring this area in the late hours). Bar Glaciar, on the uphill corner toward the Rambla, is a booming beer station for young international travelers. La Taxidermista, across the way, is the only good restaurant in the plaza; Tarantos has top flamenco performances; and Jamboree offers world-class jazz. Ⓜ *Catalunya, Liceu.*

❻ **Portaferrissa fountain.** Both the fountain and the ceramic representation of Barcelona's second set of walls and the early Rambla are worth studying carefully. If you can imagine pulling out the left side of the ceramic scene and looking broadside at the amber yellow 13th-century walls that ran down this side of the Rambla, you will see a clear picture of what this spot looked like in medieval times. The sandy Rambla ran along outside the walls, while the portal looked down through the ramparts into the city. As the inscription on the fountain explains, the *Porta Ferrica,* or Iron Door, was named for the iron measuring stick attached to the wood and used in the 13th and 14th centuries to establish a unified standard for measuring goods. ⊠ *Rambla and Carrer Portaferrissa, Rambla* Ⓜ *Liceu.*

⓬ **Sant Agustí.** This unfinished church is one of Barcelona's most unusual structures, with jagged stone sections projecting down the left side and the upper part of the front entrance on Plaça Sant Agustí waiting to be covered with a facade. Begun in 1728 and abandoned 20 years later, the projected facade, designed by Pere Costa, was to be baroque in style, but funding stopped and so did the construction. Sant Agustí comes alive on May 22, feast day of Santa Rita, patron saint of "los imposibles"—that is, lost causes. Unhappily married women, unrequited lovers, and all-but-hopeless sufferers of every stripe and spot form long lines through the square and down Carrer Hospital. Each carries a rose that will be blessed at the chapel of Santa Rita on the right side of the altar. ⊠ *Pl. Sant Agustí, Raval* ☎ *93/318–6231* Ⓜ *Liceu.*

# La Diada de Sant Jordi: Barcelona's Lovers' Day

Barcelona's best day? Easy. April 23—St. George's Day, La Diada de Sant Jordi, Barcelona's Valentine's day—a day when kissometer readings go off the charts, a day so sweet and playful, so goofy and romantic, that 6 million Catalans go giddy from dawn to dusk.

Patron saint of Catalonia, international knight-errant St. George allegedly slew a dragon about to devour a beautiful princess south of Barcelona. From the dragon's blood sprouted a rosebush, from which the hero plucked the prettiest blossom for the princess. Hence, the traditional Rose Festival celebrated in Barcelona since the Middle Ages to honor chivalry and romantic love, a day for men and mice alike to give their true loves roses. In 1923, the lovers' fest merged with International Book Day to mark the anniversary of the all-but-simultaneous April 23, 1616 deaths of Miguel de Cervantes and William Shakespeare.

More than 4 million roses and half a million books are sold in Catalonia on Sant Jordi's Day, men giving their inamoratas roses and the ladies giving books in return. Bookstalls run the length of the Rambla, and although it's an official workday, nearly all of Barcelona manages to play hooky and wander. In the city, St. George is everywhere, beginning on the facade of the Catalonian seat of government, the Generalitat. Art Nouveau master Eusebi Arnau sculpted Sant Jordi skewering the unlucky dragon on the facade of the Casa Amatller as well as on the corner of Els Quatre Gats café, while Gaudí dedicated an entire house, Casa Batlló, to the Sant Jordi theme with the cross of the saint implanted in the scaly roof and the bones of the dragon's victims framing the windows of the main facade.

A Roman soldier martyred for his Christian beliefs in the 4th century, St. George is one of the most venerated of all saints, patron of England, Greece, and Romania, among other places. Associated with springtime and fertility, Sant Jordi roses include a spike of wheat and a little red and yellow "senyera," the Catalonian flag. And the books? There's the Shakespeare and Cervantes anniversary, and Barcelona is the publishing capital of the Spanish-speaking world. Language and love have, in any case, always been closely associated.

In Barcelona and all of Catalonia, Sant Jordi's Day erupts joyfully. There is a 24-hour reading of *Don Quixote*. Authors come to bookstalls to sign books. In Sarrià, a floral artisan displays 45 kinds of roses representing 45 different kinds of love, from impossible to unrequited to filial and maternal. The *sardana* is reverently performed in Plaça Sant Jaume, while the Generalitat, its patio filled with roses, opens its doors to the public. Choral groups sing love songs in the Gothic Quarter as jazz combos play in Plaça del Pi. The Rambla is solid humanity from the Diagonal to the Mediterranean, 3 km (2 mi) of barcelonins basking in the warmth of spring and romance. Rare is the roseless woman on the streets of Barcelona.

By midnight, the Rambla, once a watercourse, is again awash with flower water and covered with rose clippings and tiny red-and-yellow–striped ribbons spelling "Sant Jordi," "Diada de la Rosa" (Day of the Rose), and "t'estimo" (I love you).

**⑩ Santa Maria del Pi.** Sister church to Santa Maria del Mar and to Santa Maria de Pedralbes, this early Catalan Gothic structure is perhaps the most fortresslike of all three, hulking dark and massive and perforated only by the main entryway and the mammoth rose window, said to be the world's largest. Try to see the window from inside in the late afternoon to get the best view of the colors. The church was named for the lone pine tree (*pi*) that stood in what was a marshy lowland outside the 4th-century Roman walls. An early church dating back to the 10th century preceded the present Santa Maria del Pi, begun in 1322 and finally consecrated in 1453. Like Santa Maria del Mar, the church of Santa Maria del Pi is one of Barcelona's many examples of Mediterranean Gothic architecture, though the aesthetic distance between the two is substantial. The church's interior is disappointingly cluttered compared with the clean and lofty lightness of Santa Maria del Mar, but the creaky choir loft and the Ramón Amadeu painting of La Mare de Deu dels Desamparats (Our Lady of the Helpless), for which the artist reportedly used his wife and children as models for the Virgin and children, are interesting. The lateral facade of the church, around to the left in Plaça Sant Josep Oriol, bears a plaque dedicated to the April 6, 1806, fall of the portly parish priest José Mestres, who slipped off the narrow catwalk circling the outside of the apse. He survived the fall unhurt, and the event was considered a minor miracle commemorated with the plaque.

The adjoining squares, **Plaça del Pi** and **Plaça de Sant Josep Oriol,** are two of the liveliest and most appealing spaces in the old quarter, filled with much-frequented outdoor cafés and used as a venue for markets selling natural products or paintings or as an impromptu concert hall for musicians. The handsome entryway and courtyard at No. 4 Plaça de Sant Josep Oriol across from the lateral facade of Santa Maria del Pi is the **Palau Fivaller,** now seat of the Agricultural Institute, an interesting patio to have a look through. From Placeta del Pi, tucked in behind the church, you can see the bell tower and the sunny facades of the apartment buildings on the north side of Plaça Sant Josep Oriol. Placeta del Pi was once the cemetery for the blind, hence the name of the little street leading in: Carrer Cecs de la Boqueria (Blind of the Boqueria). This little space with its outdoor tables is a quiet and cozy place for a coffee or excellent tapas at El Taller de Tapas. ⊠ *Pl. del Pi s/n, Rambla* ☎ *93/318–4743* ⊙ *Daily 9–1:30 and 4:30–8* Ⓜ *Liceu.*

**ALSO WORTH SEEING**

**❷ Café Zurich.** This traditional café and rendezvous point at the top of the Rambla, over the metro station, has an elegant, high-ceilinged interior. The terrace is one of the city's prime people-watching spots. ⊠ *Pl. de Catalunya 1, Rambla* ☎ *93/317–9153* ⊙ *Daily 9 AM–2 AM* Ⓜ *Catalunya.*

**⑰ Carrer Escudellers.** Named for the *terrissaires* (earthenware potters) who worked here making *escudellas* (bowls or stew pots), this colorful loop is an interesting sub-trip off the Rambla. Go left at Plaça del Teatre and you'll pass the landmark **Grill Room** at No. 8, an Art Nouveau saloon with graceful wooden decor and mediocre cuisine (still, it's a fine stop for a beverage at the ornate oaken bar). Next is **La Fonda Escudellers,**

## Barcelona: An Architectural Toy Box

The city's independent outlook has been spectacularly reflected in its anthology of architecture, which covers 2,000 years of history from classical Roman, Romanesque, Gothic, Renaissance and baroque, neoclassical, and Moderniste to the rationalist, minimalist, and postmodern solutions of Richard Meier, Santiago Calatrava, Rafael Moneo, Norman Foster, Ricardo Bofill, and Jean Nouvel.

If Madrid is about paintings, Barcelona's forte is architecture, notably the work of Antoni Gaudí (1852–1926), whose buildings are the most startling manifestations of Modernisme—the Spanish, and mainly Catalan chapter of the late-19th-century Art Nouveau movement. Other leading Moderniste architects include Lluís Domènech i Montaner and Josep Puig i Cadafalch.

The most Art Nouveau–rife area is L'Eixample (The Expansion). Barcelona's Eixample claimed as its own the artistic movement called Art Nouveau in France, Modern Style in England, Sezessionstil in Austria, Jugendstil in Germany, Liberty or Floreale in Italy, Modernisme in Catalonia, and Modernismo in Spain. Scanning these terms provides a good overview of what Art Nouveau is all about: new, modern (in the late 19th century), playful, flowery, revolutionary, and free. Art Nouveau was a reaction to the misery and massification brought about by technology and the Industrial Revolution. It is what most characterizes the city: only Barcelona has 50 cataloged Moderniste buildings as well as more than 250 private houses with Art Nouveau facades, interiors, or other elements, with the works of Gaudí providing a separate chapter.

Barcelona's Roman, Romanesque, and Gothic legacy is equally interesting. The famous Rambla separates the Gothic Quarter and its Roman core from the Raval, where the medieval hospital, the shipyards, and Sant Pau del Camp, Barcelona's oldest church, are the main attractions, along with Richard Meier's rationalist MACBA (Museu d'Art Contemporani de Barcelona) and the CCCB (Centre de Cultura Contemporània de Barcelona) next door.

The medieval intimacy of the Gothic Quarter balances the grace and distinction of the wide boulevards in the Moderniste Eixample, while Roman walls and columns provide counterpoint to sleek new 21st-century structures in the Raval or the Olympic Port. A visit to Gaudí's Sagrada Família followed by a quick hop over to the Mediterranean Gothic Santa Maria del Mar will leave your senses reeling with the gap between Catalan Art Nouveau ornamentation and the early Catalan Gothic's classical economy. Even more dramatically, proceed from Domènech i Montaner's Moderniste showstopper, the Palau de la Música Catalana, to Mies van der Rohe's minimalist masterpiece, the Barcelona Pavilion: from more and more to less and less. For a look at the future, keep an eye on Ricardo Bofill's projected hotel in the form of a sail at the base of the Rompeolas (breakwater) in the port, or take a tram ride east from Ciutadella–Vil.la Olímpica into the Diagonal Mar district, taking in, along the way, Ricardo Bofill's Teatre Nacional de Catalunya, Rafael Moneo's Auditori, Jean Nouvel's rocket ship–like Torre Agbar, and the Fòrum building by Herzog & de Meuron.

another lovely, glass- and stone-encased dining emporium best admired from afar but avoided. (The vacuum-packed, nuked risottos leave a lot to be desired.) At Nos. 23–25 is Barcelona's most comprehensive ceramics display, at **Art Escudellers,** with a branch across the street at No. 14. Next door, with chickens roasting over the corner, is **Los Caracoles,** once a not-to-be-missed Barcelona restaurant (now somewhat touristy and dated). Even now, the wooden bar, and the walk-through kitchen on the way in are picturesque, as are the dining rooms and tiny stairways within. Unfortunately, the cuisine is mediocre and expensive, and the clientele is almost entirely composed of tourists. Another hundred yards down Carrer Escudellers is **Plaça George Orwell,** named for the author of *Homage to Catalonia,* a space created to bring light and air into this traditionally squalid neighborhood. The little flea market that hums along on Saturday is a great place to browse.

Take a right on Carrer de la Carabassa and walk down this cobbled alley with graceful bridges between several houses and their former gardens. At the end of the street, looming atop her own basilica, is **Nostra Senyora de la Mercè** (Our Lady of Mercy). This giant representation of Barcelona's patron saint is a 20th-century (1940) addition to the roof of the 18th-century Església de la Mercè; the view of La Mercè gleaming in the sunlight, babe in arms, is one of the Barcelona waterfront's most impressive sights. As you arrive at Carrer Ample, note the **15th-century door** with a winged Sant Miquel archangel delivering a squash backhand to a scaly Lucifer; it's from the Sant Miquel church, formerly part of City Hall, torn down in the early 19th century. From the Mercè, a walk out Carrer Ample (to the right) leads back to the Rambla. Don't miss the grocery store on the corner of Carrer de la Carabassa—**La Lionesa,** at Carrer Ample 21, one of Barcelona's best-preserved 19th-century shops. At No. 7 is the **Solé** shoe store, with handmade shoes from all over the world. You might recognize Plaça Medinaceli, next on the left, from Pedro Almodovar's film *Todo sobre Mi Madre* (*All about My Mother*); from the scene featuring the heroine's dog and her aging father. Ⓜ*Drassanes.*

⓫ **Carrer Petritxol.** Just in from the Rambla and one of Barcelona's most popular streets, lined with art galleries, *xocolaterías* (hot chocolate shops), and bookstores, this narrow passageway dates back to the 15th century, when it was used as a shortcut through the backyard of an eponymous property owner. Working up Petritxol from Plaça del Pi, stop to admire the late-17th-

---

### LA MERCÈ VS. SANTA EULÀLIA

Barcelona's patron saint, Our Lady of Mercy, known as La Mercè, took over as the city's chief protector in 1714. Until then, La Mercè had been co-patroness with Santa Eulàlia, the beautiful daughter of a Sarrià merchant martyred for her Christian faith in the 4th century. Legend has it that the rains that fall on every late-September Mercè Festa Major are the tears of Santa Eulàlia shed in a jealous fury over her loss of municipal status. February's Santa Eulàlia fiesta is, for many faithful *eulalistes,* the true celebration of Barcelona's earliest patron saint.

century *sgraffiti* (chiseled, extruding ornamentation on walls), some of the city's best, on the facade over the **Roca** knife store, *the* place for cutlery in Barcelona. Next on the right at Petritxol 2 is the 200-year-old **Dulcinea** hot-chocolate refuge, with a portrait of the great Catalan playwright Àngel Guimerà (1847–1924) over the fireplace and plenty of cozy nooks for conversation and the house specialty, the *suizo* (literally, "Swiss": hot chocolate and whipped cream). Also at Petritxol 2 is the **Llibreria Quera,** one of the city's best hiking and mountaineering bookstores.

## GEOMETRICAL BARCELONA

Barcelona's three geometrically named communications arteries, Avinguda Diagonal, Avinguda Meridiana, and Avinguda del Paral.lel were devised by Ildefons Cerdà, the urban planner who designed the post-1860 Eixample (Expansion), as high-speed urban thoroughfares that would break and drain the checkerboard symmetry of his vast urban grid. The Paral.lel is so named because it parallels the equator. The Meridiana is perpendicular to the Paral. lel and parallels the Greenwich Meridian. And Diagonal runs at an oblique angle across the Eixample.

Note the plaque to Àngel Guimerà over No. 4 and the **Art Box** gallery at Nos. 1–3 across the street. At No. 5 is **Sala Parès,** founded in 1840, the dean of Barcelona's art galleries and the site for many important art shows, featuring artists like Isidre Nonell, Santiago Russinyol, and Picasso. Farther up are the gallery **Trama** at No. 8 and the **Galeria Petritxol** at No. 10. **Xocoa** at No. 9 is another popular chocolate spot. Look carefully at the "curtains" carved into the wooden door at No. 11 and the floral ornamentation around the edges of the ceiling inside. **Granja la Pallaresa,** yet another enclave of chocolate and *ensaimada* (a light-looking but deathly sweet Majorcan roll in the shape of a snail, with confectioner's sugar dusted on top). Finally on the left at No. 17 is the **Rigol** fine arts supply store. Ⓜ *Liceu.*

❾ **Casa Bruno Quadros.** Like something out of an amusement park, this former umbrella shop was whimsically designed (assembled is more like it) by Josep Vilaseca in 1885. A Chinese dragon with a parasol, Egyptian balconies and galleries, and a Peking lantern all bring exotic touches that were very much in vogue at the time of the Universal Exposition of 1888. Now housing the Caixa de Sabadell bank, this prankster of a building is theoretically in keeping with Art Nouveau's eclectic playfulness, though it has never been taken very seriously as an expression of Modernisme and, consequently, is generally omitted from most studies of Art Nouveau architecture. ✉ *La Rambla 82, Rambla* Ⓜ *Liceu.*

❹ **Església de Betlem.** The Church of Bethlehem is one of Barcelona's few baroque buildings and hulks stodgily on the Rambla just above the Rambla de les Flors. Burned out completely at the start of the Spanish civil war in 1936, the church lacks opulence once inside, whereas the outside, spruced up, is made of what looks like quilted stone. If you find this one of the world's more unsightly churches, don't feel bad: you're in the company of all of Barcelona with the possible exception of Betlem's parishioners. This was where Viceroy Amat claimed the hand of the young virreina (wife)-to-be when in 1780 she was left in the lurch by the viceroy's nephew. In a sense, Betlem has compensated the city with the half century of good works the young widow was able to accomplish with her husband's fortune. The Nativity scenes on display down the stairs at the side entrance on the Rambla at Christmastime are an old tradition here, allegedly begun by St. Francis of Assisi, who assembled the world's first in Barcelona in the early 13th century. ✉*Xuclà 2, Rambla* ☎*93/318–3823* Ⓜ*Catalunya.*

❸ **Font de Canaletes.** This fountain is a key spot in Barcelona, being the place where all great sports victories are celebrated by jubilant (and often unruly) *Barça* fans. It was originally known for the best water in Barcelona, brought in by *canaletes* (small canals) from the mountains. The bronze plaque on the pavement in front of the fountain explains in Catalan that if you drink from these waters, you will fall under Barcelona's spell and forever return…so beware. ✉*Top of Rambla, Rambla* Ⓜ*Catalunya.*

NEED A BREAK? **Café de l'Opera** (✉*La Rambla 74, Rambla* ☎*93/317–7585* Ⓜ*Liceu*), across from the Liceu opera house, is a favorite Barcelona hangout and a good place to people-watch and bump into someone you might not have expected to encounter—always a mixed blessing. The Thonet chairs and acid-engraved mirrors lend historic charm.

⓭ **Hotel España.** A cut alongside the jagged edge of the Sant Agustí church leads straight to the Hotel España, remodeled in 1904 by Lluís Domènech i Montaner, architect of the Moderniste flagship Palau de la Música Catalana. The interior is notable for its Art Nouveau decor. The hotel is recommendable only for aesthetes who prefer art over life (or, in any case, comfort), as the rooms are less than perfect. The sculpted marble Eusebi Arnau mantelpiece in the breakfast room and the Ramon Casas murals (with mermaids who have legs down to their flippers) in the dining room are, along with the lushly ornate dining room, the hotel's star artistic features. ✉*Carrer Sant Pau 9–11, Raval* ☎*93/318–1758* ⊕*www.hotelespanya.com* Ⓜ*Liceu.*

⓲ **Monument a Colom** *(Columbus Monument).* This Barcelona landmark to Christopher Columbus sits grandly at the foot of the Rambla along the wide harbor-front promenade of the Passeig de Colom, not far from the very shipyards (**Drassanes Reials**) that constructed two of the ships of his tiny but immortal fleet. Standing atop the 150-foot-high iron column—the base of which is aswirl with gesticulating angels—Columbus seems to be looking out at "that far-distant shore," which he was able to discover thanks to the patronage of Ferdinand and Isabella. In truth, he is pointing—with his 18-inch-long finger—in the general direction of Sicily. The monument was erected for the 1888 Universal Exposition to commemorate the "Discoverer's" commissioning, in Barcelona, by the monarchs in 1491. Since the royal court was at that time (and, until 1561, remained) itinerant, Barcelona's role in the discovery of the New World is, at best, circumstantial. In fact, Barcelona was consequently excluded from trade with the Americas by Isabella, so Catalonia and Columbus have never really seen eye to eye. For a bird's-eye view over the Rambla and the port, take the elevator to the small viewing area at the top of the column. (The entrance is on the harbor side.) ⊠ *Portal de la Pau s/n, Rambla* ☎ *93/302–5224* ☒ *€2.30* ⊙ *Daily 9–8:30* Ⓜ *Drassanes.*

❼ **Palau de la Virreina.** The neoclassical Virreina Palace, built by a viceroy to Peru in 1778, is now a major center for changing exhibitions of paintings, photography, and historical items. The building also houses a bookstore and a municipal tourist office. Beautiful accents on the exterior include the portal doorway and pediments carved with elaborate floral designs. ⊠ *Rambla de les Flors 99, Rambla* ☎ *93/301–7775* ⊕ *www.bcn.es/virreinaexposicions* ☒ *Free; €3 charge for some exhibits* ⊙ *Mon.–Sat. 11–8, Sun. 11–3* Ⓜ *Liceu.*

❺ **Palau Moja.** The first palace to occupy this corner on the Rambla was built in 1702 and inhabited by the Marquès de Moja. The present austere palace was completed in 1790 and, with the Betlem church across the street, forms a small baroque-era bottleneck along the Rambla. If there are temporary exhibitions in the Palau Moja, getting inside will also give you a look at the handsome mural and ceiling paintings by Francesc Pla, known as *el Vigatà* (with reference to his native town of Vic). In the late 19th century the Palau Moja was bought by Antonio López y López, Marquès de Comillas, and it was here that Jacint Verdaguer, Catalonia's national poet and chaplain of the marquess's multi-million-dollar Compañia Transatlántica shipping company, wrote his famous patriotic epic poem "L'Atlàntida." ⊠ *Portaferrissa 1, Rambla* ☎ *93/316–2740* ⊙ *On rare occasions for temporary exhibits* Ⓜ *Catalunya.*

❶ **Plaça de Catalunya.** Barcelona's main transport hub, Plaça de Catalunya, is the frontier between the Old City and the post-1860 Eixample. Comparable in size to Paris's Place de l'Étoile or to Rome's St. Peter's Square, Plaça de Catalunya is generally an unavoidable place to scurry across at high speed on your way to somewhere quieter, shadier, and generally gentler on the senses. The only relief in sight is the ⇨ **Café Zurich**, at the head of the Rambla and the mouth of the metro, which remains the classic Barcelona rendezvous point. The block behind the Zurich, known as El Triangle, houses a strip of megastores, including FNAC and Habitat, among others. Corte Inglés, the monstrous ocean-liner-esque department store on the northeast side of the square, offers Spanish goods at standard prices and in good quality.

The underground **tourist office** on the northeast corner is the place to pick up free maps of the city and check on walking tours, some in English, that originate there. The most interesting items in this large but mostly uncharming square are the sensual and exuberant sculptures. Starting from the corner nearest the head of the Rambla, have a close look at, first, the blocky Subirachs monument to Francesc Macià, president of the Generalitat (autonomous Catalan government) from 1934 to 1936. In the center of the reflecting pool is Clarà's stunning *Déesse* (*Goddess*), kneeling gracefully in the surface film. At the northwest

corner is Gargallo's heroic bronze of men, women, and oxen haul-
ing in the grape harvest, and at the northeast corner across from the
Corte Inglés is the Federic Marès bronze of a buxom maiden on horse-
back holding a model of Columbus's ship used to "discover" the New
World. Ⓜ*Catalunya.*

**⑲ Port.** Beyond the Columbus monument—behind the ornate Duana
(now headquarters for the Barcelona Port Authority)—is the **Rambla
de Mar,** a boardwalk with a drawbridge designed to allow boats into
and out of the inner harbor. The Rambla de Mar extends out to the
**Moll d'Espanya,** with its Maremagnum shopping center, IMAX theater, and the excellent aquarium. Next to the Duana, you can board a
Golondrina boat for a tour of the port or, from the Moll de Barcelona
on the right, take a cable car to Montjuïc or Barceloneta. You can
also take a boat to the end of the *rompeolas* (breakwater), 3 km (2
mi) out to sea, and walk back into Barceloneta. Trasmediterránea and
the fleeter Buquebus passenger ferries leave for Italy and the Balearic
Islands from the Moll de Barcelona, down to the right. At the end of
the quay is Barcelona's World Trade Center, a complex of offices, convention halls, restaurants, and a hotel. Ⓜ*Drassanes.*

# THE BARRI GÒTIC: MEDIEVAL SPLENDOR

No other city in Spain displays an ancient quarter that rivals Barcelona's Barri Gòtic in either historic atmosphere or sheer wealth of monumental buildings. The Gothic Quarter—a jumble of medieval buildings,
squares, and streets—is the name given to the area around the Catedral
de la Seu, still packed with Roman ruins and the Gothic structures of
the late Middle Ages that marked the zenith of Barcelona's power in the
15th century. On certain corners you feel as if you're making a genuine
excursion back into time, and, for a brief flash, suddenly the 21st century, not the 15th, seems like a figment of your imagination.

The Gothic Quarter rests squarely upon the first ancient Roman settlement. Sometimes referred to as the *rovell d'ou* (egg yolk), this high
ground the Romans called Mons Taber coincides almost exactly with
the early-1st- to 4th-century Roman Barcino. Plaça del Rei (considered one of Barcelona's best plazas), the Roman underground beneath
the City History Museum, Plaça Sant Jaume and the area around the
onetime Roman Forum, the medieval Jewish Quarter, or Call, and
the ancient Plaça Sant Just complete this tour. All in all, this nearly
entirely pedestrianized area contains Roman, Gothic, and even Moderniste treasures.

*Numbers in the text correspond to numbers in the margin and on the
Barri Gòtic map.*

### A GOOD WALK

Begin at Barcelona's cathedral, the **Catedral de la Seu ❶,** impressive in
its own spiky, stained-glass way but far from Barcelona's best building.
Don't miss the cathedral's Capella de Santa Llúcia (St. Lucie Chapel) or
the inside of the Roman wall visible in the Arxiu Històric de la Ciutat

in the **Casa de l'Ardiaca** ❷ across the street. Back to the left (northeast) of the cathedral is the **Museu Frederic Marès** ❸, with some superb masterpieces of devotional medieval sculpture (also enjoy the terrace café, surrounded by Roman walls). Next, pass the patio of the Arxiu de la Corona d'Aragó (Archives of the House of Aragón) in the **Palau del Lloctinent** ❹; then turn left again and down into **Plaça del Rei** ❺, the oldest and most evocative square of the Gothic Quarter.

As you leave Plaça del Rei, the **Museu d'Història de la Ciutat** ❻ is on your left. In this museum you can peruse the Roman city underground, one of Barcelona's most fascinating sites. Returning to the rear of the apse of the cathedral, walk left up Carrer Paradís to No. 4, Barcino's highest point and home of the hiking club **Centre Excursioniste de Catalunya (CEC)–Columnes del Temple d'August** ❼, outside which are the perfectly preserved 2,000-year-old pillars of the Roman temple named for emperor Caesar Augustus. Beside the cathedral cloister on Carrer del Bisbe in **Plaça de Garriga Bachs** ❽, a ceramic mural depicts the capture and execution by *garrote vil* (vile garrot) of 1818 Catalan resistance fighters. Through the narrow passageway to the right is **Plaça Sant Felip Neri** ❾, a picturesque nook, leading through to the **Baixada de Santa Eulàlia** ❿, with its overhead monument honoring one of the city's two female patron saints. Returning to the cathedral cloister past the modern-medieval Hotel Neri and tiny baroque jewel church of Sant Sever at No. 11 (open Thursday 5 PM–7 PM), go right on Carrer del Bisbe and walk under the much-derided Bridge of Sighs–like neo-Gothic bridge over the street to **Plaça Sant Jaume** ⓫. Here the seats of Catalonian and Barcelona government face each other across what was once part of the Roman Forum. Both the **Generalitat de Catalunya** ⓬ and the **Casa de la Ciutat–Ajuntament de Barcelona** ⓭ (city hall) are superb places to visit, among the best concentrations of art and architecture in Barcelona. (And don't miss the fragrant Anormis-Irene herb and medicinal-plant shop across Carrer Ciutat from the city hall.) El Call, the city's medieval Jewish Quarter, is nearby.

Back in Plaça Sant Jaume, walk in to the left of the Casa de la Vila and take your first left on Carrer d'en Hèrcules down to **Plaça Sant Just** ⓮, with its church and Gothic fountain. From Plaça Sant Just walk left out Carrer Dagueria (so named for medieval dagger makers), past Katherine McLaughlin's superb cheese store, La Seu, out to Carrer Sant Jaume, where a right leads down to Plaça del Àngel. From here, Carrer Tapineria leads around to the front of the cathedral, past the **Casa de la Pia Almoina–Museu Diocesà** ⓯. Make your way through Plaça Nova past the Col.legi d'Arquitectes (with the Picasso frieze of Sardanas on the facade facing the cathedral) and the **Reial Cercle Artístic** ⓰ with its beautiful Gothic voussoir, or keystone arch, over the door, down to Carrer Montsió, where a right takes you to the **Els Quatre Gats–Casa Martí** ⓱, from 1897 to 1903 a famous haunt for Barcelona's artistic, literary, and musical elite. Pablo Picasso had his first solo exhibition here in 1900.

TIMING    This walk covers some 3 km (2 mi) and should take about three hours, depending on stops. Allow another hour or two for the City History

Museum. Plan to visit before 1:30 or after 4:30, or you'll miss a lot of street life; some churches are closed, too.

**HOW TO GET THERE**  The best way to get to the Gothic Quarter and the cathedral is to start down the Rambla from the Plaça Catalunya metro stop. Take your first left on Carrer Canuda and walk past Barcelona's Ateneu Barcelonès at No. 6, through Plaça Villa de Madrid and its Roman tombstones, and then through Passatge and Carrer Duc de la Victoria and out Carrer Boters (named for early boot makers) to Plaça Nova.

**WHAT TO SEE: MAIN ATTRACTIONS**

**⑩ Baixada de Santa Eulàlia** *(Slope of Santa Eulàlia)*. Straight out from the side door of the cathedral cloister down Carrer Sant Sever past the Església de Sant Sever is the tiny overhead niche dedicated to Santa Eulàlia, the city's most honored martyr. You look up at this shrine, which is in a kind of alcove. Down this hill, or *baixada* (descent), Eulàlia was rolled in a barrel filled with—as the Jacint Verdaguer verse in ceramic tile on the wall reads—*glavis i ganivets de dos talls* (swords and double-edged knives), the final of the 13 tortures to which the 4th-century martyr was subjected before her crucifixion at Plaça del Pedró. ✉ *Carrer Sant Sever, past Carrer Sant Domènec del Call, Barri Gòtic* Ⓜ *Catalunya, Liceu, Jaume I.*

**2**

**② Casa de l'Ardiaca** *(Archdeacon's House).* The interior of this building, home of the municipal archives (upstairs), has superb views of the inside of the 4th-century Roman watchtowers and walls. Look at the Montjuïc sandstone carefully and you will see blocks taken from other buildings, carved and beveled into decorative shapes, proof of the haste of the Romans as the Visigoths approached from the north at the end of the Pax Romana. The marble letter box by the front entrance was designed in 1895 by Lluís Domènech i Montaner for the Lawyer's Professional Association and, as the story goes, is meant to symbolize, in the images of the doves, the lofty flight to the heights of justice and, in the images of the turtles, the plodding pace of administrative procedures. The lovely courtyard here, across from the Santa Llúcia chapel, is centered around a fountain and, on the day of Corpus Christi in June, it's one of the Gothic Quarter's most impressive *l'ou com balla,* or "dancing egg," a Barcelona tradition of placing an egg atop the spurts of water from the city's fountains to celebrate. ⊠ *Carrer de Santa Llúcia 1, Barri Gòtic* ☎ *93/318–1342* ⊕ *www.bcn.es* ⊗ *Mon.–Sat. 10–2 and 4–8, Sun. 10–2* Ⓜ *Catalunya, Liceu, Jaume I.*

**⑬ Casa de la Ciutat–Ajuntament de Barcelona.** The 15th-century city hall on Plaça Sant Jaume faces the Palau de la Generalitat across what was once the Roman Forum, with its mid-18th-century neoclassical facade. Any opportunity to spend time inside the city hall should be taken, as it is a rich repository for sensual sculptures, paintings, and historical sites. Around the corner to the left is a surprise: the early-15th-century Flamboyant Gothic facade with part of an arch superglued to the abutting neoclassical part (look carefully in the right corner). Inside is the famous Saló de Cent, from which the Council of 100 ruled Barcelona between 1249 and 1714. The Saló de les Croniques is filled with Josep Maria Sert's immense black-and-burnished-gold mural (1928) depicting the early-14th-century Catalan campaign in Byzantium and Greece under the command of Roger de Flor. Check out Sert's changing perspective technique that makes his paintings seem to follow you around the room. Endowed with art and sculptures by the great Catalan masters from Marès to Gargallo to Clarà to Subirachs, the interior of the city hall is open to visitors on Sunday and for occasional concerts or events held in the Saló de Cent. ⊠ *Pl. Sant Jaume 1, Barri Gòtic* ☎ *93/402–7000* ⊕ *www.bcn.es* ⊗ *Sun. 10–1* Ⓜ *Catalunya, Liceu.*

**★ ① Catedral de la Seu.** Barcelona's cathedral (named for La Seu, or See, the seat of the bishopric) is impressively filled with many centuries of city history and legend, even if it does fall short as a memorable work of architecture. This imposing Gothic monument was built between 1298 and 1450, with the spire and neo-Gothic facade added in 1892, and even these not completed until 1913. Historians are not sure about the cathedral architect—one name much bandied about is Jaume Fabre, a native of Majorca. The plan of the church is cruciform, with transepts standing in as bases for the great tower—a design also seen in England's Exeter Cathedral. Floodlighted in striking yellow beams at night with the stained-glass windows backlighted from inside and ghostly seagulls soaring over the spiky Gothic spires, Barcelona's main religious build-

# El Call: The Jewish Quarter

Its name derived from the Hebrew word *qahal* (meeting place, or place to be together), Barcelona's Jewish Quarter is just to the Rambla side of the Palau de la Generalitat. Carrer del Call, Carrer de Sant Domènec del Call, Carrer Marlet, and Arc de Sant Ramón del Call mark the heart of the 7th- to 14th-century quarter. Enclosed in this area at the end of the 7th century, Barcelona's Jews were the private financial resource of Catalonia's sovereign counts (only Jews could legally lend money). One reason the streets in Calls or Aljamas were so narrow was that their inhabitants could only build into the streets for more space. The Jewish community produced many leading physicians, economists, and scholars in medieval Barcelona, largely because practicing the Jewish faith required Bible study, thus ensuring a high degree of literacy. The reproduction of a plaque bearing Hebrew text on the corner of Carrer Marlet and Arc de Sant Ramón del Call was the only physical reminder of the Jewish presence here until the medieval synagogue reopened in 2003.

The **Sinagoga Major de Barcelona** ( ✉ *Carrer Marlet 2* ⊕ *www.call-debarcelona.org* ▣ *€2* ☾ *Tues.–Sat. 11–2, Sun. 4–7*), the restored original synagogue at the corner of Marlet and Sant Domènec del Call, is the principal remaining evidence of the Jewish presence in Catalonia. Tours are given in English, Hebrew, and Spanish, and a booklet in English (€5) explains the history of the community. The saga of Barcelona's Jewish community came to its culminating moment in August 1391 when, during a time of famine and pestilence, a nationwide outbreak of anti-Semitic violence reached Barcelona with catastrophic results: nearly the entire Jewish population was murdered or forced to convert to Christianity.

ing is only a bronze medalist behind the Mediterranean Gothic Santa Maria del Mar and Gaudí's Moderniste La Sagrada Família.

This is reputedly the darkest of all the world's great cathedrals—even at high noon, the nave is enveloped by shadows, which give it magically much larger dimensions than it actually has—so it takes a while for eyes to adjust to the rich, velvety pitch of the cathedral. Among the many sights worth seeking out are the beautifully carved choir stalls of the Knights of the Golden Fleece; the intricately and elaborately sculpted organ loft over the door out to Plaça Sant Iu (complete with a celebrated Saracen's Head sculpture); the series of 60-odd wood sculptures of men and women along the outside lateral walls of the choir in a nearly animated succession of evangelistic poses; the famous cloister; and, in the crypt, Santa Eulàlia's tomb.

St. Eulàlia, originally interred at Santa Maria del Mar—then known as Santa Maria de les Arenes (St. Mary of the Sands)—was moved to the cathedral in 1339 and is the undisputed heroine and patron of the Barcelona cathedral. *Eulalistas* (St. Eulàlia devotees, as opposed to followers of La Mercé, or Our Lady of Mercy, Barcelona's official patron) celebrate the fiesta of *La Laia* (the nickname for Eulàlia) February 9–15, and they would prefer that the cathedral be named for their favorite martyr. For the moment, the cathedral remains a virtual no-name cathedral, known universally as La Catedral and more rarely as La Seu.

Appropriately, once you enter the front door (there are also lateral entrances through the cloister and from Carrer Comtes down the left side of the apse), the first thing you see are the high-relief sculptures of the **story of St. Eulàlia,** on the near side of the choir stalls. The first scene, on the left, shows St. Eulàlia in front of Roman Consul Decius with her left hand on her heart and her outstretched right hand pointing at a cross in the distance. In the next scene to the right, Eulàlia is tied to a column and being whipped by Decius-directed thugs. To the right of the door into the choir the unconscious Eulàlia is being hauled away, and in the final scene on the right she is being lashed to the X-shape cross upon which she was crucified in mid-February of the year 303. To the right of this high relief is a sculpture of St. Eulàlia, standing with her emblematic X-shape cross, resurrected as a living saint.

Among the two dozen ornate and gilded chapels dedicated to all the relevant saints of Barcelona and beyond, one chapel to seek out is the **Capilla de Lepanto,** in the far right corner as you enter through the front door. The main attraction here is the Santo Cristo de Lepanto. This 15th-century polychrome wood sculpture of a somewhat battle-scarred, dark-skinned Christ, visible on the altar of this 100-seat chapel behind a black-clad Mare de Deu dels Dolors (Our Lady of Sorrow), was, according to oral legend, the bowsprit of the commanding Spanish galley at the battle fought between Christian and Ottoman fleets on October 7, 1571.

Note that the explanatory plaque next to the alms box at the right front of the chapel states that, though John of Austria was the commander-in-chief of the Holy League's fleet, the fleet captain and main battle commander was Lluís de Requesens (1528–76), a local Catalan aristocrat and prominent Spanish general during the reign of Felipe II.

Outside the main nave of the cathedral to the right you'll find the leafy, palm tree–shaded **cloister** surrounding a tropical garden and pool filled with 13 snow-white geese, one for each of the tortures inflicted upon St. Eulàlia in an effort to break her faith. Legend has it that they are descendants of the flock of geese of Rome's Capitoline Hill, whose honking alarms roused the city to ward off invaders during the ancient days of the Roman Republic. Don't miss the fountain with the bronze sculpture of an equestrian St. George hacking away at his perennial sidekick, the dragon, on the eastern corner of the cloister. On the day of Corpus Christi this fountain is one of the more-spectacular floral displays, featuring *l'ou com balla* (the dancing egg). The intimate **Santa Llúcia chapel** is at the front right corner of the block (reached by a separate entrance or from the cloister). Another Decius victim (although in this version he merely wanted her body), St. Llúcia allegedly plucked out her eyes to dampen the Roman consul's ardor, whereupon new ones were miraculously generated. Patron saint of seamstresses, of the blind, and of the light of human understanding, St. Lucía is portrayed over the altar in the act of presenting her plucked-out eyes, sunny-side-up on a plate, to an impassive Decius.

In front of the cathedral is the grand square of the **Plaça de la Seu,** where, Saturday 6 PM–8 PM, Sunday morning, and occasional evenings, Barcelona folk gather to dance the *sardana,* the somewhat dainty and understated circular dance, a great symbol of Catalan identity. Watch carefully: mixed in with heroic septuagenarians bouncing demurely are some young *esbarts* (dance troupes) with very serious coaches working on every aspect of their performance, from posture to the angle of arms to the cat's paw–like smooth footwork. The

> **L'OU COM BALLA, BARCELONA'S DANCING EGG**
>
> Barcelona's early June Corpus Christi celebration is a favorite day to visit the city's finest patios to see fountains adorned with the *ou com balla* (dancing egg) balancing miraculously atop the jet of water. The egg, in Christian ritual a symbol of fertility, represents the rebirth of life after Easter's tragic events. In the Mediterranean's megalithic religions that preceded Christianity, the dancing egg augured a successful growing season as spring turned to summer.

rings of dancers deep in concentration repeat the surprisingly athletic movements and steps that represent a thousand years of tradition. Also check out the listings for the annual series of evening organ concerts held inside the cathedral. ✉ *Pl. de la Seu, Barri Gòtic* ☎ *93/315–1554* ⊕ *www.catedralbcn.org* 🎟 *€4 for special visit* ☾ *Daily 7:45* AM*–7:45* PM*; during a special visit, 1–5* PM*, visitors can see entire cathedral, museum, bell tower, and rooftop* Ⓜ *Catalunya, Liceu, Jaume I.*

**❼ Centre Excursioniste de Catalunya (CEC)–Columnes del Temple d'August** *(Outing Center of Catalonia–Columns of the Temple of Augustus).* The highest point in Roman Barcelona is marked with a circular millstone at the entrance to the Centre Excursioniste de Catalunya, a club dedicated to exploring the mountains and highlands of Catalonia on foot and on skis. Inside this entryway on the right are some of the best-preserved 1st- and 2nd-century Corinthian Roman columns in Europe. Massive, fluted, and crowned with the typical Corinthian acanthus leaves in two distinct rows under eight fluted sheaths, these columns remain only because Barcelona's early Christians elected, atypically, not to build their cathedral over the site of the previous temple. The Temple of Augustus, dedicated to the Roman emperor Augustus, occupied the northwest corner of the Roman Forum, which coincided approximately with today's Plaça Sant Jaume. ✉ *Carrer Paradís 10, Barri Gòtic* ☎ *93/315–2311* ☾ *Mon.–Sat. 10–2 and 5–8, Sun. 11–2* Ⓜ *Catalunya, Liceu.*

**★ ⓱ Els Quatre Gats–Casa Martí.** Built by Josep Puig i Cadafalch in 1896 for the Martí family, this Art Nouveau house just three minutes' walk from the cathedral houses the Quatre Gats café and restaurant, a good place for a coffee or even a meal, and the legendary hangout of Modern-iste minds. The exterior is richly decorated with Eusebi Arnau sculptures, featuring the scene of St. George and the dragon that no Puig i Cadafalch project ever failed to include. Arnau (1864–1934) was the sculptural darling of the Moderniste movement. The interior is spectacularly hung with reproductions of some famous Ramon Casas paintings, such as the scene of the Toulouse Lautrec–ish Casas and the rangy Pere Romeu comedically teamed up on a tandem bicycle—one of the most iconic images of Barcelona. The restored (in 2000) Joseph Llimona sculpture of St. Joseph and the Infant Jesus gleaming whitely over St. George and the dragon was torn down in the anticlerical violence of July 1936. Picasso had his first opening here on February 1, 1900, and Antoni Gaudí hung out with Moderniste painters from Casas to Russinyol to the likes of Nonell and Anglada Camarassa, so the creative reverberations ought to be strong. *Quatre Gats* means "four cats" in Catalan, a euphemism for "hardly anybody," but the original four—Casas, Russinyol, and Utrillo, hosted by Pere Romeu— were all definitely somebodies. ⊠ *Carrer Montsió 3 bis, Barri Gòtic* ☎ *93/302–4140* ⊕ *www.4gats.com* ☾ *Mid-Aug.–July, daily 9* AM*–2* AM Ⓜ *Catalunya, Liceu.*

**⑫ Generalitat de Catalunya.** Housed in the Palau de la Generalitat, opposite city hall, this is the seat of the autonomous Catalan government. Through the front windows of this ornate 15th-century palace, the gilded ceiling of the Saló de Sant Jordi (Hall of St. George), named for Catalonia's dragon-slaying patron saint, gives an idea of the lavish decor within. The Generalitat opens to the public only on the Día de Sant Jordi (St. George's Day), April 23, during the Fiesta de la Mercé in late September, and on various other city or Catalonian holidays. The Generalitat hosts carillon concerts on Sunday at noon, another opportunity to see the inside of the building. ⊠ *Pl. de Sant Jaume 4, Barri Gòtic* ☎ *93/402–4600* ⊕ *www.gencat.net* ☾ *On special occasions only; to visit, check with Protocol office calling through main telephone number* Ⓜ *Catalunya, Liceu.*

**⑥ Museu d'Història de la Ciutat** *(City History Museum).* This fascinating

FodorśChoice ★

museum just off the Plaça del Rei traces the evolution of Barcelona from its first Iberian settlement to its founding by the Carthaginian Hamilcar Barca in about 230 BC to Roman and Visigothic times and beyond. Antiquity is the focus here: Romans took the city during the Punic Wars, and the striking underground remains of their *Colonia Favencia Julia Augusta Paterna Barcino* (Favored Colony of the Father Julius Augustus Barcino), through which you can roam on metal walkways, are the museum's main treasure. Archaeological finds include parts of walls and fluted columns as well as recovered busts and vases. Around ⇨ **Plaça del Rei** are the **Palau Reial Major,** the splendid **Saló del Tinell,** the chapel of **Santa Àgata,** and the **Torre del Rei Martí,** a lookout tower with views over the Barri Gòtic. ⊠ *Palau Padellàs, Carrer del Veguer 2, Barri Gòtic* ☎ *93/315–1111* ⊕ *www.museuhistoria.bcn. es* 🖾 *€5 (also covers admission to Monestir de Pedralbes, Center for the Interpretation and Welcome to Parc Güell, Museu Verdaguer–Vil. la Joana, and Museu Diocesà). Free 1st Sat. of month 4–8* ☾ *Tues.–Sat. 10–8, Sun. 10–3* Ⓜ *Catalunya, Liceu, Jaume I.*

**⑤ Plaça del Rei.** This plaza is widely considered the oldest and most beautiful space in the Gothic Quarter. Long held to be the scene of Columbus's triumphal return from his first voyage to the New World—the precise spot where Ferdinand and Isabella received him is purportedly on the stairs fanning out from the corner of the square (though evidence indicates that the Catholic monarchs were at a summer residence in the Empordá)—the **Palau Reial Major** was the official royal residence in Barcelona. The main room is the **Saló del Tinell,** a magnificent banquet hall built in 1362. Other elements around the square are, to the left, the ⇨**Palau del Lloctinent** (Lieutenant's Palace); towering overhead in the corner is the dark 15th-century **Torre Mirador del Rei Martí** (King Martin's Watchtower). The 14th-century **Capilla Reial de Santa Àgueda** (Royal Chapel of St. Agatha) is on the right side of the stairway, and behind and to the right as you face the stairs is the **Palau Clariana-Padellàs,** moved to this spot stone by stone from Carrer Mercaders in the early 20th century and now the entrance to the ⇨**Museu d'Història de la Ciutat.** Ⓜ*Catalunya, Liceu, Jaume I.*

❾ **Plaça Sant Felip Neri.** A tiny square just behind ⇨**Plaça de Garriga Bachs** off the side of the cloister of the Catedral de la Seu, this space was once the cemetery for Barcelona's executed heroes and villains, before all church graveyards were moved to the south side of Montjuïc where the municipal cemetery now resides. A favorite spot for early-music concerts, the square is centered on a fountain, whose trickling—a constant E-flat—fills the square with its own water music. A bomb explosion during the Spanish civil war caused the pockmarks on the walls of the San Felip Neri church. Ⓜ*Catalunya, Liceu.*

⓫ **Plaça Sant Jaume.** This central square behind the city cathedral houses the government buildings of Catalonia, the ⇨**Generalitat de Catalunya** in the Palau de La Generalitat, and that of Barcelona, the ⇨**Casa de la Ciutat–Ajuntament de Barcelona.** This was the site of the Roman Forum 2,000 years ago, though subsequent construction filled the space with buildings. The square was cleared in the 1840s, but the two imposing government buildings facing each other across it are much older. Ⓜ*Catalunya, Liceu, Jaume I.*

**NEED A BREAK?** If you feel inclined to take a breather in a Pakistani restaurant, where you can get a table between two 4th-century Roman watchtowers, seek out **El Gallo Kiriki** (✉*Carrer d'Avinyó 19, Barri Gòtic* ☎*93/301–0280*), just a block west of Plaça Sant Jaume, for either lunch or a beverage. **Cafè de l'Acadèmia** (✉*Carrer Lledó 18, Barri Gòtic* ☎*93/319–8253*) fills with government workers at lunchtime. If a coffee is all you need, look for the **Mesón del Café** (✉*Carrer Llibreteria 16, Barri Gòtic* ☎*93/315–0754*), where a deep breath is nearly as bracing as a cappuccino.

## ALSO WORTH SEEING

⓯ **Casa de la Pia Almoina–Museu Diocesà** *(Diocesan Museum).* This 11th-century Gothic alms house, now a museum, once served *sopa boba* (literally, "dumb soup") to 100 of the city's poor, hence its popular name, Pia Almoina (pious alms). Along with temporary art exhibits, the museum houses a permanent collection of religious sculptures and a potpourri of liturgical paraphernalia, from monstrances to chalices to the 12th-century paintings from the apse of the Sant Salvador de Polinyà chapel. Anyone beginning a tour of the Roman walls should take a look at the excellent relief map/scale model of Roman Barcelona (map and model are sold in the nearby Museu d'Història de la Ciutat, the city history museum) in the vestibule. Inside, Roman stones are clearly visible in this much-restored structure, the only octagonal tower of the 82 that ringed the 4th-century Barcino. Look for the Romanesque *Mares de Deu* (Mother of God) wood sculptures such as the one from Sant Pau del Camp church in Barcelona's Raval. The museum is behind the massive iron floral grate in the octagonal Roman watchtower to the left of the stairs of the Catedral de la Seu. ⊠ *Av. de la Catedral 4, Barri Gòtic* ☎ *93/315–2213* ⊠ *€8* ☉ *Tues.–Sat. 10–2 and 5–8, Sun. 11–2* Ⓜ *Catalunya, Liceu, Jaume I.*

**Col.legi d'Arquitectes.** Barcelona's architects' college, constructed in 1961 by Xavier Busquets, houses three important gems: a superb library (across the street) where for a small fee the college's bibliographical resources are placed at your disposal for architectural research purposes; a bookstore specializing in architecture, design, and drafting supplies; and a nonpareil restaurant (one of the city's great secrets). And let's not forget the Picasso friezes just above the college's windows, designed by the artist in 1960. Inside the building are two more Picasso friezes, one a vision of Barcelona and the other a poem dedicated to the *sardana,* Catalonia's national dance. ⊠ *Pl. Nova 5, Barri Gòtic* ☎ *93/306–7801* ⊕ *www.coac.net* ☉ *Mon.–Sat. 10–8* Ⓜ *Catalunya, Liceu.*

**OFF THE BEATEN PATH**

**Museu del Calçat.** Hunt down the tiny Shoe Museum, in a hidden corner of the Gothic Quarter between the cathedral and Carrer Banys Nous for a whimsical tour through the world of footwear. The collection includes a pair of clown's shoes and a pair of shoes worn by Pablo Casals. ⊠ *Pl. Sant Felip Neri, Barri Gòtic* ☎ *93/301–4533* ⊠ *€2.50* ☉ *Tues.–Sun. 11–2* Ⓜ *Catalunya, Liceu, Jaume I.*

❸ **Museu Frederic Marès** *(Frederic Marès Museum).* Here, in a building off the left (north) side of the cathedral, you can browse for hours among the miscellany assembled by the early-20th-century sculptor-collector Frederic Marès. Everything from paintings and polychrome wood carvings—such as Juan de Juní's 1537 masterpiece *Pietà* and the Master of Cabestany's late-12th-century *Apparition of Christ to His Disciples at Sea*—to Marès's personal collection of pipes and walking sticks is stuffed into this surprisingly rich potpourri. ⊠ *Pl. Sant Iu 5, Barri Gòtic* ☎ *93/310–5800* ⊕ *www.museumares.bcn.es* ⊠ *€3; free 1st Sun. of month and Wed. afternoon* ☉ *Tues.–Sat. 10–7, Sun. 10–3* Ⓜ *Catalunya, Liceu, Jaume I.*

❹ **Palau del Lloctinent** *(Lieutenant's Palace).* The three facades of this fine building face the Carrer dels Comtes de Barcelona on the cathedral side, the Baixada de Santa Clara, and the Plaça del Rei. Typical of late Gothic–early Renaissance Catalan design, it was constructed by Antoni Carbonell in 1557 and remains one of the Gothic Quarter's most graceful buildings. The heavy stone arches over the entry, the central patio, and the intricately carved roof over the stairs are all good examples of noble 16th-century architecture. The door on the stairway, which replaced an equestrian Sant Jordi sculpture identical to the one over the door of the Generalitat, is a 1975 Antoni Subirachs work portraying scenes from the life of Sant Jordi. The Palau del Lloctinent was inhabited by the king's official emissary or viceroy to Barcelona during the 16th and 17th centuries and is now open to the public for occasional concerts, and for the Corpus Christi celebration, when an egg is made to "dance" on the fountain amid an elaborate floral display in the patio. ⊠ *Carrer dels Comtes de Barcelona s/n, Barri Gòtic* ☎ *93/485–4285* Ⓜ *Catalunya, Liceu.*

❽ **Plaça de Garriga Bachs.** Ceramic murals depicting executions of heroes of the Catalan resistance to Napoleonic troops in 1809 flank this little space just outside the cloister of the Catedral de la Seu. The first three scenes show the five resistance leaders waiting their turns to be garroted or hanged (the *garrote vil,* or vile garrote, was reserved for the clergymen, as hanging was considered a lower and less-humane form of execution). The fourth scene depicts the surrender of three agitators who attempted to rally a general Barcelona uprising to save the first five by ringing the cathedral bells. The three are seen here, pale and exhausted after 72 hours of hiding in the organ, surrendering after being promised amnesty by the French. All three were subsequently executed. Ⓜ *Catalunya, Liceu.*

⓮ **Plaça Sant Just.** Off to the left side of city hall down Carrer Hèrcules (named for the mythical founder of Barcelona) are this square and the site of the Església de Sant Just i Pastor, one of the city's oldest Christian churches, dating from the 4th century. Christian catacombs are reported to have been found beneath Plaça Sant Just. The Gothic fountain was built in 1367 by famed Barcelona councilman Joan Fiveller. Fiveller had discovered a spring in the Collserola hills and had the water piped straight to Barcelona. The fountain bears an image of St. Just and city and sovereign count-kings' coats of arms, along with a pair of falcons. The excellent entryway and courtyard to the left of Carrer Bisbe Caçador is the Palau Moixó, the town house of an important early Barcelona family, while down Carrer Bisbe Caçador is the Acadèmia de Bones Lletres, the Catalan Arts and Letters Academy. The church is dedicated to the boy martyrs Just and Pastor; the Latin inscription over the door translates into English almost in reverse syntax as "Our pious patron is the black and beautiful Virgin, together with the sainted children Just and Pastore." Ⓜ *Catalunya, Liceu.*

⓰ **Reial Cercle Artístic.** This private fine arts society has two art galleries and a restaurant and bar open to the public; it also offers drawing and painting classes. The main entrance with its heavy keystone arch, the stone carvings inside to the right in the Sala Güell, and the sculptures along the stairway are all elegant and graceful Gothic details worth stopping for. The restaurant upstairs is intimate and inexpensive, while the terrace outside provides a semi-invisible perch over the street. The food is adequate for a light soup or salad. ⊠ *Carrer dels Arcs 5, Barri Gòtic* ☎ *93/318–7866* ⊙ *Mon.–Sat. 10–7, Sun. 10–3* Ⓜ *Catalunya, Liceu.*

# THE RAVAL: WEST OF THE RAMBLA

El Raval (from *arrabal,* meaning "suburb" or "slum") is the area to the west of the Rambla, on the right as you walk toward the port. Originally a rough outskirt of town stuck outside the second set of city walls that ran down the left side of the Rambla, the Raval used to be notorious for its Barri Xinès (or Barrio Chino) red-light district, the lurid attractions of which are known to have fascinated the young Pablo Picasso. Gypsies, acrobats, prostitutes, and *saltimbanques* (clowns and circus performers) who made this area their home soon found immortality in the many canvases Picasso painted of them during his Blue Period. It was the ladies of the night on Carrer Avinyó, not far from the Barri Xinès, who inspired one of the 20th-century's most famous paintings, Picasso's *Les Demoiselles d'Avignon,* an important milestone on the road to Cubism. Not bad for a city slum.

The Raval, though still rough and ready, has been gentrified and much improved since 1980, largely as a result of the construction of the Museu d'Art Contemporani de Barcelona (MACBA) and the other cultural institutions nearby, such as the Centre de Cultura Contemporània (CCCB) and the Convent dels Àngels. The Rambla del Raval has been opened up between Carrer de l'Hospital and Drassanes, and light and air are pouring into the streets of the Raval for the first time in a thousand years. The medieval Hospital de la Santa Creu, Plaça del Pedró, the Mercat de Sant Antoni, and Sant Pau del Camp are highlights of this helter-skelter, rough-and-tumble part of Barcelona. The only part to consider avoiding is the lower part between Carrer de Sant Pau and the back of the Drassanes Reials shipyards on Carrer del Portal Santa Madrona, and it's a good idea not to carry a backpack or a handbag.

*Numbers in the text correspond to numbers in the margin and on the Raval map.*

## A GOOD WALK

Starting from Plaça de Catalunya, take an immediate right after the Font de Canaletes into Carrer Tallers, named for butchers, tailors, or small textile factories (shops), depending on whether you're using Catalan or Spanish. Go left through Carrer de les Sitges to Plaça del Bonsuccés and take a right on Carrer Elisabets at the generally excellent Bar Castells, with its convenient marble counter outside on the corner. Stay on Elisabets past Llibreria La Central del Raval, presently a bookstore but once the chapel for the **Casa de la Misericòrdia** ❶, a former center for wayward or orphaned women, next door. Walk out into Plaça dels Àngels, where the medieval penumbra is suddenly brightened by Richard Meier's gleaming **Museu d'Art Contemporani de Barcelona** ❷, known as MACBA. To the left is the **Convent dels Àngels** ❸, while behind the MACBA is the **Centre de Cultura Contemporània de Barcelona** ❹ (CCCB), a rolling potpourri of art exhibits, musical events, lectures, and films. Beyond that is the **Casa de la Caritat–Pati Manning** ❺, yet another cultural institution. Head back toward the MACBA and take Carrer de Ferlandina out to Carrer Joaquin Costa, where you will see Bar Almirall, a landmark Art Nouveau saloon. Go left all the way down Joaquin

Costa to Carrer del Carme and turn left past an even more beautiful Art Nouveau bar, Bar Muy Buenas, with its curving wooden arches, acid-etched glass, and a marble bar that was once a codfish-salting basin.

Continuing down Carrer del Carme, you will reach the back entrance to the medieval **Antic Hospital de la Santa Creu i Sant Pau ❻**. Cut to the right into this entrance. The first door and patio to your right is the former Casa de la Convalescència (Convalescence House), now the Institut d'Estudis Catalans. Continue through the patio of the medieval hospital where you will pass the doors, on your right, to a reading room of the Biblioteca de Catalunya and, to the left, the children's library. Continue through the orange trees in the patio of the hospital. The main section of the library, one of Barcelona's finest Gothic spaces, is up the stairway to the right after the orange grove. Leaving the Escola Massana art school on your right, you will emerge through the massive wooden doors into Carrer Hospital. First, go left to look at the **Capella de l'Antic Hospital de la Santa Creu ❼**, now used as a space for art exhibits; then turn around and walk back down Carrer Hospital, past the tempting Passatge Bernardí Martorell (with a good restaurant, Casa Leopoldo, at the end of it) to **Plaça del Pedró ❽**. From here, walk out Carrer de Sant Antoni Abad, past the former Sant Antoni chapel, to the **Mercat de Sant Antoni ❾**, a combination flea, food, clothes, and (on Sunday) stamp market. From here follow the Ronda de Sant Pau east toward the port, cut left on Carrer de les Flors, and you will pass the excellent Cal Isidre restaurant before reaching Barcelona's oldest church, **Sant Pau del Camp ❿**. From here it's just 300 yards to Drassanes Reials, Barcelona's medieval shipyard, and the bottom of the Rambla.

TIMING    The Raval covers a lot of ground. Plan on a four-hour walk or break your exploration into two two-hour hikes. The cloister of Sant Pau del Camp is open only in the afternoon.

HOW TO GET    Begin this Raval exploration at Plaça Catalunya, with its convenient
THERE    metro stop. Walk down the Rambla and take your first right into Carrer Tallers, working your way through to the MACBA.

**WHAT TO SEE: MAIN ATTRACTIONS**

❻ **Antic Hospital de la Santa Creu i Sant Pau.** Founded in the 10th century,
Fodor'sChoice    this is one of Europe's earliest medical complexes and contains some of
★    Barcelona's most stunningly graceful Gothic architecture, built mostly in the 15th and 16th centuries. Approached through either the Casa de la Convalescència entry on Carrer del Carme or through the main door on Carrer Hospital, the cluster of medieval architecture surrounds a garden courtyard and a midtown orange grove. The first stone was laid by King Martí el Humà (Martin the Humane) in 1401. As you approach from Carrer del Carme, the first door on the left is the **Reial Acadèmia de Cirurgia i Medecina** (Royal Academy of Surgery and Medicine), a neoclassical 18th-century building of carved stone. On the right is the 17th-century Casa de la Convalescència, and straight ahead is the simple 15th-century Gothic facade of the hospital itself, with the light of the inner cloisters gleaming through the arched portal. The Royal Academy of Surgery and Medicine—open for visits until

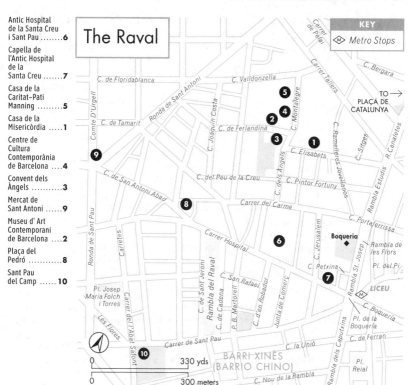

2 PM on weekdays—contains an amphitheater originally used for the observation of dissections. Across the way is the door into the patio of the **Casa de la Convalescència** (Convalescence House), with its Renaissance columns and its brightly decorated scenes of the life of St. Paul in the vestibule. The primarily blue and yellow *azulejos* (ceramic tiles) start with the image to the left of the door into the inner courtyard portraying the moment of the saint's conversion: SAVLE, SAVLE, QUID ME PERSEGUERIS (Saul, Saul, why do you persecute me?). The ceramicist, Llorenç Passolas, was also the creator of the late-17th-century tiles around the inner patio. The image of St. Paul in the center of the courtyard over what was once a well is an homage to the building's initial benefactor, Pau Ferran. Look for the horseshoes, two of them around the keyholes, on the double wooden doors in the entryway, wishing good luck to the convalescent and, again, in reference to benefactor Ferran, from *ferro* (iron), as in *ferradura* (horseshoe).

Past the door to the Biblioteca Infantil, the children's library, on both sides of the courtyard, is the 1.5-million-volume **Biblioteca de Catalunya** ( ✉*Carrer Hospital 56 or Carrer del Carme 45, Raval* ☎*93/270–2300* ⊕*www.bnc.cat* ☾ *Weekdays 9–8, Sat. 9–2*), national library of Catalunya and Spain's second in scope after Madrid's Biblioteca Nacional. The hospital patio, centered on a baroque cross, is filled with orange trees and usually also with students from the Escola Massana art school at the far end on the right. The stairway under the arch on the right leading to the main entrance of the Biblioteca de Catalunya was built in the 16th century, while the Gothic well to the left of the arch is from the 15th century, as is the little Romeo-and-Juliet balcony in the corner to the left of the Escola Massana entry. Inside the library, the wide Gothic arches and vaulting of what was once the hospital's main nave were designed in the 15th century by the architect of Santa Maria del Pi church, Guillem Abiell, who was seeking light and a sense of space. This was the hospital where Antoni Gaudí was taken after he was struck by a trolley on June 7, 1926. Among the library's collections are archives recording Gaudí's admittance and photographs of the infirmary and the private room where he died. The library's staggering resources range from silver medieval book covers to illuminated manuscripts from the *Llibre Vermell* (Red Book), the Catalonian songbook. Guided tours can be arranged at the main desk. Leaving through the heavy wooden door out to Carrer Hospital, from the far sidewalk you can see the oldest section of the medieval hospital, part of the old Hospital de Colom founded by the canon Guillem Colom in 1219 to the left of the door. The facade itself is from the 16th century. ⊠ *Carrer Hospital 56 (or Carrer del Carme 45), Raval* ☎ *93/270–2300* Ⓜ *Catalunya, Liceu.*

❹ **Centre de Cultura Contemporània de Barcelona** *(CCCB)*. No matter what's on the schedule, this multidisciplinary gallery, lecture hall, and concert and exhibition space is worth checking out. Housed in the restored and renovated Casa de la Caritat, a former medieval convent and hospital, the CCCB is, like the Palau de la Música Catalana, one of Barcelona's best combinations of contemporary and traditional architecture and design. A smoked-glass wall on the right side of the patio, designed by architects Albert Villaplana and Helio Piñon, reflects out over the rooftops of the Raval to Montjuïc and the Mediterranean beyond. ⊠ *Montalegre 5, Raval* ☎ *93/306–4100* ⊕ *www.cccb.org* 🎫 *€6; free entry to patio and bookstore* ⓢ *Tues., Thurs., and Fri. 11–2 and 4–8, Wed. and Sat. 11–8, Sun. 11–7* Ⓜ *Catalunya.*

❷ **Museu d'Art Contemporani de Barcelona** *(Barcelona Museum of Contemporary Art; MACBA).* Designed by American architect Richard Meier in 1992, this gleaming explosion of light and geometry in the darkest corner of Raval houses a permanent collection of contemporary art as well as traveling exhibits. With barely a nod to Gaudí (via the amorphous tower in front of the main facade), Meier's exercise in minimalism (resembling, to some degree, a bathroom turned inside-out) has been much debated in Barcelona. Basque sculptor Jorge Oteiza's massive bronze *La Ola (The Wave)* on the MACBA's front porch is popular with skateboard surfers, while the late Eduardo Chillida's *Barcelona* climbs the wall to the left of the main entrance in the sculptor's signature primitive blocky black geometrical patterns. The MACBA's 20th-century contemporary art collection (Calder, Rauschenberg, Oteiza, Chillida, Tàpies) is excellent, as is the guided tour carefully introducing the philosophical bases of contemporary art as well as the pieces themselves. ⊠ *Pl. dels Àngels s/n, Raval* ☎ *93/412–0810* ⊕ *www.macba.es*

FodorśChoice
★

## The Fragrances of Sant Ponç

The Raval's big day is May 11, when Carrer Hospital celebrates the Fira de Sant Ponç, a beloved Barcelona holiday. The feast day of Sant Ponç, patron saint of herbalists and beekeepers, brings Catalonia's *pagesos* (country folk) to Barcelona laden with every natural product they can haul. Everything from bees in glass cases working at their honeycombs to chamomile, rosemary, thyme, lavender, basil, pollens, mint, honeys of every kind, candied fruits, snake oil, headache remedies, and aphrodisiacs, and every imaginable condiment and savory from fennel to saffron to coriander to tarragon, takes over the city's streets and, more important, the air. The mere mention of Sant Ponç to any barcelonin is guaranteed to elicit a backward inclination of the head, closing (perhaps even fluttering) of the eyelids, and a deep and luxuriant inhalation.

Everyone seems to find time, especially if the weather is good, to take a walk from the Rambla out to Carrer Hospital to the Rambla del Raval to browse through artisanal sausage, goat cheese, wild mushrooms, cakes, jams, herbal olive oils, homemade wines, pies, cheesecakes, fig bread, hand-carved wooden spoons, knives and forks, teas, coffees, and a thousand medicinal herbal potions and lotions. In medieval times, as farmers cleared their larders for the harvest to come, medicinal herbalists and the sorceress fringe promptly hijacked this tradition and set up stalls along the walls of the 15th-century hospital (where, presumably, there was a heightened interest in their products). Today Sant Ponç is the official start of the Catalonian summer and one of Barcelona's sweetest days.

€7, €3 Wed.; temporary exhibits €4 additional ☉ Mon. and Wed.–Fri. 11–7:30, Sat. 10–8, Sun. 10–3; free guided tours daily at 6, Sun. at noon Ⓜ Catalunya.

🔟 **Sant Pau del Camp.** Barcelona's oldest church was originally outside the

Fodor's Choice

★ city walls (*del camp* means "in the fields") and was a Roman cemetery as far back as the 2nd century, according to archaeological evidence. A Visigothic belt buckle found in the 20th century confirmed that Visigoths used the site as a cemetery between the 2nd and 7th centuries. What you see now was built in 1127 and is the earliest Romanesque structure in Barcelona, redolent of the pre-Romanesque Asturian churches or of the pre-Romanesque Sant Michel de Cuxà in Prades, Catalunya Nord (Catalonia North, aka southern France). Elements of the church—the classical marble capitals atop the columns in the main entry—are thought to be from the 6th and 7th centuries. The hulking mastodonic shape of the church is a reminder of the church's defensive posture in the face of intermittent Roman persecution and, later, Moorish invasions and sackings. Check carefully for musical performances here, as the church is an acoustical gem. Note the tiny stained-glass window high on the facade facing Carrer Sant Pau. If Santa Maria del Pi's rose window is Europe's largest, this is quite probably the smallest. The tiny cloister, the only way in during afternoon opening hours, is Sant Pau del Camp's best feature, one of Barcelona's semisecret treasures. From inside the church, the right side of the altar leads out into this patio surrounded by porches or arcades. Sculpted Corinthian capitals portraying biblical scenes support triple Mudejar arches. This penumbral sanctuary is a gift from the ages barely a block from the busy Avinguda del Paral.lel. ⊠ *Sant Pau 101, Raval* ☎ *93/441–0001* ⊠ *€2* ⊙ *Cloister weekdays 4:30–7:30; Sun. mass at 10:30, 12:30, and 8* PM Ⓜ *Catalunya, Liceu, Paral.lel.*

## ALSO WORTH SEEING

❼ **Capella de l'Antic Hospital de la Santa Creu** *(Chapel of the Old Hospital of the Holy Cross).* Now an art gallery, the chapel is generally open for a browse through an art or photography exhibit and a look at the lovely vaults and arches. The sculpture over the chapel door is a baroque 18th-century representation of Charity by Pere Costa, who also did the lower part of the facade of the unfinished Sant Agustí church just down from Carrer Hospital toward the Rambla. Don't miss the ancient wooden choir loft at the back of the chapel or a look up into the cupola towering over the central nave. This quiet refuge is between the Carrer Hospital entrance to the medieval hospital and the Rambla. ⊠ *Carrer Hospital 54, Raval* Ⓜ *Catalunya, Liceu.*

❺ **Casa de la Caritat–Pati Manning.** The Centre d'Estudis i Recursos Culturals de la Diputació de Barcelona (Center for Cultural Studies and Resources of the Diputació de Barcelona) is one of the three cultural entities (the others are the **Museu d'Art Contemporani de Barcelona** and the **Centre de Cultura Contemporània de Barcelona**) that occupy what were once the grounds and buildings of a 14th-century Carthusian convent. Pati Manning–Espai Cultural (Cultural Space) includes a library, lecture halls, and exhibition galleries in which cultural and artistic initiatives of all kinds are organized. ⊠ *Carrer de Montalegre 7, Raval* ☎ *93/402–2565* ⊕ *www.diba.es/cerc/pati.asp* ⊙ *Weekdays 11–7, Sat. 10–8, Sun. 10–3* Ⓜ *Catalunya.*

❶ **Casa de la Misericòrdia.** This pretty ivy-covered courtyard with palm trees and vines was once a school and a home for female orphans and the children of the destitute. The home was founded in 1581 by theologian Don Diego Pérez de Valdivia. The excellent bookstore **La Central del Raval,** next door at Carrer Elisabets 6, was the former chapel of the Casa de la Misericòrdia. Around the corner (or through the bookstore) on Carrer dels Ramelleres at No. 17, a ring of wood in the wall just above waist level is all that remains of the ancient *torno,* or turntable, standard in early orphanages and cloistered convents. Alms, groceries, and unwanted babies alike were placed in this opening slot, to be spun anonymously into the Casa de la Misericòrdia. ⊠ *Carrer Elisabets, Raval* ☎ *93/302–1692* Ⓜ *Catalunya.*

❸ **Convent dels Àngels.** This former Augustinian convent directly across from the main entrance to the MACBA, built by Bartolomeu Roig in the middle of the 16th century, has been converted into a general cultural center with an exhibition hall (El Fòrum dels Àngels), a bookstore, a 150-seat auditorium, and a restaurant and bar. The Foment dels Arts Decoratives (FAD) now operates this handsome Raval resource.

## The Barrio Chino

Sandwiched between the Pigalle-like Avinguda del Paral.lel and the lower Rambla, Barcelona's most notorious district, the Barrio Chino, has raged raucous and unrepentant for centuries. For many years it was nearly more emblematic and characteristic of the city than, say, Gaudí or the Gothic Quarter. Local denizens inspired many of Picasso's paintings of circus acrobats and gypsies. Though all of the Raval has been commingled with the Barrio Chino (Barri Xinès in Catalan, Chinese Quarter in English, but known universally as the Barrio Chino), the authentic, hard-core "Chino" is everything between Carrer Hospital and the port on the bottom right side of the Rambla facing east.

China and the Chinese never had anything to do with all this: the Barrio Chino's name is a generic reference to all foreigners, as the area was inhabited by immigrants from other parts of Spain or from abroad. Even today, in Plaza dels Àngels in front of the MACBA, children playing soccer can be heard speaking Arabic, Urdu, and Tagalog, as well as Spanish and Catalan. French novelist Jean Genet wrote a novel (*La Marge*) about the Barro Chino, as did Pierre de Mandariargues; the prostitutes, transvestites, pimps, gypsies, and common thieves provided colorful literary textures.

Though there are pockets still used as havens for prostitutes, drug pushers, and thieves, the Barrio Chino is not nearly as dangerous as it once was. The police presence here may even make it safer than the Rambla or parts of the Gothic Quarter—but don't count on it. The Rambla del Raval runs through the middle of what used to be no-man's-land, bringing fresh air into what was once the most insalubrious and unsafe part of Barcelona.

The Forum dels Àngels is an impressive space with beautifully carved and restored sculptures of angels in the corners and at the top of the walls. ☒ *Pl. dels Àngels, Raval* ☎ *93/443–7520* ⊕ *www.fadweb.org* ☉ *Mon.–Sat. 9–9, Sun. 10–2* Ⓜ *Catalunya.*

❾ **Mercat de Sant Antoni.** An interesting spot for browsing—both for its artistic value and for its jumble of produce on sale—the Sant Antoni market is one of Barcelona's semisecret gems. This mammoth steel hangar at the junction of Ronda de Sant Antoni and Comte d'Urgell was designed in 1882 by Antoni Rovira i Trias, the winner of the competition for the planning of Barcelona's Eixample. Considered the city's greatest masterpiece of ironwork architecture, the Greek cross–shape market covers an entire block on the edge of the Eixample. A combination food, clothing, and flea market, it becomes a book, comics, stamp, and coin fest on Sunday. Though many of the food produce stalls inside remain closed, there are a few excellent bars and restaurants and some of the finest Moderniste stall facades in Barcelona. The hushed environment is reminiscent of the Boqueria market before it became Europe's most celebrated food fair. For market cuisine and good value well off the beaten tourist track, this lofty space merits a look. ☒ *Carrer Comte d'Urgell s/n, Raval* ☎ *93/443–7520* ☉ *Mon.– Sat. 9–9, Sun. 10–2* Ⓜ *Catalunya, Sant Antoni.*

**❽ Plaça del Pedró.** This landmark in medieval Barcelona was the dividing point where ecclesiastical and secular paths parted. The high road, Carrer del Carme, leads to the cathedral and the seat of the bishopric, whereas the low road, Carrer de l'Hospital, heads down to the medieval hospital and the Boqueria market, a clear choice between body and soul. Named for a stone pillar, or *pedró* (large stone), marking the fork in the road, the square became a cherished landmark for Barcelona Christians after Santa Eulàlia, co-patron of Barcelona, was crucified there in the 4th century on her distinctive X-shape cross after suffering the legendary 13 ordeals designed to persuade her to recant, which she, of course, heroically refused to do. As the story goes, an overnight snowfall chastely covered her nakedness with virgin snow. The present version of Eulàlia and her cross was sculpted by Barcelona artist Frederic Marès and erected in 1951. The bell tower and vacant alcove at the base of the triangular square are the **Sant Llàtzer** church, originally built in the open fields in the mid-12th century and used as a leper hospital and place of worship after the 15th century when Sant Llàtzer (Saint Lazarus) was officially named patron saint of lepers. Presently in the process of being rescued from the surrounding buildings that once completely obscured the church, the Sant Llàtzer chapel has a tiny antique patio and apse visible from the short Carrer de Sant Llàtzer, which cuts behind the church between Carrer del Carme and Carrer Hospital. Ⓜ *Catalunya, Liceu.*

# SANT PERE & LA RIBERA: THE MEDIEVAL TEXTILE & WATERFRONT DISTRICTS

Barcelona has rarely lain dormant architecturally, as these two districts prove. A medley of artistic styles going back centuries, this area is studded with some of the city's most iconic buildings, ranging from the light and elegant 14th-century basilica of Santa Maria del Mar—a church of the purest Catalan Gothic—to the flagship of the city's Moderniste architecture, the extraordinary Palau de la Música Catalana. Past and present collide at the Museu Picasso, where works of the great 20th-century master are displayed in three adjoining Renaissance palaces.

Sant Pere, Barcelona's old textile neighborhood, is centered on the church of Sant Pere. A half mile closer to the port, set between lower Via Laietana and the Parc de la Ciutadella, the Barri de la Ribera and the former market of El Born, now known as the Born-Ribera district, formed the hub and headquarters for Catalonia's great maritime and economic expansion of the 13th and 14th centuries. Surrounding the basilica of Santa Maria del Mar, the Born-Ribera area includes Carrer Montcada, lined with 14th- to 18th-century Renaissance palaces; Passeig del Born, where medieval jousts were held; Carrer Flassaders and the area around the early mint, La Seca, behind Carrer Montcada; the shop- and restaurant-rich Carrer Banys Vells; Plaça de les Olles; and Pla del Palau, where La Llotja, Barcelona's early maritime exchange, housed the fine arts school where Picasso, Gaudí, Domènech i Montaner, and all of Barcelona's artistic icons studied.

La Ribera began a revival in the 1980s and, with its intimate bars, cafés, taverns, and shops, continues to gain ground as one of the hottest quarters of the city for both shops and saloons. El Born, the onetime central market of Barcelona, now offers a fascinating view of pre-1714 Barcelona, dismantled by the victorious troops of Felipe V at the end of the War of the Spanish Succession. The Passeig del Born, considered the Rambla of medieval Barcelona—"*Roda al mon i torn al Born*" ("Go around the world but return to the Born") went the saying—has once again taken its place as one the city's hubs of dining, shopping, and art and architecture browsing.

*Numbers in the text correspond to numbers in the margin and on the Sant Pere, La Ribera, La Ciutadella & Barceloneta map.*

## A GOOD WALK

Sant Pere and La Ribera lie, respectively, generally to the north and east of the Gothic Quarter across Via Laietana. From the central Plaça de Catalunya, it's no more than a 15-minute walk through Portal de l'Àngel and Carrer Comtal, past the sgraffiti-adorned Casa Gremial dels Velers (the silk weavers guild) to the architectural extravaganza that is the **Palau de la Música Catalana** ❶. After taking in the Palau music hall, continue along Carrer Sant Pere Més Alt (literally, Upper St. Peter's Street) to the Plaça Sant Pere on your way past the spirit-haunted church of **Sant Pere de les Puelles** ❷. From here, cut back along Carrer Sant de Pere Més Baix (Lower St. Peter's Street) to the **Biblioteca Popular de la Dona Francesca Bonnemaison** ❸ at No. 7 before walking through Carrer Beates and across to the modernized but historic covered **Mercat de Santa Caterina** ❹. Walk through Carrer Semoleres into Plaça de la Llana, named for the wool (*llana*) industry once centered here, and turn left on Carrer Corders, named for the makers of rope (*corda*) who once worked here. The **Capella d'en Marcús** ❺ is the curious little chapel stuck in against neighboring structures at the end of Carrer Montcada.

Down Carrer Montcada across Carrer Princesa is one of the city's greatest cultural treasures, the **Museu Picasso** ❻, in five of the noble merchant mansions of the Calle Montcada. Across the street at No. 12 is the **Museu Textil i de l'Indumentària–Palau de los Marqueses de Lló** ❼, with one of Carrer Montcada's best two patios, along with **Palau Dalmases** ❽. Continue through Carrer Montcada's treasury of Renaissance palaces to the tunnel-like Arc de Sant Vicenç, where a loop through Carrer de la Seca, Carrer Cirera, **Carrer Flassaders** ❾, and back along **Passeig del Born** ❿ will get you back to Placeta Montcada and the back door of the noted sailors' church of **Santa Maria del Mar** ⓫. Walk up the right side of the church on Sombrerers (named for the medieval makers of, you guessed it, sombreros) and make an aromatic stop at the Gispert nuts, teas, coffees, spices, and herbs store, one of Barcelona's oldest and loveliest shops. Walk around the church's eastern side through the **Fossar de les Moreres** ⓬, a cemetery to **Plaça de les Olles** ⓭.

Another side trip from Santa Maria del Mar begins on the other (west) side of the church on **Carrer Banys Vells** ⓮, lined with beautiful shops and restaurants. At the end of Bany Vells, turn left on Carrer Barra de Ferro and work your way back through Carrer de la Carassa, noting the sculpted *carassa* (a stone face announcing a medieval brothel) over the corner of Carassa and Mirallers. Walk down Mirallers, taking a right on Grunyí out to Argenteria, where a left will take you back to the main facade of Santa Maria del Mar and the excellent wine-tasting bar La Vinya del Senyor. Duck through the brief 30 feet or so of Carrer Anissadeta (Barcelona's shortest street) and go left on Carrer Canvis Vells past the excellent Moroccan shop Baraka to the early maritime exchange **La Llotja ⓯**. Then go through Trompetas past the tiny door under the heavy wooden 15th-century beams and stone pillars at No. 14, said to have been an early residence of the Picasso family, to Carrer Agullers, home of two of Barcelona's best emporiums of wines and cheeses, the Viniteca, and the little Vila grocery store on the corner opposite, all run and owned by the friendly and knowledgeable Vila family.

TIMING  Depending on the number of stops, this walk can take a full day. Count on at least four hours of actual walking time. Catching Santa Maria del Mar open is key (it's closed 1:30–4:30). If you make it to Cal Pep for tapas before 1:30, you might get a place at the bar; if you don't, waiting's a pleasure. The Picasso Museum is at least a two-hour visit.

HOW TO GET  From the central Plaça Catalunya metro hub, it's just a 10-minute walk
THERE  over to the Palau de la Música Catalana for the beginning of this tour. The yellow line's Jaume I metro stop is closer to Santa Maria del Mar, but between the hassle of underground train changing and the pleasures of strolling the city streets, Plaça Catalunya is close enough.

**WHAT TO SEE: MAIN ATTRACTIONS**

⓬ **Fossar de les Moreres** (*Cemetery of the Mulberry Trees*). This low marble monument runs across the open space along the eastern side of the church of Santa Maria del Mar. It honors those defenders of Barcelona who gave their lives in the 1714 siege that ended the War of the Spanish Succession and established Felipe V on the Spanish throne. The inscription (EN EL FOSSAR DE LES MORERES NO S'HI ENTERRA CAP TRAIDOR, or "in the cemetery of the mulberry trees no traitor lies") refers to the story of the graveyard keeper who refused to bury those who had fought on the invading side, even when one of them turned out to be his son. This is the traditional gathering place for the most radical elements of Catalonia's nationalist (separatist) movement, Terra Lliura (Free Land), and the September 11 Catalonian national holiday tends to be emotional here.

From the cemetery, one of Santa Maria del Mar's most interesting peculiarities is easily visible. The lighter-colored stone on the lateral facade was left by the 17th-century Pont del Palau (Palace Bridge), erected to connect the Royal Palace (later military headquarters) in the nearby Pla del Palau with the Tribuna Real (Royal Box) over the right side of the Santa Maria del Mar altar, so that kings, queens, viceroys, and generals could get to mass without risking their lives in the streets of not-so-pacified Barcelona. The bridge, always regarded as a symbol of

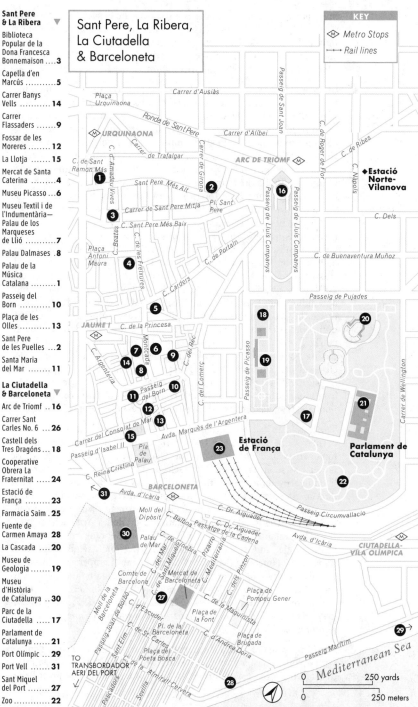

imperialist oppression, passing as it did over the Fossar de les Moreres, was finally dismantled in 1987. The controversial steel arch holding a Bunsen burner–like flame over the street, an attempt to elevate the line and intent of the war monument, was erected in 2002. ⊠ *Pl. de Santa Maria, Born-Ribera* Ⓜ *Catalunya, Jaume I.*

**⑮ La Llotja** *(Maritime Exchange).* Barcelona's Llotja, or trade center, like those of the other main commercial centers of the Corona de Aragón (Crown of Aragon, the Catalano-Aragonese confederation that dominated Mediterranean trade between the 14th and 17th century), was designed to be the city's finest example of civic architecture. Perpignan, Castelló d'Empúries, Tortosa, Valencia, Palma de Mallorca, and Zaragoza all have splendid *llotjas* dating from the 14th and 15th centuries. Originally little more than a roof to protect merchants and their wares from the elements, Barcelona's present llotja was constructed in the sweeping, wide-arched Catalan Gothic style between 1380 and 1392. At the end of the 18th century the facades were (tragically) covered in the neoclassical uniformity of the time, but the interior, the great Saló Gòtic (Gothic Hall), remained unaltered and was a grand venue for balls and celebrations throughout the 19th century. The Gothic Hall was used as the Barcelona stock exchange until 1975, and until late 2001 as the grain exchange. The hall has now been brilliantly restored, and though public visits have not been formally established, any chance to see the inside of this historic hall will reveal Gothic arches and columns and a marble floor made of light Carrara and dark Genovese marble, with little windows showing the original Montjuïc sandstone paving stones under the marble. The painted, coffered ceilings, the neoclassical patio, and the grand stairways are among La Llotja's prime treasures. ■TIP➡ **To slip into the hall, enter the Fine Arts Museum, wander over to the Saló Gòtic by walking down the stairs to the second, or main, floor and then descend the marble staircase and turn right.**

The Escola de Belles Arts (Fine Arts School) occupied the southwestern corner of the Llotja from 1849 until 1960. Many illustrious Barcelona artists studied here, including Gaudí, Miró, and Picasso, whose father was an art professor at the school. The Picasso family reportedly lived nearby under the 15th-century beams and porches at Consolat de Mar 35 (corner of Carrer Trompetes), where a half-width wooden door opens into four floors of ancient apartments with exposed ceiling beams. The **Reial Acadèmia Catalana de Belles Arts de Sant Jordi** (Royal Catalan Academy of Fine Arts of St. George) still has its seat in the Llotja, and its museum is one of Barcelona's semisecret collections of art. Nineteenth-century sculptor Damiá Campeny's voluptuous marble sculpture of a moribund Lucretia, on the main floor upstairs to the right, and the young Marià Fortuny's drawings of heroic masculine nudes are the collection's stars. ⊠ *Passeig d'Isabel II, 7, Born-Ribera* ☎ *93/319–2432 museum* ⊕ *www.racba.org* ⊠ *Museum free* ⊗ *Museum weekdays 10–2* Ⓜ *Catalunya, Jaume I.*

**❹ Mercat de Santa Caterina.** This marketplace, a splendid carnival of colors with a roller-coaster rooftop, was restored by the late Enric Miralles (though the project was finished in 2005 by his widow, architect Benedetta Tagliabue). Undulating wood and colored ceramic mosaic ceilings, recalling both Gaudí and Miró, cover a glass floor through which sections of the original building here, a 13th-century church and convent, is still visible. Alexandre Cirici i Pellicer—one of Barcelona's great art and architecture experts—identified "a certain air and aura of a North African souk." A restaurant area consisting of different bars and dining areas specializes in cuisines from Mediterranean to Asian. Typical meat and vegetable stands remain the prime attraction, though a supermarket with home delivery and an Internet ordering system have created an ultramodern facility sandwiched neatly between the neoclassical walls left standing and the medieval and Visigothic remains beneath. ⊠*Av. Francesc Cambó s/n, Born-Ribera* ☎*93/319–5740* ⊕*www.mercatsbcn.com* Ⓜ*Catalunya.*

**❻ Museu Picasso.** The Picasso Museum is housed in five adjoining palaces on Carrer Montcada, a street known for Barcelona's most elegant medieval palaces. Picasso spent his key formative years in Barcelona (1895–1904), and this collection, while it does not include a significant number of the artist's best paintings, is particularly strong on his early work. Displays include childhood sketches, works from Picasso's Rose and Blue periods, and the famous 1950s Cubist variations on Velázquez's *Las Meninas* (in Rooms 22–26). The museum was begun in 1962 on the suggestion of Picasso's crony Jaume Sabartés, and the initial donation was from the Sabartés collection. Later Picasso donated his early works, and in 1981 his widow, Jaqueline Roque, added 141 pieces. The lower-floor sketches, oils, and schoolboy caricatures and drawings from Picasso's early years in La Coruña are perhaps the most fascinating part of the whole museum, showing the facility the artist seemed to possess almost from the cradle. His *La Primera Communión (First Communion)*, painted at the age of 16, gives an idea of his early accomplishment. On the second floor you meet the beginnings of the mature Picasso and his Blue Period in Paris, a time of loneliness, cold, and hunger for the artist. ⊠*Carrer Montcada 15–19, Born-Ribera* ☎*93/319–6310* ⊕*www.museupicasso.bcn.es* 🎫*Permanent collection €6, temporary exhibits €5, combined ticket €8.50; free 1st Sun. of month* ☉*Tues.–Sat. 10–8, Sun. 10–3* Ⓜ*Catalunya, Liceu, Jaume I.*

*Fodor's*Choice
★

**❽ Palau Dalmases.** Barcelona's best 17th-century Renaissance patio is showcased here, built into a 15th-century palace. Note the heavy wooden doors leading into the patio; then take a careful look at the evocation of the Rape of Europa represented in high relief running up the baroque facade of the elegant stairway cutting across the end of the patio. Neptune's chariot, cherubic putti, naiads, dancers, tritons, and myriad musicians accompany Europa's mythological abduction by Zeus, who, in the form of a bull, carries her up the stairs and off to Crete. On either side of the door leading up the stairs, look for the minuscule representations of either putti or maidens covering their nakedness with their arms. These, along with the 15th-century Gothic chapel, with its reliefs of musical angels, and the vaulting in the reception area and in the main salon, are the only remnants of the 15th-century palace originally built here. The building is now the seat of the Omnium Cultural, a center for the diffusion of Catalan culture. Lectures, book presentations, and multiple events are open to the public. The Espai Barroc, on the ground floor, is a café with baroque-era flourishes, period furniture, and occasional musical performances. ⊠*Carrer Montcada 20, Born-Ribera* ⌷*Free* ⊗*Daily 9–2 and 4:30–7. Café Tues.–Sun. 7 PM–1 AM* Ⓜ*Catalunya, Jaume I.*

★ ❶ **Palau de la Música Catalana.** One of the world's most extraordinary music halls, with facades that are a riot of color and form, the Palau de la Música (Music Palace) is a landmark of Carrer Amadeus Vives, set just across Via Laietana, a five-minute walk from Plaça de Catalunya. From its polychrome ceramic ticket windows on the Carrer de Sant Pere Més Alt side to its overhead busts of (from left to right) Palestrina, Bach, Beethoven, and (around the corner on Carrer Amadeus Vives) Wagner, the Palau is a flamboyant tour de force designed in 1908 by Lluís Domènech i Montaner. It is today considered the flagship of Barcelona's Moderniste architecture. Originally conceived by the Orfeó Català musical society as a vindication of the importance of music at a popular level—as opposed to the Liceu opera house's identification with the Catalan (often Castilian-speaking and monarchist) aristocracy—the Palau and the Liceu were for many decades opposing cross-town forces in Barcelona's musical as well as philosophical discourse.

The exterior is remarkable in itself. The Miquel Blay sculptural group over the corner of Amadeu Vives and Sant Pere Més Alt is Catalonia's popular music come to life, with everyone included from St. George the dragon slayer (at the top) to women and children, fishermen with oars over their shoulders, and every strain and strata of popular life and music, the faces of the past fading into the background. The glass facade over the present ticket window entrance is one of the city's best examples of nonintrusive modern construction over traditional structures.

The Palau's interior is, well, a permanent uproar before the first note of music is ever heard. Wagnerian cavalry explodes from the right side of the stage over a heavy-browed bust of Beethoven; Catalonia's popular music is represented by the flowing maidens of Lluís Millet's song *Flors de Maig* (*Flowers of May*) on the left. Overhead, an inverted stained-glass cupola seems to offer the divine manna of music straight from heaven; painted rosettes and giant peacock feathers explode from the tops of the walls; and even the stage is populated with muselike Art Nouveau musicians all across the back wall. The visuals alone make music sound different here, and at any important concert the excitement is palpably thick. *Ticket office* ⊠*Sant Francesc de Paula 2 (just off Via Laietana, around corner from hall), Sant Pere* ☏*93/295-7200* ⊕*www.palaumusica.org* ⌷*Tour €9* ⊗*Tours daily 10–3:30 (10–7 July and Aug.)* Ⓜ*Catalunya.*

❿ **Passeig del Born.** Once the site of medieval jousts and Inquisitional autos-da-fé, the passeig, at the end of Carrer Montcada behind the church of Santa Maria del Mar, was early Barcelona's most important square. Late-night cocktail bars and miniature restaurants with tiny spiral stairways now line the narrow, elongated plaza. The numbered cannonballs under the public benches are the work of the "poet of space"—a 20th-century specialist in combinations of letters, words, and sculpture—the late Joan Brossa. The cannonballs evoke the 1714 siege of Barcelona that concluded the 14-year War of the Spanish Succession, when Felipe V's conquering Castilian and French troops attacked the city ramparts at their lowest, flattest flank. After their victory, the Bourbon forces obliged residents of the Barri de la Ribera (Waterfront District) to tear down nearly a thousand of their own houses, some 20% of Barcelona at that time, to create fields of fire so that the occupying army of Felipe V could better train its batteries of cannon on the conquered populace in order to repress nationalist uprisings. Walk down to the Born itself—a great iron hangar, once a produce market designed by Josep Fontseré. The initial stages of the construction of a public library in the Born uncovered the perfectly preserved lost city of 1714, complete with blackened fireplaces, taverns, wells, and the canal that brought water into the city. The Museu d'Història de la Ciutat offers free visits overlooking the ruins of the 14th- to 18th-century Barri de la Ribera on weekends 10–3. ⊠ *Born-Ribera* Ⓜ *Jaume I.*

**⑪ Santa Maria del Mar.** Ever since 1229, when Jaume I el Conqueridor
Fodor'sChoice conquered the Moors in Mallorca (to the battle cry of "Santa Maria!"),
★ his *ex voto* (pledge) was to complete a major seafarers' church in the waterfront district then known as Vilanova. The most sweepingly symmetrical and classical of all Barcelona's churches, Santa Maria del Mar is a stunning contrast to the ornate and complex architecture of later Gothic and Moderniste Barcelona. Built in a record 54 years (1329–83), the church was a stonemason's bare-bones design for a classical basilica. Santa Maria del Mar was intended to bless and protect the mighty Catalan fleet at a time when Catalonia so controlled the Mediterranean that, as the saying went, "not a fish dared swim in *Mare Nostrum* (Our Sea) without displaying the *quatre barras*" (the four stripes of the Catalan flag). Fishermen, merchant marines, stevedores, and all other seafarers were included under the patronage of Santa Maria del Mar (St. Mary of the Sea). Alfons III placed the initial stone of the long-awaited Església de la Ribera (Waterfront Church) 100 years after his great-grandfather pledged a church to protect his fleet.

The best and most beautiful existing example of early Catalan (or Mediterranean) Gothic architecture, Santa Maria del Mar is extraordinary for its unbroken lines, simplicity of form, symmetry, and elegance. The upsweeping verticality and lightness of the interior are especially surprising considering the blocky exterior surfaces. The site, originally outside the 1st- to 4th-century Roman walls at what was then the water's edge, was home to a Christian cult from the late 3rd century. In the year 303 the Christian martyr St. Eulàlia was buried at Santa Maria de les Arenes (St. Mary of the Sands). Hidden in 713 when Moors sacked the city and only recovered in 878, St. Eulàlia's remains were relocated to the Catedral de la Seu in 1339. The size of the Christian community after the mid-4th-century conversion of Emperor Constantine and the

Roman Empire's official tolerance of Christianity after the XVI Concilio de Toledo in 693 brought about the need for a larger church.

Built by a mere stonemason named Berenguer de Montagut, *magister opus* (contractor), who personally chose, fitted, and carved each stone hauled down from the same Montjuïc quarry that provided the sandstone for the 4th-century Roman walls, Santa Maria del Mar is breathtakingly, nearly hypnotically, symmetrical. The medieval numerological symbol for the Virgin Mary, the number eight (or multiples thereof) runs through every element of the basilica: The 16 octagonal pillars are 2 meters (6.5 feet) in diameter and spread out into rib vaulting arches at a height of 16 meters (52 feet). The painted keystones at the apex of the arches are 32 meters (105 feet) from the floor. Furthermore, the central nave is twice as wide as the lateral naves (8 meters each), whose width equals the difference (8 meters) between their height and that of the main nave. The result of all this proportional balance and harmony is a tonic sense of uplift that, especially in baroque and Moderniste Barcelona, is at once exhilarating and soothing.

Ironically, the church owes its present formal perfection and soaring spirituality to the anticlerical fury of the anarchists who on July 18, 1936, upon learning of the military rebellion that would plunge Spain into a bloody civil war, burned nearly all of Barcelona's churches as a reprisal against the alliance of army, church, and oligarchy. The basilica, filled with immense and ornate side chapels and mammoth wooden choir stalls, burned for 11 days, and nearly crumbled as a result of the intense heat. Restored after the end of the Spanish civil war by a series of Bauhaus-trained architects, all of whom understood the formal purity of the original design, Santa Maria del Mar has become one of the city's most universally admired architectural gems.

The interior, which should be seen when illuminated, is rich in detail. The paintings in the keystones overhead represent, from the front, the Coronation of the Virgin, the Nativity, the Annunciation, the equestrian figure of the father of Pedro IV, King Alfons, and the Barcelona coat of arms. The 34 lateral chapels are dedicated to different saints and images. The first chapel to the left of the altar (No. 20) is the Capella del Santo Cristo (Chapel of the Holy Christ), its stained-glass window an allegory of Barcelona's 1992 Olympic Games, complete with names of medalists and key personalities of the day in tiny letters. An engraved stone riser to the left of the side door onto Carrer Sombrerers commemorates the spot where San Ignacio de Loyola, founder of the Jesuit Order, begged for alms in 1524 and 1525.

The basilica's stark beauty is enhanced by a lovely southwest-facing rose window (built in 1425 and restored in 1485 after an earthquake) and unusually wide vaulting. Often compared to the German *Hallenkirche,* or single-naved church, the basilica is frequently used for choral events and early music, much of which was written precisely for this kind of space. The six-second acoustic delay, which can create mayhem in modern compositions, was planned into medieval musical scores designed to be sung or played in large spaces. Jordi Savall's Hesperion XXI early-music ensemble

CLOSE UP

## Picasso's Barcelona

The city's claim to Pablo Picasso (1881–1973) has been contested by Málaga (the painter's birthplace), as well as by Madrid, where *La Guernica* hangs, and by the town of Gernika, victim of the 1937 Luftwaffe saturation bombing that inspired the famous canvas. Picasso, an anti-Franco opponent after the war, refused to return to Franco's Spain. In turn, the regime allowed no public display of Picasso's work until 1961, when the artist's *Sardana* frieze at Barcelona's Architects' Guild was unveiled. Picasso never set foot on Spanish soil for his last 39 years.

Picasso spent a sporadic but formative period of his youth in Barcelona between 1895 and 1904, when he moved to Paris. His father was an art professor at the Reial Acadèmia de les Belles Arts in La Llotja. Picasso, a precocious draftsman, began advanced classes there at 15. The 19-year-old

Picasso first exhibited at Els Quatre Gats, a tavern still thriving on Carrer Montsió. His early Cubist painting, *Les Demoiselles d'Avignon*, was inspired not by the French town but by the Barcelona street Carrer d'Avinyó, then known for its brothel. After moving to Paris, Picasso returned occasionally to Barcelona until his last visit in 1934. Considering the artist's off-and-on tenure, it is remarkable that the city and Picasso should be so intertwined in the world's perception. The Picasso Museum, while an excellent visit, is perhaps fourth on any art connoisseur's list of Barcelona galleries.

**Iconoserveis Culturals** (✉ *Carrer Muntaner 185, Eixample* ☎ *93/410–1405* ⊕ *www.iconoserveis.com*) gives walking tours through the key spots in Picasso's Barcelona life, covering studios, galleries, family apartments, and the painter's favorite haunts and hangouts.

is always exciting to hear in this space, and any opportunity to attend a concert is highly recommended. One of Santa Maria del Mar's most magical moments is the midnight mass held on Christmas Eve, and—even more mysterious—the haunting Cant de la Sibil.la (Song of the Sibyl) sung a half hour before midnight. This pre-Christian, Mediterranean tradition dating from six centuries before Christ is performed by a countertenor and a choir of acolytes who sing an apocalyptic chant forecasting the judgment day and the coming of a messiah. Handel's *Messiah* at Christmas and Mozart's *Requiem* at Easter are annual events here, while any opportunity to hear Renaissance choral music in Santa Maria del Mar—Tomás Luís de Victoria, Guerrero, Tallis, and Byrd—especially if performed by the Sixteen or the Tallis Scholars, is an unforgettable musical feast. Santa Maria del Mar is a much-sought-after wedding spot, so you're likely to see a hopeful couple exchanging vows here on a Saturday afternoon. ✉*Pl. de Santa Maria, Born-Ribera* ⊙ *Daily 9–1:30 and 4:30–8* Ⓜ *Catalunya, Jaume I.*

NEED A
BREAK?

At **Santa Maria del Mar,** you're just a step from the best tapas in Barcelona at Cal Pep (✉*Pl. de les Olles 8, Born-Ribera* ☎*93/319–6183*). If it seems crowded, stay calm and trust Pep to seat you (preferably at the counter, where the best action occurs, from watching the chefs to meeting fellow diners) when your turn comes around. *Pan de coca* (crunchy toast with oil and fresh tomato paste), garbanzos and spinach, baby shrimp, lettuce hearts, and everything up to and including the sausage in port sauce or filet mignon is excellent.

## ALSO WORTH SEEING

**3** **Biblioteca Popular de la Dona Francesca Bonnemaison** *(Women's Public Library)*. Barcelona's (and probably the world's) first library originally established exclusively for women, this lovely spot was founded in 1909 as a female sanctuary, evidence of the city's early-20th-century progressive attitudes and tendencies. Over the opulently coffered main reading room, the stained-glass skylight reads TOTA DONA VAL MES QUAN LETRA APREN (Any woman's worth more when she learns how to read), the first line of a ballad by the 13th-century Catalan troubadour Severí de Girona. Once Franco's Spain of church, army, and oligarchy had restored law and order after the Spanish civil war, the center was taken over by Spain's one legal political party, the Falange, and women's activities were reoriented toward more domestic pursuits such as sewing and cooking. Today the library complex includes a small theater and offers a lively program of theatrical and cultural events. ⊠*Sant Pere Més Baix 7, Sant Pere* ☎*93/268–0107* ⊕*www. bonnemaison-ccd.org* ☉*Tues., Wed., and Fri. 4–9, Thurs. 10–10, Sat. 11–2* Ⓜ*Catalunya.*

**5** **Capella d'en Marcús** *(Marcús Chapel).* This Romanesque hermitage looks as if it had been left behind by some remote order of hermit-monks who meant to take it on a picnic in the Pyrenees. The tiny chapel, possibly—along with Sant Llàtzer—Barcelona's smallest religious structure, was originally built in the 12th century on the main Roman road into Barcelona, the one that would become Cardo Maximo just a few hundred yards away as it passed through the walls at Portal de l'Àngel. Bernat Marcús, a wealthy merchant concerned with public welfare and social issues, built a hospital for the poor. The chapel today known by his name was built as the hospital chapel and dedicated to the Mare de Déu de la Guia (Our Lady of the Guide). As a result of its affiliation, combined with its location on the edge of town, the chapel became linked with the Confraria del Correus a Cavall (Pony Express Guild), also known as the *troters* (trotters), and for two centuries (13th and 14th) made Barcelona the key link in overland mail between the Iberian Peninsula and Europe. ⊠*Carrer Carders 2 (Placeta d'en Marcús), Born-Ribera* ☉*Open for mass only* Ⓜ*Catalunya, Jaume I.*

**14** **Carrer Banys Vells.** This little pedestrian-only alleyway paralleling Carrer Montcada just gets better and better. Exploring Banys Vells is a delight, from the beautifully appointed and supplied Teresa Ferri restaurant **El Pebre Blau** all the way down the street past shops and the stone-vaulted **Va de Vi** (which means, in Catalan, "It's about wine") wine-tasting tavern to the **Tarannà** design and bric-a-brac shop on the corner at No. 4 Carrer Barra de Ferro. Banys Vells means "old baths," referring to the site of the early public baths. Later baths were on the street Banys Nous (New Baths) in the Gothic Quarter near the cathedral. While you're in the neighborhood, grab a beer and pick up your e-mail at the **Internet Gallery Café** at No. 3 Barra de Ferro; have a look at the medieval-vintage **La Cua Corta** restaurant (where you can roast your filet mignon at your table) on Carrer de la Carassa; and have a single-malt or a beer from Scotland at the **Clansmen** opposite Carrer Mirallers on Barra de Ferro. ⊠ *Born-Ribera* Ⓜ *Catalunya, Jaume I.*

❾ **Carrer Flassaders.** The Carrer Flassaders (named for blanket makers) loop begins on Carrer Montcada opposite La Xampanyet, one of La Ribera's favorite bars (specializing in a sticky sparkling wine best avoided—but otherwise an excellent place for tapas and ambience). Duck into the short, dark Carrer Arc de Sant Vicenç. At the end you'll find yourself face to face with **La Seca,** the Barcelona mint, where money was manufactured until the mid-19th century. Coins bearing the inscription, in Castilian, *Principado de Cataluña* (Principality of Catalonia) were minted here as late as 1836. The interior of La Seca (most of which is not open to the public) is an exquisitely restored split-level maze of wooden beams and pillars. Directly ahead in La Seca is the studio and showroom of the internationally prestigious sculptor Manel Alvarez; look for announcements of openings on the door across from the end of Arc de Sant Vicenç.

Moving left to Carrer de la Cirera, look up overhead to the left for the niche with the image of **Santa Maria de Cervelló,** one of the patron saints of the Catalan fleet, on the back side of the Palau Cervelló on Carrer Montcada. Moving down to the right on Carrer de la Cirera past the Otman shop and tearoom, you arrive at the corner of **Carrer dels Flassaders;** walk left past several impressive shops—Re-Born at Flassaders 23; the café, restaurant, and design store **Café de la Princesa** at the corner of Carrer Sabateret—and then turn back down Flassaders through a gauntlet of elegant little clothing, furnishings, and jewelry design stores past the main entry to La Seca at No. 40, with the gigantic royal Bourbon coat of arms over the imposing archway. At No. 42 is the antiques dealer **Hammam,** also occupying part of La Seca; curios and furniture from everywhere from Morocco to India fill the rambling space, and a downstairs space is used for art openings. The stylish Cortana clothing store is across the street. Look up to your right at the corner of the gated Carrer de les Mosques, famous as Barcelona's narrowest street. The mustachioed countenance peering down at you was once a medieval advertisement for a brothel. Boccabacco, at No. 44, is Barcelona's best Italian delicatessen. A right on Passeig del Born will take you back to Santa Maria del Mar. ⊠ *Born-Ribera* Ⓜ *Jaume I.*

❼ **Museu Tèxtil i de l'Indumentària–Palau de los Marqueses de Lló.** With one of Carrer Montcada's best two courtyards (the other is the Palau Dalmases at No. 20), this peaceful spot has a handy café where you can admire the 14th- to 16th-century loggia, stairway, and windows. The textile museum's displays include every imaginable piece of clothing worn from prehistoric times through the late-19th-century Art Nouveau frenzy of decorative excess. The museum store offers interesting books and artifacts, all related to the textile industry that made medieval Barcelona prosper. ⊠ *Carrer Montcada 12–14, Born-Ribera* ☎ *93/319–7603* ⊕ *www.museutextil.bcn.es* ⊠ *€3.50; free 1st Sun. of month 3–8* ☉ *Tues.–Sat. 10–8, Sun. 10–3* Ⓜ *Catalunya, Jaume I.*

┌─
│ NEED A
│ BREAK?
└─
The patio of El Café Tèxtil ( ✉ *Carrer Montcada 12, Born-Ribera* ☎ *93/268–2598*) is one of the city's best, and an ideal spot for anything from a tea to a light meal. In winter the sun manages to find its way into this quiet space; in summer you can find shade unless you happen to be there at high noon.

**⓭ Plaça de les Olles.** This pretty little square named for the makers of *olles*, or pots (as in *olla podrida*, literally, the "rotten pot Spanish stew"), has been known to host everything from topless sunbathers to elegant Viennese waltzers to tapa grazers stacked in three ranks deep at Cal Pep, where Barcelona's best delicacies are served up. The balconies at No. 6 over the Café de la Ribera are, somewhat oddly, decorated with colorful blue and yellow tile on the second and top floors. The house with the turret over the street on the right at the corner leading out to Pla del Palau (at No. 2 Plaça de les Olles) is another of Enric Sagnier i Villavecchia's retro-Moderniste works. This one, a neo-Gothic heap of conical towers and balconies, is an improvement on white elephants such as the neo-Disney Temple Expiatori del Sagrat Cor that gleams relentlessly over Barcelona from the top of Tibidabo. ✉ *Born-Ribera* Ⓜ *Jaume I.*

**❷ Sant Pere de les Puelles** *(St. Peter of the Novices).* One of the oldest medieval churches in Barcelona has been destroyed and restored so many times that there is little left to see except the beautiful stained-glass window that allows illumination of the stark interior. The word *puelles* is from the Latin *puella* (girl)—the convent here was known for the beauty and nobility of its young women and was the setting for some of medieval Barcelona's most tragic stories of impossible love. Legend has it that the *puellae*, when threatened with rape and murder by the invading Moors under Al-Mansur in 986, disfigured themselves by slicing off their own ears and noses in an (apparently futile) attempt to save themselves. ✉ *Lluís El Piadós 1, Sant Pere* ☎ *93/268–0742* ☉ *Open for mass only* Ⓜ *Catalunya, Jaume I.*

# LA CIUTADELLA & BARCELONETA: NEAR THE PORT

Now Barcelona's central downtown park, La Ciutadella was originally the site of a fortress built by the conquering troops of the Bourbon monarch Felipe V after the fall of Barcelona in the 1700–14 War of the Spanish Succession. Barceloneta and La Ciutadella fit together historically and urbanistically, as some 1,000 houses in the Barrio de la Ribera, then the waterfront neighborhood around Plaça del Born, were ordered dismantled by their owners to create fields of fire for La Ciutadella's cannon keeping watch over the rebellious Catalans. Barceloneta, then a marshy wetland, was filled in and developed almost four decades later, in 1753, to compensate families who had lost homes in La Ribera.

Barceloneta has always been a beloved and maverick escape from the formality of cosmopolitan Barcelona life, an urban fishing village barcelonins sought for Sunday paella on the beach and a stroll through what feels like a freer, more-bohemian ambience. With its tiny original houses, its abundant laundry flapping brightly over the streets, and its history of seafarers, gypsies, and all manner of other colorful characters, Barceloneta continues to seem like a world apart, an enclave of passionate Mediterranean romance with a more spontaneous, carefree flavor than Catalans are generally known for.

Open water in Roman times and gradually silted in only after the 15th-century construction of the Barcelona port, Barceloneta is Barcelona's traditional fishing and stevedores' quarter. Originally composed of 15 longitudinal and 3 cross streets and 329 two-story houses (either to allow easy access of sun and air or to avoid masking the Ciutadella's fields of fire, depending on whom you talk to, soldier or civilian), Barceloneta was Europe's earliest planned urban development, built by the military engineer Juan Martin Cermeño under the command of El Marquès de la Mina, Juan Miguel de Guzmán Dávalos Spinola (1690–1767).

*Numbers in the text correspond to numbers in the margin and on the Sant Pere, La Ribera, La Ciutadella & Barceloneta map.*

## A GOOD WALK

Starting at the **Arc de Triomf** 🔟, on Passeig de Sant Joan, built as the grand entryway for the Universal Exposition of 1888, walk down Passeig Lluís Companys and into the **Parc de la Ciutadella** 🔟, the green "lung" of downtown Barcelona. The **Castell dels Tres Dragóns** 🔟, which houses the Museu de Zoologia, is on your right. The next buildings on the right are the Hivernacle, a spectacular greenhouse converted into a restaurant and concert hall; the **Museu de Geologia** 🔟; and the Umbracle, a delicious shady iron structure with a collection of jungle plants. Turn left at the Castell dels Tres Dragons to **La Cascada** 🔟—the monument-cum-waterfall designed by Josep Fontseré i Mestres in 1881. The large building farther in to the left was the Ciutadella's arsenal and is now the home of the **Parlament de Catalunya** 🔟. La Plaça de les Armes is a former parade ground in front of the parliament with the graceful 1906 Josep Llimona sculpture *Desconsol* in the center of the pond.

To the right and behind the Parliament is Barcelona's first-rate **zoo** 🔟. Leaving the Parc de la Ciutadella on Marquès de l'Argentera, you should not miss the **Estació de França** 🔟, Barcelona's last authentic old-world railroad station, now tragically in near total disuse. Past the station, turn left and walk 300 yards across the wide Carrer Doctor Aiguader into the minidistrict of Barceloneta and down Passeig Joan de Borbó, the main thoroughfare paralleling the port. The second street on the left, Carrer de Ginebra, named for an early gin mill, leads past the excellent Lobito restaurant at No. 9 and past several bustling taverns. A cut over to Carrer Maquinista takes you past the oldest restaurant in Barceloneta, Can Ramonet, the picturesque pink house on the corner across from the newly restored and renovated Mercat de la Barceloneta in Plaça del Poeta Boscà. This modern market complex includes two fine restaurants, a pair of bars, eight fish stores, eight butcher shops, four fruit shops, a vegetable store, and a bakery. The open square on the other side has two interesting buildings on the left: No. 47 is a restored 18th-century house with a tiny no-name café on the ground floor, while No. 51 has a colorfully engraved late-19th-century facade.

Crossing to the right side of the square, look for La Cova Fumat at No. 56, a tiny restaurant and tapas sanctuary (open 1–3 and 7–9 only). Leave this delicious place through the back door into Carrer de Sevilla and turn left into Carrer de Sant Carles, where you will find a series of Barceloneta's most interesting buildings. At No. 12 is a typical early Barceloneta house of only two stories, crowned with baroque floral ornamentation and scrolls—look for the shanty on the roof. At Sant Carles 9 is the 1918 **Cooperative Obrera La Fraternitat** ㉔, Barceloneta's best Art Nouveau building and the home of one of the city's first workers' organizations. At No. 7 is the ornate **Farmacia Saim** ㉕, a stone house built over an original Barceloneta structure in 1902. On the left at **Carrer Sant Carles No. 6** ㉖ is the only completely original Cermeño-designed house left in Barceloneta, consisting only of the ground floor, originally designed for boats, nets, and equipment, and an upper floor used as a living space. At No. 4 is Can Solé, a famous restaurant that is one of Barceloneta's oldest and best. Turn right into Plaça de la Barceloneta, where you will see the baroque church of **Sant Miquel del Port** ㉗.

Return to Carrer de Sant Carles and take a left, walking all the way down to the beach, past several interesting houses with sgraffiti-covered facades at Nos. 19 and 32, to the **Fuente de Carmen Amaya** ㉘, a fountain and bas-relief sculpture dedicated to the famous Gypsy flamenco dancer, who was born in Barceloneta in 1913. Climb the stairs and cross the Passeig Maritim to the walkway over the beach. From here, to your left you will see the **Port Olímpic** ㉙ and the Frank Gehry goldfish, looking a lot better post-Guggenheim. You can also see the Olympic Port's twin skyscrapers: the Hotel Arts and the Mapfre office building looming over it. Farther left is another important Barceloneta landmark, the Catalana de Gas water tower, a colorful conical spire built by Art Nouveau architect Domènech i Estapà.

Now walk to your right up the beach past the tempting Chiringuito Silvestre, a summer (April–October) spot serving mediocre seafood at tables on the beach. A few steps farther along on the right is Can Majó, Barceloneta's premier seafood restaurant, a good place for lunch or dinner. Continue up the boardwalk past Rebecca Horn's curious tower sculpture of rusting boxes to Plaça de Mar and turn right into Passeig Joan de Borbó, where you will pass a number of excellent dining spots, principally Barceloneta, Can Costa, Suquet de l'Almirall, and Can Manel la Puda. Return to the Gothic Quarter via the Moll de la Fusta side of the Passeig Joan de Borbó, leaving the Palau de Mar and the **Museu d'Història de Catalunya** ㉚ on your right. The Roy Lichtenstein sculpture *Barcelona Head* is the roosterlike monument in front of the central post office on Passeig de Colom, while the **Port Vell** ㉛ is to the left up the grassy hill, usually dotted with lovers.

TIMING   This is a three- to four-hour walk. Add another hour or two if you're stopping for a bite. Try to time your arrival in Barceloneta so you catch the local market in full activity at midday (until 2) and get a chance to graze through the neighborhood on your way to a beachside table for paella. Can Manel la Puda serves paella until 4 in the afternoon.

HOW TO GET   The Barceloneta stop on the metro's yellow line (Line 4) is the closest
THERE   subway stop, though a walk through the Gothic Quarter from Plaça de Catalunya is the best way of reaching Barceloneta. For La Ciutadella, the Arc de Triomf stop on the red line (Line 1) is the closest.

## WHAT TO SEE: MAIN ATTRACTIONS

❷❻ **Carrer Sant Carles No. 6.** The last Barceloneta house left standing in its original 1755 two-story entirety, this low, boxlike structure was planned as a single-family dwelling with shop and storage space on the ground floor and the living space above. Overcrowding soon produced split houses and even quartered houses, with workers and their families living in tiny spaces. After nearly a century of living under Madrid-based military jurisdiction, Barceloneta homeowners were given permission to expand vertically, and houses of as many as five stories began to tower over the lowly original dwellings. The house is not open to the public. ⊠ *Carrer Sant Carles 6, Barceloneta* Ⓜ *Barceloneta.*

OFF THE
BEATEN
PATH

**Dipòsit de les Aigües–Universitat Pompeu Fabra.** The Ciutadella campus of Barcelona's private Universitat Pompeu Fabra contains a contemporary architectural gem worth seeking out. It's just two blocks up from the Ciutadella–Vil.la Olímpica metro stop where the tram line out to the Fòrum begins. Once the hydraulic cistern for the Ciutadella waterfall built in 1880 by Josep Fontseré, the Dipòsit de les Aigües was converted to a library in 1999 by contemporary architects Lluís Clotet and Ignacio Paricio. The massive, 3-foot-thick walls, perforated and crowned with arches, are striking, while the trompe l'oeil connecting corridor between the reading rooms is through-the-looking-glass perplexing. ⊠ *Ramon Trias Fargas 25–27, La Ciutadella* ☎ *93/542–1709* ⊡ *Free* ⊘ *Weekdays 8–1:30 AM, weekends 10–9* Ⓜ *Ciutadella–Vil.la Olímpica.*

❷❸ **Estació de França.** The elegantly restored Estació de França, Barcelona's main railroad station until about 1980 and still the stopping point for some trains to and from France and points along the Mediterranean, is outside the west gate of the Ciutadella. No longer very active, this mid-19th-century building is a pleasant place to get a sense of the romance of Europe's traditional railroads. The station has a café that is a good place for an espresso and a croissant or a beer (though not much else), along with the sounds and aromas of an authentic European train station. ⊠ *Marquès de l'Argentera s/n, Born-Ribera* ☎ *93/496–3464* Ⓜ *Barceloneta.*

❸⓪ **Museu d'Història de Catalunya.** Built into what used to be a port warehouse, this state-of-the-art, interactive museum makes you part of Catalonian history from prehistoric times through more than 3,000 years and into the contemporary democratic era. After centuries of "official" Catalan history dictated from Madrid (from 1714 until the mid-19th century Renaixença, and from 1939 to 1975) this is an opportunity to revisit Catalonia's autobiography. Explanations of the exhibits appear in Catalan, Castilian, and English. Guided tours are available on Sunday at noon and 1 PM. The rooftop cafeteria has excellent views over the harbor and is open to the public (whether or not you visit the museum itself) during museum hours. ⊠ *Pl. Pau Vila 1, Barceloneta* ☎ *93/225–4700* ⊕ *www.mhcat.net* ✆ *€3.50; free 1st Sun. of month* ⊙ *Tues. and Thurs.–Sat. 10–7, Wed. 10–8, Sun. 10–2:30* Ⓜ *Barceloneta.*

**ALSO WORTH SEEING**

⑯ **Arc del Triomf.** This imposing, exposed-redbrick arch was built by Josep Vilaseca as the grand entrance for the 1888 Universal Exhibition. Similar in size and sense to the traditional triumphal arches of ancient Rome, this one refers to no specific military triumph anyone can recall. In fact, Catalunya's last military triumph of note may have been Jaume I el Conqueridor's 1229 conquest of the Moors in Mallorca—as suggested by the bats (always part of Jaume I's coat of arms) on either side of the arch itself. The Josep Reynés sculptures adorning the structure represent Barcelona hosting visitors to the Exhibition on the west (front) side, while the Josep Llimona sculptures on the east side depict the prizes being given to outstanding contributors to the Universal Exhibition. ⊠ *Passeig de Sant Joan, La Ciutadella* Ⓜ *Arc de Triomf.*

⑱ **Castell dels Tres Dragons** *(Castle of the Three Dragons).* Built by Domènech i Montaner as the café and restaurant for the 1888 Universal Exposition, the building was named in honor of a popular mid-19th-century comedy written by the father of Catalan theater, Serafí Pitarra. An arresting building that greets you on the right entering the Ciutadella from Passeig Lluí Companys, it has exposed brickwork and visible iron supports, both radical innovations at the time. Domènech i Muntaner's building later became an arts-and-crafts workshop where Moderniste architects met to experiment with traditional crafts and to exchange ideas. It now holds Barcelona's **Museu de Zoologia** (Zoology Museum). ⊠ *Passeig Picasso 5, La Ciutadella* ☎ *93/319–6912* ⊕ *www.bcn.es/medciencies* ✆ *€3.75* ⊙ *Tues., Wed., Fri., and weekends 10–2:30, Thurs. 10–6:30* Ⓜ *Arc de Triomf.*

㉔ **Cooperative Obrera La Fraternitat** *(Brotherhood Workers Cooperative).* This strikingly ornate building in the otherwise humble fishermen's quarter, the only Art Nouveau building in Barceloneta, housed the progressive workers' organization, La Fraternitat, founded in 1879. Begun as a low-cost outlet to help supply workers and their families with basic necessities at cut-rate prices, the cooperative soon became a social and cultural center that included a public library. The present cooperative building was inaugurated in 1918 and is now, once again, Barceloneta's library. ⊠ *Carrer Comte de Santa Clara 8, Barceloneta* ☎ *93/225–3574* Ⓜ *Barceloneta.*

**El Transbordador Aeri del Port** This hair-raising cable-car ride over the Barcelona harbor from Barceloneta to Montjuïc (with a midway stop in the port) is spectacular, though it is not always clear whether the great views are the result of the vantage point or the rush of mortality. The cable car leaving from the tower at the end of Passeig Joan de Borbó connects the Torre de San Sebastián on the Moll de Barceloneta, the tower of Jaume I in the port boat terminal, and the Torre de Miramar on Montjuïc. Critics maintain, not without reason, that the ride is expensive, not very cool, and actually pretty scary. On the positive side, this is undoubtedly the slickest way to connect Barceloneta and Montjuïc, and the Torre de Altamar restaurant in the tower at the Barceloneta end serves excellent food and wine along with nonpareil views. ⊠*Passeig Joan de Borbó s/n, Barceloneta* ☎*93/225–2718* ☜*€9 round-trip, €7.50 one-way* ⊙*Daily 10:45–7* Ⓜ*Barceloneta.*

㉕ **Farmacia Saim.** This ornate house with floral trim around the upper balconies, griffins over the door, and the pharmacist's insignia (the serpent and amphora symbolic of the curative properties of snake oils mixed in the apothecary vial) is the still-operating successor of Barceloneta's first pharmacy. Originally situated across the street, the present house was built in 1902. One of the sturdiest houses in Barceloneta, Farmacia Saim was used as a bomb shelter during the 1936–39 Spanish civil war when Franco's bombers, in an attempt to paralyze the Barcelona port to slow down Republican resupply, frequently dumped misdirected bombs on Barceloneta. ⊠*Carrer Sant Carles 7, Barceloneta* ☎*93/221–7670* Ⓜ*Barceloneta.*

㉘ **Fuente de Carmen Amaya** *(Carmen Amaya Fountain).* Down at the eastern end of Carrer Sant Carles, where Barceloneta joins the beach, is the monument to the famous Gypsy flamenco dancer Carmen Amaya (1913–63), born in the Gypsy settlement known as Somorrostro, part of Barceloneta until 1920, when development sent the gypsies farther east to what is now the Fòrum grounds (from which they were again displaced in 2003). Amaya achieved universal fame at the age of 16, in 1929, when she performed at Barcelona's International Exposition. Amaya made triumphal tours of the Americas and starred in films such as *La hija de Juan Simón* (1934) and *Los Tarantos* (1962). The fountain, and its high-relief representations of cherubic children in the throes of flamenco, has been poorly maintained since it was placed here in 1959, but it remains an important reminder of Barceloneta's roots as a rough-and-tumble, romantic enclave of free-living sailors, stevedores, Gypsies, and fishermen. This Gypsy ambience all but disappeared when the last of the *chiringuitos* (ramshackle beach restaurants specializing in fish and rice dishes) fell to the wreckers' ball shortly after the 1992 Olympics. ⊠*Carrer Sant Carles, Barceloneta* Ⓜ*Barceloneta.*

⑳ **La Cascada.** The sights and sounds of Barcelona seem far away when you stand near this monumental, slightly overdramatized creation by Josep Fontseré, presented as part of the 1888 Universal Exhibition. The waterfall's rocks were the work of a young architecture student named Antoni Gaudí—his first public works, appropriately natural and organic, and certainly a hint of things to come. ⊠*La Ciutadella* Ⓜ*Arc de Triomf, Ciutadella.*

**⑲ Museu de la Geologia.** Barcelona's first public museum displays rocks, minerals, and fossils along with special exhibits on Catalonia and the rest of Spain. The museum is next to the Castell dels Tres Dragons, not far from the beautiful *Umbracle* (meaning a shaded place for plants), a magnificently graceful 19th-century greenhouse that showcases a collection of jungle plants that grow best in shade. ⊠*Off Passeig de Picasso, La Ciutadella* ☎*93/319–6895* ⊕*www.bcn.es/museuciencies* ⊠*€3.50; free 1st Sun. of month* ⊙*Tues., Wed., Fri., and weekends 10–2, Thurs. 10–6:30* Ⓜ*Arc de Triomf, Ciutadella.*

**☾ ⑰ Parc de la Ciutadella** *(Citadel Park).* Once a fortress designed to consolidate Madrid's military occupation of Barcelona, the Ciutadella is now the city's main downtown park. The clearing dates from shortly after the War of the Spanish Succession in the early 18th century, when Felipe V demolished some 1,000 houses in what was then the Barri de la Ribera to build a fortress and barracks for his soldiers and a glacis or open space used a buffer zone or no-man's-land to put space between rebellious Barcelona and his artillery positions. The fortress walls were pulled down in 1868 and replaced by gardens laid out by Josep Fontseré. Within the park are a cluster of museums, the Catalan parliament, and the city zoo. ⊠*La Ciutadella* Ⓜ*Arc de Triomf, Ciutadella.*

**㉑ Parlament de Catalunya.** Once the arsenal for the Ciutadella—as evidenced by the thickness of the building's walls—this is the only surviving remnant of Felipe V's fortress and now houses the Catalan Parliament. ⊠*Pl. d'Armes, La Ciutadella* ☎*93/319–5728* ⊠*€4* ⊙*Tues.–Sat. 10–7, Sun. 10–2* Ⓜ*Arc de Triomf, Ciutadella.*

**㉙ Port Olímpic.** Choked with yachts, restaurants, tapas bars, and megarestaurants serving reasonably decent fare continuously 1 PM–1 AM, the Olympic Port is 2 km (1 mi) up the beach, marked by the mammoth shimmering goldfish sculpture by Frank Gehry of Bilbao Guggenheim fame (Bilbao got a leviathan; Barcelona got a goldfish). In the shadow of Barcelona's first real skyscraper, the Hotel Arts, the Olympic Port rages on Friday and Saturday nights, especially in summer, with hundreds of young people of all nationalities contributing to a scene characterized by go-go girls (and boys), fast-food chains, ice-cream parlors, and a buzz redolent of spring break in Cancún. Ⓜ*Ciutadella, Vila Olímpica.*

**㉛ Port Vell.** From Pla del Palau, cross to the edge of the port, where the Moll d'Espanya, the Moll de la Fusta, and the Moll de Barceloneta meet ("moll" meaning docks). Just beyond the colorful Roy Lichtenstein sculpture in front of the post office, the modern Port Vell complex—an IMAX theater, aquarium, and Maremagnum shopping mall—looms seaward on the Moll d'Espanya. The Palau de Mar, with its five somewhat pricey and impersonal quayside terrace restaurants, stretches down along the Moll de Barceloneta (try Llevataps or the Merendero de la Mari; even better is El Magatzem by the entrance to the Museu de Història de Catalunya in the Palau de Mar). Key points in the Maremagnum complex are the grassy hillside (for lovers, especially, on April 23, Sant Jordi's Day, Barcelona's variant of Valentine's

Day); and the *Ictineo II* replica of the submarine created by Narcis Monturiol (1819–85)—the world's first, launched in the Barcelona port in 1862. Ⓜ*Barceloneta.*

㉗ **Sant Miquel del Port.** Have a close look at this baroque church with its modern (1992) (pseudo-bodybuilder) version of the winged archangel Michael himself, complete with sword and chain, in the alcove on the facade. One of the first buildings to be completed in Barceloneta, Sant Miquel del Port was begun in 1753 and finished by 1755 under the direction of architect Damià Ribes. Due to strict orders to keep Barceloneta low enough to fire La Ciutadella's cannon over, Sant Miquel del Port had no bell tower and only a small cupola until Elies Rogent added a new one in 1853. Along with the image of Sant Miquel, Sant Elm, and Santa Maria de Cervelló, patrons of the Catalan fleet, also appeared on the baroque facade. All three images were destroyed at the outbreak of the Spanish civil war in 1936. Interesting to note are the metopes, palm-size, gilt bas-relief sculptures around the interior cornice and repeated outside at the top of the facade. These 74 Latin-inscribed allegories each allude to different attributes of St. Michael: for example, the image of a boat and the inscription IAM IN TUTO (I am in everything), alluding to the protection of St. Michael against the perils of the sea. To the right of Sant Miquel del Port at No. 41 Carrer de Sant Miquel is a house decorated by seven strips of floral sgraffiti and a plaque commemorating Fernando de Lesseps, the engineer who built the Suez Canal, who had lived in the house when serving as French consul to Barcelona. In the square by the church, take a close look at the fountain with its Barcelona coat of arms and Can Ganassa, on the east side, a worthy tapas bar. ✉*Pl. de la Barceloneta, Barceloneta* Ⓜ*Barceloneta.*

**NEED A BREAK?** Friendly **Can Manel la Puda** (✉*Passeig Joan de Borbó 60–61, Barceloneta* ☎*93/221–5013* Ⓜ*Barceloneta*) is always good for a tasty, inexpensive feast in the sun. Serving lunch until 4 and starting dinner at 7, it's a handy and popular place for *suquets* (fish stew), paella, and *arròs a banda* (rice with shelled seafood).

㉒ **Zoo.** Barcelona's excellent zoo (supposedly moving out to the Fòrum area but as yet unmoved) occupies the whole bottom section of the Parc de la Ciutadella. There's a superb reptile house and a full complement of African animals. The dolphin show usually plays to a packed house. ✉*La Ciutadella* ☎*93/225–6780* 🌐*www.zoobarcelona.com* 💶*€14.50* 🕐*Daily 10–7* Ⓜ*Arc de Triomf, Ciutadella.*

# THE EIXAMPLE: MODERNISTE BARCELONA

Barcelona's most famous neighborhood, this gracious late-19th-century urban development is known for its dizzying unnumbered grid and dazzling Art Nouveau architecture. The district encompasses an elegant checkerboard above Plaça de Catalunya and is called the Eixample ("Expansion" in Catalan). Somewhat wide and noisy for the most comfortable walking and wandering, the area, nevertheless, has so much superlative architecture that it's easy to spend considerable time exploring this practically open-air Moderniste museum. With its hard-line street grid—though softened a bit by the *xaflanes* (chamfers), the beveled block corners at intersections—the Eixample is oddly labyrinthine for a Cartesian network (the planners forgot to number it). Many longtime Barcelona residents find it possible to get lost on its unnumbered and unalphabetized streets, though this could also be because the place is so entertaining. Divided into the onetime well-to-do Dreta (right) to the right of Rambla Catalunya looking inland, and the more working-class Ezquerra (left) to the left of Rambla Catalunya, the Eixample locations are also either *mar* (sea side of the street) or *muntanya* (mountain side).

The Eixample was created with the dismantling of the Ciutat Vella's city walls in 1860, when Barcelona embarked upon a vast expansion scheme fueled by the return of rich colonials from Central and South America, by an influx of provincial aristocrats who had sold their country estates after the second Carlist War (1847–49), and by the city's growing industrial power. The street grid was the work of urban planner Ildefons Cerdà, and much of the building was done at the height of Modernisme by a virtual who's who of the greatest Art Nouveau architects, including many landmarks by Gaudí, Domènech i Montaner, and Puig i Cadafalch. In the architectural feast these masters serve up, the pièce de résistance is Gaudí's Sagrada Família church. The Eixample's principal thoroughfares are Rambla de Catalunya and Passeig de Gràcia, where the city's most elegant shops vie for space among its best Moderniste buildings.

The Ruta del Modernisme (Moderniste Route) ticket offers coupon booklets, including discounted visits, to more than 100 Moderniste buildings in and around Barcelona. For €15, a manual published in various languages allows you to self-guide through the city's Art Nouveau architecture. Inquire at your hotel or the tourist office, or purchase tickets directly at the **Casa Amatller** ( ✉ *Passeig de Gràcia 41, Eixample* ☎ *93/488–0139* ✆ *Mon.–Sat. 10–7, Sun. 10–2* Ⓜ *Passeig de Gràcia*), which is part of the Mansana de la Discòrdia. You can also purchase tickets at the Pavellons de la Finca Güell or at the Hospital de la Santa Creu i de Sant Pau.

*Numbers in the text correspond to numbers in the margin and on the Eixample map.*

## A GOOD WALK

Starting in the Plaça de Catalunya, walk up Passeig de Gràcia until you reach the corner of Consell de Cent. Take a deep breath: you are about to enter something resembling the eye of Barcelona's Moderniste hurricane, the **Manzana de la Discòrdia** ❶. This is the "city block (or apple) of discord," where the three great figures of Barcelona's late-19th-century Moderniste movement—Domènech i Montaner, Puig i Cadafalch, and Gaudí—went head to head and toe to toe with three very different buildings: Casa Lleó Morera, Casa Amatller, and Casa Batlló, the latter one of Gaudí's most fanciful creations. The **Casa Montaner i Simó–Fundació Tàpies** ❷, with its wire sculpture *Núvol i cadira (Cloud and Chair)* by Antoni Tàpies himself, is just west, around the corner on Carrer Aragó.

Swing by **Casa Domènech i Estapà** ❸ on Carrer de Valencia, on your way up to Gaudí's greatest (although most criticized) private commission, **Casa Milà** ❹, known as *La Pedrera (The Stone Quarry)*, three blocks farther up Passeig de Gràcia. After seeing the roof (with its signature veiled or helmeted chimneys), the Gaudí museum, and the typical early-20th-century apartment here, pop into Vinçon for a look through one of Barcelona's

> **THE LABYRINTHINE EIXAMPLE**
>
> Barcelona's unnumbered Eixample (Expansion), the post-1860 grid, is a perfect place to get lost, but fear not: the Eixample, though schizophrenic, is vertebrate. Carrer Balmes divides the Eixample's working-class *Esquerra* (left, looking uphill) from its bourgeois *Dreta* (right). Even the blocks are divided into *davant* (front) or *darrera* (behind) apartments. The sides of the streets are either *mar* (sea) or *muntanya* (mountain), with south-facing muntanya facades receiving better light.

top design stores, with views into the back of Casa Milà. Just around the corner at Avinguda Diagonal 373 is Puig i Cadafalch's intricately sculpted **Casa Àsia–Palau Baró de Quadras** ❺, home of the Casa Àsia study, business, and cultural center; it's just two minutes from the architect's Nordic castle fantasy, the **Casa de les Punxes** ❻, at Nos. 416–420. From here it's only a 10-minute hike to Passeig de Sant Joan and yet another Puig i Cadafalch masterpiece, **Casa Macaia** ❼.

By this time you're only three blocks from Gaudí's **Temple Expiatori de la Sagrada Família** ❽ (plan for a half-day visit). After a tour of Gaudí's unfinished "stone Bible," stroll over to Domènech i Montaner's **Hospital de Sant Pau** ❾—another Moderniste monument. Other Eixample spots to visit, though they're widely scattered and not easily scheduled into a single walking tour, can be seen if you head back south and to the west and include Gaudí's **Casa Calvet** ❿, **Passatge Permanyer** ⓫, the **Universitat Central** ⓬, the chaletlike **Casa Golferichs** ⓭ by Rubió i Bellver, and the **Casa de la Papallona** ⓮ (the House of the Butterfly), with one of the most spectacular Art Nouveau facades in town.

TIMING Depending on how many taxis you take, this is at least a four-hour walk. Add another three hours to explore the Sagrada Família. Look for the *passatges* (passageways) through some of the Eixample blocks; Passatge Permanyer, Passatge de la Concepció, and Passatge Mendez Vigo are three of the best. Beware of the tapas emporiums lining Passeig de Gràcia; they, nearly unanimously, microwave previously prepared tapas and are not the best.

HOW TO GET THERE The metro stops at Plaça de Catalunya and Provença nicely bracket this quintessential Barcelona neighborhood, while the Diagonal and Passeig de Gràcia stops place you in the heart of the Eixample.

# The Eixample

**KEY**

◈ Metro Stops

Ⓢ FGC Stops

🛈 Tourist information

Casa Àsia-Palau Baró
de Quadras .................. **5**

Casa Calvet .................. **10**

Casa de la Papallona ...... **14**

Casa de les Punxes ........ **6**

Casa Domènech i Estapà ... **3**

Casa Golferichs .............. **13**

Casa Macaia .................. **7**

Casa Milà .................... **4**

Casa Montaner i
Simó–Fundació Tàpies ..... **2**

Hospital de Sant Pau ...... **9**

Manzana de la
Discòrdia ..................... **1**

Passatge Permanyer ...... **11**

Temple Expiatori
de la Sagrada Família ...... **8**

Universitat Central ........ **12**

0 ———— 300 yards

0 ———— 300 meters

## WHAT TO SEE: MAIN ATTRACTIONS

**5 Casa Àsia–Palau Baró de Quadras.** The neo-Gothic and plateresque (intricately carved in silversmith-like detail) facade of this house built in 1904 for Baron Quadras has one of the most spectacular collections of Eusebi Arnau sculptures in town (other Arnau sites include the Palau de la Música Catalana, Quatre Gats–Casa Martí, Casa Amatller, and Casa Lleó Morera). Look for the theme of St. George slaying the dragon once again, this one in a spectacularly vertiginous rush of movement down the facade. Don't miss the intimate-looking row of alpine chalet–like windows across the top floor. Casa Àsia, an excellent and comprehensive resource for cultural and business-related research, opened here in 2003. ✉ *Av. Diagonal 373, Eixample* ☎ *93/238–7337* ⊕ *www. casaasia.es* 🎟 *Free* ⊙ *Tues.–Sat. 10–8, Sun. 10–2* Ⓜ *Diagonal.*

★ **4 Casa Milà.** Usually referred to as **La Pedrera** (The Stone Quarry), with a wavy, curving stone facade that undulates around the corner of the block, Casa Milà is one of Gaudí's most celebrated yet initially reviled designs. Topped by chimneys so eerie they were nicknamed *espantabruxes* (witch-scarers), the building was unveiled in 1910 to the horror of local residents. The sudden appearance of these cavelike balconies on their most fashionable street led to the immediate coining of descriptions such as "the Stone Quarry"—or, better yet, "Rockpile"—along with references to the Gypsy cave dwellings in Granada's Sacromonte. Other observers were undone by the facade, complaining, as one critic put it, that the rippling, undressed stone made you feel "as though you are on board a ship in an angry sea." Seemingly defying the laws of gravity, the exterior has no straight lines and is adorned with winding balconies covered with wrought-iron seaweedlike foliage sculpted by Josep Maria Jujol.

The building was originally meant to be dedicated to the Mother of God and crowned with a sculpture of the Virgin Mary. The initial design was altered by owner Pere Milà i Camps, who, after the anticlerical violence of the Setmana Tràgica (Tragic Week) of 1909, decided that the religious theme would be an invitation for a new outbreak of mayhem. Gaudí's rooftop chimney park, alternately interpreted as veiled Saharan women or helmeted warriors, is as spectacular as anything in Barcelona, especially in late afternoon when the sunlight slants over the city into the Mediterranean. Inside, the handsome **Espai Gaudí** (Gaudí Space) in the attic has excellent critical displays of Gaudí's works from all over Spain, as well as explanations of theories and techniques, including an upside-down model (a reproduction of the original in the Sagrada Família museum) of the Güell family crypt at Santa Coloma made of weighted hanging strings. This hanging model is based on the "Theory of the Reversion of the Catenary," which says that a chain suspended from two points will spontaneously hang in the exact shape of the inverted arch required to convert the stress to compression, thus structural support. The **Pis de la Pedrera** apartment is an interesting look into the life of a family that lived in La Pedrera in the early 20th century. Everything from the bathroom to the kitchen is filled with reminders of how comprehensively life has changed in the last century. People still live in the other apartments. ✉ *Passeig de Gràcia 92, Eixample* ☎ *93/484–5995* ✉ *Espai Gaudí €5, Pis de la Pedrera €4, combined ticket €8* ⊙ *Daily 10–8; guided tours weekdays at 6. Espai Gaudí roof terrace open for drinks evenings June–Sept.* Ⓜ *Diagonal, Provença.*

**NEED A BREAK?**

If you're near Rambla Catalunya, don't hesitate to report in to the semi-sub-terranean **La Bodegueta** ( ✉ *Rambla de Catalunya 100, Eixample* Ⓜ *Proven-ça*) for some *pa amb tomaquet* (bread with olive oil and tomatoes) and bits of cheese or ham.

**❾ Hospital de Sant Pau.** Certainly one of the most beautiful hospital complexes in the world, the Hospital de Sant Pau is notable for its Mudejar motifs and sylvan plantings. The hospital wards are set among gardens under exposed brick facades intensely decorated with mosaics and polychrome ceramic tile. Begun in 1900, this monumental production won Lluís Domènech i Montaner his third Barcelona "Best Building" award, in 1912. (His previous two prizes were for the Palau de la Música Catalana and Casa Lleó Morera.) The Moderniste enthusiasm for nature is apparent here; the architect believed patients were more apt to recover surrounded by trees and flowers than in sterile hospital wards. Domènech i Montaner also believed in the therapeutic properties of form and color, and decorated the hospital with Pau Gargallo sculptures and colorful mosaics. ✉ *Carrer Sant Antoni Maria Claret 167, Eixample* ☎ *93/291–9000, 93/488–2078 for tours* ⊕ *www.sant-pau.es* ✉ *Free; tour €5* ⊙ *Daily 9–8; tours weekends 10–2, weekdays by advance arrangement* Ⓜ *Hospital de Sant Pau.*

**❶ Manzana de la Discòrdia.** The name is a pun on the Spanish word *manzana,* which means both city block and apple, alluding to the three-way architectural counterpoint on this block and to the classical myth of the Apple of Discord (which played a part in that legendary tale about the Judgment of Paris). The houses here are spectacular and encompass three monuments of Modernisme—Casa Lleó Morera, Casa Amatller, and Casa Batlló. Of the three competing buildings (four if you count Sagnier i Villavecchia's comparatively tame 1910 Casa Mulleras at No. 37), Casa Batlló is clearly the star attraction and the only one of the three offering visits to the interior.

FodorśChoice
★

The ornate **Casa Lleó Morera** (No. 35) was extensively rebuilt (1902–06) by Palau de la Música Catalana architect Domènech i Montaner and is a treasure house of Catalan Modernisme. The facade is covered with ornamentation and sculptures depicting female figures using the modern inventions of the age: the telephone, the telegraph, the photographic camera, and the Victrola. The inside is even more astounding, another anthology of Art Nouveau techniques assembled by the same team of glaziers, sculptors, and mosaicists Domènech i Montaner directed in the construction of the Palau de la Música Catalana. The Eusebi Arnau sculptures around the top of the walls on the main floor are based on the Catalan lullaby *"La Dida de l'Infant del Rei"* ("*The Nurse of the King's Baby"*), while the stained-glass scenes in the old dining room of Lleó Morera family picnics resemble Moderniste versions of impressionist paintings. The house is closed to the public, but call to check about visits.

The neo-Gothic, pseudo-Flemish **Casa Amatller** (No. 41) was built by Josep Puig i Cadafalch in 1900, when the architect was 33 years old. Eighteen years younger than Domènech i Montaner and 15 years younger than Gaudí, Puig i Cadafalch was one of the leading statesmen of his generation, mayor of Barcelona and, in 1917, president of Catalonia's first home-rule government since 1714, the Mancomunitat de Catalunya. Puig i Cadafalch's architectural historicism sought to recover Catalonia's proud past, in combination with eclectic elements from Flemish or Netherlandish architectural motifs. The Eusebi Arnau sculptures range from St. George and the dragon to the figures of a handless drummer with his dancing bear. The flowing-haired "Princesa" is thought to be Amatller's daughter, while the animals up above are pouring chocolate, a reference to the source of the Amatller family fortune. Casa Amatller is closed to the public (call or ask about any change in this situation), but a boutique and small gallery inside the entryway sells Art Nouveau objects and organizes exhibits related to Modernisme.

Gaudí at his most spectacular, the colorful and bizarre **Casa Batlló** (No. 43), with its mottled facade resembling anything from an abstract pointillist painting to a rainbow of colored sprinkles on an ice-cream cone, is usually easily identifiable by the crowd of tourists snapping photographs on the sidewalk. Nationalist symbolism is at work here: the scaly roof line represents the Dragon of Evil impaled on St. George's cross, and the skulls and bones on the balconies are the dragon's victims. These motifs are allusions to Catalonia's Middle Ages, its codes of chivalry, and religious fervor. Gaudí is said to have directed the chromatic composition of the facade from the middle of Passeig de Gràcia, calling instructions to workmen on scaffolding equipped with baskets of multicolored fragments of ceramic tiling. The interior design follows a gently swirling maritime motif in stark contrast to the terrestrial strife represented on the facade. ⊠*Passeig de Gràcia 43, between Consell de Cent and Aragó, Eixample* ☎*93/216–0306* ⊕*www.casabatllo.es* ☐*€17* ⊙*Daily 9–8* Ⓜ*Passeig de Gràcia.*

**❽** **Temple Expiatori de la Sagrada Família.** Barcelona's most emblematic

Fodor's Choice  architectural icon, Antoni Gaudí's Sagrada Família, is still under con-

★  struction 126 years after it was begun. This striking and surreal creation was conceived as nothing short of a Bible in stone, a gigantic representation of the entire history of Christianity, and it continues to cause responses from surprise to consternation to wonder. No building in Barcelona and few in the world are more deserving of investing anywhere from a few hours to the better part of a day in getting to know it well. In fact, a quick visit can be more tiring than an extended one, as there are too many things to take in at once. However long your visit, it's a good idea to bring binoculars.

Looming over Barcelona like some magical mid-city massif of needles and peaks left by aeons of wind erosion and fungal exuberance, the

*Continued on page 94*

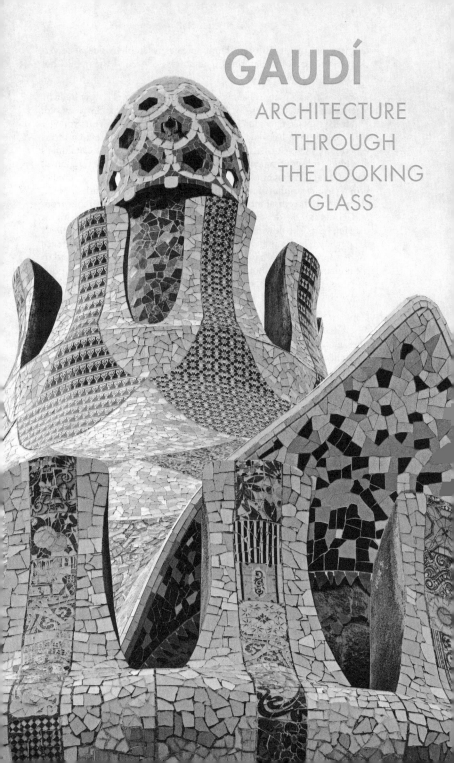

# GAUDÍ

## ARCHITECTURE THROUGH THE LOOKING GLASS

(left) The rooftop of Parc Güell's gatehouse. (top) Construction continues on la Sagrada Família.

Shortly before his 75th birthday in 1926, Antonio Gaudí was hit by a trolley car while on his way to mass. The great architect—initially unidentified—was taken to the medieval Hospital de la Santa Creu in Barcelona's Raval and left in a pauper's ward, where he died two days later without regaining consciousness. It was a dramatic and tragic end for a man whose entire life seemed to court the extraordinary and the exceptional.

Gaudí's singularity made him hard to define. Indeed, eulogists at the time, and decades later, wondered how history would treat him. Was he a religious mystic, a rebel, a bohemian artist, a Moderniste genius? Was he, perhaps, all of these? He certainly had a rebellious streak, as his architecture stridently broke with tradition. Yet the same sensibility that created the avant-garde benchmarks Parc Güell and La Pedrera also created one of Spain's greatest shrines to Catholicism, the *Temple Expiatori de la Sagrada Família* (Expiatory Temple of the Holy Family), which architects agree is one of the world's most enigmatic structures (work on the cathedral continues to this day). And while most of Gaudí's works suggest a futurist aesthetic, he also reveled in the use of ornamentation, which 20th century architecture largely eschewed.

What is no longer in doubt is Gaudí's place among the great architects in history. Eyed with suspicion by traditionalists in the 1920s and '30s, vilified during the Franco regime, and ultimately redeemed as a Barcelona icon after Spain's democratic transition in the late '70s, Gaudí's work has finally gained universal admiration.

## THE MAKING OF A GENIUS

Gaudí was born in 1852 the son of a boilermaker and coppersmith in Reus, an hour south of Barcelona. As a child, he helped his father forge boilers and cauldrons in the family foundry, which is where Gaudí's fascination with three-dimensional and organic forms began. Afflicted from an early age with rheumatic fever, the young architect devoted his energies to studying and drawing flora and fauna in the natural world. In school he was erratic: brilliant in the subjects that interested him, absent and disinterested in the others. As a seventeen-year-old architecture student in Barcelona, his academic results were mediocre. Still, his mentors agreed that he was brilliant.

Unfortunately being brilliant didn't mean instant success. By the late 1870s, when Gaudí was well into his twenties, he'd only completed a handful of projects, including the Plaça Reial lampposts, a flower stall, and the factory and part of a planned workers' community in Mataró. Gaudí's career got the boost it needed when, in 1878, he met Eusebi Güell, heir to a textiles fortune and a man who, like Gaudí, had a refined sensibility. (The two bonded over a mutual admiration for the visionary Catalan poet Jacint Verdaguer.) In 1883 Gaudí became Güell's architect and for the next three decades, until Güell's death in 1918, the two collaborated on Gaudí's most important architectural achievements, from high-profile endeavors like Palau Güell, Parc Güell, and Pabellones Güell to smaller projects for the Güell family.

(top) Interior of Casa Batlló. (bottom) Chimneys on rooftop of Casa Milà recall helmeted warriors or veiled women.

## GAUDÍ TIMELINE

**1883–1884**

Gaudí builds a summer palace, *El Capricho* in Comillas, Santander for the brother-in-law of his benefactor, Eusebi Güell. Another gig comes his way during this same period when Barcelona ceramics tile mogul Manuel Vicens hires him to build his town house, *Casa Vicens*, in the Gràcia neighborhood.

*El Capricho*

**1884–1900**

Gaudí whips up the Güell Pabellones, Palau Güell, the Palacio Episcopal of Astorga, Barcelona's Teresianas school, the Casa de los Botines in León, Casa Calvet, and Bellesguard. These have his classic look of this time, featuring interpretation of Mudéjar (Moorish motifs), Gothic, and Baroque styles.

*Palacio Episcopal*

## BREAKING OUT OF THE T-SQUARE PRISON

If Eusebi Güell had not believed in Gaudí's unusual approach to Modernisme, his creations may not have seen the light of day. Güell recognized that Gaudí was imbued with a vision that separated him from the crowd. That vision was his fascination with the organic. Gaudí had observed early in his career that buildings were being composed of shapes that could only be drawn by the compass and the T-square: circles, triangles, squares, and rectangles—shapes that in three dimensions became prisms, pyramids, cylinders and spheres. He saw that in nature these shapes are unknown. Admiring the structural efficiency of trees, mammals, and the human form, Gaudí noted ". . . neither are trees prismatic, nor bones cylindrical, nor leaves triangular." The study of natural forms revealed that bones, branches, muscles, and tendons are all supported by internal fibers. Thus, though a surface curves, it is supported from within by a fibrous network that Gaudí translated into what he called "ruled geometry," a system of inner reinforcement he used to make hyperboloids, conoids, helicoids, or parabolic hyperboloids.

These tongue-tying words are simple forms and familiar shapes: the femur is hyperboloid; the way shoots grow off a

Hyperboloid

Hyperbolic Paraboloid

Casa Batlló's scaly dragon-back roof atop a structure composed of tibias, femurs, and skulls show Gaudí's interest in anatomy and organic forms.

branch is helicoidal; the web between your fingers is a hyperbolic paraboloid. To varying degrees, these ideas find expression in all of Gaudí's work, but nowhere are they more clearly stated than in the two masterpieces La Pedrera and Parc Güell.

**1900–1917**

Gaudí's Golden Years—his most creative, personal, and innovative period. Topping each success with another, he tackles Parc Güell, the reform of Casa Batlló, the Güell Colony church, Casa Milà (AKA La Pedrera), and the Sagrada Família school.

*Casa Batlló's complex chimneys*

**1918–1926**

A crushing blow: Gaudí suffers the death of his assistant, Francesc Berenguer. Grieving and rudderless, he devotes himself fully to his great unfinished opus, la Sagrada Família—to the point of obsession. On June 10th, 1926, he's hit by a trolley car. He dies two days later.

*La Sagrada Família*

# HOW TO SEE GAUDÍ IN BARCELONA

Few architects have left their stamp on a major city as thoroughly as Gaudí did in Barcelona. Paris may have the Eiffel Tower, but Barcelona has Gaudí's still unfinished masterpiece, the Temple Expiatori de la Sagrada Família, the city's most emblematic structure. Dozens of other buildings, parks, gateways and even paving stones around town bear Gaudí's personal Art Nouveau signature, but the continuing progress on his last and most ambitious project makes his creative energy an ongoing part of everyday Barcelona life in a unique and almost spectral fashion.

(top) The serpentine ceramic bench at Parc Güell, designed by Gaudí collaborator Josep Maria Jujol, curves sinuously around the edge of the open square. (bottom) Sculptures by Josep María Subirachs grace the temple of the Sagrada Família.

In Barcelona, nearly all of Gaudí's work can be visited on foot or, at most, with a couple of metro or taxi rides. A walk from Palau Güell near the Mediterranean end of the Rambla, up past Casa Calvet just above Plaça Catalunya, and on to Casa Batlló and Casa Milà is an hour's stroll, which, of course, could take a full day with thorough visits to the sites. Casa Vicens is a half hour's walk up into Gràcia from Casa Milà. Parc Güell is another thirty- to forty-minute walk up from that. La Sagrada Família, on the other hand, is a good hour's hike from the next nearest Gaudí point and is best reached by taxi or metro. The Teresianas school, the Bellesguard Tower, and Pabellones Güell are within an hour's walk of each other, but to get out to Sarrià you will need to take the comfortable Generalitat (FGC) train.

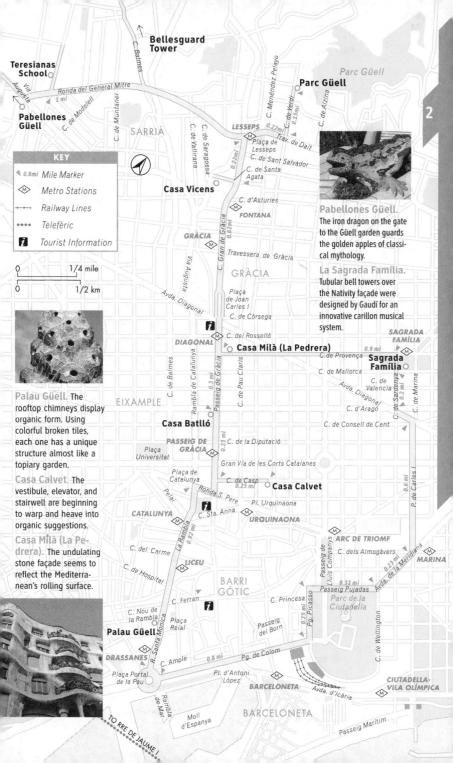

**Bellesguard Tower**

**Teresianas School**

*Via Augusta*

*Ronda del General Mitre* 1 mi

**Pabellones Güell**

*C. de Modolell*

*C. de Muntaner*

*C. de Vallirana*

*C. de Saragossa*

**SARRIÀ**

*Balmes*

*C. Menéndez Pelayo*

*C. de Verdi*

*C. de Alzira*

*Parc Güell*

**Parc Güell**

2

**LESSEPS** Ⓜ  0.22mi *Trav. de Dalt* 0.15mi

Plaça de Lesseps

0.22mi

*C. de Sant Salvador*

*C. de Santa Agata*

**Casa Vicens**

*C. d'Asturies*

**FONTANA** Ⓜ

**GRÀCIA**

*C. Gran de Gràcia*

0.82mi

*Via Augusta*

*Travessera de Gràcia*

**GRÀCIA**

*Avda. Diagonal*

Plaça de Joan Carles I

*C. de Còrsega*

Ⓘ

**DIAGONAL** Ⓜ  *C. del Rosselló*

**Casa Milà (La Pedrera)**

*C. de Balmes*

*Rambla de Catalunya*

*Passeig de Gràcia*

0.3 mi

*C. de Pau Claris*

**EIXAMPLE**

**Casa Batlló**

*PASSEIG DE GRÀCIA* Ⓜ

Plaça Universitat

0.25 mi *C. de la Diputació*

Plaça de Catalunya

*Gran Vía de les Corts Catalanes*

Plaça de Catalunya

Ⓜ

*Pelai*

Plaça de Catalunya

*C. de Casp* 0.25 mi **Casa Calvet**

*Ronda S. Pere*

Ⓘ

*C. Sta. Anna*

**CATALUNYA** Ⓜ

*Pl. Urquinaona*

**URQUINAONA** Ⓜ

*C. del Carme*

*La Rambla*

0.92 mi

**LICEU** Ⓜ

*C. de Hospital*

**BARRI GÓTIC**

*C. Ferran*

Ⓘ

*C. Princesa*

*C. Nou de la Rambla*

Plaça Reial

**Palau Güell**

**DRASSANES** Ⓜ

*R. Santa Mònica*

*C. Ample*

0.8 mi

*Passeig del Born*

*Pg. de Colom*

*Pg. Picasso*

Plaça Portal de la Pau

*Pl. d'Antoni López*

**BARCELONETA**

*Avda. d'Icària*

*Rambla de Mar*

Moll d'Espanya

**BARCELONETA**

*Passeig Marítim*

TO RRE DE JAUME I

*SAGRADA FAMÍLIA*

0.9 mi

**Sagrada Família** Ⓜ

*C. de Provença*

*C. de Mallorca*

*C. de València*

*Avda. Diagonal*

*C. d'Aragó*

*C. de Consell de Cent*

*C. de Sardenya*

0.2 mi

*C. de Marina*

*P. de Carles I*

0.6 mi

**ARC DE TRIOMF** Ⓜ

*Passeig de Lluís Companys*

*C. dels Almogàvers*

0.23 mi

*Avda. de la Meridiana*

**MARINA** Ⓜ

0.32 mi

*Passeig Pujades*

Parc de la Ciutadella

0.25 mi

*C. de Wellington*

**CIUTADELLA-VILA OLÍMPICA** Ⓜ

---

### KEY

◄ 0.8mi *Mile Marker*

◈ *Metro Stations*

⊢⊢⊢ *Railway Lines*

•••• *Telefèric*

ℹ *Tourist Information*

0 — 1/4 mile
0 — 1/2 km

---

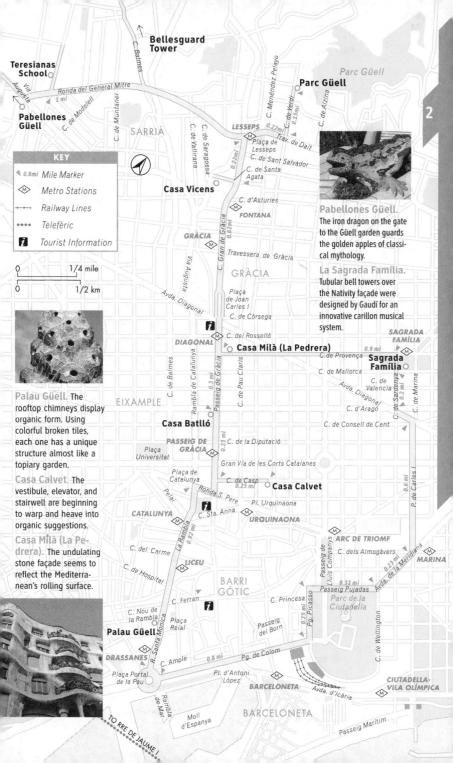

**Pabellones Güell.** The iron dragon on the gate to the Güell garden guards the golden apples of classical mythology.

**La Sagrada Família.** Tubular bell towers over the Nativity façade were designed by Gaudí for an innovative carillon musical system.

**Palau Güell.** The rooftop chimneys display organic form. Using colorful broken tiles, each one has a unique structure almost like a topiary garden.

**Casa Calvet.** The vestibule, elevator, and stairwell are beginning to warp and heave into organic suggestions.

**Casa Milà (La Pedrera).** The undulating stone façade seems to reflect the Mediterranean's rolling surface.

Sagrada Família can at first seem like piles of caves and grottoes heaped on a labyrinth of stalactites, stalagmites, and flora and fauna of every stripe and spot. The sheer immensity of the site and the energy flowing from it are staggering. The scale alone is daunting: the current lateral facades will one day be dwarfed by the main Glory facade and central spire—the **Torre del Salvador** (Tower of the Savior), which will be crowned by an illuminated polychrome ceramic cross and soar to a final height 1 yard shorter than the Montjuïc mountain (564 feet) guarding the entrance to the port (Gaudí felt it improper for the work of man to surpass that of God). Today, for a €2 additional charge, you can take an elevator skyward to the top of the **bell towers** for some spectacular views. Back on the ground, visit the **museum**, which displays Gaudí's scale models; photographs showing the progress of construction; and images of Gaudí's multitudinous funeral. In fact, the architect is buried to the left of the altar in the **crypt**, which has its own entrance through the Sagrada Família's parish church on Carrer Provença.

Soaring spikily skyward in intricately twisting levels of carvings and sculptures, part of the Nativity facade is made of stone from Montserrat, Barcelona's cherished mountain sanctuary and home of Catalonia's patron saint, La Moreneta, the Black Virgin of Montserrat. Gaudí himself was fond of comparing the Sagrada Família to the flutes and pipes of the sawtooth massif 50 km (30 mi) west of town, while a plaque in one of Montserrat's caverns reads LLOC D'INSPIRACIÓ DE GAUDÍ (Place of inspiration of Gaudí).

*History of Construction and Design.* "My client is not in a hurry," Gaudí was fond of replying to anyone curious about the timetable for the completion of his mammoth project . . . and it's a lucky thing, because the Sagrada Família was begun in 1882 under architect Francesc Villar, passed on in 1891 to Gaudí (who worked on the project until his death in 1926), and is still thought to be 20 years from completion, despite the ever-increasing velocity of today's computerized construction techniques. After the church's neo-Gothic beginnings, Gaudí added Art Nouveau touches to the crypt (the floral capitals) and in 1893 went on to begin the Nativity facade of a new and vastly ambitious project. Conceived as a symbolic construct encompassing the complete story and scope of the Christian faith, the Sagrada Família was intended by Gaudí to impact the viewer with the full sweep and force of the Gospel. For the last 15 years of his life, Gaudí became a recluse and took up residence in the church grounds. At the time of his death in 1926 only one tower of the Nativity facade had been completed.

Gaudí's plans called for three immense facades, the lateral (Nativity and Passion) facades presently visible on the north and south sides of the church, and the even larger Glory facade designed as the building's main entry, facing east over Carrer de Mallorca. The four bell towers over each facade would represent the 12 apostles, a reference to the celestial Jerusalem of the Book of Revelation, built upon the 12 apostles. The four larger towers around the central Tower of the Savior will represent the evangelists Mark, Matthew, John, and Luke. Between the central tower and the reredos at the northwestern end of the nave will rise the 18th and second-highest tower, crowned with a star, in honor of the Virgin Mary. The naves are not supported by buttresses but by treelike helicoidal (spiraling) columns. The first bell tower, in honor of Barnabas, the only one Gaudí lived to see, was completed in 1921. Presently there are eight towers standing: Barnabas, Simon, Judas, and Matthias (from left to right) over the Nativity facade and James, Bartholomew, Thomas, and Phillip over the Passion facade.

*Meaning and Iconography.* Reading the existing facades is a challenging course in Bible studies. The three doors on the **Nativity facade** are named for Charity in the center, Faith on the right, and Hope on the left. As explained by Joan Serra, vicar of the parish of the Sagrada Família and devoted Gaudí scholar, the architect often described the symbology of his work to visitors although he never wrote any of it down. Thus, much of this has come directly from Gaudí via the oral tradition. In the Nativity facade Gaudí addresses nothing less than the fundamental mystery of Christianity: Why does God the Creator become, through Jesus Christ, a creature? The answer, as Gaudí explained it in stone, is that God did this to free man from the slavery of selfishness, symbolized by the iron fence around the serpent of evil (complete with an apple in his mouth) at the base of the central column of the **Portal of Charity.** The column is covered with the genealogy of Christ going back to Abraham. To the left is a sea tortoise at the base of the parabolic arch, while to the right is a land turtle with flora and fauna from Catalonia above and behind.

Above the central column is a portrayal of the birth of Christ; above that, the Annunciation is flanked by a grottolike arch of water in a solid state: ice, another element of nature. Overhead are the constellations in the Christmas sky at Bethlehem: if you look carefully you'll see two babies, representing the Gemini, and the horns of a bull, for Taurus.

To the right, the **Portal of Faith,** above Palestinian flora and fauna, shows scenes of Christ's youth: Jesus preaching at the age of 13 and Zacharias prophetically writing the name of John. Higher up are grapes and wheat, symbols of the Eucharist, and a sculpture of a hand and eye, symbols of divine providence.

The left-hand **Portal of Hope** begins at the bottom with flora and fauna from the Nile; the slaughter of the innocents; the flight of the Holy Family into Egypt; Joseph, surrounded by his carpenter's tools, contemplating his son; the marriage of Joseph and Mary flanked by Mary's parents, the grandparents of Jesus, Joaquin and Anna. Above this is a sculpted boat with an anchor, representing the Church, piloted by St. Joseph assisted by the Holy Spirit in the form of a dove. Overhead is a typical peak or spire from the Montserrat massif.

Gaudí, who carefully studied music, planned these slender towers to house a system of tubular bells (still to be created and installed) capable of playing more complete and complex music than standard bell-ringing changes had previously been able to perform. At a height of one-third of the bell tower are the seated figures of the apostles. The peaks of the towers represent the apostles' successors in the form of miters, the official headdress of a bishop of the Western Church.

The **Passion facade** on the Sagrada Família's southwestern side, over Carrer Sardenya and the Plaça de la Sagrada Família, is a dramatic contrast to the Nativity facade. Gaudí, whose plans called for nearly everything that appears on the Passion facade, intended to emphasize the abyss between the birth of a child and the crucifixion and death of a man. In 1986, Josep Maria Subirachs (Barcelona 1927), was chosen by project director Jordi Bonet to finish the Passion facade. Subirachs was picked for his starkly realistic, almost geometrical, sculptural style, which matched Gaudí's artistic intent for the Passion facade even though his personal sculptural idiom was entirely distinct. Choosing an artist with such radically different ideas and aesthetics from those of the Sagrada Família's creator was a daring move by the project's directors, though finding a modern-day iconoclast as original and independent as Gaudí severely limited choices. Subirachs currently has a studio and living quarters (granted for life) in the Sagrada Família.

Subirachs pays double homage to the great Moderniste master in the Passion facade: Gaudí himself appears over the left side of the main entry making notes or drawings, the evangelist in stone, while the Roman soldiers farther out and above are modeled on Gaudí's helmeted, *Star Wars*–like warriors from the roof of La Pedrera.

Framed by leaning tibia-like columns, the bones of the dead, and following an S-shape path across the Passion facade, the scenes represented begin at the lower left with the Last Supper. The faces of the disciples are contorted in confusion and dismay, especially that of Judas, clutching his bag of money behind his back over the figure of a reclining hound, symbol of fidelity in contrast with the disciple's perfidy. The next sculptural group to the right represents the prayer in the Garden of Gethsemane and Peter awakening, followed by the kiss of Judas. The square numerical cryptogram behind contains 16 numbers offering a total of 310 combinations all adding up to 33, the age of Christ at his death.

In the center, Jesus is lashed to a pillar during his flagellation, a tear track carved into his expressive countenance. Note the column's top stone out of kilter, reminder of the stone soon to be removed from Christ's sepulcher. The knot and the broken reed on the base of the pillar symbolize the physical and psychological suffering in Christ's captivity and scourging. Look for the fossil imbedded in the stone on the back left corner of the pedestal, taken by Sagrada Família cognoscenti as an impromptu symbol of the martyr's ultimate victory. To the right of the door are a rooster and Peter, who is lamenting his third denial of Christ "ere the cock crows." Farther to the right are Pilate and Jesus with the crown of thorns, while just above, starting back to the left, Simon of Cyrene helps Jesus with the cross after his first fall.

Over the center is the representation of Jesus consoling the women of Jerusalem (cf., Book of Revelation): "Don't cry for me; cry for your children..." and a faceless (because her story is considered legendary, not historical fact) St. Veronica with the veil she gave Christ to wipe his face with on the way to Calvary. It was said to be miraculously imprinted with his likeness. The veil is torn in two overhead and covers a mosaic that Subirachs disliked and elected to conceal. To the left is the likeness of Gaudí taking notes, and farther left is the equestrian figure of a centurion piercing the side of the church with his spear, the church representing the body of Christ. Above are the soldiers rolling dice for Christ's clothing and the naked, crucified Christ at the center. The moon to the right of the crucifixion refers to the darkness at the moment of Christ's death and to the full moon of Easter; to the right are Peter and

> ## SUBIRACHS & GAUDÍ
>
> Josep Maria Subirachs, the sculptor finishing Gaudí's plans, is a militant atheist. Known for his hard-edged interpretations of the human form, Subirachs quickly distanced himself from Gaudí. In 1990, religious leaders called for his resignation when a naked and anatomically complete Christ on the cross was unveiled, though Subirachs defended his work as part of the stark realism of the scene. Originally contracted on condition of complete artistic freedom, Subirachs eventually prevailed, and his work is now undebated.

Mary at the sepulcher, Mary with an egg overhead symbolizing the resurrection of Christ. At Christ's feet is a figure with a furrowed brow, perhaps suggesting the agnostic's anguished search for certainty. It is thought to be a self-portrait of Subirachs, characterized by the sculptor's giant hand and an "S" on his right arm.

Over the door will be the church's 16 prophets and patriarchs under the cross of salvation. Apostles James, Bartholomew, Thomas, and Phillip appear at a height of 148 feet on their respective bell towers. Thomas, the apostle who demanded proof of Christ's resurrection (thus the expression "doubting Thomas"), is visible pointing to the palm of his hand, asking to inspect Christ's wounds. Bartholomew, on the left, is turning his face upward toward the culminating element in the Passion facade, the 26-foot-tall gold metallic representation of the resurrected Christ on a bridge between the four bell towers at a height of 198 feet.

*Future of the project.* Architect Jordi Bonet, 81, director of the work on the Sagrada Família, is the son of one of Gaudí's assistants and remembers playing among the rocks and rubble of the construction site as a child. (Indeed, with Bonet's brother Lluís as head parish priest, the Sagrada Família is virtually a family project.) On Saint Joseph's day, March 19, 2007, the 125th anniversary of the laying of the first stone of a project initially instigated by a society dedicated to Saint Joseph, the Bonet brothers presided over a celebratory mass. The apse, covered but still incomplete, will eventually have space for 15,000 people, a choir loft for 1,500, and occupy an area large enough to encompass the entire Santa Maria del Mar basilica. The towers still to be completed over the apse include those dedicated to the four evangelists–Matthew, Mark, Luke, and John—the Virgin Mary, and the highest of all, dedicated to Christ the Savior. By 2022, the 170th anniversary of the birth of Gaudí, the great central tower and dome, resting on four immense columns of Iranian porphyry, considered the hardest of all stones, will soar to a height of 561 feet, making the Sagrada Família Barcelona's tallest building. By 2026, the 100th anniversary of Gaudí's death, after 144 years of construction in the tradition of the great medieval and Renaissance cathedrals of Europe, the Sagrada Família may well be complete enough to call finished. The projected esplanade east of the Glory Facade entails the removal of a block of apartments, constructed in the early 1970s with the understanding that, eventually, expropriations and demolition would ensue. Carrer Mallorca will go underground. No dates have been set for this major urban re-engineering.

A major celebration, if not an entire year of festivities, is likely for 2026, by which time the line from John (13:27) carved into a corner of the Passion facade by Josep Maria Subirachs, who like the Bonet brothers, is currently in his late seventies, will have even more poignancy: EL QUE ESTÁS FENT, FES-HO DE PRESSA (Whatever you are doing, do it in a hurry).

English tours can be arranged with the guide organization **Guiart** (☎669/482404 ✉€3.50 plus entry fee ☉Nov.–Feb., Mon., Fri., and weekends 11 and 1; Mar., daily 11 and 1; Apr.–Oct., daily 11, 1, 3, and 5:30). ✉Pl. de la Sagrada Família, Eixample ☎93/207-3031 ⊕www. sagradafamilia.org ✉€10, bell tower elevator €2 ☉Oct.–Mar., daily 9–6; Apr.–Sept., daily 9–8 Ⓜ Sagrada Família.

### ALSO WORTH SEEING

**❿ Casa Calvet.** This exquisite but more conventional town house (for Gaudí, anyway) was the architect's first commission in the Eixample (the second was the dragonlike Casa Batlló, and the third, and last—he was never asked to do another—was the stone quarry–esque Casa Milà). Peaked with baroque scroll gables over the unadorned (no ceramics, no color, no sculpted ripples) Montjuïc sandstone facade, Casa Calvet compensates for its structural conservatism with its Art Nouveau details, from the door handles to the benches, chairs, vestibule, and spectacular glass-and-wood elevator. Built in 1900 for the textile baron Pere Calvet, the house includes symbolic elements on the facade, ranging from the owner's stylized letter "C" over the door to the cypress, symbol of hospitality, above. The wild mushrooms on the main (second) floor reflect Pere Calvet's (and perhaps Gaudí's) passion for mycology, while the busts at the top of the facade represent St. Peter, the owner's patron saint; and St. Genis of Arles and St. Genis of Rome, patron saints of Vilassar, the Calvet family's hometown in the coastal Maresme north of Barcelona. For an even more sensorial taste of Gaudí, dine in the same building's next-door **Casa Calvet restaurant,** elaborately decorated in Moderniste ornamentation. ✉Carrer Casp 48, Eixample Ⓜ Catalunya, Urquinaona.

**⓮ Casa de la Papallona.** This extraordinary apartment house crowned with an enormous yellow butterfly (*papallona*) made of *trencadis* (broken ceramic chips used by the Modernistes to add color to curved surfaces) was built in 1912 by Josep Graner i Prat. Next to Plaça Espanya, directly overlooking the Arenes de Barcelona bullring, the building displays lines of a routine, late-19th-century design—that is, until you reach the top of the facade. ⊠*Llançà 20, Eixample* Ⓜ*Plaça Espanya.*

**❻ Casa de les Punxes** *(House of the Spikes).* Also known as Casa Terrades for the family that owned the house and commissioned Puig i Cadafalch to build it, this extraordinary cluster of six conical towers ending in impossibly sharp needles is another of Puig i Cadafalch's northern European inspirations, this one rooted in the Gothic architecture of Nordic countries. One of the few freestanding Eixample buildings, visible from 360 degrees, this ersatz-Bavarian or Danish castle in downtown Barcelona is composed entirely of private apartments. Some of them are built into the conical towers themselves and consist of three circular levels connected by spiral stairways, about right for a couple or a very small family. Interestingly, Puig i Cadafalch also designed the Terrades family mausoleum, albeit in a much more sober and respectful style. ⊠*Av. Diagonal 416–420, Eixample* Ⓜ*Diagonal.*

**❸ Casa Domènech i Estapà.** This less radical example of Eixample Art Nouveau architecture is interesting for its balconies and curved lines on the facade, for its handsome doors and vestibule, and for the lovely etched designs on the glass of the entryway. Built by and for the architect Domènech i Estapà in 1908–09, eight years before his death, this building represents a more conservative interpretation of the aesthetic canons of the epoch, revealing the architect's hostility to the Art Nouveau movement. Domènech i Estapà built more civil projects than any other architect of his time (Reial Acadèmia de Cièncias y Artes, Palacio de Justicia, Sociedad Catalana de Gas y Electricidad, Hospital Clínico, Observatorio Fabra) and was the creator of the Carcel Modelo (Model Prison), considered a state-of-the-art example of penitentiary design when it was built in 1913. ⊠*Valencia 241, Eixample* Ⓜ*Passeig de Gràcia.*

**⓭ Casa Golferichs.** Gaudí disciple Joan Rubió i Bellver built this extraordinary house, known as El Xalet (The Chalet) for the Golferichs family when he was not yet 30. The rambling wooden eaves and gables of the exterior enclose a cozy and comfortable dark-wood-lined interior with a pronounced verticality. The top floor, with its rich wood beams and cerulean walls, is often used for intimate concerts; the ground floor exhibits paintings and photographs. ⊠*Gran Via 491, Eixample* ☎*93/323–7790* ⊕*www.golferichs.org* ◷ *Weekdays 9–2 and 4–8, Sat. 9–2* Ⓜ*Urgell, Rocafort.*

**❼ Casa Macaia.** This graceful Puig i Cadafalch building constructed in 1901 was the former seat of the ubiquitous Centre Cultural Fundació "La Caixa," a deep-pocketed, far-reaching cultural entity funded by the Caixa Catalana (Catalan Savings Bank). Look for the Eusebi Arnau sculptures over the door depicting, somewhat cryptically, a man mounted on a donkey and another on a bicycle, reminiscent of the similar Arnau sculptures on the facade of Puig i Cadafalch's Casa

Amatller on Passeig de Gràcia. ⊠ *Passeig de Sant Joan 108, Eixample* Ⓜ *Verdaguer.*

❷ **Casa Montaner i Simó–Fundació Tàpies.** This former publishing house—and
Fodor's Choice    the city's first building to incorporate iron supports, built in 1880—has
★    been handsomely converted to hold the work of preeminent contemporary Catalan painter Antoni Tàpies, as well as temporary exhibits.
Tàpies is an abstract painter, although influenced by surrealism, which
may account for the sculpture atop the structure—a tangle of metal
entitled *Núvol i cadira* (*Cloud and Chair*). The modern, airy split-level gallery also has a bookstore that's strong on Tàpies, Asian art,
and Barcelona art and architecture. ⊠ *Carrer Aragó 255, Eixample*
☎ 93/487–0315 ⊠ €4.50 ⊗ *Tues.–Sun. 10–8* Ⓜ *Passeig de Gràcia.*

OFF THE
BEATEN
PATH
**Museu Egipci de Barcelona.** Even though you came to Barcelona to study,
presumably, Catalonia, not ancient Egypt, you might be making a mistake
by skipping this major collection of art and artifacts. Housing what is probably Spain's most comprehensive exhibition on Egypt, this excellent museum
takes advantage of state-of-the-art museological techniques that are nearly
as interesting as the subject matter, which ranges from Egyptian mummies
to exhibits on Cleopatra. ⊠ *Fundació Arqueòlogica Clos, Valencia 284, Eixample* ☎ 93/488–0188 ⊕ www.fundclos.com ⊠ €7 ⊗ *Mon.–Sat. 10–8, Sun.
10–2; guided tour with Egyptologists Sat. at noon and 2; night visits with
actors and theatrical scenes Fri. and Sat. 9:30–11 PM by reservation; tours in
English Fri. at 5 or by previous reservation* Ⓜ *Passeig de Gràcia.*

⓫ **Passatge Permanyer.** Cutting through the middle of the block bordered
by Pau Claris, Roger de Llúria, Consell de Cent, and Diputació, this
charming, leafy mid-Eixample sanctuary is one of 46 *passatges* (alleys
or passageways) that cut through the blocks of this gridlike area.
Inspired by John Nash's neoclassical Regent's Park terraces in London
(with their formal and separate town houses), Ildefons Cerdà originally envisioned many more of these utopian mid-block gardens, but
Barcelona never endorsed his vision. Once an aristocratic enclave and
hideaway for pianist Carles Vidiella and poet, musician, and illustrator
Apel.les Mestre, Passatge Permanyer is, along with the nearby Passatge
Méndez Vigo, the best of these through-the-looking-glass downtown
Barcelona alleyways. ⊠ *Enter near Carrer Pau Claris 118, Eixample*
Ⓜ *Passeig de Gràcia.*

⓬ **Universitat Central.** Barcelona's Central University was built in 1889
by Elies Rogent. In its neo-Romanesque style alluding, no doubt, to
classical knowledge, the university's two-tiered Pati de Lletres (Literary Patio) is its most harmonious element, along with the vestibule,
gardens, and Paraninfo (main assembly hall). Originally founded as
a medical school in 1401 by King Martí I (dubbed "the Humane"),
the university was exiled to the town of Cervera 100 km (62 mi) west
of Barcelona in 1717 by Felipe V as part of his program to dismantle
Catalonia in reprisal for supporting the Habsburg contender in the
War of the Spanish Succession. The town became Catalonia's version

of Oxford or Cambridge until the university was invited back to Barcelona in 1823. ⊠*Gran Via 585, Eixample* ☎*93/402–1100* ⊕*www. ub.es* Ⓜ*Catalunya.*

# GRÀCIA: RADICAL CHIC

Gràcia is a state of mind. More than a neighborhood, a village republic that has periodically risen in armed rebellion against city, state, and country, Gràcia is a jumble of streets with names (Llibertat, Fraternitat, Progrès, Venus) that suggest the ideological history of this fierce little nucleus of working-class citizens and sentiment. The site of Barcelona's first collectivized manufacturing operations (i.e., factories) provided a dangerous precedent as workers organized and developed into radical groups ranging from anarchists to feminists to Esperantists. Once an outlying town that joined the municipality of Barcelona only under duress, Gràcia attempted to secede from the Spanish state in 1856, 1870, 1873, and 1909.

Lying above the Diagonal from Carrer de Còrsega all the way up to Parc Güell, Gràcia's lateral borders run along Via Augusta and Balmes to the west and Carrer de l'Escorial and Passeig de Sant Joan to the east. Today the area is filled with appealing bars and restaurants, movie theaters, and outdoor cafés—always alive and usually thronged by young and hip couples in the throes of romantic ecstasy or agony of one kind or another. Mercé Rodoreda's famous novel *La Plaça del Diamant* (translated by David Rosenthal as *The Time of the Doves*) begins and ends in Gràcia's square of the same name during the August Festa Major, a festival that fills the streets with the rank-and-file residents of this always lively yet intimate little pocket of general resistance to Organized Life.

*Numbers in the text correspond to numbers in the margin and on the Gràcia map.*

## A GOOD WALK

Starting in **Parc Güell ❶**—a fantastic Gaudí extravaganza of a park including the Casa-Museu Gaudí inside—find your way down through upper Gràcia along Carrer Larrard and then below Travessera de Dalt, Carrer de les Flors, to **Plaça Rovira i Trias ❷**, where a bronze effigy of architect Antoni Rovira i Trias is seated elegantly on a bench in the middle of the square. From there, continue on Carrer de las Tres Senyores over to **Plaça de la Virreina ❸**. Carrer d'Astúries leads out of Plaça de la Virreina over to **Plaça del Diamant ❹** and the Colometa bronze. From Plaça del Diamant, continue on Carrer d'Astúries out to Gran de Gràcia and walk up to Carrer de les Carolines and Gaudí's first house, **Casa Vicens ❺**, a colorful ceramic neo-Mudejar gem. Next stop, well downhill across Rambla del Prat, is the **Mercat de la Llibertat ❻**, one of Gràcia's two food markets. Cut back across Gran de Gràcia past another Berenguer creation, the **Centre Moral Instructiu de Gràcia ❼**, and on to Plaça del Sol, one of Gràcia's most popular squares. Farther east is Gràcia's other market, **Mercat de la Revolució ❽** (now officially known

as Abaceria Central). From here it's a short hike three blocks back to **Plaça Rius i Taulet** ❾, Gràcia's main square with its emblematic clock tower. From Plaça Rius i Taulet cut out to **Gran de Gràcia** for a look at more elegant Art Nouveau buildings by Berenguer, on your way to Botafumeiro for some of Barcelona's best Galician seafood, or down to the bottom of Gràcia, just above Carrer Còrsega, to Jean Luc Figueras, an exquisite restaurant just a few steps from the Gaudí-esque facade of another Art Nouveau gem, **Casa Comalat** ❿.

TIMING    This is a three- to four-hour outing that could take five with lunch included or an entire day really to get the feel of Gràcia. Evening sessions at the popular Verdi cinema (v. o.—showing films in their original language) usually get out just in time for a late-night bite at Botafumeiro, which closes at 1 AM. Güell Park is best in the afternoon, when the sun spotlights the view east over the Mediterranean. Exploring Gràcia with the Llibertat and Revolució markets closed is a major loss, so plan to reach the markets before 2 PM.

HOW TO GET    By metro, the Gràcia stop on the FGC (Ferrocarril de la Generalitat
THERE    de Catalunya) trains that connect Sarrià, Sabadell, Terrassa, and Sant Cugat with Plaça Catalunya is your best option. The metro's green line (Line 3) stops at Fontana and Lesseps drop you in the heart of Gràcia

and near Parc Güell, respectively. The yellow line (Line 4) stop at Joanic is a short walk from Gràcia's northeast side.

## WHAT TO SEE: MAIN ATTRACTIONS

★ **❺** **Casa Vicens.** Antoni Gaudí's first important commission as a young architect was begun in 1883 and finished in 1885. For this house, Gaudí had still not succeeded in throwing away his architect's tools, particularly the T-square. The historical eclecticism (that is, borrowing freely from past architectural styles around the world) of the early Art Nouveau movement is evident in the Orientalist themes and Mudejar motifs lavished throughout the facade. The fact that the house was commissioned by a ceramics merchant may explain the use of the green ceramic tiles that turn the facade into a striking checkerboard. Casa Vicens was the first polychromatic facade to appear in Barcelona. The chemaro palm leaves decorating the gate and surrounding fence are thought to be the work of Gaudí's assistant Francesc Berenguer, while the comic iron lizards and bats oozing off the facade are Gaudí's playful version of the Gothic gargoyle. The interior (in the rare event that the owners open the house to the public) is even more surprising than the outside, with its trompe-l'oeil birds painted on the walls of the salon and the intricately Mocarabe, or Moorish-style, carved ceiling in the smoking room. Gaudí's second commission, built in 1885, was in the little town of Comillas in Santander, for the Marquès de Comillas, Antonio López y López, a shipping magnate and the most powerful man of his time. Not surprisingly, the two houses bear a striking resemblance to each other. ⊠ *Carrer de les Carolines 24–26, Gràcia* ☎ *93/488–0139* Ⓜ *Gràcia, Fontana.*

★ **Gran de Gràcia.** This central artery up through Gràcia would be a lovely stroll if the car and (worse) motorcycle din weren't so overpowering. (A tunnel would do the trick nicely.) However, many of the buildings along Gran de Gràcia are of great artistic and architectural interest, beginning with **Can Fuster,** at the bottom of Gran de Gràcia 2–4. Built between 1908 and 1911 by Palau de la Música Catalana architect Lluís Domènech i Montaner in collaboration with his son Pere Domènech i Roure, the building shows a clear move away from the chromatically effusive heights of Art Nouveau. More powerful, and somehow less superficial, than much of that style of architecture, it uses the winged supports under the balconies and the floral base under the corner tower as important structural elements instead of as pure ornamentation, as Domènech i Montaner the elder might have. As you move up Gran de Gràcia, probable Francesc Berenguer buildings can be identified at No. 15; No. 23, with its scrolled cornice; and Nos. 35, 49, 51, 61, and 77. Officially attributed to a series of architects—since Berenguer lacked a formal degree (having left architecture school to become Gaudí's "right hand")—these Moderniste masterworks have long inspired debate over Berenguer's role. Ⓜ *Fontana, Gràcia.*

★ **❻** **Mercat de la Llibertat.** This uptown version of the Rambla's Boqueria market is one of Gràcia's coziest spaces, a food market big enough to roam in and small enough to make you feel at home. Built by Francesc Berenguer between 1888 and 1893, the Llibertat market reflects, in its name alone, the revolutionary and democratic sentiment strong in Gràcia's traditionally blue-collar residents. Look for Berenguer's decorative swans swimming along the roofline and the snails surrounding the coat of arms of the town of Gràcia. ⊠ *Pl. Llibertat 27, Gràcia* ☎ *93/217–0995* ⊕ *www.bcn.es/mercatsmunicipals* ⊙ *Daily 7–3* Ⓜ *Gràcia.*

❽ **Mercat de la Revolució.** Officially the Abaceria Central, the market got its early name from the nearby Plaça de la Revolució de Setembre de 1868 just a block away up Carrer dels Desamparats. Browse through and consider having something delicious such as a plate of wild mushrooms or a *tortilla de patatas* (potato omelet) at the very good bar and restaurant at the far corner on the lower east side. ⊠ *Travessera de Gràcia 186, Gràcia* ☎ *93/213–6286* ⊕ *www.bcn.es/mercatsmunicipals (look under the offical name "Abaceria Central")* ⊙ *Daily 7–3* Ⓜ *Joanic, Gràcia.*

❶ **Parc Güell.** Güell Park is one of Gaudí's, and Barcelona's, most pleasant and stimulating places to spend a few hours. Whereas Gaudí's landmark Sagrada Família can be exhaustingly bright and hot in its massive energy and complexity, Parc Güell is invariably light and playful, uplifting and restorative. Alternately shady, green, floral, or sunny, the park always has a delicious corner for whatever one needs. Named for and commissioned by Gaudí's main patron, Count Eusebi Güell, it was originally intended as a hillside garden community based on the English Garden City model, centered, amazingly enough, on an open-air theater built over a covered marketplace. Only two of the houses were ever built (one of which, designed by Gaudí assistant Francesc Berenguer, became Gaudí's home from 1906 to 1926 and now houses the park's Gaudí museum). Ultimately, as Barcelona's bourgeoisie seemed happier living closer to "town," the Güell family turned the area over to the city as a public park.

Fodor's Choice
★

An Art Nouveau extravaganza with gingerbread gatehouses topped with, respectively, the hallucinogenic red-and-white fly ammanite wild mushroom (rumored to have been a Gaudí favorite) on the right and the *phallus impudicus* (no translation necessary) on the left, Parc Güell is a perfect visit for a sunny afternoon when the blue of the Mediterranean is best illuminated by the western sun. The gatehouse on the right holds the Center for the Interpretation and Welcome to Parc Güell. The center has plans, scale models, photos, and suggested routes analyzing the park in detail. Other Gaudí highlights include the ⇨ **Casa-Museu Gaudí** (a house in which Gaudí lived), the Room of a Hundred Columns—a covered market supported by tilted Doric-style columns and mosaic-encrusted buttresses, and guarded by a patchwork lizard—and the fabulous serpentine, polychrome bench that snakes along the main square. The bench is one of Gaudí assistant Josep Maria Jujol's most memorable creations, and one of Barcelona's best examples of the *trencadis* technique of making colorful mosaics with broken bits of tile. ⊠ *Carrer d'Olot s/n; take Metro to Lesseps; then walk 10 mins uphill or catch Bus 24 to park entrance, Gràcia* ⊙ *Oct.–Mar., daily 10–6; Apr.–June, daily 10–7; July–Sept., daily 10–9* Ⓜ *Lesseps.*

★ ⑨ **Plaça Rius i Taulet.** Named for a memorable Gràcia mayor, this is the town's most emblematic and historic square, marked by the handsome clock tower in its center. The tower, built in 1862, is just over 110 feet high, has public water fountains around its base, royal Bourbon crests over the fountains, and an iron balustrade atop the octagonal brick cylinder stretching up to the clock and belfry. The symbol of Gràcia, the clock tower was bombarded by federal troops when Gràcia attempted to secede from the Spanish state during the 1870s. Always a workers' neighborhood and, as a result, prone to social solidarity, Gràcia was mobilized by mothers who refused to send their sons off as conscripts to fight for the crumbling Spanish Imperial forces during the late 19th century, thus requiring a full-scale assault by Spanish troops to reestablish law and order. Today sidewalk cafés prosper under the leafy canopy here. The Gràcia Casa de la Vila (town hall) at the lower end of the square is yet another Francesc Berenguer opus. Ⓜ *Gràcia.*

**NEED A BREAK?** The **Bar Candanchú** (⊠ *Pl. de Rius i Taulet 9, Gràcia* ☎ *93/237–7362* Ⓜ *Gràcia*), a refreshing stop, runs tables until early morning. For an upscale treat, **Botafumeiro** (⊠ *Gran de Gràcia 81, Gràcia* ☎ *93/218–4230* Ⓜ *Gràcia*) never disappoints; the counter is the place to be for icy Albariño white wine and *pop a feira* (octopus on potato slices with smoked paprika), a Galician favorite.

### ALSO WORTH SEEING

★ ⑩ **Casa Comalat.** At the bottom of Gràcia between the Diagonal and Carrer Còrsega, this often overlooked Moderniste house (not open to the public) built in 1911 is a good one to add to your collection. For a look at the best side of this lower Gràcia Art Nouveau gem, cut down past Casa Fuster at the bottom of Gran de Gràcia, take a left on Bonavista, then a right on Santa Teresa down to Casa Comalat just across Carrer Còrsega. This Salvador Valeri i Pupurull creation is one of Barcelona's most interesting Moderniste houses, especially this side of it, with its bulging polychrome ceramic balconies and its melted wax–like underpinnings. Look for the curious wooden galleries, and check out the designer bar, SiSiSi, around on the less-interesting facade at Diagonal 442. ⊠ *Carrer de Còrsega 316, Gràcia* Ⓜ *Diagonal.*

❶ **Casa-Museu Gaudí.** Within **Parc Güell,** the museum occupies a pink, ★ Alice-in-Wonderland house in which Gaudí lived with his niece from 1906 to 1926. Exhibits in this house museum include Gaudí-designed furniture and decorations, drawings, and portraits and busts of the architect. ⊠ *Parc Güell, up hill to right of main entrance, Gràcia* ☎ *93/219–3811* 💶 *€4* ⊗ *May–Sept., daily 10–8; Oct.–Feb., daily 10–6; Mar. and Apr., daily 10–7* Ⓜ *Lesseps.*

❼ **Centre Moral Instructiu de Gràcia.** Another creation by Gaudí's assistant Francesc Berenguer (Gràcia is Berenguer country), this building is one of the few in Barcelona with an exposed-brick Mudejar facade. The Centre Moral Instructiu was built in 1904 and still functions as a YMCA-like cultural institution; Berenguer was its president at one time. ⊠ *Carrer Ros de Olano 9, Gràcia* Ⓜ *Gràcia.*

## BERENGUER: GAUDÍ'S RIGHT HAND

Francesc Berenguer's role in Gaudí's work and the Moderniste movement, despite leaving architecture school prematurely to work for Gaudí, was significant (if not decisive) and has been much debated by architects and Art Nouveau scholars. If Barcelona was Gaudí's sandbox, Gràcia was Berenguer's. Although unlicensed to legally sign his projects, Berenguer is known to have designed nearly every major building in Gràcia, including the Mercat de la Llibertat. The house at Carrer de l'Or 44 remains one of his greatest achievements, a vertical exercise with pinnacles at the stress lines over rich stacks of wrought-iron balconies. The Gràcia Town Hall in Plaça Rius i Taulet and the Centre Moral Instructiu de Gràcia at No. 9 Carrer Ros de Olano are confirmed Berenguer houses, while the buildings on Carrer Gran de Gràcia at Nos. 15, 23, 35, 49, 51, 61, 77, and 81 are all either confirmed or suspected Berenguer designs. Even Gaudí's first house, Casa Vicens, owes its chemaro palm leaf iron fence to Berenguer. After Berenguer's premature death at the age of 47 in 1914, Gaudí said he had "lost his right hand." Indeed, in his last 12 years, Gaudí built nothing but the Sagrada Família and, in fact, progressed little there.

**❸ Plaça de la Virreina.** The much-punished and oft-restored church of Sant Joan de Gràcia in this square stands where the Palau de la Virreina once stood, the mansion of the same virreina (wife, in this case widow, of a viceroy) whose 18th-century palace on the Rambla (Palau de la Virreina) is now a prominent municipal museum and art gallery. The story of La Virreina, a young noblewoman widowed at an early age by the elderly viceroy of Peru, is symbolized in the bronze sculpture in the center of the square portraying Ruth (of the Old Testament), represented carrying the sheaves of wheat she was gathering when she learned of the death of her husband, Boaz. Ruth, who remained loyal to her widowed mother-in-law, Naomi, is the Old Testament paradigm of wifely faith to her husband's clan, a parallel to La Virreina's lifelong devotion to the performance of good works with her husband's fortune.

The rectorial residence at the back of the church is the work of Gaudí's perennial assistant and right-hand man Francesc Berenguer. Just across the street, the house at Carrer de l'Or 44 was built in 1909, also by Berenguer. Giddily vertical and tightly packed into its narrow slot, it demonstrates one of his best tricks: building town houses sharing walls with adjacent construction. Ⓜ*Fontana.*

**❹ Plaça del Diamant.** This little square is of enormous sentimental importance in Barcelona as the site of the opening and closing scenes of 20th-century Catalan writer Mercé Rodoreda's famous 1962 novel *La Plaça del Diamant*. Translated by the late American poet David Rosenthal as *The Time of the Doves,* it is the most widely translated and published Catalan novel of all times: a tender yet brutal story of a young woman devoured by the Spanish civil war and, in a larger sense, by life itself. A bronze statue in the square portrays Colometa, the novel's protagonist, caught in the middle of her climactic scream during which "a little bit of nothing trickled out of my mouth, like a cockroach made of spit…and that bit of nothing that had lived so long trapped inside me was my youth and it flew off with a scream of I don't know what…letting go?" The bronze birds represent the pigeons that Colometa spent her life obsessively breeding; the male figure on the left pierced by bolts of steel is Quimet, her first love and husband, whom she met at a dance in this square and later lost in the war. Ⓜ*Fontana.*

❷ **Plaça Rovira i Trias.** This charming little square and the story of Antoni Rovira i Trias shed much light on the true nature of Barcelona's eternal struggle with Madrid and Spanish central authority. Take a careful look at the map of Barcelona positioned at the feet of the bronze effigy of the architect and urban planners near the center of the square and you will see a vision of what the city might have looked like if Madrid's (and the Spanish army's) candidate for the design of the Eixample in 1860, Ildefons Cerdà, had not been imposed over the plan devised by Rovira i Trias, initial and legitimate winner of the open competition for the commission. Rovira i Trias's plan shows an astral design radiating out from a central Eixample square that military minds saw as avenues of approach; Cerdà's design, on the other hand, made the Diagonal into a natural barrier. Ⓜ*Lesseps.*

# UPPER BARCELONA: SARRIÀ & PEDRALBES

Sarrià is a 1,000-year-old village that once overlooked Barcelona from the foothills of the Collserola. Gradually swallowed up over the centuries by the westward-encroaching city, Sarrià has become a haven for petit-bourgeois merchants, writers, and artists, as well as a home for many Barcelona schools occupying what were once summer mansions for the city's commercial leaders. St. Eulàlia, Barcelona's co-patroness, is always described as "the beautiful daughter of a wealthy Sarrià merchant" who fell afoul of Roman consul Decius in the 4th century, a reminder of Sarrià's perennially well-off citizenry. J. V. Foix, the famous Catalan poet who published in France throughout the Franco regime, is an honored citizen here, his descendants the proprietors of Sarrià's two famous Foix pastry shops. Now largely a pedestrian sanctuary, Sarrià still retains much of its village atmosphere, although it is just 15 minutes by the Generalitat train from the Rambla. The miniaturesque original town houses sprinkled through Sarrià are a reminder of the not-so-distant past when this enclave was an even more bougainvillea-festooned eddy at the edge of Barcelona's roaring urban torrent.

Pedralbes clings to the beginnings of the Collserola hills above Sarrià, a neighborhood of mansions scattered around the 14th-century Monestir de Pedralbes (Pedralbes Monastery). Peripheral points of interest include some of Gaudí's most memorable works, including the Pavellons de la Finca Güell on Avinguda de Pedralbes, Torre Bellesguard above Plaça de Sant Gervasi, and the Teresianas convent and school just above the intersection of General Mitre and Ganduxer; the Palau Reial de Pedralbes is a 20-minute walk downhill on the Diagonal (just behind the Finca Güell gate and the Càtedra Gaudí), while the Futbol Club Barcelona's monstrous, 98,000-seat Nou Camp sports complex and museum are another 20 minutes' walk down below the Hotel Princesa Sofia on the Diagonal.

*Numbers in the text correspond to numbers in the margin and on the Sarrià & Pedralbes map.*

### A GOOD WALK

Because the Monestir de Pedralbes closes at 2, the best way to explore this part of town is to begin with the monastery and then head back down into Sarrià, where you can browse and graze until 4 or 4:30. From Sarrià's Reina Elisenda train stop, it's a 10-minute walk or a 2-minute cab ride to the **Monestir de Pedralbes** ❶. (If you walk, avoid noisy Passeig Reina Elisenda in favor of Carrer Ramon Miquel i Planas, one block uphill from the station leading across into lovely Carrer del Monestir.) After a tour of the monastery, take a walk down the cobblestone Baixada del Monestir alongside sumptuously sculpted and sgraffiti-covered El Conventet (Little Convent), named for an earlier Franciscan convent (one of the many luxurious private mansions in this district). Cross to the Mató de Pedralbes restaurant (named for the *mató*, or cottage cheese, for which the Clarist nuns of Pedralbes were once famous), where you might be tempted to have lunch. Back up in Plaça del Monestir, walk east on Carrer del Monestir past the ancient ficus tree in the center of Plaça Jaume II and across Avinguda Foix into Carrer Ramon Miquel i Planas. A right on Sagrat Cor will take you down to the back of the Sarrià market. The Sarrià church and **Plaça Sarrià** ❷ are just across Passeig Reina Elisenda.

After touring Sarrià, where there are numerous fine lunch and dinner options, either taxi or walk to Gaudí's convent and girls' school, **Colegio de les Teresianas** ❸ and the **Torre Bellesguard** ❹, 1 km (½ mi) or so uphill, or taxi to **Pavellons de la Finca Güell–Càtedra Gaudí** ❺ and its spectacular Gaudí gate, home of the Càtedra Gaudí study center. From here you can walk to the **Palau Reial de Pedralbes** ❻ and its decorative arts collections, and even hike or taxi over to the **Camp Nou** ❼ stadium 1 km (½ mi) downhill—home of the famed FC Barcelona team—to enjoy a soccer match or simply to visit the spectacular stadium and museum.

TIMING  This is a three-hour outing, including at least an hour in the monastery. Count four or five with lunch included. The Monestir de Pedralbes closes at 2 PM, so go in the morning. Bar Tomás serves its famous potatoes with *allioli* 1–4 and 7–10, another key timing consideration, while the Foix de Sarrià pastry emporium is open until 9.

HOW TO GET  Sarrià is best reached on the FGC (Ferrocarril de la Generalitat de
THERE  Catalunya) train line, which is part of the city metro system, though a cut above. These trains leave Plaça Catalunya every few minutes and will drop you at the Reina Elisenda or Sarrià stops in 15 minutes. Bus 64 also runs the length and width of Barcelona, from Barceloneta to Plaça Sarrià and Pedralbes.

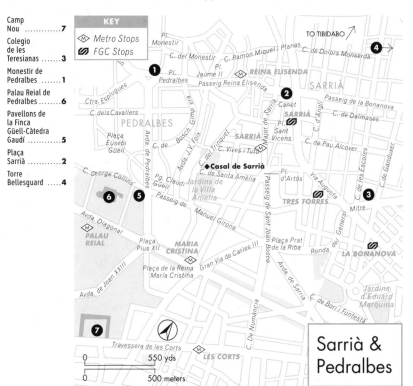

Sarrià &
Pedralbes

## WHAT TO SEE: MAIN ATTRACTIONS

**❼ Camp Nou.** If you're in Barcelona between September and June, a chance to witness the celebrated FC Barcelona play soccer (preferably against Real Madrid, if you can get in) at Barcelona's gigantic stadium, Camp Nou, is a seminal Barcelona experience. Just the walk down to the field from the Diagonal with another hundred thousand fans walking fast and hushed in electric anticipation is unforgettable. Games are played Saturday night at 9 or Sunday afternoon at 5, though there may be international Champion's League games on Tuesday or Wednesday evenings as well. Ask your hotel concierge how to get tickets, or call the club in advance. The stadium seats 98,000, and fills to capacity for big games. A worthwhile alternative to seeing a game is the guided tour of the FC Barcelona museum and facilities. The museum has a five-screen video showing the club's most memorable goals, along with player biographies and displays chronicling the history of one of Europe's most colorful soccer clubs. ⊠*Arístides Maillol, Les Corts* ☎*93/496–3608* ⊕*www.fcbarcelona.com* ☜*Museum €5.30; combined ticket including tour of museum, field, and sports complex €9.50* ☉*Museum Mon.–Sat. 10–6:30, Sun. 10–2* Ⓜ*Collblanc, Palau Reial.*

**❶ Monestir de Pedralbes.** This marvel of a monastery, named for its whitish stones (*pedres albes*), is really a convent for the Franciscan order of Poor Clares founded in 1326 by Reina Elisenda (Queen Elisenda),

FodorśChoice
★

fourth wife of Count-King Jaume II. The three-story Gothic cloister, one
of the finest in Europe, surrounds a lush garden. The day cells, where
the nuns spent their mornings praying, sewing, and studying, circle the
arcaded courtyard. Reina Elisenda's cell, the Capella de Sant Miquel,
just to the right of the entrance, has murals painted in 1346 by Catalan
master Ferrer Bassa, who imported Italian Gothic painting techniques.
Look for the letters spelling out JOAN NO M'OBLIDES (John do not forget
me!) scratched between the figures of St. Francis and St. Clare (with
book and quill), written by a forcibly incarcerated and broken-hearted
novice. Farther along, inscriptions over the tombs of nuns who died
here can be seen through the paving grates. The nuns' upstairs dormitory contains the convent's treasures: paintings, liturgical objects, and
seven centuries of artistic and cultural patrimony. Temporary exhibits
are displayed in this space. The refectory where the Poor Clares dined
in silence has a pulpit used for readings, while wall inscriptions exhort
"Silentium" (Silence), "Audi tacens" (Listening makes you wise), and
"Considera morientem" (Consider we are dying). Don't miss the fading
mural in the corner or the paving tiles broken by heavy cannon during
the 1809 Napoleonic occupation. ⊠*Baixada Monestir 9, Pedralbes*
☎*93/203–9282* ⊠*€5; free 1st Sun. of month* ☉*Oct.–May, Tues.–Sun.*
*10–2; June–Sept., Tues.–Sun. 10–5* Ⓜ*Reina Elisenda.*

**❺ Pavellons de la Finca Güell–Càtedra Gaudí.** The former stables of the Güell
family contain the Càtedra Gaudí, a Gaudí library and study center
(curiosity is the only credential required for admission) and offer a visit
to the gardens and gatehouses. This structure was crucial to Gaudí's
architectural career as one of the three Ruta del Modernisme centers
(along with Hospital de Sant Pau, and the Plaça Catalunya Tourist
Office). The fierce, wrought-iron dragon crafted by Gaudí is a reference
to national poet Jacint Verdaguer's epic poem *L'Atlàntida,* published
in 1877, in which, as per Greek mythology, the dragon Ladon guards
the garden with the tree that bore the golden apples tended by the
daughters of Atlas. To get here from Sarrià, walk through the park at
the Casal de Sarrià at the western end of Vives i Tutó and the Jardins
de la Vil.la Amèlia and then through Carrer Claudi Güell to Passeig
Manuel de Girona to Avinguda de Pedralbes. A walk through the side
entrance into the gardens of the Palau Reial de Pedralbes next door will
complete a 3-km (2-mi) sylvan excursion through upper Barcelona's
leafiest reaches and leave you just a block or two from Jean-Louis
Neichel's excellent and eponymous gourmet restaurant. ⊠*Av. Pedralbes 7, Pedralbes* ☎*93/204–5250* ☉*Daily 9–8* Ⓜ*Sarrià, Palau Reial.*

**❷ Plaça Sarrià.** The 1,000-year-old village of Sarrià was originally a cluster of farms and country houses overlooking Barcelona from the hills.
Once dismissively described as *"Sarrià: vents, torrents, i convents"*
(Sarrià: winds, brooks, and convents), this quiet enclave is now a haven
at the upper edge of the roaring metropolis. Start an exploration at the
square, which hosts an antiques and crafts market on Tuesday morning, *sardana* dances on Sunday morning, and Christmas fairs in season.
The Romanesque church tower, lighted a glowing ocher at night, looms
overhead. Across Passeig Reina Elisenda from the church (50 yards to

the left), wander through the brick-and-steel hangar **produce market** and the tiny, flower- and bougainvillea-choked **Plaça Sant Gaietà** just behind it. For a quick tour of upper Sarrià, walk behind the market along the cobbled Carrer Pare Miquel de Sarrià to Major de Sarrià, turn uphill to the left and then right into Carrer Graus past the door into the excellent garden restaurant Vivanda. A left on Carrer Avió Plus Ultra will take you past Sarrià's most wisteria- and ivy-covered house (on the right) and past the studio of floral artisan Flora Miserachs in the ancient village house at No. 21. Loop around to the left back into Major de Sarrià and walk back down (past the superb restaurant Tram-Tram on your right), past the tiny old village houses at Nos. 188 and 126 (the latter with the year 1694 engraved in the stone over the door) to return to Plaça Sarrià.

Cut through the Placeta del Roser to the left of the church to the elegant **town hall** in the Plaça de la Vila; note the buxom bronze sculpture of **Pomona,** goddess of fruit, by famed Sarrià sculptor Josep Clarà (1878–1958). After peeking in to see the massive ceiling beams (and reasonable fixed-price lunch menu) in the restaurant Vell Sarrià, at the corner of Major de Sarrià, go back to the Pomona bronze and turn left into tiny Carrer dels Paletes with its tiny niche on the corner overhead to the right. The saint in the niche is Sant Antoni, patron saint of bricklayers (*paletes*). You'll come out on Major de Sarrià. Continue down this pedestrian-only street and turn left into bougainvillea- and honeysuckle-lined **Carrer Canet,** with its diminutive, cottagelike artisans' quarters. The tiny houses at Nos. 15, 21, and 23 are some of the few remaining original village houses in Sarrià. Turn right at the first corner on Carrer Cornet i Mas and walk two blocks down to Carrer Jaume Piquet.

A quick probe to the left will take you to No. 30, Barcelona's most perfect small-format **Moderniste house,** thought to be the work of no less than Palau de la Música Catalana architect Domènech i Montaner, complete with faux-medieval upper windows, wrought-iron grillwork, floral and fruited ornamentation, and organically curved and carved wooden doors either by or inspired by Gaudí himself. The next stop down Cornet i Mas is Sarrià's prettiest square, **Plaça Sant Vicens,** a leafy space ringed by old Sarrià houses and centered on a statue of Sarrià's patron, St. Vincent, portrayed, as always, beside the millstone used to sink him to the bottom of the Mediterranean after he was martyred in Valencia in 302. Note the other versions of the saint, in the ceramic tiles and behind the glass pane of the niche over the square's upper right-hand corner. Can Pau, the café on the lower corner with Carrer Mañé i Flaquer, is the local hangout, a good place for coffee and once a haven for authors Gabriel García Marquez and Mario Vargas Llosa, who lived in Sarrià in the late 1960s and early 1970s.

Other Sarrià landmarks to look for include the two **Foix** pastry stores, one at Plaça Sarrià 9–10 and the other at Major de Sarrià 57, above Bar Tomás. Both have excellent pastries, breads, and cold *cava* (Catalan sparkling wine). The late J. V. Foix (1893–1987), son of the store's founders, was one of the great Catalan poets of the 20th century, a key player in keeping the Catalan language alive during the 40-year Franco regime. The Plaça Sarrià Foix, a good spot for homemade ice cream, has a bronze bust of the poet, whereas the Major de Sarrià location has a bronze plaque identifying the house as the poet's birthplace and inscribed with one of his most memorable verses: *Tota amor és latent en l'altra amor/tot llenguatge és saó d'una parla comuna/tota terra batega a la pàtria de tots/tota fe serà suc d'una més alta fe* (Every love is latent in the other love/every language is part of a common tongue/every country touches the fatherland of all/every faith will be the essence of a higher faith). ⊠*Pl. Sarrià (take Bus 22 from the bottom of Av. de Tibidabo, or the U-6 train on the FGC subway to Reina Elisenda), Sarrià* Ⓜ*Reina Elisenda.*

❹ **Torre Bellesguard.** For Gaudí to the last drop, climb up above Plaça de la Bonanova to this private residence built between 1900 and 1909 over the ruins of the summer palace of the last of the sovereign countkings of the Catalan-Aragonese realm, Martí I l'Humà (Martin I the Humane), whose reign ended in 1410. This homage to the king has a bell arch, tower, gargoyles, and crenellated battlements that are all Gaudí winks to Gothic architecture; the catenary arches and the puzzles of *trencadis* (broken bits of stone) of colored slate on the facade and over the windows are pure Gaudí. Built of rough slate from the Collserola hills up behind the site, Torre Bellesguard blends into the background in what seems an early example of low-impact environmental design. Look for the stained-glass red and gold markings of the Catalan *senyera* (banner) on the tower, which is topped by the typical four-armed Greek cross favored by Gaudí. Over the front door is the inscription SENS PECAT FOU CONCEBUDA (without sin was she conceived) referring to the Immaculate Conception of the Virgin Mary, while above on the facade appears a colorful Bell Esguard (beautiful view). On either side of the front door are benches with trencadis mosaics of playful fish bearing the crimson *quatre barres* (four bars) of the Catalan flag as well as the Corona d'Aragó (Crown of Aragón). The fish are a reference to Catalonia's medieval maritime empire, during which it was said that "not even a fish dared swim the Mediterranean without showing the colors of the Catalan flag." The surprisingly colorful and ornate interior of the residence is rarely viewable, though at the Càtedra Gaudí on Avinguda de Pedralbes photographic studies show the architect's interior supporting catenary arches in a number of sizes and shapes. ⊠*Bellesguard 16–20, Sant Gervasi* ☉*For visits consult the Ruta del Modernisme* ☎*93/317–7652* Ⓜ*Sarrià.*

**NEED A BREAK?**

**Bar Tomás** ( ⊠*Major de Sarrià 49, Sarrià* ☎*93/203–1077* Ⓜ*Sarrià*), on the corner of Jaume Piquet, is a Barcelona institution, home of the finest potatoes in town. Order the famous *doble mixta* of potatoes with *allioli* and hot sauce. Draft beer (ask for a *caña*) is the de rigueur beverage.

**ALSO WORTH SEEING**

❸ **Colegio de les Teresianas.** Built in 1889 for the Reverend Mothers of St. Theresa, when Gaudí was in a relatively benign creative fervor and still occasionally using straight lines, this building, still a school, showcases upper floors reminiscent of those in Berenguer's apartment house at Carrer de l'Or 44 with its steep peaks and verticality. Hired to finish a job begun by another architect, Gaudí found his freedom of movement somewhat limited in this project, both in budget and in the work completed before he started. The dominant theme here is the architect's use of steep, narrow catenary arches and Mudejar exposed-brick pillars. The most striking effects are on the second floor, where two rows of a dozen catenary arches run the width of the building, each of them unique because, as Gaudí explained, nothing in nature is identical. The brick columns are crowned with T-shape brick capitals (for St. Theresa). The tiny patios filled with plants are Gaudí's nod to the Moorish courtyard tradition. Look down at the marble doorstep for the inscription by mystic writer and poet Santa Teresa de Avila (1515–82), the much-quoted TODO SE PASA (all things pass), the letters themselves partly worn away by a century of footsteps. For visits, consult the **Ruta del Modernisme** (☎93/317–7652, 902/076621 *within Spain* ⊕*www.rutadelmodernisme.com*). ✉*Ganduxer 85, Sant Gervasi* ☎93/254–1670 Ⓜ*Les Tres Torres, Sarrià.*

❻ **Palau Reial de Pedralbes** *(Royal Palace of Pedralbes).* Built in the 1910s as the palatial estate of Count Eusebi Güell—one of Gaudí's most important patrons—this mansion was transformed into a royal palace by architect Eusebi Bona i Puig and completed in 1929. King Alfonso XIII, grandfather of Spanish king Juan Carlos I, visited the palace in the mid-1920s before its completion. In 1931, during the Second Spanish Republic, the palace became the property of the municipal government, and it was converted to a decorative arts museum in 1932. In 1936 the rambling, elegant country-manor-house palace was used as the official residence of Manuel Azaña, last president of the Spanish Republic.

Today the palace houses both the **Museu de les Arts Decoratives** and the **Museu de la Ceràmica.** The collection of decorative arts includes palace furniture and antiques from the 15th through 20th centuries, while the ceramics display covers Spanish ceramic art from the 12th century to the present, as well as ceramics by contemporary artists. The influence of Moorish design techniques in Spanish ceramics and decorative arts is carefully documented in a separate display. A good 30-minute forced march down from the Monestir de Pedralbes, the palace is good place to visit in combination with the Càtedra Gaudí study center. The best way to walk there from Sarrià's Plaça de Sant Vicens is to cut across Major de Sarrià and Oriol Mestres to Fontcoberta, take a left and then a right on Vives i Tutó, and walk to the corner of Conde del Trinquet, where you can then go through the consecutive gardens of the Casal de Sarrià and the Jardins de la Vil.la Amèlia, exiting into Passeig de Claudi Güell and cutting down to the end of Passeig Manuel Girona just across from the Càtedra Gaudí. After seeing Càtedra Gaudí, cut around the right side and walk along Carrer de Fernando Primo de Rivera, which runs along the garden walls of the palace, down to the main entrance on the Diagonal. ✉*Av. Diagonal 686, Pedralbes* ☎93/280–5024 *decorative arts museum,* 93/280–1621 *ceramic museum* ⊕*www.museuceramica.bcn.es* ⊕*www.museuartsdec-*

*oratives.bcn.cat* ✉€4 *includes both museums; free 1st Sun. of month* ⊙ *Tues.–Sat. 10–6, Sun. 10–3* Ⓜ *Palau Reial.*

# TIBIDABO, VALLVIDRERA & THE COLLSEROLA HILLS

Tibidabo is Barcelona's traditional promontory, a romantic evening and late-night promenade overlooking the city and a nonpareil point from which to watch the Mediterranean produce Technicolor dawns and blazing sunrises. The Collserola hills, Barcelona's version of the Vienna Woods out to the northwest of the city, are visible rising verdantly behind the city. Honeycombed with well-kept trails, the Parc de Collserola is a vast, 20,000-acre forest and park beyond Tibidabo and Vallvidrera, complete with wild boar and miles of wilderness. The offices of the Parc de Collserola authorities next to the Jacint Verdaguer museum at Vil.la Joana can supply detailed maps of this lush resource just 10 minutes by train from Sarrià. Vallvidrera, a busy hilltop intersection with a few markets, bars, restaurants, and several notable Moderniste houses, perches at the pinnacle overlooking both the Montserrat massif to the west and Barcelona below to the east. Return to Barcelona either by walking the Carretera de les Aigües (Water Road), so named for the canals that once carried water into downtown Barcelona from the upper Llobregat River, or from Vallvidrera's Art Nouveau funicular station.

### A GOOD TOUR

At the top of Carrer de Balmes, the U-7 FGC Generalitat Tibidabo train's run from Plaça Catalunya ends at Plaça Kennedy. The first building on the right as you start up Avinguda del Tibidabo is known as La Rotonda, notable for its Art Nouveau ceramic ornamentation on the upper part of the facade. The Tramvía Blau (Blue Trolley) sets out from just above La Rotonda and, passing the imposing white **Casa Roviralta–El Frare Blanc,** drops you at Plaça del Doctor Andreu, where the funicular climbs up to the heights of **Tibidabo.** Plaça del Doctor Andreu has several restaurants, the best of which is La Venta. From Tibidabo the road to the **Torre de Collserola** continues another 2 km (1 mi) over to **Vallvidrera,** where there are several good restaurants (such as Can Trampa in Plaça de Vallvidrera). From Vallvidrera, return to Barcelona via the funicular or on foot. The other way to approach is via the Baixador de Vallvidrera stop on the FGC Generalitat railway line to San Cugat, Sabadell, or Terrassa. A five-minute walk up to the **Museu Verdaguer** at Vil.la Joana will put you on well-marked trails through the Parc de Collserola. There are also trail markings to Vil.la Joana from the Torre de Collserola. The Barcelona train from the Baixador de Vallvidrera will drop you back in Plaça de Catalunya in 20 minutes.

TIMING   This is a four-hour outing, just to Tibidabo, Vallvidrera, and back. Add an hour or two for lunch and another three for the trek out to Vil.la Joana and back by train. A hike from Vil.la Joana all the way to the end of the *rompeolas* (breakwater) in the port could be done in four to five hours (followed by lunch in the Torre de San Sebastián at the Torre de Altamar).

HOW TO GET THERE The FGC U-7 train from Plaça Catalunya will leave you at Tibidabo's Tramvía Blau (Blue Trolley). The FGC trains that run out to Sant Cugat, Terrassa, and Sabadell stop at Peu Funicular, and the funicular up to Vallvidrera. These same trains will also leave you at the Baixador de Vallvidrera stop through the tunnel under the Collserola hills, where a two-hour hike will take you past Vil.la Joana, poet Jacint Verdaguer's last home, and into Vallvidrera and upper Barcelona.

## WHAT TO SEE: MAIN ATTRACTION

OFF THE BEATEN PATH

**CosmoCaixa–Museu de la Ciència Fundació "La Caixa"** Young scientific minds work overtime in this new and ever-more-interactive science museum, just below Tibidabo. Among the many displays designed for children seven and up are the Geological Wall, a history of rocks and rock formations studied through a transversal cutaway section; and the Underwater Forest, showcasing the climate and species of an Amazonian rain forest in a large greenhouse. Exhibits of sustainable exploitation techniques such as the Red Line: How to Make Wood Without Damaging the Forest are accompanied by explanations of environmental problems and how to correct them. ⊠ *Teodor Roviralta 55, Sant Gervasi* ☎ *93/212–6050* ⊕ *www.cosmocaixa.com* ⌚ *€3 (€2 per interactive activity inside)* ⊙ *Tues.–Sun. 10–8* Ⓜ *Avinguda de Tibidabo and Tramvia Blau at stop halfway up to Tibidabo.*

## ALSO WORTH SEEING

**Casa Roviralta–El Frare Blanc.** Gaudí disciple Joan Rubió i Bellver, author of the Gran Via's Casa Golferichs, won the Barcelona architecture prize of 1913 with this hulking interplay of exposed brick and white surfaces. The house is traditionally known as *El Frare Blanc* (The White Monk) for the *masía* (Catalan country house) that previously occupied the spot and served as home to a community of Dominican monks, who wore white habits. Now the home of the Asador de Aranda restaurant, this is a place to keep in mind for a late-winter-afternoon roast after a hike in from beyond the Collserola hills. ⊠ *Av. Tibidabo 31, La Bonanova* ☎ *93/417–0115* Ⓜ *Tibidabo.*

**Museu Verdaguer–Vil.la Joana.** Catalonian poet Jacint Verdaguer died in this house in 1902. The story of Verdaguer's reinvention of Catalan nationalism in the late 19th century, and his ultimate death in disgrace, defrocked and impoverished, is a fascinating saga. Considered the national poet of Catalonia and the most revered and beloved voice of the Catalan "Renaixença" of the 19th century, Verdaguer—universally known as *Mossèn Cinto* (Mossèn is Catalan for priest; Cinto is from Jacinto, Spanish for Jacint)—finally succumbed to tuberculosis and a general collapse triggered by economic, existential, and doctrinal religious troubles. Priest, poet, mystic, student, hiker, and lover of the Pyrenees, he was seen as a virtual saint, and wrote works of great religious and patriotic fervor such as *Idilis* and *Cants mistichs,* as well his famous long masterpiece, *Canigó* (1886). In *La Atlàntida* (1877), eventually to become a Manuel de Falla opera-oratorio, he wrote about prehistoric myths of the Iberian Peninsula and the Pyrenees. Verdaguer's death provoked massive mourning. His popularity was so enormous that violently anticlerical Barcelona anarchists in mid-uprising ceased fighting and stormed the churches to ring the bells on hearing the news of his death. The funeral was one of the greatest and most multitudinous events in Barcelona history, comparable only to Gaudí's in spontaneity and emotion.

Lines from his patriotic poem *Enyorança* (*Yearning*) are slowly and sonorously recited at Vil.la Joana every June 10 on the anniversary of his death, as the last evening sun streams in through the clouds over the Montserrat massif to the west, setting for Verdaguer's immortal poem (and song) *Virolai*.

*Sabéssiu lo catalá*
*sabríeu qué es enyorança*
*la malaltia dels cors*
*trasplantats a terra estranya…*
*aqueix mal que sols té nom*
*en nostra llengua estimada*
*aqueixa veu dels ausents,*
*aqueix sospir de la pàtria*
*que crida sos fills llunyans*
*amb amorosa recança.*

If you knew Catalan,
you would know what yearning was,
the affliction of hearts
transplanted to foreign lands…
that malady that only has a name
in our beloved tongue
the voice of those departed,
the sighing for the homeland
her distant sons lament
with loving sorrow.

✉ *Ctra. de les Planes, Vallvidrera* ☎ *93/204–7805* ⊕ *www.museuhistoria.bcn.es* 🎟 *Free* 🕐 *Oct.–Mar., Wed. 10–2, weekends 11–3; June–Sept., Wed. 10–2, Sat. 11–2 and 3–6, Sun. 11–3* Ⓜ *Baixador de Vallvidrera.*

**Tibidabo.** One of Barcelona's two promontories—the other is Montjuïc—this hill bears a particularly distinctive name, generally translated as "To Thee I Will Give" and referring to the Catalan legend that this was the spot from which Satan showed Christ, and tempted him with, all the riches of the earth (namely, Barcelona below) "if thou will fall down and worship me" or, according to the Gospel according to St. Matthew (in Latin), "Haec omnia Tibi dabo si cadens adoraberis me." When the wind blows the smog out to sea, the views from this 1,789-foot peak are legendary. Tibidabo's skyline is marked by a commercialized neo-Gothic church built by Enric Sagnier in 1902, a radio mast that used to seem tall, and—looking like something out of the 25th century—the 854-foot communications tower, the ⇨ **Torre de Collserola**, designed by Sir Norman Foster. There's not much to see here except the vista, particularly from the tower. Clear days are few and far between in 21st-century Barcelona, but if (and only if) you hit one, this two-hour excursion is worth considering. The restaurant **La Venta** ( ✉ *Pl. Doctor Andreu s/n, Vallvidrera* ☎ *93/212–6455*) at the base of the funicular is excellent and is a fine place to sit in the sun in cool weather (the establishment provides straw sun hats). **El Mirador de la Venta** ( ✉ *Pl. Doctor Andreu s/n, Vallvidrera* ☎ *93/212–6455*) has great views and contemporary cuisine to match. The bar **Mirablau** ( ✉ *Pl. Doctor Andreu s/n* ☎ *93/418–5879*), overlooking the city lights, is a popular hangout. ✉ *Take Tibidabo train (U-7) from Pl. de Catalunya; Buses 24 and 22 to Pl. Kennedy; or a taxi. At Av. Tibidabo, catch Tramvía Blau (Blue Trolley), which connects with the funicular to the summit* Ⓜ *Tibidabo.*

**Torre de Collserola.** The Collserola Tower, which unkindly dwarfs the rest of the Tibidabo promontory, was designed by Norman Foster for the 1992 Olympics amid controversy over defacement of the traditional mountain skyline. A vertigo-inducing elevator ride takes you to the observation deck atop the tower, where you can drink in a splendid panorama of the city (when weather conditions allow). Take the funicular up to Tibidabo; from Plaza Tibidabo there is free transport to the tower. ✉ *Av. de Vallvidrera, Vallvidrera* ☎ *93/406–9354* 💶 *€6* 🕙 *Wed.–Sun. 11–6* Ⓜ *Tibidabo.*

★ **Vallvidrera.** This perched village is a quiet respite from Barcelona's headlong race. Oddly, there's nothing exclusive or upmarket—for now—about Vallvidrera, as most well-off barcelonins prefer to be closer to the center of things. From **Plaça Pep Ventura,** in front of the Moderniste funicular station, there are superb views over some typical little Vallvidrera houses and the Montserrat massif hulking in the distance to the west. Vallvidrera can be reached from the Peu Funicular train stop and the Vallvidrera funicular, by road, or on foot from Tibidabo or Vil.la Joana. The cozy Can Trampa at the center of town in Plaça de Vallvidrera, and Can Martí down below, above the Carretera de les Aigües, are fine spots for lunch or dinner. Ⓜ *Peu Funicular.*

# MONTJUÏC

This hill overlooking the south side of the port is popularly said to have been named Mont Juif for the Jewish cemetery once on its slopes, though a 3rd-century Roman document referring to the construction of a road between Mons Taber (around the cathedral) and Mons Jovis (Mount of Jove) suggests that in fact the name derives from the Roman deity Jove, or Jupiter. Compared to the human warmth, hustle, and bustle of Barcelona, Montjuïc may feel remote, but its Miró Foundation, the Museu Nacional d'Art de Catalunya's Romanesque collection of Pyrenean murals and frescoes in the Palau Nacional, the minimalist Mies van der Rohe Pavilion, the lush Jardins de Mossèn Cinto Verdaguer, and the gallery and auditorium CaixaFòrum (Casaramona) are all undoubtedly among Barcelona's must-see sights. Other Montjuïc choices—the fortress, the Olympic stadium, Palau Sant Jordi, and the

Poble Espanyol—are interesting enough, though second-tier visits compared to options such as Parc Güell and the Monestir de Pedralbes.

*Numbers in the text correspond to numbers in the margin and on the Montjuïc map.*

**A GOOD TOUR**

Walking from sight to sight on Montjuïc is possible but not recommended. The walking tends to be long and, without the city's ongoing street theater, somewhat tedious. What's more, you'll want fresh feet to appreciate the museums and sights, especially the Romanesque art collection in the Palau Nacional and the Miró Foundation.

The Transbordador Aeri drops you at the Jardins de Miramar, a 10-minute walk from the Plaça de Dante; the Funicular de Montjuïc from Paral.lel Metro stops immediately beside Plaça de Dante. From here, another small cable car takes you up to the **Castell de Montjuïc** ❶. From the bottom station, the **Fundació Miró** ❷—a much-loved museum, with fine scenic vantage points, devoted to one of Barcelona's most celebrated modern artists—is just a few minutes' walk, and beyond are the **Estadi Olímpic** ❸ (Olympic Stadium) and the Palau Sant Jordi. From the stadium, walk straight down to the Palau Nacional and its **Museu Nacional d'Art de Catalunya** ❹—a colossal palace housing what is widely considered the finest collection of Romanesque art in the world. The **Museu d'Arqueologia de Catalunya** ❺ is just down to the east. From the Palau Nacional, a wide stairway leads down past the Plaça de les Cascades and the Font Màgic, past the famous **Mies van der Rohe Pavilion** ❻ and the **CaixaFòrum (Casaramona)** ❼ cultural center. **Poble Espanyol** ❽ is a few hundred yards up to the left of CaixaFòrum on Avinguda Marquès de Comillas. The Fira de Barcelona convention pavilions line either side of Avinguda de la Reina Maria Cristina, leading out through the so-called Venetian Towers to **Plaça de Espanya** ❾.

TIMING   With unhurried visits to the Miró Foundation and any or all of the Museu Nacional d'Art de Catalunya collections in the Palau Nacional, this is a four- to five-hour excursion, if not a full day. Have lunch afterward in the Poble Espanyol just up from Mies van der Rohe's Barcelona Pavilion or in the excellent restaurant at the Fundació Miró. Even better, find your way down into the Poble Sec neighborhood east of Montjuïc and graze your way back to the Rambla.

HOW TO GET   The most dramatic approach to Montjuïc is the cross-harbor cable car
THERE   (Transbordador Aeri) from Barceloneta or from the mid-station in the port; Montjuïc is accessed by taxi or Bus 61 (or on foot) from Plaça Espanya, or by the funicular that operates from the Paral.lel (Paral.lel metro stop, Line 3). The Telefèric de Montjuïc up from the funicular stop to the Castell de Montjuïc is the final leg to the top

**WHAT TO SEE: MAIN ATTRACTIONS**

★ ❼ **CaixaFòrum.** This redbrick, neo-Mudejar Art Nouveau fortress, built to house a factory in 1911 by Josep Puig i Cadafalch (architect of Casa de les Punxes, Casa Amatller, Casa Martí, and Casa Quadras), is a center for art exhibits, concerts, lectures, and cultural events. Well worth

# Montjuïc

Parc Joan Miró

Les Arenes

ROCAFORT

C. de la Creu Coberta

C. de Moianès

C. de la Bordeta

C. de la Diputació

Gran Vía de les Corts Catalanes

ESPANYA Ⓜ

**9**

Gran Vía de les Corts Catalanes

Carrer de Vilamarí

Carrer d'Entença

C. de Rocafort

C. de Calàbria

C. de Mèxic

Avda. del Marques de Comillas

**7**

**8**

Plaça de Sant Jordi

**6**

Avda. dels Montanyans

Avda. de la Reina Maria Cristina

Avda. de Rius i Taulet

Avda. de la Tècnica

Avda. del Parallel

Avda. de Mistral

C. de Tamarit

C. de Tamarit

Avda. de l'Estadi

Passeig de les Cascades

Avda. de Lleida

C. de Ricart

C. de la França Xica

POBLE SEC Ⓜ

C. de la Concòrdia

P. de Minici Natal

**4**

Passeig de Santa Madrona

Passeig de l'Exposició

C. de Blai

Carrer de Margarit

Cami del Polvorí

Jardins de Joan Maragall

**5**

C. de Magalhaes

C. d'Elkano

Passeig Olímpic

**3**

**2**

Avda. de Miramar

C. dels Tres Pins

Passeig Olímpic

Carrer del Doctor Font i Quer

Jardins de Mossèn Jacint Verdaguer

Parc d'Atraccions de Montjuïc

Jardins de Miramar

Carretera dels Mondials

Parc de Montjuïc

**Castell de Montjuïc**

**1**

Carretera de Montjuïc

TO → TELEFÉRIC STATION

C. de Miramar

| KEY | |
|---|---|
| •—•—• | Funicular |
| ◇◈◇ | Metro Stops |
| •••• | Teleféric |

0 ————— 550 yds
0 ————— 500 meters

keeping an eye on in daily listings, Casaramona, now CaixaFòrum, has come back to life as one of Barcelona's hottest art venues. The restoration work is one more example of the fusion of ultramodern design techniques with traditional (even Art Nouveau) architecture. ⊠*Av. Marquès de Comillas 6–8, Montjuïc* ☎*93/476–8600* ⊕*www. fundacio.lacaixa.es* 🔳*Free; charge for evening concerts* ⊘*Tues.–Sun. 10–8; later for concerts.*

**❷ Fundació Miró.** The Miró Foundation, a gift from the artist Joan Miró to
FodorśChoice his native city, is one of Barcelona's most exciting showcases of contem-
★ porary art. The airy, white building, with panoramic views north over Barcelona, was designed by Josep Lluís Sert and opened in 1975; an extension was added by Sert's pupil Jaume Freixa in 1988. Miró's playful and colorful style, filled with Mediterranean light and humor, seems a perfect match for its surroundings, and the exhibits and retrospectives that open here tend to be progressive and provocative. Look for Alexander Calder's fountain of moving mercury. Miró himself rests in the cemetery on Montjuïc's southern slopes. During the Franco regime, which he strongly opposed, Miró first lived in self-imposed exile in Paris, then moved to Majorca in 1956. When he died in 1983, the Catalans gave him a send-off amounting to a state funeral. ⊠*Av. Miramar 71, Montjuïc* ☎*93/443–9470* ⊕*www.bcn.fjmiro.es* 🔳*€7.50* ⊘*Tues., Wed., Fri., and Sat. 10–7, Thurs. 10–9:30, Sun. 10–2:30.*

**★ ❻ Mies van der Rohe Pavilion.** One of the architectural masterpieces of the Bauhaus School, the legendary Pavelló Mies van der Rohe—the German contribution to the 1929 International Exhibition, reassembled between 1983 and 1986—remains a stunning "less is more" study in interlocking planes of white marble, green onyx, and glass. In effect, it is Barcelona's aesthetic antonym (possibly in company with Richard Meier's Museu d'Art Contemporani de Barcelona, Rafael Moneo's Auditori, and the Mediterranean Gothic Santa Maria del Mar) for the hyper–Art Nouveau Palau de la Música and the city's myriad Gaudí spectaculars. Don't fail to note the matching patterns in the green onyx panels or the mirror play of the black carpet inside the pavilion with the reflecting pool outside, or the iconic Barcelona chair designed by Ludwig Mies van der Rohe (1886–1969); reproductions of the chair have graced Modernist and modern interiors around the world for decades. ⊠*Av. Marquès de Comillas s/n, Montjuïc* ☎*93/423–4016* ⊕*www.miesbcn.com* 🔳*€4* ⊘*Daily 10–8.*

**❹ Museu Nacional d'Art de Catalunya** *(MNAC; Catalonian National*
FodorśChoice *Museum of Art).* Housed in the imposingly domed, towered, fres-
★ coed, and columned **Palau Nacional,** built in 1929 as the centerpiece of the International Exposition, this superb museum was renovated in 1995 by Gae Aulenti, architect of the Musée d'Orsay in Paris. In 2004 the museum's three collections—Romanesque, Gothic, and the Cambó Collection, an eclectic trove, including a Goya, donated by Francesc Cambó—were joined by the 19th- and 20th-century collection of Catalan impressionist and Moderniste painters. Also now on display is the Thyssen-Bornemisza collection of early masters, with works by Zurbarán, Rubens, Tintoretto, Velázquez, and others. With

this influx of artistic treasure, the MNAC becomes Catalonia's grand central museum. Pride of place goes to the Romanesque exhibition, the world's finest collection of Romanesque frescoes, altarpieces, and wood carvings, most of them rescued from chapels in the Pyrenees during the 1920s to save them from deterioration, theft, and art dealers. Many, such as the famous *Cristo de Taüll* fresco (from the church of Sant Climent de Taüll in Taüll), have been reproduced and replaced in their original settings. ✉*Mirador del Palau 6, Montjuïc* ☎*93/622–0360* ⊕*www.mnac.es* ⊡*€9* ☾*Tues.–Sat. 10–7, Sun. 10–2:30.*

## ALSO WORTH SEEING

**❶ Castell de Montjuïc.** Built in 1640 by rebels against Felipe IV, the castle has been stormed several times, most famously in 1705 by Lord Peterborough for Archduke Carlos of Austria. In 1808, during the Peninsular War, it was seized by the French under General Dufresne. Later, during an 1842 civil disturbance, Barcelona was bombed from its heights by a Spanish artillery battery. The moat contains attractive gardens, with one side given over to an archery range, and the various terraces have panoramic views over the city and out to sea. The castle now functions as a **military museum** housing the weapons collection of early-20th-century sculptor Frederic Marès. ✉*Ctra. de Montjuïc 66, Montjuïc* ☎*93/329–8613* ⊡*€3* ☾*Tues.–Sun. 9:30–8.*

**★ ❸ Estadi Olímpic.** The Olympic Stadium was originally built for the International Exhibition of 1929, with the idea that Barcelona would then host the 1936 Olympics (ultimately staged in Hitler's Berlin). After failing twice to win the nomination, the city celebrated the attainment of its long-cherished goal by renovating the semiderelict stadium in time for 1992, providing seating for 70,000. The **Galeria Olímpica,** a museum about the Olympic movement in Barcelona, displays objects and shows audiovisual replays from the 1992 Olympics. An information center traces the history of the modern Olympics from Athens in 1896 to the present. Next door and just downhill stands the futuristic **Palau Sant Jordi Sports Palace,** designed by the noted Japanese architect Arata Isozaki. The Isozaki structure has no pillars or beams to obstruct the view and was built from the roof down—the roof was built first, then hydraulically lifted into place. ✉*Passeig Olímpic 17–19, Montjuïc* ☎*93/426–2089* ⊕*www.fundaciobarcelonaolimpica.es* ⊡*€4 gallery* ☾*Tues.–Sat. 10–2 and 4–7.*

**❺ Museu d'Arqueologia de Catalunya.** Just downhill to the right of the Palau Nacional, the Museum of Archaeology holds important finds from the Greek ruins at Empúries, on the Costa Brava. These are shown alongside fascinating objects from, and explanations of, megalithic Spain. ✉*Passeig Santa Madrona 39–41, Montjuïc* ☎*93/424–6577* ⊕*www. mac.es* ⊡*€2.50* ☾*Tues.–Sat. 9:30–7, Sun. 10–2:30.*

**❾ Plaça de Espanya.** This busy circle is a good place to avoid, but sooner or later you'll probably need to cross it to go to the convention center or to the Palau Nacional. It's dominated by the so-called Venetian Towers (they're actually Tuscan) built in 1927 as the grand entrance to the 1929 International Exposition. The fountain in the center is the work of Josep Maria Jujol, the Gaudí collaborator who designed the curvy and colorful benches in Parc Güell. The sculptures are by Miquel Blay, one of the master artists and craftsmen who put together the Palau de la Música. The neo-Mudejar bullring, Les Arenes, is now used for theater and political rallies. On the corner of Carrer Llançà, just down to the right looking at the bullring, you can just get a glimpse of the kaleidoscopic lepidopteran atop the Art Nouveau Casa de la Papallona (House of the Butterfly). From the plaza, you can take the metro or Bus 38 back to the Plaça de Catalunya.

☾ ❽ **Poble Espanyol.** Created for the 1929 International Exhibition as a sort of artificial Spain-in-a-bottle, with faithful reproductions of Spain's various architectural styles punctuated with boutiques, workshops, and studios, the Spanish Village takes you from the walls of Ávila to the wine cellars of Jerez de la Frontera. The liveliest time to come is at night, and a reservation at one of the half-dozen restaurants gets you in for free, as does the purchase of a ticket for the two discos or the Tablao del Carmen flamenco club. ✉ *Av. Marquès de Comillas s/n, Montjuïc* ☎ *93/508–6300* ⊕ *www.poble-espanyol.com* 💶 *€7.50* ☽ *Mon. 9–8, Tues.–Thurs. 9–2, Sat. 9–4, Sun. 9–noon.*

# Where to Eat

## WORD OF MOUTH

"The menu was entirely in Catalan but we figured out enough to order lunch. I had a beautiful plate of shrimp carpaccio with green pasta...It's that first meal in Europe that [made] me realize we're not in Kansas any more. By now it was after 2:30 but the place was filled with workers on their lunch break. So we were already getting into the rhythm of the Barcelona day."

—Nikki

# WHERE TO EAT PLANNER

## Dining Hours

Barcelona, like the rest of Spain, dines late. Those who try to fight this reality will not fare well. Lunch is served 2–4 and dinner 9–11. If you arrive a half hour early, you may score a table but miss the life and fun of the place. The restaurants serving continuously 1 PM–1 AM are rarely the best ones. (Botafumeiro is an exception.) Hunger attacks between meals are easily resolved in the city's numerous cafés and tapas bars, where anything from a *bocadillo de tortilla* (potato omelet sandwich) to *gambas al ajillo* (shrimp cooked in garlic) will more than stem the tide.

## Prices

Since the introduction of the euro, prices have skyrocketed in Barcelona. Whereas fixed lunch menus can be found for as little as €10, most good restaurants cost closer to €20. For serious evening dining, plan on spending €30–€50 per person, with the most expensive places costing upward of €75, and often, depending on your wine choices, over €100. Barcelona restaurants, even pricey gourmet establishments, offer a daily lunchtime menu (*menú del día*) consisting of two courses plus wine, coffee, or dessert at rock-bottom prices.

## Tipping

Tipping, though common, is not required; the gratuity is included in the check. If you do tip, as an extra courtesy, anywhere from 5% to 10% is perfectly acceptable. No one seems to care much about tipping, though all parties seem to end up happier if a small gratuity is left.

## Reservations

Nearly all of Barcelona's best restaurants require reservations. As the city has grown in popularity, more and more receptionists are perfectly able to take your reservations in English. Your hotel concierge will also be happy to call and reserve you a table. Beware of taxi drivers and hotel receptionists who try to send you to other restaurants they claim are better.

## Dress

In Barcelona there *is* an unwritten code of elegance, and tourists in short shorts and tank tops will not feel comfortable in the city's top restaurants, and some of them might not even let you in.

## Smoking

Though anti-smoking regulations and no-smoking sections in restaurants have vastly improved over the last decade, you can often count on dining next to a table of smokers.

## What it costs in Euros

|  | ¢ | $ | $$ | $$$ | $$$$ |
|---|---|---|---|---|---|
| At Dinner | Under €10 | €10–€14 | €15–€22 | €23–€29 | Over €29 |

Prices are per person for a main course at dinner.

By George
Semler

**BARCELONA'S RESTAURANT SCENE IS AN** ongoing surprise. Between the cutting-edge of avant-garde culinary experimentation and the cosmopolitan and rustic dishes of traditional Catalan fare is a fleet of inventive chefs producing some of Europe's finest Mediterranean cuisine.

**The Cuisine:** Catalans are legendary lovers of fish, vegetables, rabbit, duck, lamb, game, and natural ingredients from the Pyrenees or the Mediterranean. The *mar i muntanya* (sea and mountain—that is, surf and turf), a recipe combining seafood with upland products, is a standard. Rabbit and prawns, cuttlefish and meatballs, chickpeas and clams are just a few examples. Combining salty and sweet tastes—a Moorish legacy—is another common theme, as in duck with pears, rabbit with figs, or lamb with olives.

| TOP 5 |
| --- |
| ■ Drolma for game and white truffles in season. |
| ■ Ca l'Isidre for classical Catalan cuisine. |
| ■ Comerç 24 for clever riffs on molecular gastronomy. |
| ■ Cinc Sentits for originality. |
| ■ Cal Pep for perfect seafood and general clamor. |

3

The Mediterranean diet, which is based on olive oil, seafood, fibrous vegetables, onions, garlic, and red wine, is at home in Barcelona, and food tends to be seasoned with Catalonia's four basic sauces—*allioli* (pure garlic and olive oil), *romescu* (almonds, hazelnuts, tomato, garlic, and olive oil), *sofregit* (fried onion, tomato, and garlic), and *samfaina* (a ratatouille-like vegetable mixture).

Typical entrées include *habas a la catalana* (a spicy broad-bean stew), *bullabesa* (fish soup-stew similar to the French bouillabaisse), and *espinacas a la catalana* (spinach cooked with oil, garlic, pine nuts, raisins, and bits of bacon). Toasted bread is often doused with olive oil and spread with squeezed tomato to make *pa amb tomaquet,* delicious on its own or as a side order.

**Deals & Discounts:** *Menús del día* (menus of the day), served only at lunchtime, are good values. Beware of the *advice* of hotel concierges and taxi drivers, who have been known to warn that the place you are going is either closed or no good anymore and to recommend places where they get kickbacks.

**And to Drink:** Catalan wines from the nearby Penedès region, especially the local *méthode champenoise* (sparkling white wine known in Catalonia as cava), adequately accompany regional cuisine. Meanwhile, winemakers from the Priorat, Ampurdan, and Costers del Segre regions are producing some of Spain's most exciting new wines.

# BEST BETS FOR BARCELONA DINING

Need a cheat sheet for Barcelona's thousands of restaurants? Our Fodor's writer has selected some of his favorites by price, cuisine, and experience in the lists shown here. You can also search by neighborhood or find specific details about a restaurant in our full reviews—just peruse the following pages. Happy dining in Catalonia's capital by the sea. ¡Bon profit!

**Fodor's**Choice

Àbac, $$$$, Tibidabo

Botafumeiro, $$$$, Gràcia

Ca l'Isidre, $$$$, Raval

Cal Pep, $$, Born-Ribera

Can Majó, $$$, Barceloneta

Casa Leopoldo, $$$, Raval

Cinc Sentits, $$$, Eixample

Comerç 24, $$$$, Born-Ribera

Drolma, $$$$, Eixample

El Racó de Can Fabes, $$$$, Sant Celoni

Manairó, $$$, Eixample

Neichel, $$$$, Pedralbes

Sant Pau, $$$$, Sant Pol del Mar

Silvestre, $$, Sant Gervasi

Tapioles 53, $$, Poble Sec

Tram-Tram, $$$$, Sarrià

HIGHLY RECOMMENDED

Alkimia, $$$, Eixample

Can Gaig, $$$$, Eixample

Cata 1.81, $$, Eixample

Hispania, $$$, Arenys de Mar

Ipar-Txoko, $$, Gràcia

La Cúpula, $$$, Eixample

Roig Robí, $$$, Gràcia

Taktika Berri, $$$$, Eixample

## By Price

$

Agut, Barri Gòtic

Ca l'Estevet, Raval

Can Manel la Puda, Barceloneta

Folquer, Gràcia

$$

Café de l'Acadèmia, Barri Gòtic

Cometacinc, Barri Gòtic

El Mató de Pedralbes, Pedralbes

La Taxidermista, Rambla

Silvestre, Sant Gervasi

$$$

Can Majó, Barceloneta

Cinc Sentits, Eixample

Manairó, Eixample

Suquet de l'Almirall, Barceloneta

Tram-Tram, Sarrià

Vivanda, Sarrià

$$$$

Àbac, Tibidabo

Ca l'Isidre, Raval

Can Gaig, Eixample

Comerç 24, Born-Ribera

Drolma, Eixample

El Racó de Can Fabes, Sant Celoni

## Cuisine

TRADITIONAL SPANISH

El Asador de Aranda, $$$, Tibidabo

TRADITIONAL CATALAN

Antiga Casa Solé, $$$$, Barceloneta

Ca l'Isidre, $$$$, Raval

Can Gaig, $$$$, Eixample

Casa Leopoldo, $$$, Raval

Drolma, $$$$, Eixample

Hispania, $$$, Arenys de Mar

Neichel, $$$$, Pedralbes

Tram-Tram, $$$, Sarrià

CONTEMPORARY CATALAN

Àbac, $$$$, Tibidabo

Andaira, $$$$, Barceloneta

La Cúpula, $$$, Eixample

L'Olivé, $$$, Eixample

**Sant Pau**, $$$$, Sant Pol de Mar

LA NUEVA COCINA/ EXPERIMENTAL CUISINE

**Alkimia**, $$$, Eixample

**Cinc Sentits**, $$$ , Eixample

**Comerç 24**, $$$$, Born-Ribera

**Manairó**, $$$, Eixample

**Tapioles 53**, $$, Poble Sec

BASQUE

**Ipar-Txoko**, $$, Gràcia

**Taktika Berri**, $$$$, Eixample

TAPAS

**Cal Pep**, $$, Born-Ribera

**Casa Lucio**, $$$, Eixample

**El Vaso de Oro**, $$, Barceloneta

**Inòpia Clàssic Bar**, $$, Eixample

**Mantequeria Can Ravell**, $$, Eixample

**Sagardi**, $$, Born-Ribera

STEAK HOUSE

**El Asador de Aranda**, $$$, Tibidabo

**Gorría**, $$$, Eixample

PAELLA

**Can Majó**, $$$, Barceloneta

**Suquet de l'Almirall**, $$$, Barceloneta

SEAFOOD

**Antiga Casa Solé**, $$$$, Barceloneta

**Botafumeiro**, $$$$, Gràcia

**Fishhh!**, $$$, Sant Gervasi

# By Experience

BEST BANG FOR YOUR BUCK

**Barceloneta**, $$, Barceloneta

**Cal Pep**, $$, Born-Ribera

**Mantequeria Ya Ya Amelia**, $$, Eixample

**Silvestre**, $$, Sant Gervasi

**Vivanda**, $$$, Sarrià

QUAINT AND COZY

**Agut**, $, Barri Gòtic

**Antiga Casa Solé**, $$$$, Barceloneta

**Ca l'Estevet**, $, Raval

**Casa Lucio**, $$$, Eixample

YOUNG AND HAPPENING

**Cinc Sentits**, $$$ , Eixample

**Comerç 24**, $$$$, Born-Ribera

**Manairó**, $$$, Eixample

**Nonell**, $$$, Barri Gòtic

**Shunka**, $$, Barri Gòtic

SUMMER DINING

**Can Majó**, $$$, Barceloneta

**Tram-Tram**, $$$, Sarrià

**Vivanda**, $$$, Sarrià

3

## CIUTAT VELLA (OLD CITY)

Ciutat Vella includes the Rambla, Barri Gòtic, Ribera, and Raval districts between Plaça de Catalunya and the port. Chic new restaurants and cafés seem to open daily in Barcelona's Old City.

### BARRI GÒTIC

CATALAN  ✕ **Café de l'Acadèmia.** With wicker chairs, stone walls, and background
$$  classical music, this place is sophisticated-rustic, and the excellent contemporary Mediterranean cuisine specialties such as *timbal d'escalibada amb formatge de cabra* (roast vegetable salad with goat cheese) or *crema de pastanaga amb gambes i virutes de parmesá* (cream of carrot soup with shrimp and Parmesan cheese shavings) make it more than a mere café. Politicians and functionaries from the nearby Generalitat frequent this dining room, which is always boiling with life. Be sure to reserve at lunchtime. ⊠*Lledó 1, Barri Gòtic* ☎*93/319–8253* ▭*AE, DC, MC, V* Ⓜ*Jaume I.*

$$  ✕ **Cometacinc.** This stylish place in the Barri Gòtic, an increasingly chic neighborhood of artisans and antiquers, is a fine example of Barcelona's new-over-old architecture and interior design panache. Although the 30-foot floor-to-ceiling wooden shutters are already a visual feast, the carefully prepared interpretations of old standards, such as the *carpaccio de toro de lidia* (carpaccio of fighting bull) with basil sauce and pine nuts, awaken the palate brilliantly. ⊠*Carrer Cometa 5, Barri Gòtic* ☎*93/310–1558* ▭*AE, DC, MC, V* ⊘*Closed Tues.* Ⓜ*Jaume I.*

$-$$  ✕ **Agut.** Wainscoting and 1950s canvases are the background for the mostly Catalan crowd in this homey restaurant in the lower reaches of the Gothic Quarter. Agut was founded in 1924, and its popularity has never waned—after all, hearty Catalan fare at a fantastic value is always in demand. In season (September–May), try the *pato silvestre agridulce* (sweet-and-sour wild duck). There's a good selection of wine, but no frills such as coffee or liqueur. ⊠*Gignàs 16, Barri Gòtic* ☎*93/315–1709* ▭*AE, MC, V* ⊘*Closed Mon. and July. No dinner Sun.* Ⓜ*Jaume I.*

$-$$  ✕ **Pla.** Filled with young couples night after night, this combination music, drinking, and dining place is candlelit and sleekly designed in glass over ancient stone, brick, and wood. The cuisine is light and contemporary, featuring inventive salads and fresh seafood. Open until 3 AM (kitchen open until 1) on Friday and Saturday, Pla is a good postconcert option. ⊠*Carrer Bellafila 5, Barri Gòtic* ☎*93/412–6552* ▭*AE, DC, MC, V* ⊘*Closed Tues. No lunch* Ⓜ*Jaume I.*

ECLECTIC  ✕ **Cuines Santa Caterina.** A lovingly restored market designed by the
$$-$$$  late Enric Miralles and completed by his widow Benedetta Tagliabue provides a spectacular setting for one of the city's most original dining operations. With a breakfast and tapas bar open from dawn to midnight and a variety of culinary specialties cross-referenced by cultures (Mediterranean, Asian) and products (pasta, rice, tapas) all served on sleek counters and long wooden tables under the undulating wooden superstructure of the market, this is an exciting place to dine. ⊠*Av.*

*Francesc Cambó, Barri Gòtic* ☎*93/268–9918* ⊟*AE, DC, MC, V* Ⓜ*Catalunya, Liceu, Jaume I.*

**$$–$$$** ✗**Nonell.** Chef Oliver Balteo draws from his experiences as a culinary professor in Venezuela as well as on his Lebanese roots to produce excellent, eclectic cuisine in this recent addition to the city's gastronomic scene. Dishes range from classic Mediterranean to Castilian roast suckling pig to Middle Eastern creams and sauces. The wine list is entirely original, featuring labels you may have never heard of but will be glad to get to know; service is impeccable and delivered with panache and wit—and all in perfect English. ⊠*Pl. Isidre Nonell, Barri Gòtic* ☎*93/301–1378* ⊟*AE, DC, MC, V* Ⓜ*Catalunya, Liceu.*

JAPANESE **$$** ✗**Shunka.** Widely regarded as Barcelona's finest Japanese restaurant, this cozy hideaway behind the Hotel Colón serves straight across the counter from the burners to the diners. Mediterranean and Japanese cuisines have much in common (such as raw fish dishes); at Shunka, the Asian-European fusion creations are peerlessly crafted and wholly delectable. ⊠*Sagristans 5, Barri Gòtic* ☎*93/412–4991* ⊟*AE, DC, MC, V* Ⓜ*Liceu.*

### BORN-RIBERA

CARIBBEAN **$–$$** ✗**La Habana Vieja.** If you've got an itch for a taste of Old Havana—*ropa vieja* (shredded beef) or *moros y cristianos* (black beans and rice) with *mojitos* (a sweet cocktail of rum, mint, and sugar) or a round of *plátanos a puñetazos* (punched plantains)—this is your Barcelona refuge. The upstairs tables overlooking the bar are cozy little crow's nests, and the neighborhood is filled with quirky dives and saloons for pre- and post-dinner carousing. ⊠*Bany Vells 2, Born-Ribera* ☎*93/268–2504* ⊟*AE, DC, MC, V* ☉*Closed Sun.* Ⓜ*Jaume I.*

ECLECTIC **$–$$** ✗**El Foro.** This hot spot near the Born is always full to the rafters with lively young and not-so-young people. Painting and photographic exhibits line the walls, and the menu is dominated by meat cooked over coals, pizzas, and salads. Flamenco and jazz performances downstairs are a good post-dinner option. ⊠*Princesa 53, Born-Ribera* ☎*93/310–1020* ⊟*AE, DC, MC, V* ☉*Closed Mon.* Ⓜ*Jaume I.*

LA NUEVA COCINA **$$$–$$$$** Fodor'sChoice ★ ✗**Comerç 24.** Artist, aesthete, and chef Carles Abellán playfully reinterprets traditional Catalan favorites at this minimalist treasure. Try the *arròs a banda* (paella with peeled mollusks and crustaceans), *tortilla de patatas* (potato omelet), and, for dessert, a postmodern version of the traditional after-school snack of chocolate, olive oil, salt, and bread. The menu is pretty far out, yet it always hits the mark. ⊠*Carrer Comerç 24, Born-Ribera* ☎*93/319–2102* ⚞*Reservations essential* ⊟*AE, DC, MC, V* ☉*Closed Sun.* Ⓜ*Jaume I.*

MEDITERRANEAN **$–$$** ✗**El Pebre Blau.** This handsome space, surrounded by centuries-old wooden doors and shutters, offers an ever-changing selection of dishes collected from all over the Mediterranean. A sybaritic bonanza on the site of the early baths (*banys vells*) of the waterfront district this is a soothing setting for contemporary dining at reasonable prices. ⊠*Bany Vells 21, Born-Ribera* ☎*93/319–1308* ⊟*AE, DC, MC, V* ☉*No lunch* Ⓜ*Jaume I.*

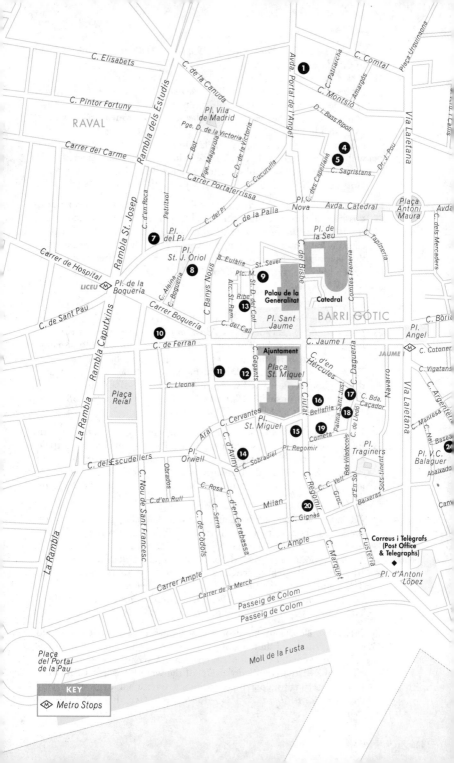

# Where to Eat in the Barri Gòtic & Born-Ribera

3

Carrer d' Ausias March

Carrer de Brun
C. Bou de St. Pere
C. Sant Pere Més Alt
M. del Pilar
2
3
C. Sant Pere Mitjà
C. Sant Pere Més Baix
Llàstics
C. Metges
C. de Castro
C. P. de la Figuera
C. de Jaume Giralt
C. del Portal Nou
C. de fonollar
Francesc Cambó
6
C. Freixures
C. de Tarrós
C. G. Pellisser
C. Colomines
Tiradors
C. del Comerç
Passeig de Pujades
40
C. Corders
39
Assaonadors
Tantarantana
C. de la Princesa
38
C. Barra de Ferro
C. Cremat Gran
26
Pl. Jaume Sabartes
C. Cremat Xic
Banys Vells
27
C. Montcada
37
C. Sabateret
C. Fusina
Grunyi
Brosoli
Arc St. Vincents
33
C. Flassaders
C. del Rec
Passeig de Picasso
Rossic
25
Miralles
29
31
32
Secca
C. de Mosques
C. del Comerç
C. Comercial
Sombrerers
30
35
36
Passeig del Born
Espartería
Plaça Santa Maria
23
C. Bonaire
C. de Ribera
Plaça de les Olles
Nous
34
C. A. de St. Joan
Pescateria
BORN-RIBERA
22
Vidriería
Calle del Mar
Avda. Marquès de l'Argentera
Passeig d'Isabel II
Plaça del Palau
21
C. Gen. Castaños
Passeig Circumval·lació
C. Reina Cristina
Avda. d'Icària
BARCELONETA

0                    100 yds
0                    100 meters

SEAFOOD
$$$$

✕**El Passadís d'en Pep.** Squirreled away through a tiny passageway off the Pla del Palau near the Santa Maria del Mar church, this lively bistro serves a rapid-fire succession of delicious seafood tapas and wine as soon as you appear. Sometime later in the proceedings you may be asked to make a decision about your main course, usually fish of one kind or another. Feel free to stop at this point. And avoid *bogavante* (lobster) unless you're on an expense account. ⊠*Pla del Palau 2, Born-Ribera* ☎*93/310–1021* ⊟*AE, DC, MC, V* ✆*Closed Sun. and last 2 wks of Aug.* Ⓜ*Jaume I.*

### RAMBLA

MEDITERRANEAN
$$–$$$

✕**La Taxidermista.** Don't worry: you won't dine surrounded by stuffed squirrels. A former natural-science museum and taxidermy shop (Dalí once purchased 200,000 ants and a stuffed rhinoceros here), this is the only recommendable restaurant in the sunny Plaça Reial. Decorator Beth Gali designed the interior around original beams and steel columns. Delicacies such as *bonito con escalibada y queso de cabra* (white tuna with braised aubergines, peppers, and goat cheese) are served at outside tables best enjoyed in the winter sun. ⊠*Pl. Reial 8, Rambla* ☎*93/412–4536* ⊟*AE, DC, MC, V* ✆*Closed Mon.* Ⓜ*Liceu.*

CATALAN
$$–$$$

✕**Can Culleretes.** Tucked away just off the Rambla in the Gothic Quarter, this family-run restaurant founded in 1786 breathes tradition in both decor and culinary offerings. As Barcelona's oldest restaurant (as listed in the Guinness Book of Records) generations of the Manubens and Agut families have kept this unpretentious spot at the forefront of the city's dining options for over two centuries. Wooden beams overhead and bright paintings of sea- and landscapes on the walls surround a jumble of tables served by legions of descendents of the founding families. Traditional Catalan specialties such as spinach cannelloni with cod, wild boar stew, or the classic white beans with botifarra sausage are impeccably prepared by a fleet of skilled family chefs. ⊠*Carrer Quintana 5, Rambla/Barri Gòtic* ☎*93/317–6485* ⊟*AE, DC, MC, V* ✆*Closed Mon. and July. No dinner Sun.* Ⓜ*Catalunya, Liceu.*

### RAVAL

CATALAN
$$$–$$$$
Fodor'sChoice
★

✕**Ca l'Isidre.** A favorite with Barcelona's art mob, this place is shellacked with pictures and engravings, some original, by Dalí and other art stars. Just inside the Raval from Avinguda del Paral.lel, the restaurant relies on fresh produce from the nearby Boqueria for its traditional Catalan cooking. Isidre's wines are invariably novelties from all over the Iberian Peninsula; ask for his advice and you will get a great wine as well as an enology, geography, and history course delivered with charm, brevity, and wit. The slight French accent in cuisine is evident in superb homemade foie gras. Come and go by cab at night; the area can be shady. ⊠*Les Flors 12, Raval* ☎*93/441–1139* ✍*Reservations essential* ⊟*AE, MC, V* ✆*Closed Sun., Easter wk, and mid-July–mid-Aug.* Ⓜ*Paral.lel.*

$$$–$$$$
Fodor'sChoice
★

✕**Casa Leopoldo.** Hidden in a dark Raval pocket west of the Rambla, this restaurant owned by the Gil family serves fine seafood and Catalan fare. To get here, approach along Carrer Hospital, take a left through the Passatge Bernardí Martorell, and go 50 feet right on Sant Rafael to

## On the Menu

Be prepared for tongue-twisting specialties such as the *minimandonguilles amb tomaquet concassé* (mini-meatballs with crushed tomato) and the *llom de xai al cardomom amb favetes a la menta* (lamb with cardamum and broad beans with mint). Menus in Catalan are as musical as they are aromatic, with rare ingredients such as *salicornia* (seawort, or sea asparagus) with *bacalao* (cod) or fragrant wild mushrooms such as *rossinyols* (chanterelles) and *moixernons* (field agaric) accompanying dishes such as *mandonguilles amb sepia* (meatballs with cuttlefish).

Four diverse sauces come to the classical Catalan table: *sofregit* (fried onion, tomato, and garlic used as a base for nearly everything); *samfaina* (a ratatouille-like sofregit with eggplant and sweet red peppers); *picada* (a paste of garlic, almonds, bread crumbs, and olive oil, that can also include pine nuts, parsley, saffron, or chocolate); and *allioli* (pounded garlic and olive oil).

The three e's deserve a place in any Catalan culinary anthology: *escalivada* (roasted red peppers, eggplants, and tomatoes served in garlic and olive oil); *esqueixada* (shredded salt-cod salad served raw with onions, peppers, olives, beans, olive oil, and vinegar); and *escudella* (a winter stew of meats and vegetables with noodles and beans).

Universal dishes, if somewhat old-fashioned, are *pa amb tomaquet* (toasted bread with squeezed tomato and olive oil), *espinacas a la catalana* (spinach cooked with raisins, garlic, and pine nuts), and *botifarra amb mongetes* (pork sausage with white beans). The *mar i muntanya* (sea and mountain, or Catalan surf 'n' turf), such as stewed chicken and prawns or meatballs and cuttlefish, has been a standard since Roman times. Rice dishes are called *arròs* and range from the standard seafood paella to the *arròs a banda* (paella with shelled prawns, shrimp, and mussels), to *arròs negre* (paella cooked in cuttlefish ink), to *fideuà* (paella made of vermicelli noodles) or *arròs caldoso* (a brothy risotto-like dish made with lobster).

Fresh fish such as *llobarro* (sea bass, *lubina* in Spanish) or *dorada* (gilthead bream) cooked *a la sal* (in a shell of salt) are standards, as are *llenguado* (sole) and *rodaballo* (turbot). Duck, goose, chicken, and rabbit frequent Catalan menus, as do *cabrit* (kid or baby goat), *xai* (lamb), *llom* (pork), and *bou* (beef). Finally, come desserts, the two Catalan classics, *mel i mató* (honey and fresh cream cheese) and *crema catalana* (a crème brûlée, sweet custard with a caramelized glaze).

A typical session *à table* in Barcelona might begin with *pica-pica* (hors d'oeuvres), a variety of delicacies such as *jamón ibérico de bellota* (acorn-fed ham), *xipirones* (baby squid), *pimientos de Padrón* (green peppers, some piquante), or *bunyols de bacallà* (cod fritters or croquettes), and pa amb tomaquet (bread with tomato). From here you can order a starter such as *canelones* (cannelloni) or *esqueixada* (shredded salt-cod salad served raw with onions, peppers, olives, beans, olive oil, and vinegar), or you can go straight to your main course.

the Gil front door. Try the *revuelto de ajos tiernos y gambas* (eggs scrambled with young garlic and shrimp) or the famous *cap-i-pota* (stewed head and hoof of pork). Albariños and Priorats are among Rosa Gil's favorites. ⊠ *Sant Rafael 24, Raval* ☎ *93/441–3014* ▭ *AE, DC, MC, V* ☾ *Closed Mon. No dinner Sun.* Ⓜ *Liceu.*

¢–$   ✕ **Ca l'Estevet.** Journalists, students, and artists haunt this romantic little spot near the MACBA (contemporary art museum), across the street from Barcelona's journalism school, and around the block from Barcelona's *La Vanguardia* daily. Estevet and family are charming, and the carefully elaborated Catalan cuisine sings, especially at these prices. Try the asparagus cooked over coals, the *chopitos gaditanos* (deep-fried baby octopus), or the *magret de pato* (duck breast). The house wine is inexpensive, light, and perfectly drinkable. ⊠ *Valdoncella 46, Raval* ☎ *93/302–4186* ▭ *AE, DC, MC, V* ☾ *Closed Sun.* Ⓜ *Catalunya.*

> ### TAPAS IN CATALONIA
>
> Catalonia was always too busy making and marketing things to have any time for tapas or the leisurely lifestyle that comes with wandering from bar to bar grazing on small portions—that is until the tourist industry made it clear that tapas were profitable. Curiously, what began as a lagniappe provided gratis with drinks, only made sense in Catalonia when attached to a price tag. Barcelona, once nearly barren of quality tapa opportunities, presently boasts some of Spain's finest and most creative miniature cuisine.

ECLECTIC
$$–$$$
Fodor'sChoice
★

✕ **Tapioles 53.** A former umbrella factory beyond the Raval on the hillside descending from Montjuïc, this little gem of a restaurant in a loftlike ground floor has become a big favorite of English-speaking visitors to Barcelona and local food fanatics alike. Aussie Sarah Stothart's three-course menu with some choice for less then €40 and a five-course set taster's menu at under €60 are what you get, and all of it is original and delicious. Everything from the spinach gnocchi made with goat cheese from Ronda (that people describe as "like eating clouds") to the *dhoa*, an Egyptian speciality made of ground almonds, coriander, cumin, cinnamon, and several other ingredients that may vary according to the weather (literally, from winter to summer, ingredients change with the climate) is as light, fresh, and filled with taste. ⊠ *Carrer Tapioles 53, Poble Sec* ☎ *93/329–2238* ▭ *AE, DC, MC, V* ☾ *Closed Sun. and Mon. No lunch* Ⓜ *Paral.lel-Poble Sec.*

MEDITERRANEAN
$$–$$$

✕ **El Cafetí.** Candlelit and romantic, this little hideaway at the end of the passageway in from Carrer Hospital is an intimate bistro with a menu encompassing various ingredients from foie gras to cod to game in season. Try the *ensalada tibia de queso de cabra* (warm goat cheese salad) or the *solomillo de corzo al foie* (roebuck filet mignon with foie gras). ⊠ *Hospital 99 (at end of Passatge Bernardí Martorell), Raval* ☎ *93/329–2419* ▭ *AE, DC, MC, V* ☾ *Closed Mon. No dinner Sun.* Ⓜ *Liceu.*

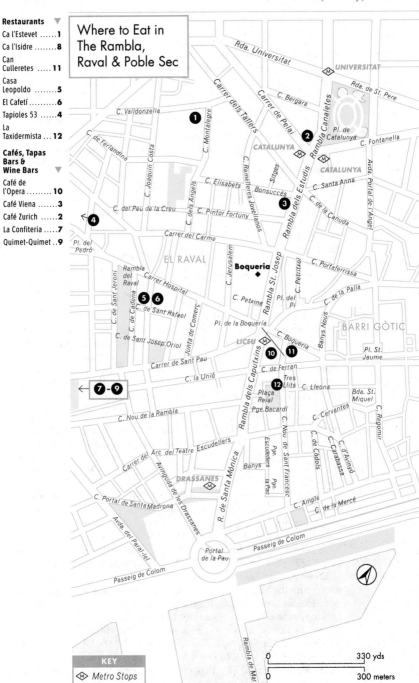

**Restaurants** ▼
Ca l'Estevet ......**1**
Ca l'Isidre ........**8**
Can
Culleretes .....**11**
Casa
Leopoldo ........**5**
El Cafetí ..........**6**
Tapioles 53 ......**4**
La
Taxidermista ...**12**

**Cafés, Tapas
Bars &
Wine Bars** ▼
Café de
l'Opera .........**10**
Café Viena .......**3**
Café Zurich ......**2**
La Confiteria .....**7**
Quimet-Quimet ..**9**

Where to Eat in
The Rambla,
Raval & Poble Sec

**KEY**
◈ Metro Stops

0        330 yds
0        300 meters

## BARCELONETA & THE PORT OLÍMPIC

Barceloneta and the Port Olímpic (Olympic Port) have little in common beyond their seaside location. The Olympic Port offers a somewhat massified and modern environment with a crazed disco strip, while Barceloneta has retained its traditional character as a sailors' and fishermen's neighborhood.

> **LA BARCELONETA, LAND OF PAELLA**
>
> Sunday paella in La Barceloneta is a classic Barcelona family outing. Paella or, in Catalan, *arròs* (rice), comes in various forms. *Paella marinera* is a seafood rice boiled in fish stock, made with arroz bomba (especially absorbent rice ideal for paella), and seasoned with clams, mussels, prawns, and jumbo shrimp. *Arròs negre* (black rice) is rice cooked in squid ink. *Arròs a banda* presents the ingredients without shells. *Fideuá* is made with vermicelli noodles mixed with the standard ingredients. Paella is for a minimum of two diners, and is usually enough for three.

MEDITERRANEAN   ✕**Agua.** With views through gnarled
$$$–$$$$   and ancient olive trees over the beach into the Mediterranean, this sleek slot hidden "under the boardwalk" near Frank Gehry's gleaming goldfish may not be classical Barceloneta in decor or cuisine, but it's an exciting place to dine, whether on the terrace on warm summer nights or sunny winter days, or inside the immense bay windows. Seafood is the main draw and value on the menu here, but risottos, steaks, and lamb are also equally available. Expect action, bustle, streamlined design surroundings, beautiful people, and acceptable-if-not-spectacular fare at this very popular tourist favorite. Be sure to reserve in advance. ✉*Passeig Marítim de la Barceloneta 30 (Marina Village), Port Olímpic* ☎*93/225–1272* ▤*AE, DC, MC, V* Ⓜ*Ciutadella–Vila Olímpica, Barceloneta.*

$$$–$$$$   ✕**Mondo.** Just off Barceloneta in the port's Maremagnum complex on the upper level of the IMAX theater, Mondo has gained fame for fine seafood in a contemporary design setting overlooking Barcelona's yachting marina and, not coincidentally, the afternoon fish auction by the clock tower over on the Moll dels Pescadors. Original creations such as *foie con albaricoque y pétalos de tomate seco* (duck liver with apricot and julienned sun-dried tomatoes) join seafood classics such as *caldoso de bogavante* (lobster bouillabaisse) on an inventive and original menu that stops well short of molecular gastronomy. Mondo morphs into a fashionable dance club and disco after the dinner hour. ✉*Moll d'Espanya s/n (IMAX bldg.), Maremagnum, Barcelona* ☎*93/221–3911* ▤*AE, DC, MC, V* Ⓜ*Drassanes, Barceloneta.*

$$$–$$$$   ✕**Torre d'Altamar.** Seafood of every stripe, spot, fin, and carapace emanates from the kitchen here, but the filet mignon under a colossal slab of foie is a tour de force. Housed inside the cable-car tower over the far side of the port, this restaurant has spectacular views of Barcelona as well as far out into the Mediterranean. ✉*Passeig Joan de Borbó 88–Torre de San Sebastián, Barceloneta* ☎*93/221–0007* ▤*AE, DC, MC, V* ⊘*Closed Sun. No lunch Mon.* Ⓜ*Barceloneta.*

$–$$   ✕**Can Manel la Puda.** The first choice for a paella in the sun, year-round, Can Manel is near the end of the main road out to the Barceloneta beach. Any time before 4 o'clock will do; it then reopens at 7 PM. *Arròs a banda* (rice with peeled shellfish) and paella *marinera* (with seafood) or *fideuá* (with noodles) are all delicious. The paella, prepared for a minimum of two diners, will easily feed three (or even four if you're planning to dine a few more times that day). ⊠ *Passeig Joan de Borbó 60, Barceloneta* ☎ *93/221–5013* ⊟ *AE, DC, MC, V* ✆ *Closed Mon.* Ⓜ *Barceloneta.*

SEAFOOD ✕ **Andaira.** New flavors and innovative, contemporary cooking distin-
$$$–$$$$ guish this restaurant from the standard Barceloneta dining panorama. It's not that Andaira doesn't do the traditional waterfront rice and fish dishes, but that they do them with a sleek, modern flair, all within sight of the Mediterranean from a contemporary streamlined second-floor dining room surrounded by picture windows. ⊠ *Vila Joiosa 52–54, Barceloneta* ☎ *93/221–1616* ⊟ *AE, DC, MC, V* Ⓜ *Barceloneta.*

$$$–$$$$ ✕ **Antiga Casa Solé.** Just two blocks from Barceloneta's prettiest square, the charming Plaça de Sant Miquel, this traditional midday-Sunday pilgrimage site occupies a typical waterfront house and serves fresh, well-prepared, piping-hot seafood. Whether it's *llenguado a la plancha* (grilled sole) or the exquisite *arròs negre amb sepia en su tinta* (black rice with squid in its ink), everything here comes loaded with taste. In winter try to get close to the open kitchen for the aromas, sights, sounds, and warmth. ⊠ *Sant Carles 4, Barceloneta* ☎ *93/221–5012* ⊟ *AE, DC, MC, V* ✆ *Closed Mon. and last 2 wks of Aug. No dinner Sun.* Ⓜ *Barceloneta.*

$$–$$$ ✕ **Barceloneta.** This enormous riverboat-like building at the end of the yacht marina in Barceloneta is hardly an intimate space where the chef greets every patron. On the other hand, the food is delicious, the service impeccable, the hundreds of fellow diners make the place feel like a cheerful New Year's Eve celebration, and, all in all, a bad time has never been had here. Rice and fish dishes are the house specialty, and the salads are excellent. ⊠ *L'Escar 22, Barceloneta* ☎ *93/221–2111* ⊟ *AE, MC, V* Ⓜ *Barceloneta.*

$$–$$$ ✕ **Can Majó.** This is one of Barcelona's premier seafood restaurants
Fodor'sChoice located right on the beach in Barceloneta. House specialties are *caldero*
★ *de bogavante* (a cross between paella and lobster bouillabaisse) and *suquet* (fish stewed in its own juices), but whatever you choose will be excellent. In summer, the terrace overlooking the Mediterranean is the closest you can now come to the Barceloneta *chiringuitos* (shanty restaurants) that used to line the beach here. ⊠ *Almirall Aixada 23, Barceloneta* ☎ *93/221–5455* ⊟ *AE, DC, MC, V* ✆ *Closed Mon. No dinner Sun.* Ⓜ *Barceloneta.*

$$–$$$ ✕ **El Lobito.** Although it can get filled to the gills with diners in full feeding frenzy spilling out onto a terrace in summer, the only thing really wrong with this place is that they serve you too much. Pure fish and seafood flows out of this kitchen, and the uproar tells you everyone's definitely here to have fun. The wine list meets the standards of the savvy seafood. ⊠ *Ginebra 9, Barceloneta* ☎ *93/319–9164* ⊟ *AE, DC, MC, V* ✆ *Closed Mon.* Ⓜ *Barceloneta.*

☺ $$–$$$ ✕ **Els Pescadors.** A kilometer northeast of the Olympic Port in the interesting Sant Martí neighborhood, this handsome late-19th-century bistro-style dining room has a lovely terrace on a little square shaded by immense ficus

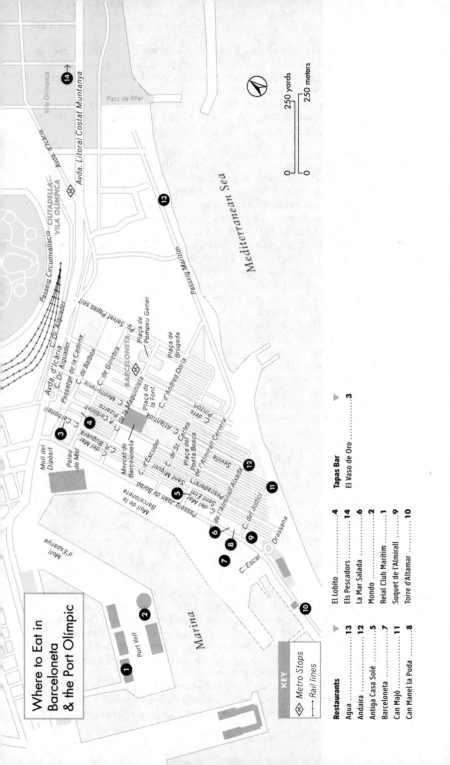

# Where to Eat in Barceloneta & the Port Olímpic

Mediterranean Sea

Parc de Mar

Vila Olímpica

**KEY**

⬨ Metro Stops
⊢⊣ Rail lines

**Restaurants** ▶

| | |
|---|---|
| Agua | 13 |
| Andaira | 12 |
| Antiga Casa Solé | 5 |
| Barceloneta | 7 |
| Can Majó | 11 |
| Can Manel la Puda | 8 |
| El Lobito | 4 |
| Els Pescadors | 14 |
| La Mar Salada | 6 |
| Mondo | 2 |
| Reial Club Marítim | 1 |
| Suquet de l'Almirall | 9 |
| Torre d'Altamar | 10 |

**Tapas Bar** ▶

| | |
|---|---|
| El Vaso de Oro | 3 |

## CLOSE UP

## Refuel Around Town

Barcelona's best quick bites may be the falafel and shawarma vendors that have sprung up all over town. Then again, any of the "uninterrupted service" restaurants that have bars, including the Basque bars along the Rambla, offer tapas and small rations of everything from *tortilla de patata* (potato omelet) to *riñones al jerez* (kidneys cooked in sherry). Tapas, in fact, were and are Iberian fast food for the ages. While the prefab, microwaving tapas emporiums along Passeig de Gràcia are far from the city's best cuisine, they'll do for a quick bite.

Barcelona's produce markets such as the Boqueria or the Mercat de Santa Caterina, or the two markets in the village of Gràcia, are excellent places for a restorative coffee, soft drink, or beer, and a sandwich. The heaps of colorful produce always whet the appetite. A perch on a bar stool for a delicious *ración de tortilla* (a wedge

of potato omelet) is about as typically Spanish as you can get. Other options include chorizo, ham, or cheese sandwiches.

The typical Barcelona *bar de toda la vida*, the day in, day out, standard-issue bar, invariably serves up a perfectly good *bocadillo de lomo* (pork loin sandwich) at the bar or on the sidewalk terrace. The standard bocadillo is made of baguette-style bread and is simply stuffed with anything from calamari to cheese or ham. Butter is never present unless requested.

Another option is the take-out *pollo al ast* (roast chicken) that many delicatessens and butchers display in the process of roasting in front of or inside their stores. Marinated in a special barbecue sauce, these chickens are always tasty, though the chances of not covering yourself with the sauce are minimal.

trees. Kids can range freely in the traffic-free square while their parents concentrate on well-prepared seafood specialties such as *fideuá* (paella made with noodles), paella, or fresh fish. ⊠*Pl. de Prim 1, Sant Martí* ☎*93/225–2018* ⊟*AE, MC, V* ⊘*Closed Mon.* Ⓜ*Poblenou.*

$$–$$$ ✕**Reial Club Marítim.** For harbor views at sunset, excellent maritime fare, and a sense of escape from urban chaos, hit Barcelona's yacht club, El Marítim, just around the harbor through Barceloneta. Highlights are *paella marinera* (seafood paella), *rodaballo* (turbot), *lubina* (sea bass), and *dorada* (sea bream). Or just ask for the freshest fish and you won't be disappointed. ⊠*Moll d'Espanya, Barceloneta* ☎*93/221–7143* ⊟*AE, DC, MC, V* ⊘*No dinner Sun.* Ⓜ*Barceloneta.*

$$–$$$ ✕**Suquet de l'Almirall.** With a handy terrace for alfresco dining in summer, "The Admiral's Fish Stew" indeed serves fare fit for the admiralty. Specialists in rice dishes and *caldoso de bogavante*, an abundantly brothy rice dish with lobster, this is one of Barceloneta's best. ⊠*Passeig Joan de Borbó 65, Barceloneta* ☎*93/221–6233* ⊟*AE, DC, MC, V* ⊘*Closed Mon. No dinner Sun.* Ⓜ*Barceloneta.*

$–$$ ✕**La Mar Salada.** A handy alternative next door to the sometimes-crowded Can Manel la Puda, this little seafood and rice restaurant has a sunny restaurant and whips up excellent paella, black rice, *fideuá* (paella made of vermicelli noodles), bouillabaisse, and fresh fish. Order an Albariño white wine from Galicia's Rias Baixas and a mixed salad—

you can't do much better for value and quality in Barceloneta. ⊠*Passeig Joan de Borbó 58, Barceloneta* ☎*93/221–2127* ⊟*AE, MC, V* ⊘*Closed Tues.* Ⓜ*Barceloneta.*

## EIXAMPLE

Eixample dining, invariably upscale and elegant, ranges from traditional cuisine in Moderniste houses to designer fare in sleek minimalist-experimental spaces.

BASQUE ✕**Beltxenea.** Long one of Barcelona's top restaurants, Beltxenea is
$$$$ ornamented with carved-wood columns in the hall, grand oak fireplaces, elegant Isabelline high-back chairs, and chandeliers all recalling the past glories of this lovely town house. In summer you can dine outdoors in the formal garden. Chef Miguel Ezcurra's Basque cuisine is exquisite; a specialty is *merluza con kokotxas y almejas* (hake simmered in stock with clams and barbels). Try the house wines—all excellent. ⊠*Mallorca 275, Eixample* ☎*93/215–3024* ⚞*Reservations essential* ⊟*AE, DC, MC, V* ⊘*Closed Sun. and Aug. No lunch Sat.* Ⓜ*Passeig de Gràcia.*

$$$–$$$$ ✕**Gorría.** Fermin Gorría's place, now run by his son Javier, is quite simply the best straightforward Basque cooking in Barcelona. Everything from the stewed *pochas* (white beans) to the heroic *chuletón* (steak) is as clean, clear, and pure as the Navarran Pyrenees. The Castillo de Sajazarra reserva '95, a semisecret brick-red Rioja, provides the perfect accompaniment at this delicious pocket of Navarra in the Catalan capital. ⊠*Diputació 421, Eixample* ☎*93/245–1164* ⊟*AE, DC, MC, V* ⊘*Closed Sun.* Ⓜ*Monumental.*

$$$–$$$$ ✕**Lasarte.** Martin Berasategui's landing in the Catalan capital comes at a moment when Spain's great chefs, for better or for worse, are opening more and more branch operations around the peninsula. Berasategui has left his kitchen in the capable hands of Alex Garés, who trained with the best (Pellicer of Àbac and Manolo de la Osa in Cuenca's Las Rejas) and serves an eclectic selection of Basque, Mediterranean, market, and personal interpretations and creations. Expect whimsical aperitifs and surprising and serious combinations such as foie and smoked eel or simple wood pigeon cooked to perfection. (For a lighter, more economical Berasategui-directed experience, try Loidi, recently opened next door, with a prix fixe €32 four-course menu of appetizer, fish, meat, and dessert.) ⊠*Mallorca 259, Eixample* ☎*93/445–0000* ⊟*AE, DC, MC, V* ⊘*Closed weekends* Ⓜ*Provença.*

★ $$$–$$$$ ✕**Taktika Berri.** Specializing in San Sebastián's favorite dishes, the only drawback for this Basque restaurant is that a table is hard to score unless you call weeks in advance (an idea to consider before you hit the airport). The tapas served over the first come, first served bar, however, are of such a high quality that you can barely do better à table, though there is a theory that dining well precludes seeing your feet. The charming family that owns and runs this semisecret gem is the definition of hospitality. ⊠*Valencia 169, Eixample* ☎*93/453–4759* ⚞*Reservations essential* ⊟*AE, DC, MC, V* ⊘*Closed Sun. No dinner Sat.* Ⓜ*Provença.*

*Continued on page 146*

El Bulli's Letter Soup

# SPAIN'S FOOD REVOLUTION

If milkshake waterfalls, bite-sized soup squares, and smoking cocktails sound like mouthwatering menu items, you may be ready to pull up a chair at the adventurous table of *la nueva cocina*. You won't be sitting alone: Foodies worldwide are lining up for reservations at Spain's hottest restaurants.

The movement, variously termed "*la nueva cocina*" (the new kitchen), "molecular gastronomy," or "avant-garde cooking," is characterized by the exploration of new techniques, resulting in dishes that defy convention. By playing with the properties of food, chefs can turn solids into liquid, and liquid into air. Olive oil "caviar," hot ice cream, and carrot-juice noodles are just a few of the alchemic manifestations of taste, texture, and temperature that have emerged.

Ferran Adrià of El Bulli in Roses is widely credited as the creative force behind Spain's new culinary movement, but chefs throughout the country have followed his lead. Beyond Spain, the movement is already having a seismic impact on the international culinary scene. Chefs from other European countries and the Americas have shifted their focus, looking beyond France—long esteemed as the world's culinary vanguard—to Spain for new techniques and inspiration.—*Erica Duecy*

# FERRAN ADRIÀ — *LA NUEVA COCINA'S* VISIONARY

(clockwise from top left): Adrià's spiral of black sesame-seed crunch with coconut ice cream; razor-clam sushi with ginger spray; curry-glazed kaffir lime leaves; beet chips with vinegar powder; the El Bulli kitchen; Adrià in his Barcelona workshop.

Adrià has often been called the world's top chef, but his rise to fame didn't happen overnight. Adrià was an emerging talent in 1987 when he attended a cooking demonstration by legendary French chef Jacques Maximin who spoke about his belief that "creativity means not copying." By Adrià's account, that statement transformed his approach to cooking.

The changeover to conceptual cuisine—where techniques and concepts became the driving force for Adrià's creativity—occurred in 1994, when he developed a technique for producing dense foam from various liquids. A handful of new techniques emerged in those early years, but "nowadays, that process is accelerated," he says. "Within one year, I am working with several types of techniques."

Some of Adrià's most famous dishes include puffed rice paella, Parmesan marshmallows, a cocktail of frozen gin and hot lemon fizz, mini cuttlefish ravioli with bursting pockets of coconut and ginger, and almond ice cream swirled with garlic oil and balsamic vinegar. These creative concoctions are served at El Bulli in meals of 25 to 30 courses, with each course no more than a few bites.

## GETTING THERE

Reservations are booked a year in advance for Ferran Adrià's El Bulli restaurant in Roses, located about 175 km north of Barcelona, set on an isolated beach. The El Bulli Web site features a comprehensive photo catalog of Ferran Adrià's creations from 1985 to present: ⊕ www.elbulli.com ⊠ El Bulli, Cala Montjoi. Ap. 30 17480. Girona. ☎ 972/150457.

## TRICKS OF THE TRADE

### HOW DO THEY DO IT?

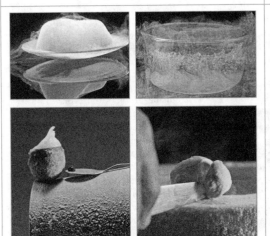

Daniel Garcia at El Calima using liquid nitrogen.

(clockwise from top left): Dry ice changes from a solid directly to a gas without becoming liquid; liquid nitrogen boils in a glass container at room temperature; a nitro-cooled pistachio truffle; a nitro-cooled caipirinha with tarragon essence.

Many techniques of *la nueva cocina* are borrowed from the food processing industry, including the use of liquid nitrogen, dry ice, and gellifying agents. This technological approach to cooking may seem like a departure from Spain's ingredient-driven cuisine, but avant-garde chefs say their creations are no less rooted in Spanish culture than traditional fare like paella.

One leading chef, Juan Mari Arzak, describes his approach as "not traditional Basque cooking, but rather culturally influenced cooking from the region, using the products of the region," he says. "We are doing things that haven't been done before." Using *lyophilization*, a freeze-drying technique, Arzak makes powders from peanuts and licorice. "You use the powder to add flavor to things," he says. "If you dust tuna with peanut powder and salt, it concentrates the underlying flavors to make the tuna taste like a more intense version of tuna."

Additionally, an unprecedented spirit of collaboration has defined the movement. "It is true that in other culinary movements chefs have been reluctant to share their knowledge," Adrià says. "Some people ask us, why do you share everything? Why do you share your secrets? The answer is that that's the way we understand cooking—that it's meant to be shared."

Liquid nitrogen: Just a small amount of this cryogenic fluid can be used to make instant ice cream from any liquid, including olive oil. Because liquid nitrogen can cause frostbite if it touches exposed skin, excess amounts of the substance must be allowed to evaporate before the food is served.

Dry ice: Bubbling sauces and cascading milk shakes can be made by adding dry ice to a liquid so it bubbles over the rim of its container.

Gellifiers: Fruit and vegetable juices can be used to make noodles with this technique. When juice is mixed with methylcellulose, a thickening compound derived from cellulose, it solidifies and can be extruded through a thin tube to form noodles.

Freeze-drying: The technique behind freeze-dried ice cream and soups is used to create concentrated powders from items like ham and berries. First, the substance is frozen in a controlled environment. Then, the pressure is lowered while applying heat so the frozen water in the substance becomes a gas.

## THE SPANISH ARMADA

Among the most recognized contributors to *la nueva cocina* are Juan Mari Arzak, Martín Berasategui, Alberto Chicote, Quique Dacosta, Daniel García, Joan Roca, and Paco Roncero.

Chef Juan Mari Arzak and his daughter Elena.

**Juan Mari Arzak** is recognized for modernizing and reinvigorating Basque cuisine at Restaurante Arzak in San Sebastián, which he now operates with his daughter Elena, who represents the fourth generation of Arzak restaurateurs. Despite his deep culinary roots and decades-long career, Arzak says he works to maintain a fresh perspective. "It's important to look at the world through a cook's eyes, but to think like a little kid," he says. "Because when you are a boy, you have the capacity to be amazed and surprised." Restaurante Arzak, ⊠ Avda. Alcalde Jose Elosegui, 273 / 20015 Donostia / San Sebastian. ☎ 943/278465. ⊕ www.arzak.info.

At his eponymous fine-dining restaurant in Lasarte, **Martín Berasategui** is known for his dedication to local products and fresh flavors. Notable dishes have included foie gras, smoked eel, and apple terrine; and *percebes*, goose barnacles served with fresh peas in vegetable broth. Martín Berasategui, ⊠ Calle Loidi, 4 / E-20160 Lasarte-Oria. ☎ 943/366471. ⊕ www.martinberasategui.com.

The cuisine at **Alberto Chicote's** Nodo fuses Spanish and Japanese ingredients and techniques. His version of tuna tataki, for example, features seared tuna, which is macerated in soy sauce and rice vinegar then chopped and served with chilled garlic cream, and garnished with drops of olive oil and black olive powder. Nodo, ⊠ Calle Velázquez 150, Retiro/Salamanca, Madrid. ☎ 915/644044.

**Quique Dacosta** is the inventive self-taught chef at the helm of El Poblet in Dénia, a coastal town in the Alicante region. The restaurant specializes in contemporary seafood but can veer also into highly conceptual fare like his "Guggenheim Bilbao oysters," a dish of shimmering oysters in barnacle stock, glazed with a sauce made from aloe vera, agar agar (a seaweed-based gellifier), and powdered silver. El Poblet, ⊠ Ctra Les Marines, km. 3, Dénia. ☎ 965.784179. ⊕ www.elpoblet.com.

### IT'S AN ADVENTURE

Puffed-rice paella may not be a dish that appeals to every diner. But try to view the experience as an exploration of the palate, and a teaser for the mind. Practitioners of *la nueva cocina* typically serve their creative concoctions in small servings over several courses, a presentation style meant to stimulate a thoughtful, conscious eating experience. Sure, customers may not like everything they put into their mouths, but still they come to be dazzled by the bold flavors and unexpected textures. Don't be surprised to see diners exclaim in delight and awe as they dive into these new sensory experiences.

In his early 30s, Daniel García is one of the younger practitioners of *la nueva cocina*, as well as head chef at El Calima, the restaurant in the Hotel Don Pepe in Marbella. "My cultural inspiration comes from the area where I work, in Andalusia, the south of Spain," he says. Acclaimed dishes include gazpacho with anchovies and *queso fresco* snow, and a passion fruit flan with herb broth and eucalyptus-thyme essence. Hotel Gran Meliá Don Pepe, ✉ Ave. José Meliá, Marbella. ☏ 952/764252.

Joan Roca is chef at El Celler de Can Roca in Girona, which he runs with his two brothers, Josep and Jordi. Roca is known for his work exploring the intersection between aroma and flavor, with dishes such as his "Adaptation of the Perfume *Angel* by Thierry Mugler," featuring cream of toffee, chocolate, gelée of violet and bergamot, and red fruits ice cream with vanilla. Savories include smoked lemon prawn with green peas and liquorice, and white and green asparagus with cardamom oil and truffles. El Celler de Can Roca, ✉ Carretera de Taialá. ☏ 972/222157. ⊕ www.cellercanroca.com.

Chefs in action, demonstrating their creativity in the kitchen: (top) Alberto Chicote with his assistants; (bottom) Martín Berasategui.

Paco Roncero is chef at La Terraza del Casino in Madrid, one of the city's most acclaimed establishments. He is considered one of Ferran Adrià's most outstanding students. "When I started working with Ferran (in 1998), my whole concept of cuisine changed," he says. "I started researching and trying to do new things. Now my cuisine is modern, *vanguardia*, without losing sight of tradition."

## Barcelona's "Must-Eat"

Your top priorities for a trip to Barcelona might just read: see great art and architecture, enjoy the nightlife, eat ham. In all seriousness, you shouldn't pass up the opportunity to eat Spain's exquisite artisanal ham made from acorn-fed native black pigs whose meat is salt-cured and then air-dried for two to four years. The best kind, jamón ibérico *de bellota*, comes from carefully managed and exercised pigs fed only on acorns. This lengthy process results in a silky, slightly sweet and nutty meat that is contradictorily both light and intensely rich.

You can casually approach the quest for ham at many bars or restaurants across Barcelona, feasting on different qualities of hams, including jamón ibérico's lesser but still stellar cousin, jamón serrano. Or you can do it purposefully, seeking out the very best the country has to offer. For that, there's really only one place,

**Jamonísimo** (✉ 85 Provenza, Eixample ☎ 93/439–0847 Ⓜ Entença).

This small and modern store and café is like a museum of ham. Here you can learn Ham 101: staff teach that it matters not only what the pig ate, but also which part of Spain's southwestern *dehesa* (a rolling oak forest) it was raised in. You'll even discover which particular cut from the ham is the most flavorful. For a full lesson, sit in the café with a tasting plate of "las texturas de ibérico" (approx. €24).

Jamonísimo will vacuum seal packages for you to take home, but be aware that Spanish meats are still illegal to bring through U.S. customs. So be prepared to swallow your stash on the spot at customs, or enjoy it in your hotel room or while traveling around Catalonia.

—Nina Callaway

---

$$–$$$ ✕**Sagardi Muntaner.** Basque favorites from *alubias de Tolosa* (diminutive but potent black beans from Tolosa) to *pimientos de piquillo* (sweet red bell peppers) to *txuletón de buey* (ox steak) are on the menu at this mid-Eixample address open from noon to midnight every day of the week. The bar displays the full range of typical Basque tapas and serves freezing *txakolí* (a young white wine from the Basque Country) for openers. ✉ *Muntaner 70–72, Eixample* ☎ 93/902–520–522 ☰ AE, DC, MC, V Ⓜ *Universitat, Provença*.

CATALAN    ✕**Can Gaig.** This Barcelona favorite is justly famous for combining
★ $$$$    superb interior design with carefully prepared cuisine. Market-fresh ingredients and original combinations are solidly rooted in traditional recipes from Catalan home cooking, while the menu balances seafood and upland specialties, game, and domestic raw materials. Try the *perdiz asada con jamón ibérico* (roast partridge with Iberian ham), or, if it's available, *becada* (woodcock), in which Carles Gaig is a recognized master. ✉ *Carrer d'Aragó 214, Eixample* ☎ 93/429–1017 ⌲ *Reservations essential* ☰ AE, DC, MC, V ☉ *Closed Mon., Easter wk, and Aug.* Ⓜ *Passeig de Gràcia*.

★ $$$–$$$$    ✕**La Cúpula.** Start your engines! In the midst of a collection of seven antique Hispano-Suiza automobiles, this unusual spot—superbly helmed by Carles Gaig—serves contemporary Catalan and Mediterranean cuisine. Everything from *guisantes estofados con gambas* (peas stewed with shrimp) to *arroz negro cremoso con chipirones y Torta del Casar* (creamy black rice with squid and Torta del Casar cheese) appears on this fine menu. ⊠*Sicilia 255, Eixample* ☎*93/208–2061* ⌔*Reservations essential* ▤*AE, DC, MC, V* ⊗*No dinner Sun.* Ⓜ*Sagrada Família.*

$$$–$$$$ ✕**L'Olivé.** Comforting Catalan home cooking means this busy and attractive spot is always packed with trendy diners having a great time. Excellent hearty food, smart service, and some of the best *pa amb tomaquet* (toasted bread with olive oil and squeezed tomato) in town leaves you wanting to squeeze in, too. ⊠*Balmes 47, Eixample* ☎*93/452–1990* ▤*AE, DC, MC, V* ⊗*No dinner Sun.* Ⓜ*Provença.*

LA NUEVA ✕**Alkimia.** Chef Jordi Vilà is making news here with his inventive cre-
COCINA ations and tasting menus at €40 and €54 that pass for a bargain in
★ $$$–$$$$ top Barcelona culinary culture. It's usually packed, but the alcoves are intimate and the stark decor is parceled out among them. Vilà's deconstructed *pa amb tomaquet* (in classical usage, toasted bread with olive oil and squeezed tomato) in a shot glass give a witty culinary wink (as it were) before things get deadly serious with raw tuna strips, baby squid, or turbot. A dark-meat course, venison or beef, brings the taste progression to a close before dessert provides more comic relief. Alkimia, as its name suggests, is magic. ⊠*Indústria 79, Eixample* ☎*93/207–6115* ▤*AE, DC, MC, V* ⊗*Closed Sat. lunch, Sun., Easter wk, and Aug. 1–21* Ⓜ*Sagrada Família.*

$$$–$$$$ ✕**Manairó.** A *manairó* is a mysterious Pyrenean elf who helps make
Fodor'sChoice things happen, and Jordi Herrera may be a culinary one. A demon with
★ everything from blowtorch-fried eggs to meat cooked *al clavo ardiente* (à la burning nail), fillets warmed from within by red-hot spikes producing meat both rare and warm and never undercooked, Jordi also cooks cod under a lightbulb at 220°F (*bacalao iluminado*—illuminated codfish) and serves a palate-cleansing gin and tonic with liquid nitrogen, gin, and lime. The intimate though postmodern-edgy design of the dining room is a perfect reflection of the cuisine. ⊠*Diputació 424, Eixample* ☎*93/231–0057* ⌔*Reservations essential* ▤*AE, DC, MC, V* ⊗*Closed Sun., Mon., and last 3 wks of Aug.* Ⓜ*Monumental.*

$$$–$$$$ ✕**Saüc.** Named for the curative elderberry plant, Saüc's avant-garde decor is the first hint that the fare here is far from standard. This postmodern *cuina d'autor* (original cuisine) run by an enterprising young couple, Xavi Franco and Anna Donate, uses fine ingredients and combines them in flavorful and original (yet artifice-free) surprises such as scallops with cod tripe and black sausage or monkfish with snails. The taster's menu is an unbroken series of unusual combinations of standard products, none of which fail to please. Try the *coulant de chocolate y maracuyá* (chocolate pudding with passion fruit) for dessert. ⊠*Pje. Lluís Pellicer 12 baixos, Eixample* ☎*93/321–0189* ▤*AE, DC, MC, V* ⊗*Closed Sun., Mon., holidays, Jan. 1–8, and Aug. 1–15* Ⓜ*Provença.*

$$–$$$ ✕**Cinc Sentits.** The engaging Artal family—maître d' and owner Rosa,
Fodor'sChoice server and eloquent food narrator Amy, and chef Jordi—a Catalan fam-
★ ily with a couple of decades in Canada and the United States, offers

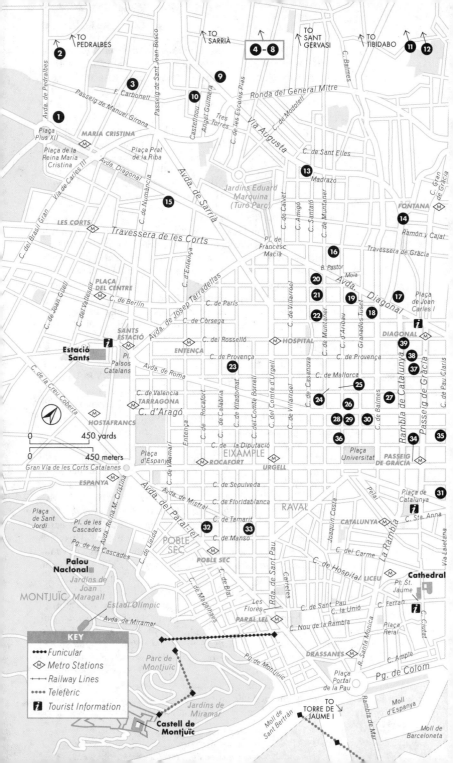

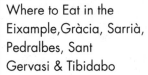

## Where to Eat in the Eixample, Gràcia, Sarrià, Pedralbes, Sant Gervasi & Tibidabo

a unique Barcelona experience: cutting-edge contemporary *cuina d'autor* in a minimalist setting, and explained in detail in native English. Three fixed menus—light, tasting, and *omakase* (a "trust the chef" surprise menu, including wine pairings of the chef's choice)—provide a wide range of tastes and textures. At the end of the meal, a special printout reprises the nine mini-courses and seven wines that have just crossed your palate. This is foodie nirvana. ⊠*Aribau 58, Eixample* ☎93/323–9490 ⊟*AE, DC, MC, V* ⊗*Closed Sun. No dinner Mon.* Ⓜ*Provença.*

> ### CALÇOTS FROM HEAVEN
>
> Since the late 19th century, calçots, long-stemmed white onions cooked over grapevine clippings have provided a favorite early-spring outing from Barcelona. Restaurants now serve calçots in the Collserola hills or on the beaches of Gavá and Casteldefells from November to April. Some in-town restaurants also serve calçots, always consumed with romescu sauce and accompanied by lamb chops, botifarra sausage, and copious quantities of young red wine poured from a long-spouted porrón held overhead. Wear dark (and preferably expendable) clothing.

MEDITERRANEAN
**$$$$**
Fodor'sChoice
★

✕**Drolma.** Named (in Sanskrit) for Buddha's female side, Fermin Puig's intimate perch in the Hotel Majestic was an instant success. The *menú de degustació* (taster's menu) might have pheasant cannelloni in foie-gras sauce with fresh black truffles or giant prawn tails with *trompettes de la mort* (black wild mushrooms) with *sôt-l'y-laisse* (free-range chicken nuggets). Fermin's foie gras *a la ceniza amb ceps* (cooked over wood coals with wild mushrooms)—a recipe rescued from the chef's boyhood farmhouse feasts—is typical of Drolma's signature blend of tradition and inspiration. ⊠*Passeig de Gràcia 70, Eixample* ☎93/496–7710 ⚐*Reservations essential* ⊟*AE, DC, MC, V* ⊗*Closed Sun. and Aug.* Ⓜ*Provença, Passeig de Gràcia.*

**$$$–$$$$**

✕**Casa Calvet.** It's hard to pass up the opportunity to break bread in one of the great Moderniste's creations. Designed by Antoni Gaudí from 1898 to 1900, the Art Nouveau Casa Calvet includes this graceful dining room decorated in Moderniste ornamentation from looping parabolic door handles to polychrome stained glass, etched glass, and wood carved in floral and organic motifs. The Catalan and Mediterranean fare is light and contemporary, though refreshingly innocent of *nueva cocina* influence. ⊠*Casp 48, Eixample* ☎93/412–4012 ⊟*AE, DC, MC, V* ⊗*Closed Sun. and last 2 wks of Aug.* Ⓜ*Urquinaona.*

**$$$–$$$$**

✕**Jaume de Provença.** Locals come here because they want to discover more of famed chef Jaume Bargués's haute-cuisine repertoire. Winning dishes include *lenguado relleno de setas* (sole stuffed with mushrooms) and the *lubina* (sea bass) soufflé. The traditionally designed restaurant, complete with a bar and a spacious yet intimate dining room, is in the Hospital Clinic part of the Eixample. ⊠*Provença 88, Eixample* ☎93/430–0029 ⚐*Reservations essential* ⊟*AE, DC, MC, V* ⊗*Closed Mon., Aug., Easter wk, and Dec. 25 and 26. No dinner Sun.* Ⓜ*Entença.*

**$$–$$$**

✕**Tragaluz.** *Tragaluz* means skylight—literally, "light-swallower"—and this is an excellent choice if you're still on a design high from Vinçon or Gaudí's Pedrera. The sliding roof opens to the stars in good weather, while the chairs, lamps, and fittings by Javier Mariscal (creator of 1992 Olympic mascot Cobi) reflect Barcelona's passion for whimsy and playful design. The Mediterranean cuisine remains light and innovative. ✉*Passatge de la Concepció 5, Eixample* ☎*93/487–0196* ▤*AE, DC, MC, V* ⊘*Closed Jan. 5. No lunch Mon.* Ⓜ*Diagonal.*

$$ ✕**Mantequeria Ya Ya Amelia.** Delicatessen and wine emporium, this *mantequeria* (literally, "buttery") two blocks uphill from Gaudí's Sagrada Família church serves lovingly prepared and clued-in dishes ranging from warm goat-cheese salad to foie (duck or goose liver) to beef. The wine list, of course, is exquisite and the service is cheerful. The original Ya Ya Amelia ("Ya Ya" is a nickname for grandma), around the corner at Sardenya 364, closes Sunday, so one or the other is always open. Both restaurants serve continuously from midday (1 PM) to midnight. The Mantequeria is usually fresher, less smoky, and less crowded. Ask for the chef's table by the kitchen for a closer look at the action. ✉*Còrsega 537, Eixample* ☎*93/435–8048* ▤*AE, DC, MC, V* ⊘*Closed Mon.* Ⓜ*Sagrada Família.*

## GRÀCIA

This lively, young, and intimate neighborhood has restaurants encompassing everything from the most sophisticated cuisine to simply good food at affordable prices.

BASQUE
★ $$-$$$
✕**Ipar-Txoko.** This excellent little enclave has managed to stay largely under the radar, and for that reason, among others, the cuisine is authentic, the prices are fair, and the service is personal and warm. A balanced menu offers San Sebastián specialties such as *txuleta de buey* (beef steak) or *besugo* (sea bream) flawlessly, while the wine list offers classic Riojas and Txomin Etxaniz txakolí. ✉*Carrer Mozart 22, Gràcia* ☎*93/218–1954* ⌔*Reservations essential* ▤*AE, DC, MC, V* ⊘*Closed Sun., Mon., and last 3 wks of Aug.* Ⓜ*Gràcia, Diagonal.*

CATALAN
★ $$$-$$$$
✕**Roig Robí.** Rattan chairs and a garden terrace characterize this simple-yet-polished dining spot in the bottom corner of Gràcia just above the Diagonal (near Via Augusta). Rustic and relaxed, Roig Robí (ruby red in Catalan, as in the color of certain wines) maintains a high level of culinary excellence, serving market cuisine with original personal touches directed by chef Mercé Navarro. Try the *arròs amb espardenyes i carxofes* (rice with sea cucumbers and artichokes). ✉*Seneca 20, Gràcia* ☎*93/218–9222* ⌔*Reservations essential* ▤*AE, DC, MC, V* ⊘*Closed Sun. and 3 wks in Aug. No lunch Sat.* Ⓜ*Gràcia, Diagonal.*

$-$$
✕**Folquer.** This little hideaway just above the Diagonal in the lower reaches of Gràcia is a good way to end a tour of this village-within-a-city. With one of the best-value taster's menus in Barcelona, Folquer has creatively prepared traditional Catalan specialties using first-rate ingredients. The dining room is a traditional and intimate space, with tables set close together and a warm French bistro–like atmosphere. ✉*Torrent de l'Olla 3, Gràcia* ☎*93/217–4395* ▤*AE, DC, MC, V* ⊘*Closed Sun. and last 2 wks of Aug. No lunch Sat.* Ⓜ*Diagonal.*

## With Children?

Children are often seen *and* heard in Barcelona restaurants for lunch, a bit less so for dinner. Many restaurants have a children's menu, usually consisting of some form of roast chicken, canelones, or the old faithful *botifarra amb mongetes* (pork sausage with white beans).

Barceloneta's beachfront paella specialists are great favorites for Sunday lunches, with children free to get up and run, skate, cycle, or generally race up and down the boardwalk while their parents linger over brandies and coffee. **Els Pescadors,** a seafood restaurant, has a lovely terrace opening onto a little square that is very handy for children letting off steam.

Serving coffee and light meals, **Aula Zero** is a popular upper Barcelona spot with outdoor tables. Parents peruse the newspapers while children race around the gardens and play on the jungle gyms and slides.

For sandwiches on the go, served in fresh, warm bread, an inexpensive and very respectable snack, try the **Pans & Company** stores all over town. Children will always gobble the Catalan staple *pa amb tomaquet* (toasted bread with olive oil and squeezed tomato), and most cafés, bars, and terraces can whip up a plate on short notice. And for dessert, Barcelona's ubiquitous ice-cream parlors and vendors are another favorite.

**Aula Zero** ( ⊠ *Carrer del Desert s/n, Jardines de Can Sentmenat* ☎ *93/597–1313* Ⓜ *Reina Elisenda).*
**Els Pescadors** ( ⊠ *Pl. de Prim 1, Port Olímpic* ☎ *93/225–2018* ⊘ *Closed Mon.* Ⓜ *Poblenou).*

---

LA NUEVA COCINA
$–$$

✕**Ot.** Don't worry. The dismal facade here hides a delicious taster's menu (the only choice, actually). Original dishes change monthly and encompass creatively combined market specialties that surprise and delight. This is one of Barcelona's best opportunities to experience contemporary *cuina d'autor* at prices that don't dent your wallet. ⊠ *Torres 25, Gràcia* ☎ *93/284–7752* ▤ *AE, DC, MC, V* ⊘ *Closed Sun., last 3 wks of Aug., and Dec. 25. No lunch Sat.* Ⓜ *Joanic.*

MEDITERRANEAN
¢–$

✕**Bilbao.** A cheery bistro near the bottom of Gràcia, this place is always packed with hungry epicureans having a festive time. Unpretentious, straightforward, Mediterranean market cuisine is well prepared and sold at reasonable prices here, but the best feature is the generally gleeful din—a good sign. Try the fried egg with black truffles and look for the Montsant red wines, always great values. ⊠ *Perill 33, Gràcia* ☎ *93/458–9624* ▤ *AE, DC, MC, V* ⊘ *Closed Sun. and holidays* Ⓜ *Diagonal, Joanic.*

MIDDLE EASTERN
¢–$

✕**Amrit.** The delicious Syrian cuisine here is usually a "double feature" combined with catching a flick at the Verdi movie theater a couple of doors down. *Hummus, baba ghanouge* (baba ghanoush), *bulgar* (minced meat with bulgar wheat), and *shawarma* (mutton with flat Syrian bread) are all light and tasty dinner options. ⊠ *Verdi 18, Gràcia* ☎ *93/217–6550* ▤ *AE, DC, MC, V* ⊘ *Closed Sun.* Ⓜ *Fontana.*

SPANISH ✕**Botafumeiro.** On Gràcia's main thoroughfare, Barcelona's finest Gali-
$$$$ cian restaurant has maritime motifs, snowy tablecloths, wood paneling,
Fodor'sChoice and fleets of waiters in spotless white outfits all moving at the speed of
★ light. The bank-breaking *Mariscada Botafumeiro* is a seafood medley
from shellfish to fin fish to cuttlefish to caviar. An assortment of *media
ración* (half-ration) selections is available at the bar, where *pulpo a
feira* (squid on slices of potato), *jamón ibérico de bellota* (acorn-fed
ibérico ham), and *pan con tomate* (toasted bread topped with olive oil
and tomato) make peerless late-night snacks. People-watching is tops,
and the waiters behind the counter could double as late-night talk show
hosts. ⊠ *Gran de Gràcia 81, Gràcia* ☎ *93/218–4230* ⊟ *AE, DC, MC,
V* Ⓜ *Gràcia.*

## SARRIÀ, PEDRALBES & SANT GERVASI

Take an excursion to the upper reaches of town for an excellent selection of restaurants, along with cool summer evening breezes and a
sense of village life in Sarrià.

CATALAN ✕**Tram-Tram.** At the end of the old tram line above the village of Sar-
$$$–$$$$ rià, Isidre Soler and his beautiful wife, Reyes, have put together one of
Fodor'sChoice Barcelona's finest culinary offerings. Try the *menú de degustació* and
★ you might be lucky enough to get marinated tuna salad, cod medal-
lions, and venison filet mignon, among other tasty creations. Perfectly
sized portions and a streamlined reinterpretation of space within this
traditional Sarrià house—especially in the garden out back—make
this a memorable dining experience. ⊠ *Major de Sarrià 121, Sarrià*
☎ *93/204–8518* ⊟ *AE, DC, MC, V* ☽ *Closed Sun. and late Dec.–early
Jan. No lunch Sat.* Ⓜ *Reina Elisenda.*

$$–$$$ ✕**Acontraluz.** A stylish covered terrace in the leafy upper-Barcelona
neighborhood of Tres Torres, Acontraluz, so named for its translucent
ceiling, has a strenuously varied menu ranging from game in season,
such as *rable de liebre* (stewed hare) with chutney, to the more northern
*pochas con almejas* (beans with clams). All dishes are prepared with
care and talent, and the lunch menu is a bargain. ⊠ *Milanesat 19, Tres
Torres* ☎ *93/203–0658* ⊟ *AE, DC, MC, V* ☽ *Closed middle 2 wks of
Aug.* Ⓜ *Tres Torres.*

$–$$ ✕**El Mató de Pedralbes.** Named for the *mató* (cottage cheese) traditionally prepared by the Clarist nuns across the street in the Monestir de
Pedralbes, this is a fine stop after touring the monastery, which closes at
2 PM. It also has one of the most authentically Catalan menus at a great
value. Look for *sopa de ceba gratinée* (onion soup), *trinxat* (chopped
cabbage with bacon bits), or *truite de patata i ceba* (potato and onion
omelet). ⊠ *Bisbe Català 10, Pedralbes* ☎ *93/204–7962* ⊟ *AE, DC,
MC, V* ☽ *Closed Sun.* Ⓜ *Reina Elisenda.*

FRENCH ✕**Gouthier.** Thierry Airaud's attractive, minimalist dining space at the
$–$$ bottom of Plaça Sant Vicenç de Sarrià specializes in oysters, caviars,
foies (duck and goose livers), and cavas and champagnes to go with
these exquisite products. Fortunately, the tasting portions allow you
to indulge your wildest food fantasies without sustaining massive

financial damage. ⊠*Carrer Mañé i Flaquer 8, Sarrià* ☎*93/205–9969* ▤*AE, DC, MC, V* ☯*Closed Sun. and Mon.* Ⓜ*Sarrià.*

ITALIAN
$$$–$$$$

✕**Le Quattro Stagioni.** For excellent, streamlined Italian cuisine that will remind you more of postmodern urban cooking than of *The Godfather,* this chic spot just down from the Bonanova metro stop on the Sarrià line is a winner. It's always filled with intriguing-looking bon vivants evenly balanced between hip locals and clued-in tourists, and the garden is cool and fragrant on summer nights. ⊠*Dr. Roux 37, Sant Gervasi* ☎*93/205–2279* ▤*AE, DC, MC, V* Ⓜ*Tres Torres.*

> ## A MARKET FOR EVERY MOOD
>
> Beginning with the Rambla's Boqueria, now closely pursued in prestige by the Mercat de Santa Caterina, Barcelona's 40 semi-open-air, steel hangar-covered produce markets are increasingly treasured as neighborhood attractions. Each market has its own flavor and personality, from upper Barcelona's Mercat Galvany, known as the Mercat de los Bisones (market of the mink coats) for its elegantly clad bourgeois clientele, to the maritime-flavored, fishermen's-quarter market in Barceloneta.

LA NUEVA
COCINA
$$$$

✕**El Racó d'en Freixa.** Chef Ramó Freixa, one of Barcelona's established culinary luminaries, is taking founding father José María's work to another level in a polished, minimalist, designer space that serves as a perfect metaphor for his cuisine. His clever reinterpretations of traditional recipes, all made with high-quality raw ingredients, have qualified the younger Freixa's work as *cuina d'autor.* One specialty is *peus de porc en escabetx de guatlle* (pig's feet with quail in a garlic-and-parsley gratin). ⊠*Sant Elíes 22, Sant Gervasi* ☎*93/209–7559* ▤*AE, DC, MC, V* ☯*Closed Mon., Easter wk, and Aug. No dinner Sun.* Ⓜ*Sant Gervasi.*

MEDITERRANEAN
$$$$
Fodor'sChoice
★

✕**Neichel.** Originally from Alsace, chef Jean-Louis Neichel skillfully navigates a wide variety of exquisite ingredients such as foie gras, truffles, wild mushrooms, herbs, and the best seasonal vegetables. His flawless Mediterranean delicacies include *ensalada de gambas de Palamós al sésamo con puerros* (shrimp from Palamós with sesame-seed and leeks) and *espardenyes amb salicornia* (sea slugs and sea asparagus) on sun-dried tomato paste. The dining room is contemporary decor muffled by thick carpets and heavy drapes. ⊠*Carrer Bertran i Rózpide 1 (off Av. Pedralbes), Pedralbes* ☎*93/203–8408* ⌂*Reservations essential* ▤*AE, DC, MC, V* ☯*Closed Sun., Mon., and Aug.* Ⓜ*Maria Cristina.*

$$–$$$

✕**Fishhh!** Everyone needs to go to a shopping mall sooner or later, and at L'Illa Diagonal, a mile west of Plaça Francesc Macià, you can shop *and* dine on some of Barcelona's best seafood at Lluís Genaro's first-rate fish emporium. Long a major seafood supplier of Barcelona's top restaurants (his seafood-central command post off the southeast corner of the Boqueria market, with massive Doric columns framing a world of fish, is worth a look), Genaro and his staff have put together a lively and popular dining space that exudes Boqueria market-style excitement in the midst of a busy shopping venue. ⊠*Av. Diagonal 557, Sant*

*Gervasi, Les Corts* ☎*93/444–1139* 🗖*AE, DC, MC, V* ⊙*Closed Sun.*
Ⓜ*Les Corts.*

**$$–$$$** ✕**Vivanda.** Just above the Plaça de Sarrià, this leafy garden is espe-
cially wonderful between May and mid-October, when outside din-
ing is a delight. The menu has Catalan specialties such as *espinacas
a la catalana* (spinach with raisins, pine nuts, and garlic) and inventive combinations of seafood and inland products. ✉*Major de Sarrià 134, Sarrià* ☎*93/203–1918* 🗖*AE, DC, MC, V* ⊙*Closed Sun.*
Ⓜ*Reina Elisenda.*

**$–$$** ✕**Silvestre.** This young constellation in Barcelona's culinary universe
FodorśChoice serves modern cuisine to some of Barcelona's most distinguished din-
★ ers. Just below Via Augusta, a series of intimate dining rooms and cozy
corners are carefully tended by chef Guillermo Casañé and his charming wife, Marta Cabot, a fluent English–speaking maître d' and part-
ner. Look for fresh market produce lovingly prepared in dishes such
as tuna tartare or noodles and shrimp. ✉*Santaló 101, Sant Gervasi*
☎*93/241–4031* 🗖*AE, DC, MC, V* ⊙*Closed Sun., middle 2 wks of
Aug., and Easter wk. No lunch Sat.* Ⓜ*Muntaner.*

## TIBIDABO

CATALAN ✕**Àbac.** In the tradition of Catalonia's finest restaurants, Xavier Pellicer
**$$$$** leaves no detail to chance here. Innovative canons learned from Europe's
FodorśChoice top chefs are converted into original recipes. The taster's menu is the
★ only reasonable choice here: trust Xavi (and any attempt at economy is
roughly analogous to quibbling about deck chairs on the Titanic). Àbac
is now an uptown boutique hotel as well as a gourmet pilgrimage. For
fine feasting no more than a convenient crawl from your luxury suite
(with spa facilities on hand to help repair the damage), this is one of
Barcelona's most exciting new combinations of superb dining with top
accommodations. ✉*Av. del Tibidabo 1–7, Tibidabo* ☎*93/319–6600*
⚘*Reservations essential* 🗖*AE, DC, MC, V* ⊙*Closed Sun. and Aug.
No lunch Mon.* Ⓜ*Tibidabo.*

SPANISH ✕**El Asador de Aranda.** Designed by Art Nouveau architect Rubió i Bell-
**$$$–$$$$** ver, this immense palace 1,600 feet above the Avenida Tibidabo metro
station is a hike but worth remembering if you're in upper Barcelona.
The kitchen specializes in *cordero lechal* (roast lamb); try *pimientos de
piquillo* (hot, spicy peppers) on the side. The dining room has a terra-
cotta floor and a full complement of Art Nouveau ornamentation rang-
ing from intricately carved wood trimmings to stained-glass partitions,
with acid-engraved glass, and Moorish archways. ✉*Av. del Tibidabo
31, Tibidabo* ☎*93/417–0115* 🗖*AE, DC, MC, V* ⊙*Closed Easter wk
and Sun. in Aug. No dinner Sun.* Ⓜ*Tibidabo.*

## OUTSKIRTS OF BARCELONA

With the many fine in-town dining options available in Barcelona, any
out-of-town recommendations must logically rank somewhere in the
uppermost stratosphere of gastronomic excellence. These three, all

rated among the top five or six establishments below the Pyrenees (one at the foot of Montseny, the other on the coast) undoubtedly do.

CATALAN    ✕**Sant Pau.** Carme Ruscalleda's Sant Pol de Mar treasure, one of the six
**$$$$**    top restaurants below the Pyrenees (and maybe the best of the six, if
Fodor'sChoice    you lean toward modern yet classical) is a scenic 40-minute train ride
★    along the beach from Plaça Catalunya's RENFE station: the Calella
train stops at the door. Inside are a warm glow and clean, spare lines, with a garden overlooking the Mediterranean. Dishes change with the seasons, but be alert for *vieiras* (scallops) with crisped artichoke flakes on roast potato, and *lubina* (sea bass) on baby leeks and chard in *garnatxa* (sweet Catalan wine) sauce. If you're there for Sant Jordi, Barcelona's Valentine's Day, you might score a *misiva de amor* (love letter), a pastry envelope containing julienned berries and peaches. ⊠ *Carrer Nou 10, Sant Pol de Mar* ☎ *93/760–0662* ▤ *AE, DC, MC, V* ☉ *Closed Mon., 2 wks in Mar., and 2 wks in Nov. No dinner Sun.*

**$$$–$$$$**    ✕**El Racó de Can Fabes.** Santi Santamaria's master class in Mediterra-
Fodor'sChoice    nean cuisine merits the 45-minute train ride (or 30-minute drive) north
★    of Barcelona to Sant Celoni, a good jumping-off point for a Montseny
hiking excursion. One of the four top-rated restaurants in Spain (along with El Bulli in Roses, and Arzak and Berasategui in San Sebastián), this is a must for anyone interested in fine dining. Every detail, from the six flavors of freshly baked bread to the cheese selection, is superb. The taster's menu is the wisest solution. The RENFE stations are at Passeig de Gràcia or Sants (the last train back is at 10:24 PM, so this is a lunchtime or early-dinner transport solution). Fortunately, there are five rooms available here just a few steps from your last glass of wine. ⊠ *Carrer Sant Joan 6, Sant Celoni* ☎ *93/867–2851* ▤ *AE, DC, MC, V* ☉ *Closed Mon., 1st 2 wks of Feb., and late June–early July. No dinner Sun.*

★ **$$$–$$$$**    ✕**Hispania.** This famous pilgrimage—one of the best restaurants in Cat-
alonia for the last 50 years—is just 39 km (24 mi) north of Barcelona, easily reached by the Calella train from the RENFE station in Plaça Catalunya. The sisters Reixach continue to turn out the same line of classical Catalan cuisine that, despite the name Hispania, has characterized this graceful dining room from the start. *Faves amb butifarra negre* (fava beans with with black sausage) rank high on the list of signature dishes here, but the fresh fish and seafood from the Arenys de Mar fish auction are always excellent as well. ⊠ *Carrer Real 54, Arenys de Mar* ☎ *93/791–0457* ▤ *AE, DC, MC, V* ☉ *Closed Tues., Easter wk, and Oct. No dinner Sun.*

## CAFÉS & TAPAS BARS

Barcelona may have more bars and cafés per capita than any other place in the world. In a culture where it is important to flaunt the fact that you are a man or woman of leisure—even in frantic, business-obsessed Barcelona—cafés serve an important function: safety valve, outdoor living room, meeting place, and a giant cocktail party to which everyone in the world is invited. Combining the Vienna coffeehouse concept (an isolated refuge with others) and mixing it with a natu-

## Ground Rules for Coffee

Coffee culture in Barcelona has certain linguistic peculiarities. A normal espresso, black coffee, is simply *un café*. Try saying *café solo*, Madrid-style, and observe the looks you get. A *tallat*, from the verb, in Catalan, *tallar* (to cut) is coffee with just a little milk (*café cortado* in the rest of Spain). For the very best-tasting coffee, nearly rivaling the aroma of fresh-ground coffee beans, order the *café corto*, a true espresso with less liquid and more taste. *Café amb llet* is Catalan for café con leche or coffee with milk.

If you really want to see the waiter's eyes glaze over, order a *café descafeinado de maquina con leche desnatada natural* (decaffeinated coffee made in the espresso machine with skimmed milk applied at room temperature).

And a word of warning for those who prefer their java to-go: coffee is still, for the most part, a sit-down affair. So take time to stop and smell the fresh roast.

ral southern European talent for joyful and boisterous improvisation, Barcelona offers a thousand intimate yet hyperactive nooks that seem designed both for lovers searching for a hideaway or for partyers out for a good time.

Be advised: the sidewalk cafés along the Rambla are noisy, dusty, overpriced, and overexposed to thieves and pickpockets; the Rambla isn't for sitting anyway. Bars and cafés close at varying hours, though most of the hot spots in and around the Born are good until about 2:30 AM.

Cafés and tapas bars are shown on the maps for the corresponding neighborhoods.

## CAFÉS

**Café de l'Opera.** Directly across from the Liceu opera house, this high-ceilinged Art Nouveau interior has welcomed opera-goers and performers for more than 100 years. It's a central point on the Rambla traffic pattern, and de rigueur; locals know that just about any Barcelona resident passes through this much-frequented haunt. ⊠*Rambla 74, Rambla* ☎*93/317–7585* ⊗*Daily 9:30* AM–*2:15* AM Ⓜ*Liceu.*

**Café Textil.** Set in one of the Ribera neighborhood's prettiest Renaissance courtyards, this is a sunny place to have coffee, tea, or a light lunch. The Picasso Museum across the street provides a certain continual buzz, but the hush of this space is a peaceful break in Barcelona's frenetic rhythm. ⊠*Carrer Montcada 12, Born-Ribera* ☎*93/268–2598* ⊗*Daily 10* AM–*12* PM Ⓜ*Jaume I.*

**Café de la Princesa.** One street in behind Carrer Montcada and the Picasso Museum, this little boutique, restaurant, and café is a unique space dedicated to design, crafts, books, and wine and food tastings. The ancient exposed-brick walls and cozy nooks in this lovely spot merit a visit. ⊠*Flassaders 21, Born-Ribera* ☎*93/268–2181* ⊗*Daily 9* AM–*2* PM *and 4:30* PM–*8* PM Ⓜ*Jaume I.*

**Café Paris.** Always a popular place to kill some time, the lively Café Paris hosts everyone from Prince Felipe, heir to the Spanish throne, to poets and pundits of all spots and stripes. The tapas are excellent, the beer is cold, and the place is open 365 days a year. ⊠ *Carrer Aribau 184, at Carrer Paris, Eixample* ☎ *93/209–8530* ☉ *Daily 6* AM*–2* AM Ⓜ *Provença.*

**Café Viena.** The rectangular perimeter of this classic bar is always packed with local and international travelers in a party mood. A pianist upstairs lends it a cabaret touch. ⊠ *Rambla dels Estudis 115, Rambla* ☎ *93/349–9800* ☉ *Daily 9* AM*–2* AM Ⓜ *Catalunya.*

**Café Zurich.** Of key importance to Barcelona rank-and-file society, this classical café, sitting at the top of the Rambla, remains the city's prime meeting point. The outdoor tables offer peerless people-watching; the interior is high-ceilinged and elegant. ⊠ *Pl. Catalunya 1, Rambla* ☎ *93/317–9153* ☉ *Daily 9* AM*–2* AM Ⓜ *Catalunya.*

**Dole Café.** Just a slender slot on the corner of Capitan Arenas and Manuel de Falla, this famous upper Barcelona café is absolutely vital to the Sarrià and Capitan Arenas neighborhoods. Along with extraordinarily good coffee, sandwiches and pastries here are uncannily well made and tasty. ⊠ *Manuel de Falla 16–18, Sarrià* ☎ *93/204–1120* ☉ *Weekdays 6* AM*–6* PM, *Sat. 6* AM*–1:30* PM Ⓜ *Sarrià, Maria Cristina.*

**Els Quatre Gats.** A mythical artists' café, this is where Picasso had his first exhibition in 1899. Surrounded by colorful Toulouse Lautrec–like paintings by Russinyol and Casas, the café offers variations of *pa torrat* (slabs of country bread with tomato, olive oil, and anything from anchovies to cheese to cured ham or omelets), while the restaurant serves the full gamut of fish and meat dishes. The building itself, Casa Martí, by Moderniste master Puig i Cadafalch and sculptural detail by Eusebi Arnau, is the best treat of all. ⊠ *Montsió 3, Barri Gòtic* ☎ *93/302–4140* ☉ *Daily 8* AM*–1* AM Ⓜ *Catalunya.*

**Espai Barroc.** This unusual baroque *espai* (space) is in Carrer Montcada's most beautiful patio, the 15th-century Palau Dalmases (one of the many houses built by powerful Barcelona families between the 13th and 18th century). The stairway, decorated with a bas-relief of the rape of Europa and Neptune's chariot, leads up to the Omnium Cultural, a key center for the study and dissemination of Catalonian history and culture. The patio merits a look even if you find the café too lugubrious. ⊠ *Carrer Montcada 20, Born-Ribera* ☎ *93/310–0673* ☉ *Tues.–Sun. 8* PM*–2* AM Ⓜ *Jaume I.*

**La Báscula.** This cozy café is on one of the Born area's most picturesque streets. Curiously, the building, the next over from the medieval mint (La Seca) at Carrer Flassaders 42, was the main candy factory in 19th- and early-20th-century Barcelona. Look up outside this artistic café and study the sign still engraved into the concrete: FÁBRICA DE DULCES— CARAMELOS–CONSERVAS–TURRONES–CHOCOLATES–GRAGEAS–PELADILLAS: the entire gamut of Barcelona bonbons. Sandwiches, cakes, pies, coffee, tea, and juices are served in this gracefully decorated, peaceful spot tucked in on the street behind Carrer Montcada and the Picasso Museum. ⊠ *Flassaders 30 bis, Born-Ribera* ☎ *93/319–9866* ☉ *Mon.– Sat. 9:30* AM*–11:30* PM Ⓜ *Jaume I.*

**La Bodegueta.** If you can find this dive (literally: it's a short drop below sidewalk level), you'll find a warm and cluttered space with a dozen small tables, a few spots at the marble counter, and lots of happy couples drinking coffee or beer, usually accompanied by the establishment's excellent *pa amb tomaquet* (toasted bread with squeezed tomato and olive oil) and either Manchego cheese, Iberian cured ham, or *tortilla de patatas* (potato-and-onion omelet). ⊠ *Rambla de Catalunya 100, Eixample* ☎ *93/215–4894* ⊘ *Daily 8* AM*–2* AM Ⓜ *Provença.*

**La Cerería.** Tucked in at the corner of Baixada de Sant Miquel and Passatge de Crèdit, this ramshackle little hangout has a charm all its own. The tables in the Passatge itself are shady and breezy in summer; look for the plaque at No. 4 commemorating the birth there of Catalan painter Joan Miró (1893–1983). ⊠ *Baixada de Sant Miquel 3–5, Barri Gòtic* ☎ *93/301–8510* ⊘ *Daily 10* AM*–1* AM Ⓜ *Liceu.*

**La Confiteria.** This beautifully restored bakery just off Avinguda del Paral. lel serves drinks and light tapas in an intimate and artistic environment that shows photographs and occasionally has live music. ⊠ *Sant Pau 128, Raval* ☎ *93/443–0458* ⊘ *Tues.–Sun. 9* AM*–2* AM*, Mon. 6* PM*–2* AM Ⓜ *Paral.lel.*

**Laie Librería Café.** Much than a mere bookstore, the café and restaurant serves dinner until 1 AM. Readings, concerts, and book presentations round out an ample program of events. ⊠ *Pau Claris 85, Eixample* ☎ *93/302–7310* ⊘ *Mon.–Sat. 9* AM*–1* AM Ⓜ *Urquinaona.*

**Schilling.** Near Plaça Reial, Schilling is always packed to the point where you'll have difficulty getting a table. It's a good place for coffee by day, drinks and tapas by night. ⊠ *Ferran 23, Barri Gòtic* ☎ *93/317–6787* ⊘ *Daily 10* AM*–2* AM Ⓜ *Liceu.*

**Venus.** Pivotally placed on the corner of Comtessa de Sobradiel, Escudellers, and Avinyó in the Barri Gòtic, this cozy delicatessen, restaurant, and café has an ideal location. The window overlooking Comtessa de Sobradiel seems perfectly designed for reading, writing, and people-watching in the best tradition of sidewalk cafés. ⊠ *Avinyó 25, Barri Gòtic* ☎ *93/301–1585* ⊘ *Daily 9* AM*–2* AM Ⓜ *Liceu.*

## TAPAS BARS

The *tapa* (literally, "lid")—originally a piece of cheese or ham covering a glass of wine and one of Spain's major contributions to world culinary culture—is not traditionally a Catalonian custom. Even now, San Sebastián, Seville, Cádiz, Bilbao, and Madrid are all considered superior to Barcelona in tapa culture, but this is changing: astute Catalans and Basque chefs are transforming Barcelona into an emerging tapa capital. Especially around Santa Maria del Mar and the Passeig del Born area, migratory wine tippling and tapa grazing are prospering and proliferating. Beware of the tapas in places along Passeig de Gràcia, which, while minimally acceptable, are microwaved and far from Barcelona's best.

**Adarra.** In Gràcia not far from the Plaça del Diamant, this wood-paneled Basque tavern is handy for the Verdi movie theaters as well as the Teatre Lliure. A good selection of *pintxos* (single tapas) and *cazuelitas* (little earthenware casseroles) is well accompanied by cider, txakolí, Rioja wines, and draft beer. ⊠ *Torrent de l'Olla 148, Gràcia* 🕾 *93/218–9237* ⊘ *Daily 6 PM–1 AM* Ⓜ *Fontana.*

**Bar Tomás.** Famous for its *patatas amb allioli* (potatoes with a sauce of pounded garlic and olive oil) and refreshingly chilly beers, this narrow, old-fashioned Sarrià classic is a place to seek out. On Wednesday, when Bar Tomás is closed, its patrons crowd Iborra (just behind it on Carrer d'Ivorra), which serves the same legendary fare. ⊠ *Major de Sarrià 49, Sarrià* 🕾 *93/203–1077* ⊘ *Thurs.–Tues. 6 PM–1 AM* Ⓜ *Sarrià.*

★ **Cal Pep.** Cal Pep is in permanent feeding frenzy and has been this way for a quarter century. Two minutes' walk east from Santa Maria del Mar toward the Estació de França, Pep's has Barcelona's best and freshest selection of tapas, cooked and served piping hot in this boisterous space. ⊠ *Pl. de les Olles 8, Born-Ribera* 🕾 *93/319–6183* ⊘ *Tues.–Sat. 1 PM–4 PM and 8–midnight, Mon. 8 PM–midnight* Ⓜ *Jaume I.*

**Can Paixano.** Famous for its cheap (and awful) rosé house cava (stick with beer here, or order a decent bottle of wine) and sausage sandwiches, this cavernous place is an ongoing brawl that the predominantly young crowd that comes here seems to love. The delicatessen-like emporium in the back room selling cheeses, wines, and sausages is the best part of the operation, not counting the massive and beautiful wooden doors onto the street. ⊠ *Reina Cristina 7, Born-Ribera* 🕾 *93/310–0839* ⊘ *Mon.–Sat. 9 AM–10:30 PM* Ⓜ *Jaume I.*

**Casa Lucio.** With preserved and fresh ingredients and original dishes flowing from the kitchen, this miniaturesque and handsome (though expensive) dazzler just two blocks south of the Mercat de Sant Antoni is well worth tracking down. Lucio's wife, Maribel, is relentlessly inventive. Try the *tastum albarole* (cured sheep cheese from Umbria) or the *pochas negras con morcilla* (black beans with black sausage). ⊠ *Viladomat 59, Eixample* 🕾 *93/424–4401* ⊘ *Mon.–Sat. 1–4 PM and 8–11 PM* Ⓜ *Sant Antoni.*

**Cerveseria La Catalana.** This bright and booming bar with a few tables on the sidewalk is packed for a reason: excellent food at fair prices. Try the small *solomillos* (filet mignons), mini-morsels that will take the edge off your carnivorous instincts without undue damage. ⊠ *Mallorca 236, Eixample* 🕾 *93/216–0368* ⊘ *Daily 8 AM–1:30 AM* Ⓜ *Provença.*

**Ciudad Condal.** This long wooden bar covered with an anthology of tapas is always filled with a discerning throng of hungry clients. ⊠ *Rambla de Catalunya 18, Eixample* 🕾 *93/318–1997* ⊘ *Daily 7:30 AM–1:30 AM* Ⓜ *Passeig de Gràcia.*

**El Bitxo.** An original wine list and ever-rotating choices of interesting cava selections accompany creative tapas and small dishes from foie (duck or goose liver) to ibérico hams and cheeses, all in a rustic wooden setting 50 yards from the Palau de la Música. ⊠ *Verdaguer i Callis 9, Sant Pere* 🕾 *93/268–1708* ⊘ *Daily 7 PM–12 PM* Ⓜ *Catalunya.*

**El Irati.** There's only one drawback to this lively Basque bar between Plaça del Pi and the Rambla: it's narrow and harder to squeeze into than the Barcelona metro at rush hour. Try coming at 1 PM or 7:30 PM. The excellent tapas should be accompanied by txakolí. The tables in

# Tapas: The Ultimate Movable Feast

Visitors to Spain didn't use to rank food, especially tapas, ahead of, say, Gaudí in the greater scheme of their travel ambitions, but all this has changed in recent years. Travelers are finding that the food is as good a reason for exploring Spain as any other. This is especially true when it comes to that most Spanish of all creations, the most paradigmatic celebration of the make-it-up-as-you-go-along quality of life south of the Pyrenees—the *tapa* (small morsel or hors d'oeuvre; derived from the verb *tapar,* meaning "to cover"). An evening weaving from one tapas bar to another can make a delightful dining adventure in Barcelona, and needn't preclude a late dinner.

The history of tapas goes back to the 781-year (7th- to 15th-century) Moorish presence on the Iberian Peninsula. The Moors brought with them exotic ingredients such as saffron, almonds, and peppers; introduced sweets and pastries; and created refreshing dishes such as cold almond- and vegetable-based soups still popular today. The Moorish taste for small and varied delicacies has become Spain's best-known culinary innovation. The term *tapa* itself is said to have come from pieces of ham or cheese laid across glasses of wine, both to keep flies out and to keep stagecoach drivers sober.

It is said that as far back as the 13th century, ailing Spanish king Alfonso X El Sabio ("The Learned") took small morsels with wine on his doctor's advice and so enjoyed the cure that he made it a regular practice in his court. Even Cervantes refers to tapas as *llamativos* (attention getters), for their stimulating properties, in *Don Quixote.* Often miniature versions of classic Spanish dishes, tapas allow

you to sample different kinds of food and wine with minimal alcohol poisoning, especially on a *tapeo*—the Spanish version of a pub crawl: you walk off your wine and tapas as you move around.

A few standard tapas to watch for: *calamares fritos* (fried squid or cuttlefish, often mistaken for onion rings), *pulpo a feira* (octopus on slices of potato), *chopitos* (baby octopuses), *chistorra* (fried spicy sausage), *chorizo* (hard pork sausage), *champiñones* (mushrooms), *setas* (wild mushrooms), *gambas al ajillo* (shrimp cooked in parsley, oil, and garlic), *langostinos* (jumbo shrimp or prawns), *patatas bravas* (potatoes in spicy sauce), *pimientos de Padrón* (peppers, some very hot, from the Galician town of Padrón), *sardinas* (fresh sardines cooked in garlic and parsley), *chancletes* (whitebait cooked in oil and parsley), and *salmonetes* (small red mullet).

Just to complicate things, the generic term *tapas* covers various forms of small-scale nibbling. *Tentempiés* are small snacks designed to "keep you on your feet." *Pinchos* are bite-size offerings impaled on toothpicks; *banderillas* are similar, so called because the toothpick is wrapped in colorful paper resembling the batons used in bullfights. *Montaditos* are canapés, innovative combinations of delicacies "mounted" on toast; *raciones* (rations, or servings) are hot tapas served in small earthenware casseroles.

The preference for small quantities of different dishes also shows up in restaurants, where you can often order a series of small dishes *para picar* (to pick at).

3

the back serve full meals as well. ✉ *Cardenal Casañas 17, Barri Gòtic* ☎ *93/302–3084* ✆ *Tues.–Sat. noon–midnight, Sun. noon–4* Ⓜ *Liceu.*

**El Vaso de Oro.** A favorite with young food lovers from Barcelona and beyond, this slender and often overcrowded little counter serves some of the best beer and tapas in town. ✉ *Balboa 6, Barceloneta* ☎ *93/319–3098* ✆ *Daily 9 AM–midnight* Ⓜ *Barceloneta.*

**El Xampanyet.** Just down the street from the Picasso Museum, hanging *botas* (leather wineskins) announce one of Barcelona's liveliest and prettiest *xampanyerias* (champagne bars), usually stuffed to the gills with a rollicking mob of local and out-of-town celebrants. The oversweet house sparkling wine (to be avoided) and *pa amb tomaquet* (toasted bread with squeezed tomato and olive oil) are served on marble-top tables near walls decorated with *azulejos* (glazed tiles). ✉ *Montcada 22, Born-Ribera* ☎ *93/319–7003* ✆ *Tues.–Sat. noon–4 PM and 6:30 PM–midnight; Sun. noon–4* Ⓜ *Jaume I.*

**Euskal Etxea.** This elbow-shape, pine-paneled space is one of the best of the Basque bars around the Gothic Quarter. The tapas and canapés will speak for themselves. An excellent and usually completely booked restaurant and a Basque cultural circle and art gallery round out this social and gastronomical oasis. ✉ *Placeta de Montcada 13, Born-Ribera* ☎ *93/310–2185* ✆ *Mon.–Sat. 9 AM–1 AM, Sun. 9 AM–4:30 PM* Ⓜ *Jaume I.*

**Inòpia Clàssic Bar.** Albert Adrià, younger brother and chief culinary researcher for his hyper-famous brother Ferran Adrià (of El Bulli fame), has opened his own tapas bar just a few blocks west of the Mercat de Sant Antoni. Products and preparations are uniformly interesting and excellent at this faux-industrial designer corner, from the fragrant Torta del Casar cheese to the olive sampler served in a ceramic flute. ✉ *Tamarit 104, Eixample* ☎ *93/424–5231* ✆ *Tues.–Sat. 7:30 PM–11 PM, Sun. 1–4 PM* Ⓜ *Rocafort, Poble Sec.*

**Jaizkibel.** One of Barcelona's off-the-beaten-track secrets, this bright and cheery proto-Basque enclave is six blocks from the Sagrada Família, five from the Casa Macaia Fundació La Caixa art gallery and concert hall, three from the Monumental bullring, and just three from the Auditori, all proving this to be a handy place to catch a bite while on the run. *Xipirones* (baby squid) and *calamares* (cuttlefish rings) are all well prepared here, and served with a fine selection of Albariños, Ruedas, and Penedès wines. ✉ *Sicília 180, Eixample* ☎ *93/245–6569* ✆ *Sept.–July, Tues.–Sun. 8 AM–2 AM* Ⓜ *Arc de Triomf.*

**La Flauta.** Both branches of this excellent and boisterous tapas/dining location are equally good. The name of the restaurant refers to the staple flutelike sandwiches that are the house specialty, but there is also an infinite number of tapas and small portions of everything from wild mushrooms in season to wild asparagus or *xipirones* (baby octopuses) served in this vast counter space flanked with dozens of tables. Try a *sobrassada* (pork paste with paprika from Majorca) *flauta* (thin, flutelike sandwich). ✉ *Carrer Balmes 171, Eixample* ☎ *93/415–5186* ✆ *Mon.–Sat. 1–4 and 8–midnight* Ⓜ *Provença* ✉ *Carrer Aribau 23, Eixample* ☎ *93/323–7038* ✆ *Daily noon–midnight* Ⓜ *Provença.*

**La Palma.** Behind the Plaça Sant Jaume's *ajuntament* (city hall), toward the post office, is this cozy and ancient café with marble tables, wine barrels, sausages hanging from the ceiling, and newspapers to linger over. ⊠*Palma Sant Just 7, Barri Gòtic* ☎*93/315–0656* ⊙*Daily 8 AM–3 PM and 7–10 PM* Ⓜ*Jaume I.*

**Mantequeria Can Ravell.** Lovers of exquisite wines, hams, cheeses, oils, whiskies, cigars, caviars, baby eels, anchovies, and any other delicacy you can think of, this is your spot. The backroom table open from midmorning to early evening is first come, first served; complete strangers share tales, tastes, and textures at this foodie forum. The upstairs dining room serving lunch (and dinners Thurs. and Fri.), through the kitchen and up a spiral staircase, has a clandestine, through-the-looking-glass vibe. ⊠*Carrer Aragó 313, Eixample* ☎*93/457–5114* ⊙*Mon. 10AM–7p[m], Tues., Wed. 10AM–9 PM, Thurs.–Fri. 10AM–10 PM, Sat. 10AM–6PM.* Ⓜ*Passeig de Gràcia.*

**Moncho's Barcelona.** One of José Ramón Neira's (aka Moncho) many establishments (including the upscale Botafumeiro), this rangy bar and café serves very respectable cazuelitas (small earthenware dishes), offering minitastes of Gallego and Catalan classics such as *alubias* (kidney beans) and *calamares en su tinto* (squid stewed in its own ink). ⊠*Travessera de Gràcia 44–46, Eixample* ☎*93/414–6622* ⊙*Daily noon–1:30 AM* Ⓜ*Gràcia.*

**Paco Meralgo.** The name, a pun on *para comer algo* (to eat something), may be only marginally amusing, but the tapas here are excellent: from the classical *calamares fritos* (fried squid rings) to the *pimientos de Padrón* (green peppers, some fiery, from the Galician town of Padrón.) ⊠*Carrer Muntaner 171, Eixample* ☎*93/430–9027* ⊙*Mon.–Sat. 1–4 and 8–midnight* Ⓜ*Provença.*

**Piratas.** This extraordinary little slot (so-named for Roman Polanski's film of the same name) just a block away from the Auditori de Barcelona is an excellent choice for a pre- or post-concert taste of Luis Ortega's improvisational cuisine, all prepared behind the bar as if by magic. Cheeses, hams, potatoes, foies, caviars, olives, anchovies, and tuna, as well as excellent wines, all flow freely here. Space is limited, so reservations are essential. ⊠*Carrer Ausiàs Marc 157, Eixample* ☎*93/245–7642* ⌕*Reservations essential* ⊙*Weekdays 1 PM–1 AM, Sat. 8–1* Ⓜ*Marina.*

**Quimet-Quimet.** A foodie haunt, this tiny place lined with wine and whiskey bottles is stuffed with products and people. If you come too late, you might not be able to get in. Come before 1:30 PM and 7:30 PM and you will generally find a stand-up table. Chef-owner Quimet improvises ingenious canapés. All you have to do is orient him toward cheese, anchovies, or whatever it is you might crave, and Quimet does the rest, *and* recommends the wine to go with it. ⊠*Poeta Cabanyés 25, Poble Sec* ☎*93/442–3142* ⊙*Weekdays noon–4 and 7–10:30, Sat. noon–4* Ⓜ*Paral.lel.*

**Sagardi.** This attractive, wood-and-stone cider house comes close to re-creating its Basque prototype. Cider shoots from mammoth barrels; piping-hot tapas make the rounds; and the restaurant prepares *txuletas de buey* (beefsteaks) over coals. ⊠*Carrer Argenteria 62, Born-Ribera* ☎*93/319–9993* ⊙*Daily 1:30 PM–3:30 PM and 8 PM–midnight* Ⓜ*Jaume I.*

**Santa Maria.** A combination of cutting-edge industrial design with medieval stone walls and innovative tapa creations keeps Santa Maria thriving. Leading chefs are likely to turn up here for anything from *espardenyes* (sea cucumber) to *escamarlans amb salicornia* (prawns with saltwort). ⊠ *Comerç 17, Born-Ribera* ☎ *93/315–1227* ⊘ *Tues.– Sat. 1:30 PM–3:30 PM and 8:30 PM–12:30; closed last 2 wks of Aug.* Ⓜ *Jaume I.*

**Taberne Les Tapes.** Proprietors and chefs Barbara and Santi offer a special 10-selection tapa anthology at this narrow, cozy, cheery place, just behind the town hall and just seaward of Plaça Sant Jaume. Barbara, originally from Worcestershire, England, takes especially good care of visitors from abroad. ⊠ *Pl. Regomir 4, Barri Gòtic* ☎ *93/302–4840* ⊘ *Mon.–Sat. 9 AM–midnight; closed Aug.* Ⓜ *Jaume I.*

**Taller de Tapas.** Next to Plaça del Pi, facing the eastern lateral facade of Santa Maria del Pi, this tapas specialist has it all: cheery young staff, traditional Catalan dishes in single-bite format, and service from midday to midnight. The other Taller de Tapas at Argenteria 51 near Santa Maria del Mar is equally good. ⊠ *Pl. de Sant Josep Oriol 9, Barri Gòtic* ☎ *93/302–6243* ⊘ *Daily noon–midnight* Ⓜ *Liceu* ⊠ *Argenteria 51, Born-Ribera* ☎ *93/268–8559* ⊘ *Daily noon–midnight* Ⓜ *Jaume I.*

**Tapaç 24.** Carles Abellán has done it again. His irrepressibly creative Comerç 24 has been a hit since the day it opened, and his new tapas emporium is headed in the same direction. Here Abellán shows us how much he admires traditional Catalan and Spanish bar food, from *patatas bravas* (potatoes in hot sauce) to *croquetas de jamón ibérico* (croquettes made of ibérico ham). ⊠ *Carrer Diputació 269, Eixample* ☎ *93/488–0977* ⊘ *Mon.–Sat. 8 AM–midnight* Ⓜ *Passeig de Gràcia.*

**Taverna del Born.** All manner of tapas and cazuelitas with everything from stewed lentils to *pulpo a feira* are served at this terrace, bar, and restaurant overlooking the Born market. The tables outside manage to be breezy in summer and sunny in winter, and the intersection is one of the Born area's liveliest. ⊠ *Passeig de Born 27–29, Born-Ribera* ☎ *93/315– 0964* ⊘ *Tues.–Sat. 11 AM–12:30 AM, Sun. 11 AM–5 PM* Ⓜ *Jaume I.*

**Udala.** This double-ended gem—restaurant at one end and tapas bar at the other—serves some of the best *montaditos* (canapés) and cazuelitas in Barcelona in a bright, wood-lined bar that is usually well attended by lovers of fine dining. ⊠ *Sicília 202, Eixample* ☎ *93/245–2165* ⊘ *Tues.–Sun. 8 AM–2 AM; closed Aug.* Ⓜ *Tetuan.*

# WINE BARS

Barcelona's wine culture (and that includes cava, Catalonia's *méthode champenoise* sparkling wine) has taken off in the last decade. Young food and wine connoisseurs, resonating from the relatively recent *glamour* of Ferran Adrià's Nueva Cocina rage, have taken to drinking wine for quality rather than quantity, much as agronomists and enologists are cultivating smaller grapes with less juice and more taste in vineyards around the Iberian Peninsula. Bars and taverns dedicated partly or exclusively to wine tasting, nearly unknown in Barcelona before the beginning of the millennium, are proliferating. Happily, tapas and smallish rations of delicacies are keeping up with the wine offerings, and wine-tasting taverns are an increasingly viable option for combining a light dinner with bacchic investigation.

**Ateneu Gastronòmic.** Across the parking lot from the town hall in what was once the site of the Roman baths, this restaurant-*enoteca* (wine library) with an outdoor terrace in summer offers a wide selection of wines and fine meals to go with them. ⊠ *Pl. de Sant Miquel 2 bis, Barri Gòtic* ☎ *93/302–1198* ☉ *Tues.–Sat. 1:30 PM–3:30 PM and 8:30 PM–12:30 AM* Ⓜ *Liceu.*

★ **Cata 1.81.** Wine tasting (*La Cata*) in this contemporary design space comes with plenty of friendly advice about enology and some of the world's most exciting new vintages. Small delicacies such as truffle omelets and foie gras make this streamlined sliver of a bar a gourmet haven as well. ⊠ *Valencia 181, Eixample* ☎ *93/323–6818* ☉ *Mon.–Sat. 6 PM–1 AM* Ⓜ *Provença.*

**La Barcelonina de Vins i Esperits.** This vast room surrounded by several hundred bottles of wine and cava (Catalan sparkling wine) on the shelves overhead is an excellent choice for evening wine tastings accompanied by light tapas. ⊠ *Carrer Valencia 304, Eixample* ☎ *93/215–7083* ☉ *Weekdays 6 PM–2 AM, Sat. 7:30 PM–2 AM, Sun. 8 PM–2 AM* Ⓜ *Provença.*

**La Cave.** With 450 wines from around the world arranged according to price and taste thermometers around a wine barrel–like basement, this *enoteca* (wine library) is a wine-lovers paradise. Selected dishes from *magret de pato* (duck breast) to French cheeses ranging from Reblochon to Cabecou to Pont l'Évêque make this an ideal wine cellar for tastings and a light dinner. ⊠ *Av. Josep Vicenç Foix 80, Sarrià* ☎ *93/206–3846* ☉ *Mon.–Sat. 1:30–5 PM and 8 PM–midnight* Ⓜ *Sarrià.*

**La Taverna del Palau.** Behind a glass facade facing the Palau de la Música, this sleek little tavern is perfect for a hit of cava during intermission or a beer and a *flauta* (thin, flutelike sandwich) of cured ham. ⊠ *Sant Pere més Alt 8, Sant Pere* ☎ *93/268–8481* ☉ *Mon.–Sat. 8AM–midnight* Ⓜ *Catalunya.*

**La Tinaja.** Part wine bar, part tapas emporium, this handsome cavern just around the corner from that other tapas favorite, Cal Pep, offers a good selection of wines from all over Spain and fine acorn-fed Iberian ham to go with it. The salads are excellent, and the tone of La Tinaja is refined and romantic. ⊠ *L'Esparteria 9, Born-Ribera* ☎ *93/310–2250* ☉ *Tues.–Sat. noon–4 PM and 6:30 PM–midnight* Ⓜ *Jaume I.*

**La Vinateria del Call.** Just a block and a half from the cathedral cloister in the heart of the *Call*, Barcelona's medieval Jewish Quarter, this dark and candlelit spot serves a wide variety of well-thought-out wines, tapas, and full meals. ⊠ *Sant Domènec del Call 9, Barri Gòtic* ☎ *93/302–6092* ☉ *Mon.–Sat. 6 PM–1 AM* Ⓜ *Liceu.*

**La Vinya del Senyor.** Ambitiously named "The Lord's Vineyard," this excellent wine bar directly across from the entrance to the lovely church of Santa Maria del Mar changes its list of international wines every week. ⊠ *Pl. de Santa Maria 5, Born-Ribera* ☎ *93/310–3379* ☉ *Tues.–Sun. noon–1 AM* Ⓜ *Jaume I.*

**Terrabacuş 24.** A sleek new tapas idea: combine an extensive wine list offering 250 different wines (50 served by the glass) with a wide variety of tapas from Catalonia, Spain, and beyond. With the advice of a sommelier, various different wines are recommended for specific tapas, be they seafood, sashimi, or ibérico ham. The result is an exciting and different tapas and wine-tasting emporium with a happening young buzz. ⊠*Carrer Muntaner 185, Eixample* ☎*93/410–8633* ⊘*Mon.– Sat. 1:30–4 and 9–midnight* Ⓜ*Provença.*

**Va de Vi.** This beautifully restored (excavated, really) spot in the stables of what was once an aristocratic house is so entertaining to the eye it's hard to decide where to look. Meanwhile, the selection of wines (*Va de Vi* means "It's about wine") and artisanal cheeses and hams is first rate. ⊠*Banys Vells 16, Born-Ribera* ☎*93/319–2900* ⊘*Daily 6 PM– 2 AM* Ⓜ*Jaume I.*

**Viníssim.** Down the street from the Vinateria del Call, this is a fine wine bar and restaurant serving excellent vintages and small portions of Catalan delicacies and Mediterranean cooking. ⊠*Sant Domènec del Call 12, Barri Gòtic* ☎*93/301–4575* ⊘*Mon.–Sat. noon–midnight, Sun. noon–5 PM* Ⓜ*Liceu.*

# Where to Stay

**WORD OF MOUTH**

"I stayed at a great hotel (hotel Granvia) off the Gran Via in the Eixample area. This was a nice, safe area and I felt fine walking around alone, even up until 11:30 PM or so. The cool thing about my location is that it was only 2 blocks from El Corte Inglés (major department store with everything you could possibly need), and 2 blocks from Plaça de Catalunya (city center)."

–Magellan_5

# BARCELONA LODGING PLANNER

## Facilities

Hotel entrances are marked with a plaque bearing the letter H and the number of stars. The letter R (standing for *residencia*) after the letter H indicates an establishment with no meal service. The designations *fonda* (F), *pensión* (P), *hostal* (Hs), and *casa de huéspedes* (CH) indicate budget accommodations. In most cases, especially in smaller villages, the rooms will be clean but basic. In larger cities, they can be downright dreary.

Barcelona's hotel offerings at the top end are as good as any in the world. There is greater quality at lower prices in the mid-range hotels. Hotel ratings used by the Turisme de Barcelona are based on stars, with five stars as the highest rating. Two stars and above are dependable ratings, while one-star ratings should be considered budget options. You should specify when reserving whether you prefer two beds or one double bed. Single rooms (*habitación sencilla*) are usually available, but often on the small side. You might prefer to pay a bit extra for single occupancy in a double room (*habitación doble uso individual*).

Note that it's a good idea to reserve well ahead and check if there will be a major convention in the city during your visit. Also note that high-season rates prevail during Holy Week.

## Cutting Costs

Room rates are often negotiable if hotels are not booked solid. Business travelers may be able to arrange a 20%–40% discount, just by asking. Booking months in advance often will turn up better rates, especially if you reserve via the Internet or fax, rather than by calling. Ask about weekend rates, which are as much as half off regular prices. October to June prices may plunge or soar depending on the number of conventions or special events taking place; negotiate the best rate you can get.

## Prices

Budget travelers, backpackers, and students will all find affordable options throughout the Ciutat Vella; just look up and you will see survivable *pensiones* and *hostales*, which usually have vacancies, announced on balconies. But for the discerning traveler, Barcelona's finer hotels are, alas, as expensive as those of any other cosmopolitan city.

Most of the pricing include a V.A.T. (Value Added Tax) of 7%. Many hotels operate on the European Plan (EP, with no meals) and some on the Breakfast Plan (BP, with a full breakfast) or Continental Plan (CP, with a continental breakfast). Breakfast can vary from packaged juice, coffee, rolls, and butter to a generous buffet. Price categories are assigned based on the range between least- and most-expensive standard double rooms in nonholiday high season.

## What It Costs in Euros

|        | ¢         | $       | $$        | $$$       | $$$$     |
|--------|-----------|---------|-----------|-----------|----------|
| Hotels | Under €75 | €75–€124 | €125–€174 | €175–€225 | Over €225 |

Hotel prices are for two people in a standard double room in high season.

## WHERE TO STAY IN BARCELONA

| | Neighborhood Vibe | Pros | Cons |
|---|---|---|---|
| Rambla | A solid stream of humanity around the clock, the Rambla is always alive and palpitating. A promenade that is chock full of every type of street life, this is where you can feel the city's pulse. | The Rambla is the city's most iconic runway and always an exciting strip. The Boqueria market, the flower stalls, the opera house, and Plaça Reial are all quintessential Barcelona. | The incessant crush of humanity can be overwhelming, especially if FC Barcelona wins a championship and the entire city descends upon the Rambla. |
| Gothic Quarter & Ribera-Born | With 19th-century gaslight-type lamps glowing in the corners of Roman and Gothic areas, this is a romantic part of town. The Picasso Museum and Santa Maria del Mar basilica sit nearby. | The architecture of the Gothic Quarter is tangible evidence of the city's past. Plaça Sant Jaume, the cathedral, Plaça del Rei, and the Born-Ribera district are the main reasons to visit the city. | Echoes reverberate around this ancient sound chamber and, while there is little serious noise, what there is goes a long way. |
| Raval | The Raval has always been a rough and tumble part of town. But the nightlife is exciting and the diversity of the neighborhood is exemplary. Bonus: living behind the Boqueria market. | For the closest thing to Marrakesh in Barcelona, the Raval has a buzz all its own. A contemporary art museum, the medieval hospital, and the Mercat de Sant Antoni offer plenty to explore. | The Raval can seem dangerous, whether it is or not. Certain corners teem with prostitutes, drug dealers, and Barcelona's seamiest elements. |
| Eixample | Some of Gaudí's best buildings line the sidewalks and many of the city's finest hotels and restaurants are right around the corner. And then there's the shopping… | Eixample remains the world's only Art Nouveau neighborhood, constantly rewarding to the eye. Gaudí's unfinished masterpiece La Sagrada Família is within walking distance. | A bewildering grid without numbers or alphabetization, the Eixample can seem hard-edged compared to the older, quirkier, parts of Barcelona. |
| Barceloneta & Olympic Port | The onetime fisherman's quarter, Barceloneta retains its informal and working-class ambience, with laundry flapping over the streets and sidewalk restaurants lining Passeig Joan de Borbó. | Living near the beach gives the city a laid-back feel. The Olympic Port is a world apart, but Barceloneta is brimming with the best seafood dining spots in town. | Barceloneta offers few hotel opportunities, while the Olympic Port offers only one: the monolithic Hotel Arts, which, for all its quality, seems a tourist colony away from the rest of town. |
| Pedralbes, Sarrià & Upper Barcelona | Upper Barcelona is leafy and residential and the air is always a few degrees cooler. Pedralbes holds Barcelona's finest mansions; Sarrià is a rustic village suspended in the urban sprawl. | Getting above the madding fray and into better air has distinct advantages and the upper reaches of Barcelona offers them. A 15-minute train ride connects Sarrià with the Rambla. | The only drawback to staying in upper Barcelona is the 15-minute commute to the most important monuments and attractions. After midnight on weeknights this will require a taxi. |

4

By George
Semler

**BARCELONA'S HOTELS OFFER CLEAR DISTINCTIONS.** Hotels in the Ciutat Vella (Old City)—the Gothic Quarter and along the Rambla—are charming and convenient for sightseeing, though sometimes short on peace and quiet. Relative newcomers such as the Neri, the Duquesa de Cardona, the Banys Orientals, and the Casa Camper Barcelona are contemporary-design standouts inhabiting medieval architecture, a combination at which Barcelona architects and decorators are peerless. Eixample hotels (including most of the city's best) are late-19th- or early-20th-century town houses restored and converted into exciting modern environments. Downtown hotels, including the Palace (former Ritz), the Claris, the Majestic, the Condes de Barcelona, and the Hotel Omm, best combine style and luxury with a sense of place, and the peripheral palaces (the Hotel Arts, the Eurostar Grand Marina, and the Rey Juan Carlos I) are less about Barcelona and more about generic luxury. Sarrià and Sant Gervasi upper-city hotels get you up out of the urban crush, and Olympic Port and Diagonal Mar hotels are in high-rise towers (requiring transport to and from the real Barcelona). Smaller budget hotels are less than half as expensive as some of the luxury addresses and more a part of city life.

## CIUTAT VELLA (OLD CITY)

The Ciutat Vella includes the Rambla, Barri Gòtic, Born-Ribera, and the Raval districts between Plaça de Catalunya and the port.

### BARRI GÒTIC

$$$–$$$$
Fodor's Choice
★

**Hotel Neri.** Built into a 17th-century palace over one of the Gothic Quarter's smallest and most charming squares, Plaça Sant Felip Neri, the Neri is a singular counterpoint of ancient and avant-garde design. The facade and location are early Barcelona, but the cavernous interior spaces are unfailingly contemporary and edgy. Rooms stress straight lines, sheer and angular precision, and expanses of wood and stone. **Pros:** central location, design, roof terrace for cocktails and breakfast. **Cons:** can be noisy at night, edgy design feels chilly to some. ⊠*St. Sever 5, Barri Gòtic, 08002* ☎*93/304–0655* ⊕*www.hotelneri.com* 🛏*22 rooms* ⋔*In-room: Wi-Fi, refrigerator. In-hotel: Wi-Fi, public internet, restaurant, bar* ⊟*AE, DC, MC, V* ⓇⓄⓁ*EP* Ⓜ*Liceu, Catalunya.*

$$$
**Gran Hotel Barcino.** Appropriately named for the ancient Roman settlement of Barcelona that once surrounded this hotel (this site is about in the middle of where the Roman Forum once was), the Barcino offers nearly unparalleled ease for exploring the Gothic Quarter and Born-Ribera. Rooms are small but well planned, and sparsely filled with modern furniture with

---

**TOP 5**

■ Hotel Neri for its Gothic stone surroundings and edgy design.

■ Hotel Majestic as a hub of mid-city Passeig de Gràcia elegance.

■ Turó de Vilana for leafy upper Barcelona peace and quiet.

■ Hotel Claris for superior service and technology in an historic structure.

■ Hotel Omm for postmodern originality in design and cuisine.

designer details. The concierge will advise you about not-to-miss events in either the City Hall or the Catalan seat of government, the Generalitat. **Pros:** central location, bright contemporary design, friendly staff. **Cons:** small rooms, on a busy street in the dead center of town, not a lot of amenities, no room service. ⊠*Jaume I 6, Barri Gòtic, 08002* ☎*93/302–2012* ⊕*www.gargallo-hotels.com* ↩*53 rooms* ☐*In-hotel: bar* ☐*AE, DC, MC, V* ⏸*EP* Ⓜ*Jaume I.*

**\$\$–\$\$\$**

Fodor'sChoice

★

▦**Colón.** There's something clubby about this elegant Barcelona standby, surprisingly intimate and charming for such a sizable operation. The location is ideal—directly across the plaza from the cathedral, overlooking weekend *sardana* dancing, Thursday antiques markets, and, of course, the floodlit cathedral by night. Rooms are comfortable and furnished with traditional pieces, some of them antiques; try to get one with a view of the cathedral. The Colón was a favorite of the artist Joan Miró. **Pros:** walking distance from all of central Barcelona, views of cathedral, friendly staff. **Cons:** slightly old-fashioned, low tech. ⊠*Av. Catedral 7, Barri Gòtic, 08002* ☎*93/301–1404* ⊕*www. hotelcolon.es* ↩*140 rooms, 5 suites* ☐*In-room: Wi-Fi, safe, refrigerator. In-hotel: restaurant, bar* ☐*AE, DC, MC, V* ⏸*EP* Ⓜ*Catalunya.*

**\$\$**

▦**Hesperia Metropol.** A block in from the port and midway between the Rambla and Via Laietana, this modestly priced hotel has a central location on a quiet street and cheerful guest rooms. A bright, upbeat lobby and sliding-glass entryway display the reigning aesthetic here. **Pros:** central location, the beach a 15-minute walk away, friendly staff. **Cons:** not the most elegant part of town, missing atmosphere. ⊠*Ample 31, Barri Gòtic, 08002* ☎*93/310–5100* ⊕*www.hesperia-metropol.com* ↩*68 rooms* ☐*In-room: safe. In-hotel: bar, parking (fee)* ☐*AE, DC, MC, V* ⏸*EP* Ⓜ*Drassanes, Jaume I.*

**\$–\$\$**

▦**Regencia Colon.** Tucked behind the Colón hotel, and with just about all the same conveniences (minus the cathedral view) at half the price, the Regencia Colon is a solid option to consider. It may even be a little quieter back here, where you're not listening to street minstrels on the main drag. Rooms are unexceptional, with standard wood furnishings. Note that the restaurant does not serve dinner. **Pros:** central location near cathedral, near excellent restaurants. **Cons:** small lobby, no bar, lacks its own scene. ⊠*Sagristans 13, Barri Gòtic, 08002* ☎*93/318–9858* ⊕*www.hotelregenciacolon.com* ↩*51 rooms* ☐*In-room: safe. In-hotel: restaurant* ☐*AE, DC, MC, V* ⏸*EP* Ⓜ*Catalunya.*

**\$–\$\$**

▦**Rialto.** With its glass-walled reception area on the corner of Pas de l'Ensenyança and Carrer Ferran, this bright, spotless, well lighted place gives way to more subdued rooms with wooden floorboards, white walls, patterned gray drapes and bedspreads, and solid walnut doors. Passatge del Crèdit, on the other side of the hotel, was where iconic Catalan painter Joan Miró was born. Miró's birth room is now the Rialto's suite 330 (€210), a perfect spot for dreams filled with shooting red and blue stars. **Pros:** central location, friendly staff. **Cons:** one of the busiest streets in the city, no room service. ⊠*Ferran 42, Barri Gòtic, 08002* ☎*93/318–5212* ⊕*www.gargallo-hotels.com* ↩*197 rooms, 1 suite* ☐*In-room: safe. In-hotel: restaurant, bar, laundry service* ☐*AE, DC, MC, V* ⏸*EP* Ⓜ*Liceu, Catalunya.*

**$–$$**   ⊞ **Suizo.** The lobby and public rooms in this Barcelona classic have sweeping spaces around a curving reception desk, modern furniture, and good views over the busy square just east of Plaça del Rei. Guest rooms have gleaming whitewashed walls set off by mustard- and coffee-colored drapes, bedspreads, and wood: colorful but soothing and sober at the same. time. The location places you in the middle of most of Ciutat Vella's most important attractions: the Picasso Museum, Santa Maria del Mar, and the bustling Born-Ribera neighborhood are all a two-minute walk away, and the City History Museum is across the street. **Pros:** central location over a subway stop, cheerful and sunny new rooms, friendly staff. **Cons:** a maelstrom of tourists and pedestrians passes the door, short on amenities. ⊠ *Pl. del Àngel 12, Barri Gòtic, 08002* ☎ *93/310–6108* ⊕ *www.gargallo-hotels.com* ⤶ *59 rooms* ⌂ *In-room: safe. In-hotel: bar, laundry service* ⊟ *AE, DC, MC, V* ⊺⊙*EP* Ⓜ *Jaume I.*

**$**   ⊞ **Jardí.** Perched over the traffic-free and charming Plaça del Pi and

Fodor's Choice   Plaça Sant Josep Oriol, this chic budget hotel has rooms with views

★   of the Gothic church of Santa Maria del Pi and outfitted with modern pine furniture. The in-house breakfast (€6) is excellent, and the alfresco tables at the Bar del Pi, downstairs, are ideal in summer. There are five floors—the higher, the quieter—and an elevator. It's not the Ritz, and it can be noisy in summer, but all in all the Jardí is great value. **Pros:** central location, good value, impeccable bathrooms. **Cons:** flimsy beds and furnishings, no amenities, including no room service. ⊠ *Pl. Sant Josep Oriol 1, Barri Gòtic, 08002* ☎ *93/301–5900* ⊕ *www.hoteljardi-barcelona.com* ⤶ *40 rooms* ⊟ *AE, DC, MC, V* ⊺⊙*EP* Ⓜ *Liceu, Catalunya.*

### BORN-RIBERA

**$$$–$$$$**   ⊞ **Grand Hotel Central.** At the edge of the Gothic Quarter, very near the Barcelona cathedral, this hot new midtown hideaway is becoming a magnet for the hip and hot-to-trot. Rooms are flawlessly furnished and equipped with high-tech design features, from flat-screen TVs to DSL hookups. The restaurant, supervised by internationally acclaimed chef Ramón Freixa, is bound for glory, and the top-floor pool offers a unique perch over the city's 2,000-year-old Roman and Gothic central nucleus. The higher the better is the rule here, as street level can be noisy, soundproofing or not. **Pros:** excellent location between the Gothic Quarter and the Born, attentive service, full gamut of high-tech amenities. **Con:** the street outside is noisy and fast. ⊠ *Via Laietana 30, Barri Gòtic, 08003* ☎ *93/295–7900* ⊕ *www.grandhotelcentral.com* ⤶ *147 rooms* ⌂ *In-room: Ethernet, Wi-Fi. In-hotel: restaurant, bar, public Internet, public Wi-Fi, pool, gym, parking (fee)* ⊟ *AE, DC, MC, V* ⊺⊙*EP* Ⓜ *Catalunya.*

**$$–$$$**   ⊞ **Hotel Chic & Basic Born.** A revolutionary concept best illustrated by the middle-of-your-room glass shower stalls, the Chic & Basic is a hit with young hipsters looking for a Barcelona combo package of design, surprise, and originality at less-than wallet-rocking prices. The restaurant, called the White Bar for its completely albino decor, serves excellent Mediterranean cooking. Designer Xavier Claramunt has come up with a winner here. **Pros:** perfectly situated for Barcelona's

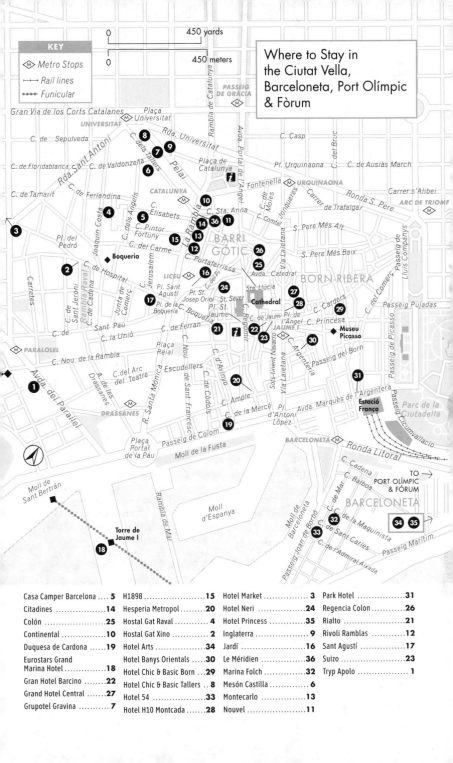

## KEY

◈ Metro Stops
⊢—→ Rail lines
•••• Funicular

## Where to Stay in the Ciutat Vella, Barceloneta, Port Olímpic & Fòrum

Casa Camper Barcelona .... **5**
Citadines ................. **14**
Colón .................... **25**
Continental .............. **10**
Duquesa de Cardona ..... **19**
Eurostars Grand
Marina Hotel ............. **18**
Gran Hotel Barcino ...... **22**
Grand Hotel Central ..... **27**
Grupotel Gravina ......... **7**

H1898 ..................... **15**
Hesperia Metropol ........ **20**
Hostal Gat Raval .......... **4**
Hostal Gat Xino .......... **2**
Hotel Arts ............... **34**
Hotel Banys Orientals .... **30**
Hotel Chic & Basic Born .. **29**
Hotel Chic & Basic Tallers .. **8**
Hotel 54 ................. **33**
Hotel H10 Montcada ...... **28**

Hotel Market .............. **3**
Hotel Neri ............... **24**
Hotel Princess ........... **35**
Inglaterra ............... **9**
Jardí .................... **16**
Le Méridien .............. **36**
Marina Folch ............. **32**
Mesón Castilla ........... **6**
Montecarlo ............... **13**
Nouvel ................... **11**

Park Hotel ............... **31**
Regencia Colon ........... **26**
Rialto ................... **21**
Rivoli Ramblas ........... **12**
Sant Agustí .............. **17**
Suizo .................... **23**
Tryp Apolo ............... **1**

hot Born-Ribera scene, clean-lined sleek and impeccable design. **Cons:** noisy nightlife around the hotel requires closed windows on weekends, rooms and spaces are small. ⊠ *Carrer Princesa 50, Born-Ribera, 08003* ☎ *93/295–4652* ⊕ *www.chicandbasic.com* ☞ *31 rooms* ⟡ *In-room: Wi-Fi. In-hotel: restaurant, bar, public Internet, public Wi-Fi* ▤ *AE, DC, MC, V* ⧫ *EP* Ⓜ *Jaume I.*

$$–$$$     ⊞ **Hotel H10 Montcada.** Übermodern, this high-tech hotel at the edge of the Gothic Quarter (part of the sleek H10 chain popping up all over Spain) is a sure bet for contemporary design and comfort—though the minimalist decor can leave you starved for visual stimulation. A five-minute walk from some of Barcelona's most medieval corners, the rooms, though small, are efficient and offer every state-of-the-art commodity you could ask for. **Pros:** central location, high-tech amenities. **Cons:** no restaurant or bar, no scene of its own, no room service. ⊠ *Via Laietana 24, Born-Ribera, 08003* ☎ *93/268–8570* ⊕ *www.h10. es* ☞ *87 rooms* ⟡ *In room: Wi-Fi, safe, refrigerator. In-hotel: restaurant, bar, gym* ▤ *AE, DC, MC, V* ⧫ *EP* Ⓜ *Jaume I.*

$–$$     ⊞ **Park Hotel.** Backing into some of Barcelona's prime art, architecture, and wine and tapa territory, this hotel offers sleek rooms and modernized comforts across the street from the Estació de França. It's modest but efficient and looking better all the time. **Pros:** central location, good value, friendly staff. **Cons:** small rooms, no glamour, no room service. ⊠ *Av. Marquès de l'Argentera 11, Born-Ribera, 08003* ☎ *93/319–6000* ⊕ *www.parkhotelbarcelona.com* ☞ *91 rooms* ⟡ *In room: Wi-Fi, refrigerator. In-hotel: restaurant, bar* ▤ *AE, DC, MC, V* ⧫ *EP* Ⓜ *Barceloneta.*

$     ⊞ **Hotel Banys Orientals.** This contemporary design hotel presents innovative lighting and imaginative touches, such as four-poster beds and Gaudí-esque chairs. (Despite its name, the "Oriental Baths" has, for the moment, no spa.) With the popular Senyor Parellada restaurant downstairs, rooms overlooking the street can be noisy, not from traffic but from the flow of humanity moving up and down Carrer Argenteria, one of the city's liveliest arteries. Two steps from Santa Maria del Mar and the Born area, this is a good base camp for most of early Barcelona's finest treasures. **Pros:** central location, interesting design, recent technology. **Cons:** noisy nightlife thoroughfare, mediocre restaurant. ⊠ *Argenteria 37, Born-Ribera, 08003* ☎ *93/268–8460* ⊕ *www. hotelbanysorientals.com* ☞ *43 rooms, 7 suites* ⟡ *In-hotel: restaurant, bar, public Internet* ▤ *AE, DC, MC, V* ⧫ *EP* Ⓜ *Jaume I.*

### EL RAVAL

$$$     ⊞ **Casa Camper Barcelona.** The mutual brainchild of the Camper footwear empire and Barcelona's nonpareil Vinçon design store, this 21st-century hotel sits halfway between the Rambla and the MACBA (Museum of Contemporary Art). No smoking, no tips, a free 24-hour snack facility where you can invite your friends, ecologically recycled residual waters, children up to 12 staying free of charge, and the Foodball restaurant next door serving spheroids of natural ingredients such as garbanzo beans and spinach all add up to a brave new world in the formerly dark and scary Raval. **Pros:** handy location in mid-Raval just off the Rambla, ultra-modern technology and concept. **Cons:** snacking

## GOURMET HOTELS

Hotels with stellar restaurants have proliferated in Barcelona over the last decade. Whereas in the early '90s top hotel dining opportunities were scarce, there are now a dozen Barcelona hotels offering distinguished cuisine: The Hotel Majestic, with its restaurant Drolma, is the leader of the pack and probably the hotel that sparked the fin-de-20th-siècle hotel restaurant revival. Later, the Hotel Arts and Ferran Adrià disciple Sergi Arola teamed up as did the Palace (former Ritz) and its restaurant Caelis under French chef Romain Fornell. The Hotel Omm placed Girona's Roca brothers at the culinary helm of its restaurant Moo; The Basque Country's Martin Berasategui opened Lasarte at the Hotel Condes de Barcelona; Carles Gaig moved his Barcelona classic to the midtown Hotel Cram; and the Hotel Claris signed Daniel Padró to direct their restaurant, East 47. Meanwhile, Hotel Hesperia Tower's Evo, under acclaimed chef Santi Santimaria, is one of the hot newcomers, while the Hotel Eurostars Grand Marina's Aire de Mar, led by Miquel Fuxá, Gran Hotel la Florida's Orangerie directed by Cesar Palomeque, and the Grand Hotel Central's restaurant, Actual, under the direction of Ramon Freixa, also rate food visits whether you are staying under the roof or not.

temptation, area can be sketchy late at night. ⊠*C. Elisabets 11, Raval, 08001* ☏*93/342–6280* ⊕*www.casacamper.com* ⊃*20 rooms, 5 suites* ⚲*In-room: Wi-Fi, safe. In-hotel: restaurant, 24-hour buffet, parking (fee), no-smoking rooms* ▤*AE, DC, MC, V* ⍾❘*BP* Ⓜ*Catalunya.*

$$$ ⌸**Inglaterra.** A welcoming Moderniste stairway in this neoclassical building leads to sleek guest rooms decorated in light-color wood with Japanese motifs. The cafeteria-restaurant-library is an experimental multiuse space designed as a refuge for rest and reflection at the edge of the Ciutat Vella. **Pros:** central location, modern facilities, near the Raval and the MACBA. **Cons:** noisy avenue in front of hotel, in the epicenter of Barcelona. ⊠*Pelai 14, Raval, 08001* ☏*93/505–1100* ⊕*www.hotel-inglaterra.com* ⊃*55 rooms* ⚲*In-room: Wi-Fi, safe. In-hotel: restaurant, bar, laundry service* ▤*AE, DC, MC, V* ⍾❘*EP* Ⓜ*Catalunya.*

$$–$$$ ⌸**Tryp Apolo.** The Apolo is a massive modern business hotel—rooms are impeccable, but impersonal—in the middle of the traditional cabaret and theater district, not far from Drassanes, the Columbus monument at the end of the Rambla, and the port. The location is handy for Montjuïc and the Fira de Barcelona; however, the 15-minute walk over to the Rambla and the Gothic Quarter takes you through the heart of the Raval's notorious Barrio Chino, one of Barcelona's most rough-and-tumble neighborhoods. A 10-minute walk down Carrer Nou de la Rambla is your best route across to the Rambla, but the metro will safely whip you around from the Paral.lel to the Liceu stop in three minutes. **Pros:** central location for the Raval, high-tech, large and lively. **Cons:** noisy thoroughfare at the door, high-rise and impersonal building. ⊠*Av. del Paral.lel 57, Raval, 08002* ☏*93/443–1122* ⊕*www.sol-melia.com* ⊃*290 rooms, 24 suites* ⚲*In-room: Wi-Fi, safe. In-hotel: restaurant, parking (fee)* ▤*AE, DC, MC, V* ⍾❘*EP* Ⓜ*Paral.lel.*

**$$**   ☷**Mesón Castilla.** A few steps up Carrer Tallers from the top of the Rambla, this little hotel is well positioned for exploring medieval Barcelona and the Moderniste Eixample. Just around the corner from the MACBA and the rest of the Raval, rooms here are quiet and, though slightly old-fashioned, a good value for the price. **Pros:** central location, comfortable public rooms and furnishings. **Cons:** on a busy street, very mid-city without green spaces. ⊠*Valdoncella 5, Raval, 08001* ☎*93/318–2182* ⊕*www.mesoncastilla.com* ⤳*56 rooms* ⚭*In-hotel: bar* ▭*AE, DC, MC, V* ⏀*EP* Ⓜ*Catalunya.*

**$$**   ☷**Sant Agustí.** In a leafy square just off the Rambla, the Sant Agustí has long been popular with musicians performing at the Liceu opera house. Rooms are small but pleasantly modern, with plenty of light wood and clean lines. **Pros:** central location near the Boqueria market, the Rambla, and the opera house; cozy traditional design. **Cons:** noisy square requiring closed windows, short on amenities and room service. ⊠*Pl. Sant Agustí 3, Raval, 08001* ☎*93/318–1658* ⊕*www.hotelsa. com* ⤳*77 rooms* ⚭*In-room: safe. In-hotel: bar* ▭*AE, DC, MC, V* ⏀*EP* Ⓜ*Liceu.*

Fodor'sChoice   ★

**$**   ☷**Hostal Chic & Basic Tallers.** Another sleek budget choice in the upper Raval, this even-more-economic version of the Hotel Chic & Basic over in the Born has a living room called Chill & Basic with Wi-Fi access and free snacks. Other surprising assets include in-room music speakers that allow you to listen to the mix created by the hotel's music director or plug in your own iPod. **Pros:** perfectly designed and situated for an exciting, low-cost Barcelona experience; young and friendly staff. **Cons:** the streets in the Raval can reverberate noisily at night, space is tight in these rooms. ⊠*Carrer Tallers 82, Raval, 08001* ☎*93/302– 5183* ⊕*www.chicandbasic.com* ⤳*14 rooms* ⚭*In-room: Wi-Fi, refrigerator. In-hotel: public Internet, public Wi-Fi* ▭*AE, DC, MC, V* ⏀*EP* Ⓜ*Catalunya, Universitat.*

**$**   ☷**Hostal Gat Xino.** A cheery space in what was once the darkest Raval, Gat Raval's sister location places the adventurous traveler in the middle of what may seem more like a North African souk than a modern textile and design metropolis. Near the intersection of Carrers Carmen and Hospital, the Gat Xino gives you an up-close look at one of Barcelona's most cosmopolitan and traditionally tumultuous neighborhoods. Rooms are decorated in bright colors, and the value is unbeatable. In the bargain, you may discover that the Raval and its raucous street life are inhabited by Barcelona's friendliest citizens. **Pros:** central location, smart and sassy design, up-to-date technology, hostel-like friendly clients and staff. **Cons:** busy and noisy section of the Raval, small rooms and public spaces. ⊠*Hospital 155, Raval, 08001* ☎*93/324–8833* ⊕*www.gataccommodation.com* ⤳*35 rooms* ⚭*In-room: Wi-Fi. In-hotel: public internet, Wi-Fi* ▭*AE, DC, MC, V* ⏀*BP* Ⓜ*Sant Antoni.*

**$**   ☷**Hotel Market.** A wallet-friendly boutique hotel and yet another Barcelona design triumph, the Hotel Market is so named for the Mercat de Sant Antoni. On a little alleyway a block from the market and walking distance from all of the Raval and Gothic Quarter sites and attractions, this ultramodern, high-tech, designer lodging opportunity is one of Barcelona's best bargains. Rooms are simply but solidly furnished with dark-wood trim and beams setting off bright white bedspreads and surfaces. The hotel restaurant offers superlative fare and excellent value. **Pros:** well equipped, designed, and positioned for a low-cost Barcelona visit; young and friendly staff. **Con:** rooms are a little cramped. ⊠*Carrer Comte Borrell 68 (entrance on Passatge Sant Antoni Abat 10), Raval, 08001* ☎*93/325–1205* ⊕*www.markethotel.com.es* ⬚*37 rooms* ⌂*In-room: Wi-Fi, refrigerator. In-hotel: restaurant, bar, public Internet, public Wi-Fi* ⊟*AE, DC, MC, V* ⭐*EP* Ⓜ*Sant Antoni.*

¢–$    🖫**Hostal Gat Raval.** This hip little hole-in-the-wall opens into a surprisingly bright and sleekly designed modern space with rooms that come in different shapes, styles, and number of beds, all cheerily appointed and impeccably maintained. Just around the corner from the MACBA, the Gat Raval seems to have been influenced by Richard Meier's shining contemporary structure, though you'd never guess it from the street. **Pros:** central location in the deepest Raval, contemporary design, recent technology. **Cons:** noisy street at threshold, somewhat cramped rooms and public spaces, few amenities. ⊠*Joaquin Costa 44, Raval, 08001* ☎*93/481–6670* ⊕*www.gataccommodation.com* ⬚*22 rooms* ⌂*In-room: Wi-Fi. In-hotel: public Internet, public Wi-Fi* ⊟*AE, DC, MC, V* ⭐*BP* Ⓜ*Universitat.*

Fodor'sChoice
★

### THE RAMBLA

$$$$    🖫**Le Méridien.** Le Méridien vies with the Rivoli Ramblas as the premier hotel in the Rambla area. Guest rooms are bright, spacious, and colorful, with pastel-hue walls. Rooms are filled with top-quality furnishings, from the beds to the flat-screened TVs, and sumptuously decorated in bright colors and rich wood trim with marble bathrooms and, from the top floors, terrific views over the city. The hotel is very popular with businesspeople—fax machines and computers for your room are available on request—and has hosted its share of celebrities as well. Rooms overlooking the Rambla are completely soundproof. **Pros:** central location, amply endowed with amenities of all kinds, great views over the Rambla from some rooms. **Con:** if your face hasn't appeared recently on the cover of *Us Weekly,* hotel service can be a little perfunctory and impersonal. ⊠*Rambla 111, Rambla, 08002* ☎*93/318–6200* ⊕*www. lemeridien-barcelona.com* ⬚*390 rooms* ⌂*In-room: safe. In-hotel: restaurant, bar, parking (fee)* ⊟*AE, DC, MC, V* ⭐*EP* Ⓜ*Catalunya.*

$$$–$$$$    🖫**Duquesa de Cardona.** This refurbished 16th-century town house overlooking the port has ultracontemporary facilities with designer touches, all housed in an early-Renaissance structure. The exterior rooms have views of the harbor, the World Trade Center, and the passenger boat terminals. The hotel is a 10-minute walk from everything in the Gothic Quarter or Barceloneta, and no more than a 30-minute walk from the main Eixample attractions. The miniature rooftop pool, more for a dip than a swim, is cooling in summer. **Pros:** at a key spot over the port, contemporary technology in a traditional palace. **Cons:** rooms on the small side, roof terrace tiny, views over port blocked by Maremagnum complex. ⊠*Passeig de Colom 12, Rambla, 08002* ☎*93/268–9090* ⊕*www.hduquesadecardona.com* ⬚*44 rooms* ⌂*In-room: dial-up. In-hotel: restaurant, pool* ⊟*AE, DC, MC, V* ⭐*EP* Ⓜ*Drassanes.*

Fodor'sChoice
★

# Lodging Alternatives

### APARTMENT RENTALS

If you want a home base that's roomy enough for a family and comes with cooking facilities, consider a furnished rental. These can save you money, especially if you're traveling with a group. Apartment rentals are increasingly popular in Barcelona these days. Aparthotels rent apartments in residences subdivided into small living spaces at prices generally more economical than hotel rates. Rentals by the day or week can be arranged, though prices may rise for short stays. Prices range from €100 to €300 per day depending on the quality of the accommodations, but perfectly acceptable lodging for four can be found for around €150 per night. Apartment accommodations can be arranged through any of the agencies listed below.

### LOCAL APARTMENT AGENCIES

**Aparthotel Bertran** ( ⊠ *Bertran 150, Eixample, 08023* ☎ *93/212–7550* ⊕ *www.hotelbertran.com*). **Aparthotel Bonanova** ( ⊠ *Bisbe Sivilla 7, Eixample, 08022* ☎ *93/253–1563*). **Aparthotel Nàpols** ( ⊠ *Napols 116, Eixample, 08013* ☎ *93/246–4573* ⊕ *www.napols.net*). **Apartment Barcelona** ( ⊠ *Valencia 286, Eixample, 08022* ☎ *93/215–7934* ⊕ *www.apartmentbarcelona.com*). **Apartments Ramblas** ( ☎ *93/301–7678* ⊕ *www.apartmentsramblas.com*). **BarcelonaForrent** ( ☎ *93/457–9329* ⊕ *www.barcelonaforrent.com*). **Barcelona Rentals/Atlanta-Ads** ( ☎ *404/849–5827* ⊕ *www.atlanta-ads.com*). **Barceloneta Suites** ( ☎ *93/221–4225* ⊕ *www.barcelonetasuites.com*). **Feel Barcelona** ( ⊠ *Balmes 28, 08007* ☎ *93/301–9341* ⊕ *www.feelbarcelona.com*). **Flats By Days** ( ☎ *93/342–6481*

⊕ *www.flatsbydays.com*). **Friendly Rentals** ( ⊠ *Pasaje Sert 8 Bis, 08003* ☎ *93/268–8051* ⊕ *www.friendly-rentals.com*). **Goben Apartments** ( ⊠ *Selva de Mar 202, Eixample, 08020* ☎ *93/278–1156* ⊕ *www.gobcn.com*). **Lofts & Apartments** ( ⊠ *Allada i Vermell 6–8, Eixample, 08003* ☎ *93/342–7300* ⊕ *www.lofts-apartments.com*). **Oh-Barcelona** ( ⊠ *Fontanella 20, Eixample, 08023* ☎ *93/302–0379* ⊕ *www.oh-barcelona.com*). **Rent a Flat in Barcelona** ( ⊠ *Fontanella 18, Eixample, 08013* ☎ *93/342–7300* ⊕ *www.rentaflatinbarclona.com*)

### INTERNATIONAL AGENTS

**Hideaways International** ( ⊠ *767 Islington St., Portsmouth, NH 03801* ☎ *603/430–4433 or 800/843–4433* 🖷 *603/430–4444* ⊕ *www.hideaways.com*); annual membership $185.

### HOME EXCHANGES

If you would like to exchange your home for someone else's, join a home-exchange organization, which will send you its updated listings of available exchanges for a year and will include your own listing in at least one of them. It's up to you to make specific arrangements. Home-exchange directories sometimes list rentals as well as exchanges.

### EXCHANGE CLUB

**HomeLink International** ( ⊠ *Box 47747, Tampa, FL 33647* ☎ *813/975–9825 or 800/638–3841* 🖷 *813/910–8144* ⊕ *www.homelink.org*); $110 yearly for a listing, online access, and catalog; $75 without catalog.

### HOSTELS

No matter how old you are, you can save on lodging costs by staying at hostels (*albergue juvenil,* and not a *hostal,* a popular term for a modest hotel without major facilities, signaled by a small "s" next to the "H" on the hotel doorway's blue plaque).

In some 4,500 locations in more than 70 countries around the world, Hostelling International (HI), the umbrella group for a number of national youth-hostel associations, offers single-sex, dorm-style beds and, at many hostels, rooms for couples, and family accommodations. Membership in any HI national hostel association, open to travelers of all ages, allows you to stay in HI-affiliated hostels at member rates; one-year membership is about $28 for adults; hostels charge about $10–$30 per night. Members have priority if the hostel is full.

Turisme Juvenil Catalunya (TUJUCA) can help you locate youth hostels in Barcelona. Many of these hostels happily take people of all ages, though you may have to pay an extra fee to become a card-carrying member. Many elderly youth-hostel fans find hostels, where people tend to exchange tips and chat freely, friendlier and more inclusive than hotels, where speaking to a stranger seems all but taboo. Nearly all Barcelona hostels offer common rooms for television, card games, and general socializing, dining rooms for meals, and sleeping accommodations ranging from double bedrooms to dormitories, the latter arrangement more frequent.

### ORGANIZATIONS

**Hostelling International—USA** ( ⊠ *8401 Colesville Rd., Suite 600, Silver Spring, MD 20910* ☎ *301/495–1240* 🖷 *301/495–6697* ⊕ *www.hiusa. org*). **Turisme Juvenil Catalunya (TUJUCA)** ( ⊠ *Rocafort 116–122, Eixample, 08015* ☎ *93/483–8339* ⊕ *www.tujuca.com*).

### HOSTELS

**Alberg Abba** ( ⊠ *Passeig de Colom 9, Barri Gòtic, 08002* ☎ *93/319–4545* ⊕ *www.abbayouthostel.com*). **Alberg Kabul** ( ⊠ *Pl. Reial 17, Rambla, 08002* ☎ *93/318–5190* ⊕ *www.kabul.es*). **Alberg Palau** ( ⊠ *Palau 6, Barri Gòtic, 08002* ☎ *93/412–5080* ⊕ *www. bcnalberg.com*). **Alberg-Residencia La Ciutat** ( ⊠ *Ca l'Alegre de Dalt 66, Eixample, 08024* ☎ *93/213–0300*). **Gothic Point** ( ⊠ *Vigatans 5, Born-Ribera, 08024* ☎ *93/268–7808* ⊕ *www.gothicpoint.com*). **Ideal Youth Hostel** ( ⊠ *Carrer Unió 12, Raval, 08024* ☎ *93/342–6177* ⊕ *www.ideal-hostel.com*). **Sea Point** ( ⊠ *Pl. del Mar 1–4, Barceloneta, 08024* ☎ *93/224–7075* ⊕ *www.seapointhostel.com*).

4

**$$$–$$$$** 🖫**H1898.** This elegant, if somewhat impersonal, hotel overlooking the Rambla occupies a building with an illustrious history as the headquarters of the Compañia de Tabacos de Filipinas. Named for the fateful year when Spain was stripped of its final colonial possessions, the Philippines among them, the hotel's elegance is an homage to bygone glories as well as a sign of the city's present opulence. Rooms are superbly equipped with state-of-the-art appliances (such as flat-screen plasma TVs), and the location is unbeatable. **Pros:** central location on the Rambla, state-of-the-art design and technology. **Con:** noisy Rambla thronging by at your threshold. ☒ *La Rambla 109, Rambla, 08002* 🕾*93/552–9552* ⊕*www.nnhotels.es* 🖘*166 rooms, 3 suites* ⚒ *In-room: Ethernet. In-hotel: restaurant, bar, pool, gym, parking (fee)* ☰*AE, DC, MC, V* ⦿*EP* Ⓜ*Catalunya.*

**$$$–$$$$** 🖫**Montecarlo.** The ornate, illuminated entrance takes you from the Rambla through an enticing marble hall; upstairs, you enter a sumptuous reception room with a dark-wood Art Nouveau ceiling. Rooms, which vary wildly in size and facilities, are modern and bright; many overlook the Rambla, a debatable bonus depending on your susceptibility to noise. Some of the back rooms overlook the moist and intimate palm-shaded *jardín romántico* of the Ateneu Barcelonès, Barcelona's literary club and library, all to the tune of the hotel's waterfall, reminiscent of the Rambla's early days as a spate river. **Pros:** centrally positioned, top new equipment and furnishings. **Cons:** on the tumultuous Rambla, slightly impersonal in design and service. ☒ *Rambla 124, Rambla, 08002* 🕾*93/412–0404* ⊕*www.montecarlobcn.com* 🖘*55 rooms, 1 suite* ⚒ *In-hotel: restaurant, bar, parking (fee)* ☰*AE, DC, MC, V* ⦿*EP* Ⓜ*Catalunya.*

**$$–$$$** 🖫**Rivoli Ramblas.** Behind this traditional upper-Rambla facade lies a surprisingly original marble-floored interior equipped with state-of-the-art facilities. The rooms are pastel in hue and contemporary in design, with avant-garde details. Guests range from hip honeymooners to discerning retirees. The roof-terrace bar has panoramic views. **Pros:** good location on the Rambla, all top-notch comfort and facilities present and accounted for. **Cons:** somewhat large and impersonal, noisy and tumultuous Rambla at the doorstep. ☒ *Rambla 128, Rambla, 08002* 🕾*93/481–7676* ⊕*www.rivolihotels.com* 🖘*81 rooms, 9 suites* ⚒ *In-hotel: restaurant, bar, gym, parking (fee)* ☰*AE, DC, MC, V* ⦿*EP* Ⓜ*Catalunya.*

**$$** 🖫**Citadines.** This Rambla hotel is bright, modern, and soundproof. Lodgings range from apartments with sitting rooms to one-room studios with kitchenettes and small dining areas. The rooftop solarium has views of Montjuïc and the Mediterranean. Across the Rambla is the tower over the Poliorama theater where George Orwell, author of *Homage to Catalonia*, was posted during the Spanish civil war. Ask for a back room over Plaça Villa de Madrid for a quieter spot set over a leafy square with a 3rd-century Roman roadway and tombs. **Pros:** central location, facilities and technology perfect. **Cons:** noisy Rambla a constant hubbub, apartments small and motel-like. ☒ *Rambla 122, Rambla, 08002* 🕾*93/270–1111* ⊕*www.citadines.com* 🖘*115 studios, 16 apartments* ⚒ *In-room: kitchen. In-hotel: bar* ☰*AE, DC, MC, V* ⦿*EP* Ⓜ*Catalunya.*

$$ [🏨]**Nouvel.** White marble, etched glass, elaborate plasterwork, and carved, dark woodwork blend into a handsome Art Nouveau interior here. Rooms have marble floors, firm beds, and chic bathrooms. The narrow street, just below Plaça de Catalunya, is pedestrian-only and therefore quiet. **Pros:** centrally positioned, charming Moderniste details, quiet pedestrianized street. **Cons:** rooms on the small side, not especially high tech. ⊠ *Santa Anna 18–20, Rambla, 08002* ☎ *93/301–8274* ⊕ *www.hotelnouvel.com* ↗ *71 rooms* ⟨In-room: safe. In-hotel: restaurant, bar* ☰ *AE, DC, MC, V* ¶○IEP Ⓜ *Catalunya.*

$–$$ [🏨]**Grupotel Gravina.** Near Plaça de Catalunya and just five minutes from the MACBA and the Raval, this slick hotel decorated in glass and marble offers comfort and modern appointments on a quiet street tucked in away from all hubbub. **Pros:** pivotally placed, first-rate facilities. **Cons:** small spaces and public rooms. ⊠ *Gravina 12, Rambla, 08001* ☎ *93/301–6868* ⊕ *www.grupotel.com* ↗ *84 rooms* ⟨In-hotel: restaurant, bar, no-smoking rooms* ☰ *AE, DC, MC, V* ¶○IEP Ⓜ *Catalunya.*

$ [🏨]**Continental.** This modest hotel stands at the top of the Rambla, just below Plaça de Catalunya. Space is tight, but the rooms manage to accommodate large, firm beds. It's high enough over the Rambla to escape street noise, so ask for a room overlooking Barcelona's most emblematic street. This is a good place to read *Homage to Catalonia*, as George Orwell stayed here with his wife in 1937 after recovering from a bullet wound. **Pros:** in the heart of the city, historically significant, high enough over Rambla to be quiet, with balconies from which to admire the human flow below. **Cons:** slightly old-fashioned and down at the heel, low tech, small rooms. ⊠ *Rambla 138, Rambla, 08002* ☎ *93/301–2570* ⊕ *www.hotelcontinental.com* ↗ *35 rooms* ⟨In-room: Wi-Fi, safe* ☰ *AE, DC, MC, V* ¶○IEP Ⓜ *Catalunya.*

## BARCELONETA, PORT OLÍMPIC & FÒRUM

$$$$ [🏨]**Eurostars Grand Marina Hotel.** A cylindrical tower built around a central patio, the Grand Marina offers maximum luxury just two minutes from the Rambla over Barcelona's port. With stunning views of the city or the Mediterranean, this ultracontemporary monolith is in the middle of, though well above, Barcelona's best sights. Rooms are bright and comfortable, albeit somewhat generic, and the public spaces are geometrical expanses of sleek glass and steel. Guests tend to be conventioneers and business travelers. **Pros:** centrally positioned over the port and the Rambla, great views out to sea, excellent restaurant. **Cons:** high-rise impersonal construction, primarily a convention center and business hotel. ⊠ *Moll de Barcelona (World Trade Center), Port Olímpic, 08039* ☎ *93/603–9000* ⊕ *www.grandmarinahotel.com* ↗ *291 rooms* ⟨In-room: safe, Wi-Fi, refrigerator. In-hotel: 3 restaurants, bar, pool, gym, parking (fee)* ☰ *AE, DC, MC, V* Ⓜ *Drassanes* ¶○IEP.

★ $$$$ [🏨]**Hotel Arts.** This luxurious Ritz-Carlton-owned monolith overlooks Barcelona from the Olympic Port, providing unique views of the Mediterranean, the city, and the mountains behind. The hotel's main drawback is that it's somewhat in a world of its own, a short taxi ride from the center of the city. That said, its world is an exciting one.

True to its name, fine art—from Chillida drawings to Susana Solano sculptures—hangs everywhere. Sergi Arola's restaurant is a chic, postmodern culinary playground. **Pros:** excellent views over Barcelona; first-rate, original art all over the halls and rooms; fine restaurants; general comfort and technology. **Cons:** a 30-minute hike from the nearest point of Barcelona, hotel feels like a colony of (mostly American) tourists apart from local life. ⊠ *Calle de la Marina 19, Port Olímpic, 08005* ☎*93/221–1000* ⊕*www.hotelartsbarcelona.es* ⚓*397 rooms, 59 suites, 27 apartments* ⟁ *In-room: safe, Wi-Fi, refrigerator. In-hotel: 3 restaurants, room service, bar, pool, beachfront, parking (fee)* ☰*AE, DC, MC, V* ⎮OⓘEP Ⓜ*Ciutadella–Vil.la Olímpica.*

**$$$$** ⛫**Hotel Princess.** Designed by architect Óscar Tusquets, this skyscraper towers over the 2004 Fòrum de les Cultures complex at the eastern end of the Diagonal, Barcelona's major crosstown avenue. If this sort of urban jamboree (tall buildings and thousands of people) appeals to you, then don't miss this spectacularly equipped spa-like environment, with a hot tub in every room and endless views out over the 2004 Fòrum site and the Mediterranean. **Pros:** the ultimate high-tech hotel, bubbling in-hotel action for conventioneers. **Cons:** a half-hour taxi ride from the center of town, impersonal architecture. ⊠ *Av. Diagonal 1, Diagonal Mar, 08019* ☎*93/356–1000* ⊕*www.princess-hotels.com* ⚓*364 rooms* ⟁ *In-room: Wi-Fi. In-hotel: restaurant, bar, pool, gym* ☰*AE, DC, MC, V* ⎮OⓘEP Ⓜ*Maresme–Fòrum.*

**$$–$$$** ⛫**Hotel 54.** With rooms overlooking the Barceloneta port and just a few minutes' walk from the beach, this modern, minimalist newcomer to the Barcelona hotel scene offers much for travelers seeking location, comfort, and economy. The sleek lines and a blue-curtained facade announce the property's brash and sassy attitude, and the interior lives up to the space-age starkness on the outside. **Pros:** well positioned for the nearby Born-Ribera neighborhood, latest technology and equipment. **Cons:** buses roar back and forth around the clock on Passeig Joan de Borbó, rooms are minimalist almost to a fault, a little chilly and mechanical. ⊠ *Passeig Joan de Borbó 54, Barceloneta, 08003* ☎*93/225–0054* ⊕*www.hotel54barceloneta.com* ⚓*28 rooms* ⟁ *In-room: Wi-Fi, refrigerator. In-hotel: restaurant, bar, public Internet, public Wi-Fi* ☰*AE, DC, MC, V* ⎮OⓘEP Ⓜ*Barceloneta.*

**¢–$** ⛫**Marina Folch.** This little Barceloneta hideaway is crisp and contemporary. Rooms are small and equipped with somewhat matchstick furnishings, but most have views over the Barcelona harbor. Five minutes from the beach and with an excellent restaurant and a generous, caring family at the helm, it's a budget winner. **Pros:** great value, five minutes from the beach, surrounded by fine tapas and dining opportunities, good value. **Cons:** furnishings light and flimsy, spaces cramped, no in-hotel Internet connection. ⊠ *Carrer Mar 16 pral., Barceloneta, 08003* ☎*93/310–3709* 📠*93/310–5327* ⚓*11 rooms* ⟁ *In-hotel: restaurant* ☰*AE, DC, MC, V* ⎮OⓘEP Ⓜ*Barceloneta.*

## EIXAMPLE

**$$$$**   ⊞**Alexandra.** Behind a reconstructed Eixample facade, everything here is slick and contemporary. The rooms are spacious and attractively furnished with dark-wood chairs, and those that face inward have thatch screens on the balconies for privacy. From the airy marble hall on up, the Alexandra is a dependable mid-Eixample lodging option. **Pros:** central to the Eixample and a 20-minute walk from the port, light and upbeat contemporary. **Con:** rooms seem constricted after all the space in the lobby. ⊠*Mallorca 251, Eixample, 08008* ☎*93/467–7166* ⊕*www.hotel-alexandra.com* ☞*95 rooms, 5 suites* ⚲*In-hotel: restaurant, bar, laundry service, parking (fee)* ▭*AE, DC, MC, V* ⊙|*EP* Ⓜ*Provença.*

**$$$$**   ⊞**Avenida Palace.** At the bottom of the Eixample, between the Rambla de Catalunya and Passeig de Gràcia, this hotel conveys elegance and antiquated style despite dating from only 1952. The lobby is wonderfully ornate, with curving staircases spinning off in many directions. Everything is patterned, from the carpets to the plasterwork, a style largely echoed in the bedrooms. If you want contemporary minimalism, stay elsewhere. **Pros:** prime location; facilities and technology perfect. **Cons:** old-fashioned and overly ornate; no trace of cutting-edge, design-happy Barcelona here. ⊠*Gran Via 605–607, Eixample, 08007* ☎*93/301–9600* ⊕*www.avenidapalace. com* ☞*146 rooms, 14 suites* ⚲*In-hotel: restaurant, bar* ▭*AE, DC, MC, V* ⊙|*EP* Ⓜ*Passeig de Gràcia.*

**$$$$**   ⊞**Claris.** Widely considered Barcelona's best hotel, the Claris is a fascinating mélange of design and tradition. Rooms come in 60 different
Fodor'sChoice   modern layouts, some with restored 18th-century English furniture and
★   some with contemporary furnishings from Barcelona's playful legion of designers. Lavishly endowed with wood and marble, the hotel also has a Japanese water garden, a rooftop cocktail terrace and pool, and two first-rate restaurants, including East 47, which has become one of the most admired dining spots in Barcelona. **Pros:** elegant service and furnishings, central location for shopping and Moderniste architecture, facilities and technology perfect. **Con:** hard on the credit card. ⊠*Carrer Pau Claris 150, Eixample, 08009* ☎*93/487–6262* ⊕*www. derbyhotels.es* ☞*80 rooms, 40 suites* ⚲*In-hotel: 2 restaurants, bar, pool, gym, laundry service, parking (fee)* ▭*AE, DC, MC, V* ⊙|*EP* Ⓜ*Passeig de Gràcia.*

**$$$$**   ⊞**Fira Palace.** Close to the Palacio de Congressos (aka Fira de Barcelona), the city Convention Palace and with easy access to Montjuïc and its attractions, the massive and somewhat impersonal Fira Palace is one of Barcelona's leading business and convention havens. It's modern to a fault, and a solid choice for generic creature comforts rather than local color. **Pros:** good location for conventions and congresses, facilities and technology perfect. **Cons:** somewhat impersonal, lacking charm. ⊠*Av. Rius i Taulet 1, Eixample, 08004* ☎*93/426–2223* ⊕*www.fira-palace. com* ☞*258 rooms, 18 suites* ⚲*In-room: dial-up. In-hotel: restaurant, bar, pool, gym, parking (fee)* ▭*AE, DC, MC, V* ⊙|*EP* Ⓜ*Poble Sec.*

4

$$$$   ⛨**Gallery.** In the upper part of the Eixample below the Diagonal, this modern hotel offers impeccable service and a central location for middle and upper Barcelona. (In the other direction, you're only half an hour's walk from the waterfront.) It's named for its proximity to the city's prime art-gallery district, a few blocks away on Rambla de Catalunya and Consell de Cent. Rooms are comfortable, contemporary in decor, spotless, largely characterless, but perfectly adequate. **Pros:** well located for Eixample shopping and Moderniste architecture, intimate enough to feel a personal touch. **Cons:** slightly cold and high-tech, minimalist lines and ambience. ⊠*Roselló 249, Eixample, 08008* ☎*93/415–9911* ⊕*www.galleryhotel.com* ⇆*108 rooms, 5 suites* ☖*In-room: dial-up. In-hotel: restaurant, bar, gym, parking (fee)* ⊟*AE, DC, MC, V* ⏐⚭⏐*EP* Ⓜ*Provença.*

$$$$   ⛨**Hotel Omm.** Another on Barcelona's lengthening list of design hotels,
Fodor'sChoice   this postmodern architectural tour de force was conceived by a team
★   of designers who sought to create, in a playful way, a mystic sense of peace mirroring its mantra. Minimalist rooms, a soothing reception area, and even the pool all contribute to this aura. The upper rooms overlook the roof terrace of Gaudí's Casa Milá. The restaurant, Moo, serves modern cuisine orchestrated by the Roca brothers—Joan, Josep, and Jordi—who achieved international prestige with their Celler de Can Roca near Girona. **Pros:** a perfect location for the upper Eixample, a design triumph, a sense of being at the epicenter of style, great nightlife scene around the bar on weekends. **Cons:** slightly pretentious staff; the restaurant, Moo, is pricey and a little precious. ⊠*Roselló 265, Eixample, 08008* ☎*93/445–4000* ⊕*www.hotelomm.es* ⇆*58 rooms, 1 suite* ☖*In-hotel: restaurant, bar, pool, parking (fee)* ⊟*AE, DC, MC, V* ⏐⚭⏐*EP* Ⓜ*Diagonal, Provença.*

★ $$$$   ⛨**Hotel Palace (former Ritz).** Founded in 1919 by Caesar Ritz, this is the grande dame of Barcelona hotels, renamed in 2005. The imperial lobby is at once loose and elegant; guest rooms contain Regency furniture, and some have Roman-style mosaics in the baths. Service is generally excellent. The restaurant, Caelis, serves first-rate French cuisine. **Pros:** equidistant from Gothic Quarter and central Eixample, elegant and polished service, consummate old-world luxury in rooms. **Cons:** a little stuffy, painfully pricey. ⊠*Gran Via 668, Eixample, 08010* ☎*93/318–5200* ⊕*www.hotelpalacebarcelona.com* ⇆*122 rooms* ☖*In-hotel: restaurant, bar, gym* ⊟*AE, DC, MC, V* ⏐⚭⏐*EP* Ⓜ*Passeig de Gràcia.*

$$$$   ⛨**Majestic.** With an unbeatable location on Barcelona's most stylish
Fodor'sChoice   boulevard, surrounded by fashion emporiums of every denomination,
★   the Majestic is a near-perfect place to stay. The building is part Eixample town house and part modern extension, but pastels and Mediterranean hues warm each room. The superb restaurant, Drolma, is a destination in itself. **Pros:** perfectly placed in the center of the Eixample, good balance between technology and charm, one of Barcelona's best restaurants. **Con:** facing one of the city's widest, brightest, noisiest, most commercial thoroughfares. ⊠*Passeig de Gràcia 68, Eixample, 08008* ☎*93/488–1717* ⊕*www.hotelmajestic.es* ⇆*273 rooms, 30 suites* ☖*In-room: Wi-Fi. In-hotel: 2 restaurants, bar, pool, gym, parking (fee)* ⊟*AE, DC, MC, V* ⏐⚭⏐*EP* Ⓜ*Passeig de Gràcia.*

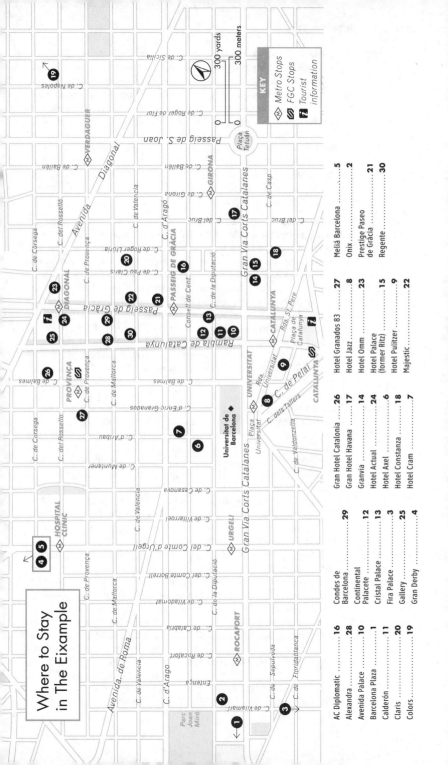

# Where to Stay
in The Eixample

## KEY

◇ Metro Stops

Ⓢ FGC Stops

🛈 Tourist
Information

300 yards

300 meters

$$$–$$$$ **Barcelona Plaza.** A modern, unsurprising business hotel with a vaguely industrial air about it, this well-operated place is in a location convenient for visitors participating in congresses at the Fira de Barcelona convention grounds; it is also nicely placed for efficient airport runs. Rooms are decorated in grey tones and are of ample size, efficiently appointed, and generally impeccable, if unremarkable. **Pro:** handy for the airport, the convention center, and CaixaFòrum. **Cons:** far from Barcelona's main attractions and overlooking a hectic square usually clogged with overstressed drivers. ✉*Pl. Espanya 6–8, Eixample, 08014* ☎*93/426–2600* 🌐*www.hoteles-catalonia.es* *338 rooms, 9 suites* *In-hotel: restaurant, bar, pool, parking (fee)* *AE, DC, MC, V* *EP* Ⓜ*Espanya.*

$$$–$$$$ Fodor's Choice ★ **Condes de Barcelona.** Reserve well in advance—this is one of Barcelona's most popular hotels, and early reservations score bargain rates. Its pentagonal lobby has a marble floor and the original columns and courtyard from the 1891 building. The newest rooms have hot tubs and terraces overlooking interior gardens. An affiliated fitness club around the corner offers golf, squash, and swimming. Chef Martín Berasategui's restaurant, Lasarte, is one of Barcelona's most sought after dining spots. **Pros:** elegant Moderniste building with chic contemporary furnishings, prime spot in the middle of the Eixample. **Cons:** too large for much of a personal touch, staff somewhat overextended, restaurant Lasarte difficult to book. ✉*Passeig de Gràcia 75, Eixample, 08008* ☎*93/467–4780* 🌐*www.condesdebarcelona.com* *181 rooms, 2 suites* *In-room: safe, Wi-Fi. In-hotel: restaurant, bar, pools, gym, parking (fee)* *AE, DC, MC, V* *EP* Ⓜ*Passeig de Gràcia.*

$$$–$$$$ **Cristal Palace.** Just off Rambla Catalunya and near the gardens of Barcelona's University, this hotel is in the middle of the art-gallery district and within walking distance of the Rambla, the Ciutat Vella, and the Moderniste architecture of the Eixample. Guest rooms are modern and decorated in wood, marble, and bright colors. **Pros:** well positioned for exploring both the Eixample and the Gothic Quarter on foot, handy for making the university patios your private garden. **Con:** street side over Carrer Diputació can be noisy. ✉*Diputació 257, Eixample, 08007* ☎*93/487–8778* 🌐*www.hotelcristalpalace.com* *147 rooms, 1 suite* *In-hotel: restaurant, bar, public Internet, parking (fee)* *AE, DC, MC, V* *EP* Ⓜ*Passeig de Gràcia.*

$$$–$$$$ **Gran Hotel Catalonia.** A modern glass, stone, and steel structure just two blocks from Passeig de Gràcia, this hotel has rooms that are soundproofed to combat the roaring, traffic-flooded Balmes, in additional to being cheery, ultramodern, and bright; and the direct garage entrance will instantaneously solve your what-to-do-with-this-rental-car problem. Staff is extremely helpful with suggestions and arrangements. **Pro:** good for exploring the Eixample and the old part of the city. **Con:** Balmes is the city's main up-and-down artery and traffic is intense day and night. ✉*Balmes 142, Eixample, 08008* ☎*93/415–9090* 🌐*www.hoteles-catalonia.es* *75 rooms, 10 suites* *In-room: safe, dial-up. In-hotel: restaurant, room service, bar, laundry service, public Internet, parking (fee)* *AE, DC, MC, V* *EP* Ⓜ*Provença.*

$$$–$$$$   ☷ **Gran Hotel Havana.** Both a business and pleasure operation, the Havana may not remind you at all of the Greater Antilles, but the efficient service, the lofty patio with its rooftop skylight, and the bustling, busy feel of the place will help to boost your biorhythms to those of energetic Barcelona. This hotel is about equidistant from everything in the city, and its soundproofed rooms provide the refuge you need from the roaring Gran Via. **Pros:** lively lobby filled with savvy clients from all over the world, well positioned, friendly staff. **Con:** on a major crosstown artery where traffic is usually frantic all day. ⊠ *Gran Via 647, Eixample, 08010* ☎ *93/412–1115* ⊕ *www.hoteles-silken.com* ⬚ *141 rooms, 4 suites* ⌂ *In-hotel: restaurant, bar, gym, parking (fee)* ☰ *AE, DC, V* ⑩ *EP* Ⓜ *Passeig de Gràcia.*

$$$–$$$$   ☷ **Hotel Cram.** A laundry list of famous interior decorators had a hand in assembling this Eixample design hotel. Just a block behind the leafy, orange tree–filled patio of the University of Barcelona's philology and letters school, a short walk from the central Eixample and the Rambla, home of Carles Gaig's famous restaurant (Can Gaig), the Cram is good place to keep in mind for impeccable accommodations in midtown Barcelona. **Pros:** dazzlingly designed, well positioned for the Eixample and Rambla, smart and friendly staff. **Cons:** Aribau is a major uptown artery and traffic careens through at all hours, rooms are not spacious. ⊠ *Carrer Aribau 54, Eixample, 08008* ☎ *93/216–7700* ⊕ *www.hotelcram.com* ⬚ *67 rooms* ⌂ *In-room: Wi-Fi, refrigerator. In-hotel: restaurant, bar, public Internet, public Wi-Fi* ☰ *AE, DC, MC, V* ⑩ *EP* Ⓜ *Universitat.*

$$$–$$$$   ☷ **Hotel Granados 83.** Constructed with an exposed brick, steel, and
Fodor'sChoice  glass factory motif with Buddhist and Hindu art giving the hotel a Zen
   ★  tranquillity, this relative newcomer to the local hotel panorama has established itself as one of Barcelona's best design hotels. A few steps below the Diagonal and well situated for exploring the Eixample and the rest of the city, the hotel, named for Barcelona's famous composer and pianist Enric Granados, is an interesting compendium of materials and taste. The first-rate Mediterranean restaurant and the rooftop pool and solarium provide the cherry on top of this sundae. **Pros:** quiet semipedestrianized street; elegant building with chic design in wood, marble, and glass; polished service. **Con:** room prices here vary wildly according to availability and season. ⊠ *Carrer Enric Granados 83, Eixample, 08008* ☎ *93/492–9670* ⊕ *www.derbyhotels.es* ⬚ *70 rooms, 7 suites* ⌂ *In-room: safe, Wi-Fi, refrigerator. In-hotel: restaurant, bar, pools, spa, gym, parking (fee)* ☰ *AE, DC, MC, V* ⑩ *EP* Ⓜ *Provença.*

$$$–$$$$   ☷ **Meliá Barcelona.** The lobby here has a waterfall with a hydraulic rush that dominates the reception and the piano bar (aptly christened Drinking in the Rain). Dark-wood shelves and dressers line amply sized rooms equipped with top-of-the-line technology from flat-screen TV to high-speed Internet and Wi-Fi. Although the hotel is hardly convenient to the sights you come to Barcelona to see, its famous brunches are gigantic feasts, an unecessary extra with all the city's dining options, but for serious breakfast lovers, this may be Barcelona's best. **Pros:** relaxed and restful lobby, with ample spaces and abundant; friendly and helpful staff. **Cons:** far from most of Barcelona's main attractions,

4

on a roaring avenue generally clogged with traffic. ⊠*Av. de Sarrià 50, Eixample, 08029* ☎*93/410–6060* ⊕*www.solmelia.es* ⇨*299 rooms, 15 suites* ⅄*In-room: dial-up. In-hotel: restaurant, room service, bar, gym* ⊟*AE, DC, MC, V* ⏀*EP* Ⓜ*Hospital Clinic, Muntaner.*

**$$$** ⬚**Gran Derby.** Contemporary and sleek, this Eixample hotel is ideal for families, since it's composed entirely of suites and duplexes with sitting rooms. Rooms are decorated in crisp tones and lined with lavish leather or leather-like fabrics and zebra patterns, while baths are lined with coffee-colored tiles. Only the location is less than ideal; for sightseeing purposes, it's a bit out of the way, but a 20-minute march down the Diagonal puts you right on Passeig de Gràcia. **Pros:** the rooms and suites are spacious and well equipped, on a quiet side street off Avinguda Sarrià, friendly service. **Con:** far from the city's main attractions. ⊠*Loreto 28, Eixample, 08029* ☎*93/322–2062* ⊕*www.derbyhotels. es* ⇨*29 rooms, 12 suites* ⅄*In-hotel: restaurant, bar, pool, parking (fee)* ⊟*AE, DC, MC, V* ⏀*EP* Ⓜ*Muntaner, Hospital Clinic.*

**$$–$$$** ⬚**AC Diplomatic.** On the corner of Consell de Cent and just a block from Barcelona's busiest explosion of Moderniste architecture, the Manzana de la Discòrdia on Passeig de Gràcia, this hotel is also midway between the Eixample's two best mid-block passageways, Mendez Vigo and Passatge Permanyer. Decorated in pastel tones and sweeping economical lines, the Diplomatic offers good value and comfort for a central Eixample address. Rooms are bright, deocrated with contemporary furnishings and heavy drapes. Some have views over Carrer Pai Claris. **Pros:** bright contemporary lobby, friendly staff, high-tech equipment, well soundproofed. **Con:** somewhat antiseptic airport-waiting-room design. ⊠*Pau Claris 122, Eixample, 08009* ☎*93/272–3810* ⊕*www. ac-hotels.com* ⇨*211 rooms* ⅄*In-room: Wi-Fi. In-hotel: restaurant, bar, pool, gym, parking (fee)* ⊟*AE, DC, MC, V* ⏀*EP* Ⓜ*Diagonal.*

**$$–$$$** ⬚**Calderón.** On the chic and leafy Rambla de Catalunya, this modern high-rise has facilities normally found in hotels farther out of town. Public rooms are huge, with cool, white-marble floors, and the bedrooms follow suit. Aim high: the views from sea to mountains and over the city on top floors are stunning. **Pros:** upbeat, bright, contemporary design, ample public spaces, friendly service. **Con:** the antiseptic, glass-and-steel tower can seem impersonal and generic. ⊠*Rambla de Catalunya 26, Eixample, 08007* ☎*93/301–0000* ⊕*www.nh-hoteles.es* ⇨*224 rooms, 29 suites* ⅄*In-hotel: restaurant, bar, pools, gym, parking (fee)* ⊟*AE, DC, MC, V* ⏀*EP* Ⓜ*Passeig de Gràcia.*

**$$–$$$** ⬚**Hotel Axel.** This hotel catering primarily (but by no means exclusively) to gays has spacious and spotless rooms with every possible comfort, a mid-Eixample location in what has come to be known as the "Gayxample." Rooms are soundproof and luminous. Free bottled water is available in every corridor. The hotel restaurant is excellent, and the rooftop Skybar has wonderful views over the city. **Pros:** exciting minimalist contemporary design, graceful public spaces and lighting, friendly service. **Con:** erotic in-room art could be outside some guests' comfort zone. ⊠*Aribau 33, Eixample, 08011* ☎*93/323–9393* ⊕*www.hotelaxel.com* ⇨*66 rooms* ⅄*In-room: Wi-Fi. In-hotel: restaurant, bar, gym, spa, pool, public Internet, public*

Wi-Fi, parking (fee), no-smoking rooms, refrigerator ⊟AE, DC, MC, V ⵔOⵔEP Ⓜ Universitat.

$$-$$$ ⬚ **Hotel Jazz.** Bright wood and plenty of glass give this mid-city new-comer a contemporary, hip feel—and the young party animals from around the world walking through the lobby do nothing to dispel the notion that something very clued-in must be going on here. Rooms are pristine, if a little sterile, with state-of-the-art bathrooms and light, sleek furnishings. A step from the Rambla at the lower edge of the Eixample, the location is dead center in the heart of Barcelona. **Pros:** exciting and sleek lobby, design hipsters clientele, smart and friendly staff. **Con:** tucked into the point of a triangle too close to the raging Carrer Pelai, inner-city brouhaha only a few feet away. ⊠ *Pelai 3, Eixample, 08001* ☎ *93/552–9696* ⊕ *www.nnhotels.es* ⤶ *29 rooms* ⬙ *In-room: safe. In-hotel: restaurant, bar, pool* ⊟AE, DC, MC, V ⵔOⵔEP Ⓜ *Catalunya.*

$$-$$$ ⬚ **Hotel Pulitzer.** Built squarely over the metro's central hub and walking distance from everything in town, this elegant new hotel could not be better located to take advantage of Barcelona's many attractions. With ultramodern, high-tech equipment of every stripe and spot—from DSL Internet and Wi-Fi hookups to hot tubs—the Pulitzer combines smart service with chic decor at moderate prices. **Pros:** surprisingly quiet and collected sanctuary considering the central location, well-equipped bar and public Internet rooms, breakfast room bright and cheery. **Con:** too large and busy for intimacy or much personal attention from staff. ⊠ *Vergara 8, Eixample, 08002* ☎ *93/481–6767* ⊕ *www.hotelpulitzer. es* ⤶ *91 rooms* ⬙ *In-room: safe, Ethernet. In-hotel: restaurant, bar, public Internet, public Wi-Fi* ⊟AE, DC, MC, V ⵔOⵔEP Ⓜ *Catalunya.*

$$-$$$ ⬚ **Prestige Paseo de Gràcia.** A triumph of design built around a (mostly original) 1930s staircase, this hotel offers purity of line and minimal-ist sleekness as the reigning aesthetic principles, especially inside the rooms. The roof terrace is a tour de force, the different sections divided by contrasting colors and textures. **Pros:** ideally positioned in the middle of the Eixample, superbly balanced minimalist design, elegant service. **Cons:** opens onto Barcelona's main shopping street, wide, bustling, and loud. ⊠ *Passeig de Gràcia 62, Eixample, 08008* ☎ *93/272–4180* ⊕ *www.prestigehotels.com* ⤶ *45 rooms* ⬙ *In-room: Ethernet, Wi-Fi. In-hotel: 2 restaurants, bar, pool, gym, public Internet, public Wi-Fi, parking (fee)* ⊟AE, DC, MC, V ⵔOⵔEP Ⓜ *Passeig de Gràcia.*

$$-$$$ ⬚ **Regente.** Moderniste style and copious stained glass lend glamour and appeal to this smallish hotel. The cozy hotel bar has colorful stained-glass windows, while guest rooms are elegantly restrained. A verdant roof terrace (with a pool) and a prime position on the Rambla de Catalunya seal the positive verdict. **Pros:** intimate hotel with traditional furnishings, leafy Rambla Catalunya is a quiet but lively promenade. **Con:** small public rooms. ⊠ *Rambla de Catalunya 76, Eixample, 08008* ☎ *93/487–5989* ⊕ *www.hcchotels.com* ⤶ *79 rooms* ⬙ *In-room: safe. In-hotel: restaurant, bar, pool* ⊟AE, DC, MC, V ⵔOⵔEP Ⓜ *Passeig de Gràcia.*

$$ ⬚ **Granvia.** A 19th-century town house and Moderniste enclave with a hall-of-mirrors breakfast room and an ornate staircase, the Granvia

allows you to experience Barcelona's Art Nouveau even while you're sleeping. (To stay in character, go around the block to Gaudí's Casa Calvet, at No. 48 Carrer de Casp, for lunch or dinner.) Guest rooms have plain alcoved walls, bottle-green carpets, and Regency-style furniture; those overlooking Gran Via itself have better views but are quite noisy. **Pro:** waking up surrounded by Barcelona's famous Modern-iste design. **Cons:** somewhat antiquated, service a little tourist-weary. ⊠ *Gran Via 642, Eixample, 08007* ☎ *93/318–1900* ⊕ *www.nnhotels. es* ⊠ *53 rooms* ⌂ *In-hotel: Wi-Fi, parking (fee)* ☱ *AE, DC, MC, V* ⍾ *EP* Ⓜ *Passeig de Gràcia.*

$$ **Hotel Actual.** This good-value hotel between Passeig de Gràcia and Pau Claris offers contemporary technology, minimalist design, and a central Eixample location. Small rooms have plenty of light and are appointed with crisp furnishings. The owners are the Gimeno sisters of the nearby Gimeno design store, so it's no wonder the place is sleek and hip. Some rooms have views of Gaudí's La Pedrera rippling around the corner of Passeig de Gràcia. **Pros:** a contemporary design triumph with smart public spaces, helpful and friendly service. **Cons:** rooms are small, and those on the street side can be noisy. ⊠ *Rosselló 238, Eixample, 08008* ☎ *93/552–0550* ⊕ *www.hotelactual.com* ⊠ *29 rooms* ⌂ *In-room: Wi-Fi, safe* ☱ *AE, DC, MC, V* ⍾ *EP* Ⓜ *Diagonal.*

$$ **Hotel Constanza.** This contemporary boutique hotel offers top value along with cool white surfaces punctuated with the occasional slash of fire-engine-red sofas and chairs. Burgundy hallways and rooms furnished in woods and leathers, along with well-equipped and designed bathrooms, complete the sense of postmodern chic. **Pros:** well positioned for walking the Eixample or the Gothic Quarter, contemporary design worthy of Barcelona's design legacy, friendly service. **Con:** rooms on the Carrer Bruc side can be noisy. ⊠ *Bruc 33, Eixample, 08008* ☎ *93/270–1910* ⊕ *www.hotelconstanza.com* ⊠ *29 rooms* ⌂ *In-room: safe* ☱ *AE, DC, MC, V* ⍾ *EP* Ⓜ *Urquinaona.*

$$ **Onix.** This hotel is next to the Montjuïc convention center and other attractions such as the Miró Foundation and the Romanesque collection; Sants train terminal is within a 15-minute walk; it overlooks Barcelona's onetime-bullring-now-concert-venue Les Arenes as well as the Parc Joan Miró. Three buildings away is the Casa de la Papallona (House of the Butterfly), one of Barcelona's most spectacular Art Nouveau facades. Add to this the hotel's multilingual staff and fresh rooms, and the result is an impressive small though inexpensive hotel.

> **BARCELONA'S TOP DESIGN**
>
> Since Antoni Gaudí changed all the rules, Barcelona architects have freely followed their instincts. Barcelona decorators and architects relentlessly produce novelties such as the Hotel Omm, the Hotel Claris, or the Princess. Cristina Gabás redesigned an 18th-century palace at the Hotel Neri; La'zaro Rosa's Hotel Banys Orientals placed a contemporary interior in an ancient building. Hotel Granados 83 has joined this group of design stars, while the new Chic & Basic Hotels concocted by Xavier Claramunt may be the most surprising of all.

**Pros:** near some of Barcelona's best art venues on Montjuïc, bright and contemporary design, cheerful service. **Cons:** far from the city's main attractions in the Gothic Quarter and the central Eixample, beds and furnishings modern but flimsy. ⊠*Llançà 30, Eixample, 08015* ☎*93/426–0087* 📞*80 rooms* 🛏*In-hotel: bar, pool, parking (fee)* ⊟*AE, DC, MC, V* ⦿*EP* Ⓜ*Espanya.*

★ $–$$ 🏨**Continental Palacete.** This former in-town mansion, or *palacete*, provides a splendid drawing room, a location nearly dead center for Barcelona's main attractions, views over the leafy tree-lined tunnel of Rambla Catalunya, and a 24-hour free buffet. Ask specifically for one of the exterior rooms; the interior rooms on the elevator shaft can be noisy. **Pros:** elegant town house with abundant ornamentation, around-the-clock food and drink at the open buffet, attentive owners and staff. **Con:** rooms on the elevator shaft can be noisy. ⊠*Rambla de Catalunya 30, Eixample, 08007* ☎*93/445–7657* ⊕*www.hotelcontinental.com* 📞*17 rooms, 2 suites* 🛏*In hotel: open 24-hour buffet, Wi-Fi, parking (fee)* ⊟*AE, DC, MC, V* ⦿*BP* Ⓜ*Passeig de Gràcia.*

$ 🏨**Colors.** This friendly little hotel in Horta, formerly an outlying village like Gràcia and Sarrià, is an intimate residence with simple but well-cared-for rooms. It's a good budget choice, named for its Crayola-color range of decors on different floors of the hotel. **Pros:** small enough for intimacy and personalized, friendly service; bright and modern design. **Cons:** a long way (20 minutes by subway) from the Gothic Quarter and the Eixample, spaces small and economy-minded. ⊠*Campoamor 79, Eixample, 08031* ☎*93/274–9920* ⊕*www.hotelcolors.com* 📞*25 rooms* 🛏*In-room: safe* ⊟*AE, DC, MC, V* ⦿*EP* Ⓜ*Valldaura.*

## GRÀCIA

$$$$ 🏨**Casa Fuster.** Casa Fuster is one of two chances (the other is the España hotel) to stay in an Art Nouveau building designed by Lluís Domènech i Montaner, architect of the retina-rattling Palau de la Música Catalana. His last project, built in 1911, this elegant hotel at the bottom of the village of Gràcia shows a tendency toward the more classical Noucentisme that followed the decorative delirium of the Moderniste movement. The rooms and public spaces reinforce the Moderniste theme with Gaudí-designed chairs, *trencadís* (broken tile) floors and door handles, and Art Nouveau–inspired lamps and fixtures. The hotel restaurant serves fine Mediterranean cuisine, while the sumptuously decorated Café Vienés was a historic meeting place for Barcelona's movers and shakers of the early 20th century. **Pros:** well placed for exploring Gràcia as well as the Eixample, equidistant from the port and upper Barcelona's Tibidabo. **Con:** the design can feel a little heavy and mournful. ⊠*Passeig de Gràcia 132, Gràcia, 08008* ☎*93/255–3000* ⊕*www.hotelescenter.es* 📞*78 rooms, 18 suites* 🛏*In-hotel: restaurant, room service, public Wi-Fi, bar, pool, gym, laundry service, parking (fee)* ⊟*AE, DC, MC, V* ⦿*EP* Ⓜ*Diagonal.*

$$ 🏨**Hotel Confort.** This hotel offers rooms equipped with new and functional equipment, streamlined contemporary furnishings at the edge of Gràcia just a few minutes' walk from the Eixample. The service

FodorsChoice

★

4

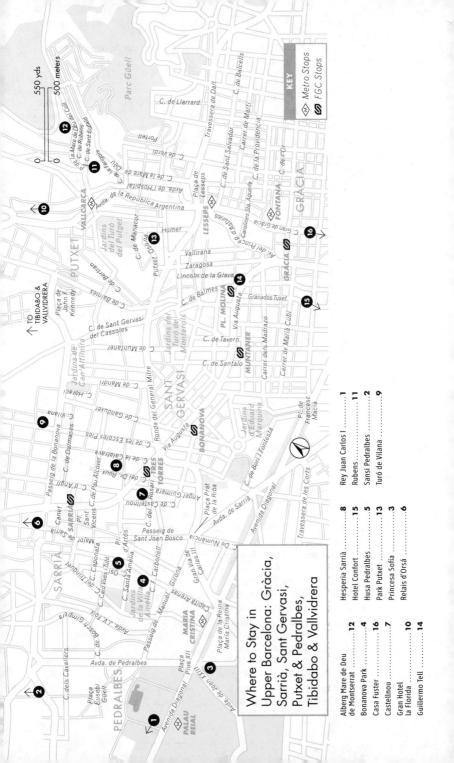

# Where to Stay in
# Upper Barcelona: Gràcia,
# Sarrià, Sant Gervasi,
# Putxet & Pedralbes,
# Tibidabo & Vallvidrera

Alberg Mare de Deu
de Montserrat ............ **12**
Bonanova Park ............ **4**
Casa Fuster ............ **16**
Castellnou ............ **7**
Gran Hotel
la Florida ............ **10**
Guillermo Tell ............ **14**

Hesperia Sarrià ............ **8**
Hotel Confort ............ **15**
Husa Pedralbes ............ **5**
Park Putxet ............ **13**
Princesa Sofía ............ **3**
Relais d'Orsá ............ **6**

Rey Juan Carlos I ............ **1**
Rubens ............ **11**
Sansi Pedralbes ............ **2**
Turó de Vilana ............ **9**

## KEY
Metro Stops
FGC Stops

550 yds
500 meters

is cheerful and efficient, and the accommodations, while modest in size, are impeccably maintained. **Pros:** small and intimate, cheerful service, modern design. **Cons:** not in a beautiful part of the city, close to the high-speed Carrer Balmes, far from the city's top attractions. ✉*Travessera de Gràcia 72, Gràcia, 08006* ☎*93/238–6828* ⊕*www. hotel-confort.com* ⟿*36 rooms* ♿*In-hotel: Wi-Fi, parking (fee)* ⊟*AE, DC, MC, V* †⊙†*EP* Ⓜ*Gràcia.*

**$–$$**   🍽 **Guillermo Tell.** Stashed away between Via Augusta and the village of Gràcia, this is about as close to sleeping in Gaudí's first house, Casa Vicens, as you can get. Rooms are amply sized, if a little plain, while the bathrooms are lavishly outfitted in marble. **Pros:** a quiet street, not far from the village of Gràcia, small enough for friendly and personalized service. **Cons:** a short subway ride to Plaça Catalunya, building of scant architectural interest or value. ✉*Guillem Tell 49, Gràcia, 08006* ☎*93/415–4000* ⊕*www.hotel-guillermotell.com* ⟿*61 rooms* ♿*In-room: safe. In-hotel: bar, parking (fee)* ⊟*AE, DC, MC, V* †⊙†*EP* Ⓜ*Sant Gervasi, Gràcia.*

## SARRIÀ, SANT GERVASI, PUTXET & PEDRALBES

**$$$$**   🍽 **Princesa Sofía.** Twenty-five years ago, this was Barcelona's most modern luxury hotel. Today, however, because of its location—somewhat out of the way on Avinguda Diagonal near the Barcelona soccer stadium—this towering high-rise is not a top choice since there are equally grand options with convenient locations. However, when other options are booked, the comforts and commodities at the Princess Sofía are still unquestionably impeccable, with soothing guest rooms decorated in soft colors, a long list of facilities, and everything from shops to three different restaurants. **Pros:** luxurious, comfortable, and completely equipped for all your needs, near the Barcelona soccer stadium and only a 20-minute walk from Sarrià. **Con:** far from the Gothic Quarter and the Eixample. ✉*Pl. Pius XII 4, Diagonal, 08028* ☎*93/508–1000* ⊕*www. expogrupo.com* ⟿*475 rooms, 25 suites* ♿*In-hotel: 3 restaurants, bar, pools, gym, parking (fee)* ⊟*AE, DC, MC, V* †⊙†*EP* Ⓜ*Maria Cristina.*

**$$$$**   🍽 **Rey Juan Carlos I.** This skyscraper is an exciting commercial complex as well as a luxury hotel, with sleek, contemporary rooms. Glass elevators whip up and down the space ship–like atrium. Here you can buy jewelry, furs, art, fashions, flowers, caviar, and even limousines. The lush garden, which includes a pond with swans, has an Olympic-size swimming pool, and the green expanses of Barcelona's finest in-town country club, El Polo, spread like a verdant blanket. There are two restaurants: Chez Vous serves French cuisine, and Café Polo has a sumptuous buffet as well as an American bar. **Pros:** 10 minutes from the airport, supremely comfortable and complete, various restaurants and everything you might need without ever leaving the hotel, polished and attentive service. **Con:** well removed (at least 20 minutes by taxi) from all of Barcelona's main sites. ✉*Av. Diagonal 661–671, Diagonal, 08028* ☎*93/364–4040* ⊕*www.hrjuancarlos.com* ⟿*375 rooms, 37 suites* ♿*In-room: dial-up. In-hotel: 2 restaurants, bars, tennis court, pool, gym, spa, parking (fee)* ⊟*AE, DC, MC, V* †⊙†*EP* Ⓜ*Zona Universitària.*

$$–$$$ 🏨**Hesperia Sarrià.** Well connected to downtown Barcelona by the Sarrià train, this is a modern hotel set on a leafy street just a block up from Via Augusta. The rooms are medium to small in size but well designed. The service is crisp and friendly, and the general demeanor of the place is smart and efficient. **Pros:** on a quiet street in a quiet neighborhood, walking distance from Sarrià and its two or three excellent restaurants. **Cons:** 20 minutes by subway from the Gothic Quarter and the Eixample, small rooms and public spaces. ⊠*Vergós 20, Sarrià, 08017* ☎*93/204–5551* ⊕*www.hesperia-sarria.es* ⟿*134 rooms* ⅋*In-room: safe. In-hotel: restaurant, bar, parking (fee), no-smoking rooms* ▤*AE, DC, MC, V* ⎥◎⎢*EP* Ⓜ*Tres Torres.*

$$–$$$ 🏨**Sansi Pedralbes.** A contemporary polished-marble and black-glass box overlooking the gardens of the Monestir de Pedralbes, this hotel may seem out of place, but the views up into the Collserola hills and over Barcelona are splendid. Rooms are impeccable in equipment and design, and the air in this part of town can be a welcome relief from steamy port-side Barcelona. It's only a 15-minute climb to the Carretera de les Aigües (water road), Barcelona's best running track, across the side of the mountain behind the city. **Pros:** small and intimate, excellent and friendly service, ultramodern design. **Con:** the nearest subway, the Sarrià train, is a 20-minute hike away, plan on plenty of taxi time. ⊠*Av. Pearson 1–3, Pedralbes, 08034* ☎*93/206–3880* ⊕*www.sansihotels.com* ⟿*70 rooms* ⅋*In-room: Wi-Fi. In-hotel: restaurant, bar, pool, public Wi-Fi, parking (fee)* ▤*AE, DC, MC, V* ⎥◎⎢*EP* Ⓜ*Reina Elisenda.*

$$ 🏨**Castellnou.** A little gem of a hotel, Castellnou is just two steps from the train that can whisk you to the middle of town. It's also not far from the freeway to the Pyrenees and handy to upper Barcelona's attractions in Sarrià, Pedralbes, and Sant Gervasi. The restaurant is intimate, but there are also a dozen good places to dine within easy walking distance. The service is warm and friendly, and the rooms are contemporary with sleek new furnishings. **Pros:** a refuge from the city, small enough for personalized service, modern design. **Cons:** a long way from the Gothic Quarter and the Eixample, rooms and public spaces cramped. ⊠*Castellnou 61, Tres Torres, 08017* ☎*93/203–0550* ⊕*www.hoteles-catalonia.es* ⟿*49 rooms* ⅋*In-hotel: restaurant, room service* ▤*AE, DC, MC, V* ⎥◎⎢*EP* Ⓜ*Tres Torres.*

$$ 🏨**Turó de Vilana.** Surrounded by bougainvillea-festooned villas and
Fodor'sChoice  mansions above Barcelona's Passeig de la Bonanova, this shiny new
★  penny has a hot tub in every room, immaculate and gleaming halls, and public areas of stone, steel, and glass, run by a pleasant staff. Rooms are polished, bright, and will lighted. In summer, upper Barcelona is noticeably cooler, not to mention quieter at night. The Turó de Vilana is a 10-minute walk from the Sarrià train that connects you with the city center in a quarter of an hour. **Pros:** new furnishings and latest technology in rooms, bright and cheery service and design, verdant and refreshing surroundings. **Con:** in upper Sarrià and a long way (30 minutes in all) from the center of town. ⊠*Vilana 7, Sant Gervasi, 08017* ☎*93/434–0363* ⊕*www.turodevilana.com* ⟿*20 rooms* ⅋*In-hotel: restaurant, room service, public Wi-Fi* ▤*AE, DC, MC, V* ⎥◎⎢*EP* Ⓜ*Sarrià.*

**$–$$**  🏨**Bonanova Park.** In upper Barcelona near Sarrià, this somewhat bare-bones dormitory-like hotel provides a break from the downtown crush at a moderate cost. Several good restaurants are within walking distance in Sarrià, as are the metro stops of Sarrià and the green line's Maria Cristina, each five minutes walk away. The rooms are bright and breezy, and the predominantly residential neighborhood is quiet. For children, there is the Quinta Amelia park a block west of the hotel. **Pros:** a good budget choice, small enough for personalized service. **Cons:** a long way from the center of town, rooms are small and lackluster, amenities nonexistent. ⊠*Capità Arenas 51, Sarrià, 08034* ☎*93/204–0900* ⊕*www.husa.es* ⬧*60 rooms* ♿*In-hotel: bar* ▭*AE, DC, MC, V* ⎮◯⎮*EP* Ⓜ*Sarrià, Maria Cristina.*

**$–$$**  🏨**Husa Pedralbes.** The two best things about this simple hotel are its location on the edge of leafy Sarrià (a 20-minute walk from the Monestir de Pedralbes and 5 minutes from the Sarrià train stop) and its intimate, personal atmosphere. Rooms are modern and elegant, though somewhat cramped. **Pros:** intimate and friendly service, bright and modern design. **Cons:** a long way (20 minutes by subway) from the Gothic Quarter and the Eixample, rooms and public spaces small. ⊠*Fontcoberta 4, Sarrià, 08034* ☎*93/203–7112* ⊕*www.husa.es* ⬧*30 rooms* ♿*In-hotel: restaurant, parking (fee)* ▭*AE, DC, MC, V* ⎮◯⎮*EP* Ⓜ*Sarrià, Maria Cristina.*

**$–$$**  🏨**Park Putxet.** Next to some overgrown, junglelike parks and private enclaves, this hideaway in upper Barcelona has the advantage of being far enough from the Rambla to provide a sense of rest, relaxation, and refuge. Park Putxet offers above-average comforts and particularly elegant bathrooms at reasonable prices. Walking distance from Gràcia and just a few minutes by train or taxi from the center of town, this is a good choice if you like to stroll and would prefer to sleep away from the city's roar. **Pros:** next to a leafy park and not far from Parc Güell, well connected with the center of town by subway. **Cons:** well removed from the city's main attractions, rooms and public spaces neither large nor especially interestingly designed. ⊠*Putxet 68, Sant Gervasi, 08023* ☎*93/212–5158* ⊕*www.hoteles-catalonia.es* ⬧*141 rooms* ♿*In-hotel: restaurant, laundry service, parking (fee)* ▭*AE, DC, MC, V* ⎮◯⎮*EP* Ⓜ*El Putxet.*

**$**  🏨**Rubens.** A little out of the way above Plaça Lesseps, this hotel has easy access to Güell Park—a few minutes' walk away—and to downtown Barcelona by taxi or public transportation. Rooms are streamlined, with attractive wooden furniture. **Pros:** good value, better and cooler air above the hue and cry of the city, friendly service. **Cons:** far from the center of town, plainly decorated. ⊠*Passeig de la Mare de Déu del Coll 10, Sant Gervasi, 08023* ☎*93/219–1204* ⊕*www.hoteles-catalonia.es* ⬧*139 rooms* ♿*In-hotel: restaurant, laundry service, parking (fee)* ▭*AE, DC, MC, V* ⎮◯⎮*EP* Ⓜ*Vallcarca.*

**¢**  🏨**Alberg Mare de Deu de Montserrat.** This youth hostel accepts guests over 25 with youth hostel cards (€3.50 per night for first six nights, available at check-in desk). The lobby, a Moderniste exhibition featuring Moorish horseshoe arches and polychrome marquetry right out of the Arabian Nights, has been featured in Barcelona art books.

This is one of the city's great bargains—shared rooms and bathrooms notwithstanding—overlooking the city near Gaudí's Güell Park. Bus 28 from the Rambla and the green line's Vallcarca metro station get you home. Doors close at midnight but open every 30 minutes for late arrivals, i.e., everyone. **Pros:** excellent budget choice, takes all ages, friendly service, lavish design. **Cons:** accommodations vary from dormitory-like multiple-bed rooms to smaller singles, front door opens only at intervals after midnight, far from downtown Barcelona and popular landmarks. ⊠*Passeig de la Mare de Déu del Coll 41–51, Vallcarca, 08023* ☎*93/210–5151* ⊕*www.tujuca.com* ⤳*223 beds in rooms of 6, 8, and 12* ⟨In-room: no TV. In-hotel: restaurant, bar, parking (fee)* ☰*AE, DC, MC, V* ¶⧀*EP* Ⓜ*Vallcarca.*

## TIBIDABO & VALLVIDRERA

★ $$$$   📷 **Gran Hotel la Florida.** With nonpareil views over Barcelona, water sculptures everywhere but in your bed, a superb restaurant (L'Orangerie), and designer suites that are difficult to leave behind, it's easy to forgive the 20 minutes' (and euros) taxi drive from the port to reach this gem. The L-shape horizon pool is a delight, as are the spas and exercise facilities. Originally opened in 1925, this design hotel has roared back to the forefront of Barcelona's most stylish lodging. **Pros:** cool air and panoramic views, artistic design, horizon pool, friendly and attentive service. **Con:** a half-hour taxi ride from the center of town. ⊠*Crtra. Vallvidrera al Tibidabo 83–93, Tibidabo, 08035* ☎*93/259–3000* ⊕*www.hotellaflorida.com* ⤳*74 rooms, 22 suites* ⟨In-room: safe, Wi-Fi. In-hotel: restaurant, bar, public Internet, public Wi-Fi, pool, gym, spa, parking (fee)* ☰*AE, DC, MC, V* ¶⧀*EP* Ⓜ*Tibidabo.*

$$$$   📷 **Relais d'Orsà.** A neoclassical mansion built in 1900, this unique inn overlooking Barcelona has been lavishly decorated in French and Scandinavian provincial styles, along with antiques from Asia and Morocco. Restful trees and gardens surround the house, while a swimming pool under the pines has panoramic views out over Barcelona and the Mediterranean. Perched next to the sleepy hilltop village of Vallvidrera, this unusual refuge is a 10-minute drive up from Sarrià at the uphill edge of Barcelona (20–30 minutes from the port). The FCG train and the funicular can get you back to the hotel just as quickly until 1 ᴀᴍ on weekdays and all night on Friday and Saturday. **Pros:** superb views and a sense of intimacy in an unusual boutique hotel. **Cons:** well outside the city's upper edge overlooking Barcelona and a long taxi ride from the center of town. ⊠*Mont d'Orsá 35, Tibidabo, 08017* ☎*93/406–9411* ⊕*www.relaisdorsa.com* ⤳*6 rooms* ⟨In-hotel: bar, pool, parking (no fee)* ☰*AE, DC, MC, V* ¶⧀*EP* Ⓜ*Peu Funicular, Vallvidrera Superior.*

# Nightlife & the Arts

**WORD OF MOUTH**

"A flamenco concert at the Palau de la Música Catalana with a tapa before and a light but delicious dinner at Cal Pep afterwards did it for me: Barcelona rocks."

–Susan

By George
Semler

**BARCELONA'S NOCTURNAL ROLL CALL,** from art openings and concerts to tapas bars, music bars, and clubbing, offers a wild mix of options. From the early-evening browsing and tapa-grazing through the area around the Born to stand-up howling and drinking at the Universal or Mas i Mas pub, to the late live and recorded music at Bikini, Danzatoria, or Luz de Gas, Barcelona offers a thousand and one ways to make it through the night without resorting to slumber.

Daily events in the arts scene race headlong from 7 o'clock lectures and book presentations, *inauguraciones* and *vernissages* (art show openings), to 9 o'clock concerts, theater, and dance performances. And then, sometime after 1 or 2 in the morning, the *real* nightlife kicks in.

To find out what's on, check *"agenda"* listings in Barcelona's leading daily newspapers *El País, La Vanguardia,* or *El Periódico de Catalunya* or the weekly *Guía del Ocio,* available at newsstands all over town. *Activitats* is a monthly list of cultural events, published by the *ajuntament* and available from its information office in Palau de la Virreina (Rambla 99). *Metropolitan* magazine, published monthly in English, is given away free in English-language bookstores and hotel lobbies.

# NIGHTLIFE

Barcelona nights are long and as wild as you want, filling all of the hours of darkness and often rolling until dawn. Most of the best clubs don't even open until well after midnight, but cafés and music bars serve as recruiting venues for the night's mission. The classical progression begins with drinks (wine or beer), tapas and dinner, a jazz or flamenco concert around 11 PM, then a pub or a music bar or two, and then, if the body can keep up with the spirit, dancing. Strutting your stuff on the dance floor can be done in a variety of locales, from clubs to ballroom dance halls, and is apt to continue until the sun comes up. Late-night bars and early-morning cafés provide an all-important break to refresh and refuel before doing another round of moves.

## BARS

There aren't just bars in Barcelona, but a suite of subcatergories for drinks: *coctelerías* (cocktail bars), *whiskerias* (often singles bars with professional escorts), *xampanyerias* (champagne—actually *cava,* Catalan sparkling wine—bars), *cerveserias* (beer halls), and wine-tasting cellars. A *bar musical* is defined in Spain as any bar with music loud enough to drown out conversation. *Xampanyerias, wine bars, and cerveserias are often spots for a meal. See Chapter 3, Where to Eat, for details on those.*

New wine bars, cafés, music bars, and tiny live-music clubs are constantly scraping plaster from 500-year-old brick walls to expose medieval structural elements that offer striking backdrops for postmodern people and conversations. The most common closing time for 90% of Barcelona's nocturnal bars is 3 AM, though this may vary according to clientele flow.

The area around the Passeig del Born, in medieval times the jousting grounds for knights in shining armor, is alive with bars, cafés, and small clubs. The Raval, not too long ago a lowlife scene, is now merely dive-bar-chic, with hip saloons along Nou de la Rambla and Carrer del Carme. Along Carrer Marià Cubí and between Carrers Aribau and Calvet above the Travessera de Gràcia is a series of lively bars and terraces. Port Olímpic and Port Vell's Maremagnum area, generally avoidable, seem to attract the nocturnal dregs, though CDLC (Carpe Diem Lounge Club) rises above the fray.

> **TOP 5**
>
> ■ Concerts in the Palau de la Música Catalana followed by drinks at the Botafumeiro bar.
>
> ■ Red-hot salsa at Antilla BCN Latin Club or Salsabor.
>
> ■ Movies at the Verdi multi-cine and nomadic dinners in Gràcia.
>
> ■ Concerts and early-morning boogie at Bikini.
>
> ■ The sun rising out of the Mediterranean from bar Mirablau on Tibidabo.

## TAVERNS, PUBS, & BARS

**Bar Almirall.** The twisted wooden fronds framing the bar's mirror and Art Nouveau touches from curvy door handles to organic-shape table lamps to floral chair design make this one of the prettiest bars in Barcelona. Dating from 1860, this is the second-oldest bar in Barcelona after the Marsella, another Raval favorite. It's near the MACBA (Museu d'Art Contemporani de Barcelona). ⊠*Joaquín Costa 33, Raval* ☎*93/412–1535* Ⓜ*Universitat.*

**Bar Muy Buenas.** This Art Nouveau gem just behind the medieval hospital has curvaceous wooden framing and a balcony overlooking the bar that mark this historic saloon as one of the city's finest Moderniste bars. The codfish basins at the edge of the counter are the original soaking and cleaning sinks once used here when the place was a fish market. ⊠*Carme 63, Raval* ☎*93/442–5053* Ⓜ*Catalunya, Universitat.*

★ **Bar Pastis.** Near the bottom of the Rambla just above the Santa Mònica art center, this tiny hole-in-the-wall has live performances Sunday (French singers), Tuesday (tango), and Wednesday (singer-songwriters). When singers are not on stage, clients are treated to an encyclopedic tour of every Edith Piaf song ever recorded. There is no cover charge. ⊠*Santa Mònica 4, Rambla* ☎*93/318–7980* Ⓜ*Drassanes.*

**George & Dragon.** Named for Barcelona's ubiquitous symbols of good and evil, the city's virtual yin and yang, this is a rollicking English pub just off Passeig de Gràcia with live music on Saturday night (no cover charge) and a full offering of international rugby, soccer, and NFL games. The menu combines standard English pub fare with Spanish tapas specialties. ⊠*Diputació 269, Eixample* ☎*93/488–1765* Ⓜ*Passeig de Gràcia.*

★ **Glaciar.** This simple, old-fashioned bar in the southwest corner of Plaça Reial is *the* spot for young travelers, especially in summer. The crowd spills out into the square's smoke-free air, making a rolling block party under the palm trees and the stars beyond. ⊠*Pl. Reial 13, Rambla* ☎*93/302–1163* Ⓜ*Liceu.*

**La Sede.** A simple saloon in the Marià Cubí–Aribau area, this is a music bar with no extravagant design on display, just good cheer and good music at an endurable decibel level. Like nearby The End, La Sede serves as respite from the crush of the madding crowd over on Marià Cubí. ✉*Laforja 140, Eixample* ☎*93/319–2314* Ⓜ*Muntaner.*

**Les Gens que J'aime.** This time-warp salon seems to have reproduced a Bohemian fantasy from a late-19th-century novel. A simple living room neatly tucked under the sidewalk, this bar is saturated in the yellow glow of lighting and the deep reds and ochers of the sofas and armchairs, all suggesting a luxury smoking car on the *Orient Express:* perfect for an intimate *tête à tête.* ✉*Carrer València 286, Eixample* ☎*93/215–6879* Ⓜ*Passeig de Gràcia.*

**London Bar.** The trapeze (often in use) suspended above the bar adds even more flair to this Art Nouveau circus haunt in the Barrio Chino. Stop in at least for a look, as this is one of the Raval's old standards, which, despite the wholly unbreathable air, has entertained generations of Barcelona visitors and locals. ✉*Nou de la Rambla 34, Raval* ☎*93/302–3102* Ⓜ*Liceu.*

**L'Ovella Negra.** With heavy wooden tables, stone floors, and some cozy nooks and crannies to drink in, the Black Sheep is the city's top student tavern, especially for the barely legal. Aromas of brews gone by never completely abandon the air in this cavernous hangout, and the troglodytic behavior is usually a good match for the surroundings. ✉*Sitges 5, Raval* ☎*93/317–1087* Ⓜ*Catalunya.*

**Marsella.** French poet and playwright Jean Genet was known to have been a regular here while "researching" and writing *La Marge,* his novel set in Barcelona's steamily picturesque Raval. A cross between a speakeasy and a Euro-bohemian café and beer hall, the Marsella serves cold beer that goes down exceptionally well. ✉*Sant Pau 65, Raval* ☎*93/442–7263* Ⓜ*Liceu.*

**Mas i Mas.** Well-heeled patrons flock here, guaranteeing a certain social intimacy by mere proximity. This is one of the few music bars that has figured out how to play the music loud enough to give the clientele a buzz, yet still allow them to communicate, at least at a rudimentary level. Masters of mixology as well as acoustical engineers, the Mas brothers put together accomplished cocktails ranging from manhattans to Singapore Slings. ✉*Marià Cubí 199, Eixample* ☎*93/209–4502* Ⓜ*Muntaner.*

**Michael Collins Irish Pub.** This congenial Irish pub near Gaudí's unfinished masterpiece has a strong international following, though the majority are English-speakers. International sporting events with everything from steeplechase to yacht racing find their way onto one of the multiple screens. Live Irish music takes the stage Thursday–Sunday. A traditional Irish lunch is the star attraction on Sunday at 1 PM. ✉*Plaza Sagrada Família 4, Eixample* ☎*93/459–1964* Ⓜ*Sagrada Família.*

**Mirablau.** This bar is a popular hangout for evening drinks, but it's even more frequented as a romantic late-night and dawn vantage point for watching the city lights down below and, eventually, the sunrise gathering over the Mediterranean horizon to the east. Take Tibidabo train (U-7) from Pl. de Catalunya or buses 24 and 22 to Pl. Kennedy.

## CLOSE UP

# Care to Order a Beer?

The standard local beers made by the venerable Damm company are basically two: Estrella Dorada and Voll Damm. The darker Voll Damm bock beer is a potent, highly alcoholic brew. The lighter Estrella Dorada (translatable as "Golden Star"), normally ordered as simply "*una Estrella*," is a cleansing lager with some bite to it (as opposed to the watery San Miguel, another less-common option). "*Una mediana*" is a middle-size bottled beer, as opposed to "*un quinto*," which is a small bottle, a fifth of a liter, or "*una litrona*," a full liter. "*Una caña*" is a draft beer drawn from the *caña* (cane, or tap). The standard choice for most Barcelona beer drinkers is "una caña," but ask for "*una caña pequeña*" (a small draft) or you might get a stein

of the stuff, known as "*una jarra.*" Some places serve "*zurritos*" (literally, a little slap, a hit)—shallow glasses with a couple of inches of beer splashed in the bottom. Watch out for an insidious new invention: a caña or tap with a small sign on it saying "*limón*," meaning lemon beer, a disappointingly sweet premixed shandy. If you want a shandy, a mix of beer and lemon-flavored fizzy water, order a "*clara*" and mix it yourself. This brew is sometimes served in a glass *porrón*, a jar with a slender spout designed to be poured from overhead at full arm's length and passed around. This is best attempted while wearing clothes you don't mind soaking with a little Bacchian overflow.

At Av. Tibidabo, catch Tramvía Blau (Blue Trolley), which connects with funicular to summit. ⊠*Plaça del Doctor Andreu s/n, Tibidabo* ☎*93/418–5879* Ⓜ*Tibidabo.*

**Nick Havanna.** Open Thursday–Saturday only, this mid-Eixample uproar is a favorite with university students primed to boogie until dawn. With a consistently hot program of recorded music ranging from rock to pop to house, nonstop action is guaranteed here, as well as Barcelona's only looking-glass urinals. ⊠*Rosselló 208, Eixample* ☎*93/215–6591* Ⓜ*Provença.*

**Opiniao.** In the upper reaches of Barcelona's Sant Gervasi district, this taste of Brazil above Via Augusta offers a low-key, quiet, and intimate sanctuary filled with booths and tables tucked into corners with occasional live performances for graduates and postgraduates still actively on the hunt. ⊠*Ciutat de Balaguer 67, Bonanova* ☎*93/418–3399* Ⓜ*Tibidabo.*

**Salero.** This café-restaurant-bar always packs in rows and ranks of gorgeous young models of both sexes and the accompanying pilot fish that bask in their reflected light. The menu is light and inventive Mediterranean fare, and the charged energy is generally that of a feeding frenzy. ⊠*Carrer del Rec 60, Eixample* ☎*93/318–4399* Ⓜ*Jaume I.*

**Sherlock Holmes.** Above Via Augusta sits a corner of Barcelona that will forever be England, with live musical performances (no cover charge) and darkly intimate nooks. As with most English and Irish pubs in Barcelona, sports broadcasts from all over the world are a staple. ⊠*Copernic 42–44, Eixample* ☎*93/414–2184* Ⓜ*Diagonal.*

**The End.** This bar is one of the most popular in the area, with a cool, breezy terrace for summer evenings. After a tour through the more populous and jam-packed saloons along Marià Cubí, The End is a relatively quiet refuge for conversations and carousing alike. ⊠ *Santaló 34, Eixample* ☎ *93/200–3942* Ⓜ *Muntaner.*

**Universal.** From early evening to late night, the Universal has been the hottest music bar in town for 30 years running. Dim lighting and music played at a level where you can still converse make this a perfect meet-up area for late nocturnal activities ahead. ⊠ *Marià Cubí 182–184, Eixample* ☎ *93/200–7470* Ⓜ *Muntaner.*

**Velodrom.** High ceilings, billiards, tapas, and a solid community of prowling and procrastinating students contribute to the laid-back scene at this popular spot just below the Diagonal. ⊠ *Muntaner 211–213, Eixample* ☎ *93/230–6022* Ⓜ *Diagonal.*

## COCTELERÍAS (COCKTAIL BARS)

**Boadas.** A small, rather formal saloon near the top of the Rambla, Boadas is emblematic of the Barcelona *coctelería* concept, which usually entails an air of decorum, expensive mixed drinks, wood and leather surroundings, and an impenetrable curtain of cigar smoke. ⊠ *Tallers 1, Rambla* ☎ *93/318–9592* Ⓜ *Catalunya.*

**Dry Martini Bar.** The namesake drink of this stately and discreet establishment is the best bet here, if only to partake of the ritual. This is a popular hangout for mature romantics: husbands and wives (though not necessarily each other's) in an environment of genteel wickedness. ⊠ *Aribau 162, Eixample* ☎ *93/217–5072* Ⓜ *Provença.*

**El Born.** This former codfish emporium is now an intimate haven for drinks, raclettes, and fondues. The marble cod basins in the entry and the spiral staircase to the second floor are the quirkiest details, but everything seems devised and designed to charm the eye. ⊠ *Passeig del Born 26, La Ribera* ☎ *93/319–5333* Ⓜ *Jaume I.*

**El Copetín.** Right on Barcelona's best-known cocktail avenue, this bar catering to young professionals in the thirty- to fifty-year-old range has good cocktails and Irish coffee. It's dimly lighted and romantic, with South Seas motifs. ⊠ *Passeig del Born 19, La Ribera* ☎ *93/319–4496* Ⓜ *Jaume I.*

**Harry's.** This is Barcelona's version of the Parisian "sank roo-doe-noo" (5, rue Daunou) favorite that intoxicated generations of American literati, faux and otherwise, in Paris. While the formal art of mixology remains somewhat alien to the Barcelona scene, those in need of a serious drink will find it here at Harry's. ⊠ *Aribau 143, Eixample* ☎ *93/430–3423* Ⓜ *Provença.*

**Miramelindo.** Famed for caipirinhas and a Brazil–meets–South Pacific stylistic confusion designed to liberate the Catalan yuppie from his mercantile moorings, this venerable bar has survived for three decades and appears to be moving forward without missing a bossa nova beat. The musical buzz ranges from Latin jazz to samba. ⊠ *Passeig del Born 15, La Ribera* ☎ *93/310–3727* Ⓜ *Jaume I.*

## CASINOS

**Casino Castell de Peralada.** An hour north of Barcelona near Figueres in Catalunya's Empordá region, this opulent den opens daily 1 PM–5 AM. Equipped with four restaurants, the Peralada Casino offers fine dining and a full range of gambling options. ⊠ *Del Castell 2/n* ☎ *972/538125* ⊕ *www.casino-peralada.com.*

**Casino Lloret.** On the coast 67 km (42 mi) north of Barcelona, the Lloret casino provides full gaming opportunities and fine dining as well. Open daily 5 PM–4 AM, this is an ideal opportunity to combine beach and bankruptcy. ⊠ *Dels Esports 1, Lloret de Mar* ☎ *972/366116* ⊕ *www. casino-lloret.com.*

**Gran Casino de Barcelona.** Open daily 1 PM–5 AM, this casino under the Hotel Arts has everything from slot machines to roulette, a dance club, floor shows, ballroom dancing, tango, line dancing, and a restaurant. ⊠ *Calle de la Marina, Port Olímpic* ☎ *93/225–7878* Ⓜ *Ciutadella–Vil. la Olímpica.*

## CLUBS & DJ VENUES

Some clubs have a discretionary cover charge that ranges €3–€15, depending on the live music offering or merely on the law of supply and demand. Bouncers like to inflict this cover charge on unsuspecting foreigners, so dress up and be prepared to talk your way in. Any story can work: for example, you own a chain of nightclubs and are on a world research tour. The party won't really get started until 1:30 or 2 AM. For a guide to Barcelona's after-dark activities check out ⊕ *www. bcn-nightlife.com*

**Agua de Luna.** Open Wednesday–Sunday, this seriously hip club with top DJs and everything from salsa to hip-hop entertains until dawn on the western side of the Eixample. The Sunday session begins at 8 PM, whereas Friday and Saturday dancing doesn't start until 11 PM or so, though you'll probably have the place to yourself if you show up before 1 AM. ⊠ *Viladomat 211, Eixample* ☎ *93/410–0440* ⊕ *www. aguadeluna.com* Ⓜ *Urgell.*

**Antilla BCN Latin Club.** This exuberantly Caribbean spot sizzles with salsa, son cubano, and merengue from opening time at 11 PM until dawn. Dance instructors "teach you the secrets of the hips" during the first opening hours. The self-proclaimed "Caribbean cultural center" cranks out every variation of salsa ever invented as well as its own magazine, *Antilla News,* to keep you abreast of the latest happenings in the world of Latin moves and grooves in the Mediterranean. ⊠ *C. Aragó 141, Eixample* ☎ *93/451–2151* ⊕ *www.antillasalsa.com* Ⓜ *Urgell.*

**Barcelona City Hall.** Wednesday-night Pigs & Diamonds parties starring electro house music and red-hot guest DJs from neighboring clubs guarantee dancing till you drop at this raging mid-city favorite. Deep, tech, groove, and microfunk are just some of the musical specialties you will experience in this party powder keg. ⊠ *Rambla Catalunya 2–4, Eixample* ☎ *93/238–0722* ⊕ *www.cityhall-bcn.com* Ⓜ *Catalunya.*

5

**Bikini.** This haven for postgraduates offers three ecosystems: Espai BKN with music from the '80s and '90s along with funk, dance-pop, and house; Espai Arutanga with salsa and Latin fusion; and Dry Bikini, which serves cocktails, sandwiches, and, of course, *bikinis* (Spanish for grilled-cheese sandwiches). Bikini opens at midnight and charges a cover of €11 with your *second* drink included. ⊠ *Deu i Mata 105, at Entença, Eixample* ☎ *93/322–0005* ⊕ *www.bikinibcn.com* Ⓜ *Les Corts.*

**Búcaro.** This straight-up disco rocks till dawn, especially on weekends when it remains open until 5 AM. The floor-to-ceiling mirrors seem to elongate the human form marvelously, encouraging a narcissistic rush that can lead to erotic mayhem. Carefully evaluate your options here, as the very young can pass for grown-ups in the cacophony of music and inventive lighting. The DJs embrace everything: house, ska, electropop, hip-hop, and funk. ⊠ *Aribau 195, Eixample* ☎ *93/209–6562* ⊕ *www.grupocostaeste.com* Ⓜ *Gràcia.*

**Buda Barcelona.** The hottest nightspot in the Eixample, Buda Barcelona is a magnet for Spanish and international celebrities. Local guests have included flamenco dancer Joaquín Cortés and actress Penelope Cruz. Even Hollywood casting legend Gretchen (Grudles) Rennell has been spotted on the prowl for new talent. Unabashedly claiming to be Barcelona's beautiful-people hangout, Buda Barcelona packs in glamorous personnel who, when not basking in the gold wallpaper, are prone to dancing on the bar. ⊠ *Pau Claris 92, Eixample* ☎ *93/318–4252* ⊕ *www.budarestaurante.com* Ⓜ *Catalunya.*

**CDLC.** The Carpe Diem Lounge Club—in case you are marooned out near the Olympic Port, staying at the Hotel Arts, or looking for post-cinema action—is the best and glitziest of the clubs out this way, complete with conveniently compartmentalized *sofa-camas* (sofa beds of a sort) for horizontal time. ⊠ *Passeig Maritim 32, Port Olímpic* ☎ *93/224–0470* ⊕ *www.cdlcbarcelona.com* Ⓜ *Ciutadella–Vil.la Olímpica.*

**Costa Breve.** Open Thursday–Saturday midnight–dawn, this hip and happening disco just above the Diagonal has DJs that spin pop, funk, and dance music until 6 AM. Though popular with the young college crowd, postgraduates still manage to find some dance-floor turf. ⊠ *Aribau 230, Eixample* ☎ *93/414–2778* ⊕ *www.grupocostabreve.com* Ⓜ *Provença.*

**Danzatoria.** Stunning models and the men that orbit them fill this club's various spaces (restaurant, disco, dance floor, chill-out space, garden) in a lavishly restored town house overlooking Barcelona. Sofas suspended from ceilings, gardens looking out over the city, a top-floor restaurant: why go anywhere else? ⊠ *Av. Tibidabo 61, Tibidabo* ☎ *93/211–6261* ⊕ *www.danzatoria-barcelona.com* Ⓜ *Tibidabo.*

**DosTrece.** A popular Raval nightspot, this multisensory redoubt composed of restaurant, bar, club, music venue, and movie theater packs in an international crew of creative carousers from actors and movie directors to journalists and musicians. Students and random young rakes, roués, and bons vivants are scattered throughout as filling. The vibe, somehow, is friendly and inclusive: strangers chat freely. Downstairs musical performances run from jazz groups to tango, son, or samba, with jam sessions erupting regularly. ⊠ *Carme 40, Tibidabo* ☎ *93/301–7306* ⊕ *www.dostrece.net* Ⓜ *Liceu.*

**Elephant.** It could be a catwalk, with models showing off the latest fashions and strutting their stuff at Elephant's Lust & Luxury Nights all in a graceful Pedralbes terrace and chalet. The 23 June Sant Joan midsummer eve party is not to be missed. (If you come dressed all in white you get in free.) ⊠*Passeig dels Til.lers 1, Pedralbes* ☎*93/334–0258* ⊕*www.elephantbcn.com* Ⓜ*Maria Cristina.*

**La Paloma.** Wonderfully peculiar and kitschy 1950s furnishings fill this old-fashioned *sala de baile* (dance hall) that dates to 1903. The balcony is a great place to view both the dance floor and the frescoed ceiling. A live orchestra plays big-band tango, mambo, bolero, cha-cha, and different genres of ballroom music until 1 or 2 AM on weekends. Later, a DJ takes over until 5 AM. La Paloma is open Thursday–Sunday. ⊠*Tigre 27, Raval* ☎*93/301–6897* ⊕*www.lapaloma-bcn.com* Ⓜ*Universitat.*

**Loft.** An offshoot of Sala Razzmatazz, this funky space dedicated to house and electronic music draws an edgy crowd in their twenties and thirties. The club opens at 1 AM on Friday and Saturday, and the energy generated between then and dawn could provide electricity for the entire city if someone could figure out how to harness the stuff. ⊠*Pamplona 88, Poble Nou* ☎*93/272–0910* ⊕*www.salarazzmatazz. com* Ⓜ*Marina, Bogatell.*

**Luz de Gas.** This always-wired hub of musical and general nightlife activity has something going on every night, from live performances to wild, late-night dancing. Though the weekly schedule may vary with the arrival of famous international names, you can generally plan for Monday blues; Tuesday jazz; Wednesday, Saturday, and Sunday cover bands; Thursday soul; and rock on Friday. ⊠*Muntaner 246, Eixample* ☎*93/209–7711* ⊕*www.luzdegas.com* Ⓜ*Muntaner, Provença.*

**Luz de Luna.** This torrid Latin specialist puts out compelling Caribbean rhythms for a crowd that knows exactly what to do with them. Like snooty ski instructors, the professional *salseros,* straight in from "the pearl of the Antilles" (aka Cuba), offer their skills to beginners and experts alike for tours of an endless repertory of moves and maneuvers straight from Havana. ⊠*Comerç 21, Born-Ribera* ☎*93/310–7542* ⊕*www.salsapower.com* Ⓜ*Jaume I.*

**Otto Zutz.** Just off Via Augusta above the Diagonal, this nightclub and disco is a perennial Barcelona favorite that keeps attracting a glitzy mix of Barcelona movers and shakers, models, ex-models, wannabe models, and the hoping-to-get-lucky mob that predictably follows this sort of pulchritude. Music is usually recorded, with occasional live performers. ⊠*Lincoln 15, Eixample* ☎*93/238–0722* ⊕*www.ottozutz.com* Ⓜ*Sant Gervasi, Plaça Molina.*

**Pachá.** First famous in Ibiza as the wildest club in Europe, Pachá has hit the ground running in Barcelona. A half a dozen bars, two VIP areas, a chill-out room, and a breezy terrace all equipped with supersonic sound gear and the latest in avant-garde decor entertain a heterogeneous crowd checking each other out with gleeful prurience. Open Friday, Saturday, and nights before holidays, Pachá's keeps the music hot with DJs, and groups from around the world spice up the live entertainment. ⊠*Av. Gregorio Maranon 17, Les Corts* ☎*93/334–3233* ⊕*www.clubpachabcn.com* Ⓜ*Zona Universitària.*

**Rat King Retro Lounge.** Wired with rockabilly and swing music and oozing bourbon on the rocks, this is an irresistible upper Eixample dive with live music on Thursday nights, when well-known guitarist Ignasi Corominas organizes a jam session after 10 PM with the help of a stand-up base and vibraphone. ⊠ *Passatge de Marimon 17, Eixample* ☎ *93/414–2456* ⊕ *www.rockabillyrules.com* Ⓜ *Gràcia.*

**Sala Razzmatazz.** Razzmatazz stages weeknight concerts featuring international draws such as Alanis Morissette and Ani DiFranco. The small-format environment is extraordinarily intimate and beats out sports stadiums or the immense Palau Sant Jordi as a top venue for concerts. It shares its Friday and Saturday club madness with neighboring sister-venture the Loft around the corner. ⊠ *Almogavers 122, Poble Nou* ☎ *93/320–8200* ⊕ *www.salarazzmatazz.com* Ⓜ *Marina, Bogatell.*

**Salsabor.** Popular with Barcelona's Latin Kings and Queens Cultural Association and their president Erika Jaramillo, this Latin American favorite cranks out salsa, merengue, and bachata (among other Latin dance sensations) for a young crowd that knows exactly how to groove to these incandescent rhythms. Simply joining the ranks of awed spectators to watch world-class salsa athletically performed is worth the price of admission, which, incidentally is free on Thursday, otherwise €10 with a drink included. ⊠ *Carrer Moiá 1, Eixample* ☎ *676/694477* ⊕ *www.salsabor.es* Ⓜ *Gràcia, Provença.*

**Salsitas.** Both restaurant and Latin dance club, this red-hot joint just off the Rambla and practically smack across from Gaudí's Palau Güell packs in a happy crowd of hard partyers. Models and the generally babelicious come here decked out in sleek and chic designer kit to shake to house music laid on by star DJs. Alabaster pillars are disguised as date palms, and a range of exotic touches go for the extreme opposite of rustic. ⊠ *Nou de la Rambla 22, Raval* ☎ *93/318–0840* Ⓜ *Liceu.*

**Up and Down.** Locally pronounced "Pen-*dow,*" this has been a classic for well-heeled party animals for more than 30 years, and it's still kicking out the jams. The club is so named for its two separate spaces, one downstairs for younger carousers and one upstairs for more mature and accomplished night owls. The FC Barcelona soccer team is apt to let off steam here after great triumphs, while upper-Barcelona's beautiful people make this their downhill base camp for nocturnal pursuits. ⊠ *Numancia 179, Les Corts–Diagonal* ☎ *93/280–2922* Ⓜ *Maria Cristina.*

## THE GAY SCENE

Barcelona's gay culture is alive and booming, with part of the Eixample (the area bordered by the streets of Diputació and Aragó, Balmes and Villarroel) rechristened as the *Gaixample.* Hetero-friendly gay restaurants include Le Lacydon, Domèstic, Azul Azul, and Colby. There are also saunas, bookstores, sex shops (Blue Box, D-arness, and Nostromo), at least one hotel (Hotel Axel), and a movie theater all aligned with the city's gay population.

*The Guía del Ocio* ( ⊕ *www.guiadelociobcn.com*), in its *"tardenoche"* (evening–night) section devotes a full page (following the nightclub section under the heading "Ambiente") to listings for gay establishments as well as addresses and phone numbers for gay collective groups in the city.

**Dietrich Gay Teatro Café.** With a gorgeous terrace and interior garden, expanses of glass separating contiguous spaces, a minimum of one drag-queen show nightly, and a jumping dance floor, this cabaret and disco dedicated to Marlene Dietrich is proving to be one of Barcelona's busiest gay discos. ⊠ *Consell de Cent 255, Eixample* ☎ *93/451–7707* Ⓜ *Urgell, Universitat.*

**Metro Disco.** Two dance floors offer a choice of disco history or Latin rhythms for a somewhat older set of men here, though all ages are represented. Porno on the tiny screens over the urinals and a solid party vibe keep this place filled to the gills and rocking. ⊠ *Sepúlveda 185, Eixample* ☎ *93/323–5227* Ⓜ *Urgell, Universitat.*

**New Chaps.** This off-Gaixample address has steer horns mounted on the walls, plenty of racy videos, and a labyrinthine dark room downstairs for a more mature gay crowd. ⊠ *Av. Diagonal 365, Eixample* ☎ *93/215–5365* Ⓜ *Diagonal, Verdaguer.*

**Space Barcelona.** Touted as the most daring club in Barcelona's gay scene, this is the place to go on Sunday when much of the competition is closed. Between Plaça Espanya and Sants train station, Space Barcelona is known for superb music, top DJs, and its superior sound system. Four different bars surround the giant stage, which is usually heavily populated with dancers and vocalists. ⊠ *Carrer Tarragona 141–147, Sants-Plaça Espanya* ☎ *93/426–8444* Ⓜ *Plaça Espanya.*

**Punto BCN.** A musical bar with billiards tables, this mid-Eixample hub is a clearing house for all persuasions and tastes, with women often outnumbering the men, pool tables or not. ⊠ *Carrer Muntaner 63–65, Eixample* ☎ *93/453–6123* Ⓜ *Universitat.*

## JAZZ & BLUES

Jazz in Barcelona owes much to native son and jazz and bop pianist Tete Montoliu (1933–97). Today's jazz scene revolves around pianist and percussionist Jordi Rossy and tenor saxophonist Llibert Fortuny. Manhattan names such as Billy McHenry and Ben Waltzer play annually in Barcelona, while Barcelona's jazz festival convenes top artists from around the world. The Palau de la Música Catalana hosts an **international jazz festival** ( ☎ *93/481–7040*) in November.

**Harlem Jazz Club.** Good jazz and country singers perform at this small but exciting music venue just a five-minute walk from Plaça Reial. Cece Gianotti and Joan Vinyals are regular country guitarists and vocalists here. ⊠ *Comtessa de Sobradiel 8, Barri Gòtic* ☎ *93/310–0755* Ⓜ *Jaume I, Liceu.*

**Jamboree-Jazz & Dance-Club.** This pivotal nightspot, another happy fiefdom of the imperial Mas siblings, is a center for jazz, rock, and flamenco in the evening's early stages (11 PM) and turns into a wild and woolly dance club after performances. Jazz greats Joe Smith, Jordi Rossy, Billy McHenry, Gorka Benítez, and Llibert Fortuny all perform here regularly, while in Los Tarantos, the upstairs space, some of Barcelona's finest flamenco can be heard. ✉ *Pl. Reial 17, Rambla* ☎ *93/301–7564* Ⓜ *Liceu.*

**Jazz Sí Club.** Run by the Barcelona contemporary music school next door, this workshop and (during the day) café is a forum for musicians, teachers, and fans to listen and debate their art. There is jazz on Monday; pop, blues, and rock jam sessions on Tuesday; jazzmen jamming on Wednesday; Cuban salsa and son on Thursday; flamenco on Friday; and rock and pop on the weekends. If the entrance isn't free, the small cover charge includes a drink. ✉ *Requesens 2, Raval* ☎ *93/329–0020* ⊕ *www.tallerdemusics.com* Ⓜ *Sant Antoni.*

**La Cova del Drac-Jazzroom.** An emblematic jazz venue dating back to Barcelona's very first jazz performances, La Cova de Drac (The Dragon's Cave) was revived in this new location by the ubiquitous Mas family of Mas i Mas fame. Jordi Rossy, Llibert Fortuny, Joe Smith, Billy McHenry, Ben Waltzer, and a long list of jazz greats perform here over the course of the year. The upper Barcelona address makes La Cova an easy stroll for Sarrià and Sant Gervasi jazz aficionados, though downtown connections on the FCG train or by taxi are also quick and painless. ✉ *Carrer Vallmajor 33, Sant Gervasi* ☎ *93/245–7396* ⊕ *www.masimas.com* Ⓜ *Muntaner, Pàdua.*

**Nao Colón/Club Bamboo.** Across from the Estació de França, this hot spot serves contemporary Mediterranean cuisine and presents concerts Tuesday–Thursday at 10 PM. Anything from jazz and blues to flamenco fusion might take the stage here, but at midnight Nao Colón turns into a pumpkin and Club Bamboo materializes with sounds from Latin house and funk to Brazilian and Cuban Afro rhythms. ✉ *Av. Marquès de l'Argentera 19, Born-Ribera* ☎ *93/268–7633* Ⓜ *Jaume I.*

**Zacarías.** Folk, rock, blues and a wide variety of musical attractions keep Zacarías on the cutting edge of Barcelona's live-music scene. Well positioned near the center of the Diagonal, this veteran nightlife hub has entertained barcelonins for several generations. Upcoming attractions include stars ranging from Sam Lardner's country-flamenco fusion group Barcelona to flamenco master Enrique Morente and his daughter Estrella Morente. ✉ *Av. Diagonal 477, Eixample* ☎ *93/207–5643* ⊕ *www.masimas.com* Ⓜ *Provença.*

---

**BARCELONA JAZZ**

Barcelona has loved jazz ever since Sam Wooding and his Chocolate Kiddies triumphed here in 1929. Jack Hilton's visits in the early '30s paved the way for Benny Carter and the Hot Club of Barcelona in 1935 and 1936. In the early years of the post–Spanish civil war Franco dictatorship, jazz was viewed as a dangerous influence from beyond, but by 1969 Duke Ellington's Sacred Concerts smuggled jazz into town under the protective umbrella of the same Catholic Church whose conservative elements cautioned the Franco regime against the perils of this "degenerate music."

# THE ARTS

A glance through the daily agenda page of *La Vanguardia* or *El País* will remind you, every day, that it will be physically impossible to make it to all the art-exhibit openings, concerts, book presentations by famous authors, lectures, free films, or theatrical events that you would like to attend in Barcelona that day. Gallery openings and book presentations alone, many of which serve drinks and canapés, could probably eliminate any need for a food or party budget in Barcelona's boiling cultural scene. The comprehensive *Guía del Ocio* (⊕*www.guiadelociobcn.com*), which includes a brief but well-researched and well-written English section, comes out Thursday for the following week, costs €1, and includes all musical listings, restaurants, bars, nightclubs, and novelties of the week.

## FESTIVALS

**El Grec** (*Festival del Grec* ☎*93/301–7775* ⊕*www.bcn.es/grec*), Barcelona's annual summer arts festival, runs from late June to the end of July. Many of the concerts and theater and dance performances take place outdoors in such historic places as Plaça del Rei and the Teatre Grec, as well as in the Mercat de les Flors.

The **Festival de Música Antiga** (*Early Music Festival* ☎*93/404–6000*) brings the best early-music groups from all over Europe to town from late April to mid-May. Concerts are held all over town, though most lectures and performances are at the **CaixaFòrum** (✉*Av. Marquès de Comillas 6–8, Eixample* Ⓜ*Espanya*).

The **Festival Internacional de Poesia** (☎*93/301–7775* ⊕*www.bcn. es/icub*), sponsored by the Institut de Cultura in May, is one of the city's most extraordinary and exciting events, with poets from places as disparate as Ethiopia, China, Poland, Ireland, and Canada joining local Catalan, Basque, Gallego, and Spanish poets reciting their work, always in the original languages. The Palau de la Música is sold out for the final recital, after a week of events in Barcelona's finest architectural gems. The festival is directly descended from Barcelona's *Jocs Florals* (Floral Games) first held in 1393, so it's no wonder that emotions run high.

The **International Music Festival** (☎*93/301–7775*), in late September, forms part of the feast of Nostra Senyora de la Mercè (Our Lady of Mercy), Barcelona's patron saint. The main venues are Palau de la Música, Mercat de les Flors, and Plaça del Rei.

## ART GALLERIES

*For art-gallery shopping, see Chapter 7.*
**CaixaFòrum.** The building itself, a restored textile factory, is well worth exploring (and is directly across from the Mies van der Rohe Pavillion on Montjuïc at the bottom of the steps up to the Palau Nacional). Temporary exhibits show the work of major artists from around the

world, while the Músics del Món (Musicians of the World) series stages everyone from Renaissance lutist Hopkinson Smith to sitar master Ravi Shankar in the intimate auditorium. ⊠ *Av. Marquès de Comillas 6–8, Montjuïc* ☎ *902/223040* ⊕ *www.fundacio.lacaixa.es* Ⓜ *Espanya.*

**Cajamadrid.** On the last corner of Rambla Catalunya overlooking Plaça de Catalunya, Cajamadrid has art shows and free concerts featuring performers such as Arianna Savall, daughter of early-music virtuoso Jordi Savall. ⊠ *Pl. de Catalunya 9, Eixample* ☎ *93/301–4494* Ⓜ *Catalunya.*

**Centre Cultural Metropolità Tecla Sala.** Some of the most avant-garde exhibits and installations that come through Barcelona find their way to this cultural powerhouse, a 15-minute metro ride away in the suburb of Hospitalet de Llobregat. (Note that the Josep Tarradellas address is not the in-town Barcelona street that runs between Estació de Sants and Plaça Francesc Macià). ⊠ *Av. Josep Tarradellas 44, Hospitalet* ☎ *93/338–5553* ⊕ *www.tallerdemusics.com* Ⓜ *La Torrasa.*

**Centre D'Art Santa Mònica.** Near Drassanes at the bottom of the Rambla, this public art-exhibit space shows a variety of work, usually by contemporary artists such as Joan Pere Viladecans or Miquel Barceló. The bar and restaurant under the ramp up to the gallery is booming. ⊠ *La Rambla 7, La Rambla* ☎ *93/316–2810* ⊕ *www.cultura.gencat. net/casm* Ⓜ *Drassanes.*

**Col.legi Oficial d'Arquitectes de Catalunya.** Architectural exhibits here are always interesting, as is the excellent restaurant just down the stairs. The Picasso frieze around the facade was the first Picasso work allowed in Spain after the 1936–39 Spanish civil war. ⊠ *Plaza Nova 5, Barri Gòtic* ☎ *93/301–5000* ⊕ *www.coac.net* Ⓜ *Liceu, Catalunya.*

**Fundació La Caixa.** La Caixa's various galleries are all important for seeing local contemporary art or for the excellent touring art shows, from Córdoba's Julio Romero de Torres to the Flemish Brueghels, that come through Barcelona regularly. *La Pedrera* ⊠ *Provença 261–265, Eixample* ☎ *93/484–5979* Ⓜ *Provença Centre Cultural* ⊠ *Passeig Sant Joan 108, Eixample* ☎ *93/476–8600* Ⓜ *Jaume I Sala Montcada* ⊠ *Carrer Montcada 14, Born-Ribera* ☎ *93/310–0699* Ⓜ *Diagonal* ⊕ *www.caixacatalunya.es.*

**La Capella de l'Antic Hospital de la Santa Creu.** Here in this chapel, as in many Barcelona art galleries, the space itself is half the show. The choir loft, the inside of the cupola, and the vaulting in the side chapels are all lovely, while the exhibits and installations are invariably young artists showing experimental works. ⊠ *Hospital 56, Raval* ☎ *93/442–7171* ⊕ *www.bcn.es/virreinaexposicions* Ⓜ *Liceu.*

**Palau de la Virreina.** With the Espai Xavier Miserachs showing photography and two other spaces and the patio available for other temporary exhibits, this is an important Barcelona art resource in a convenient location next to the Boqueria market. ⊠ *La Rambla 99, Rambla* ☎ *93/316–1000* Ⓜ *Catalunya, Liceu.*

**Palau Moja.** Periodic exhibits offer a golden opportunity to see the inside of one of Barcelona's finest *palacetes* (stately town houses), once the home of early-20th-century shipping magnate Marquès de Comillas. One recent show displayed the recovered personal files returned to Barcelona from Salamanca 70 years after they were removed during the 1936–39 Spanish civil war. ⊠ *Portaferrissa 1, Rambla* ☎ *93/316–2740* Ⓜ *Catalunya.*

## CONCERTS

For details on concerts throughout the year, check the *"agenda"* page in either *La Vanguardia* or *El País,* buy the handy *Guia del Ocio* published every Thursday, or call the tourist information office's English line (☏010) and ask for information. **Cultural information** (☏906/427017) is another way to find out if and when events are taking place, along with the city Web site at www.bcn.es. For tickets to many events, call **Servicaixa** (☏902/101212) to order in Spanish with a credit card, or stop by the tourist office in Plaça de Catalunya.

Fodor'sChoice ★ **Auditori de Barcelona.** Minimal, like the inside of a guitar, the Auditori schedules a full program of classical music with occasional jazz or pop concerts near Plaça de les Glòries. Orchestras that perform here include the Orquestra Simfònica de Barcelona i Nacional de Catalunya (OBC) and the Orquestra Nacional de Cambra de Andorra. ⊠*Lepant 150, Eixample* ☏*93/317–1096* Ⓜ *Glòries.*

**Auditori Winterthur.** Behind the L'Illa Diagonal shopping mall, this intimate, 650-seat venue places you close to major artists such as Austrian mezzo-soprano Angelika Kirschlager and Yo-Yo Ma. ⊠*Av. Diagonal 547, Eixample* ☏*93/290–1090* Ⓜ *Les Corts.*

Fodor'sChoice ★ **CaixaFòrum.** A beautifully restored and converted former textile mill, this neo-Mudéjar Puig i Cadalfalch structure is one of the city's newest venues for cultural events from concerts to art openings to lectures. Concerts here range from the Musics del Mon series with European early music to master baroque lutist Hopkinson Smith or India's legendary santoor (hammer dulcimer) player Shiv Kumar. ⊠*Av. Marquès de Comillas 6–8, Montjuïc* ☏*93/476–8600* Ⓜ*Espanya.*

**Gran Teatre del Liceu.** Barcelona's famous opera house on the Rambla runs a full season from September through June combining the Liceu's own chorus, orchestra, and players with first-tier invited soloists from June Anderson to Plácido Domingo or Barcelona's own Montserrat Caballé. In addition, touring dance companies— ballet, flamenco, and modern dance—appear here. The downstairs foyer holds early-evening recitals, puppet shows for children on weekends, and occasional analytical discussions. The Espai Liceu café under the opera house includes (along with excellent light fare) a store filled with music-related gifts, instruments, and knickknacks, and a tiny 50-seat theater projecting fragments of operas and a video of the history of the Liceu opera house. Seats can be expensive and hard to get (reserve

### MUSIC & ARCHITECTURE

Saint Augustine's dictum on music and architecture as twin arts suits Barcelona. Viola da gamba master Jordi Savall regularly combines Renaissance music with the Gothic spaces for which it was written with his Hesperion XXI concerts at the Reial Drassanes (the medieval shipyards), Santa Maria del Mar basilica, or the Monestir de Pedralbes. The Saló del Tinell in Plaça del Rei, the diminutive Sant Pau del Camp church in the Raval, or the pre-Romanesque Església de Santa Anna tucked away between Plaça Catalunya and Carrer de Santa Anna are all semi-secret acoustical gems.

well in advance), but occasionally a cheap seat or two may become available. ⊠*La Rambla 51–59, La Rambla* ☎*93/485–9913* ⊕*www. liceubarcelona.com* Ⓜ*Liceu.*

Fodor'sChoice ★ **Palau de la Música Catalana.** Barcelona's most spectacular concert hall is a Moderniste masterpiece in the Ciutat Vella, off the Barri Gòtic. Performances run September–June, with Sunday-morning concerts at 11 AM a popular tradition. The calendar here is packed—everyone from Madredeus to the Buena Vista Social Club has performed here, while the house troupe, the Orfeó Catalá, holds choral concerts several times a year. Tickets range €6–€90, and are best purchased well in advance. The ticket office is open weekdays 11–1 and 5–8, Saturday 5–8 only. ⊠*Sant Francesc de Paula 2, Sant Pere* ☎*93/295–7200* Ⓜ*Catalunya.*

**Palau Sant Jordi.** Arata Isozaki's huge macro-venue hosts massively attended pop concerts for stars like Bruce Springsteen or Paul McCartney, though occasional operas and other musical events are also presented here. ⊠*Palau Sant Jordi, Passeig Olímpic 5–7, Montjuïc* ☎*93/426–2089* Ⓜ*Espanya.*

**Saló de Cent.** Check for occasional free ceremonies and performances that allow you to visit this incomparable setting, the first protodemocratic municipal parliament (dating from 1274) in Europe. ⊠*Pl. Sant Jaume s/n, Barri Gòtic* ☎*93/402–7000* Ⓜ*Jaume I.*

## DANCE

Barcelona's dance scene has become more and more about flamenco as this Andalusian art form has gained popularity in Catalonia over the last decade. Ballet troupes, both local and from abroad, perform at the Liceu opera house with some regularity, while contemporary dance troupes such as those of Cesc Gelabert and Nacho Duato are often performing in a variety of theaters around town. L'Espai de Dansa i Música de la Generalitat de Catalunya is the city's main dance center. Most venues that host dance primarily feature theater productions.

**L'Espai de Dansa i Música de la Generalitat de Catalunya.** Generally listed as L'Espai, or "The Space," this is one of the city's prime venues for ballet and modern dance, as well as occasional musical offerings. ⊠*Travessera de Gràcia 63, Eixample* ☎*93/241–6810* Ⓜ*Gràcia.*

Fodor'sChoice ★ **Mercat de les Flors.** Near Plaça de Espanya, this theater makes a traditional setting for modern dance as well as theater. ⊠*Lleida 59, Eixample* ☎*93/426–1875* ⊕*www.mercatflors.com* Ⓜ*Poble Sec.*

**Teatre Apolo.** This historic player in Barcelona's theater life stages light opera and dance spectacles ranging from flamenco to ballet to contemporary. ⊠*Av. del Paral.lel 59, Raval* ☎*93/441–9007* ⊕*www. teatreapolo.com* Ⓜ*Paral.lel.*

**Teatre Tívoli.** One of the city's most beloved traditional theater and dance venues, the Tívoli has staged everything from the Ballet Nacional de Cuba to flamenco. It's just above Plaça de Catalunya. ⊠*Casp 10, Eixample* ☎*93/412–2063* ⊕*www.grupbalana.com* Ⓜ*Catalunya.*

FLAMENCO

Barcelona's flamenco scene is surprisingly vibrant for a culture so far removed from Andalusia. Los Tarantos, in Plaça Reial, regularly stages authentic flamenco performances.

**El Cordobés.** A magnet for tour groups in search of flamenco, the professionalism of the touring performers ensures technical proficiency, though the emotion is often absent. ⊠*Rambla 35, Rambla* ☎*93/317–5711* Ⓜ*Liceu.*

**El Patio Andaluz.** This flamenco standard has rather touristy flamenco shows, with or without dinner included, twice nightly (10 PM and 1 AM). ⊠*Aribau 242, Eixample* ☎*93/209–3378* Ⓜ*Provença.*

**El Tablao de Carmen.** Large tour groups come here to see touring flamenco troupes that are technically excellent but fall flat on passion. ⊠*Poble Espanyol, Montjuïc* ☎*93/325–6895* ⊕*www.tablaodecarmen.com* Ⓜ*Espanya.*

The **Festival de Flamenco de Ciutat Vella** (☎*93/443–4346* ⊕*www.tallerdemusics.com*), organized by the Taller de Músics (Musicians' Workshop) and based in and around the Raval's CCCB (Centre de Cultura Contemporani de Barcelona), offers a chance to hear the real thing and skip the often disappointing tourist fare available at most of the formal flamenco dinner-and-show venues around town

> ## CATALAN FLAMENCO
>
> Considered—like bullfighting—a foreign import from Andalusia, Catalonia and flamenco may sound incongruous, but Barcelona has a burgeoning and erudite flamenco audience. For the best flamenco available in Barcelona, consult listings and hotel concierges. Estrella Morente and her father Enrique, Chano Domínguez, Farruquito, Sara Baras, Paco de Lucía, and local *cantaora* Mayte Martín have had big successes in Barcelona.

**Los Tarantos.** This standby spotlights some of Andalusia's best flamenco and has been staging serious artists in a largely un-touristy environment for the last quarter century. The flamenco shows upstairs give way to disco action downstairs at the Jamboree Dance Club by 1 AM or so. ⊠*Pl. Reial 17, Barri Gòtic* ☎*93/318–3067* Ⓜ*Liceu.*

**Pisamorena.** Serving dinner and copas as well, this little restaurant and club is known for its flamenco performances and genuine flamenco character. ⊠*Consolat de Mar 37–41, Born-Ribera* ☎*93/268–0904* Ⓜ*Jaume I.*

**Soniquete.** A minuscule flamenco purists' haven tucked between the post office and Plaça Reial, Soniquete resonates with stamping feet Thursday–Sunday 9 PM–3 AM. ⊠*Milans 5, Barri Gòtic* ☎*93/351–8757* Ⓜ*Jaume I.*

**TiriTiTran.** This *colmado flamenco* (an antique term for a place where flamenco was sung and danced, with trade taking place as well) offers sherries and hams while improvised flamenco may erupt at any moment.

■ TIP➔ **Keep a discreet profile here if you want to see any action; the Catch-22 of flamenco for foreigners is that if potential performers feel that tourists are prominently present, they won't perform.** ⊠*Buenos Aires 28, Eixample* ☎*93/363–0591* Ⓜ*Provença, Hospital Clínic.*

# FILM

Though some foreign films are dubbed, Barcelona has a full assortment of original-language cinema; look for listings marked VOS (*Versión original subtitulada*). Yelmo Cineplex Icària near the Vil.la Olímpica is the main movie mill, with 30 films, all in VOS playing daily. Films in VOS are shown at the following theaters.

**Alexandra.** Conveniently placed on Rambla Catalunya, the Alexandra runs recent releases in their original language. ⊠ *Rambla de Catalunya 90, Eixample* ☎ *93/215–0503* Ⓜ *Provença.*

**Casablanca-Kaplan.** A satisfyingly quirky movie house, the Casablanca plays art-house flicks in their original language. ⊠ *Passeig de Gràcia 115, Eixample* ☎ *93/218–4345* Ⓜ *Diagonal.*

**Filmoteca de Catalunya.** This Generalitat cultural resource has VOS films and specializes in international documentaries and films made by and about women. ⊠ *Av. Sarrià 33, Eixample* ☎ *93/410–7590* Ⓜ *Hospital Clinic.*

**Icària Yelmo.** This complex near the Carles I metro stop has the city's largest selection of English-language films. ⊠ *Salvador Espriu 61, Port Olímpic* ☎ *93/221–7585* ⊕ *www.yelmocineplex.com* Ⓜ *Carles I.*

**Renoir Floridablanca.** A quick walk from the Rambla, this downtown theater just across Ronda de Sant Antoni from the Raval shows recent releases in English with subtitles. ⊠ *Floridablanca 135, Eixample* ☎ *902/221622* ⊕ *www.cinesrenoir.com* Ⓜ *Universitat.*

**Renoir-Les Corts.** Convenient to Sarrià and Sant Gervasi dwellers, this cinema behind Diagonal's El Corte Inglés is a good choice for recently released English-language features of all kinds. ⊠ *Eugeni d'Ors 12, Diagonal/Les Corts* ☎ *93/490–5510* ⊕ *www.cinesrenoir.com* Ⓜ *Maria Cristina.*

**Rex.** Not far from Plaça Espanya on the Gran Via, the Rex has occasional VOS films. ⊠ *Gran Via 463, Eixample* ☎ *93/423–1060* ⊕ *www.grupbalana.com* Ⓜ *Rocafort.*

**Verdi.** Gràcia's movie center and a great favorite for the pre- and post-show action, the Verdi unfailingly screens recent releases in their original-language version. ⊠ *Carrer Verdi 32, Gràcia* ☎ *93/238–7990* ⊕ *www.cines-verdi.com* Ⓜ *Gràcia, Fontana.*

**Verdi Park.** You can actually exit the Verdi movie theater via the back door and report in for another feature at the Verdi Park—and probably snag a beverage in the process. ⊠ *Torrijos 49, Gràcia* ☎ *93/238–7990* ⊕ *www.cines-verdi.com* Ⓜ *Gràcia, Fontana.*

# OPERA

Fodor'sChoice ★ **Gran Teatre del Liceu.** Myriad events from October through mid-July—including 10 operas, four dance productions, five concerts, and 10–15 recitals—take place in this opulent setting. It was brilliantly restored to its former glory and much more following the 1994 fire that gutted the original building. Tickets range €10–€150. In addition, a series of small concerts in the foyer promotes and enhances comprehension of the operas performing during the season. The *Sesiones Golfas* (after-hour sessions) are late-night (10 PM) entertainment events. Tickets are hard to get; reserve well in advance for all events. ⊠*Rambla 51–59, Rambla* ☎*93/485–9913 box office, 902/332211 for tickets through Servicaixa* ⊕*www.liceubarcelona.com* Ⓜ*Liceu.*

## THEATER

Most plays are performed in Catalan, though some are performed in Spanish. Barcelona is well known for avant-garde theater and for troupes that specialize in mime, large-scale performance art, and special effects (La Fura dels Baus, Els Joglars, Els Comediants in Catalan). Several theaters along Avinguda del Paral.lel specialize in musicals. The city also hosts a Festival de Títeres (Puppet Festival) in April.

**Espai Lliure.** Near Plaça and Montjuïc, this Fundació Teatre Lliure theater offers theater and dance performances. ⊠*Pl. Margarida Xirgu 1, Montjuïc* ☎*93/289–2770* ⊕*www.teatrelliure.cat* Ⓜ*Poble Sec.*

☾ **La Puntual Putxinel.lis de Barcelona.** The city's dedicated puppet (in Catalan, *putxinel.li*) theater is in the off-Born area just off Carrer del Comerç. Weekend matinee performances are major kid magnets. ⊠*Allada-Vermell s/n, Born-Ribera* ☎*639/305353* ⊕*www.lapuntual. info* Ⓜ*Jaume I.*

**Mercat de les Flors.** Near Plaça de Espanya, this is one of the city's most traditional dance and theater venues. ⊠*Lleida 59, Montjuïc* ☎*93/426–1875* ⊕*www.mercatflors.org* Ⓜ*Poble Sec.*

**Nou Tantarantana Teatre.** Just off the Ronda Sant Pau, this avant-garde theater usually has some thought-provoking production on the boards. Plays directed by Boris Rotstein, a Russian expat who has worked at the forefront of Barcelona theater for over a decade, are regular attractions here. ⊠*Carrer de les Flors 22, Raval* ☎*93/441–7022* ⊕*www. tantarantana.com* Ⓜ*Paral.lel.*

**Teatre Grec.** *(Greek Theater)* The open-air summer festival in July and August takes place here; plays, music, and dance are also presented in Plaça del Rei and Mercat de les Flors. ⊠*Santa Madrona 36, Montjuïc* ☎*93/316–1000* ⊕*www.bcn.es/grec* Ⓜ*Espanya.*

**Teatre Lliure.** Gràcia's branch of the Fundació Teatre Lliure stages theater, dance, and musical events. ⊠*Montseny 47, Gràcia* ☎*93/218– 9251* ⊕*www.teatrelliure.cat* Ⓜ*Fontana.*

Fodor's Choice ★ **Teatre Nacional de Catalunya.** Near Plaça de les Glòries, at the eastern end of the Diagonal, this glass-enclosed classical temple was designed by Ricardo Bofill, architect of Barcelona's airport. Programs cover everything from Shakespeare to ballet to avant-garde theater. ⊠*Pl. de les Arts 1, Eixample* ☎*93/306–5700* ⊕*www.tnc.cat* Ⓜ*Glòries.*

**Teatre Poliorama.** Just below Plaça de Catalunya, this famous and traditional theater nearly always has a hot-ticket show. ⊠*Rambla 15, Rambla* ☎*93/317–7599* ⊕*www.teatrepoliorama.com* Ⓜ*Catalunya.*

**Teatre Romea.** Behind the Boqueria market just off Plaça Sant Agustí, the Romea has been entertaining barcelonins for a century with everything from avant-garde Els Joglars to Shakespeare in Catalan. ⊠*Hospital 51, Raval* ☎*93/301–5504* ⊕*www.teatreromea.com* Ⓜ*Liceu.*

5

**Victòria.** This venerable theater in the heart of Barcelona's show district is a historic venue for musicals, reviews, and dance productions. ⊠ *Av. del Paral.lel 67–69, Raval* ☎ *93/443–2929* ⊕ *www.teatrevictoria.com* Ⓜ *Paral.lel.*

# Sports & the Outdoors

**WORD OF MOUTH**

"The [soccer] game started right at 5 PM and was a real experience. Those fans make our hockey or football fans look tame. 86,000 screaming people and we were right in the middle…"

—cmeyer54

By George
Semler

**ANY TALK OF SPORT IN** Barcelona is inevitably going to revolve around Futbol Club Barcelona (Barça), the local soccer team that, during the Franco regime, was the only legal means of expressing Catalan nationalism. Barça won the European Championship in 2006, and will be a leading contender for top national and international titles year in year out. Passion for Barça is so powerful that the emcee of a recent Barcelona poetry festival found it necessary to publicly thank the Barcelona soccer team for *not* reaching the European Cup finals, thus allowing the festival's closing ceremony an audience. Where else in the world are even poets unabashed soccer fans? In case Barça is playing away, R.C.D. (Reial Club Deportiu) Espanyol is also a first-division soccer team. Barcelona's Conde de Godó tennis tournament brings the world's best rackets here every April, while the Spanish Grand Prix at Mont Meló draws the top Formula One racing teams. As for keeping active yourself, there are diving, windsurfing, surfing, sailing, and water-sports activities in Barceloneta and all along the coast north and south of Barcelona. Tennis and squash courts are available in various public and semiprivate clubs around town, and Barcelona now has a dozen golf courses less than an hour away from town. Bicycle tracks run the length of the Diagonal and bike-rental agencies are popping up everywhere. Jogging the Carretera de les Aigües, the water road (named for the aqueduct that used to run across the hillside over the city) is a popular activity and a good reason runners may prefer staying in a hotel in the upper part of the city.

## BEACHES

Barcelona's *platjas* (beaches) have improved and multiplied in number from Barceloneta north to the Fòrum site at the northeastern end of the Diagonal. At Barceloneta's southwestern end is the Platja de Sant Sebastià, followed northward by the platjas de Sant Miquel, Barceloneta, Passeig Marítim, Port Olímpic, Nova Icària, Bogatell, Mar Bella, and La Nova Mar Bella (the last football-field length of which is a nudist enclave), and Llevant. The Barceloneta beach is the most popular stretch, easily accessible by several bus lines, notably the No. 64 bus (which runs all the way from Pedralbes at the top of the city) and by the L4 metro stop at Barceloneta or at Ciutadella–Vil.la Olímpica (for the northernmost beaches such as Mar Bella). The best surfing stretch is at the northeastern end of the Barceloneta beach, and the boardwalk itself offers miles of turf for walkers, skaters, bicyclers, and joggers. Topless bathing is the norm on all beaches in and around Barcelona. There are public toilet facilities, but people often stop into a nearby bar to use the facilities. There are showers (free) at the edge of the beach.

### NORTH OF BARCELONETA

Running north of Barceloneta, the first beaches are Montgat, Ocata, Vilasar de Mar, Arenys de Mar, Canet de Mar, and Sant Pol de Mar, all accessible by train from the RENFE station in Plaça de Catalunya. Sant Pol is a good pick, with clean sand, a lovely old town, and the gourmet restaurant Sant Pau (popularly called La Ruscalleda after its chef, Carmen Ruscalleda), one of the best restaurants in Catalonia (or, for that matter, Europe). Another beach with a top-notch gastronomical opportunity is Arenys de Mar with the famous Hispania restaurant a minute's walk from the beach across the NII road. Canet de Mar's beach extends for 10 km (6 mi) and offers rental options for surfboards or Windsurfers, as well as beach restaurants such as (in summer) La Roca or (all year) El Parador. The farther north you go, toward the Costa Brava, the more pristine the beaches tend to be, though this rocky coast specializes in tiny *calas* (coves or inlets) rather than lengthy strands.

> **TOP 5**
>
> ■ Watching Futbol Club Barcelona play in Camp Nou.
>
> ■ Playing the PGA Catalunya golf course in the Empordà.
>
> ■ Scuba diving in the Isles Medes off the Costa Brava.
>
> ■ Jogging the Carretera de les Aigües over Barcelona.
>
> ■ Watching Rafa Nadal win his next Conde de Godó championship.

#### SOUTH OF THE CITY

Ten kilometers (6 mi) south of Barcelona is the popular day resort **Castelldefels,** with a long, sandy beach and a series of happening bars and restaurants. A 15-minute train ride from the Passeig de Gràcia RENFE station to Gavà or Castelldefels (be sure your train actually stops at these stations, or you'll go much farther than you intended) deposits you on a 10-km (6-mi) beach. In winter, this makes for a unbeatable walk: from November through March the sun sets into the Mediterranean, thanks to the westward slant of the coastline here. There are several good places in Castelldefels for lamb chops, *calçots* (spring onions), and paella; the best, Can Patricio, serves lunch until 4:30.

**Sitges,** 43 km (27 mi) south of Barcelona, is a popular resort with good sand and clear water. Trains from Passeig de Gràcia RENFE station head here.

## BICYCLES & IN-LINE SKATES

Cruising Barcelona on wheels, whether by bike or skate, is a good way to see a lot, and save on transport. Bicycle lanes run along most major arteries.

**Barcelona Bici.** Barcelona's tourist office rents bicycles at various points around the edges of Ciutat Vella: the sea end of the Rambla, the top of the Rambla at Plaça Catalunya, and in Barceloneta. ✉*Pl. Portal de la Pau 1, Rambla* ☎*93/285–3832* ✉*Pl. Catalunya 9, Eixample* ☎*93/285–3832* Ⓜ*Catalunya* ✉*Passeig Joan de Borbó 45, Barceloneta* ☎*93/285–3832* ⊕*www.barcelonaturisme.com* Ⓜ*Barceloneta.*
**Bike Tours Barcelona.** This company offers a three-hour bike tour (in English) for €22, with a drink included. Just look for the guide with a bike and red flag at the northeast corner of the Town Hall in Plaça Sant Jaume, outside the Tourist Information Office at 11 AM daily or 4:30 PM (Monday, Wednesday, Friday) or 5:30 PM (Tuesday, Thursday, Satur-

day). ⊠*Carrer Esparteria 3, Barri Gòtic* ☎*93/268–2105* ⊕*www. biketoursbarcelona.com.*

**Bikes de Cool.** Just across from the Estació de França, this shop rents bikes and skates on weekends only. ⊠*Passeig Picasso 44, Born-Ribera* ☎*636/401997 mobile phone.*

**Classic Bikes.** Just off pivotal Plaça Catalunya, bicycles are available for rent here every day of the week from 9:30 to 8. The 24-hour rate is €17; half-day costs €11; 2 hours cost €6. ⊠*Tallers 45, Raval* ☎*93/317–1970.*

**Los Filicletos.** Whether bikes, skates, or bicycles built for two, you can rent wheels for every taste and task here. ⊠*Passeig Picasso 40, Born-Ribera* ☎*93/319–7885.*

**Scènic.** Bicycles, skates, and guided tours can be rented here weekdays until 2 PM, with an afternoon drop-off time to be specified. ⊠*Balboa 3, Barceloneta* ☎*93/319–2835.*

> CATALONIA, SPORTS MICROCOSM
>
> With skiing available in the Pyrenees from December to May, golf courses and tennis courts playable year-round, good trout streams flowing out of the mountains, and regattas of sailboats in the Mediterranean around the calendar, Barcelona and Catalonia offer many more sporting and outdoors activities than most visitors are prepared to tackle in much less than a lifetime. Spring combinations of skiing and golfing or even skiing, golfing, and fly fishing are perfectly feasible for the ambitious and adventurous, while Pyrenean hiking trails may be the best game in town.

**Un Cotxe Menys.** "*One Car Less*" in Catalan—meaning one less automobile on the streets of Barcelona—organizes various kinds of guided tours (including some in English) and bicycle outings. ⊠*Esparteria 3, Born-Ribera* ☎*93/268–2105.*

## GOLF

Weekday golf outings to one of the 22 golf courses within an hour of Barcelona are a good way to exercise and see the Catalonian countryside. Midweek greens fees range €50–€85; weekend prices double. Midweek availability is excellent except during Easter vacation and August. Call ahead to confirm a tee time, and remember to bring proof of your USGA handicap or membership in a golf club.

### AROUND BARCELONA

**Club de Golf de Sant Cugat.** This hilly 18-hole course, par 68, costs €65 Monday–Thursday and €150 Friday–Sunday. ⊠*Sant Cugat del Vallès* ☎*93/674–3958.*

**Club de Golf Terramar.** On this breezy seaside 18-hole course—par 72—you'll pay weekday greens fees of €70, and €110 on weekends and holidays. ⊠*Sitges* ☎*93/894–0580.*

**Club de Golf Vallromanes.** Thirty kilometers (19 mi) north of Barcelona between Masnou and Granollers, this challenging 18-hole, par-72 course requires a handicap of 28 or less to play. The club is closed Tuesday. Greens fees are €80 weekdays and €132 weekends. ⊠*Vallromanes* ☎*93/572–9064.*

**Reial Club de Golf El Prat.** In its new location near Terrassa, 30 km (19 mi) north of Barcelona, Reial Club de Golf El Prat is a lovely but extremely difficult 18-hole, par-72 course. It's open to nonmembers only on non-holiday weekdays for €100. ⊠ *Terrassa* ☎ *93/728–1000.*

**FARTHER AFIELD**

**Club de Golf Costa Brava.** This 18-hole, par-70 course, costs €47 during the week and €76 on weekends. ⊠ *La Masía, Santa Cristina d'Aro* ☎ *972/837150.*

**Club de Golf Pals.** An 18-hole, par-73 seaside course, Club de Golf Pals costs €50 during the week and €85 on weekends. ⊠ *Platja de Pals, Pals* ☎ *972/637009.*

**Peralada.** With 18 holes and par 71, this is a relatively flat course built around the luxurious Golf Peralada hotel on the alluvial plain of the Empordà. Greens fees are €48 on Monday, €56 Tuesday–Friday, and €75 on weekends. ⊠ *Paraje La Garriga, Peralada* ☎ *972/538287* ⊕ *www.golfperalada.com.*

★ **PGA Catalunya.** A mountainous marvel an hour from Barcelona, PGA Catalunya is ranked one of Europe's top 10 courses. With plenty of water hazards in addition to the 7,160-meter (7,032 yards) length, this 18-hole, par-72 course is always a challenge, if not an outright beating. Greens fees are €51 during the week and €70 on weekends and in summer (June 15–September 15). ⊠ *Caldes de Malavella, Girona* ☎ *972/472577* ⊕ *www.pgacatalunya.com.*

**Torremirona.** This 18-hole, par-72 rolling, inland course is in the town of Navata, an hour north of Barcelona, just southwest of Figueres. Greens fees are €50 weekdays and €68 weekends. ⊠ *Navata* ☎ *972/553737.*

## GYMS & SPAS

For more complete listings, look in the *Páginas Amarillas/Pàgines Grogues* (*Yellow Pages*) under *Gimnasios/Gimnasis.*

**Club Esportiu Femení Iradier.** Just above the Passeig de la Bonanova in the upper part of Barcelona, this sleek, exclusive club for women offers pilates, yoga, and original combinations of fitness programs, as well as squash, a gym, sauna, and pool. A day membership costs €22. ⊠ *Carrer Iradier 18 bis, Sant Gervasi* ☎ *93/254–1717* ⊕ *www.iradier.com.*

**Crack.** Off Passeig de Gràcia near the hotel Condes de Barcelona, this winner has a gym, sauna, pool (summer only), squash courts, and paddle tennis. Day membership here costs €15 for 24 hours (so it can work for two days if you time it right), with a small supplement for the squash and paddle-tennis courts. ⊠ *Passatge Domingo 7, Eixample* ☎ *93/215–2755.*

**DiR.** The DiR network has branches all over Barcelona. The minimum one-week membership costs €100 and includes fitness classes and the use of the sauna, steam room, swimming pool, and squash courts. Those working out with the equipment can pump in time to the videos playing on MTV. ☎ *901/304030 for general information Main branch Diagonal,* ⊠ *Ganduxer 25–27, Sant Gervasi* ☎ *93/202–2202* ⊕ *www.dirfitness.es.*

**02 Centro Wellness.** A minimalist-design triumph created by Alonso Balaguer in lower Sarrià, this streamlined glass-and-steel hydrotherapy spa cures whatever might be ailing you. ✉ *Carrer Eduardo Conde 2–6, Sarrià, Sant Gervasi* ☎93/205–3976.

## HIKING

The Collserola hills behind the city offer well-marked trails, fresh air, and lovely views. Take the San Cugat, Sabadell, or Terrassa FFCC train from Plaça de Catalunya and get off at Baixador de Vallvidrera; the information center, 10 minutes uphill next to Vil.la Joana (now the Jacint Verdaguer Museum), has maps of this mountain woodland just 20 minutes from downtown. The walk back into town can take from two to five hours depending on your speed and the trails you choose. For longer treks, try the 15-km (9-mi) Sant Cugat–to–Barcelona hike, or take the train south to Sitges and make the three-day walk to Montserrat.

**Associació Excursionista, Etnográfica i Folklorica** advises on and organizes outings of all kinds. ✉ *Avinyó 19, Barri Gòtic* ☎93/302–2730.
**Club Excursionista de Catalunya** has information on hiking far afield, including in the Pyrenees. ✉ *Paradis 10, Barri Gòtic* ☎93/315–2311.

## SCUBA DIVING

The Costa Brava's Illes Medes underwater nature preserve offers some of the Mediterranean's finest diving adventures. Seven tiny islands off the coastal town of L'Estartit are the home of some 1,400 species of flora and fauna and an underwater wonderland of tunnels and caves. Colorful fish, crabs, squid, and diverse plant life are observable before wetting a toe (for non-swimmers or those reluctant to dive), and deeper there are lobsters, gilthead bream, grouper, and a dazzling range of fish and marine life of all kinds. Dives of over 150 ft. may reveal rays. Other diving options are available at the Illes Formigues off the coast of Palamós and Els Ullastres off Llafranc.

**Aquàtica – Centro de Buceo** teaches diving, rents equipment, and organizes outings to the Illes Medes. With top safety-code requirements in place and certified instructors and biologists directing the programs in English, French, Catalan, or Spanish, this is one of Estartit's best diving opportunities. ✉ *Camping Rifort,* ☎972/75–06–56 ⊕ *www. aquatica-sub.com.*

## SAILING & WINDSURFING

On any day of the week in Barcelona you can see midday regattas taking place off the Barceloneta beaches or beyond the *rompeolas* (breakwater) on the far side of the port. Believe it or not, Olympic-level sailors are being trained for competition just a stone's throw (or two) from the Rambla.

**Proa 7.** Part of the Barceloviatjes agency, Proa 7 charters riverboats, catamarans, power yachts, and canal tours, and arranges all manner of fluvial boating opportunities. ✉ *Consell de Cent 344, Eixample* ☎ *93/487–0920.*

**Reial Club Marítim de Barcelona.** Barcelona's most exclusive and prestigious yacht club can advise visitors on matters maritime, from where to charter yachts and sailboats to how to sign up for sailing programs. ✉ *Moll d'Espanya 1, Port Vell* ☎ *93/221–4859* ⊕ *www.maritimbarcelona.org.*

**Ronáutica.** Rent a sailboat, power craft, or windsurfing equipment here. ✉ *Moll de la Marina 11, Port Olímpic* ☎ *93/221–0380.*

## SOCCER

**Futbol Club Barcelona,** almost 110 years old, is Real Madrid's perennial nemesis (and vice-versa) as well as a sociological and historical phenomenon of deep significance in Catalonia. Supported by more than 200,000 season ticket holders, the team was the only legal outlet for Catalan nationalist sentiment during the 40-year Franco regime. Despite giant budgets and the world's best players, Barcelona's results never seemed to live up to full potential, an anomaly Catalans were quick to blame on Madrid and the influence and manipulation, real or imagined, of the Franco regime. This all changed after 1975, with Barcelona winning four consecutive league titles and 10 of the last 27. Nevertheless, Madrid's nine European cups (to Barcelona's two) are still a sore point for long-suffering Barcelona soccer fans. Ticket windows at Access 14 to the stadium are open Mon.–Sat. and game-day Sundays 10–2 and 5–8; you can also buy tickets at Servicaixa, an ATM at Caixa de Catalunya bank entrances and elsewhere. ✉ *Camp Nou, Arístides Maillol, Les Corts* ☎ *93/496–3600* ⊕ *www.fcbarcelona.com.*

> ### EL BARÇA: MORE THAN A CLUB
>
> *El Barça: més qu'un club* is the motto for this soccer superpower out to win every championship. Basketball, roller-skate hockey, and team handball have all won national and European titles, while the club's star-studded soccer team has conquered dozens of Spanish Leagues and European championships in 1992 and 2006. "More than a club" refers to FC Barcelona's key role in Catalonian nationalism. With teams at all levels, el Barça is financed by 500,00 season ticket holders generating an annual operating capital of more than 100 million euros.

**RCD Espanyol,** another local first-division team, attracts somewhat less attention. You can purchase tickets at the stadium or at Servicaixa machines. ✉ *Olympic Stadium, Passeig Olímpic 17–19, Montjuïc* ☎ *93/425–1482* ⊕ *www.rcdespanyol.com.*

The **Spain Ticket Bureau,** not far from the Columbus monument on Rambla dels Caputxins, can score seats for home FC Barcelona games as well as any other event in Spain. ✉ *Rambla 31, Rambla* ☎ *902/903912* ⊕ *www.spainticketbureau.com* Ⓜ *Liceu.*

## SWIMMING

All fees are €8–€10 per day.

**Club Natació de Barceloneta.** Also known as Complex Esportiu Municipal Banys Sant Sebastià, this club has an indoor pool that overlooks the beach. It's open daily 7 AM–11 PM. ✉ *Passeig Joan de Borbó, Barceloneta* ☎ *93/221–0010* ⊕ *www.cnb.es.*

**Parc de la Creueta del Coll.** This huge outdoor pool is uphill from Parc Güell. It's open daily from 8 AM to 11 PM. ✉ *Castellterçol, Vall d'Hebron* ☎ *93/219–3589.*

**Dir Diagonal.** This center in upper Barcelona has indoor and outdoor pools. Opens daily from 8 AM to 11 PM. ✉ *Ganduxer 25–27, Sant Gervasi* ☎ *93/202–2202* ⊕ *www.dirfitness.es* .

**Piscines Bernat Picornell.** The daily fee at this swimming center with indoor and outdoor pools includes use of a sauna, gymnasium, and fitness equipment. It's open daily 7 AM–midnight. ✉ *Av. del Estadi 30–40, Montjuïc* ☎ *93/423–4041* ⊕ *www.picornell.com.*

## TENNIS

**Trofeo Godó – Open Seat.** Barcelona's main tennis tournament, held in late April, is a clay court event long considered a French Open warmup. For tickets to this event, consult with the Real Club de Tenis de Barcelona or the tournament Web site listed below beginning in late February. Tickets may also be obtained at www.servicaixa. com. ✉ *Carrer de Bosch i Gimpera 21, Pedralbes* ☎ *902–33–22–11* ⊕ *www.openseatbarcelona.com/en/tickets.*

**Centre Municipal Tennis Vall d'Hebron.** The Olympic tennis facilities here are open daily 8 AM–11 PM; clay costs €18 per hour, hard courts €14. ✉ *Passeig Vall d'Hebron 178–196, Vall d'Hebron* ☎ *93/427–6500* ⊕ *www.fctennis.org.*

**Complex Esportiu Municipal Can Caralleu.** A 30-minute walk uphill from the Reina Elisenda subway stop (FFCC de la Generalitat), this center offers hard courts and clean air. It's open daily 8 AM–11 PM and costs €10 per hour by day, €12 by night. *(Can Caralleu Sports Complex)* ✉ *Carrer Esports 2–8, Pedralbes* ☎ *93/203–7874* ⊕ *www.claror.org.*

# Shopping

**WORD OF MOUTH**

"You might be surprised that the shopping is so good [in Barcelona]. There are some great Spanish labels (Zara, of course, for affordable trendy clothes, but also Camper for funky shoes...)."

–Kate_W

By George
Semler

**DEFINED BY ORIGINALITY AND RELATIVE** affordability on local products, shopping in Barcelona has developed into a roaring fashion, design, gourmet-food, and crafts fair that expands daily. The fact that different parts of town provide distinct contexts for shopping makes exploring the city and browsing boutiques inclusive activities. The Ciutat Vella, especially the Born-Ribera area, is rich in small-crafts shops, young designers, and an endless potpourri of artisans and merchants operating in restored medieval spaces that are often as dazzling as the wares on sale. Even (perhaps especially) the pharmacies and grocery stores of Barcelona are often sumptuous aesthetic feasts, filled with Art Nouveau effects or Gothic details.

Shopping for design objects and chic fashion in the Eixample is like buying art supplies at the Louvre: it's an Art Nouveau architecture park filled with its own children—textiles, furnishings, curios, and knick-knacks of every kind. Wherever you go, expect surprises; a search for any specific shop or boutique will inevitably lead you past a dozen emporiums that you didn't know were there (probably because they weren't, as hot new shops open daily). Original and surprising, yet wearable clothing items—what one indefatigable shopper described as "elegant funk"—are Barcelona's signature contribution to fashion. Rather than copying the runways, Barcelona designers are relentlessly daring (naturally, as heirs of Gaudí, Dalí, and Miró) and innovative, combining fine materials with masterful workmanship in fresh ways.

Browsing through shops in this originality-obsessed metropolis feels more like museum hopping than a shopping spree, although it can, of course, be both. Design shops like Vinçon and BD Ediciones de Diseño delight the eye and stimulate the imagination, while the Passeig del Born is attracting hip young designers from all corners of the globe. Passeig de Gràcia has joined the ranks of Paris's Champs Elysées as one of the great shopping avenues in the world, with the planet's fashion houses amply represented, from Armani to Zara. Exploring Barcelona's antiques district along Carrer Banys Nous and Carrer de la Palla (some of these shops are built up against 4th-century Roman walls) is always an adventure. The shops opening daily around Santa Maria del Mar in the Born-Ribera district range from Catalan and international design retailers to shoe and leather-handbag designers, to T-shirt decorators, to dealers in nuts and spices or coffee emporiums. The megastores in Plaça de Catalunya, along the Diagonal, and in L'Illa Diagonal farther west are commercial cornucopias selling fashions, furniture, furs, books, music, and everything else under the sun. The villagelike environment of both Sarrià and Gràcia lends an intimate warmth to antiques or clothes shopping, with friendly boutique owners and sales personnel adding a personal touch often lost in the mainstream commerce of some of the city's high-end fashion icons.

Barcelona's tourist offices in the airport and in Plaça de Catalunya give away a free shopping guide booklet (updated annually) with an accompanying map and complete instructions and advice on everything from how to get your value-added tax refund at the airport to how to use the special BSL (Barcelona Shopping Line) bus that covers the length of the city's 5-km (3-mi) shopping circuit. With an all-day T-shopping Card ticket (€10), you can hop and off the shuttle and its leather seats until it (and you) are done (weekday service 7:30 AM–9:45 PM, Saturday 9 AM–9:20 PM). Stops are served about every seven minutes. Most stores are open Monday–Saturday 9–1:30 and 5–8, but some close in the afternoon. Virtually all close Sunday.

## SHOPPING DISTRICTS

### BARRI GÒTIC

The Rambla and the Gothic Quarter have shops along Carrer Ferran and Carrer Portaferrissa (one long shop, with shoe stores, clothing designers, and a chaotic range of goods from acorn-fed hams to wide-brimmed hats). The always-bustling Porta de l'Àngel, where El Corte Inglés has its music and books department on the corner of Carrer de Santa Ana, is a frenzy of consumerism. The streets around Plaça de Pi and along Carrer del Pi and Carrer Petritxol are lined with every type of store, shop, and boutique. Carrer Canuda and Carrer de Santa Ana are peppered with bookstores, jewelry stores, and gift shops. Antiques shopping alone could keep you busy for days in the Gothic Quarter, with some two dozen of the best shops along Carrer Banys Nous, Baixada de Santa Eulàlia, and, especially, Carrer de la Palla.

### BORN-RIBERA

The Ribera and Born neighborhoods, the old waterfront district around the Santa Maria del Mar basilica, seem to breed boutiques and shops of all kinds continuously. Design and clothing shops are the main draw. Check along Carrer Banys Vells and, one street north of Carrer Montcada, Carrer Flassaders for design items, jewelry, and knickknacks of all kinds. Carrer Vidrieria is lined with shops beginning with Atalanta Manufactura's silk-printing shop and ending in Plaça de les Olles, where hometown clothing designer Custo Barcelona owns the corner across from the wildly popular tapas bar Cal Pep. The aromatic Casa Gispert, just behind the Santa Maria del Mar basilica on Carrer Sombrerers, is not to be missed, nor is Baraka, the Moroccan goods expert on Carrer Canvis Vells. Vila Viniteca up Carrer Agullers near Via Laietana is always an interesting Bacchic browse.

### EIXAMPLE

Beginning with the Triangle d'Or at the top of the Rambla and up the Passeig de Gràcia, now rightly considered one of the world's greatest shopping streets, the Eixample is a compendium of design and fashion stores that could take years to fully explore. Eixample means "Expansion" (from the Spanish verb *ensanchar*) and, indeed, not only is this neighborhood immensely wide,

> ## TOP 5
>
> ■ Saffron: the lightest, most aromatic, and best-value buy left in all of Spain.
>
> ■ Rope-soled espadrilles from La Manual Alpargatera.
>
> ■ Avarca sandals (also called Menorquinas) from Menorca.
>
> ■ Custo Barcelona's ever-original tops.
>
> ■ Ceramics from all over Spain at Art Escudellers.

## BLITZ TOURS

### ARCHITECTURE, DESIGN & SHOPPING TOUR

Start at Gaudí's **La Pedrera** (aka Casa Milà), on the corner of Passeig de Gràcia and Carrer Provença. Take a walk through the attic display and the rooftop with the iconic hooded warrior chimneys. **Vinçon,** Barcelona's best design store, is a few steps up the street. The design store **Gimeno 102** is just a couple of buildings farther up the street. Around the corner on the Diagonal is **Casa Baró de Quadras,** now home of the cultural and business center Casa Àsia, at No. 373. Sweep farther east and down Carrer Roger de Llúria. To the left on Carrer Mallorca, two blocks down, you will see Casa Thomas, home of **BD Ediciones de Diseño,** Barcelona's *other* top design emporium. By this time, you might be needing refreshment. **Mantequeria Can Ravell,** at Carrer d'Aragó No. 313, a nonpareil foodie haven, will provide a place to sit and an unforgettable cornucopia of Catalan flavors. From here, move back toward Passeig de Gràcia past **La Mansana de la Discòrdia,** where the three key architects of Barcelona's mid-19th-century Art Nouveau epidemic squared off, and pop into **Bagués Joieria** in Puig i Cadafalch's Casa Amatller for a gander at some jewelry design. Just down the sidewalk under Domènech i Montaner's Casa Lleó Morera is **Loewe,** for some men's and women's fashions. Next corner down is **Hermès** on Consell de Cent with myriad fashion outlets nearby, among them **Purificación García,** famous for fabrics and treatment thereof and **Montblanc Boutique** for leather goods. At the next corner, Carrer Diputació, either way you turn, you will find more shopping opportunities. Another block down and across the street is **Zara,** on the corner of Gran Via de les Corts Catalanes and Passeig de Gràcia. Next down are **Furest** and **Gonzalo Comella,** with a restorative break at the perennial favorite caffeine stop **Bracafé** just to your left off Passeig de Gràcia on Carrer Casp. Now you're only two blocks from Gaudí's Casa Calvet at Carrer Casp No. 48.

### GOTHIC QUARTER ART & ANTIQUES

Start at the Plaça del Pi. A brief jaunt up Carrer Petritxol offers a look at **Sala Parés,** dean of Barcelona art galleries. Back through Plaça Sant Josep Oriol and up Carrer de la Palla, you will find numerous antiques stores and art galleries. The intersection with Carrer Banys Nous is surrounded by unusual flavors: **Caelum** offers teas, pastries, honeys, and candied egg yolks. Moving left down Carrer de la Palla, following the curve of the 4th-century Roman walls, you'll find a dozen more antiques emporiums, including **Erika Neidermeier** and **Artur Ramón.** An about-face back up Carrer Banys Nous will bring you past **L'Arca de l'Àvia** along with a handful of antiques shops all the way up to the Baixada de Santa Eulàlia coming in from the left. Here, overhead to the right, look for the tiles of the Jewish baths that occupied this street. A little farther along Banys Nous is **Heritage,** a vintage-clothing specialist. For a browse through several more antiques stores, walk up the Baixada de Santa Eulàlia through Carrer de Sant Sever all the way to the cathedral cloister.

stretching from Plaça de les Glòries all the way out to Plaça Francesc Macià, but it can cut a wide swathe through your bank statement before you know it. (For those with a fiscal death wish, Fermin Puig's nonpareil Drolma restaurant in the Hotel Majestic is the place to taste Barcelona's finest cuisine).

The Diagonal is lined with fashion denizens ranging from Adolfo Domínguez and Antonio Miró to Mango and Zara. Vinçon and BD Ediciones de Diseño are the chief design stores, while the Moderniste grocery store Murria, or Mantequeria Can Ravell, will keep foodies dazzled. Other targets of opportunity would include Carrer Tuset north of the Diagonal, with a Habitat store and a handful of small boutiques including the perennial tailor Conti. But this is just the tip of the shopping iceberg: turn yourself loose and discover the factory outlet stores along Carrer Girona or wander into the Bermuda Triangle of antiques shopping at the Gothsland Galeria d'Art in the Bulevard dels Antiquaris at Passeig de Gràcia 55–57.

## EL RAVAL

The Raval has traditionally held a reputation for separating you from your possessions rather than for adding to them (and you should still stay alert here for pickpockets)—but the MACBA, Barcelona's Richard Meier–designed contemporary art museum, has brought with it an upsurge of jewelry, art, and design shops in and around Plaça dels Àngels and the upper part of the neighborhood between Carrer Pelai and Carrer Hospital. Carrer Tallers, just below Plaça Catalunya, is the recorded music street of Barcelona, even spilling around the corner into Carrer Bonsuccès. The bookstore Central del Raval on Carrer Elisabets is a wonderful place to spend time, with lunch available in its excellent restaurant. Carrer Doctor Dou, once famous only for the police station students fervently hoped never to see the inside of, now has a handsome array of design and crafts shops, while Carrer Notariat is the home of an interesting collection of crafts and gift shops.

## GRÀCIA

The onetime outlying village of Gràcia is increasingly interesting for shoppers, with design stores and galleries and crafts studios along Carrer Verdi, Carrer Torrijos, and around the Mercat de la Llibertat. Plaça del Sol and Plaça Rius i Taulet abound in fashion and jewelry shops, along with arty cafés and taverns. On Plaça de la Revolució de Setembre de 1868, several boutiques specialize in everything from products from India to children's fashions.

## SARRIÀ

Even farther uphill than Gràcia, the formerly independent village of Sarrià is filling with antiques stores and indie clothing and fashion designers, so a trip through this charming neighborhood, which retains much of its small-town character, is hardly the shopping boondocks. Antiques shops can be found on Carrer de la Creu, Carrer Cornet i Mas, Plaça Artós, and Major de Sarrià, and there are more on the way. In addition, there are two branches of the famous Foix pastry store in Plaça de Sarrià and Major de Sarrià and two excellent wine stores: Iskia on Major de Sarrià, and La Cave on the corner of Carrer de la Creu and Avinguda Foix. Worth seeking out is the master florist's shop, the appropriately named Flora Miserachs at No. 27 Carrer Avió Plus Ultra.

## BOUTIQUES & SPECIALTY STORES

### ANTIQUES

Antiques shopping is centered in the Barri Gòtic, where Carrer de la Palla, Carrer Banys Nous, and the Baixada de Santa Eulàlia are lined with shops full of prints, maps, books, ceramic tiles, paintings, and furniture. An antiques market is held in front of the cathedral every Thursday 10–8. The Bulevard dels Antiquaris at Passeig de Gràcia 55 concentrates 73 antiques shops, while the end of the Rambla and Port Vell have outdoor markets on Sunday. In upper Barcelona, the village of Sarrià is becoming an antiquer's destination, with shops along Cornet i Mas, Pedró de la Creu, and Major de Sarrià.

**Acanto.** This shop, in the pivotal Bulevard dels Antiquaris, is a major clearinghouse for buying and selling a wide range of items from paintings, furniture, silver, sculpture, and bronzes to wood carvings, marble, clocks, watches, tapestries, porcelain, and ceramics. ⊠*Passeig de Gràcia 55–57, Eixample* ☎*93/215–3297* Ⓜ*Passeig de Gràcia.*

**Antigüedades Erika Niedermeier.** Near the Carrer Banys Nous end of Carrer de la Palla, Erika Niedermeier trades in collectors' items or objects dating from the 14th to the 18th century. Ceramics, painted copper, silver, ivory, stained glass, wrought iron, and tooled leather from the Middle Ages and from the Renaissance (much of it crafted by Islamic or Jewish artisans) find their way through this hands-on, history book of a store. ⊠*Carrer de la Palla 11, Barri Gòtic* ☎*93/412–7924* Ⓜ*Liceu.*

**Antigüedades Fernández.** Bric-a-brac is piled high in this workshop near the middle of this slender artery in the medieval Jewish Quarter. This master craftsman restores and sells antique furniture of all kinds. Stop by and stick your head in for the fragrance of the shellacs and wood shavings and a look at one of the last simple carpentry and woodworking shops you'll encounter in contemporary, design-mad, early-21st-century Barcelona. ⊠*Carrer Sant Domènec del Call 9, Barri Gòtic* ☎*93/301–0045* Ⓜ*Liceu.*

**Centre d'Antiquaris.** Look carefully for the little stairway leading into this 73-store mother ship of all antiques arcades off Passeig de Gràcia. You never know what you might find here in this eclectic serendipity: dolls, icons, Roman or Visigothic objects, paintings, furniture, cricket kits, fly rods, or toys from a century ago. ⊠*Passeig de Gràcia 55, Eixample* ☎*93/215–4499* Ⓜ*Passeig de Gràcia.*

**Gothsland.** Art Nouveau furniture, art objects, and decorative paraphernalia share space here with sculpted terra-cotta figures, vases, mirrors, and furniture, nearly all in Barcelona's signature Moderniste style. Paintings by Art Nouveau stars from Santiago Rusiñol to Ramón Casas might turn up here, along with lamps, clocks, and curios of all kinds. ⊠*Consell de Cent 331, Eixample* ☎*93/488–1922* Ⓜ*Passeig de Gràcia.*

**L'Arca de L'Àvia.** As the name of the place ("grandmother's trunk") suggests, this is a miscellaneous potpourri of ancient goods of all kinds, especially period clothing from shoes to gloves to hats and hairpins. Despite the found-object attitude and sense of the place, they're not giving away these vintage baubles, so don't be surprised at the costumes' cost. ⊠ *Banys Nous 20, Barri Gòtic* ☎ *93/302–1598* ⊕ *www. larcadelavia.com* Ⓜ *Liceu.*

**Novecento.** A standout primarily for being so out of place among all the design emporiums and fashion denizens on this great white way of high commerce, Novecento is an antique-jewelry store with abundant items from all epochs and movements from Victorian to Art Nouveau to Belle Epoque. ⊠ *Passeig de Gràcia 75, Eixample* ☎ *93/215–1183* Ⓜ *Passeig de Gràcia.*

## ART GALLERIES
*For art-gallery nightlife, see the Nightlife & the Arts chapter.*

Art openings and gallery browsing are a way of life in Barcelona. Any time you see wine being consumed in an art gallery, assume that you are invited and have a look around. A key cluster of art galleries is lined up on Carrer Consell de Cent between Passeig de Gràcia and Carrer Balmes and around the corner on Rambla de Catalunya. In the Gothic Quarter, Carrer Petritxol, Carrer de la Palla, and Carrer Banys Nous have several interesting galleries. The Born-Ribera quarter is another art destination, with Carrer Montcada and the parallel Carrer Banys Vells the top streets to prowl.

**Antonio de Barnola.** Installations with an architectural bent are the regulars here, with work by Catalan conceptualist Margarita Andreu, and Basques such as Itziar Okariz and José Ramón Amondarain among the regular artists. ⊠ *C/Palau 4, Barri Gòtic* ☎ *93/412–2214* Ⓜ *Jaume I, Liceu.*

**Artur Ramón—Espai Col.leccionisme.** Artur Ramon shows paintings, sculptures, and drawings, such as those by 18th-century engraver and architect Giovanni Battista Piranesi. In addition, antiques, glass, and ceramics find their way to this very seriously orchestrated collector's haven. ⊠ *Carrer de la Palla 23 and 25, Barri Gòtic* ☎ *93/302–5970* Ⓜ *Liceu.*

**Artur Ramón—Espai Contemporani.** An eclectic selection of young artists from Catalonia, Spain, France, Germany, and beyond usually hovers near the edge of the latest vanguards. Notable shows here have exhibited the fascinating Spanish-Argentinian abstractionist Esteban Lisa, the realist paintings of the Santilari brothers from Barcelona, and the colorist work of German artist Anke Blaue. ⊠ *Carrer de la Palla 10, Barri Gòtic* ☎ *93/302–5970* Ⓜ *Liceu.*

**Galeria Aunkan.** Located near the MACBA, Barcelona's contemporary art museum, Galeria Aunkan showcases contemporary and avant-garde installations from artists ranging from Jesus Vilallonga to Tom Carr and Joan Pere Viladecans. ⊠ *Ferlandina 32-D, Raval* ☎ *93/301–3027* Ⓜ *Catalunya.*

**Galeria Carles Taché.** An always-busy exhibition space with shows ranging from Alexis de Villar's African prints to Lawrence Carroll's colorful cre-

**CLOSE UP**

# Move Over, Milan

Ever since the 1992 Olympic Games blew the lid off any lingering doubts about Barcelona's contemporary creative potential, new clothing designers and boutiques have been proliferating. Barcelona Fashion Week (BFW) has now taken its place as one of Europe's most important fashion meets alongside those of Paris, London, and Milan. Meanwhile, the Pasarel.la Gaudí, formerly Barcelona's main event, has become Barcelona Bridal Week, a runway dedicated to nuptial styles. Barcelona Fashion Week, largely stripped of public financing, has forged a path of its own, relying largely on young local designers as well as traditional heavyweights such as Antonio Miró, Armand Basi, Gonzalo Comellas, and Adolfo Domínguez. Even top-name Madrid designers such as Victorio & Lucchino, Miriam Ocáriz, and Soul Aguilar, citing the Catalan capital's innovative image, prefer to show in Barcelona instead of at Madrid's own Cibeles fashion event.

Meanwhile, those hot street styles admired around town for so long have jumped to center stage. Bread & Butter Barcelona (BBB), begun in Berlin and described as a street-fashion trade show, has been so successful in Barcelona that winter and summer events are now built into the city calendar for the foreseeable future. The July 2007 conclave brought over 1000 designers from 105 countries and more than 75,000 visitors to multifaceted proceedings encompassing art, architecture, music, dance, catwalks, tastings, piercings, body art, and frenzied spates of sponsored parties. The B&B Brand Bible lists over a thousand designers from Custo and Desigual to undergrounders such De Puta Madre, Kult, and System5.

Not without a sense of humor and delight, some events take on *Zoolander*-proportions, with ever-zanier happenings such as Antonio Miró's BFW 2006 catwalk held in Barcelona's infamous Carcel Modelo, the model prison constructed in the early 20th century, or his January 2007 runway featuring illegal immigrants. The semispontaneous fringe Fashion Freak gatherings in different venues around town culminate with the Freak Boutique in the Café Noir. "Coolhunters," undercover style sleuths, prowl the back alleys looking for details of urban chic that could go from Raval to runway to rack in a matter of weeks.

Oh, and the shops! From local clothing stars Zara and Custo to whimsical design objects at BD (Barcelona Design) or Vinçon, to old crafts standbys such as La Manual Alpargatera or Cereria Subirà, Barcelona is becoming as famous for shopping as for architecture and design. El Born, the old waterfront district tucked in behind Santa Maria del Mar in the Barri de la Ribera, teems with young artisans and designers; the Eixample, the midtown grid labyrinth of Art Nouveau architecture, is rife with innovatively designed shops selling equally original items of all kinds; and the outlying villages of Gràcia and Sarrià are becoming bite-size boutique havens with much more to admire than quiet streets and leafy palms.

ations, Carles Taché displays painting and photography by established artists ✉ *Consell de Cent 290, Eixample* ☎ *93/487–8836* ⊕ *www.carlestache.com* Ⓜ *Passeig de Gràcia.*

**Galeria Claramunt.** Another gallery that seems to have sprung up in the reflected light of the Richard Meier–designed Museu d'Art Contemporani de Barcelona, a stop here is a good postscript to an exploration of the museum's treasures. ✉ *Ferlandina 27, Raval* ☎ *93/442–1847* Ⓜ *Catalunya.*

**Galeria Joan Prats.** "La Prats" has been one of the city's top galleries since the 1920s, showing international painters and sculptors from Henry Moore to Antoni Tàpies. Barcelona painter Joan Miró was a prime force in the founding of the gallery when he became friends

FASHION MEETS INTERIOR DESIGN

As if attempting to compete with Barcelona's landmarks, many of the best boutiques here have had leading contemporary interior decorators and merit visits whether purchases materialize or not. Emporiums such as Vinçon, BD (Barcelona Design), Habitat, and stores such as Arkitektura, Ras Gallery, or Greek display furnishings and interior-design objects in designer settings. And Sita Murt, the bookshop Central del Raval, Le Boudoir, La Carte des Vins, Xocoa, or Julie Sohn are as much about the space's interior design as the merchandise on sale.

with Joan Prats. The motifs of bonnets and derbies on the gallery's facade attest to the trade of Prats's father. José Maria Sicilia and Juan Ugalde have shown here, while Perejaume and Eulàlia Valldosera are regulars. ✉ *Rambla de Catalunya 54, Eixample* ☎ *93/216–0284* Ⓜ *Passeig de Gràcia.*

**Galeria Maeght.** The Paris-based Maeght gallery is not as prestigious in Barcelona, but the Renaissance palace it inhabits is spectacular. The list of superstar artists who have hung work here ranges from Antoni Tàpies to the late Pablo Palazuelo to the late Eduardo Chillida. It's usually a good idea to drop in during any Born-Ribera browsing and grazing tour to have a look at the permanent works downstairs or the current exhibit up on the first floor. ✉ *Montcada 25, Born-Ribera* ☎ *93/310–4245* ⊕ *www.maeght.com* Ⓜ *Jaume I.*

**Galeria Maria Villalba.** In the Eixample's *Dreta* (right side, looking away from the sea), this gallery is a Barcelona mainstay and well worth seeking out if you're in the neighborhood. A contemporary painting and sculpture specialist, Maria Villalba has shown abstract sculptures by Lilia Luján and Marisa Ordóñez and paintings by Sophie Dumont, Eloisa Ibarra, and Francisco Castillo Real. ✉ *Bailèn 110, Eixample* ☎ *93/457–5177* ⊕ *www.galeriamariavillalba.com* Ⓜ *Verdaguer, Girona.*

**Galeria Sargadelos.** A Galician porcelain store with an exhibition space dedicated to showing ceramicists and young artists from Spain's northwestern region of Galicia, Sargadelos is an interesting and unusual point of reference in the upper Eixample. ✉ *Provença 276, Eixample* ☎ *93/215–0368* ⊕ *www.sargadelos.com* Ⓜ *Provença.*

**Galeria Toni Tàpies.** The son of Barcelona's most esteemed living painter Antoni Tàpies, Toni Tàpies shows young artists from Catalonia, visiting painters from as far away as Canada, and even his father's recent work.

✉ *Consell de Cent 282, Eixample* ☎ *93/487–6402* ⊕ *www.tonitapies. com* Ⓜ *Catalunya.*

**Joan Gaspar.** One of Barcelona's most prestigious galleries, Joan Gaspart and his father before him brought Picasso and Miró back to Catalunya during the '50s and '60s, along with other artists considered politically taboo during the Franco regime. These days you'll find leading contemporary lights such as Joan Pere Viladecans, Rafols Casamada, or Susana Solano here. ✉ *Pl. Letamendi 1, Eixample* ☎ *93/323–0748* Ⓜ *Passeig de Gràcia.*

**Metrònom.** Radical performance and installation art, erotic photography, and video work inevitably make their way to this gallery at the uptown end of the Born. ✉ *Carrer Fussina 4, Born-Ribera* ☎ *93/268– 4298* Ⓜ *Jaume I.*

**Sala Dalmau.** Part of the always-boiling Consell de Cent scene, Sala Dalmau shows an interesting and heterodox range of Catalan and international artists. ✉ *Consell de Cent 347, Eixample* ☎ *93/215–4592* Ⓜ *Passeig de Gràcia.*

**Sala Parés.** The dean of Barcelona's art galleries, Sala Parés has shown every Barcelona artist of note since it opened in 1840. Picasso and Miró showed here, as did Casas and Rossinyol before them. ✉ *Petritxol 5, Barri Gòtic* ☎ *93/318–7008* Ⓜ *Liceu, Catalunya.*

**Sala Rovira.** Both established and up-and-coming artists, including local stars Tom Carr and Blanca Vernis, have shown their work at this upper Rambla de Catalunya gallery. ✉ *Rambla de Catalunya 62, Eixample* ☎ *93/215–2092* Ⓜ *Provença.*

**Taller 164.** For a change of pace, this one-man, one-woman gallery shows works and works-in-progress by the American artists who live and labor on their craft there. Just up from Sarrià's Tram-Tram and Vivanda restaurants, take a peek in if you're in the neighborhood. ✉ *Major de Sarrià 164, Sarrià* ☎ *93/205–6338* Ⓜ *Sarrià.*

**Trama.** Another Petritxol favorite, Trama, with occasional exceptions, tends to hang paintings that look as if they might be happier in low-price hostelry establishments, but the gallery merits a look if you find yourself on this picturesque little passageway. ✉ *Petritxol 8, Barri Gòtic* ☎ *93/317–4877* Ⓜ *Liceu, Catalunya.*

## BOOKS

Bookstore browsing in Barcelona is always quiet and curiosity-provoking. Besides the stores listed below, El Corte Inglés department stores stock a limited selection of English guidebooks and novels. FNAC, in L'Illa Diagonal, also has English titles available.

**Altair.** Barcelona's premier travel and adventure bookstore stocks many titles in English. Book presentations and events scheduled here feature a wide range of interesting authors from Alpinists to Africanists. ✉ *Gran Via 616, Eixample* ☎ *93/342–7171* Ⓜ *Catalunya.*

**BCN Books.** This midtown Eixample bookstore is a prime address for books in English. ✉ *Roger de Llúria 118, Eixample* ☎ *93/476–3343* Ⓜ *Passeig de Gràcia.*

**Casa del Llibre.** This central location on Barcelona's most important shopping street is a major book feast with a wide variety of English titles. ⊠*Passeig de Gràcia 62, Eixample* ☎*93/272–3480* Ⓜ*Passeig de Gràcia.*

**FNAC.** For musical recordings and the latest book publications, this is one of Barcelona's most dependable and happening addresses. Regular concerts, presentations of new recordings, and art exhibits take place in FNAC. Much more than a bookstore, it's an important cultural resource. ⊠*Centre Comercial L'Illa, Av. Diagonal 555–559, Eixample* ☎*93/444–5900* ⊕*www.fnac.es* Ⓜ*Maria Cristina, Les Corts* ⊠*Pl. Catalunya 4, Eixample* ☎*93/344–1800* Ⓜ*Catalunya.*

FodorśChoice **La Central.** Hands-down, Barcelona's best bookstore for years, La Cen-
★ tral has creaky, literary wooden floors and piles of recent publications with many interesting titles in English. ⊠*Carrer Mallorca 237, Eixample* ☎*93/487–5018* Ⓜ*Provença.*

**La Central del Raval.** This luscious bookstore in the former chapel of the Casa de la Misericòrdia sells books amid stunning architecture and offers an excellent restaurant as well. ⊠*Carrer Elisabets 6, Raval* ☎*93/317–0293* Ⓜ*Catalunya.*

**Laie.** A café, restaurant, jazz-performance, and cultural-events space, Laie is rimmed with stacks of books, creating the perfect sanctuary. ⊠*Pau Claris 85, Eixample* ☎*93/318–1357* Ⓜ*Catalunya.*

**Palau de la Virreina.** The bookstore in this cultural center and art gallery stocks good titles (some in English) on art, design, and Barcelona in general. ⊠*Rambla 99, Rambla* ☎*93/301–7775* Ⓜ*Liceu.*

**Quera.** This is the bookstore to seek out if you're interested in the Pyrenees or in exploring any part of the Catalonian hinterlands. Maps, charts, and books detailing everything from Pyrenean ponds and lakes to Romanesque chapels are available in this diminutive giant of a resource. ⊠*Petritxol 2, Barri Gòtic* ☎*93/318–0743* Ⓜ*Liceu.*

**Ras Gallery.** Specialized in books and magazines on art, architecture, design, and photography with a store design by Jaime Salazar, Ras neatly connects with the gallery's main theme. ⊠*Carrer Doctor Dou 10, Raval* ☎*93/412–7199* Ⓜ*Catalunya, Liceu.*

## CERAMICS

Although perusing the smaller establishments is always worthwhile, Barcelona's big department stores, including El Corte Inglés, FNAC, and Habitat, are good bets for ceramics shoppers.

FodorśChoice **Art Escudellers.** Ceramic pieces from all over Spain converge here at both
★ of these stores across the street from the restaurant Los Caracoles; more than 140 different artisans are represented, with maps showing what part of Spain the work is from. There are wine, cheese, and ham tastings downstairs, and you can even throw a pot yourself in the display workshop. ⊠*Carrer Escudellers 23–25, Barri Gòtic* ☎*93/412–6801* Ⓜ*Liceu, Drassanes.*

**Baraka.** Barcelona's prime purveyor of Moroccan goods, ceramics chief among them, Baraka is the city's general cultural commissar for matters relating to Spain's neighbor to the south. The pre-haggled goods here are generally cheaper (and the quality better) than you could bring back from Morocco. ⊠*Canvis Vells 2, Born-Ribera* ☎*93/268–4220* ⊕*www.barakaweb.com* Ⓜ*Jaume I.*

**Caixa de Fang.** Glazed tiles, glass objects, and colorful sets of cups and saucers are on sale at this little shop just off Plaça Sant Jaume. Translatable as "Box of Mud" in Catalan, Caixa de Fang shows handmade earthenware cooking vessels from all over Spain as well as boxwood and olive-wood kitchen utensils. ⊠*Freneria 1, Barri Gòtic* ☎*93/315–1704* Ⓜ*Jaume I.*

**Espai Vidre.** Glass is the thing here. This gallery allows you to admire, study, research, and buy a wide range of this ancient yet innovative material. ⊠*Carrer dels Àngels 8, Raval* ☎*93/318–9833* Ⓜ*Catalunya.*

**Itaca.** Everything from Lladró porcelain to standard ceramic plates, bowls, and inspired objects of all kinds, including pottery from Talavera de la Reina and La Bisbal, finds its way to the surface here. ⊠*Carrer Ferrán 26, Barri Gòtic* ☎*93/301–3044* Ⓜ*Liceu, Catalunya.*

**Lladró.** This Valencia company is famed worldwide for the beauty and quality of its figures. Barcelona's only Lladró factory store, this location has exclusive pieces of work, custom-designed luxury items of gold and porcelain, classic and original works, and a video explaining the Lladró production process in their Valencia factory. Fans of this idiosyncratic porcelain can even organize factory visits. The store guarantees all of its products for a full year after purchase. ⊠*Passeig de Gràcia 11, Eixample* ☎*93/270–1253* ⊕*www.lladro.com* Ⓜ*Catalunya.*

**Molsa—Nou i Vell.** An address you will almost certainly pass, at the beginning of Carrer del Pi next to the Santa Maria del Pi church, this is a long-standing Barcelona ceramics institution, with, as the name suggests, both old pieces and new. Lladró, ceramics, tiles, and pottery are all colorfully stacked in this attractive space. ⊠*Pl. Sant Josep Oriol 1, Barri Gòtic* ☎*93/302–3103* Ⓜ*Liceu.*

**Neoceramica.** This is the store to visit if you need an order of handsome tiles for your kitchen back home. With some truly striking patterns and the shipping system to get them to you in one piece (each tile, that is), you can trust the Vidal-Quadras clan for care and quality. ⊠*Mandri 43, Sarrià* ☎*93/211–8958* Ⓜ*Sarrià, El Putxet.*

## CIGARS

**Gimeno 102.** Smoking items of every kind along with pipes and cigarettes of all sorts are sold in this tobacco sanctuary, but cigars from Havana are the top draw. ⊠*Rambla 100, Barri Gòtic* ☎*93/302–0983* Ⓜ*Liceu.*

**L'Estanc de Laietana.** Famous for its underground cave and humidor at sea level, this is a shrine to the Cuban cigar unparalleled in Barcelona. Cigarettes and rolling tobacco in an all-but-infinite variety of brands are also staples here. ⊠*Via Laietana 4, Barri Gòtic* ☎*93/310–1034* Ⓜ*Catalunya.*

## CLOTHING

Savvy international clothing shoppers and fashion mavens all seem to agree that Barcelona women of all ages and the designers who dress them have a special knack for throwing themselves together with elegant nonchalance, an uncanny talent best termed as "funky grace." Spain's Milan-with-an-attitude, Barcelona remains on the cutting edge of a booming national fashion front. Clothing, jewelry, footwear, leather, and lingerie shops have proliferated in all parts of town, from the Born-Ribera district around Santa Maria del Mar to Passeig de Gràcia and out to the Diagonal in both directions, east and west

**Adolfo Domínguez.** One of Barcelona's longtime fashion giants, this is one of Spain's leading clothes designers, with four locations around town. Famed as the creator of the Iberia Airlines uniforms, Adolfo Domínguez has been in the not-too-radical mainstream and forefront of Spanish clothes design for the last quarter century. ⊠*Passeig de Gràcia 89, Eixample* ☎*93/272–0492* Ⓜ*Diagonal* ⊠*Passeig de Gràcia 32, Eixample* ☎*93/487–4170* Ⓜ*Catalunya* ⊠*Diagonal 490, Eixample* ☎*93/215–1339* Ⓜ*Muntaner* ⊠*Pau Casals 5, Eixample* ☎*93/414–1177* ⊕*www.adolfo-dominguez.com* Ⓜ*La Bonanova.*

**Ágatha Ruiz de la Prada.** An Eixample address not to miss, Ágatha Ruiz de la Prada is a Madrid-born, Barcelona-educated design Vesuvius whose bright-color motifs in men's, women's, and children's clothing as well as furniture, carpets, ceramics, lamps, pens, pencils, towels, sheets—even Band-Aids—are characterized by Miró-like stars, suns, moons, hearts, or bright polka dots. ⊠*Consell de Cent 314–316, Eixample* ☎*93/487–1667* Ⓜ*Passeig de Gràcia.*

**Anna Povo.** This stylish boutique near Plaça de les Olles displays an elegant and innovative selection of designer knits for women. In general, Anna Povo's designs are sleek and minimalist, more influenced by Mies van der Rohe than Gaudí. Colors follow this aesthetic, with cool tones in gray and beige. ⊠*Carrer Vidrieria 11, Born-Ribera* ☎*93/319–3561* Ⓜ*Jaume I.*

**Antonio Miró.** With his Miró jeans label making major inroads with the young and fashionably adventurous, classicist Toni Miró is known for the very upper stratosphere of Catalan haute couture, with clean lines fortified by blacks and dark grays for both men and women. Miró's look is, in fact, so unisex that couples of similar sizes could probably get away with sharing some androgynous looks and saving closet space. ⊠*Consell de Cent 349, Eixample* ☎*93/487–0670* Ⓜ*Passeig de Gràcia* ⊠*Valencia 272, Eixample* ☎*93/272–2491* Ⓜ*Passeig de Gràcia* ⊠*Vidrieria 5, Born-Ribera* ☎*93/268–8203* Ⓜ*Jaume I* ⊠*Carrer del Pi 11, Barri Gòtic* ☎*93/342–5875* ⊕*www.antoniomiro.es* Ⓜ*Liceu.*

**Atalanta Manufactura.** Gorgeous hand-painted and silk-screened shawls and scarves tie up this skilled artisan's studio and shop at the corner of Passeig del Born and Carrer Vidrieria; special orders are accepted. ⊠*Passeig del Born 10, Born-Ribera* ☎*93/268–3702* Ⓜ*Jaume I.*

**Benetton.** This international youth favorite and paladin for social freedoms and racial tolerance has three stores in the Eixample showing off their brightly colored threads. ⊠*Passeig de Gràcia 49, Eixample* ☎*93/216–0983* Ⓜ*Catalunya* ⊠*Passeig de Gràcia 69, Eixample* ☎*93/505–2560* Ⓜ*Passeig de Gràcia* ⊠*Rambla de Catalunya 118, Eixample* ☎*93/218–4179* ⊕*www.benetton.com* Ⓜ*Provença.*

**Carolina Herrera.** Originally from Venezuela but professionally based in New York, Carolina Herrera and her international CH logo have become Barcelona mainstays. (Daughter Carolina Herrera Jr. is a Spain resident and married to former bullfighter Miguel Baez.) Fragrances for men and women and clothes with a simple, elegant line—a white blouse is the CH icon—are the staples here. Herrera's light ruffled dresses and edgy urban footwear add feminine flourishes. ☒*Passeig de Gràcia 87, Eixample* ☎*93/272–1584* ⊕*www.carolinaherrera.com* Ⓜ*Diagonal.*

**Conti.** A favorite men's fashions outlet, Conti stocks top international designers such as Armani, Cerruti, Armand Basi, Tommy Hilfiger, Polo Jeans, and Lacoste and serves up everything from suits to shorts. ☒*Av. Diagonal 512, Eixample* ☎*93/416–1211* Ⓜ*Muntaner* ☒*Av. Pau Casals 7, Eixample* ☎*93/201–1933* Ⓜ*La Bonanova* ☒*Carrer Tuset 30, Eixample* ☎*93/217–4954* Ⓜ*Gràcia.*

**Cortana.** A sleek and breezy Balearic-island look for women is what this young designer from Majorca brings to the steamy alleyways of urban Barcelona. The contrast is a refreshing lift in the confines of this narrow street. ☒*Flassaders 43, Born-Ribera* ☎*93/310–3112* Ⓜ*Jaume I.*

**Custo Barcelona.** Ever since Custido Dalmau and his brother David returned from a round-the-world motorcycle tour with visions of California surfing styles dancing in their heads, Custo Barcelona has been a runaway success with coveted clingy cotton tops in bright and cheery hues. Now scattered all over Barcelona and the globe, Custo is scoring even more stratospheric triumphs by expanding into footwear and denim. ☒*Pl. de les Olles 7, Born-Ribera* ☎*93/268–7893* Ⓜ*Jaume I* ☒*Carrer Ferran 36, Barri Gòtic* ☎*93/342–6698* Ⓜ*Liceu* ☒*Av. Diagonal 557, Les Corts* ☎*93/322–2662* ⊕*www.custo-barcelona.com* Ⓜ*Maria Cristina.*

**Furest.** This centenary menswear star, with four stores in town and another at the airport, markets its own designs as well as selections from Armani Jeans, Ralph Lauren, Boss Hugo Boss, Brooksfield, and others. ☒*Passeig de Gràcia 12–14, Eixample* ☎*93/301–2000* Ⓜ*Catalunya* ☒*Av. Diagonal 468, Eixample* ☎*93/416–0665* Ⓜ*Muntaner* ☒*Av. Diagonal 609–615, Eixample* ☎*93/419–4006* Ⓜ*Maria Cristina* ☒*Av. Pau Casals, Eixample* ☎*93/201–2599* ⊕*www.furest.com* Ⓜ*La Bonanova.*

**Giorgio Armani.** The 2,000-square-feet floor space here guarantees plenty of privacy while exploring offerings for men and women. Armani's minimalist esthetic is a good chaser for Barcelona's unabashed baroque cocktail. ☒*Av. Diagonal 620, Eixample* ☎*93/414–6077* ⊕*www.giorgioarmani.com* Ⓜ*Maria Cristina.*

**Gonzalo Comella.** Since 1970, Gonzalo Comella has known how to stock his stores with top men's and women's fashions, from Armani Jeans to Polo Ralph Lauren to Antonio Miró or Ermenegildo Zegna. ☒*Passeig*

---

### CUSTO GUSTO

Only Barcelona could come up with Custo, an idiosyncratic fashion line created by a couple of motorcycling brothers. Since their 1980s start, the brothers Dalmau—Custido and David—have parlayed their passion for colorful and original tops into an empire that now includes footwear, denims, handbags, knits, and more. With stores scattered around Barcelona and the world (30 countries and counting), Custo's quirky embroidery and metallic graphic prints have become nearly as iconic as Gaudí's organic stalagmites or Miró's colorful asteroids.

*de Gràcia 6, Eixample* ☎93/412–6600 ⊕*www.gonzalocomella.com* Ⓜ*Passeig de Gràcia.*

**Heritage.** A compilation of retro clothing matches the handsome antique storefront in this Gothic Quarter classic just a few steps from Plaça del Pi. Balenciaga, Yves Saint Laurent, and the 1950 Spanish Pertegaz label are just a few of the stars of yesteryear back in the limelight here. ✉*Carrer Banys Nous 14, Barri Gòtic* ☎93/317–8515 ⊕*www.heritage. com* Ⓜ*Passeig de Gràcia.*

**Julie Sohn.** A rehabilitated industrial space with a dropped and vaulted ceiling now holds Julie Sohn's collection of women's clothing and accessories. Korean-born and Barcelona-based Sohn creates clothing that combines elegance and edginess. The store design (by Sohn's husband Conrado Carrasco's firm, CCT Arquitectos) manages to do the same with this handsome space. ✉*Carrer Diputació 299, Eixample* ☎93/487–5796 Ⓜ*Passeig de Gràcia* ✉*Carrer Joan d'Austria 126, Eixample* ☎93/309–0653 Ⓜ*Marina* ✉*Carrer Mestre Nicolau 8, Sarrià, Sant Gervasi* ☎93/446–6957 Ⓜ*Muntaner.*

**Kukuxumusu.** As with more and more of Barcelona's boutiques, this one comes with a worldview. T-shirts, mugs, hats, pencils, notebooks, handkerchiefs, and just about anything you can apply a design to is decorated with Mikel Urmeneta's zany zoological characters in the throes of love. ✉*Argenteria 69, Born-Ribera* ☎93/310–3647 Ⓜ*Jaume I* ✉*Arcs 6, Barri Gòtic* ☎93/342–5789 Ⓜ*Catalunya* ✉*Passeig de Gràcia 55–57, Eixample* ☎93/487–2238 ⊕*www.kukuxumusu.com* Ⓜ*Catalunya.*

**La Marthe.** Hidden up the Baixada de Santa Eulàlia in the Gothic quarter, this young designer of clean-lined yet ethereal clothes for women is making her mark on the Barcelona fashion world. Classical yet contemporary, La Marthe is attracting women looking for a soft chiffon-y look with a designer edge. ✉*Sant Sever 1, Barri Gòtic* ☎93/318–8177 Ⓜ*Liceu.*

**Le Boudoir.** Women's lingerie and intimate garments, erotic cosmetics, toys and books and all manner of wicked artifacts are sold in this attractive space designed by Mónica Sans, Julie Potter, and Paul Reynolds. The period furniture is as handsome and valuable looking as anything for sale here. ✉*Carrer Canuda 21, Barri Gòtic* ☎93/302–5281 ⊕*www.leboudoir net* Ⓜ*Catalunya.*

**Loewe.** Occupying the ground floor of Lluís Domènech i Montaner's Casa Lleó Morera, Loewe is Spain's answer to Hermès, a classical Barcelona clothing and leather emporium for men's and women's fashions and luxurious handbags that whisper status. ✉*Passeig de Gràcia 35, Eixample* ☎93/216–0400 Ⓜ*Passeig de Gràcia* ✉*Av. Diagonal 570, Eixample* ☎93/200–0920 Ⓜ*Maria Cristina* ✉*Av. Diagonal 606, Eixample* ☎93/240–5104 ⊕*www.loewe.es* Ⓜ*Passeig de Gràcia.*

**Mango.** With 10 stores (and counting) around Barcelona, Mango shares hegemony with the ubiquitous Zara over shoppers young and old, male and female. The four locations listed here will orient you toward the other stores, however many there might be by the time you hit Barcelona. Smart lines and superior tailoring are trademarks at this Barcelona favorite. ✉*Passeig de Gràcia 65, Eixample* ☎93/216–0400

Ⓜ*Passeig de Gràcia* ✉*Passeig de Gràcia 12–14, Eixample* ☎*93/240–5104* Ⓜ*Catalunya* ✉*Carrer Portaferrissa 16, Barri Gòtic* ☎*93/301–8483* Ⓜ*Catalunya* ✉*Av. Diagonal 280, Eixample* ☎*93/486–0310* ⊕*www.mango.es* Ⓜ*Glòries.*

**Otman.** With a branch in Morocco, this little groove between Carrer Montcada and Carrer Flassaders specializes in light frocks, belts, blouses, and skirts made in North Africa. Sit down for a mint tea in the back of this mysteriously illuminated shop and imagine Arabian nights. ✉*Carrer Cirera 4, La Ribera* ☎*93/310–2265* Ⓜ*Jaume I.*

**Purificación García.** Known as a gifted fabric expert whose creations are invariably based on the qualities and characteristics of her raw materials, Purificación García enjoys solid prestige in Barcelona as one of the city's fashion champions. Understated hues and subtle combinations of colors and shapes place this contemporary designer squarely in the camp of the less-is-more school of a Barcelona aesthetic movement that departs radically from the over-ornamentation of the city's Art Nouveau past. ✉*Passeig de Gràcia 21, Eixample* ☎*93/487–7292* Ⓜ*Passeig de Gràcia* ✉*Av. Pau Casals 4, Eixample* ☎*93/200–6089* Ⓜ*Muntaner* ✉*Diagonal 557, Eixample* ☎*93/444–0253* ⊕*www.purificaciongarcia.es* Ⓜ*Maria Cristina.*

**RqueR.** Conxa Jofresa stocks local Spanish and Catalan designers including Sybilla, Sita Murt, Juan Pedro Lopez, David Valls, and Viviana Uribe, among others. The name of the store, a play on the Spanish expression *erre que erre* (stubbornly, pigheadedly) can be taken as a statement of Conxa's fidelity to her founding idea of sticking with home-born designers through thick and thin. ✉*Carrer del Rec 75, Born-Ribera* ☎*93/315–2391* Ⓜ*Jaume I.*

**Sita Murt.** Local Catalan and Spanish clothing designers from Julie Sohn to Rutzü, Paul & Joe, and Anna Pianura to the Sita Murt home label hang in this cavelike space near Plaça Sant Jaume in the center of the Gothic Quarter. Colorful chiffon dresses and light, gauzy tops characterize this popular young line of clothing. ✉*Carrer Avinyó 18, Barri Gòtic* ☎*93/301–0006* Ⓜ*Liceu.*

**Tüsetú.** One street east of Santa Maria del Mar, this tiny hole-in-the-wall is a showroom for eclectic yet elegant collections by Zoe and other young innovators in women's fashions. ✉*Ases 1, Born-Ribera* ☎*93/268–3890* Ⓜ*Jaume I.*

**Zara.** Zara, partly for its affordability in Barcelona, has become second nature to barcelonins and visitors alike for its cool and casual styles for men, women, and children. There are Zara stores throughout the city, but the Passeig de Gràcia store is the most central and generally frequented, for better or for worse. Hot new styles rematerialize here in affordable form. Be prepared for sizes that run small and pants made for legs that go on forever. Zara's recipe for success has won over the world, but items are cheaper on its home turf. Well-executed, affordable copies of catwalk styles appear on the rails in a fashion heartbeat. The women's section is the front runner, but the men's and kid's sections cover good ground too. The introduction of the "Zara Home" department has also been a success. ✉*Passeig de Gràcia 16, Raval* ☎*93/318–7675* Ⓜ*Catalunya* ✉*Carrer Pelai 58, Eixample*

☎93/301–0978 Ⓜ*Passeig de Gràcia* ✉*Rambla de Catalunya 67, Eixample* ☎93/216–0868 ⊕*www.zara.com* Ⓜ*Passeig de Gràcia.*

## DESIGN & INTERIORS

Near the Pedrera on Passeig de Gràcia are Barcelona's two top design sanctuaries: Vinçon and BD. Habitat has stores on Tuset at the Diagonal and in the Plaça de Catalunya Triangle complex behind Bar Zurich at the head of the Rambla. The area around the basilica of Santa Maria del Mar and the Passeig del Born, an artisans' quarter since medieval times, is now chock-full of textile and leather design stores and gift shops with attitudes.

**Arkitektura.** Lighting design and kitchen and bathroom fixtures along with furniture and diverse objects by acclaimed architects and designers are on display here in this clean-lined upper Barcelona shop designed by architects and interior designers Marta Ventós, Carlos Tejada, and Conrado Carrasco. ✉*Via Augusta 185, Eixample* ☎93/362–4720 ⊕*www.arkitekturabcn.com* Ⓜ*Muntaner.*

**Gimeno.** Items from clever suitcases to the latest in furniture or sofas all display an innovative flair here. Household necessities, decorative goods, and gifts ranging from bags to benches share a hallmark of creativity and quality, nearly always with an edge. ✉*Passeig de Gràcia 102, Eixample* ☎93/237–2078 Ⓜ*Diagonal.*

**Habitat Barcelona.** British designer Terence Conran's emporium of beautiful objects, household items, and home furnishings is a hit with the design-appreciative denizens of Barcelona. The Habitat line of goods is produced by Conran's team of designers and is more affordable than those in his higher-end Conran Shop. ✉*Av. Diagonal 514, Eixample* ☎93/415–2992 Ⓜ*Passeig de Gràci* ✉*Pl. Catalunya, 2–4, Eixample* ☎93/301–7484 ⊕*www.habitat.net* Ⓜ*Diagonal, Catalunya.*

**MDM.** Reasonably priced household gear and design furnishings make this an interesting store to explore. Stainless steel from Rosle, WMF implements from Germany, Danish brands such as BUM and Eva Solo, and French home goods from Le Creuset are just a few of the prestigious international brand names in wood, stainless steel, and porcelain available here. ✉*Av. Diagonal 405 bis, Eixample* ☎93/238–6767 Ⓜ*Diagonal.*

Fodor'sChoice ★ **Vinçon.** A design giant some 50 years old, Vinçon steadily expanded its chic premises through a rambling Moderniste house that was once the home of Art Nouveau poet-artist Santiago Rusiñol and the studio of the painter Ramón Casas. It stocks everything from Filofaxes to handsome kitchenware. If you can tear your eyes away from all the design, seek out the spectacular Moderniste fireplace designed in wild Art Nouveau exuberance with a gigantic hearth in the form of a stylized face. The back terrace is a cool respite and a breath of fresh air with views up to the next-door rooftop warriors of Gaudí's Casa Milà. ✉*Passeig de Gràcia 96, Eixample* ☎93/215–6050 Ⓜ*Diagonal.*

## FINE FOODS & WINES

Food items can be some of the best buys in Barcelona, but be sure to check the ever-changing customs restrictions in your home country before purchasing edibles. Spanish wines from La Rioja are world renowned, but Ribera de Duero, Priorat, and other areas are producing the modern "high expression" wines popularized by American wine critic Robert Parker. Lavinia is an omnipresent wine emporium found in Barcelona and Bilbao, and will help you find a drinkable, affordable modern wine. Spain's wines are matched by its superb cured hams, generically called jamón serrano, which simply means "mountain ham." The finest cured ham is *jamón ibérico de bellota* (Iberian free-range, acorn-fed, black pig). Top-notch ham shops in Barcelona sell vacuum-sealed packets of sliced, cured ham that pack easily and make a tasty souvenir, though there is no guarantee that U.S. customs will not kidnap this precious product. Where there are fine wines and hams, cheeses cannot be far behind, with Extremadura's Torta del Casar making international headlines and on sale in specialized shops in Barcelona. Spanish saffron is possibly the last of the great foodstuff bargains available worldwide: light, legal, and cheap, while dried wild mushrooms are another aromatic favorite.

**Born Cooking.** Christine Zois has made this rustic café and bakery and barbecue shop one of Barcelona's fastest up-and-coming enterprises. If you're homesick for a taste of American homemade products such as New York style cheese cake, cookies, brownies, or cakes miscellaneous, this is your spot. ⊠ *Carrer Corretger 9, Born-Ribera* ☎ *93/310–5999* ⊕ *www.borncooking.com* Ⓜ *Jaume I.*

**Caelum.** At the corner of Carrer de la Palla and Banys Nous, this tearoom and coffee shop sells crafts and foods such as honey and preserves made in convents and monasteries all over Spain. The café and tearoom section extends neatly out into the intersection of Carrer Banys Nous (which means "new baths") and Carrer de la Palla, directly over the site of the medieval Jewish baths. ⊠ *Carrer de la Palla 8, Barri Gòtic* ☎ *93/302–6993* Ⓜ *Liceu, Catalunya.*

Fodor's Choice
★

**Casa Gispert.** On the inland side of Santa Maria del Mar, this is one of the most aromatic and picturesque shops in Barcelona, bursting with teas, coffees, spices, saffron, chocolates, and nuts. The star element in this olfactory and aesthetic feast is an almond-roasting stove in the back of the store dating from 1851, like the store itself. But don't miss the acid engravings on the office windows or the ancient wooden back door. ⊠ *Sombrerers 23, La Ribera* ☎ *93/319–7547* Ⓜ *Jaume I.*

**El Magnífico.** This coffee emporium just up the street from Santa Maria del Mar is famous for its sacks of coffee beans from all over the globe. A couple of deep breaths here will keep you caffeinated for hours. ⊠ *Carrer Argenteria 64, Born-Ribera* ☎ *93/310–3361* Ⓜ *Jaume I.*

**Foix de Sarrià.** Pastry and poetry under the same roof merit a stop. The verses of J. V. Foix, a major Catalan poet who managed to survive the Franco regime with his art intact, are engraved in bronze on the outside wall of the Major de Sarrià location, where he was born. Excellent pastries, breads, wines, cheeses, and cavas, all available on Sunday, have made Foix de Sarrià a Barcelona landmark. ⊠ *Pl. Sarrià 9–10, Sarrià* ☎ *93/203–0473* Ⓜ *Reina Elisenda* ⊠ *Major de Sarrià 57, Sarrià* ☎ *93/203–0714* Ⓜ *Sarrià.*

**Formatgeria La Seu.** Scotswoman Katherine McLaughlin has put together the Gothic Quarter's most delightful cheese-tasting sanctuary on the

CLOSE UP

# Savory Souvenirs

In Barcelona, a food lovers' city, the wide variety of gourmet and local foodstuffs available make souvenir shopping for yourself or loved ones a delicious detour.

## WHAT TO BUY

*Easy Crowd Pleasers.* Highly addictive **Marcona almonds** are soft and luscious nuts available raw, but better fried and salted. Spain has an amazing variety of **cheeses.** U.S. customs will allow hard-cured cheeses, such as Idiazabal—smoky sheep's milk cheese great melted on burgers. Bringing home wine such as sparkling **cava** is popular, but choose carefully—customs regulations only allow 1 liter of alcohol and on-board liquids restrictions require carrying wine in checked luggage. Stock up on **Catalonian olive oil** made from arbequina olives with a faint almond flavor.

*For Cooks.* Intriguing spices are perfect as souvenirs; they're light and won't take up much suitcase space. You can't go wrong with **pimentón** (Spanish smoked paprika) in three varieties—*dulce* (sweet and mild), *agridolce* (bittersweet, moderately spicy), and *picante* (hot). Gourmets will love **saffron,** the world's most expensive spice, much cheaper in Spain than in the United States.

*For Sweets Lover.* Don't miss Barcelona's superlative sweet shops. Especially look for **turrón,** a traditional Christmas candy now available year-round. You'll see "Turrón de Alicante" (hard nougat), "Jijona" (soft), as well as varieties with almonds, hazelnuts, or even burned cream. Kids will like tins of **xocolata,** a thick hot chocolate-like drink.

*For Entertainers.* Spain is famous for its canned hors d'oeuvres. Stash these in the pantry and be ready for company anytime. Don't miss excellent stuffed **olives** or the delicious **seafood,** such as tuna belly preserved in olive oil. (If you've only had American brands of tuna, you're in for a revelation.)

## WHERE TO SHOP

**Boqueria.** With more than 30,000 products, this covered market is a vibrant mecca. ⊠ *Rambla 91, Rambla* ☎ *93/318–2584* Ⓜ *Catalunya.*

**Caelum.** Bring home a piece of *caelum* (Latin for "heaven") with ornately packaged pastries and sweets handmade in Spanish convents. ⊠ *Carrer de la Palla 8, Barri Gòtic* ☎ *93/302–6993* Ⓜ *Catalunya.*

**Colmado Quilez.** Floor to ceiling, this charming grocer is packed full of gourmet goods from all over Europe. ⊠ *Rambla de Catalunya 63, Eixample* ☎ *93/215–8785* Ⓜ *Provença.*

**El Corte Inglés.** At the sprawling supermarket of this centrally located department store, you can shop like a barcelonin. ⊠ *Pl. de Catalunya 14, Eixample* ☎ *93/306–3800* Ⓜ *Catalunya.*

**Fargas** or **Xocoa.** Chocolate-lovers have choices to make—old-fashioned or modern? Fargas ( ⊠ *Carrer del Pi 16, Barri Gòtic* ☎ *93/302–0342* Ⓜ *Catalunya*) sells everything from slabs of chocolate to handmade bonbons. Xocoa's main store ( ⊠ *Carrer Petritxol 11, Barri Gòtic* ☎ *93/301–1197* Ⓜ *Catalunya*) offers myriad adventures in chocolate flavoring.

—Nina Callaway

7

site of an ancient buttery. (A 19th-century butter churn is visible in the back room.) A dozen artisanal cow, goat, and sheep cheeses from all over Spain, and olive oils can be tasted and taken home. La Seu is named for a combination of La Seu cathedral, as the "seat" of cheeses, and for cheese-rich La Seu d'Urgell in the Pyrenees. Katherine's wrapping paper, imaginatively chosen sheets of newspaper, give a final flourish to purchases. ⊠*Carrer Dagueria 16, Born-Ribera* ☎*93/412–6548* ⊕*www.formatgerialaseu.com* Ⓜ*Jaume I.*

**Iskia.** Good wine advice and a perenially renewing stock of new values to try make Iskia one of upper Barcelona's best wine emporiums. The proprietors speak English and are glad to talk about latest wine trends or explain their products at length. ⊠*Major de Sarrià 132, Sarrià* ☎*93/205–0070* ⊕*www.iskiavins.com* Ⓜ*Sarrià.*

**Jobal.** Long known as the secret saffron outlet around the corner from the Picasso museum, this fragrant spice emporium sells the full range of spices and savory items from cumin to coriander, along with teas from every corner of the globe. ⊠*Carrer Princesa 38, Born-Ribera* ☎*93/319–7802* Ⓜ*Jaume I.*

**La Botifarreria de Santa Maria.** This booming pork merchant next to the church of Santa Maria del Mar offers excellent cheeses, hams, pâtés, and homemade *sobrassadas* (pork pâté with paprika). *Botifarra*, Catalan for sausage, is the main item here, with a wide range of varieties including egg sausage for meatless Lent and sausage stuffed with spinach, asparagus, cider, cinnamon, and Cabrales cheese. ⊠*Carrer Santa Maria 4, La Ribera* ☎*93/319–9784* Ⓜ*Jaume I.*

**La Carte des Vins.** Enological books and accessories, and a carefully selected list of top international vintages fill this gorgeous wine shop decorated in fresh wood tones, many of them coming from tops of wine crates arranged around the tops of the display racks. Architect Daniel Nassat and interiorist Laurent Godel, authors of this graceful space, seem to have studied nearby Santa Maria del Mar to come up with a line so pure. ⊠*Sombrerers 1, Born-Ribera* ☎*93/268–7043* Ⓜ*Jaume I.*

**La Casa del Bacalao.** This cult store decorated with cod-fishing memorabilia specializes in salt cod and books of codfish recipes. Slabs of salt and dried cod, used in a wide range of Catalan recipes such as *esqueixada*, in which shredded strips of raw salt cod are served in a marinade of oil and vinegar, can be vacuum-packed for portability. ⊠*Comtal 8, just off Porta de l'Àngel, Barri Gòtic* ☎*93/301–6539* Ⓜ*Catalunya.*

**La Cave.** When in Sarrià, have a stop at this original wine cellar and restaurant. With every wine color-coded by taste, price, and geography, you are brilliantly rescued from pandemic wine store bewilderment. La Cave also provides a printout of tasting notes and technical data for every bottle, so that you not only know what you're getting, but what you've had and why. In addition, co-owner and manager Claude Cohen is an English-French-Spanish linguist and can dispense expert advice and plenty of humor as well. ⊠*Av. J. V. Foix 80, Sarrià* ☎*93/206–3846* Ⓜ*Sarrià.*

**Mantequeria Can Ravell.** Arguably Barcelona's best all-around fine-food and wine emporium, Can Ravell is a cult favorite with a superb selection of everything you ever wanted to savor from the finest anchovies from La Scala to the best cheese from Idiazabal. Through the kitchen and up the tiny spiral staircase, the dining room offers one of Barcelona's best lunch menus. The tasting table downstairs operates on a first come, first served basis and brings together foodies from all over the world to swap tasting tales. It's closed Sunday and Monday. ⊠ *Aragó 313, Eixample* ☎ *93/457–5114* Ⓜ *Passeig de Gràcia, Girona.*

**Orígens 99.9%.** Restaurant and delicatessen Orígens 99.9% occupies a former glassblowing shop with the original wooden balcony overhead beautifully restored and conserved. Olive oils, wines, and cheeses— all organically grown products from Catalonia—are the specialties in this *espai gastrònomic* (gastronomical space) and restaurant. Over the store's main produce display, don't miss the wood carving of San Antonio de Padua, patron saint of lost objects. ⊠ *Vidrieria 6–8, Born-Ribera* ☎ *93/310–7531* Ⓜ *Jaume I.*

**Queviures Murria.** Founded in 1890, this historic Moderniste shop, its windows decorated with Ramón Casas paintings and posters, has a superb selection of some 200 cheeses, sausages, wines, and conserves from Spain, Catalunya, and beyond. The ceramic Casas reproductions lining the interior walls are eye candy, as are all the details in this work of art–cum–grocery store (*queviures* means foodstuffs, literally, "things to keep you alive"). ⊠ *Roger de Llúria 85, Eixample* ☎ *93/215–5789* Ⓜ *Diagonal.*

**Tea Shop.** Earl Grey, black, white, red, green: every kind of tea you've ever heard of and many you probably haven't are available at this encyclopedic tea repository on Gràcia's main drag. The Taller de Cata (Tasting Workshop) held Thursday 5:30–7:30 PM will stimulate your tea culture in the event that you are interested in learning how to distinguish a Pai Mu Tan (white tea) from a Lung Ching (green tea) or how to correctly prepare and serve different varieties of this universal world brew and beverage. ⊠ *Gran de Gràcia 91, Gràcia* ☎ *93/217–4923* Ⓜ *Passeig de Gràcia.*

**Tot Formatge.** This small but chock-full and bustling shop in the Born-Ribera district manages to fit cheeses from all over Spain and the world onto its shelves. Specializing in local Catalan, French, and Spanish produce, this is the place for a comprehensive cheese tour of the Iberian Peninsula or across the length of the Pyrenees. The staff can provide fascinating explanations of the geographical and social histories behind the methods used by different regions to prepare and produce their respective cheeses. ⊠ *Passeig del Born 13, La Ribera* ☎ *93/319–5357* Ⓜ *Jaume I.*

**Tutusaus.** With an anthological selection of cheeses, hams, pastries, and delicacies of all kinds, this famous café, restaurant, and delicatessen is a hallowed upper Barcelona hangout just off Turo Park. Whether for coffee, a taste of cheese or foie, or a full meal composed of a selection of delicacies, this little hideaway is superb. ⊠ *Francesc Perez Cabrero 5, Sant Gervasi* ☎ *93/209–8373* Ⓜ *La Bonanova.*

**Vilaplana.** Just up the street from Tutusaus next to Turo Park, this is a famous address for Barcelona food lovers, known for its pastries, cheeses, hams, pâtés, caviars, and fine deli items. ⊠ *Francesc Perez Cabrero, Eixample* ☎ *93/201–1300* Ⓜ *La Bonanova.*

Fodor'sChoice **Vila Viniteca.** Near Santa Maria del Mar, this is the best wine treasury ★ in Barcelona, with tastings, courses, and events meriting further investigation. The tiny family grocery store across the street offers exquisite artisanal cheeses ranging from French goat cheese to Extremadura's famous Torta del Casar. ⊠ *Carrer Agullers 7, Born-Ribera* ☎ *93/268–3227* Ⓜ *Jaume I.*

### FOOD & FLEA MARKETS

Besides the Boqueria, other spectacular food markets include two in Gràcia—the Mercat de la Llibertat (near Plaça Gal.la Placidia) and the Mercat de la Revolució (on Travessera de Gràcia)—the Mercat de Sarrià (near Plaça de Sarrià and the Reina Elisenda train stop), the Merca de la Concepció on Carrer Aragó, and the Mercat de Santa Caterina across Via Laietana from the cathedral.

★ **Boqueria.** The oldest of its kind in Europe, Barcelona's most colorful and bustling food market appears here on the Rambla between Carrer del Carme and Carrer de Hospital. Open Monday–Saturday, it's most active before 3 PM, though many of the stands remain open all day. Standout stalls include Petràs, the wild mushroom guru in the back of the market on Plaça de la Gardunya, and Juanito Bayen of the world-famous collection of bar stools known as Pinotxo. ⊠ *Rambla 91, Rambla* ☉ *Mon.–Sat. 8–4* ☎ *93/318–2017* Ⓜ *Liceu, Catalunya.*

**Els Encants.** Barcelona's biggest flea market, an event with distinctly Bohemian allure, spreads out at the end of Carrer Dos de Maig. The center of the circular Plaça de les Glòries Catalanes also fills with ill-gotten goods of all kinds. Keep close track of your wallet or you might come across it as an empty item for sale. ⊠ *Carrer Dos de Maig 177, Eixample* ☉ *Wed.–Sat. 9–2* ☎ *93/246–3030* Ⓜ *Glòries.*

**Mercat Gòtic.** A browser's bonanza, this antique-books and art objects market occupies the Plaça de la Seu, in front of the cathedral, on Thursday. ⊠ *Pl. de la Catedral s/n, Barri Gòtic* ☉ *Thurs. 9–9* Ⓜ *Catalunya.*

**Mercat de Sant Antoni.** Just outside the Raval at the end of Ronda Sant Antoni, this steel hangar colossus is an old-fashioned, food and second-hand clothing and books (many in English) market. Sunday morning is the most popular time to browse through the used-book and video game market. ⊠ *Carrer del Comte d'Urgell 1, Raval* ☉ *Sun. 9–2, Tues.–Sat. 8–2.* Ⓜ *Sant Antoni.*

**Plaça del Pi.** This little square fills with the interesting tastes and aromas of a natural-produce market (honeys, cheeses) on Thursday, while neighboring Plaça Sant Josep Oriol holds a painter's market every Sunday. ⊠ *Pl. del Pi s/n, Barri Gòtic* ☉ *Fri.–Sun. 1st and 2nd weekends of the month and special holidays 8–8* Ⓜ *Catalunya, Liceu.*

**Plaça Reial.** The nightlife in this area has just barely evaporated off the streets on Sunday morning when a stamp and coin market sets up. Not far away, there's a general crafts and flea market near the Columbus monument at the port end of the Rambla. ⊠*Pl. Reial s/n, Rambla* ☉*Sun. 9–2* Ⓜ*Liceu.*

**Sarrià.** Tuesday antiques markets in Sarrià's town square provide another good reason to explore this charming onetime outlying village in the upper part of the city. The nearby produce market, a mini-Boqueria, is the place for coffee, while Tram-Tram, Vivanda, and Vell Sarrià, just downhill in front of the town hall, are excellent choices for lunch after a hike over to the Monestir de Pedralbes and back. ⊠*Pl. de Sarrià, Sarrià* ☉*Tues. 9–3* Ⓜ*Sarrià, Reina Elisenda.*

## GIFTS, SOUVENIRS & STATIONERY

**Cereria Subirà.** Known as the city's oldest shop, having remained open since 1761 (though it was not always a candle store), this "waxery" (*cereria*) offers candles in all sizes and shapes ranging from wild mushrooms to the Montserrat massif, home of the Benedictine abbey dear to the heart of every barcelonin. ⊠*Baixada Llibreteria 7, Barri Gòtic* ☎*93/315–2606* Ⓜ*Jaume I.*

**Natura.** A gracefully decorated store in the Natura chain, this crafts specialist stocks a good selection of global trifles, including pieces from India and North Africa. Incense, clothing, tapestries, candles, furniture, and surprises of all kinds appear in this cross-cultural craft shop. ⊠*Argenteria 78, Born-Ribera* ☎*93/268–2525* Ⓜ*Jaume I.*

**Papers Coma.** On Barcelona's most artistic street, Papers Coma offers inventive gadgets and knickknacks, most of them related to stationery. ⊠*Montcada 20, La Ribera* ☎*93/319–7601* Ⓜ*Jaume I.*

Fodor'sChoice ★ **Papirum.** Exquisite hand-printed papers, marbleized blank books, and writing implements await you and your muse at this tiny, medieval-tone shop. ⊠*Baixada de la Llibreteria 2, Barri Gòtic* ☎*93/310–5242* Ⓜ*Jaume I.*

Fodor'sChoice ★ **Pepa Paper.** Barcelona's most famous paper and stationery store, Pepa Paper (Pepa is a nickname for Josefina and Paper, Catalan for—you guessed it—paper) carries a gorgeous selection of cards, paper, and myriad objects and paraphernalia related to correspondence. ⊠*Carrer Valencia 266, Eixample* ☎*93/215–9223* Ⓜ*Provença, Passeig de Gràcia* ⊠*Carrer Paris 167, Eixample* ☎*93/494–8420* Ⓜ*Provença* ⊠*Av. Diagonal 557–575, Sarrià, Sant Gervasi* ☎*93/405–2478* Ⓜ*Maria Cristina.*

## JEWELRY

**Bagués Joieria.** An iconic Barcelona jeweler with its main headquarters on the Rambla at the corner of Carrer del Carmen, Bagués has bejeweled barcelonins since 1839. His Lluís Masriera line of Art Nouveau jewels, intricate flying nymphs, and lifelike golden insects are his most recognizable creations. The location on Moderniste architect Puig i Cadafalch's Casa Amatller in the famous Mansana de la Discòrdia on Passeig de Gràcia is worth the visit just to get a closer look at the house. ⊠*La Rambla 105, Rambla* ☎*93/481–7050* Ⓜ*Catalunya* ⊠*Passeig de Gràcia 41, Eixample* ☎*93/216–0174* ⊕*www.bagues.es* Ⓜ*Catalunya.*

**Forum Ferlandina.** A wide gamut of creations by some 50 international designers of jewelry is on display in this slender slot directly across the street from the MACBA. ⊠*Ferlandina 31, Raval* ☎*93/441–8018* Ⓜ*Catalunya.*

**Majoral/Alea Galeria de Joies.** Enric Majoral's jewelry design takes inspiration from organic and natural shapes such as pea pods. With gold and pearl creations that seem to have sprouted from the forest floor, this collection makes even the most hard-core urbanite appreciate nature. ⊠ *Carrer Argenteria 66, Born-Ribera* ☎ *93/310–1373* ⊕ *www. sargantana.net* Ⓜ *Jaume I.*

**Puig Doria.** This popular jeweler, with two locations in town and another in the airport, sells a full range of personal accessories of great style and taste, from neckties and watches to items in silver and gold. ⊠ *Av. Diagonal 612, Eixample* ☎ *93/201–2911* Ⓜ *Diagonal* ⊠ *Rambla de Catalunya 88, Eixample* ☎ *93/215–1090* Ⓜ *Passeig de Gràcia.*

**Zapata Joyero.** The Zapata family, with three stores around town, has been prominent in Barcelona jewelry design and retail for the last half century. With original designs of their own and a savvy selection of the most important Swiss and international watch designers, this family business is now in its second generation and makes a point of taking good care of clients with large or small jewelry needs. Their L'Illa store, for example, specializes in jewelry accessible to the budgets of younger clients. ⊠ *Av. Diagonal 557, Eixample* ☎ *93/430–6238* Ⓜ *Provença* ⊠ *Mandri 20, Sant Gervasi* ☎ *93/211–6774* Ⓜ *Sarrià* ⊠ *L'Illa, Diagonal 557 (stores No. 126 and 133), Diagonal* ☎ *93/444–0063* Ⓜ *Maria Cristina.*

### SHOES

**Camper.** Just off Plaça Catalunya and not far from the 25-room boutique hotel of the same name (and company) this internationally famous Spanish shoe emporium offers a comprehensive line of funky boots, heels, and shoes of all kinds. Both men and women's shoes, all in line with the company's rugged outdoor philosophy, are displayed against a rocky mountainous background deisgned by Martí Guixé and the Camper Studio. ⊠ *Carrer Pelai 13–37, Raval* ☎ *93/302–4124* Ⓜ *Catalunya.*

**Casas International.** This is one of the city's best shops for browsing through a wide range of international trendsetting footwear. Sister stores at Porta de l'Àngel 40 and Portaferrissa 25 show surprising and original in-house designs, but this branch on the Rambla is predominantly Italian, with heels high and low, round and stiletto, and square toes and a savvy mix of stylish shoes for men and women. ⊠ *Rambla 125, Barri Gòtic* ☎ *93/302–4598* Ⓜ *Liceu.*

FodorsChoice **Farrutx.** Shoes, including sandals and espadrilles, made in the tradition
★ of the Balearic Islands for the dynamic modern woman are the specialty here. Brilliantly designed, these kicks will set you back plenty but the quality is undeniable. ⊠ *Roselló 218, Eixample* ☎ *93/215–0685* Ⓜ *Provença* ⊠ *Pau Casals 18–20, Sarrià, Sant Gervasi* ☎ *93/200– 6920* Ⓜ *Muntaner, La Bonanova.*

FodorsChoice **La Manual Alpargatera.** If you appreciate old-school craftsmanship in
★ footwear, visit this boutique, just off Carrer Ferran. Handmade rope-sole sandals and espadrilles are the specialty, and this shop has sold them to everyone—including the Pope. The beribboned espadrilles model used for dancing the sardana is also available, but these artisans are capable of making any kind of creation you can think of. ⊠ *Avinyó 7, Barri Gòtic* ☎ *93/301–0172* Ⓜ *Liceu.*

**Noel Barcelona.** Cowboy boots of every imaginable style and color are on display at this stupendous surprise in midtown Barcelona. High heel, low heel, stilletto toe, round toe, higher, lower, hand-tooled or plain leather, this is said to be the finest collection of cowboy boots in Europe. Espadrilles and other kind of shoes are also available. ⊠ *Carrer Pelai 48, Raval* ☎ *93/317–8638* Ⓜ *Catalunya.*

Fodor'sChoice **S'avarca de Menorca.** For a range of
★ handmade leather sandals (often referred to as Abarcas) with straps across the heels in an infinity of variations and colors, this is Barcelona's finest store for footwear from the Balearic Isles. Abarcas come with thicker soles for city walking or lighter ones for wearing around the house. ⊠ *Capellans 2, Barri Gòtic* ☎ *93/342–5738* Ⓜ *Catalunya, Jaume I.*

**Solé.** One of Barcelona's most original shoemakers, this artisan makes footwear by hand, imports handmade shoes from all over Spain, and sells other models from Indonesia and Morocco. With boots, sandals, and a wide range of selections for both men and women, the rugged, rustic look prevails. ⊠ *Carrer Ample 7, Barri Gòtic* ☎ *93/301–6984* Ⓜ *Drassanes.*

**Tascón.** International footwear designers and domestic shoemakers alike fill these stores with solid urban footwear and brands such as Panama Jack, Timberland, Camper, and Doc Martens. These walking and hiking shoes are for people with miles on their minds. ⊠ *Av. Diagonal 462, Eixample* ☎ *93/415–5616* Ⓜ *Diagonal* ⊠ *Passeig de Gràcia 64, Eixample* ☎ *93/487–4447* Ⓜ *Passeig de Gràcia* ⊠ *Passeig del Born 8, Born-Ribera* ☎ *93/268–7293* Ⓜ *Jaume I.*

## DEPARTMENT STORES & MALLS

**Bulevard Rosa.** This alleyway off Passeig de Gràcia, as much a social event as a shopping venue, is composed of more than 100 clothing, jewelry, perfume, and footwear shops. Lunch is a major element in the shopping process, and the Jardí del Bulevard restaurant down the stairway under this raging commercial maelstrom is an opportunity to see and be seen and recharge acquisitive batteries. ⊠ *Passeig de Gràcia 53–55, Eixample* ☎ *93/378–9191* Ⓜ *Passeig de Gràcia.*

**El Corte Inglés.** Otherwise known as ECI, this iconic and ubiquitous Spanish department store has its main Barcelona branch on Plaça Catalunya, with a books and music annex 100 yards away in Porta de l'Àngel. Spain's most powerful and comprehensive clothing and general goods emporium (its name means "The English Cut") can be tedious,

but you can find just about anything you're looking for. The encyclopedic range of quality items here can save you hours of questing around
town. ✉ *Pl. de Catalunya 14, Eixample* ☎ *93/306–3800* Ⓜ *Catalunya*
✉ *Porta de l'Àngel 19–21, Barri Gòtic* ☎ *93/306–3800* Ⓜ *Catalunya*
✉ *Pl. Francesc Macià, Av. Diagonal 471, Eixample* ☎ *93/419–2020*
Ⓜ *La Bonanova* ✉ *Av. Diagonal 617, Diagonal, Les Corts* ☎ *93/419–*
*2828* Ⓜ *Maria Cristina.*

**El Triangle.** The Triangle d'Or or Golden Triangle at the top end of the
Rambla on Plaça Catalunya is a stylish and popular complex and home
for, among other stores, FNAC, where afternoon book presentations
and CD launches bring together crowds of literati and music lovers.
✉ *Pl. Catalunya 4, Rambla* ☎ *93/344–1800* Ⓜ *Catalunya.*

**L'Illa Diagonal.** A rangy complex buzzing with shoppers swarm-
ing through 100 stores and shops ranging from food specialists to
Decathlon sports gear to Bang & Olufsen sound systems, FNAC, or
the Zapata jewelers downstairs. ✉ *Av. Diagonal 545–57, Eixample*
☎ *93/487–1699* Ⓜ *Maria Cristina.*

**Pedralbes Centre.** A conglomeration just a few blocks west of L'Illa Diagonal includes a Lavinia wine store and ends with the Diagonal branch
of the ubiquitous El Corte Inglés. ✉ *Av. Diagonal 609–615, Eixample*
☎ *93/410–6821* Ⓜ *Maria Cristina.*

# Catalonia: The Costa Brava to Tarragona

## WORD OF MOUTH

"If you have a car, I would definitely explore the Costa Brava region. My husband and I spent three days there last fall…Calella de Palafrugell, Llafranc, Tamariu, Begur, Pals, Peratallada, Girona…there's so much to experience, with the sea and small medieval villages everywhere. It's a beautiful area in which to relax and explore!"

—strass

By James C.
Townsend
Updated
by George
Semler

**THE CHALLENGE OF TOURING CATALONIA**—the nation within a nation (officially, Autonomous Community) that forms the northeast shoulder of Spain—is simplified by the fact that all roads lead to or from Barcelona. Planes and ships land and dock there, and all highways and railways entering this corner of Spain are headed for Barcelona. But although Barcelona is the capital of Catalonia (to use the English spelling; it's Cataluña in Castilian, Catalunya in Catalan), the city is too cosmopolitan to be thought of as its authentic "soul." To find the *real* Catalonia, you must remember that all roads also lead *from* Barcelona and take you to the hinterlands. And, in fact, many barcelonins do exactly that every time they get a chance. It is widely known that Barcelona is a city of second sons who left their country roots to seek fame and fortune in the metropolis. Today even the city's hippest artists and most modern entrepreneurs still flee the capital every summer to return to the timeless inland villages and picturesque coastal hamlets of Catalonia.

In fact, the sea and the sierra—*mar i muntanya* in Catalan—are the two primal forces that define the spirit of Catalonia. The Mediterranean borders one side of the region and the Pyrenees the other, and legend ascribes the birth of Catalonia's very heart to the love of a shepherd for a mermaid (the region known as the Empordà). The result, so to speak, scattered Catalonia's landscape with memorable sights and places. The Costa Brava, a celebrated resort area, extends along nearly a hundred miles of coast from Blanes, at the mouth of the Tordera River some 65 km (40 mi) north of Barcelona, up to Port Bou on the French border. It contains Catalonia's most idyllic *platjes* (beaches), often separated by rocky salients threaded by *cales* (creeks), and indented by innumerable coves. Crowded with fig trees and vineyards, cacti and mimosa, eucalyptus trees, pines, birches, and its famous cork oak trees; and perfumed by the scents of lavender, thyme, and rosemary, this coast has both hidden, unspoiled villages, like Calella de Palafrugell, and resorts like Lloret de Mar, overrun with tourists working on their suntans. The glory of the Costa Brava Catalana—to use its full name—remains in those villages and hamlets where the outside walls of houses (owing to phosphorus in the whitewash) glow like mother-of-pearl in the sun and take on sharp, purple shadows. Such towns are a source of infinite pleasure to anyone with an eye for aesthetic beauty, so it's little wonder that the surrealist master Salvador Dalí embraced Cadaqués as home, or that Marc Chagall found his "blue paradise" at Tossa de Mar. In unspoiled spots along this coast traditional and iconic scenes remain: fishing boats painted green and blue—the favorite color of Catalonia—drawn up on the sandy beach, women mending nets, wine being sipped in small bars and taverns.

Those in search of more historical glamour will want to head inland to Girona, the biggest city of Northern Catalonia (population 82,000) and an amalgam of many ages and styles, symbolized by its cathedral, first built in splendid Romanesque and then transformed in willowy Gothic and overlaid in florid Catalan baroque. Arab, Christian, and Jewish communities all lived side by side in Girona, so you can wander down arcaded alleyways and along the Onyar River to discover not only the cathedral complex but the Banys Arabs (Arab Baths) and El Call, the most fully preserved historic Jewish neighborhood in Spain. All three are remnants of Girona's medieval golden age. A university town, Girona also has fashionable cafés, fine bookstores, and a full cultural calendar. Not far to its north lies another cultural must-do: Figueres and its spectacular Teatre-Museu Dalí , the leading shrine to the region's most famous native son.

> **TOP 5**
>
> ■ Cadaqués: Art and nature in Dalí's "most beautiful place on earth"
>
> ■ Girona's *Call* or Jewish Quarter
>
> ■ The Alberes range from Puig Neulós to Cap de Creus
>
> ■ The Dalí Triangle: Figueres, Púbol, Port Lligat
>
> ■ Tarragona's Roman walls and amphitheater

Heading inland, you can see some of Catalonia's most extraordinary landscapes in the pillowy hills of Montseny or the eerie, volcanic Garrotxa region. Northwest of Barcelona is the most revered pilgrimage spot in Catalonia, the "sawtooth mountain" shrine of Montserrat—monastery of La Moreneta (the "Black Virgin") and legendarily the site where Parsifal found the Holy Grail. Montserrat is as memorable for its setting as for its religious treasures, so you will want to explore its strange pink hills, jagged peaks, and crests dotted with hermitages (with funiculars offering breathtaking views). To the southwest are several other historic spiritual sanctuaries, including the Cistercian monasteries of Santes Creus and Santa Maria de Poblet, characterized by monolithic Romanesque architecture and beautiful cloisters. More worldly pleasures await along the Costa Daurada (Golden Coast) in the smart resort town of Sitges, while a stop in the city of Tarragona will bear witness to Catalonia's 2,000-year-old history amid the city's extensive collection of Roman ruins. Whether you're out to enjoy the sun-and-sand combo on the Costa Brava or follow the trail of the Greek colonists or the Roman emperors, be sure to enjoy some Catalan blackberries with fresh oranges squeezed over them, a treat "of ambrosial sweetness" as 4th-century Roman author Avienus noted.

## EXPLORING CATALONIA: THE COSTA BRAVA TO TARRAGONA

In the northeast corner of the Iberian Peninsula, Catalonia spreads out north, south, and west of the city of Barcelona, over four provinces: Tarragona, Barcelona, and Girona—which run from south to north along the coastline of the Mediterranean Sea—and Lleida, which is landlocked. The provinces are, in turn, subdivided into *comarques*, or counties—for example, the Alt (upper) and Baix (lower) Empordà, in the upper northeast part of the province of Girona, both famed for their landscape and cuisine, are two comarques. Barcelona, the capital of Catalonia, is centered in Barcelona province and has the best communication links. Just a day trip away (no destination is more than a five-hour excursion by bus) are dazzling sights. Moving north to Girona province, you'll find both the Costa Brava—Spain's rocky

## GREAT ITINERARIES

If you're out to explore Catalonia, who can resist waking up in Barcelona and heading first to the Costa Brava? From the metropolis you can drive just about anywhere in Catalonia in two hours (even to the higher reaches of the Pyrenees), but to get a good impression of the countryside a trip of several days is advisable. In three days you can head north from Barcelona to see a good slice of Catalonia and get a real taste of the country. In 10 days, you can contemplate seeing most of Catalonia's highlights, from beaches to mountains to monasteries.

### IF YOU HAVE 3 DAYS

Starting from Barcelona, make your first stop in the central Costa Brava at ⬚ **Tossa de Mar**, with its walled medieval town perched next to the sea. On Day 2, drive inland and explore ⬚ **Girona ❶– ⓫**, with its Gothic cathedral and Jewish Quarter, which still preserves an ancient heritage. On Day 3, drive north to **Figueres** and visit the Teatre-Museu Gala-Salvador Dalí. Have lunch at one of the town's many choice restaurants, and in the evening you can

return to Barcelona in under two hours down the A7 highway.

### IF YOU HAVE 5 DAYS

On the first day, drive two hours to the Iberian Peninsula's easternmost point, Cap de Creus, just north of ⬚ **Cadaqués**, and see Dalí's house at Port Lligat. On Day 2, start working back toward Barcelona and points south. Stop in **Figueres** to visit the Dalí museum, then continue south to the history-rich city of ⬚ **Girona ❶– ⓫**. On Day 3, have lunch at the medieval village of **Peratallada** and see the Iberian ruins of **Ullastret** before driving south past Barcelona to the monastery at ⬚ **Santa Maria de Poblet**. Spend the night there after exploring the medieval town of Montblanc and the Cistercian triangle of monasteries completed by Santes Creus and Vallbona de les Monges. On Day 4, head for ⬚ **Tarragona** for a browse through the ruins of what was the Roman Empire's capital of Hispania Citerior. On the last of this five-day tour, relax at the seaside resort of ⬚ **Sitges**, where the sun setting into the Mediterranean is an unforgettable sight.

response to the Côte d'Azur and the Amalfi Coast—and the historic city of Girona. Tarragona province is the farthest south, famous for its Roman capital city of Tarragona.

### ABOUT THE RESTAURANTS

Catalonia's restaurants, especially in Barcelona's outskirts, are increasingly and deservedly famous. From El Bulli (Cala Montjoi, near Roses) to the Celler de Can Roca (Girona), La Cuina de Can Simon (Tossa de Mar), the Mas de Torrent (La Bisbal), and a host of other first-rate establishments, fine dining in Catalonia, which began in the hinterlands at the legendary Hotel Empordà, seems to have remained and proliferated in the country. But don't get the idea that you need to go to an internationally acclaimed restaurant to dine well. It's well known that El Bulli's star chef Ferran Adrià dines regularly at the no-frills Barretina in Roses, where straight-up fresh fish is the day-in, day-out attraction. Northern Catalonia's Empordà region is known not only for seafood but for a rich assortment of inland and upland products as well. Beef from Girona's verdant pastureland is prized throughout Catalonia, while wild mushrooms from the Pyrenees and game from the Alberes range offer seasonal depth and breadth to menus across the region. From a simple beachside paella or *llobarro* (sea bass) at a *chiringuito* (shack) with tables on the sand, to the splendor of a meal at Celler de Can Roca or Mas de Torrent, playing culinary hopscotch through Catalonia is a good way to organize a tour.

Mealtimes in Spain are among the latest in Europe. Lunch starts at 2–2:30, and dinner starts between 8 and 10, more usually between 9 and 11 in urban centers. In areas that cater to foreign visitors, particularly the Costa Brava, restaurants open for lunch and dinner much earlier (noon–1 for lunch, 7–8 for dinner). In well-touristed areas, some restaurants open early for dinner, but note that many of these may be overpriced and not authentically Spanish; still, they can help in a pinch. The best solution for hunger pangs in the early evening is to do as Spaniards do and stop in for tapas, which are usually served throughout the day.

## ABOUT THE HOTELS

Lodgings on the Costa Brava range from the finest, most sophisticated hotels to spartan *pensions* that are no more than a place to sleep and change clothes between beach, bar, restaurant, and disco outings. The better accommodations are usually well situated and have splendid views of the seascape. Many simple, comfortable hotels provide a perfectly adequate stopover and decent dining. If you plan to visit during the high season (July and August), be sure to book reservations well in advance at almost any hotel in this area, especially the Costa Brava, which remains one of the most popular summer resort areas in Spain. Many Costa Brava hotels close down in the winter season, between November and March.

Another alternative is to stay at one of Catalonia's medieval monasteries, which offer serene, if spartan, rooms at nice prices. Full board, with breakfast, lunch, and dinner, is usually included in the price, which ranges €25–€45 per person. You generally don't have to belong to any religious group, but you do need to respect the monastery and its occupants. The Catalonia tourist office in Barcelona and local tourist offices have information on these accommodations.

Finally, you may consider *paradores*, Spanish government-subsidized chains of what are essentially four- and five-star hotels. Rates are reasonable, and the paradors are invariably immaculate and tastefully furnished, often with antiques or reproductions. All paradors have fine restaurants specializing in regional products and dishes, and you can stop in for a meal or a drink without spending the night. Because paradors are extremely popular with foreigners and Spanish travelers alike, make reservations well in advance.

| WHAT IT COSTS IN EUROS | | | | | |
|---|---|---|---|---|---|
| | ¢ | $ | $$ | $$$ | $$$$ |
| RESTAURANTS | under €10 | €10–€15 | €16–€20 | €21–€25 | over €25 |
| HOTELS | under €85 | €85–€120 | €121–€150 | €151–€175 | over €175 |

Restaurant prices are for a main course for one person at dinner. Hotel prices are for two people in a standard double room in high season.

### TIMING

Any time of the year is suitable to enjoy the beauty of the Costa Brava, but for sun and swimming in the Mediterranean (often the main lure) late spring to early autumn is prime time. Starting in mid-May, the weather gets warm enough to take that first dip, though the water will still be cold. The weather keeps getting warmer until torrid temperatures arrive in late July and most of August. Unfortunately, it's difficult to find a place to lie down on a beach in August, when all of Europe is on vacation. Late summer and early fall are perfect times to enjoy the pleasures of the Catalan coast without either excessive heat or people. The local bounty of seasonal wild mushrooms and game is at its best from mid-October to mid-January. Winters are usually brisk but stimulating, a good time for hiking and visiting cultural sights.

# THE COSTA BRAVA

Fierce, beautiful, and wild—but never dull—the Costa Brava is one of Spain's most bewitching places. The name means "rugged coast," a description first coined in 1905 by Catalan journalist Ferran Agulló to describe one of Europe's most abrupt and rocky coastlines. The Costa Brava is a nearly unbroken series of sheer rock cliffs dropping down to crystalline waters, capriciously punctuated with innumerable coves and tiny beaches on narrow inlets, each of which is called a *cala*. Hundreds of bays and peninsulas calm the waters before they hit land, allowing fishermen to make a living and also, in centuries gone by, pirates to gain plunder. When pirates plied the Mediterranean in the 16th and 17th centuries and threatened the Catalan coast, towns were built inland away from danger and the coastline was all but deserted. Miguel de Cervantes, the author of *Don Quixote,* was captured by Barbary pirates in 1575 and held for five years in Algiers (recent scholarship has concluded that he was captured on the Costa Brava's Bay of Roses). Today the only plundering is done by hotel owners, who make fortunes every summer from the busloads of tour groups that swamp the Costa in high season.

This Costa Brava is a comparatively recent discovery. The first tourists arrived at the beginning of the 20th century: well-to-do families from Barcelona, who came to escape the ovenlike temperatures of the big city by bathing along the shore. They were trailed, in turn, by artists and bohemians. Picasso, Marc Chagall, Santiago Rusiñol, and Salvador Dalí all came and were swiftly conquered by the coast's natural charms

## PLEASURES & PASTIMES

### BEACHES

Jagged rocky cliffs shimmer around you, and the deep blue of the Mediterranean sea extends to the horizon as sailboats and sailboards cut through the swells. On one of Europe's most famous resort coastlines, your expectations have been met. The fact remains, however, that much of this "rugged" coast is not given over to first-class beaches but to sharp ridges that jut out, creating deep coves or headlands where pine forest reaches the very edge of the water. Still, you can find extensive sand beaches at Blanes and Lloret, and around the Bay of Roses, as well as many secluded expanses of sand where people can, if so disposed, bask in the sun, alone and undisturbed. Note that parking is available at many beaches for a small fee of about €3.75 per day.

If you see a blue flag flying at a beach, you know it has received the approval of the European Environmental Education Foundation. One obvious beach rule: the closer they are to town, the more crowded they will be. The most popular beaches are those at Platja d'Aro, Lloret de Mar, Tossa de Mar, and Roses. All these fly blue flags. But the secret of finding a wonderful beach is to get to those where few, if any, people go, such as the Cala del Senyor Ramon, between Sant Feliu de Guíxols and Tossa de Mar, or Platja Castell in Palamós. Other out-of-the-way beaches are Cala Montjoi and Cala Jóncols between Roses and Cadaqués. Ask the locals or do your own exploring, and when you find a pristine spot with no one around, don't tell anybody.

### FIESTA

Each town or village in Catalonia celebrates its yearly *Festa Major,* or festival, in honor of its patron saint. The dates of these festivities will vary, but many of them are held at the height or end of summer. They are richly celebrated with dances, parades, athletic events, religious services, and general fun-making. The leading festivals, however, are the *verbenes,* the festivities of the eves of St. John and St. Peter, on June 24 and 29, celebrated with fireworks and bonfires that send flames leaping up high into the night sky, followed by riotous dancing till dawn. The biggest *verbena* welcomes the eve of *Sant Joan* (St. John) on June 24, or Midsummer Night's Eve. This celebration recalls the ancient pagan festivities of the summer solstice and the agricultural cycle of the end and rebirth of the year. Nearly every town throws a party on this night, and there are hundreds of private ones you just might get yourself invited to. Bring a bottle of *cava* (the native bubbly) and you'll be more than welcome. June 29 is *Sant Pere* (St. Peter), the patron saint of fishermen. The fishermen of Roses invite all to try suquet fueled with plenty of cold rosé wine.

Easter is the time for religious processions and performances, some dating back to the Middle Ages. A chilling reminder of the transience of life is the *Dansa de la Mort* (Dance of Death) on Holy Thursday (the Thursday before Easter Sunday) at Verges, northeast of Girona. Men and boys dressed as skeletons maneuver eerily through the streets to the ominous beat of the drum.

8

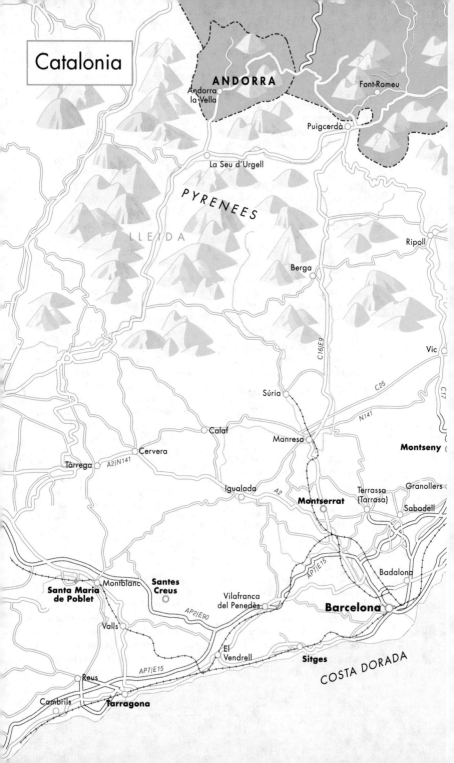

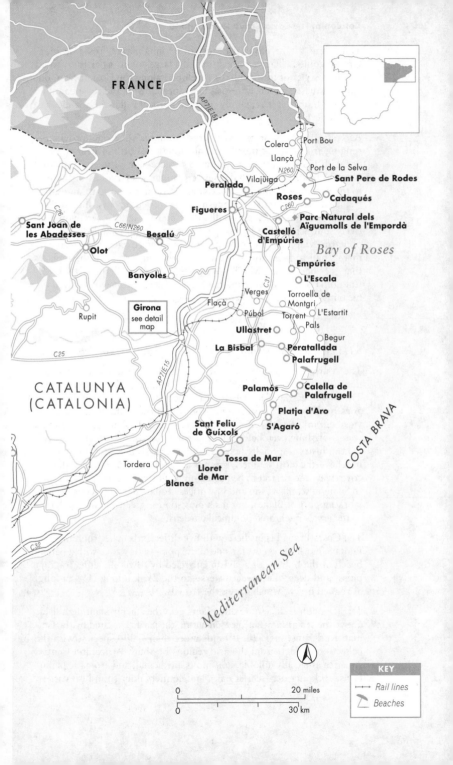

as much as by the physical beauty of its inhabitants (Tossa de Mar's Greek-profiled villagers once attracted a large colony of artists). Today different styles of tourism have developed along the Costa Brava: one aimed at mass tourism, at resorts like Lloret de Mar and Roses, another found at more selective, family-oriented ports of call like Cadaqués and Tossa de Mar.

Ascending the coast of Northern Catalonia's Girona province— ranging from Blanes (north of Barcelona) to Portbou near the border with France—the Costa Brava is a succession of inlets, bays, and coves. A landscape of lush deep-green mountains serves as a backdrop to the rocky shore and aquamarine foreground of the coast and sandy beaches, many dotted by modern tourist developments. Inland there is more tranquillity, with small towns and villages that remain relatively untouched. The landscape is one of carefully tended fields and orchards, vineyards and olive groves, and tree-covered hills. Here and there small fortified towns recall the turbulent history of these places that goes back to the Middle Ages or earlier. You will quickly see why Catalonia acquired its name from the ancient Latin word *castellum,* meaning "fortified settlement."

## BLANES

*60 km (37 mi) northeast of Barcelona, 45 km (28 mi) south of Girona.*

The southernmost outpost of the Costa Brava, Blanes was first settled by Iberian tribes, followed by the Romans in the 1st century BC. The town's castle of Sant Joan, on a mountain overlooking the town, goes back to the 11th century. The watchtower along the coastline was built in the 16th century to protect against Barbary pirates. Blanes was flourishing even before the tourism boom of the late 1950s, with light industry (especially textiles) and a large fishing fleet. But its long beaches—the most southerly strands in Girona province—and adjacent coves were too perfect to be passed up by northern Europeans flocking to Spain in search of sun and low prices. Today many travelers skip the working port of Blanes, but it's a must-do for green-thumbers, thanks to the area's celebrated botanical gardens.

The Costa Brava begins here with five different beaches running from Punta Santa Anna on the far side of the port—a tiny cove with a pebbly beach at the bottom of a chasm encircled by towering cliffs, fragrant pines, and deep blue-green waters—to the 2½-km-long (1½-mi-long) S'Abanell beach, which draws the crowds.

★ Terrace upon terrace of exotic plants grip the steeply slanting hillside above the sea at **Jardí Botànic Marimurtra,** the garden created by the German Karl Faust in 1928. It holds more than 7,000 species, with the collection of cacti from the arid regions of South Africa and Central America especially notable. Poisonous, medicinal, and aromatic plants, ferns, cork, kermes (scarlet oak), and conifers flourish in lush variety.

⊠*Passeig Karl Faust 10* ☎*972/330826* ⌧€5 ⊗*Apr.–Oct., daily 9–6; Nov.–Mar., weekdays 10–5, weekends 10–2.*

★ The impressive **Jardí Botànic Pinya de Rosa** contains some 4,000 plant species. Created in 1945 by industrial engineer Dr. Fernando Riviere de Caralt at the foot of the sea, the botanical garden is noted for its collection of cacti (some as tall as 50 feet), aloe, century, and yucca plants. American botanists consider its collection of more than 600 species of *Opuntia* (prickly pear) one of the finest in the world. ⊠*Platja de Santa Cristina* ☎*972/355290* ⌧€5 ⊗*Daily 9–6.*

☾ The summer event in Blanes that everyone waits for is the **fireworks competition,** held every night at 10:30 July 21–27; it coincides with the town's yearly festival. The fireworks are launched over the water from a rocky outcropping in the middle of the seaside promenade known as Sa Palomera, while people watch from the beach and surrounding area as more gunpowder is burned in a half hour than at the battle of Trafalgar.

Launches from **Dofijets Boats** (☎*609/356301*) and "**Viajes Marítims** (☎*616/909100*) on the harbor front can take you up the coast to neighboring towns and beaches from May through September.

### WHERE TO EAT & STAY

¢–$  ✕⌧ **Horitzó.** Overlooking the main Blanes beach, this is the town's best hotel. Though far from luxurious, rooms are adequate and the balconies overlooking the Mediterranean give the place its main charm. Thirty minutes from Barcelona by car and an hour via a panoramic railroad along the edge of the beach, this is an economical and viable alternative for visiting the Costa Brava and Barcelona as well. **Pros:** handy to Barcelona by railroad, a peaceful beach hideaway. **Cons:** Blanes can be over-touristed in summer, not really far enough from Barcelona to get a sense of what the Costa Brava is really all about. ⊠*Passeig Marítim S'Abanell 11, 17320* ☎*972/330400* ⊕*www.hotel horitzo.com* ⌧*118 rooms* ⌂*In-hotel: restaurant* ▤*AE, DC, MC, V* ⊗*Closed Nov.–Mar.* ℿ*EP.*

8

## LLORET DE MAR

*10 km (6 mi) north of Blanes, 67 km (42 mi) northeast of Barcelona, 43 km (27 mi) south of Girona.*

The Costa Brava officially begins at Lloret de Mar, but one look at it and you might be tempted to head back to Barcelona. The many concrete-tower hotels fill up with thousands of young people on a tight budget out to drink, dance, and work on a tan. Of course, if you're looking for that spring-break atmosphere—this is the place. Swamped by faux English pubs and German beer gardens, the town also offers quiet pedestrian zones and some gorgeous architecture to admire. The town's cultural opportunities range from concerts and art openings to the Iberian ruins at Turó Rodó and the medieval castle of Sant Joan.

If you want nothing between you and the sun, head to the *cala* (cove) near Lloret de Mar called Boadella and reserved for nudists. Given the heavy tourist buildup, the beach that stretches along the promenade is Lloret de Mar's main attraction, but it's usually packed and you'll probably have to put up with your neighbor's boom box. At the northern end of this strand is Sa Caleta, a cove that offers more sheltered swimming. On the twisting scenic road between Lloret and Tossa de Mar is the small pristine Cala Morisca (Moorish Cove).

Three kilometers (2 mi) south of Lloret is **Santa Cristina** ( ⊠*Signposted off Ctra. de Blanes*), a sheltered sandy cove with an 18th-century chapel amid soaring pine and eucalyptus trees that grow to the shore. The allegorical mural painting by Joaquín Sorolla entitled *Catalunya* on view at the Hispanic Society of America in New York City was purportedly modeled in part on this landscape. Every July there is a pilgrimage by boat to the chapel. You can take a break for lunch to enjoy a succulent fish paella at one of the beach's three *chiringuitos* (makeshift beach restaurants under awnings).

The **Jardins de Santa Clotilde,** neo-Renaissance gardens designed in 1919 by architect Nicolau Maria Rubió i Tudurí and based on Florence's Boboli gardens, are characterized by an emphasis on plants and shrubbery—flower lovers should look elsewhere. ⊠*Ctra. de Blanes, Km 652* ☎*972/364735* ⊠*€5* ☉*June–Oct., Tues. 4–7, Wed.–Sun. 10:30–1 and 4–7.*

## WHERE TO EAT & STAY

**$–$$** ×⊡ **Husa Roger de Flor.** Short on services and amenities but long on traditional Costa Brava elegance, this dignified villa stands in stark contrast to the cookie-cutter concrete columns of Lloret. On the eastern edge of town, it has the finest panoramic views of any lodging in the vicinity. The gardens, with a saltwater pool and geraniums, bougainvillea, and palms, add an elegant touch. High-ceilinged, though somewhat threadbare, rooms and furnishings are simple yet comfortable. L'Estelat restaurant is a prime spot for gazing at the Mediterranean—and dining on local fare such as *ensalada de bacalao con habas* (cod salad with broad beans). **Pros:** unbeatable views and traditional surroundings. **Cons:** short on technology and state-of-the-art equipment such as Wi-Fi or flat-screen TVs. ⊠*Turó de l'Estelat, Apartat 66, 17320* ☎*972/364800* ⊕*www.hotel-husarogerdeflor.com* ↙*87 rooms* ᗰ*In-hotel: public Internet, restaurant, tennis court, pool* ⊟*AE, DC, MC, V* ☉*Closed Nov.–Mar.* ⼝*EP.*

## NIGHTLIFE

Notorious as the Costa Brava's hottest nightlife destination, Lloret de Mar explodes after dark. Foreigners and locals of all ages rage until dawn at the happening **Moby's** ( ⊠*Av. Just Marlès* ☎*972/364214*). Around the corner is **Tropics** ( ⊠*Carrer Ferran Agulló 47* ☎*972/364214*), an electronically laser-lighted and audio-powered brawl with two dance floors and five bars. **Bumper's** ( ⊠*Pl. del Carme 4* ☎*972/362071*) is another hot music bar and disco. **Hollywood Disco** ( ⊠*Ctra. de Tossa 5* ☎*972/643693*) may be the wildest scene of all, with go-go dancers and strippers, while the **St. Trop** ( ✉*Baixada de la Riera 16* ☎*972/365051*) completes this quintet of Lloret's top clubs.

## TOSSA DE MAR

*11 km (7 mi) north of Lloret de Mar, 80 km (50 mi) northeast of Barcelona, 41 km (25 mi) south of Girona.*

Set around a blue buckle of a bay, Tossa de Mar is a symphony in two parts: the Vila Vella, or the Old Town—a knotted warren of steep, narrow, cobblestone streets with many restored buildings (some dating back to the 14th century)—and the Vila Nova, or the New Town. The former is encased in medieval walls and towers, but the New Town is open to the sea and is itself a lovely district threaded by 18th-century lanes. Girdling the Old Town, on the Cap de Tossa promontory that juts out into the sea, the 12th-century walls and towers at water's edge are a local pride and joy, considered the only example of a fortified medieval town on the entire Catalan coast.

Artist Marc Chagall vacationed in Tossa de Mar for four decades, and called it his "blue paradise." Ava Gardner filmed the 1951 Hollywood extravaganza *Pandora and the Flying Dutchman* here (a statue dedicated to her stands on a terrace on the medieval walls); today the film is compelling for its location scenes of an untouched Costa Brava. Things may have changed since those days, but all in all, this beautiful village retains much of the magic of the unspoiled Costa Brava. The primary beach at Tossa de Mar is the Platja Gran (Big Beach) in front of the town beneath the walls, and just next to it is Mar Menuda (Little Sea). Small, fat, colorfully painted fishing boats—maybe the same ones that caught your dinner—are pulled up onto the beach, heightening the charm.

The main bus station (the local tourist office is here) is on Plaça de les Nacions Sense Estat. Take Avinguda Ferran and Avinguda Costa Brava to head down the slope to the waterfront and the Old Town, which is entered by the Torre de les Hores, and head to the Vila Vella's heart, the Gothic church of Sant Vicenç. Then just saunter around and take a dip in the Middle Ages.

The Romans knew a good place when they saw it, as Turissa's (the name they gave Tossa de Mar) famous ancient villa, uncovered in 1914, proves. At *Els Ametllers* (the Almond Trees), near the back of the town and bounded on one side by Avinguda Pelegrí, are the ruins of the **Vila Romana,** which include an oil press, warehouses, and several rooms with magnificent mosaic pavements (one of which bears the owner's name: Salve Vitale). Additional discoveries revealed a sunken swimming pool, a hot-air heating system, and a monumental fountain—all indications this family lived in imperial luxury. The villa is not open to public view, but you can see many of the excavated finds in the Museu Municipal de Tossa de Mar.

The **Museu Municipal de Tossa de Mar,** housed in the Palau Batlle, a 12th-century palace named for the Batlle family, displays ancient Roman objects and mosaics from the Vila Romana. It also has paintings by 19th-century Catalan painters and by Marc Chagall, Foujita, Masson, and others. ⊠ *Pl. del Pintor Roig i Soler 1* ☎ *972/340709* ✂ *€3* ⊘ *Mid-June–mid-Sept., daily 10–8; mid-Sept.–mid-June, Tues.–Sun. 11–1 and 3–5.*

## WHERE TO EAT & STAY

$$–$$$ ✕ **La Cuina de Can Simon.** Elegantly rustic, this restaurant right beside the old walled city serves a combination of classical cuisine with very up-to-date touches. The service is top-shelf, from the welcoming tapa with a glass of *cava* (sparkling wine) to the little pastries accompanying coffee. ⊠ *Portal 24* ☎ *972/341269* ▭ *AE, DC, MC, V* ⊘ *Closed last 2 wks of Nov.; last 2 wks of Jan.; and Mon. and Tues. Oct.–May. No dinner Sun.*

$–$$ ✕ **Bahia.** An institution for years, this place is known for its authentic home cooking. Dishes such as *cim-i-tomba* (a kind of *suquet*, Catalan fish-and-potato stew, typical of Tossa), *brandade* (puree) of cod, and great desserts are all revelations. ⊠ *Passeig del Mar 19* ☎ *972/340322* ▭ *AE, DC, MC, V* ⊘ *No dinner mid-Oct.–Easter.*

★ $$$–$$$$ ⬚ **Gran Hotel Reymar.** Built in the unornamented rationalist style in the 1960s on a spectacular rocky promontory at the edge of the sea, this hotel has graceful modern lines that contrast with the jagged rocks around it—and it's just a 10-minute walk from the historic walls of the Old Town. Reymar has fairly dazzling restaurants and bars. Rooms have satellite TV, marble-covered bathrooms, fine modern furniture, and seafront balconies. **Pro:** long on comforts and technology. **Con:** short on charm and architectural grace. ⊠ *Platja de Mar Menuda s/n, 17320* ☎ *972/340312* ⊕ *www.TossaGranHotelReyMar.com* ✂ *148 rooms, 18 suites* ⅄ *In-hotel: 4 restaurants, bars, tennis court, pools, some pets allowed* ▭ *AE, DC, MC, V* ⊘ *Closed Nov.–Apr.* ⦿*EP.*

$–$$ ⬚ **Hotel Diana.** Built by the Moderniste architect Antoni Falguera, this Art Nouveau gem is one of the finest places on the Costa Brava to cozy up with a glass of sherry and while away the early evening. Overlooking a beach, the Diana also contains an enticing inner courtyard—a lush garden with palm trees, flowers, and fountains, and inside, a stunning Art Nouveau fireplace that incorporates a bust by Frederic Marés of Falguera's wife. Guest rooms have contemporary furnishings. **Pros:** first-rate art and architecture, verdant surroundings. **Cons:** somewhat lacking in amenities, no public Internet. ⊠ *Pl. de Espanya 6, 17320* ☎ *972/341886* ⊕ *www.diana-hotel.com* ✂ *20 rooms, 1 suite* ⅄ *In-hotel: Wi-Fi, bar, some pets allowed* ▭ *AE, DC, MC, V* ⊘ *Closed Nov.–Easter* ⦿*BP.*

¢–$ ⬚ **Hotel Capri.** Maria Eugènia Serrat, a native Tossan, displays local hospitality at her small family hotel. Set on the beach with the medieval walls looming behind it, the hotel has a super location. Rooms are individually decorated in different styles and colors. **Pros:** very warm and personal hostessing, good combination of medieval surroundings and modern technology. **Cons:** tight quarters in general, rooms a little small. ⊠ *Passeig del Mar 17, 17320* ☎ *972/340358* ⊕ *www. hotelcapritossa.com* ✂ *22 rooms* ⅄ *In-hotel: Wi-Fi, some pets allowed* ▭ *MC, V* ⊘ *Closed Nov.–Mar.* ⦿*BP.*

¢ 📺**Hotel Sant March.** This family hotel in the center of town, run by Francesc Zucchitello, is just two minutes from the beach. His wife and mother-in-law care for an interior garden that is the envy of many. All rooms open onto the garden—making for much-appreciated tranquillity in a sometimes hectic town. **Pros:** intimate, family run hotel with a warm personal touch. **Cons:** though the rooms are largely shielded from the midtown din, the location is at the very eye of the storm. ✉*Av. del Pelegrí 2, 17320* ☎*972/340078* ⊕*hotelsantmarch. en.eresmas.com* 🛏*29 rooms* ♿*In-hotel: Wi-Fi, bar* 🟰*AE, DC, MC, V* �><*Closed Oct.–Mar.* 🍴*BP.*

## SANT FELIU DE GUÍXOLS

*23 km (14 mi) north of Tossa de Mar, 100 km (62 mi) northeast of Barcelona, 37 km (23 mi) southeast of Girona.*

In this fishing and shipping town set in a small bay, handsome Moderniste mansions line the seafront promenade, recalling the town's former wealth from the cork industry. In front of that, an arching beach of fine white sand leads around to the fishing harbor at its north end. Behind the promenade, a well-preserved old quarter of narrow streets and squares leads to a 10th-century gateway with horseshoe arches (all that remains of a pre-Romanesque monastery); nearby, a church still stands that combines Romanesque, Gothic, and baroque styles.

Indeed, the next time you open a bottle of vintage champagne, you might say a little prayer for this venerable town. Surrounded by dark-green cork forests (as is much of northeastern Catalonia), it first found its place in the sun during the 17th century when French abbot Dom Pérignon, on a trip to the Benedictine monastery of Sant Pere de Rodes, 64 km (40 mi) north of here, discovered that the properties of cork allow it to contain the high pressure that builds up inside a champagne bottle. Before long, the cork forests of this town became famous, with the stripped bark of the cork oak (*quercus suber*) used to make cork stoppers (and other products such as insulation). Before the Dom's discovery, hemp plugs soaked in oil or wooden bungs had been used. At first, corks were made by hand, with each cork cut to shape by a craftsman. It was a good job, and cork makers, paid by the piece, enjoyed a certain social standing. Eventually, of course, power-driven blades and punches took over, but not before founding the fortunes of many Sant Feliu de Guíxols residents.

The **Museu d'Història de la Ciutat** has interesting exhibits about the town's cork and fishing trades. It also displays local archaeological finds. ✉*Carrer Abadia s/n* ☎*972/821575* 🎫*Free* �><*July–Sept., Tues.–Sat. 11–2 and 5–8, Sun. 11–2; Oct.–June, Tues.–Sat. 11–2 and 4–7, Sun. 11–2.*

### WHERE TO EAT & STAY

★ $$–$$$ ✕**El Dorado Mar.** Around the southern end of the beach perched over the entrance to the harbor, this superb family restaurant offers fine fare at unbeatable prices. Whether straight seafood such as *lubina* (sea bass) or *dorada* (gilthead bream) or *revuelto de setas* (eggs scrambled with wild mushrooms), everything served here is fresh and filled with taste. ✉*Passeig Irla 15* ☎*972/326286* ▤*AE, DC, MC, V* ⊙*No dinner mid-Oct.–Easter.*

★ $$ ✕**Eldorado.** Lluis Cruanya, who once owned Barcelona's top restaurant and another in Manhattan, has done it again with Eldorado. With his daughter Suita running the dining room and Iván Álvarez as chef, this contemporary-lined and smartly designed restaurant a block back from the beach serves taste-filled morsels from *llom de tonyina a la plancha amb tomàquets agridolços, ceba i chíps d'escarchofa* (grilled tuna with pickled tomato, baby onions, and artichoke chips) to *Llobarro rostít amb emulsió de cítrics i espàrrecs trigueros* (roast sea-bass with a citric emulsion and wild asparagus), all cooked to perfection. Try the *patates braves* (new potatoes in allioli and hot sauce), as good as any in Catalonia. ✉*Rambla Vidal 19* ☎*972/821414* ▤*AE, DC, MC, V* ⊙ *Closed Tues. Oct.–Easter.*

★ ¢ ✕▥**Can Segura.** Half a block in from the beach, Can Segura is the best deal in town, with home-cooked seafood and upland specialties. The dining room is always full, with customers waiting their turn in the street, but the staff is good at finding spots at the jovially long communal tables. Small but proper rooms are available for overnight sojourns. **Pros:** two minutes from the beach with great value dining downstairs. **Cons:** no Wi-Fi or public Internet, weak on technology and amenities, a budget choice. ✉*Carrer de Sant Pere 11, 17220* ☎*972/321009* 🖷*972/321101* ⇆*11 rooms* ⌂*In-hotel: restaurant, bar* ▤*AE, DC, MC, V* ⊙*Closed Nov.–Easter (except New Year's Eve weekend)* ⦿*EP.*

## S'AGARÓ

★ *3 km (2 mi) north of Sant Feliu, 103 km (64 mi) northeast of Barcelona, 42 km (26 mi) south of Girona.*

S'Agaró is one of the Costa Brava's most elegant clusters of villas and seaside mansions, built up around S'Agaró Vell, a fashionable private development that often hosted the likes of John Wayne and Cole Porter. Set by the sea, S'Agaró itself has a delightful promenade walk along the seawall from La Gavina—the noted hotel in S'Agaró Vell—to Sa Conca beach.

S'Agaró Vell, by the beach of Sant Pol, is one of the earliest examples in Spain of a tourist resort created specifically as such. It was designed by poet and architect Rafael Masó i Valentí in the fashionable style of the time known as Noucentisme: an alluring post–Art Nouveau return to a more classical style. The promoter was the visionary Josep Ensesa, son of a wealthy Girona industrialist, who in the 1920s created S'Agaró Vell as a luxury residential resort aimed exclusively at the pleasures of summer. Today more than 50 homes have been built—all with the well-proportioned, subdued lines that Noucentisme derived from Greek and Roman classical architecture, each required to adhere to the stylistic specifications originally established by Masó.

## WHERE TO EAT & STAY

★ $$–$$$  ✕**Villa Mas.** For excellent dining at nonstratospheric costs in S'Agaró, this Moderniste villa with a lovely turn-of-the-20th-century zinc bar inside works with fresh products recently retrieved from the Mediterranean. The terrace is a popular and shady spot just across the road from the beach, and the clientele is predominantly young and savvy. ⊠*Platja de Sant Pol 95* ☎*972/822526* ▭*AE, DC, MC, V* ⊘*Closed Mon. Oct.–Mar. and Dec. 12–Jan 12. No dinner weekdays Oct.–Mar.*

$$$$  ✕▦**L'Hostal de la Gavina.** This is the place for the last remnants of

Fodor's Choice  Costa Brava chic. Big rollers such as Cole Porter followed upper-class

★  couples from Barcelona who began honeymooning here in the 1930s. In S'Agaró Vell, on the eastern corner of Sant Pol beach, the hotel is an outstanding display of design and cuisine (don't miss the fresh fish and seafood), opened in 1932 by Josep Ensesa. Guest rooms have fine wood furniture and Oriental rugs. Tennis, golf, and riding are nearby, and on a summer evening the loggia overlooking the sea is sublime. **Pros:** superbly decorated and appointed, wonderful traditonal European environment. **Cons:** hard on the budget *and* habit-forming. ⊠*Pl. de la Rosaleda s/n, 17248* ☎*972/321100* ⊕*www.lagavina.com* ⇆*58 rooms, 16 suites* ⚷*In-room: safe. In-hotel: restaurant, pool, gym, some pets allowed* ▭*AE, DC, MC, V* ⊘*Closed Nov.–Easter (except New Year's Eve weekend)* ¶⊙*EP.*

## PLATJA D'ARO

*3 km (2 mi) north of S'Agaró, 108 km (64 mi) northeast of Barcelona, 39 km (24 mi) southeast of Girona.*

Platja d'Aro has 3 km (2 mi) of splendid beach to recommend it, though it is heavily built up. Like many other places on the coast, it was a knot of fishing shacks attached to the inland main town of Castell d'Aro, but tourist development changed that.

## WHERE TO EAT & STAY

$–$$  ✕**Aradi.** This typical Costa Brava tavern and restaurant serves fare based on market products bought daily. Try the *esparracat d'ous amb patates i gambes a l'all* (fried eggs with potatoes and garlic shrimp), a star dish. The terrace is the place to be year round, when the weather is good. ⊠*Av. Cavall Bernat 78* ☎*972/817376* ▭*AE, DC, MC, V* ⊘*Closed Mon.*

★ $$  ✕▦**Costa Brava.** Built on the rocks over the beach, this family-run hotel and restaurant offers splendid views from comfortable (though not luxurious) rooms facing the sea as well as from the bar and sitting room. Rooms are bright and airy and, while contemporary in design and furnishings, undistinguished. The restaurant, Can Polda, is a traditional dining space with sea views. **Pros:** right *in* the Mediterranean over the beach, great panoramas. **Cons:** the design of the building itself and of the rooms and furnishings is unremarkable. ⊠*Crtra. de Palamós – Punta d'en Ramis 17250* ☎*972/817308* ⊕*www.hotelcostabrava. com* ⇆*57 rooms* ⚷*In-hotel: restaurant, bar, terrace* ▭*AE, DC, MC, V* ⊘*Restaurant closed Nov. 21–Mar.4* ¶⊙*BP.*

Come summer, Platja d'Aro is a major party hub on the Costa Brava, overflowing with young foreigners and Spaniards who carouse at the many nightclubs and discos and then crash on the beach or in pensions. One of the most popular—and pulsating—discos in town is **Ithaka** (⊠ *Parc d'Aro* ☎ *972/826537*) in the new Parc d'Aro residential neighborhood and raging in summer. Crowds of people seek out the **Ático** (⊠ *Av. Cavall Bernat 44* ☎ *972/819152*) for dancing and partying. **Carroll's** (⊠ *Av. S'Agaró* ☎ *972/818410*), a standout for its antique-car DJ booth, tends to fill with a young crowd in the early evening.

## PALAMÓS

*7 km (4 mi) north of Platja d'Aro, 109 km (68 mi) northeast of Barcelona, 46 km (29 mi) southeast of Girona.*

Facing south, Palamós is a working harbor town sited on a headland that protects it from the prevailing north wind. The town was founded in 1277 by the king of Aragón, Peter II, as a royal port, and the Old Quarter remains well preserved, although its walls (built in the 16th century as protection against pirates) are no longer standing.

Palamós has the second-largest fishing fleet on the Costa Brava. The **fish market** is highly esteemed, and Palamós shrimp are among the most prized in Spain. Sleek sea bass, gargoyle-ish anglerfish, hefty grouper, and colorful rockfish are auctioned, making the market an exciting place to visit when the fishing boats begin to come in around six o'clock in the early evening.

★ To see what the Costa Brava looked liked before development, visit the beach of **Castell,** north of Palamós and the better-known La Fosca beach. As the road emerges from a thick green Mediterranean forest of evergreen oak, pine, and spiny underbrush you are greeted by 280 yards of wide, sandy beach. At one end are several fishing shacks, with a couple of tumbledown restaurants, their awnings scattered along the beach. No other buildings, let alone apartments or hotels, block the sight, so it's no wonder Castell has been praised for its scenic beauty. The Catalan government purchased a part of the Castell area and declared it to be a "place of natural interest," with an eye to keeping developers out.

On the southern end of the beach overlooking the cove is **Mas Juny,** the (still privately owned) farmhouse that once belonged to Josep Maria Sert (1874–1945), the Catalan mural painter who was one of the most acclaimed painters of the 1930s and '40s. With the money he received for decorating New York City's Waldorf-Astoria hotel he bought Mas Juny in 1929 for his third wife and transformed this typical Catalan stone farmhouse into an elegant retreat. The Serts' extravagant parties drew the likes of Marlene Dietrich and Baron Rothschild. At the northern end of the beach, atop the rocky promontory of Agulla (Needle) del Castell, are extensive, partially excavated **Iberian ruins.** Unlike other such remains uncovered in urban settings, these ruins are set in the natural habitat where the people lived 2,600 years ago.

Hidden in the woods a 10-minute walk behind the beach is a studio that painter Salvador Dalí designed and had built. It has an irregularly shaped door and is known as **La Barraca de la Porta Torta** (The Shack of the Crooked Door). The studio is open to the public.

To get to Castell, take the road north from Palamós's small port and look for signs to La Fosca; Castell is past La Fosca, on a sand road. This will bring you there in a few minutes. Arrive early; it gets crowded in summer.

## CALELLA DE PALAFRUGELL

*11 km (7 mi) north of Palamós, 120 km (74 mi) north of Barcelona, 44 km (27 mi) east of Girona.*

A pretty fishing village that has managed to retain some of its original charm, Calella de Palafrugell is especially popular for its July *habanera* song festival. With an arcaded seafront—called Les Voltes (the vaults)—and with fishing boats pulled up onto the beach, this is but the first of a series of one small *cala* (cove) after another with tiny fishing villages offering secluded places to swim. They're all worth a stop, if only to imagine what the Costa Brava was like before the tourist boom. Other coves or inlets include Sa Riera, Aiguablava, Sa Tuna, Tamariu, and Llafranc. The sheer cliffs, transparent waters, and abundant vegetation in this region make this the quintessential Costa Brava.

Evidence of the isolation of this stretch of the coast is its own dialect. Note the feminine article "sa" or masculine "es," as in Sa Riera or Es Pianc, in front of many place-names of the area—a feature of the *salat,* or salty, Catalan variant spoken along this coast. In earlier times locals rarely traveled inland and this isolation preserved this archaic usage, which locals as far south as Tossa de Mar and as far north as Cadaqués use in their daily speech.

This stretch of coast claims the promontory of **Cap Roig,** with panoramic views of the soaring Formigues (Ants) Isles. The islands were the site of a decisive battle in 1285, in which the Catalan fleet, led by the great Catalan admiral Roger de Llúria, destroyed the French fleet sailing to supply Felipe the Bold's siege of Girona. The battle ended, temporarily, French aspirations in the Mediterranean. Cap Roig is less than 2 km (1 mi) south of Callela de Palafrugell and makes for an enchanting half-hour walk from town.

### WHERE TO EAT & STAY

★ $$$$ ✕⌂ **El Far de Sant Sebastiá.** A 17th-century hermitage attached to a 15th-century watchtower, this jumble of elegant stairways and terraces overlooking the Mediterranean lavishes visitors with a full complement of sensorial rewards and pleasures. Overlooking the Bay of Llafranc from a rocky aerie leading down to a sandy beach, El Far (lighthouse or watchtower) is an hour and a half from Barcelona at the heart of the Costa Brava. Rooms are high-ceilinged and breezy with sea views, and the restaurant specializes in local Empordà and Mediterranean cuisine. **Pros:** one of the best combinations of graceful architecture and spectacular views on the Costa Brava. **Cons:** somewhat isolated from Costa Brava village life. ✉ *Platja de Llafranc, Llafranc–Palafrugell 17211* ☎ *972/301639* 🖷 *972/304328* ⊕ *www.elfar.net* ↩ *9 rooms* 🛆 *In-hotel: restaurant, no elevator, public Wi-Fi* ☰ *AE, DC, MC, V.*

★ $$$–$$$$    ✕🖬 **Hotel Aigua Blava.** What began as a small *hostal* in the mid-1920s is now a full-fledged luxury hotel, run by the fourth generation of the same family. Traditional touches—rocking chairs and wooden furniture in the sitting rooms, black-and-white photos tracing the evolution of the hotel—blend pleasantly with the breezy pastel decoration of the rooms and the luscious sea views. The bright, sun-filled restaurant overlooks the water and serves traditional Mediterranean fish dishes, including *bacalao* (cod) and *merluza* (hake). Hotel Aigua Blava is about 9 km (6 mi) north of Calella de Palafrugell. **Pros:** personalized, family-run environment, comfortable and traditional design, surrounded by gardens and greenery. **Cons:** equipment and furnishings are somewhat antique, not a state-of-the-art Jacuzzi and flat-screen TV kind of operation. ✉ *Platja de Fornells, Begur 17255* ☎ *972/622058* 🖷 *972/622112* ⊕ *www.aiguablava.com* ↩ *85 rooms* 🛆 *In-hotel: restaurant, bar, tennis court, pool, public Wi-Fi, no elevator* ☰ *AE, DC, MC, V.*

★ $$–$$$    ✕🖬 **Parador de Aiguablava.** The vista from this modern, blindingly white parador, 9 km (6 mi) north of Calella de Palafrugell, is the classic postcard Costa Brava: the rounded Cala d'Aiguablava wraps around the shimmering blue Mediterranean. On the terrace you can bask in the sun while waves break at the rocky shore and dissolve into white froth below. The parador maximizes its cliff-top perch with large windows everywhere—in the cool-tone rooms, the bright and airy restaurant, and the many comfortable sitting rooms. The restaurant serves fine Costa Brava favorites, including the much-heralded *anchoas* (anchovies) from nearby L'Escala. **Pros:** being in it, you see the magnificent views around the parador. **Cons:** the barracks-like alabaster structure atop the cliffs is something of an eyesore. ✉ *Platja d'Aiguablava, Begur 17255* ☎ *972/622162* 🖷 *972/622166* ⊕ *www.parador.es* ↩ *78 rooms* 🛆 *In-hotel: restaurant, pool, gym, public Internet* ☰ *AE, DC, MC, V.*

## NIGHTLIFE & THE ARTS

A throwback to the romantic 19th century is the lingering presence on Costa Brava of the *habanera,* a musical lament strummed on a guitar in a swaying Cuban rhythm and sung mostly in Spanish, though some songs are in Catalan. Telling of longing for the homeland and the hard conditions of life in the colonies, these popular songs are performed by groups at events and clubs throughout summer.

The Calella de Palafrugell *habanera (songfest* ☎ *972/614475 for information from tourist office)* takes place on the first Saturday in July. The festival is held in the cozy *plaça* (plaza) of Port Bo; tickets cost €18.

## PALAFRUGELL

*5 km (3 mi) west of Calella de Palafrugell, 123 km (76 mi) north of Barcelona, 39 km (24 mi) east of Girona.*

This busy inland market town has preserved its Catalan flavor with the old streets and shops around its 16th-century church. Palafrugell is indelibly connected with the Catalan writer Josep Pla (1897–1981), who was a chronicler of daily life in Catalonia, especially that of his home turf. His works can be considered vast memoirs that cover a half century of Catalan life, seen through the eyes—sometimes ironic, and sometimes pained—of a man who laments the collapse of the rural world. Though he sided with the Franco regime during the Spanish civil war (something that was held against him by many Catalan intellectuals), he published his books in Catalan rather than Spanish in 1947, which was anathema to the Franco regime. Pla is omnipresent in Palafrugell: bookstores, posters, even "Josep Pla" menus in restaurants. In an effort to expand the resort image of the Costa Brava, Palafrugell sponsors cultural events and festivals outside the summer season.

The **Fundació Josep Pla** is the best place to get information on local activities; there is also a large library. You can pick up a map (€6) with Josep Pla places of interest for a do-it-yourself tour of the town. Guided Pla walks (€5) can be scheduled on Saturday mornings for groups of 15 or more or by individuals by calling to reserve ahead. ⊠ *Carrer Nou 51* ☎ *972/305577* ⊕ *www.fundaciojoseppla.cat* ☜ *€3* ⊗ *Mid-June–mid-Sept., Tues.–Sat. 10–1 and 5–8:30, Sun. 10–1; mid-Sept.–mid-June, Tues.–Fri. 5–8, Sat. 9:30–1 and 5–8, Sun. 10–1.*

8

## LA BISBAL

*8 km (5 mi) northwest of Palafrugell, 125 km (78 mi) northeast of Barcelona, 28 km (18 mi) east of Girona.*

An inland town, La Bisbal has been famous since the 16th century as a pottery-producing center. The land around the town conceals clay deposits from thousands of years of alluvial remains.

### WHERE TO STAY

**$$$$**
Fodor's Choice
★

**Mas de Torrent.** In the tiny village of Torrent, but very close to La Bisbal, lies one of Spain's most refined retreats. A vision of easy elegance and rustic Catalan style, this converted 18th-century *masia* (farmhouse) resembles something from a sumptuous coffee-table art book. The stylish suites are in the hotel's gardens; the bungalows overlook the gardens. The panache carries over to its restaurant, which serves the best of sea and land from the Baix (Lower) Empordà. For total idleness, tempt yourself with the summer poolside buffet; the more active will utilize the sports facilities—golf, riding, deep-sea fishing, tennis, water sports—nearby. **Pros:** fine cuisine, impeccable design and decor, superior service. **Cons:** isolated from easy access to local life, slightly redolent of a gated tourist community. ⊠ *Afores s/n, Torrent 17123* ☎ *972/303292* ⊕ *www.mastorrent.com* ↵ *32 rooms, 7 suites* ☝ *In-hotel: restaurant, pool, some pets allowed* ▤ *AE, DC, MC, V* ▯*EP.*

### SHOPPING

Pottery shops line **Carrer de l'Aigüeta,** where you can find everything from the kitschy to the simply elegant. In antiques shops you can discover sought-after (and expensive) beautiful, old Catalan pottery. You can go directly to the pottery makers at several local factories, but the best outlet in town is **Terrisseria Salamó** ( ⊠ *Carrer del Padró 54* ☎*972/640255*); for five generations this small crafts center has been producing sets of china from the most traditional to the latest marbled designs.

## PERATALLADA

*5 km (3 mi) east of La Bisbal, 11 km (7 mi) north of Palafrugell, 128 km (80 mi) northeast of Barcelona, 31 km (19 mi) east of Girona.*

Medieval and miniaturistic Peratallada (population 400) is an enchanting town that seems quite happily stuck in the Middle Ages. Its beautifully preserved ancient buildings, narrow cobbled streets, arched walkways, and tiny hidden squares invite you to lose yourself in another century. A spectacular moat carved entirely out of rock encircles the town—hence its name, which means "carved rock."

### WHERE TO EAT & STAY

$–$$ ✕**Can Nau.** Overlooking the Plaça Esquiladors in the heart of town, this restaurant in a snug *casa de pagès* (country house) exudes warmth and rustic charm, from its sturdy wooden tables to the bright paintings of the local landscape. The menu stars simple, time-honored Catalan comfort food such as *conill amb salsa d'ametlles* (rabbit in almond sauce) and *botifarra dolç amb compota de poma* (sweet country sausage with stewed apples). ⊠*Pl. Esquiladors 2* ☎*972/634035* ⊕*www.cannau. iespana.es* ☰*MC, V* ☾*Closed Wed. except holidays; mid-June–mid-July; and Dec. 18–27. No dinner Sun.(except in Aug.)*

★ ¢ ☖**Ca L'Aliu.** Antique furniture and comfortable beds with thick quilts and plump pillows fill the fresh-smelling rooms of this soothing, small country house. The owners, a friendly family, can fill you in on what's going on around town and will even lend you a bicycle for a tour of the nearby countryside. **Pros:** rustic, medieval furnishings and structure fit perfectly with the town's ancient aesthetic. **Cons:** rooms are small, privacy is limited. ⊠*Roca 617113* ☎*972/634061* ⊕*www.calaliu.com* ⤶*7 rooms* ☖*In-room: no a/c, no phone. In-hotel: bicycles, no elevator* ☰*MC, V* ◑*BP.*

### NIGHTLIFE & THE ARTS

Peratallada has its share of sprightly festivals, such as the **Festa Medieval** on the first weekend in October. Everyone dresses up in medieval costume and parades through the streets. The **Fira Peratallada,** the last Sunday in April, includes a bustling cheese market and arts-and-crafts stands in the main square.

## ULLASTRET

*4 km (2½ mi) north of Peratallada, 130 km (81 mi) northeast of Barcelona, 35 km (22 mi) east of Girona.*

For anyone unaccustomed to seeing massive Iberian stonework other than Greek or Roman ruins, the vast dimensions of Ullastret can be a surprising experience. With a rural setting about 2 km (1 mi) north of the village of Ullastret, in the direction of Torroella de Montgrí, the archaeological site of Ullastret contains the remains of houses, temples, cisterns, grain silos, and burial sites. A sense of calm pervades the carefully tended and landscaped site, while soaring, fragrant cypress trees shade and cool you.

The people who lived at Ullastret were the *Indiketes,* an aboriginal Iberian civilization already long settled here when the first Phoenician traders arrived in about 600 BC. The Greeks landed at nearby Empúries in about 630 BC; the temples built at the highest point of the village display an example of their Hellenizing influence. Start your visit by first following the outside wall; then enter the fortress through the main door. At the top of the rise, the **Museu d'Arqueologia de Catalunya–Ullastret** (archaeological museum) contains a collection of Attic (Athenian) pottery, another example of how the Greeks influenced the Iberians. On the first Sunday of the month from April to September, a young woman called Indiketa, dressed in native Iberian costume, gives guided tours of the site at noon. With a prior reservation you can take this tour in English. ⊠ *Puig de Sant Andreu s/n* ☎ *972/179058* ⊕ *www.mac.es/ullastret* ⌸ *€3.50* ☉ *Oct.–May, Tues.–Sun. 10–2, 3–6; June–Sept 30 and Easter Week, Tues.–Sun. 10–8. (Closes 1 Jan. and 25, 26 Dec.).*

## L'ESCALA

*10 km (6 mi) north of Ullastret, 135 km (84 mi) northeast of Barcelona, 39 km (24 mi) northeast of Girona.*

On the beautiful Bay of Roses, L'Escala faces north and feels the full effects of the *tramuntana,* the blustery northwest wind that affects the Girona and Empordà area of Catalonia and is particularly strong in fall. With that in mind, and with more than a touch of irony, the Catalan writer Josep Pla said of L'Escala's natives, "The inhabitants of this village have, for the mere fact of living in it, a certain merit." Like many others, this fishing village has felt the effects of tourism, tacky souvenir stands and all. But the beach, the Greek ruins of Empúries (best explored from here), and the divine anchovies make a trip to L'Escala worthwhile. Instead of shipping the local anchovies to the market, the fishermen of L'Escala kept these little treasures for themselves at home. In due time, these sublimely salted morsels were discovered by the earliest tourists and what had been a cottage industry became a small industrial operation. Today five shops selling the anchovies have obtained quality certificates. Be sure to stop at any restaurant in town to try this treat as an appetizer—a slice of crisp toast with anchovies dripping

**8**

olive oil, accompanied by a glass of freezing white wine, amounts to nirvana on the Costa Brava.

### WHERE TO EAT & STAY

$–$$  ✕**El Roser 2.** All the tables have views of the spectacular Bay of Roses at this edge-of-town restaurant, which serves blissful nouvelle seafood cuisine. Salads include *bogavant amb pernil i salsa de safrà* (lobster with ham and saffron sauce) and *barat amb melmelada de tomàquet* (mackerel with tomato jam). One of the most succulent dishes is *turbot rostit amb favetes a la catalana i espaguetis de calamar* (roasted turbot with stewed *faves*—a lima-bean-like legume—and squid spaghetti). ⊠*Passeig Lluís Albert 1* ☎*972/771102* ▤*AE, DC, MC, V* ☉*Closed Feb. and Mon. Sept.–June. No dinner Sun.*

$–$$  ✕▦**Nieves–Mar.** This bright, modern family hotel on the seafront is famous for its Ca la Neus restaurant, which offers up all the usual suspects: suquet (Catalan fish-and-potato stew), *llamantol al forn* (baked lobster), and paella. They also make a smashing bouillabaisse. The suites and many guest rooms have fine views of the Bay of Roses and some have balconies. **Pros:** bright, well lighted place with unforgettable views. **Con:** when the powerful northwest tramuntana is blowing out of the Pyrenees, expect a mild sandstorm. ⊠*Passeig Marítim 8, 17130* ☎*972/770300* ⊕*www.nievesmar.com* ⬦*65 rooms, 10 suites* ⚬*In-hotel: tennis court, pool, executive floor, some pets allowed* ▤*AE, DC, MC, V* ☉*Closed Nov.–Mar.* �*BP.*

## EMPÚRIES

★ *1 km (½ mi north of L'Escala, 135 km (84 mi) northeast of Barcelona, 39 km (24 mi) northeast of Girona.*

Empúries is the only Greek city still in existence on the Iberian Peninsula; the exact location of others has never been established. Back in the days when the *Odyssey* was the first travel guidebook of note, the Greeks settled here from Massalia (modern Marseilles), for trading purposes, in the 6th century BC. Originally hailing from Phocaea in Ionia (today's western coast of Turkey), they set sail as part of the colonial expansion of the Greek city-states. They founded a city whose very name, Emporion or Emporium (which translates to "market"), symbolized prosperity, exports, and commerce, and whose site—on the south shore of the Bay of Roses, near L'Escala—was a promising one. This scenic site backdropped by the sea has more than 30 acres of excavations to explore (including some beautiful mosaic floor remnants) and a fascinating museum.

When Scipio landed in Emporium in 218 BC, he found a vigorous Greek settlement, comprising two towns: Paleopolis, the Old City, and Neapolis, the new one. Paleopolis was where the modern walled village of Sant Martí d'Empúries is today (if you want a quick lunch, head here; once an island, it has been united with the mainland by the sedimentation of the Ter River, which empties into the Bay of Roses. Work on Neapolis, begun by Barcelona archaeologists some 80 years ago, revealed that Emporium was made up of two separate towns, housing

Greeks and Iberians. Greeks had access to the Iberian ghetto, but not vice-versa probably due to security considerations. The arrangement—Greeks on the island, Iberians on the mainland with no access to the sea, enabled the Greeks to monopolize trade. The Greeks eventually moved to the mainland where they founded Neapolis and continued their prosperous trade with the natives, as attested by the abundant finds of Greek pottery in the surrounding area.

In 218 BC the Romans landed at Empúries as a result of the Second Punic War against the Carthaginians (who were led by Hannibal), inaugurating a period of Roman occupation of the Iberian Peninsula that lasted several centuries (and served as the basis of the languages and culture of Spain and Portugal). The Romans added their own town to the place named, in the plural, Emporiae. Empúries eventually declined as other Roman cities, such as Tarragona, gained importance. It was abandoned in the 4th century AD and rediscovered only in the 19th century.

Highlights of the site—many structures have nothing remaining but their foundations—include the defensive walls, the open Agora marketplace, and the site of the Asklepion, the temple of the Greek god of medicine. In 1909 a statue of Asclepius was uncovered in a cistern in front of this temple, dated to the 4th century BC, and promptly moved to the Archaeological Museum in Barcelona (there are copies on-site). Recent excavations have uncovered the Roman baths of Empúries, but only 10%–15% of the Roman city is excavated. What you see today above ground is mostly the later Roman city, although the street grid is of the Greek settlement; beneath lie much of the Greek ruins, which probably will remain where they are. Enter the excavations from the seafront pedestrian promenade (most people find this by walking along the coast for 15 minutes from L'Escala or hopping the little Carrilet train that departs from L'Escala on the hour) from mid-June to mid-September; at other times, the only access is via a road on the main Figueres route.

Further digging is likely to reveal important new discoveries in addition to the previously excavated goodies, including mosaic floors and phallic icons, that are now on view in the small **Museu d'Arqueologia de Catalunya–Empúries** here. ⊠ *Ctra. del Museu s/n, L'Escala* ☎ *972/770208* ⊕ *www.mac.es/empuries* ⊠ *€5* ⊙ *June–Sept. and Easter wk, Tues.–Sun. 10–8; Oct.–May, Tues.–Sun. 10–2 and 3–6.*

## CASTELLÓ D'EMPÚRIES

*11 km (7 mi) northwest of Empúries, 139 km (86 mi) northeast of Barcelona, 47 km (29 mi) northeast of Girona.*

The seignorial silhouette of the cathedral of Santa Maria rises majestically above the Empordà plain, a particularly impressive picture from the fields east of town. Castelló d'Empúries is fundamentally an agricultural town but has an adjacent, self-contained, and not terribly appealing resort development on the Bay of Roses known as Empuriabrava. Castelló itself is a handsomely historic town with Gothic palaces and an intricate warren of cobbled streets; its heart is the Plaça dels Homes, where a tourist office can provide a town map. Marshes surround the town, which now lies several miles inland, but in the Middle Ages ships (and Viking raiders) sailed up the Muga River from the sea to dock here.

Outside the **cathedral of Santa Maria** ( ⊠ *Pl. Mosén Cinto Verdaguer s/n* ☎*972/158019*), dating to the 13th and 14th centuries, pride of place is given to the Romanesque bell tower and the portal sculpted with figures of the apostles and the Epiphany. In the spacious building, a fine 15th-century alabaster altar has delicate, highly detailed expressive figures.

## PARC NATURAL DELS AÏGUAMOLLS DE L'EMPORDÀ

*Less than 1 km (½ mi) east of Castelló d'Empúries, 139 km (86 mi) north of Barcelona, 47 km (29 mi) northeast of Girona.*

It's almost a miracle that this natural refuge has survived. Set beside the modern resort of Empuriabrava—which was carved out of the same terrain in the mid-'60s—this parcel of land was scheduled for development when a conservation movement was founded in 1976 to save it. In 1983 the Catalan parliament declared the area a nature preserve, and it has since become a haven for birds migrating from northern Europe to Africa. Thanks to this sanctuary, the bird population of all the Empordà plain continues to prosper. Hundreds of species flock here, including avocets, black-winged stilts, ringed plovers, common sandpipers, water rails, hoopoes, purple gallinules, rollers, marsh harriers, and Montagu's harrier. In addition, otters, marine cows, Camargue horses, and fallow deer have been reintroduced to this habitat. Fittingly, park administrators like to stress that silence is one of their most valued resources. There's an information center in Castelló d'Empúries. ⊠*Entrance off Ctra. de Sant Pere Pescador, Castelló d'Empúries* ☎*972/454222* ⊕*www.roses.cat/en/turisme/natura/aiguamollsemporda.aspx* ⊠*Free* ☼*Daily dawn–dusk.*

## ROSES

*9 km (5½ mi) northeast of Castelló de Empúries, 153 km (95 mi) northeast of Barcelona, 56 km (35 mi) northeast of Girona.*

The opening lines of C. S. Forester's Horatio Hornblower novel *Flying Colors* read, "Captain Hornblower was walking up and down along the sector of the ramparts of Rosas.... Overhead shone the bright autumn sun of the Mediterranean, hanging in a blue Mediterranean sky, and shining on the Mediterranean blue of Rosas Bay—the blue water fringed with white where the little waves broke against the shore of golden sand and grey-green cliff." It's not surprising Forester raised the curtain here, as the Golf de Roses has often been called the most splendid gulf on the Costa Brava. Today you can still visit those ramparts—which surround the remains of the old Greek, Roman, and

## On the Menu

Filled with superior restaurants and with more than 2,000 years of culinary tradition, Catalonia is a foodie's delight. Critic Ferran Agulló once said, "Catalan cuisine is essentially natural; it is not expensive, and it is easy." Chefs hold that the success of the local cuisine comes not only from the quality of the ingredients but also from its great variety. Fish from the Mediterranean, produce from the farmlands of the interior, and lamb and game from the Pyrenees all mean that just about any good restaurant can offer an excitingly varied menu. Furthermore, as a Mediterranean crossroads, Catalonian cuisine has been influenced by Moorish, French, and Italian culinary canons—and before that by Roman and Greek traditions.

What is generally recognized as the Catalan cuisine of today originated in Girona at the Motel (now Hotel) Ampurdán in Figueres under the direction of chef Josep Mercader. Beginning with French-influenced or "Spanish" cuisine, Mercader simplified and creatively transformed traditional Catalan cuisine. Ever since his establishment opened in 1961, Mercader's influence has been felt all over Spain, and many restaurants in Girona have incorporated his recipes.

The dish that best defines this area is the *platillo*. Difficult to define, the word is Castilian in origin and means "little plate." Some say these dishes were based on poor cuts or leftovers simmered with fresh seasonal vegetables. From the Mercader kitchen emerged recipes such as the *platillo de pollastres amb bolets* (chicken with mushrooms), a recipe that calls for range-fed chickens that have led a "happy life." Others hold that slow cooking and dramatic combinations rather than poverty of ingredients define the *platillo*. Other dishes to look for are *ànec amb peres* (duck with pears); *conill amb prunes* (rabbit with prunes); *sèpia amb verdures* (cuttlefish with vegetables); *pesols amb sèpia* (peas with cuttlefish); and *sèpia amb tripa de bacallà* (cuttlefish with cod innards). All can make for a hearty and stimulating meal. That Catalan staple, *pa amb tomàquet*, deserves a special mention. It consists of thick slices of bread, sometimes toasted, on which open tomatoes are rubbed, leaving the inner pulp. Sprinkled with olive oil and lightly salted, *pa amb tomàquet* accompanies countless Catalan dishes.

You cannot visit the Costa Brava and not try the fish. One of the best things to order is *suquet*. Originally, suquet was a very simple soup that fishermen made on their boats with little more than oil, water, onions, green peppers, garlic, tomatoes, potatoes, and whatever portion of the catch was too rough and plain for sale. Today, it's an upscale dish and everybody has his or her own opinion about who makes it best. A highly prized fish is the *llobarro* (sea bass), best eaten with as few complications as possible, preferably grilled with a sprinkling of fennel and served with a tangy mayonnaise.

Costa Brava seafood delicacies change by the season. In December restaurants serve *El Niu* (the nest), a local casserole with cod, hake, cuttlefish, egg, and potatoes. From January through March a winter specialty is *eriço* (sea urchin). There is a sweet spot in April when *xipirones* (baby octopuses) and *habitas tiernas* (tiny fava beans) are both at their finest.

8

medieval cities of Roses—and take in the view of the town, sitting at the head of the bay. Roses may not excel in scenic beauty any longer— many modern hotels, discos, and modern boats have intruded—but it's loaded with history.

Roses began as a Greek colony from the island of Rhodes (hence, its name) and was a branch of the big Empúries settlement down the coast. The Roman writer Cato states that the Greeks settled here in 776 BC, although archaeological excavations have not found any evidence earlier than 600 BC. But the Greeks were simply the first in a long line of settlers.

Unfortunately, the little that remains of old Roses is swamped in summer, when the native population of 13,500 booms to over 120,000. To serve these teeming numbers, the town has countless restaurants, discotheques, and amusement parks for the young. Almost everyone's main activity is going to the immense beaches that line the Bay of Roses. If you head out along the coast between Roses and the next village to the north, Cadaqués, you'll discover an enchanting continuum of steep and bare rocky mountains covered with spiny underbrush. Although the Mediterranean sun beats down mercilessly in summer, coves ringed by towering red pines dip into sheltered sandy beaches, allowing all to sunbathe, swim, and play. The last two coves before Cadaqués, Cala Montjoi and Cala Jònculs, are relatively free of development, with only a couple of hotels and restaurants (one of them the famous El Bulli). Between these two inlets, the jagged cliffs of the Norfeu headlands tumble into the unruly sea. Motorboats and sailboats cruise this coast, anchoring in the shelter of coves and inlets to spend the day on the water before heading back to Roses and its ongoing fiesta.

The historical concentration of civilizations inside Roses's **Ciutadella** (citadel) is unlike any other in Spain. Within these walls, settlements of Greeks, Romans, and Visigoths followed each other in turn, with a residential quarter here up to the late 19th century. Inside the citadel is the Romanesque Benedictine **monastery and cloister of Santa Maria,** a pentagonal structure begun in 1543. Walls were important back then: much of Roses's strategic importance lay in the fact that its site offered ships a safe haven from the coast's blustery *tramuntana* wind. An archaeologist gives free guided visits inside the citadel on Sunday and Wednesday mornings at 11 AM in winter and 10 AM in summer; it's open to the public from 9 AM until dark. The Museu Històric i Arqueològic, opened in 2004, and the Sala de Exposiciones, with temporary exhibits, complete the offerings available here. ⊠ *Av. de Rhodes s/n* ☎ *972/151466* ⊡ *€3* ⊙ *Apr.–Sept., daily 10–8; Oct.–Mar., daily 10–6.*

## WHERE TO EAT & STAY

**$$$$** ✕ **El Bulli.** A gastronomic Disney World, this seaside hideaway has become a sacrosanct foodie pilgrimage—just don't show up without reservations: getting a table requires calling months (or years) in advance. If you do manage to get to the top of the waiting list, be prepared for a bizarre culinary spectacle. El Bulli, named for the original owner's toy bulldogs, has become one of the world's most famous restaurants, the Formula One of cuisine. Chef Ferran Adrià will make your palate his playground with a 35-course taster's menu that has been known in the past to feature concoctions such as *espuma de humo* (foam of smoke), rosewater bubbles, and *aire de zanahoria con coco amargo* (air of carrot with bitter coconut), faux caviar made of congealed melon drops, or rabbit ear chips. Don't come here planning on having anything resembling a feast or a big meal; this is just a joyride for the senses. Do plan on spending at least €200 per person. ⊠ *Cala Montjoi, Roses, Girona* ☎ *972/150457* 🖶 *972/150717* ⊕ *www.elbulli. com* ⚖ *Reservations essential* ▭ *AE, DC, MC, V* ⊘ *Closed Oct.–Mar. No lunch.*

★ $$$-$$$$ ✕ **La Barretina.** One of the best places for fresh fish in the area, this spot named for the typical Catalan headgear is a big favorite among hyper-creative local chefs longing for a simple and satisfying meal of traditional cuisine. ⊠ *Carrer Cap Norfeu 29, 17480* ☎ *972/256123* ▭ *AE, DC, MC, V* ⊘ *Closed Tues.*

★ $$$-$$$$ ✕▥ **Almadraba Park Hotel.** This stunning hotel run by Jaume Subirós, proprietor of the Hotel Empordà in Figueres, sits on a bluff overlooking the horseshoe-shape Cala Almadraba—a cove about a half mile wide, 4 km (2½ mi) from Roses—with access to a white-sand beach. The Figueres hotel is considered the cradle of Catalan cuisine, and the kitchen here offers the same level of sophisticated cooking, so try one of the fine rice-dish specialties on the terrace with an incomparable view of the entire Bay of Roses. The hotel's look and style throughout are modern, clean-lined, and angular. **Pros:** polished, highly professionalized service, excellent views and sense of getting away to a secluded refuge. **Cons:** somewhat isolated from anything else, Roses is a long, winding (though scenic) 5-kilometer drive away. ⊠ *Platja de l'Almadraba s/n, 17480* ☎ *972/256550* ⊕ *www.almadrabapark.com* ⥲ *60 rooms, 6 suites* ⚐ *In-hotel: restaurant, bar, Wi-Fi, tennis court, pool* ▭ *AE, DC, MC, V* ⊘ *Closed mid-Oct.–mid-Mar.* ¹⊘¹ *BP.*

$$$-$$$$ ▥ **Vistabella.** Small and elegant, this quiet hotel is placed high up on a cliff overlooking the cove of Canyelles Petites, 2½ km (1½ mi) up the coast from Roses. It has excellent service and there are opportunities to pursue many water sports. The kitchen serves international cuisine. **Pros:** self-sufficient complex offering everything you need from sailboats to supper, nonpareil Mediterranean panoramas. **Cons:** almost too peaceful, somewhat removed from the lively vibe of a Costa Brava village resort. ⊠ *Av. Díaz Pacheco 26, 17480* ☎ *972/256200* ⊕ *www. vistabellahotel.com* ⥲ *23 rooms, 8 suites* ⚐ *In-hotel: 2 restaurants, pool, gym, beachfront, some pets allowed* ▭ *AE, DC, MC, V* ⊘ *Closed mid-Oct.–mid-Mar.* ¹⊘¹ *BP.*

$$-$$$ ▥ **Terraza.** Lovely views straight out to the sea and a swimming pool overlooking the beach make this semi-secluded address on the way into Roses a natural stopping place. In the kitchen, chef Toni Gotanegra ensures a high gastronomical level at this traditional yet modernized Roses hotel, one of the deans of Empordà hospitality. **Pros:** a 15-minute walk down the beach from the town of Roses, with its lively bars, shops, restaurants, and nightlife. **Cons:** just off the main drag into

town, the hotel lacks the remote refuge feel of other Roses lodging options. ⊠*Passeig Marítim 16, 17480* ☎*972/256154* ⊕*www.hotel-terraza.com* ⤶*110 rooms* ⚐*In-hotel: restaurant, pool, Wi-Fi* ⊟*AE, DC, MC, V* ⊘*Closed Jan.1–Mar. 7.* ⦅◎⦆*BP.*

### NIGHTLIFE

Roses and the area ringing the Golf de Roses have a multitude of booming nightspots, especially in summer—but keep in mind that until 1 AM or so these are ghost towns. For a quiet start, everyone's favorite bar is **La Sirena** (⊠*Pl. Sant Pere 7* ☎*972/257294*). All of the Plaça Sant Pere terrace bars and cafés are, in fact, an ongoing street party. Nearby is **Barbarosa** (⊠*Carrer Sant Isidre 3* ☎*972/255507*), a music bar that fills with potential miscreants as the sunset dies. **Si Us Plau** (⊠*Av. de Rhode 58* ☎*972/254264*) is a small villa near the beach that rocks during summer evenings. From there people head out to the big discos in Empuriabrava, starting with **Bananas** (⊠*Ctra. Figueres–Roses, Km 38.5* ☎*972/452121*). **Pasarela** (⊠*Passeig Marítim s/n* ☎*972/452097*) is another action-packed nightclub.

## CADAQUÉS

★ *17 km (11 mi) northeast of Roses, 167 km (104 mi) northeast of Barcelona, 70 km (43 mi) northeast of Girona.*

Cadaqués (pronounced cada-*kess*) has been called the most beautiful village on the Costa Brava. Its jumble of white houses, roofed with red tiles, massed upon each other, and capped by the church of Santa Maria—which seems suspended in the air—has been immortalized by hundreds of artists. A full list of the writers, musicians, and artists who stayed here at one time or another would be encyclopedic—Federico García Lorca, Luis Buñuel, Marcel Duchamp, Salvador Dalí, John Cage, and Pablo Picasso are just a few of the greatest names. Dalí—the founder of Spanish surrealism and the man who created the *Persistence of Memory* (housed in New York City's Museum of Modern Art) and those melting watches—spent many childhood summers here, and Picasso may have been inspired by the boxlike, whitewashed houses of the Costa Brava (and France's nearby Côte Vermeille) to create Cubism.

Today Cadaqués has been discovered: the horse-drawn carts that threaded their way up and down the mountain of El Pení have long ago been traded in for Mercedes, and there are more expensive art galleries than impoverished artists. Still, the town is off the beaten highway and can only be reached by one snaking road that travels over the Serra de Rodes range. (For years, many couples had wedding pictures taken in Sardinia, as it was easier to sail there than to go to Figueres overland.) Thanks to this seclusion, Cadaqués remains one of the most unspoiled and lovely towns of the coast.

The village is a labyrinth of steep and narrow pebble-paved streets. Its serpentine waterfront is lined with whitewashed private homes and inlets where small fishing boats have been pulled up onto the black, slate sand. The social center is the *rambla*, a street promenade crowded with outdoor cafés. When the sun goes down, these fill up with people having a few drinks before going off to dinner, and they fill up again in the late hours with people as eager to talk the night away as to catch the sea breezes. At the Bar Melitón on this waterfront, a plaque commemorates the many hours Marcel Duchamp spent here playing chess.

If you don't want to gallery-hop, head for the town's small museum, the **Museu Municipal d'Art,** which entices with its temporary collections of landscape and seascape paintings inspired by the scenery of the Costa Brava. In summer the museum showcases art by Dalí. ⊠ *Carrer Narcís Monturiol 15* ☎ *972/258877*

> ### DALÍ DALLIANCES
>
> Salvador Dalí was as notorious for his bizarre life as for his paintings. In his twenties, he was sentimentally involved with Federico García Lorca, though their passion remained unconsummated. Luis Buñuel, author of the surrealist film *Un Chien Andalou* (An Andalusian Dog), was another Dalí fizzled romance. When surrealist poet Paul Éluard visited Port Lligat in 1929, Dalí fell for Éluard's Russian-born wife Gala, his muse and lover—of sorts—for life. According to Dalí biographer Ian Gibson, in *The Shameful Life of Salvador Dalí*, the artist's sense of shame, a "pathological shyness", both drove his art and blocked his love life.

🎫€5 ⌚ *Easter–mid-Nov., daily 10:30–1:30 and 3–8; mid-Nov.–Easter, Mon.–Sat. 10:30–1:30 and 4–8.*

One cove up the coast from Cadaqués—just a 15-minute walk away—is **Port Lligat,** where Salvador Dalí (1904–89) built his famous house in the 1930s, which became a love nest for him and his adored wife and model Gala (who left famed surrealist poet Paul Éluard to become Madame Dalí).

★ At the **Casa Museu Salvador Dalí,** tours in English, French, and Catalan escort you through the artist's abode and his many "wonders": the stuffed polar bear hung with turquoise jewels, the dismembered mannequins, the dressing area filled with photos of the artist and celebrities, the bedroom with the panoramic view over Cap de Creus, the easternmost point on the Spanish peninsula (Dalí liked to boast he was the first man in Spain to see the sun every morning), and the swimming pool designed to look like either a phallus or the floor plan of the Alhambra, Granada's iconic Moorish palace (depending on who was asking the question). The view from the garden—which is full of amazing egg-shape sculptures—will be familiar, as it was a prevalent backdrop in Dalí's paintings. Note that the tour takes 40 minutes and must be booked in advance. ⊠ *Port Lligat* ☎ *972/251015* ⊕ *www.salvador-dali.org* 🎫 *€10* ⌚ *By appointment Mar. 15–June 14 and Sept. 16–Jan. 6, Tues.–Sun. 10:30–5:10; June 15–Sept. 15, daily 9:30–8:10.*

★ Dalí called **Cap de Creus,** the headland to the north of Port Lligat, "a grandiose geological delirium"—a fairly apropos description, since the rocky mineral formations of this cape twist and curl in the most extraordinary way, as if the earth had been convulsed, then wrung out and dropped into the sea and battered by surging waves. The area was declared a maritime and terrestrial natural park in 1998. To continue the Dalí theme, opt for a cruise out to Cap de Creus on the *Gala*, now helmed by Senyor Caminada, the son of a longtime Dalí employee; it is moored at Port Lligat's shore and excursions are offered daily to the cape and back for about €8 per person.

**NEED A BREAK?** Gaze down at heart-knocking views of the craggy coast and crashing waves with a warm mug of coffee in hand or fine fare on the table at **Bar Restaurant Cap de Creus** ( ⊠ *Ctra. Cap de Creus* ☎ *972/199005*), which sits on a rocky crag above the Cap de Creus.

## WHERE TO EAT & STAY

★ $$    ✕ **Es Trull.** Some people consider this cedar-shingled cafeteria on the harbor side street in the center of town the best kitchen in town. An ancient olive press in the interior gave Es Trull its name. It specializes in fish dishes such as *escórpora* (scorpion fish) and rice dishes, such as the star player, *arròs de calamar i gambes* (rice with squid and shrimp), or *arròs negre amb calamar i sèpia* (rice in ink of squid and cuttlefish). ⊠ *Port Ditxós s/n* ☎ *972/258196* ▭ *AE, MC, V* ☉ *Closed Nov.–Easter.*

$-$$    ✕ **Can Pelayo.** This family-run button of a place serves excellent fish. It's hidden behind Plaça Port Alguer, a few minutes' walk south of the town center. ⊠ *Carrer Nou 11* ☎ *972/258356* ▭ *AE, DC, MC, V* ☉ *Closed weekdays Oct.–May.*

¢–$    ✕ **Casa Anita.** Simple, fresh, and generous cuisine is the draw at this **Fodor's Choice** tiny place on the street that leads to Port Lligat and Dalí's house. The ★ crowd's *couleur locale* includes hippies, down-and-outs, beachcombers, and other riffraff on a budget. Try the salads and the sardine, mussel, and sea bass dishes, and get there early. ⊠ *Carrer Miquel Rosset 16* ☎ *972/258471* ▭ *AE, DC, MC, V* ☉ *Closed Mon. Sept.–May; last 2 wks of Nov.; and mid-Jan.–mid-Feb.*

$$–$$$    🏨 **Playa Sol.** Open for more than 40 years, this hotel has the experience that comes with age. The rooms are done tastefully in red and ocher; some overlook the sea. The Playa Sol is in the cove of Es Pianc on the left side of the bay of Cadaqués as you face the sea, a five-minute walk from the village center. Boaters will love this place—all types of craft tie up here, as Catalan writer Josep Pla spread its fame as the best place to drop anchor in Cadaqués. **Pros:** powerful historic vibrations and a cozy, refuge-in-the-eye-of-the-maelstrom feel. **Cons:** rooms on the small side, public spaces constricted. ⊠ *Platja Es Pianc 3, 17488* ☎ *972/258100* ⊕ *www.playasol.com* ⊷ *49 rooms* ⚹ *In-hotel: restaurant, bar, Wi-Fi, pool* ▭ *AE, DC, MC, V* ☉ *Closed mid-Nov.–mid-Feb.* ⓄⒺP.

$–$$    🏨 **Llané Petit.** An intimate, typically Mediterranean bay-side hotel, Llané Petit caters to people who want to make the most of their stay in the village and don't want to spend too much time in their hotel rooms. Rooms are simple and serene—as is the cuisine, which uses lots of grilled meats and fish. **Pros:** the semi-private beach next to the hotel is less crowded that the main Cadaqués beach. **Cons:** rooms on the small side, somewhat lightweight beds and furnishings. ⊠ *Carrer Dr. Bartomeus 37, 17488* ☎ *972/251020* ⊕ *www.llanepetit.com* ⊷ *37* rooms ♿ *In-hotel: restaurant, public Internet, Wi-Fi.* ⊟*AE, MC, V* ⊘*Closed 2 wks in Dec.* ⦿*EP.*

## SHOPPING

Cadaqués is all about art, and there are quite a few galleries—most active June–September, December, and around Easter—worth visiting. **Galeria de la Riba** ( ⊠*Riba Pianc s/n* ☎*972/159273*) handles well-known Spanish, Catalan, and international artists. The village social center, **L'Amistat** ( ⊠*Dr. Trèmols 1* ☎*972/258800*), is a good place to start; in addition to being the place where villagers bide their time playing cards, it regularly holds art exhibitions of local and international artists with homes in Cadaqués. **L'Ateneu** ( ⊠*Av. Caritat Serinyana 8* ☎*972/159209*), a nonprofit organization, regularly exhibits Catalan, Spanish, and international artists; once a year it holds a three-day collective fund-raiser exhibition at Cap de Creus. **Port Doguer** ( ⊠*Guillem Bruguera 10* ☎*972/258910*) has managed such established artists as the Moscardó brothers, Japanese painter Shigeyoshi Koyama, Sabala, Vilallonga, and Roca-Sastre, with exhibitions in a wonderful space—an old olive press. **Taller Fort** ( ⊠*Hort d'en Sanés* ☎*972/258549*) deals in international small-format art and also sponsors an annual painting competition. **Galeria Carlos Lozano** ( ⊠*Riba Pianc 2* ☎*972/159209*), founded by a Dalí crony and pivotal force in the Cadaqués art scene until his death in 2000, remains a key gallery, showing, among other prestigious artists, the work of Miguel Condé.

## NIGHTLIFE

The owner of the dark, wood-paneled **Bar Anita Nit** ( ⊠*Miquel Rosset 6* ☎*972/258471*) calls it his *whiskeria* because of the excellent selection of old whiskeys on offer. The cavernous **L'Hostal** ( ⊠*Passeig 8* ☎*972/258000*) is an institution and a draw for Dalí fans. The great man used to hang out here and lent a hand in redesigning it in 1975. As you walk in, look down: Dalí designed the "eye"-tiled floor. German-born owner Marci has played host to everyone from Mick Jagger to Gabriel García Marquez. The latter left a pen-and-ink sailboat drawing inscribed "*Para Marci, Con un Barco—Gabriel*," ("To Marci, With a Boat—Gabriel") on display in the bar.

# SANT PERE DE RODES

Fodor'sChoice ★ *18 km (11 mi) west of Cadaqués, 170 km (105 mi) northeast of Barcelona, 67 km (42 mi) northeast of Girona.*

Once commanding territory and power on both sides of the Pyrenees, the Benedictine monastery of Sant Pere de Rodes rises majestically on a steep mountainside overlooking Cap de Creus. The dignity of its architecture and the beauty of its view—which overlooks the Creus Peninsula and the waters of the Mediterranean—make it a must-visit. First built in 878 and reformed and expanded between the 9th and 12th centuries, it is one of the finest examples of Romanesque architecture in Spain, with exceptional examples of masonry laid in the *opus spicatum* (herringbone) pattern. Particularly notable are the church, with its two-tiered ambulatory, 12th-century bell tower, and defense tower. On the left-hand side of the church's altar as you enter, a winding stairway barely wide enough for one person leads to the second level. Also note the nave's 11th-century columns, decorated with wolf and dog heads.

Repeatedly sacked over the centuries, Sant Pere de Rodes lost most of its influence in the 18th century. The monastery contains a study center for the Cap de Creus nature preserve. Sant Pere de Rodes can be reached from the village of Vilajuïga or from Port de la Selva. The road winding up from Vilajuïga passes several groups of prehistoric dolmens, all signposted. Megaliths are very common in this area, more than 130 of them having been counted to date in the *comarca* (county) of the Alt Empordà alone. ✉ *Port de la Selva* ☎ *972/387559, 972/193192 for study center* ⊕ *www.mhcat.net/oferta_museal/monuments/comarques_ de_girona/monestir_de_sant_pere_de_rodes* 💶 *€3.75* ☽ *Oct.–May, Tues.–Sun. 10–5:30; June–Sept., daily 10–8. Closed Monday (unless it's a holiday), 25 and 26 Dec., 1 and 6 Jan.*

## FIGUERES

*23 km (14 mi) southwest of Sant Pere de Rodes, 42 km (26 mi) north of Girona, 150 km (93 mi) northeast of Barcelona.*

Figueres is the capital of the *comarca* (county) of the Alt Empordà, the bustling county seat of this predominantly agricultural region. Local people come from the surrounding area to shop at its many stores and stock up on farm equipment and supplies. Thursday is market day, and farmers gather at the top of the Rambla to do business and gossip, taking refreshments at cafés and discreetly pulling out and pocketing large rolls of bills, the result of their morning transactions. But among the tractors and mule carts is the main reason tourists come to Figueres: the jaw-dropping Dalí museum, one of the most-visited museums in Spain.

Painter Salvador Dalí is Figueres's most famous son. With a painter's technique that rivaled that of Jan van Eyck, a flair for publicity so aggressive it would put P.T. Barnum in the shade, and a penchant to shock (he loved telling people Barcelona's historic Gothic Quarter should be knocked down), Dalí scaled the ramparts of art history as one of the foremost proponents of surrealism, the art movement launched in the 1920s by André Breton. His most lasting image may be the melting watches in his iconic 1931 painting, *The Persistence of Memory.* The artist, who was born in Figueres (1904) and was to die here (1989), decided to create a museum-monument to himself during the last two decades of his life. Dalí often frequented the Cafeteria Astòria at the top of the Rambla (still the center of social life in Figueres), signing autographs for tourists or just being Dalí: he once walked down the street with a French omelet in his breast pocket instead of a handkerchief.

★   A museum was not a big enough word for Dalí, so he christened his monument the **Teatre-Museu Dalí.** Theater it is, as this was the Old Town theater, once reduced to a ruin in the Spanish civil war. Now topped with a glass geodesic dome and studded with Dalí's iconic egg shapes, the multilevel museum pays homage to his fertile imagination and artistic creativity. It includes gardens, ramps, and a spectacular drop cloth Dalí painted for Les Ballets de Monte Carlo. Don't look for his greatest paintings here, although there are some memorable images, including *Gala at the Mediterranean,* which takes the body of Gala (Dalí's wife) and morphs it into the image of Abraham Lincoln once you look through coin-operated viewfinders. The sideshow theme continues with other coin-operated pieces, including *Taxi Plujós* (Rainy Taxi), in which water gushes over the snail-covered occupants sitting in a Cadillac once owned by Al Capone, or *Sala de Mae West,* a trompe-l'oeil vision in which a pink sofa, two fireplaces, and two paintings morph into the face of Hollywood sex symbol Mae West. Fittingly, another "exhibit" on view is Dalí's own crypt. When his friends considered what flag to lay over his coffin, they decided to cover it with an embroidered heirloom tablecloth instead. Dalí would have liked this unconventional touch, if not the actual site: he wanted to be buried at his castle of Púbol next to his wife, Gala, but the then mayor of Figueres took matters into his own hands. All in all, the museum is a piece of Dalí dynamite. The summer night session is a perfect time for a postprandial browse through the world's largest surrealist museum. ⊠*Pl. Gala-Salvador Dalí 5* ☎*972/677500* ⊕*www.salvador-dali.org* 🎫*€12* ☉*Oct.–June, Tues.–Sun. 10:30–5:15; July–Sept., daily 9–7:15; special summer nighttime visits July 28–Sept.2, 10 PM–1AM.*

The collections at the **Museu de l'Empordà** range from the Roman era to the Catalan Renaixença. ⊠*Rambla 2* ☎*972/502305* 🎫*€2.50* ☉*July–Sept., Tues.–Sat. 11–7, Sun. 11–2.*

**8**

☪ The **Museu del Joguet de Catalunya,** displaying childhood playthings pre-Toys 'R' Us, is Spain's only toy museum. Hundreds of antique dolls are on display. The museum possesses collections of toys owned by, among others, Salvador Dalí, Federico García Lorca, and Joan Miró. It also hosts Catalonia's only *caganer* exhibit, from mid-December to mid-January on odd-numbered years. These playful little figures of guys (and gals) answering nature's call have long had a special spot in the Catalan *pessebre* (Nativity scene). Farmers are the most traditional figures, squatting discreetly behind the animals, but these days you'll find Barça soccer players and politicians, too. Check with the museum for exact dates. ⊠*Hotel de Figueres, Carrer de Sant Pere 1* ☎*972/504508* ⊕*www.mjc.cat* 🎫*€5.50* ☉*July–Sept., daily 10–1 and 4–7; Oct.–mid-Jan. and mid-Feb.–June, Tues.–Sat. 10–1 and 4–7, Sun. 10–1.*

The imposing **Castell de Sant Ferran,** an 18th-century fortified castle that is one of the largest in Europe, stands 1 km (½ mi) northwest of town. Only when you start exploring the castle grounds (and walking around its perimeter of roughly 4 km [2½ mi]) can you appreciate how immense it is. The parade grounds extend for acres, and the arcaded stables can hold more than 500 horses. This castle was the site of the last official meeting of the Republican parliament (on February 1, 1939) before it surrendered to Franco's forces. The army still uses the castle, and there may be times when you cannot enter, so call ahead. ⊠*Pujada al*

*Castell s/n* ☎*972/506094* ☜*€2.50* ⊙*Mar.–June and mid-Sept.–Oct.,*
*daily 10:30–2 and 4–6; July–mid-Sept., daily 10:30–8; Nov.–Feb., daily*
*10:30–2. Last admission 1 hr before closing.*

**OFF THE**
**BEATEN**
**PATH**

**Casa-Museu Gala Dalí.** The third point of the Dalí triangle is the medieval
castle of Púbol, where the artist's wife Gala is buried in the crypt. During
the 1970s this was Gala's residence, though Dalí also lived here in the early
1980s. It contains paintings and drawings, Gala's haute-couture dresses,
elephant sculptures in the garden, furniture, and other objects chosen by
the wcouple. Púbol, roughly between Girona and Figueres, is near the C255
and is not easy to find. If you are traveling by train, get off at the Flaçà station on the Barcelona-Portbou line of RENFE railways; walk or take a taxi 4
km (2½ mi) to Púbol. By bus the Sarfa bus company has a stop in Flaçà and
on the C255 road, some 2 km (1 mi) from Púbol. ⊠*Púbol* ☎*972/677500*
⊕*www.salvador-dali.org* ☜*€6* ⊙*Mid-Mar.–mid-June and mid-Sept.–Oct.,*
*Tues.–Sun. 10:30–6; mid-June–mid-Sept., daily 10:30–8. Last admission 45*
*mins before closing.*

**WHERE TO EAT & STAY**

**$–$$**
Fodor's Choice
★

✕▥**Hotel Empordà.** Just a mile north of town, this hotel and elegant
restaurant ($$–$$$) run by Jaume Subirós is hailed as the birthplace
of modern Catalan cuisine and has become a pilgrimage destination
for foodies seeking superb Catalan cooking. Try the *terrina calenta de
lluerna a l'oli de cacauet* (hot pot of gurnard fish in peanut oil) or, if
it's winter, *llebre a la Royal* (boned hare cooked in red wine). Guest
rooms have parquet floors and sparkling bathrooms, and you can sit
in the sun and have a drink on the terrace. The hotel is 1½ km (1 mi)
north of town. **Pros:** historic culinary destination and, of course, great
cuisine. **Cons:** the hotel occupies an unprepossessing roadside lot beside
the busy Nll highway. ⊠*Ctra. NII, Km 1.5, 17600* ☎*972/500562*
⊕*www.hotelemporda.com* ⏎*42 rooms* ⌂*In-hotel: restaurant, bar,
some pets allowed* ▤*AE, DC, MC, V* ⑩*BP.*

**$**

✕▥**Hotel Duràn.** Once a stagecoach relay station, the Duràn is now a
well-known hotel and restaurant. Salvador Dalí had his own private
dining room here, and you can still have dinner with the great surrealist, or at least with pictures of him. Try the *mandonguilles amb sèpia a
l'estil Anna* (meatballs and cuttlefish), a *mar i muntanya* (surf-and-turf)
specialty of the house. The elegant, classic guest rooms are outfitted
with wooden furniture; some overlook the Rambla. You can relax in
the good-size sitting room on the first floor. **Pro:** handy location at the
nerve center of pretty rural town. **Con:** both rooms and public spaces
over-cluttered with rustic furnishings and artifacts. ⊠*Carrer Lasauca
5, 17600* ☎*972/501250* ⊕*www.hotelduran.com* ⏎*65 rooms* ⌂*In-
hotel: restaurant, bar, parking (fee)* ▤*AE, MC, V* ⑩*EP.*

## PERALADA

*12 km (7 mi) northeast of Figueres, 47 km (29 mi) north of Girona.*

This small, quiet village has a fine glassware museum, a noted summer music festival, and—of all things—a casino. The village's history goes back at least to the 9th century, and the counts of Peralada, one of the noblest titles of Catalonia, originated here. Ramon Muntaner, the great 13th-century Catalan chronicler, was from Peralada; his *Chronicle* describes how the town was put to the torch in 1285 by the Almogàvers, Catalan soldiers of fortune who carved out an empire in Greece. Archaeological excavations have uncovered signs of this great fire.

The **Museu del Castell de Peralada,** in the old Convent del Carme, houses the best glassware museum in Spain, a library with more than 70,000 volumes, and a wine museum. The park is one of the finest English-style gardens in the region, with a lake in which swans glide back and forth. ⊠*Pl. del Carme s/n* ☎*972/538125* 💶*€40* ☉*July–mid-Sept., daily tours (in English) on the hr 10–noon and 5–8; mid-Sept.–June, Tues.–Sat. tours on the hr 10–noon and 4:30–5:30, Sun. 10–noon.*

### WHERE TO EAT & STAY

$–$$ ✕**Cal Sagristà.** This neo-rustic space greets you warmly with aged brick walls and contemporary paintings. A former convent-school of Augustinian nuns, the restaurant has an arbored terrace with a view encompassing the Alberes range. For openers, the *amanida amb bolets confitats* (salad with preserved mushrooms) is a treat. Other delights include *magret de anec amb salsa de gerds* (duck with raspberry jam) and *cua de bou amb cebetes* (oxtail with shallots), all accompanied by the local Castell de Peralada Blanco Seco. ⊠*Rodona 2* ☎*972/538301* ▤*AE, MC, V* ☉*Closed last 2 wks of Nov. and last 2 wks of Jan. No dinner Sun. or Tues. Sept.–June.*

$$$$ ▦**Golf Peralada.** Surrounded by an often windswept 18-hole golf course, this graceful upper Empordà refuge has become a point of reference in Peralada. Equipped with every luxury, from hydrotherapy to state-of-the-art fitness and sauna equipment, this pleasure palace is a little redolent of a Las Vegas spa dropped into Northern Catalonia, but if that's what you're looking for, here it is. **Pros:** impeccable and encyclopedic list of amenities, resources, and comforts. **Cons:** excessively ultra-modern and impersonal. ⊠*Av. Rocaberti s/n, 17491* ☎*972/538830* ⊕*www.golfperalada.com* ⤵*53 rooms, 2 suites* ♿*In-hotel: restaurant, bar, public Internet, Wi-Fi, golf course, pool, gym, spa, executive floor, parking (fee), some pets allowed* ▤*AE, DC, MC, V* ⊚*EP.*

$ ▦**Hostal de la Font.** This solid stone house in the center of town was once a convent. Enric Serraplana, the proprietor, is also an antiques dealer, to the hotel's benefit. Rooms have wooden floors and handsome, sometimes antique, furnishings with contemporary, renovated baths. The interior patio was once the convent cloister. The dining room is wood-paneled and gracefully decorated with antiques and has a communal table where guests have breakfast together. **Pros:** the midtown location allows you to get the feel of life in this small rural town. **Cons:** rooms are not spacious and sometimes overfurnished. ⊠*Carrer*

8

*de la Font 15–19, 17491* ☎*972/538507* ⊕*www.hostaldelafont.com.*
*es* ⌂*12 rooms* ⌂*In-hotel: public Internet, Wi-Fi, some pets allowed*
⊟*AE, DC, MC, V* ⦿*EP.*

### NIGHTLIFE & THE ARTS

The **Casino Castell de Peralada** occupies the Castell de Perelada, a 19th-century re-creation (complete with crenellated battlements) of an original medieval castle. Games include French and American roulette, black-jack, and slot machines. A valid ID (proving you are over 21) is neces-sary for admission. ⊠*Carrer Sant Joan s/n, 17491* ☎*972/538125* 🎫*€4* ⊙*Mon.–Thurs. 7 PM–4 AM, Fri. and Sat. 7 PM–5 AM, Sun. 5 PM–4 AM.*

The Castell de Peralada is the main site of the **Festival Internacional de Música,** a music festival held in its gardens every July and August. The world's finest artists perform in the town castle, and original works are especially composed for this event. ⊠*Carrer Sant Joan s/n* ☎*93/280–5868 or 972/538292* ⊕*www.festivalperalada.com.*

# INLAND TO GIRONA

Northern Catalonia contains the soft, green hills of the Ampurdan (in Catalan, Empordà) farm country and the Alberes mountain range, the eastern tip of the Pyrenees. The ancient city of Girona, often ignored by people who bolt from its airport to the resorts of the Costa Brava (about an hour away), is an easy and interesting day trip from Barce-lona. Much of this city's charm comes from its narrow medieval streets, historic buildings, fine restaurants, and a community of students and scholars drawn by the local university. To the west you can discover a region that, studded with historic and picturesque towns such as Besalú and Olot, calls to mind Italy's Tuscany or France's Lubéron. Sprinkled across these landscapes are *masies* (farmhouses) with austere, grayish or pinkish staggered-stone rooftops and ubiquitous square towers that make them look like fortresses. Even the tiniest village has its church, arcaded square, and *rambla,* where villagers take their evening stroll. Around Olot, the volcanic region of the Garrotxa, with more than 30 now-extinct volcanoes (the last eruption was at least 9,500 years ago, though experts say new activity cannot be discounted), is a striking landscape, with—amid lush forests of beech, oak, and pine—barren moonscapes worthy of *Star Wars*. Heading back south from Girona, nature lovers can also make a stop at the pristine Montseny wilderness park before entering the tumultuous rhythm of Barcelona once again.

## GIRONA

*97 km (60 mi) northeast of Barcelona.*

Girona (Gerona in Castilian), a city of more than 70,000 inhabit-ants, keeps intact the magic of its historic past. In fact, with its brood-ing hilltop castle, soaring cathedral, and dreamy riverside setting, it resembles a vision from the Middle Ages. Once called a "Spanish Ven-ice"—although there are no real canals here, just the confluence of four

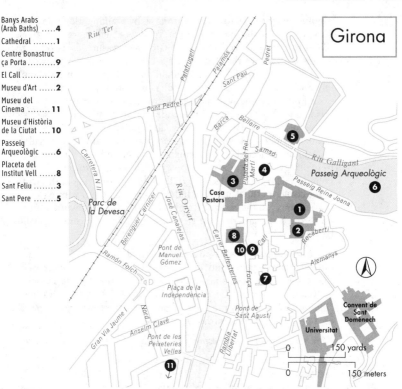

rivers—the city is almost as evocative as that city on the lagoon. With El Call, one of Europe's best-preserved Jewish communities dating from the Middle Ages, and the Arab Baths, lovely Girona is a reminder that Spain's Jewish and Islamic communities both thrived here for centuries. Today, as a university center, it combines past and vibrant present—art galleries, chic cafés, and trendy boutiques have set up shop in many of the restored buildings of the Old Quarter.

The Romans founded Gerunda in the 1st century AD at a convenient ford that spanned the confluence of four rivers: the Ter, Onyar, Güell, and Galligants. Nearby stone quarries supplied building material, and the mountain on which the Old City sits is known as Les Pedreres (the quarries). The Old Quarter of Girona, called the Força Vella (old force, or fortress), is built on the side of the mountain and is a tightly packed labyrinth of fine buildings, monuments, and steep, narrow cobblestone streets, linked with frequent stairways. You can still see vestiges of the Iberian and Roman walls in the cathedral square and in the patio of the old university. Head over from modern Girona (on the west side of the Onyar) to the Old Quarter on the east side. The main street of the Old Quarter is Carrer de la Força. It follows the old Via Augusta, the Roman road that connected Rome with its provinces.

The best way to get to know Girona is by walking along its streets. As you wander through the Força Vella, you will be repeatedly surprised by new discoveries. One of Girona's treasures is its setting, as it rises high above the Riu Onyar, where that river merges with the Ter. (The Ter flows from a mountain waterfall that can be glimpsed in a gorge above the town.) Regardless of your approach to the town, walk first along the west-side banks of the Onyar, between the train trestle and the Plaça de la Independència, to admire the classic view of the Old Town, with its pastel yellow, pink, and orange waterfront facades. Windows and balconies are always draped with colorful drying laundry reflected in the shimmering river and often adorned with fretwork grilles of embossed wood or delicate iron tracery. Cross the Pont de Sant Agustí bridge over to the Old City from under the arcades in the corner of the Plaça de la Independència and find your way to the tourist office, to the right at Rambla Llibertat 1. Then work your way up through the labyrinth of steep streets, using the cathedral's huge baroque facade as a guide.

A special Girona visitor's card allowing free admission to some museums and monuments and discounts at others can be purchased at the tourist-office welcome station. Look for the **Punt de Benvinguda** (⊠ *Carrer Berenguer Carnicer 3* ☎ *972/211678* ⊕ *www.girona-net. com/puntb*), at the entrance to Girona from the town's main parking area on the right bank of the Onyar River.

*Numbers in the text correspond to numbers in the Girona map.*

❶ At the heart of the Old City, Girona's **cathedral** looms above 90 steps and is famous for its nave—at 75 feet, the widest in the world and the epitome of the spatial ideal of Catalan Gothic architects. Since Charlemagne founded the original church in the 8th century, it has been through many fires, changes, and renovations, so you are greeted by a rococo-era facade—"eloquent as organ music" and impressively set off by a spectacular flight of 17th-century stairs, which rises from its own plaça. Inside, three smaller naves were compressed into one gigantic hall by the famed architect Guillermo Bofill in 1416. The change was typical of Catalan Gothic "hall" churches, and it was done to facilitate preaching to crowds. Note the famous silver canopy, or *baldaquí* (baldachin). The oldest part of the cathedral is the 11th-century Romanesque **Torre de Carlemany** (Charlemagne Tower).

The cathedral has an exquisite 12th-century cloister, which has an obvious affinity with the cloisters in the Roussillon area of France; you can visit them with a ticket to the cathedral's **Museu Capitular,** or Tresor, indeed filled with treasures. They include a 10th-century copy of Beatus's manuscript *Commentary on the Apocalypse*—one of the famous 10th-century manuscripts illuminated in the dramatically primitive Mozarabic style—the Bible of Emperor Carlos V, and the celebrated *Tapís de la Creació* (*Tapestry of the Creation*), considered by most experts to be the finest tapestry surviving from the Romanesque era (and, in fact, thought to be the needlework of Saxons working in England). It depicts the seven days of the Creation as told in Genesis

FodorśChoice
★

in the primitive but powerful fashion of early Romanesque art, and looks not unlike an Asian mandala. Made of wool, with predominant colors of green, brown, and ocher, the tapestry once hung behind the main altar as a pictorial Bible lesson. The four seasons, the stars, winds, months of the year and days of the week, plants, animals, and elements of nature circle round a central figure, likening paradise to the eternal cosmos presided over by Christ. In addition to its intrinsic beauty, along the bottom band (which appears to have been added at a later date) another significant detail is the depiction of two *iudeis*, or Jews, dressed in the round cloaks they were compelled to wear to set them apart from Christians. This scene is thought to be the earliest portrayal of a Jew (other than biblical figures) known in Christian art. ☒*Pl. de la Catedral* ☎*972/214426* ⊕*www.lacatedaldegirona.com* ☒*€4; free Sun.* ⊙*Nov.–Mar., weekdays 10–7, Sat. 4:30–7, Sun. 10–2, 4:30–7; Apr.–Oct., weekdays 10–8 , 4:30–8, Sat. 4:30–8, Sun. 2–8.*

**❷** The Episcopal Palace near the cathedral contains the wide-ranging collections of the **Museu d'Art,** Girona's main art museum. You'll see everything from superb Romanesque *majestats* (carved wood figures of Christ) to reliquaries from Sant Pere de Rodes, and illuminated 12th-century manuscripts to works of the 20th-century Olot school of landscape painting. ☒*Pujada de la Catedral 12* ☎*972/203834* ⊕*www. museuart.com* ☒*€3* ⊙*Tues.–Sat. 10–7, Sun. 10–2.*

**NEED A BREAK?**

Fortify yourself for sightseeing with some superb tea and plump pastries at **La Vienesa** ( ☒*Carrer La Pujada del Pont de Pedra 1* ☎*972/486046*). One of the town's best-loved gathering points for conversation, this cozy spot is good place to regroup and re-navigate.

**❸** The vast bulk of the church of **Sant Feliu** is landmarked by one of Girona's most distinctive belfries, topped by eight pinnacles. One of Girona's most beloved churches, it was repeatedly rebuilt and altered over four centuries and stands today as an amalgam of Romanesque columns, Gothic nave, and baroque facade. It was founded over the tomb of St. Felix of Africa, a martyr under the Roman emperor Diocletian. ☒*Pujada de Sant Feliu* ☎*972/201407* ⊙*Daily 9–10:30, 11:30–1, and 4–6:30.*

**❹** The **Banys Arabs** are misnamed, since they were actually built by Morisco (workers of Moorish descent who remained in Spain after the 1492 Expulsion Decree) craftsmen in the late 12th century, long after Girona's Islamic occupation (795–1015) had ended. Following the old Roman model that had disappeared in the West, the custom of bathing publicly may have been brought back from the Holy Land with the Crusaders. These baths are sectioned off into three rooms in descending order; a *frigidarium*, or cold bath, a square room with a central octagonal pool and a skylight with cupola held up by two stories of eight fine columns; a *tepidarium*, or warm bath; and a *caldarium*, or steam room, beneath which is a chamber where a fire was kept burning. Here the inhabitants of the old Girona came to relax, exchange gossip, or do business. It is known from another public bathhouse in Tortosa, Tarragona, that the various social classes came to bathe by sexes on fixed days of the week; Christian men on one day, Christian women on another, Jewish men on still another, Jewish women (and prostitutes) on a fourth, Muslims on others. ✉ *Carrer Ferran el Catòlic s/n* ☎ *972/213262* ⊕ *www. banysarabs.org* 💶 *€2.50* ⊙ *Apr.– Sept., Tues.–Sat. 10–2 and 4–7, Sun. 10–2; Nov.–Apr., Tues.–Sun. 10–1.*

**❺** The church of **Sant Pere** *(St. Peter)*, across the Galligants River, was finished in 1131 and is notable for its octagonal Romanesque belfry and the finely detailed capitals atop the columns in the cloister. The church now houses the **Museu Arqueològic** (Museum of Archaeology), which documents the region's history since Paleolithic times and includes some artifacts from Roman times. ✉ *Carrer Santa Llúcia s/n* ☎ *972/202632* 💶 *€3* ⊙ *Church and museum daily 10–1 and 4:30–7.*

> ### VERGES : HALLOWEEN MEETS EASTER
>
> The village of Verges, northeast of Girona, holds one of Spain's most macabre and unusual Easter celebrations, La Dansa de la Mort (The Dance of Death), a tribute to mortality that seems more Halloween than Easter. Descended from medieval tradition, the Dance of Death is part of the procession commemorating the life and death of Christ. Five luminous skeletons painted over black leotards create a life- (that is, death-) like effect of dancing bones. Props include a scythe, a handless clock suggesting death's unknowable hour, and a bowl of ashes symbolizing mortal decay.

**❻** The landscaped gardens of the stepped **Passeig Arqueològic,** an archaeological walk, run below the restored walls of the Old Quarter (which you can walk, in parts) and have good views from belvederes and watchtowers. From there, climb through the Jardins de la Francesa to the highest ramparts for a view of the cathedral's 11th-century Charlemagne Tower.

**❼** Girona is especially noted for **El Call,** its 13th-century Jewish Quarter, which can be found branching off Carrer de la Força, south of the Plaça Catedral. The word *call* (pronounced "kyle" in Catalan) may come from an old Catalan word meaning "narrow way" or "passage," derived from the Latin word *callum* or *callis*. Others suggest that it comes from the Hebrew word *Qahal*, meaning "assembly" or "meeting of the community." Owing allegiance to the Spanish king (who exacted tribute for this distinction) and not to the city government, this once prosperous Jewish community—one of the most flourishing in Europe during the Middle Ages—was, at its height, a leading center of learning. An important school of the Kabala was centered here. The most famous teacher of the Kabala from Girona was Rabbi Mossé ben Nahman (also known as Nahmànides and by the acronym—taken from the first letters of his title and name, RMBN—Ramban), who is popularly believed to be one and the same as Bonastruc ça Porta. Nahmànides wrote an important religious work based on meditation and the reinterpretation of the Bible and the Talmud.

The earliest presence of Jews in Girona is uncertain, but the first historical mention dates from 982, when a group of 25 Jewish families moved to Girona from nearby Juïgues. Jews may have been already present in the region for several hundred years, however. Today the layout of El Call bears no resemblance to what this area looked like in the 15th century, when Jews last lived here. Space was at a premium inside the city walls in Girona, and houses were destroyed and built higgledy-piggledy one atop the other. The narrow streets, barely wide enough for a single person to pass (they have now been widened slightly), crisscrossed one above the other.

**8** In the **Placeta del Institut Vell,** a small square on Carrer de la Força, you can study a tar-blackened 3-inch-long, half-inch-deep groove carved shoulder-high into the stone of the right door post as you enter the square. It indicates the location of a mezuzah, a small case or tube of metal or wood in which a piece of parchment with verses from the Torah (declaring the essence of Jewish belief in one God) was placed. When someone went through the doorway, the mezuzah was touched as a sign of devotion. Evidence of the labyrinthical layout of a few street ruts in the Old Quarter may still be seen inside the antiques store Antiguitats la Canonja Vella at Carrer de la Força 33.

**9** The **Centre Bonastruc ça Porta,** housed in a former synagogue and dedicated to the preservation of the Jewish heritage of Girona, organizes conferences, exhibitions, and seminars. The **Museu de Història dels Jueus** (Museum of Jewish History) contains 21 stone tablets, one of the finest collections in the world of medieval Jewish funerary slabs. These came from the old Jewish cemetery of Montjuïc, revealing when the railroad between Barcelona and France was laid out in the 19th century. Its exact location, about 1½ km (1 mi) north of Girona on the road to La Bisbal and known as La Tribana, is being excavated. The center also holds the **Institut d'Estudis Nahmànides,** with its extensive library of Judaica. ✉ *Carrer de la Força 8* ☎ *972/216761* ⊕ *www. ajgirona.org/call* 🎫 *€3* ⊙ *Mon.–Sat. 10–6, Sun. 10–3.*

**10** The **Museu d'Història de la Ciutat,** a fascinating museum on Carrer de la Força, is filled with memorabilia from Girona's long and embattled past. From pre-Roman objects to paintings and drawings from the notorious siege at the hands of Napoleonic troops to the early municipal lighting system and the medieval printing press, there is plenty to see here. You will definitely come away with a clearer idea of Girona's past. ✉ *Carrer de la Força 27* ☎ *972/222229* ⊕ *www.ajuntament.gi/museu_ciutat* 🎫 *€3* ⊙ *May–Sept., Tues.–Sat. 10–2 and 5–7, Sun. 10–3.*

**11** The **Museu del Cinema,** an interactive cinema museum, has artifacts and movie-related paraphernalia going all the way back to Chinese shadows, the first rudimentary moving pictures. The Cine Nic toy filmmaking machines, originally developed in 1931 by the Nicolau brothers of Barcelona and now being relaunched commercially, allow even novices to put together their own movies. ✉ *Carrer Sèquia 1* ☎ *972/412777* ⊕ *www.museudelcinema.org* 🎫 *€4* ⊙ *May–Sept., Mon.–Sat. 10–8, Sun. 10–3; Oct.–Apr., Mon.–Sat. 10–6, Sun. 10–3.*

8

**NEED A BREAK?**

Dig into piping-hot crepes or fresh salads at the inviting **Cafè Bistrot** (✉ *Pujada Sant Domènec 4* ☎ *972/218803*), where you can kick back at an outside table or sit in the dark, classy interior. Among the savory favorites are spinach with béchamel; chocoholics may make a beeline for the warm Nutella crepes.

A five-minute walk uphill behind the cathedral leads to a park and the **Torre de Gironella**, a four-story tower (no entry permitted) dating from the year 1190 that marks the highest point in the Jewish Quarter. Girona's Jewish community took refuge here in early August of 1391, emerging 17 weeks later to find their houses in ruins. Even though Spain's official expulsion decree did not go into effect until 1492, this attack effectively ended the Girona Jewish community. Destroyed in 1404, reconstructed in 1411, and destroyed anew by retreating Napoleonic troops in 1814, the Torre de Gironella was the site of the celebration of the first Hanukkah ceremony in 607 years held on December 20, 1998, with Jerusalem's chief Sephardic rabbi Rishon Letzion presiding. ✉ *Ctra. Sant Gregori 91.*

## WHERE TO EAT & STAY

$$$–$$$$

**Fodor's**Choice
★

✕ **Celler de Can Roca.** One of the dozen top restaurants below the Pyrenees, just a mile and a half northwest of town, this is a must-stop for any self-respecting foodie. You can survey the kitchen from the dining room and watch the Roca brothers in the act of creating their masterful *arròs amb garotes i botifarra negre* (rice with urchins and black sausage) and *cua de bou farcida amb foie gras* (oxtail stuffed with foie gras). For dessert try the *pastel calent de xocolata i gingebre* (hot chocolate cake with ginger) or jasmine tea ice cream. Don't be embarrassed to ask the sommelier for guidance through the encyclopedic wine list. ✉ *Ctra. Taialà 40* ☎ *972/222157* ⌂ *Reservations essential* ☰ *AE, DC, MC, V* ⊘ *Closed Sun., Mon., and first 2 wks of July.*

$$–$$$

✕ **Albereda.** Excellent Catalan cuisine with exotic touches is served here in an elegant setting under exposed brick arches. Try the *galeta amb llagostins glaçada* (zucchini bisque with prawns) or the *amanida tèbia d'espàrrecs naturals amb bacallà i cansalada ibérica* (warm asparagus salad with codfish and ibérico ham) for a mar i muntanya (surf & turf) with the garden thrown in as well. Wild mushrooms, truffles, foie gras, and fresh fish vie for space on this rich menu. ✉ *Carrer Albereda 7 bis* ☎ *972/226002* ☰ *AE, DC, MC, V* ⊘ *Closed Sun.*

★ $–$$

✕ **Cal Ros.** Tucked under the arcades just behind the north end of Plaça de la Llibertat, this restaurant combines ancient stone arches with crisp, contemporary furnishings and cheerful lighting. The cuisine is flavorful: hot goat-cheese salad with pine nuts and *garum* (black-olive and anchovy paste, a delicacy dating back to Roman times), *oca amb naps* (goose with turnips), and a blackberry sorbet should not to be missed. ✉ *Carrer Cort Reial 9* ☎ *972/217379* ☰ *AE, DC, MC, V* ⊘ *Closed Mon. No dinner Sun.*

$

✕ **Penyora.** Here you'll find both good local fare and, if you order from the prix-fixe menu, a bargain. The menu lists daily-changing meat, fish, and vegetarian options, including *lasanya de verdures* (vegetarian lasagna), generously layered with mushrooms, spinach, carrots, and beans,

CLOSE UP

## Farmhouse Stays

Dotted throughout Catalonia are farmhouses (*casas rurales* in Spanish, and *cases de pagès* or *masies* in Catalan), where you can spend a weekend or longer. Accommodations vary from small, rustic homes to spacious, luxurious farmhouses with fireplaces and pools. Sometimes you stay in a guest room, as at a B&B; in other places you rent the entire house and do your own cooking. Most tourist offices, including the main Catalonia Tourist Office in Barcelona, have info and listings for the *cases de pagès* of the region. You can peruse listings

of farmhouses on ⊕ *www.gencat.net.* Several organizations in Spain also have detailed listings and descriptions of Catalonia's farmhouses, and it's best to book through one of these.

**LOCAL AGENTS**

**Federació d'Agroturisme i Turisme Rural Comarques de Tarragona** ( ⊠ Sant Francesc 1, Cornudella de Montsant43360 ☎ 977/821082 ⊕ www.agroturisme.org). **Tural** ( ⊠ Carrer Aragó 359, Eixample, Barcelona08009 ☎ 93/539–4678 ⊕ www.tural.org).

---

and tasty pumpkin stuffed with vegetables. ⊠ *Carrer Nou del Teatre 3* ☎ *972/218948* ☐ *AE, DC, MC* ⊗ *Closed Tues.*

★ $–$$   🛏 **Hotel Històric y Apartaments Històric Girona.** This boutique hotel has one room (the suite) with views of the cathedral and Gothic vaulting overhead. The apartment accommodations are in a 9th-century house, with remnants of a 3rd-century Roman wall and a Roman aqueduct on the ground floor and in one of the apartments. One dining room even contains a wall made in the pre-Romanesque *opus spicatum* herringbone pattern. Wooden furniture fills the simply but pleasantly furnished rooms. Casilda Cruz rents these good-value apartments in the Old Quarter for as many days as you'd like, from one day to one month. **Pros:** ideal environment for a visit to Europe's best-preserved medieval Jewish Quarter, with top technology and comforts. **Cons:** rooms and apartments are a little cramped. ⊠ *Carrer Bellmirall 4A, 17004* ☎ *972/223583* ⊕ *www.hotelhistoric.com* ⇄ *8 rooms, 7 apartments, 1 junior suite, 1 suite* ⚿ *In-room: Wi-Fi, kitchens in apartments* ☐ *AE, DC, MC, V* 🍴 *EP.*

¢–$   🛏 **Bellmirall.** This pretty little hostel across the Onyar in the Jewish Quarter, despite its scarcity of amenities, offers top value in the heart of Girona's most historic section. **Pros:** a budget choice, this hostel provides the basics with perfect aesthetic taste as well. **Cons:** rooms are small, and—cut off from Internet, TV, telephone—slightly claustrophobia inducing. ⊠ *Carrer Bellmirall 3, 17001* ☎ *972/204009* ⇄ *7 rooms* ⚿ *In-room: no a/c, no phone, no TV* ☐ *No credit cards* ⊗ *Closed Jan. and Feb.* 🍴 *EP.*

★ ¢   🛏 **Hotel Peninsular.** In a handsomely restored centenary structure, this hotel occupies a strategic spot at the end of the Pont de Pedra (the stone bridge), a Girona landmark in the center of the shopping district. **Pros:** a good location over the river Onyar and at the hub of Girona life. **Cons:** smallish rooms and sometimes noisy on Friday and Saturday nights. ⊠ *Carrer Nou 3, 17002* ☎ *972/203800* ⊕ *www.novarahotels.*

*com* ✈*68 rooms* &*In-room: Wi-Fi, safe. In-hotel: public internet, bar.* ▤*AE, DC, MC, V* †◎|*EP.*

### NIGHTLIFE & THE ARTS

Girona is a university town, so the night scene is especially lively during the school year. Trendy young people flock to **Accés 21** ( ⊠*Carrer Bonaventura Carreres Peralta 7* ☎*972/213708*). The older crowd goes to **La Via** ( ⊠*Pedret 66* ☎*972/410461*), on the road going to Palamós. A popular nightspot for the young, hip set is **Platea** ( ⊠*Carrer Geroni Real de Fontclara 4* ☎*972/227288*).

In summer, nighttime action centers on **Les Carpes de la Devesa** ( ⊠*Passeig de la Devesa*), a park on the west side of the Onyar River in the modern city. From June to September 15, three awnings, or *carpes,* are set up here so that people can sit outside in the warm weather until the wee hours, enjoying drinks and listening to music.

### SHOPPING

If it's jewelry you're looking for, head to **Anna Casals** ( ⊠*Carrer Ballesteries 33* ☎*972/410227*). For interior decoration, plastic arts, religious paintings, and sculptures, stop at **Dolors Turró** ( ⊠*Ballesteries 19* ☎*972/410193*). **Gluki** ( ⊠*Carrer Argenteria 26* ☎*972/201989*) has made chocolate since 1880. Candles are the specialty at **Karla** ( ⊠*Carrer Ballesteries 21* ☎*972/227210*). All manner of masks, dolls, pottery, and crafts are available at **La Carpa** ( ⊠*Carrer Ballesteries 37* ☎*972/212002*). **Turrons Candela** ( ⊠*Carrer Argenteria 3* ☎*972/220938*) specializes in tasty nougat.

**Codina** ( ⊠*Carrer Santa Clara 20* ☎*972/219880*) sells lovely women's clothes. Young people stock up on threads at **Desideratum** ( ⊠*Carrer Migdia 30* ☎*972/221448*). Men will find fine garb at **Falcó** ( ⊠*Carrer Maluquer Salvador 16* ☎*972/207156*). For shoes, go to **Peacock** ( ⊠*Carrer Nou 15* ☎*972/226848*).

Girona's best bookstore, with a large travel-guide section and a small section of English fiction, is **Llibreria 22** ( ⊠*Carrer Hortes 22* ☎*972/212395*). For travel books and other editions in English, try **Ulysus** ( ⊠*Carrer Ballesteries 22* ☎*972/221773*).

## BANYOLES

*19 km (12 mi) north of Girona, 116 km (72 mi) northeast of Barcelona.*

If Girona has cosmopolitan pleasures, Banyoles, with its lovely lake, makes a pleasant escape into the Catalan countryside. The town itself has a graceful historic quarter, complete with the Monestir de Sant Esteve (usually locked, but ask around for admittance) and an arcaded Plaça Major. If you wish to stay over (most people make this a day trip from Girona), inquire about accommodations at the local Turismo office at Passeig de la Industria 25.

The spring-fed **Estany de Banyoles,** the lake where rowing contests were held for the 1992 Olympic Games, is known for its natural beauty.

Swimming, rowing, picnicking, and fishing for the lake's famous carp draw many people here. Although there is no Loch Ness monster here, some say the lake holds a fabled carp called *La Ramona,* which weighs more than 33 pounds and eats peanuts from your hand. You can try to spot her by renting a rowboat for €3 per hour per person, or taking the scenic cruiser around the lake for the same price.

The local **Museu d'Arqueològic** holds intriguing finds from the archaeo-logical site of La Draga, next to the lake and a 10-minute walk from town. Catalan archaeologists working at the Neolithic lakeshore site found a wooden tool at least 7,000 years old, the oldest wooden arti-fact ever found in the Mediterranean area, and one of the oldest in the world. You can also see the bones of ancient mastadons found in the area, and a copy of the famous Banyoles Jaw, discovered in 1887 and believed to be more than 100,000 years old, making it one of the earliest known human jawbones. Items from the Serinyà Caves are exhibited as well. ⊠*Pl. de Font 11,* ☏*972/572361* ⛁*€2 includes nat-ural history museum, €3 includes natural history museum and Serinyà Caves* ☉*Sept.–June, Tues.–Sat. 10:30–1:30 and 4–6:30, Sun. 10:30–2; July and Aug., Tues.–Sat. 11–1:30 and 4–8, Sun. 10:30–2.*

Regional treasures of natural history are on view at the **Museu Munici-pal Darder d'Història Natural,** near the archaeology museum. It displays taxidermic animals from the area (and the world), including croco-diles, ducks, bears, and sheep, as well as regional plants. ⊠*Pl. dels Estudis s/n* ☏*972/574467* ⛁*€2 includes archaeology museum, €3 includes archaeology museum and Serinyà Caves* ☉*Sept.–June, Tues.–Sat. 10:30–1:30 and 4–6:30, Sun. 10:30–2; July and Aug., Tues.–Sat. 11–1:30 and 4–8, Sun. 10:30–2.*

You can visit the **Cuevas de Serinyà** *(Serinyà Caves),* 8 km (5 mi) north of Banyoles, where many of the artifacts in the local archaeological museum were unearthed. In July and August, guided tours (though usually not in English) take you through the series of small caves every hour on the hour; during the rest of the year, guided tours are only on weekends, every hour on the hour. ⊠*Ctra. de Serinyà s/n* ☏*972/593310* ⛁*€3 includes archaeology and natural history muse-ums* ☉*Mar.–June, Tues.–Fri. 10–4, weekends 11–6; July–Sept., daily 11–7; Oct.–Feb., Tues.–Fri. 10–3, weekends 11–5.*

## BESALÚ

*25 km (15 mi) north of Banyoles, 34 km (21 mi) north of Girona.*

Besalú, once the capital of a feudal county until power was transferred to Barcelona at the beginning of the 12th century, remains one of the best-preserved and evocative medieval towns in Catalonia. Among its main sights are two churches, Sant Vicenç (set on an attractive, café-lined plaza) and Sant Pere, and the ruins of the convent of Santa Maria on the hill above town.

This ancient town's most emblematic feature is its Romanesque **Pont Fortificat,** an 11th-century fortified bridge with crenellated battlements that spans the Fluvia River.

One unusual sight is the mikvah, unusual 13th-century **Jewish ritual baths** discovered in the 1960s; see the tourist office for keys.

The **tourist office** ( ⊠ *Pl. de la Llibertat* ☎ *972/591240*), open June–September, can provide current opening hours for Sant Pere and keys to various town sights. The arcaded square is also the site of a Tuesday market.

The mikvah is a key resource for attaining ritual purity through immersion in running water in Orthodox Judaism. To visit the mikvah (Jewish ritual baths) and the churches (usually closed otherwise), there are guided tours organized by the tourist office. During the Jewish Festival (first week of March) and the Medieval Festival (first weekend in September ) there are special visits to the historic quarter led by residents and costumed actors. The 11th century seems little more than a heartbeat away as a rabbi (an actor) from the old Jewish community shows the mikvah. A walk through the Call, or Jewish Quarter, follows. At the church of Sant Pere, with its 13th-century ambulatory, you may hear Gregorian chant. Book at the tourist office. ⊠ *Pl. de la Llibertat* ☎ *972/591240* 🖭 *€3* 🕑 *Tours July and Aug., Wed. at 11.*

### WHERE TO EAT

★ $$-$$$ ✕**Els Fogons de Can Llaudes.** A faithfully restored 11th-century Romanesque chapel holds proprietor Jaume Soler's outstanding restaurant, one of Catalonia's best. A typical main dish is *confitat de bou amb patates al morter i raïm glacejat* (beef confit with glacé grapes, served with mashed potatoes with nutmeg). The *menú de degustació* (taster's menu) is recommended; call at least one day in advance to reserve this menú. ⊠ *Prat de Sant Pere 6* ☎ *972/590858* 🔊 *Reservations essential* 🗐 *AE, MC, V* 🕑 *Closed Tues. and last 2 wks of Nov.*

## OLOT

*21 km (13 mi) west of Besalú, 55 km (34 mi) northwest of Girona.*

Capital of the Garrotxa area, Olot is famous for its 19th-century school of landscape painters and has several excellent Art Nouveau buildings, including one with a facade by Domènech i Montaner.

The **Museu Comarcal de la Garrotxa** *(County Museum of La Garrotxa)* contains works of Catalan Modernisme (a variant of Art Nouveau) as well as sculptures by Miquel Blai, creator of the long-tressed maidens who support the balconies along Olot's main boulevard. ⊠ *Carrer Hospici 8* ☎ *972/279130* 🖭 *€3* 🕑 *Mon. and Wed.–Sat. 10–1 and 4–7, Sun. 10–1:30.*

### WHERE TO EAT & STAY

$$-$$$ ✕**Restaurante Ramón.** Ramón is so exclusive that he adamantly refuses to be in this book, so please don't let him see it. His restaurant, Olot's culinary treasure, is the opposite of rustic: sleek, modern, refined. The

*cuina de la terra* (home cooking of regional specialties) includes *patata de Olot* (potato stuffed with veal) and *cassoleta de judias amb xoriç* (white haricot beans with sausage). ⊠*Carrer Bolós 22* ☏*972/261001* ⚓*Reservations essential* ☰*AE, DC, MC, V* ⊘*Closed Thurs.*

¢ 🖬**La Perla d'Olot.** Known for its friendly family ambience, this hotel is always the first in Olot to fill up. On the edge of town toward the Vic road, it's within walking distance of two parks. Rooms are classic and unsurprising, though well equipped and comfortable. **Pros:** relaxed and unpretentious, an easy stop with comfortable rooms and personalized service. **Cons:** a little far from the center of Olot where the locals live. ⊠*Av. Santa Coloma 97, 17800* ☏*972/262326* ⊕*www.laperlahotels.com* ⟟*30 rooms, 37 apartments* ⚓*In-room: Wi-Fi. In-hotel: restaurant, bar, public Internet, some pets allowed* ☰*AE, DC, MC, V* �Ⓧ*EP.*

**NIGHTLIFE**

Local art hangs on the wall and small marble café tables fill **Bar Cocodrilo** (⊠*Sant Roc 5* ☏*972/263124*), a hip and happening nightspot. You can watch the world go by from the outdoor tables at **Cafè Europa** (⊠*Pl. Major s/n* ☏*972/273113*) or duck inside and nurse your drink at the bar to the sounds of rock and *pop espanyol* (Spanish pop).

**EN ROUTE** The villages of Vall d'En Bas lie south of Olot off Route A153. A freeway cuts across this countryside to Vic, but you'll miss a lot by taking it. The twisting old road leads you through rich farmland past farmhouses whose dark wooden balconies are bedecked with bright flowers. Turn off for Sant Privat d'En Bas and Els Hostalets d'En Bas.

## MONTSENY

*75 km (47 mi) south of Olot, 60 km (37 mi) northeast of Barcelona.*

Montseny is Barcelona's mountain retreat and refuge, a highland forest less than an hour north of the city, and the highest mountain range in Catalonia outside the Pyrenees. Its softly undulating slopes sweep up to the massif's main peaks at Turó de l'Home (5,656 feet), les Agudes (5,633 feet), Matagalls (5,590 feet), and Calma i Puigdrau (4,455 feet). In summer and in good weather they are a fairly easy climb. The almost overwhelming view at the top of the Turó de l'Home stretches to the Pyrenees in the north and far past Barcelona in the south. Known as one of the great *pulmons* (lungs) of Europe for its forests of oxygen-producing beech, pine, oak, and fir trees, Montseny may, in the long run, be even more important to Catalonia's spiritual health than to its physical well-being. Montseny's mountain villages, such as Montseny itself, or Mosqueroles, Riells, Campins, Viladrau, and El Brull, are rustic sanctuaries with delightful little inns and farmhouses to admire and to dine at or stay in. It has been a protected park area since 1978, and is also part of UNESCO's world network of biosphere reserves.

The **Servei de Parcs Naturals** ( ☎93/340–2541 ⊕*www.diba.es/parcs/ montseny/montseny.htm*) organizes excursions along the many rivers and streams draining the Montseny massif.

**WHERE TO EAT & STAY**

$   ✗⬚**Can Barrina.** Splendid views over the Montseny massif enhance this comfortable stone country house, built in 1620 and reconstructed in 1988. The menu focuses on local products ranging from wild mushrooms such as *rossinyols* (chanterelles) and *múrgules* (morels) to wild boar, rabbit, duck, and venison. The roaring fireplace in the restaurant can be complemented by another in your room (if you can manage to secure either Room D or F). In summer you can relax in the garden or on the terraces after a day of hiking the crests. **Pro:** comfortable and rustic base camp for hiking in the Montseny massif. **Con:** can get overpopulated if a wedding reception happens to be scheduled while you are there. ⊠*Ctra. Palautordera, Km 1.2, 08460* ☎*93/847–3065* ⊕*www.canbarrina.com* ⊷*14 rooms* ⌂*In-hotel: restaurant, pool* ⊟*AE, DC, MC, V* ⦿*EP.*

$$$$   ⬚**Hotel Monestir de Sant Marçal.** Jordi Tell runs this small, very exclusive hotel high up in the Montseny massif. In an 11th-century monastery with adjacent chapel (where mass can be celebrated), it offers a personalized sanctum sanctorum with cozy, rustic rooms. Some people will appreciate its library; others, its private honey-based cosmetic line, Sant Marçal del Montseny. You can arrange guided excursions on foot or by bike. **Pro:** exquisite rustic and aristocratic highland refuge. **Con:** weekend can be crowded, better during the week when you have the hotel, and the Montseny, to yourself. ⊠*Ctra. de Sant Celoni a Sant Marçal, Km 28, 08460* ☎*93/847–3043* ⊕*www.hotel-santmarcal.com* ⊷*12 rooms* ⌂*In-room: no a/c. In-hotel: restaurant, Wi-Fi, bar, pool, no elevator* ⊟*AE, DC, MC, V* ⦿*BP.*

# SOUTHERN CATALONIA

Barcelona is surrounded by scenic landscapes and ancient architecture—Sant Cugat del Vallés, with a lovely Benedictine abbey; Terrassa with its notable examples of Romanesque architecture; Llobregat, with a Roman bridge. The world-famous monastery of Montserrat is where medieval legend placed the Holy Grail (a claim contested by many other places). From Montserrat you can move south of Barcelona and continue backward in time, with a pleasure stop in Sitges, the prettiest and most popular resort in Barcelona's immediate environs, with an excellent beach, an attractive Old Quarter, and some interesting Moderniste details. In from the coast lies the "Cistercian triangle," with celebrated historic monasteries at Poblet, Santes Creus, and Vallbona de les Monges. The walled town at Montblanc is also a lovely sight. Farther south, along the coast, the time machine zooms back to the days of ancient Rome when you arrive in Tarragona, in Roman times regarded as one of the empire's finest creations. Its wine was already famous and its population was the first *gens togata* (literally, the toga-clad race) in Spain, which conferred on them equality with the citizens of Rome. Roman relics, with the Circus Maximus heading the list, are still the stamp of Tarragona's grandeur, and to this the Middle Ages added wonderful city walls and citadels.

## MONTSERRAT

★ *50 km (31 mi) northwest of Barcelona.*

You don't have to be a believer to visit the Benedictine monastery of Montserrat. A traditional side trip from Barcelona is the shrine of La Moreneta, the Black Virgin of Montserrat, high in the crags of the Montserrat massif. These jagged, sawtooth peaks have given rise to countless legends: here St. Peter left a statue of the Virgin Mary carved by St. Luke, Parsifal found the Holy Grail, and Wagner sought inspiration for his opera. Whatever the truth of such mysteries, Montserrat has long been considered Catalonia's spiritual heart. A monastery has stood on this site since the early Middle Ages, though the present 19th-century building replaced the rubble left by Napoléon's troops in 1812. Honeymooning couples flock here by the thousands seeking La Moreneta's blessing. Twice a year, on April 27, Our Lady of Montserrat's name day, and September 8 (which celebrates the *verges trobades,* (found virgins) of Catalonia, statues of Our Lady discovered by shepherds in remote places and venerated all over the country), the diminutive statue of Montserrat's Black Virgin becomes the object of one of Spain's greatest pilgrimages.

While the Montserrat complex is vast, most architectural historians excoriate its modern renovation. Note, however, the Gothic portal of the Twelve Apostles. At the monastery, only the basilica and museum are regularly open to the public. The **basilica** is dark and ornate, its blackness pierced by the glow of hundreds of votive lamps. Above the high altar stands the famous polychrome statue of the Virgin and Child, to which the faithful can pay their respects by way of a separate door. The statue is black due to centuries of incense and candle smoke, not because the face and hands were ever painted black. Another treasure found here is the **Escolania,** the monastery's famous boys' choir, founded in the 13th century and now known internationally through concert tours and recordings. The boys receive intense musical training from an early age and a general education; some of them later enter the monastery as monks. At 1 PM daily they sing the *Salve regina* and the *Virolai,* the hymn of Our Lady of Montserrat. In the evening after vespers, at 7:10 PM, they sing, together with the monks, the *Salve montserratina,* alternating between polyphony and Gregorian chant. On Sunday and holidays they take part in the mass at Montserrat and in vespers. In July and at Christmas the choir is away from Montserrat.

The monastery's **museum** has two sections: the Secció Antiga (open Tuesday–Saturday 10:30–2) contains old masters, among them paintings by El Greco, Correggio, and Caravaggio, and the amassed gifts to the Virgin; the Secció Moderna (open Tuesday–Saturday 3–6) concentrates on more recent artists. This impressive art collection is the

8

result of private bequests. Xavier Busquets, one of Barcelona's most important architects, left many impressionist and Moderniste paintings to Montserrat on his death in 1990, including works by Monet, Sisley, Degas, Pissarro, Rouault, Sargent, Sorolla, and Zuloaga. Other donors have left examples by lesser-known masters of 19th- and 20th-century Catalan painting: Martí Alsina, Joaquim Vayreda, Francesc Gimeno, Santiago Rusiñol, Ramon Casas, Isidre Nonell, Joaquim Mir, Hermen Anglada-Camarassa, plus works by Picasso and Dalí.

Montserrat is as memorable for its setting as for its artistic and religious treasures, so be sure to explore its strange, pink hills, many of whose crests are dotted with hermitages. The hermitage of **Sant Joan** can be reached by funicular. The views over the mountains to the Mediterranean and, on a clear day, to the Pyrenees are breathtaking. Montserrat's rocky masses are of stone conglomerate, which, over thousands of years, have been molded into bizarre shapes by tectonic movements, climatic changes, and erosion. In the deep, humid shades between the stony outcroppings, vegetation is exuberant. Many trails and paths crisscross these formations; there are many routes good for short walks of a half day or more. Expert climbers will be challenged by the difficulty of the pinnacles and spires, but play it safe—every year climbers are killed or injured. The countless legends that surround the monastery are undoubtedly rooted in the strangely unreal appearance of these peaks of San Jerónimo, some of which jut up abruptly 3,725 feet above the valley of the Llobregat River and are outlined with monoliths, which, from a distance, look like immense stone figures. Look especially for La Momia and her "daughter" La Momieta. El Massif de Sant Salvador crowns all. Also remarkable are the six colossal rocks called Les Santes Magdalenes, which have been compared to everything from Henry Moore sculptures to a Victorian tea party. In 1987, Montserrat's mountain range was declared a national park.

If all this sounds intriguing, you may even want to consider staying overnight in the monastery's simple lodgings. To get to Montserrat from Barcelona, follow the AP2/AP7 *autopista* on the upper ring road (Ronda de Dalt), or from the western end of the Diagonal as far as Sortida (Exit) 25 to Martorell. Bypass this industrial center and follow AP18 and the signs to Montserrat. You can also take a train from Barcelona's Plaça Espanya metro station, which takes you to Monistrol de Montserrat (where you can catch the funicular up to the monastery), or a guided tour with Pullmantur or Julià. ☏ 93/877–7777, 93/877–7701 *for accommodations.*

## SITGES

*81 km (50 mi) south of Montserrat, 43 km (27 mi) southwest of Barcelona.*

Sitges is the prettiest and most popular resort in Barcelona's immediate environs, with an excellent beach, an attractive Old Quarter, and some interesting Moderniste architecture. It's also one of Europe's premier gay resorts. In summer this action-packed town never sleeps—its nightlife, especially along Primer de Maig street, known as Carrer del Pecat ("street of sin"), is famous. The old part of Sitges still retains its narrow streets and fishermen's houses, although apartment developments spread in all directions. Beautiful but overgrown, the village has long been nicknamed Blanca Subur for its whitewashed houses. The easily recognizable 18th-century parish church of Sant Bartomeu and Santa Tecla, sitting on the promontory of La Punta over the sea, is a scene endlessly painted by artists. Today Sitges has almost become a suburb of Barcelona, just 20 to 30 minutes away from the city.

There's always been an artistic climate in Sitges. At the end of the 19th century followers of the Moderniste movement flocked here, led by Santiago Rusiñol, to celebrate the Festes Modernistes, a bonding of like-minded artists. American millionaire Charles Deering, heir to the farm-machinery fortune of his father, William Deering, stayed here from 1910 to 1921 and was a friend of the Modernistes, playing a leading role in stimulating the arts in Sitges.

Natives of Sitges emigrated to America in the 19th century, especially to Cuba and Puerto Rico, many returning with great fortunes that they quickly spent on splendid homes that are still standing. You can see the elegant Vidal-Quadras homes at Carrer del Port Alegre 9 and Carrer Davallada 12, as well as many others around the town. February is Carnival time, and Sitges hosts thousands of people who come to see the parades and outrageous costumes.

If you're traveling to Sitges by car from Barcelona, head southwest along Gran Via or Passeig Colom to the Ronda Litoral and the freeway that passes the airport on its way to Castelldefels. From here, the AP16 freeway and tunnels will get you to Sitges in 20 to 30 minutes. Regular trains leave Sants and Passeig de Gràcia for Sitges; the ride takes half an hour. To get from Montserrat to Sitges you don't have to go back to Barcelona; take local road C1411 south from Montserrat to get on the AP7. Continue south on the AP7 to Vilafranca del Penedès, where you exit and take local road B211 to Sitges.

Of the three Sitges museums (the other two are Maricel de Mar, exhibiting Gothic and Renaissance works, and the Museu Romàntic—Can Lllopis, a look at 18th- and 19th-century bourgeois family life), the most interesting is **Cau Ferrat**, founded by the artist Santiago Rusiñol (1861–1931). The museum is a compendium of Rusiñol's Arte Total philosophy and covers ceramics, wrought iron, stained glass, carvings, furniture, and works by Rusiñol contemporaries Casas, Utrillo, Clarasó, Mas i Fondevila, Regoyos, Zuloaga, Picasso, Pitchot, and Anglada Camarasa, as well as several Rusiñols and two El Grecos. Connoisseurs of wrought iron will appreciate the beautiful collection of *creus terminals*, crosses that once marked town boundaries. ✉*Fonollar s/n* ☎*93/894–0364* ⊕*www.diba.es* ☎*€4, valid for all 3 museums; free 1st Wed. of month* ☾*June 14–Sept. 30, Tues.–Sat. 9:30–2 and 4–7; Oct. 1–June 13, Tues.–Sat. 9:30–2 and 3:30–6:30, Sun. 10–2.*

**OFF THE
BEATEN
PATH**

Fodor'sChoice
★

**Museu Pau Casals.** On the beach at Sant Salvador, just east of the town of El Vendrell, the former home of renowned cellist Pablo (Pau in Catalan) Casals (1876–1973), who left Spain in 1939 in self-imposed exile after Franco's rise to power, holds a museum with his belongings. You can see several of his cellos, original musical manuscripts, personal letters, and works of (mostly Moderniste) art. Other exhibits describe the Casals campaign for world peace. Across the street, the Auditori Pau Casals holds frequent concerts and, in July and August, a classical music festival. In El Vendrell, 18 km (11 mi) west of Sitges, you can also visit the Casa Nadiua Pau Casals (birthplace of Pau Casals) (Carrer Santana 6 ☎977/665642). ⊠ *Av. Palfuriana 67, El Vendrell 43880* ☎*977/684276* ⊕ *www.paucasals.org* ⊡*€5* ☉ *Mid-June–mid-Sept., Tues.–Sat. 10–2 and 5–9, Sun. 10–2; mid-Sept.–mid-June, Tues.–Sat. 10–2 and 4–6, Sun. 10–2.*

## WHERE TO EAT & STAY

$–$$  ✕ **Can Pagès.** Snug and family-owned, this restaurant in the heart of the Old Town serves hearty regional fare amid colorful tiles, sturdy wooden tables and chairs, and brick-red walls lined with works by local artists. The menu, adorned with the painting of a grizzled *pagès* (farmer), created by Aragonese artist and longtime Sitges resident Manuel Blesa, promises down-home Catalan cuisine, including the restaurant's signature dish, *bacallà Can Pagès* (cod with lobster and aioli) and *carxofes a la brasa* (grilled artichoke). ⊠ *Sant Pere 24–26* ☎*93/894–1195* ⊟*AE, DC, MC, V* ☉*Closed Mon. in Dec.*

$–$$  ✕ **La Nansa.** Now in its fifth generation and run by Antoni Rafecas, this family restaurant on a narrow street in the Old Quarter is famous for having brought back traditional recipes such as *arròs a la sitgetana* (Sitges-style rice, a rice broth with meats and seafood). La Nansa (named for the basket fish traps seen adorning the restaurant) also makes an outstanding *suquet de lluerna* (stew of gurnard fish). For openers try their homegrown tangy *escabetx de bonítol* (pickled bonito). ⊠ *Carrer de la Carreta 24* ☎*93/894–1927* ⊟*AE, DC, MC, V* ☉*Closed Tues. and Wed. in Jan.*

$–$$  ✕ **La Torreta.** An understated waterfront gem, this longtime favorite beckons with its excellent seafood, low whitewashed ceilings, and pale yellow walls hung with maritime paintings and old maps. Owner Josep Amigo, whose mother opened the restaurant in 1962, delivers a menu based on the freshest seasonal ingredients and "fruits of the sea," including such dishes as *cargols de puntxes* (sea snails in a vinaigrette sauce) and *calamars a la planxa amb all i julivert* (grilled squid with garlic and parsley). In summer, diners flock to the outdoor patio that overlooks the teeming boardwalk and a beach. ⊠ *Port Alegre 17* ☎*93/894–5253* ⊟*AE, DC, MC, V* ☉*Closed Tues. and Nov. 15–Dec. 15.*

$$$–$$$$  ⊞ **San Sebastián Playa.** At stage center directly over the Platja de Sant Sebastiá this alabaster elephant is widely recognized as the best place to stay in Sitges. Ample windows with vistas of frothy waves and the beach front this gleaming facade. Rooms, done in bright white with wood trimming and furnishings, have elegant white-balustraded balconies, where you can soak up the rays before joining the milling

crowds in summer or, in winter, spreading out in lonely splendor on the sand. **Pros:** dead center in the middle of the action, top technology, nonpareil views. **Con:** book well in advance, even in winter, as corporate groups favor this hotel. ☒*Port Alegre 53, 08870* ☎*93/894–8676* ⊕*www.hotelsansebastian.com* ↪*48 rooms, 3 suites* ⚲*In-hotel: cafeteria, bar, Wi-Fi, public internet, meeting rooms, pool* ▤*AE, DC, MC, V* ⦿*EP.*

$$ ▥**Terramar.** This splendid hotel built in the 1930s sits at the end of the long beachside promenade. Some rooms, with drab orange-and-brown color schemes, still show the effects of a 1960s renovation. Ongoing refurbishment is producing a brighter look, so do ask for a new room. The terrace is great for people-watching. Guests have a 50% discount at the excellent golf course behind the hotel. **Pros:** good-size balconied rooms with large windows and panoramic views out to sea. **Con:** some rooms have dated decor. ☒*Passeig Marítim 80, 08870* ☎*93/894–0050* ⊕*www.hotelterramar.com* ↪*204 rooms* ⚲*In-hotel: restaurant, Wi-Fi, tennis courts, pool* ▤*AE, DC, MC, V* ⦿*BP.*

**EN ROUTE** **Upon leaving Sitges, make straight for the AP2** *autopista* **by way of Vilafranca del Penedès, where you can taste the excellent Penedès wines and tour the Bodega Miguel Torres (** ☒*Comercio 22* ☎*93/890–0100***).**

The interesting **Museu del Vi** *(Wine Museum)* in the 14th-century former royal palace at Vilafranca del Penedès explores wine-making history. ☒*Pl. Jaume 1* ☎*93/890–0582* ⊠*€5* ⊗*Tues.–Sun. 10–2 and 4–7.*

## SANTES CREUS

8

*50 km (31 mi) southwest of Sitges, 95 km (59 mi) west of Barcelona.*

Founded in 1157 by Ramon Berenguer IV, the Cistercian monastery of Santes Creus has three austere aisles and an unusual 14th-century apse that connects with the cloisters and the courtyard of the royal palace. The cloister was designed by Reinard des Fonoll, probably an Englishman, who stayed on to live for 30 years at the monastery. The columns, originally a symbol of simplicity with leaf or plain motifs, are here a veritable zoo in stone: griffins, mermaids, and all types of mythological animals accompany Adam and Eve, elephants, monkeys, dogs, and lions. There is even the exotic face of a Viking and the Green Man, a Celtic representation of nature. From Sitges, drive inland toward Vilafranca del Penedès and the A7 freeway; then take the A2 (Lleida). To get to Santes Creus by train from Sitges, take the Lleida line to L'Espluga de Francolí, 4 km (2½ mi) from Poblet. ☒*Off the A2* ☎*977/638329* ⊠*€5* ⊗*Mid-Mar.–mid-Sept., Tues.–Sun. 10–1:30 and 3–7; mid-Sept.–mid-Jan., Tues.–Sun. 10–1:30 and 3–5:30; mid-Jan.–mid-Mar., Tues.–Sun. 10–1:30 and 3–6.*

**EN ROUTE** **The walled town of Montblanc is off the A2 at Salida (Exit) 9, its ancient gates too narrow for cars. A walk through its tiny streets reveals Gothic churches, a 16th-century hospital, and medieval mansions.**

## SANTA MARIA DE POBLET

*25 km (19 mi) west of Santes Creus.*

This splendid Cistercian foundation at the foot of the Prades Mountains is one of the great masterpieces of Spanish monastic architecture. The cloister is a stunning combination of lightness and size; on sunny days the shadows on the yellow sandstone are extraordinary. Founded in 1150 by Ramon Berenguer IV in gratitude for the Christian Reconquest, the monastery first housed a dozen Cistercians from Narbonne. Later, the Crown of Aragón used Santa Maria de Poblet for religious retreats and burials. The building was damaged in an 1836 anticlerical revolt, and monks of the reformed Cistercian Order have managed the difficult task of restoration since 1940.

Today monks and novices again pray before the splendid retable over the tombs of Aragonese rulers, restored to their former glory by sculptor Frederic Marés; sleep in the cold, barren dormitory; and eat frugal meals in the stark refectory. If you would like to join the monks—18 comfortable rooms are available, for men only—call **Pare Benito** (☎977/870089) to arrange a stay of up to 10 days within the stones and silence of one of Catalonia's gems. There has always been a sharp rivalry between the monasteries of Montserrat and Poblet, which often took opposing sides in the many quarrels that plagued Catalonia in its history. The last coup may have been won by Poblet. In 1980, Josep Tarradellas, the first president of the restored Generalitat, Catalonia's autonomous government, left his library and papers to Poblet and not to Montserrat. To get to Poblet from Sitges by train, take the Lleida line to L'Espluga de Francolí, 4 km (2½ mi) from Poblet. You can also take the train to Tarragona and catch a bus to the monastery ( ✉ *Autotransports Perelada* ☎973/202058). Be sure to reserve your one-hour guided tour of the monastery at least a few days in advance. ✉ *Off A2* ☎977/870254 ✆€5 ⊙ *Guided tours by reservation Apr.–Sept., daily 10–12:30 and 3–6; Oct.–Mar., daily 10–12:30 and 3–5:30.*

## TARRAGONA

*50 km (30 mi) southeast of Poblet, 98 km (61 mi) southwest of Barcelona.*

Set on a rocky hill overlooking the sea, the ancient Roman stronghold of Tarragona is a bracing architectural mix of past and present. Roman pillars rise amid modern apartment buildings, and a Roman amphitheater shares the city coastline with trawlers and tugboats. Though the modern city is very much an industrial town, with a large port and thriving fishing industry, it has preserved its heritage superbly. Stroll along the town's cliff-side perimeter and you'll see why the Romans set up shop here: Tarragona is strategically positioned at land's edge, its lookout points commanding unobstructed sea views. As capital of the Roman province of Tarraconensis (from 218 BC), Tarraco, as it was then called, formed the empire's principal stronghold in Spain, and by the 1st century BC the city was regarded as one of the empire's finest urban creations. Its wine was already famous, and its people were the first in Spain to become Roman citizens. St. Paul preached here in AD 58, and Tarragona became the seat of the Christian church in Spain until it was superseded by Toledo in the 11th century.

Entering the city from Barcelona, you'll pass the **triumphal arch of Berà,** dating from the 3rd century BC, 19 km (12 mi) north of Tarragona; and from the Lleida (Lérida) road, or *autopista,* you can see the 1st-century **Roman aqueduct** that helped carry fresh water 32 km (19 mi) from the Gaià River. Tarragona is divided clearly into old and new by the Rambla Vella; the Old Town and most of the Roman remains are to the north, while modern Tarragona spreads out to the south. You could start your visit to Tarragona at the acacia-lined Rambla Nova, at the end of which is a balcony overlooking the sea, the **Balcó del Mediterràni.** Then walk uphill along the Passeig de les Palmeres; below it is the ancient amphitheater, and the modern, semicircular Imperial Tarraco hotel on the passeig artfully echoes the amphitheater's curve.

★ The remains of Tarragona's Roman **amphitheater,** built in the 2nd century AD, have a spectacular view of the sea. This arena with its tiered seats was the site of gladiatorial and other contests. You're free to wander through the access tunnels and along the seating rows. Sitting with your back to the sea, you might understand why Augustus favored Tarragona as a winter resort. In the center of the theater are the remains of two superimposed churches, the earlier of which was a Visigothic basilica built to mark the bloody martyrdom of St. Fructuós and his deacons in AD 259. ⊠ *Passeig de les Palmeres* 🖼 *€2, €8 combination ticket valid for all Tarragona museums and sites* ☉ *June–Sept., Tues.– Sat. 9–9, Sun. 9–3; Oct.–May, Tues.–Sat. 9–5, Sun. 10–3.*

Students have excavated the vaults of the 1st-century Roman **Circus Maximus,** near the amphitheater. The plans just inside the gate show that the vaults now visible formed only a small corner of a vast arena (350 yards long), where 23,000 spectators gathered to watch chariot races. As medieval Tarragona grew, the city gradually swamped the circus. ⊠ *Pl. del Rei* 🖼 *€2, €8 combination ticket* ☉ *June–Sept., Tues.– Sat. 9–9, Sun. 9–3; Oct.–May, Tues.–Sat. 9–5, Sun. 10–3.*

The former **Praetorium,** a towering building, was Augustus's town house and is reputed to be the birthplace of Pontius Pilate. Its Gothic appearance is the result of extensive alterations in the Middle Ages, when it housed the kings of Catalonia and Aragón during their visits to Tarragona. The Praetorium is now the city's **Museu d'Història** (History Museum), with plans showing the evolution of the city. The museum's highlight is the **Hippolytus Sarcophagus,** which bears a bas-relief depicting the legend of Hippolytus and Fraeda. You can also access the remains of the Circus Maximus from the Praetorium. ⊠ *Pl. del Rei* ☎ *977/241952* 🖼 *€2, €8 combination ticket* ☉ *June–Sept., Tues.–Sat. 9–9, Sun. 9–3; Oct.–May, Tues.–Sat. 9–7, Sun. 10–3.*

★ A 1960s neoclassical building contains the **Museu Nacional Arqueològic de Tarragona** and the most significant collection of Roman artifacts in Catalonia. Among the items are Roman statuary and domestic fittings such as keys, bells, and belt buckles. The beautiful mosaics include a head of Medusa, famous for its piercing stare. Don't miss the video on Tarragona's history. ⊠*Pl. del Rei 5* ☎*977/236209* ⌨*€2.40; free Tues.* ☺*June–Sept., Tues.–Sat. 10–8, Sun. 10–2; Oct.–May, Tues.–Sat. 10–1:30 and 4–7, Sun. 10–2.*

The **Catedral,** built between the 12th and 14th centuries on the site of a Roman temple and a mosque, shows the changes from the Romanesque to Gothic style. The initial rounded placidity of the Romanesque apse, begun in the 12th century, later gave way to the spiky restlessness of the Gothic; the result is somewhat confused. If no mass is in progress, enter the cathedral through the cloister. The main attraction here is the 15th-century Gothic alabaster altarpiece of St. Tecla by Pere Joan, a richly detailed depiction of the life of Tarragona's patron saint. Converted by St. Paul and subsequently persecuted by local pagans, St. Tecla was repeatedly saved from demise through divine intervention. ⊠*Pla de la Seu,* ☎*977/221736* ⌨*€2.40* ☺*July–mid-Sept., Mon.–Sat. 10–7; mid-Sept.–mid-Nov., Mon.–Sat. 10–5; mid-Nov.–mid-Mar., Mon.–Sat. 10–2; mid-Mar.–June, Mon.–Sat. 10–1 and 4–7; open for services Sun. only.*

Now a museum, the **Casa Castellarnau,** a Gothic *palauet,* or town house, built by Tarragona nobility in the 18th century, includes stunning furnishings from the 18th and 19th centuries. The last member of the Castellarnau family vacated the house in 1954. ⊠*Carrer Cavallers* ☎*977/242220* ⌨*€2, €8 combination ticket* ☺*June–Sept., Tues.–Sat. 9–9, Sun. 9–3; Oct.–May, Tues.–Sat. 9–7, Sun. 10–3.*

The **Passeig Arqueològic** ( ⊠*access from Via de l'Imperi Romà*) is a 1½-km (1-mi) circular path skirting the surviving section of the 3rd-century BC Ibero-Roman ramparts, built on even earlier walls of giant rocks. On the other side of the path is a glacis, a fortification added by English military engineers in 1707 during the War of the Spanish Succession. Look for the rusted bronze of Romulus and Remus.

**El Serrallo.** The always entertaining fishing quarter and harbor is below the city near the bus station and the mouth of the Francolí River. Attending the afternoon fish auction is a golden opportunity to see how choice seafood starts its journey toward your table in Barcelona or Tarragona. For seafood closer to its source, restaurants in the port such as **Estació Marítima** ( ⊠*Moll de Costa, Tinglado 4* ☎*977/232100*)or **Manolo** ( ⊠*Carrer Gravina 61* ☎*977/223484*)are excellent choices for no-frills fresh fish in a rollicking environment.

Just uphill from the fish market is the fascinating early Christian necropolis and museum **Necrópolis i Museu Paleocristià** (Cemetery and Paleochristan Museum). ⊠*Av. Ramon y Cajal 80* ☎*977/211175* ⌨*€2.40, €8 combination ticket; free Tues.* ☺*June–Sept., Tues.–Sat. 10–1 and 4:30–8, Sun. 10–2; Oct.–May, Tues.–Sat. 10–1:30 and 3–5:30, Sun. 10–2.*

### WHERE TO EAT & STAY

$–$$ ✕**Les Coques.** If you have time for only one meal in the city, take it at this elegant little restaurant in the heart of historic Tarragona. The menu is bursting with both mountain and Mediterranean fare. Meat lovers should try the *costelles de xai* (lamb chops in a dark burgundy sauce); seafood fans should ask for *calamarsets amb favetes* (baby calamari sautéed in olive oil and garlic and served with legumes). ⊠*Baixada Nova del Patriarca 2 bis* ☎*977/228300* ▤*AE, DC, MC, V* ✆*Closed Sun., 10 days in Feb., and mid-July–mid-Aug.*

★ $–$$ ✕**Les Voltes.** Built into the vaults of the Roman Circus Maximus, this out-of-the-way spot serves a hearty cuisine. You'll find Tarragona specialties, mainly fish dishes, as well as international recipes, with *calçotada* (spring onions) in winter. (If you want to try calçotadas, you must call to order them a day in advance.) ⊠*Carrer Trinquet Vell 12* ☎*977/230651* ▤*MC, V* ✆*Closed July and Aug. No dinner Sun., no lunch Mon.*

OFF THE BEATEN PATH ★ **Joan Gatell.** A short 15-minute hop down the coast to Cambrils will offer a memorable chance to try one of the most famous restaurants in southern Catalonia. The Gatell sisters used to run two restaurants side by side; Fanny now carries on the tradition of exquisite local meals by herself in this one, named after their founding father Joan. Try the *fideus negres amb sepionets* (noodle paella with baby squid cooked in squid ink) or *lubina al horno con cebolla y patata* (roast sea bass with onion and potato). Cambrils is 18 km (11 mi) southwest of Tarragona. ⊠*Passeig Miramar 26, Cambrils* ☎*977/360057* ▤*AE, DC, MC, V* ✆*Closed Mon., Oct., and late Dec.–Jan. No dinner Sun.*

$–$$ ▦**Imperial Tarraco.** Large and white, this half-moon-shape hotel has a superb position overlooking the Mediterranean. The large public rooms have cool marble floors, black-leather furniture, marble-top tables, and Oriental rugs. Guest rooms are plain but comfortable, and each has a private balcony. Insist on a sea view. **Pros:** facing the Mediterranean looking over the fishing port and the Roman amphitheater, a privileged spot. **Con:** occupies a very busy Tarragona intersection with heavy traffic. ⊠*Passeig Palmeres, 43003* ☎*977/233040* ⊕*www.husa. es* ⇒*170 rooms* ⚙*In-hotel: restaurant, bar, tennis court, pool* ▤*AE, DC, MC, V* ⊙*EP.*

¢ ▦**Làuria.** Simple modern furnishings fill the spacious rooms at this hotel, the most pleasant place to stay in downtown Tarragona. Room terraces overlook the serene pool and patio area, the Rambla Nova, or the sea. **Pros:** easy on the wallet and comfortable. **Cons:** as a budget choice it's a little threadbare and modest in appearance. ⊠*Rambla Nova 20, 43004* ☎*977/236712* ⊕*www.hlauria.es* ⇒*72 rooms* ⚙*In-hotel: bar, public Internet, pool* ▤*AE, DC, MC, V* ⊙*EP.*

### NIGHTLIFE & THE ARTS

Nightlife in Tarragona takes two forms: older and quieter in the upper city, younger and more raucous down below. There are some lovely rustic bars in the Casc Antic, the upper section of old Tarragona. Port

Esportiu, a pleasure-boat harbor separate from the working port, has another row of dining and dancing establishments; young people flock here on weekends and summer nights. For a dose of culture with your cocktail, try **Antiquari** ( ✉ *Santa Anna 3* ☎ *977/241843*), a laid-back bar that hosts readings, art exhibits, and occasional screenings of classic or contemporary films. At **Museum** ( ✉ *Carrer Sant Llorenç s/n* ☎ *977/240612*) you can relax and have a peaceful drink.

The **Teatre Metropol** ( ✉ *Rambla Nova 46* ☎ *977/244795*) is Tarragona's center for music, dance, theater, and cultural events ranging from *castellers* (human-castle formations), usually performed in August and September, to folk dances.

## SHOPPING

**Antigüedades Ciria** ( ✉ *Pla de la Seu 2* ☎ *977/248541*), like other shops in front of the cathedral and in the Pla de la Seu, has an interesting selection of antiques. You have to haggle for bargains, but **Carrer Major** has some exciting antiques stores. They're worth a thorough rummage, as the gems tend to be hidden away.

# CATALONIA ESSENTIALS

*To research prices, get advice from other travelers, and book travel arrangements, visit www.fodors.com.*

## AIR TRAVEL

### AIRPORTS

Girona's airport, alternately referred to as Girona–Costa Brava, Barcelona–Girona, or, simply Girona Airport, about 13 km (8 mi) south of the city, has become Catalonia's low-cost flight hub. Ryanair and other carriers fly regularly from this handy terminal an hour north of Barcelona. There is bus transportation between the airport and both Girona and Barcelona (**Barcelonabus** ( ✉ *Passeig de Sant Joan 52, Girona* ☎ *902/130014*)). Buses take an average of 75 minutes and cost €12 one-way, €21 round-trip. **Sagales** ( ☎ *902/130014*, ⊕ *www.sagales. com*) runs buses to various points along the coast from Girona–Costa Brava Airport.

**Airport Information Girona–Costa Brava Airport** ( ✉ *Afores s/n, Vilobí d'Onyar* ☎ *972/186600*).

### CARRIERS

Besides the major Spanish carrier Iberia, Girona Airport serves a large number of charter and low-cost airlines, many of which are centralized under a single telephone number with the name Service Air.

**Airlines & Contacts Air Europa** ( ✉ *Afores s/n, Vilobí d'Onyar* ☎ *972/474014* ⊕ *www.aireuropa.com*). **Iberia** ( ✉ *Pl. Marqués de Camps 8, Girona* ☎ *972/474192*). **Monarch** ( ✉ *Afores s/n, Vilobí d'Onyar* ☎ *972/474017* ⊕ *www.monarch.com*). **Ryanair** ( ✉ *Afores s/n, Vilobí d'Onyar* ☎ *902/361550 or 807/220220* ⊕ *www.ry-anair.com*). **Service Air** ( ☎ *972/186697* ⊕ *www.serviceair.com*). **Spanair** ( ✉ *Afores s/n, Vilobí d'Onyar* ☎ *902/131415* ⊕ *www.spanair.com*).

## CAR RENTALS AT GIRONA-COSTA BRAVA AIRPORT

**Agencies Avis** ( ✉ *Girona–Costa Brava Airport, Vilobí d'Onyar* ☎ *972/474333*). **Europcar** ( ✉ *Girona–Costa Brava Airport, Vilobí d'Onyar* ☎ *972/209946*). **Hertz** ( ✉ *Girona–Costa Brava Airport, Vilobí d'Onyar* ☎ *972/186619*).

### BIKE TRAVEL

Most Spanish biking is done on road bikes. Watch out for the lack of a shoulder on many Spanish roads. Cars travel very fast, and though drivers are used to encountering bikers they do not go out of their way to make you feel safe and cared for. Spain's numerous nature areas are perfect for mountain biking; many have specially marked trails.

Catalonia's alternating lush and rugged terrain has become more accessible to mountain bikers with the advent of *Centres BTT* ("BTT" stands for *bicicleta tot terreny*, Catalan for "mountain bike"; in Castilian, it's *bicicleta todo terreno*). BTT Centers are natural areas where a minimum of 100 km (62 mi) of biking trails have been—and continue to be—created. The bike circuits are signposted and marked according to difficulty, so families with kids and pros alike can access the trails. Overseen by the Federació Catalana de Ciclisme (Catalan Cycling Federation), these biking areas have information centers where you can pick up maps and tourist information; bicycle services, from rentals to repair; and showers and bathrooms. There are presently 14 BTT Centers all over Catalonia. A map pinpointing these centers and including contact information is available at the Generalitat de Catalunya BTT Web site (www.gencat.net/turistex_nou/btt/uk/bttabiertos.htm).

It is better to rent a bike locally, rather than facing the logistics and complications of bringing your own bike with you. Bikes are usually not allowed on trains; they have to be packed and checked as luggage. Most Spanish nature areas have at least one agency offering mountain bikes for rent and, in many cases, guided biking tours. Check with park visitor centers for details. In addition, hotels in rural areas often have bikes available for guests, either for rent or for free.

**Information Centres BTT/FCC Catalunya** ( ✉ *Passeig de la Generalitat 21, Banyoles* ☎ *972/580639* ⊕ *www.gencat.es/turisme/btt*).

### BIKE RENTALS

**Alberg de Joventut Cerverí** ( ✉ *Carrer Ciutadans 9, Girona* ☎ *972/218003*). **Cicles Empordà** ( ✉ *Av. Gola Estany 33, Roses* ☎ *972/152478*). **Trafalch Bikes** ( ✉ *Carrer Major 14, Salt (2 km [1 mi] from Girona center)* ☎ *972/234943*). **The World Rent a Bike** ( ✉ *Camprodon i Artesa 14, Lloret de Mar* ☎ *636/302112*).

### BOAT & FERRY TRAVEL

Many short-cruise lines along the coast give you a chance to get a view of the Costa Brava from the sea. Visit the port areas in the main towns listed below and you will quickly spot several tourist cruise lines. Plan on spending around €6–€8. The glass-keeled Nautilus boats for observation of the Islas Medes underwater park cost €15 and run on weekends only between October and March.

**Boat & Ferry Information** Creuers Badia de Roses ( ⊠ *Passeig Marítim s/n, Roses* ☎ *972/255499*). **Marina Princess** ( ⊠ *Passeig Marítim 34, L'Estartit* ☎ *972/750643* ⊕ *www.marinaprincess.com*). **Nautilus** ( ⊠ *Passeig Marítim 23, L'Estartit* ☎ *972/751489* ⊕ *www.nautilus.es*). **Roses Serveis Marítims** ( ⊠ *Passeig Marítim s/n, Roses* ☎ *972/152426*). **Viajes Marítimos** ( ⊠ *Passeig Sant Pere 5, Lloret de Mar* ☎ *972/369095* ⊕ *www.viajesmaritimos.com*). **Viatges Marítims Costa Brava** ( ⊠ *Aquarium, L'Estartit* ☎ *972/750880*).

## BUS TRAVEL

Sarfa operates buses to Lloret, Sant Feliu de Guíxols, S'Agaró, Platja d'Aro, Palamós, Begur, Roses, Cadaqués, and other destinations on the Costa Brava. The bus line Barna Bus overlaps and complements some of these services; buses leave from the same Estació del Nord in Barcelona as Sarfa buses. Buses can also be caught at the Estació del Nord if you're heading south to destinations like Tarragona and Sitges. Teisa handles buses inland from Girona city and is next to the Girona train station. Other bus transportation hubs are Lloret de Mar and Figueres.

### FARES & SCHEDULES

Only Girona and Tarragona have a major municipal bus transportation service. The Old Quarter of Girona does not have bus service through its narrow streets. City TMG (Transporte Municipal Girona) buses in Girona run daily 7 AM–10 PM. The fare is €1.15; for multiple journeys you can purchase a ticket for 10 rides for €8.40. Route maps are displayed at bus stops. In Tarragona, which is more spread out, city buses run daily from about 7 AM until after 10 PM. Extra lines in summer take people to the beaches. The fare is €1.10; for multiple journeys you can purchase a ticket for 10 rides for €5.40.

**Bus Information** Barna Bus ( ☎ *93/232–0459*). **Figueres** ( ⊠ *Pl. de l'Estació s/n* ☎ *972/673354*). **Girona** ( ⊠ *Pl. d'Espanya s/n* ☎ *972/212319*). **Lloret de Mar** ( ⊠ *Ctra. Hostalric a Tossa s/n* ☎ *972/365788*). **Sarfa** ( ⊠ *Estació del Nord, Alí Bei 80, Eixample, Barcelona* ☎ *93/265–1158 or 902/302025* Ⓜ *Arc de Triomf*). **Tarragona** ( ⊠ *Polígon Industrial Francolí, Tarragona* ☎ *977/254–9480* ⊕ *www.fut.es/emt*). **Teisa** ( ⊠ *Estació d'Autobusos, Pl. d'Espanya s/n, Girona* ☎ *972/200275*).

## CAR RENTAL

**Agencies** Atesa ( ⊠ *Ctra. Barcelona 204–206, Girona* ☎ *972/217274 or 902/100101*). **Avis** ( ⊠ *Barcelona 25, Girona* ☎ *972/206933* ⊠ *Enric Granados 24, Lloret de Mar* ☎ *972/373023* ⊠ *España 24, Sitges* ☎ *93/894–0287*). **Europcar** ( ⊠ *Carrer del Freu s/n, L'Estartit* ☎ *972/751731* ⊠ *Pl. de l'Estació s/n, Figueres* ☎ *972/673434* ⊠ *Ctra. Blanes a Tossa s/n, Lloret de Mar* ☎ *972/363366*). **Hertz** ( ⊠ *Pl. de l'Estació s/n, Girona* ☎ *972/210108* ⊠ *Pl. de l'Estació s/n, Figueres* ☎ *972/672801* ⊠ *Artur Carbonell 27, Sitges* ☎ *93/894–8986*).

## CAR TRAVEL

The proximity of the towns and villages of northeastern Catalonia and good modern roads make for easy access to the many sights and points of interest. From Barcelona, the fastest way to the Costa Brava is to start up the inland AP7 *autopista* tollway toward Girona and then take Sortida (Exit) 10 for Blanes, Lloret de Mar, Tossa de Mar, Sant Feliu de Guíxols, S'Agaró, Platja d'Aro, Palamós, Calella de Palafrugell, and Palafrugell. From Palafrugell, you can head inland for La Bisbal, and from there on to the city of Girona. From Girona you can easily travel to the inland towns of Banyoles, Besalú, and Olot. To head to the middle section of the Costa Brava, get off at Sortida 6, the first exit after Girona; this will point you directly to the Iberian ruins of Ullastret. To reach the northern part of the Costa Brava, get off the AP7 before Figueres at Sortida 4 to get to L'Estartit, L'Escala, Empúries, Castelló d'Empúries, Aïguamolls de l'Empordà, Roses, Cadaqués, Sant Pere de Rodes, and Port Bou. Sortida 4 will also take you directly to Figueres, Peralada, and the Alberes range. If you prefer, you can also take national road N11 north, but it is heavily traveled, especially in summer.

To reach Sitges from Barcelona, take the autopista C32 south along the coast; the AP7–E15 highway also runs south inland to Tarragona. To head west toward Lleida and the monasteries of Santes Creus and Santa Maria de Poblet and the medieval town of Montblanc, and on to Madrid, take the A7 south from Barcelona and turn west onto the A2–E90 at L'Arboç. To get to Montserrat, take highway A18 off the A7 from Barcelona.

## ROAD CONDITIONS
Catalonia is a geographically undulating country with a few interspersed mountain ranges such as the Montseny, just north of Barcelona; only the Pyrenees mountains are especially rugged. Here roads twist and turn, and to get anywhere takes considerable time. All the towns on the Costa Brava are interconnected by a road network that is very congested in summer; traffic can be slow and frustrating.

## TOURS
For tours to Montserrat, contact Julià Tours or Pullmantur.

**Fees & Schedules** **Julià Tours** ( ✉ *Ronda Universitat 5, Eixample, Barcelona* ☎ *93/317–6454* ⊕ *www.juliatravel.com*). **Pullmantur** ( ✉ *Gran Via de les Corts Catalanes 645, Eixample, Barcelona* ☎ *93/317–1297* ⊕ *www.pullmantur-spain.com*).

## TRAIN TRAVEL
The Spanish railroad company is called RENFE, which stands for *Red Nacional de Ferrocarriles Españoles (⇨ By Train in Barcelona Essentials)*. Most of the Costa Brava is *not* served directly by railroad. A local line heads up the coast from Barcelona but takes you only to Blanes; from there it turns inland and connects at Maçanet-Massanes with the main line up to France. Direct trains only stop at major towns, such as Girona, Flaçà, and Figueres. If you want to get off at a small town, be sure to take a local train; or you can take a fast direct train to, let's say, Girona and get off and wait for a local to go by (the words for local, express, and direct are basically the same in Spanish as in English). The stop on the main line for the middle section of the Costa Brava is Flaçà, where you can take a bus or taxi to your final destination. Girona and Figueres are two other towns with major bus stations that feed out to the towns of the Costa Brava. The train does serve the last three towns on the north end of the Costa Brava, Llançà, Colera, and Port Bou. In the southern direction, Sitges and Tarragona are also served directly by

8

train. A short railroad line serves Montserrat and takes you to Monistrol, where you can catch the funicular to the monastery.

The Estació de França near the port, Barcelona's original train terminal, handles only certain local trains since Sants-Estació became the main station in the late 1980s.

Train Information **Estació de França** ( ✉ *Marquès de l'Argentera s/n, Born-Ribera, Barcelona* ☎ *93/496–3464).* **Passeig de Gràcia** ( ✉ *At Aragó, Eixample, Barcelona* ☎ *902/240202).* **Sants-Estació** ( ✉ *Pl. dels Països Catalans s/n, Eixample, Barcelona* ☎ *902/240202* ⊕ *www.renfe.es).*

## TRAVEL AGENCIES

Local Agents **Alfa Tours** ( ✉ *Pl. de Francesc Calvet i Rubalcaba 5, Girona* ☎ *972/220381).* **Crom Raid & Adventure** ( ✉ *Av. de les Alegries 12, Lloret de Mar* ☎ *972/365412).* **Viatges Berga** ( ✉ *Carrer Sant Agustí 11, Tarragona* ☎ *977/252610).*

## VISITOR INFORMATION

The tourist offices throughout this area are very helpful and well informed. Don't hesitate to go to one if you have any problem or question about any place you will be visiting. The Patronat de Turisme Costa Brava Girona, a consortium that deals with all tourist activities in northeastern Catalonia, has a useful Web site.

Tourist Information **Patronat de Turisme Costa Brava Girona** ( ☎ *972/208401* ⊕ *www.costabrava.org).* **Blanes** ( ✉ *Pl. de Catalunya s/n* ☎ *972/330348).* **Cadaqués** ( ✉ *Cotxe 2-A* ☎ *972/258315).* **Figueres** ( ✉ *Pl. del Sol s/n* ☎ *972/503155).* **Girona** ( ✉ *Rambla de la Llibertat 1* ☎ *972/226575).* **Lloret de Mar** ( ✉ *Pl. de la Vila s/n* ☎ *972/364735).* **Palafrugell** ( ✉ *Pl. de la Església s/n* ☎ *972/611820).* **Palamós** ( ✉ *Passeig de Mar s/n* ☎ *972/600550).*

**Platja d'Aro** ( ✉ *Mossèn Jacint Verdaguer 4* ☎ *972/817179).* **Roses** ( ✉ *Av. de Rhode 101* ☎ *972/257331).* **Sant Feliu de Guíxols** ( ✉ *Pl. Monestir s/n* ☎ *972/820051).* **Sitges** ( ✉ *Carrer Sínia Morera 1* ☎ *93/894–4251).* **Tarragona** ( ✉ *Carrer Major 39* ☎ *977/250795).* **Tossa de Mar** ( ✉ *Av. de Pelegrí 25* ☎ *972/340108).*

# Excursion to Bilbao

## WORD OF MOUTH

"What impressed me about [Bilbao] is that they have taken urban renewal and design seriously. . . . There is a lot of really beautiful contemporary design and architecture in the city, something you don't see as often in Europe."

—MikeT

By George
Semler

**TIME IN BILBAO CAN BE IDENTIFIED AS BG OR AG** (Before Guggenheim, After Guggenheim). Frank O. Gehry's stunning Museo Guggenheim Bilbao opened in 1997, and no single monument of art and architecture has ever so radically changed a city—or, for that matter, a nation, and in this case two: Spain and Euskadi. Euskadi is the term for the Basque Country—a world apart with its own language, gastronomy, sports, and rural culture. Even the Basque Country's longtime political and social conflict came to a temporary halt after the Guggenheiming of Bilbao. The city once known as a steel and boatbuilding giant reinvented itself as a cultural capital not only with this art museum, but with a sleek subway system by Norman Foster, a glass footbridge by Santiago Calatrava, and the urban landscape of César Pelli's Abandoibarra project. Residents of the inner city recently numbered 373,000, but greater Bilbao (Bilbo, in Euskera, the Basque language) now encompasses almost 1 million inhabitants. That gives Bilbao, the capital of the province of Vizcaya, nearly half the total population of the Basque Country and makes it the fourth-largest urban population in Spain. Until relatively recently a smoke-stained industrial soot bowl—though never lacking a sparkling cultural and culinary tradition—Bilbao has made a brilliant investment in art and tourism and led the entire Basque Country into a new era of economic and spiritual regeneration, suggesting that life can indeed, to some degree, imitate art (or at least an art museum).

Gehry's gleaming titanium whale of a museum hovers alongside the estuary of the Nervión River, connects Bilbao's 700-year-old Casco Viejo (Old Quarter) with the 19th-century Ensanche (Widening), and seems to collect and reflect light throughout Bilbao. For starters, from the central atrium of the Guggenheim you can look both east up into Bilbao's most urban streets or above to the hills to the west, where farmers and grazing livestock continue about their age-old business. Meanwhile, churches in Bilbao's Casco Viejo are emerging from centuries of industrial grime, while parks and gardens are being reclaimed from what were once rusting shipyards and steel mills. Bilbao now seems a happy version of Hieronymous Bosch's *Garden of Earthly Delights* triptych, on view in Madrid's Prado, a virtual anthill of commerce and endeavor. And as the saying goes, "As Bilbao goes, so goes Euskadi."

Bilbao is a scenic and easy drive from Barcelona that can be accomplished in five hours or less. Thanks to the prohibition on highway advertising and the lack of forestation along major highways, driving in Spain is a superb way to see the geography of the Iberian Peninsula.

## EXPLORING BILBAO

Surrounded by the green promontories of Artxanda, Bérriz, Abril, Artagan, Malmasin, Arnótegui, Pagasarri, Arraiz, and Cobetas, Bilbao has suddenly become more famous for its emblematic "Bilbao blue" skies of deep cerulean than for its traditional *siri-miri* drizzle or the rusting remains of its once opulent shipyards. Bibao, once written off as a gloomy, factory-ridden seaport, is now a city made for strolling through lush green parks, along the river, through art museums, and across architecturally poetic footbridges.

Though Bilbao's new attractions get more press, the city's old treasures still quietly line the banks of the rust-color Nervión River. The Casco Viejo (Old Quarter)—also known as Siete Calles (Seven Streets)—is a charming jumble of shops, bars, and restaurants on the river's right bank above the Puente del Arenal. In the early-20th-century Ensanche (Widening) on the left bank of the Nervión, broad boulevards such as Gran Vía and Alameda Mazarredo, provide Bilbao's more formal face.

Flaviobriga, as the Romans called what they described as a bustling hub filled with a remarkable quantity and quality of iron ore, women, and foodstuffs, has always been prosperous. The modern city of Bilbao, founded in 1300 by a Vizcayan noble, Diego López de Haro, was Spain's main northern port for the wool exports that represented the Iberian Peninsula's most important source of medieval wealth. Later Bilbao became an industrial and mining center, thanks mainly to the abundance of minerals in the surrounding hills. An affluent industrial class developed here, as did the working-class suburbs (like Portugalete and Barakaldo) that line the Margen Izquierda (Left Bank) of the Nervión estuary. Agriculture and fishing made way for shipbuilding, coal mining, and steel manufacturing, as Bilbao and the Industrial Revolution embraced each other in the 19th century. The Universidad Comercial de Deusto, founded by the Jesuit Order in 1886, was one of the first business-management schools in the world. Meanwhile, early banking moguls such as Carlos Jacquet and Pedro McMahon y Aguirre developed expertise and power in this area that led to the early Banco de Vizcaya and eventually to today's giant Banco de Bilbao-Vizcaya-Argentaria.

Over the course of the 20th century the iron and coal mines began to fail; by the '60s the heavy steel industry was becoming technologically obsolete, though by that time Bilbao's expertise in banking and commerce was solidly established. When steel giant Altos Hornos closed and the mills along the Nervión became a Basque version of Chicago's rust belt, business and commerce continued. Nevertheless, the numbers tell their story: Bilbao's population doubled between 1950 and 1975 but has remained static at 1 million since.

## TOP 5

■ Siete Calles : a joyous street party with happy Basques out de txiquiteo (bar hopping).

■ Mercado de la Ribera: a triple-decker market resembles an ocean liner parked in the Nervión.

■ Museo de Bellas Artes: Bilbao's superb fine arts museum provides a traditional counterpoint to the Guggenheim's postmodern glitter.

■ San Mamés : Bilbao's soccer stadium offers top European teams in an emotion-charged and historic environment.

■ Cider Houses: cider houses and their typical fare are a must for visitors.

## GREAT ITINERARIES

### IF YOU HAVE 1 DAY

Begin at the Guggenheim in the morning and continue by taking a stroll (or a tram ride) up the river to the Mercado de la Ribera for a look at the vast and spectacular triple-tier display of food products. With a whetted appetite, allow yourself a light midday tapeo and txikiteo run through the Casco Viejo's taverns followed by lunch at El Perro Chico. The next move is to walk across the Ensanche to the Museo de Bellas Artes for a look at the Zurbaráns and El Grecos and the Basque collection of Zuloaga. Dinner might take you through a Licenciado Poza tavern or two on your way to Guria or Etxanobe, or back to the Guggenheim for some serious Bilbao cuisine.

### IF YOU HAVE 3 DAYS

For the three-day Bilbao, start with the Guggenheim in the morning on Day 1, visit the Mercado de la Ribera, and dive into the Casco Viejo for a tapa at Xukela and another at Victor Montes in Plaza Nueva before crossing the Puente del Mercado footbridge to Perro Chico for lunch. In the afternoon, see more of the Guggenheim and eventually have dinner at Guria or Zortziko or Etxanobe. On Day 2, see the Museo de Bellas Artes and walk across the Ensanche for one of Ander Calvo's designer sandwiches at his Taberna de los Mundos before hopping the Eusko Tren from Estación de Atxuri to Mundaka and Bermeo for sunset over the Urdaibai nature preserve at the mouth of the Ría de Gernika. The relentless will find a way to swing a late dinner at Goizeko Kabi. Day 3 would start with a walk through the Doña Casilda de Iturrizar Park, a look through the fascinating Museo Vasco in the Casco Viejo, and a funicular ride to Artxanda and the Txakolí de Artxanda for lunch overlooking the city. Visit the Museo Marítimo in the afternoon and have dinner in the excellent Casa Rufo or the postmodern Aizian in the Sheraton Bilbao.

Many of the wealthy left during the last quarter of the 20th century, driven out by the fear of kidnapping and the extortion of the so-called revolutionary tax of ETA (Euskadi Ta Askatasuna, or Basque Homeland and Liberty) separatist terrorists. The Right Bank suburb of Getxo, for instance, has been remarkable for its abandoned mansions, many of which are now being restored as descendants of the original owners move back. Between the upsurge of ETA and the industrial "reconversion" (layoffs, or downsizing), Vizcaya was at a standstill until the early '90s, when the Basque and Bilbao governments, along with Guggenheim Museum director Thomas Krens and architect Frank Gehry, concocted an unlikely scheme designed to inject confidence and hope into an unraveling socioeconomic panorama.

### GETTING YOUR BEARINGS

Though the Bilbao "Metropoli" ranges for miles up and down the Ría de Bilbao (the estuary of the Nervión), the part of the city you will be exploring comprises under 3 km (2 mi), from the downstream Palacio de Euskalduna to the upstream Mercado de la Ribera. The subway can be handy for a quick shot from one end of town to the other, but is not a necessity for getting around unless you need to make an opera curtain or soccer kickoff.

A 20-minute excursion on Norman Foster's designer subway will get you close to the beach at Getxo, while a train ride from the narrow-gauge Atxuri station through the Urdaibai natural park reaches Mundaka and Bermeo in under an hour.

## ALONG THE NERVIÓN RIVER

Walking the banks of the Nervión is a satisfying jaunt. After all, this was how—while out on a morning jog—the Guggenheim's director, Thomas Krens, first discovered the perfect spot for his project, nearly opposite the Right Bank's Deusto University. From the Palacio de Euskalduna upstream to the colossal Mercado de la Ribera, parks and green zones line either side of the river. An amble here will offer even more when César Pelli's Abandoibarra project fills in the half mile between the Guggenheim and the Euskalduna bridge with a series of parks, the Deusto University library, the Sheraton Bilbao Hotel, and a major shopping center.

### A GOOD WALK

Starting at the shiplike **Palacio de Euskalduna** ❶—a music venue and convention hall—and the **Museo Marítimo de Bilbao** ❷, walk up through the botanical bonanza **Parque de Doña Casilda de Iturrizar** ❸ to Bilbao's excellent **Museo de Bellas Artes** ❹, where the El Greco and Goya masterworks share wall space with lesser-known but wonderful painters like Sorolla and Zuloaga. Then walk five minutes through the modern Abandoibarra gardens or along Alameda Mazarredo to the **Museo Guggenheim Bilbao** ❺—with luck the sun will be giving a shine to its titanium-covered walls. Continue to the river and turn right to reach and cross Santiago Calatrava's **Puente de Zubi-Zuri** ❻. From the bridge you will have a view of Arata Isozaki's giant skyscraper, Torre Isozaki, probably still under construction. Continue up the Right Bank of the river past Bilbao's **Ayuntamiento** ❼ (City Hall) to the linden tree–lined Paseo del Arenal. From there continue walking up the river past the **Teatro Arriaga** ❽—a reconstructed Belle Epoque theater—and the **Mercado de la Ribera** ❾ for a look at one of the largest covered food markets in Europe. From there, walk farther for a good look at the church of **San Antón** ❿. Backtrack to cross the river on the **Puente de la Ribera** ⓫ and turn left for lunch at El Perro Chico.

TIMING    Depending on how long you spend snoozing in the park or browsing through the market, this is at least a three-hour walk. Add anywhere from three hours to a full day for a Guggenheim visit.

### WHAT TO SEE

❼ **Ayuntamiento** *(City Hall)*. Architect Joaquín de Rucoba built this city hall in 1892, on the site of the San Agustín convent destroyed during the 1836 Carlist War. Sharing the Belle Epoque style of de Rucoba's Teatro Arriaga, the Ayuntamiento is characterized by the same brash, slightly aggressive attitude to which most bilbaínos confess without

## PLEASURES AND PASTIMES

### ART & ARCHITECTURE

The Bilbao Guggenheim rivals Madrid's Prado Museum as Spain's most-visited art venue, and Bilbao's Museo de Bellas Artes is one of the top-ranked art museums in the country. Frank Gehry's design for the Guggenheim made the building an attraction in itself. The city's other architectural highlights include Santiago Calatrava's soaring Loiu airport terminal and his Zubi-Zuri footbridge, Norman Foster's subway system running throughout greater Bilbao, the Palacio de Euskalduna music and convention complex by Federico Soriano and Dolores Palacios, César Pelli's skyscraper under construction on the bank of Bilbao's Nervión, and Arata Isozaki's tower rising floor by floor just upriver from the Guggenheim. Between the Guggenheim and the Palacio de Euskalduna, the Abandoibarra project is converting the riverside space into a series of gardens, shops, hotels, and libraries.

### SPAIN'S BEST CUISINE

Bilbao is deeply, purely, and seriously committed to culinary excellence. Long before the Guggenheim opened, those in the know knew that downtown Bilbao contained some of the Basque Country's and Spain's most superb dining establishments. The Basque cuisine in and around Bilbao and San Sebastián is generally considered the best food in Spain, combining the fresh fish of the Atlantic and upland vegetables, beef, and lamb with a love of sauces that is rare south of the Pyrenees. The now 20-year-old *nueva cocina vasca* (new Basque cooking) movement, as described by Basque chef and cooking academy director Luis Irizar, was simply an adaptation of ancient canons to contemporary life: "Fishermen still want their marmitako (tuna stew) as powerful and stick-to-your-ribs as ever, but the rest of us, working at computers or behind the wheel of a car, need lighter interpretations of the traditional recipes." In Bilbao, as throughout Euskadi, it's nearly impossible to avoid a great meal. Specialties include *kokotxas* (nuggets of cod jaw), *besugo a la parrilla* (sea bream grilled over coals), *chuleta* (or *txuleta*, in Euskera) *de buey* (garlicky beefsteak grilled over coals), and the deservedly ubiquitous *bacalao al pil-pil*—cod-flank fillets cooked very slowly in a boiled emulsion of garlic and gelatin from the cod itself, so that the oil makes a popping noise ("pil-pil") and a white sauce is created.

Though the local Basque wine, *txakolí*, a young, white brew made from tart green grapes, is refreshing with tapas and first courses, serious dining in the Basque Country is usually accompanied by wines from La Rioja, which *bilbainos* consider all but a colony of the great metropolis. Just an hour south of Bilbao, La Rioja and its wines are part of daily life in Bilbao. Many of the vineyards are, in fact, owned by old Bilbao families. La Rioja Alta produces the finest wines in Spain, but purists insisting on sipping a Basque wine with their Basque cuisine could choose a Rioja Alavesa, from the north side of the Ebro in the Basque province of Alava. Navarra also produces some fine vintages, especially rosés and reds—and in such quantity that some churches in Allo, Peralta, and other towns were actually built with a mortar mixed with wine instead of water.

undue embarrassment. The Salón Árabe, the highlight of the interior, was designed by the same architect who built the Café Iruña, as their mutual neo-Mudéjar motifs suggest. ☒*Paseo Campo de Volantín s/n, El Arenal* ☏*94/420–4200, 94/420–5298 for tours* ☜*Tour free* ⊙*Tours weekdays 9–11 by special request* Ⓜ*Abando.*

**❾ Mercado de la Ribera.** This triple-decker ocean liner with its prow headed down the estuary toward the open sea is one of the best markets of its kind in Europe, as well as one of the biggest, with more than 400 retail stands covering 37,950 square feet. Like the architects of the Guggenheim and the Palacio de Euskalduna nearly 75 years later, the architect was not unplayful with this well-anchored ocean-going grocery store in the river. From the stained-glass entryway over Calle de la Ribera to the tiny catwalks over the river or the diminutive restaurant on the second floor, the market is an inviting place. Look for the farmer's market on the top floor, and down on the bottom floor, ask how fresh a fish is some morning and you might hear, "Oh, that one's not too fresh: caught last night." ☒*Calle de la Ribera 20, Casco Viejo* ☏*94/415–3136* ⊙*Mon.–Sat. 8 AM–1 PM* Ⓜ*Casco Viejo.*

**★ ❹ Museo de Bellas Artes** *(Museum of Fine Arts).* Considered one of the top five museums in a country that has a staggering number of museums and great paintings, the Museo de Bellas Artes is like a mini-Prado, with representatives from every Spanish school and movement from the 12th through the 20th centuries. The museum's fine collection of Flemish, French, Italian, and Spanish paintings includes works by El Greco, Goya, Velázquez, Zurbarán, Ribera, Gauguin, and Tàpies. One large and excellent section traces developments in 20th-century Spanish and Basque art alongside works by better-known European contemporaries, such as Léger and Bacon. Look especially for Zuloaga's famous portrait of La Condesa Mathieu de Moailles and Sorolla's portrait of Basque philosopher Miguel de Unamuno. A statue of Basque painter Ignacio de Zuloaga outside greets visitors to this sparkling collection at the edge of Doña Casilda Park and on the Left Bank end of the Deusto bridge, five minutes from the Guggenheim. Three hours might be barely enough to fully appreciate this international and pan-chronological painting course. The museum's excellent Arbolagaña restaurant offers a stellar lunch break to break up the visit. ☒*Parque de Doña Casilda de Iturrizar, El Ensanche* ☏*94/439–6060* ⊕*www.museobilbao.com* ☜*€5.50; Bono Artean combined ticket with Guggenheim (valid 1 yr) €12 plus €2 additional on admittance to 2nd museum; free Wed.* ⊙*Tues.–Sat. 10–1:30 and 4–7:30, Sun. 10–2* Ⓜ*Moyúa.*

**❺ Museo Guggenheim Bilbao.** Described by Spanish novelist Manuel Vazquez Montalban as a "meteorite," the Guggenheim, with its eruption of light in the ruins of Bilbao's failed shipyards and steelworks, has dramatically reanimated this onetime industrial city. How Bilbao and the Guggenheim met is in itself a saga: Guggenheim director Thomas Krens was looking for a venue for a major European museum, having found nothing acceptable in Paris, Madrid, or elsewhere, and glumly accepted an invitation to Bilbao. Krens was out for a morning jog when he found it—the empty riverside lot once occupied by the Altos Hornos

Fodor'sChoice ★

9

# Bilbao

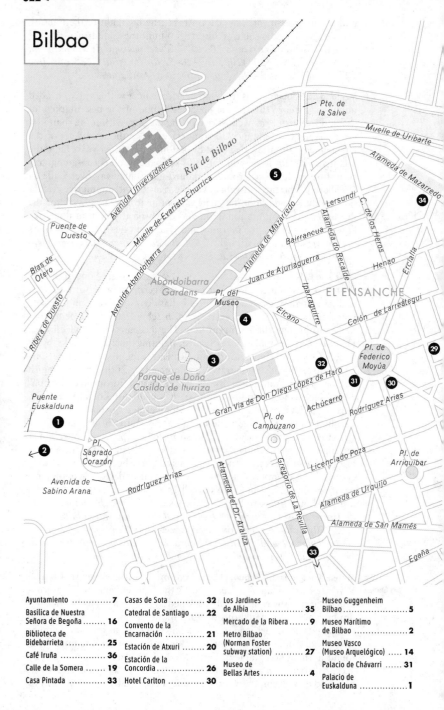

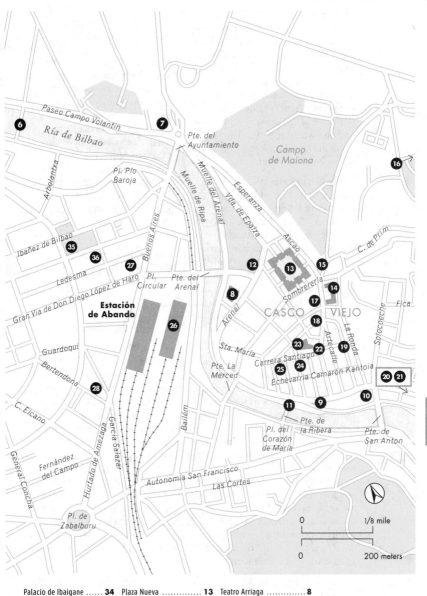

9

de Vizcaya steel mills. The site, at the heart of Bilbao's traditional steel and shipping port, was the perfect place for a metaphor for Bilbao's macro-reconversion from steel to titanium, from heavy industry to art, as well as a nexus between the early-14th-century Casco Viejo and the new 19th-century Ensanche and between the wealthy Right Bank and working-class Left Bank of the Nervión River.

Frank Gehry's gleaming brainchild, opened in 1997 and hailed as "the greatest building of our time" by architect Philip Johnson and "a miracle" by Herbert Muschamp of the *New York Times,* has sparked an economic renaissance in the Basque Country after more than a half century of troubles. In its first year, the Guggenheim attracted 1.4 million visitors, three times the number expected and more than both Guggenheim museums in New York during the same period.

> ### THE GUGGENHEIM AND MARILYN MONROE
>
> "What twins the actress and the [Guggenheim]…is that both of them stand for an American style of freedom. That style is voluptuous, emotional, intuitive, and exhibitionist. It is mobile, fluid, material, mercurial, fearless, radiant, and as fragile as a newborn child. It can't resist doing a dance with all the voices that say 'No.' It wants to take up a lot of space. And when the impulse strikes, it likes to let its dress fly up in the air."
>
> —The late Herbert Muschamp (*New York Times* architecture critic)

At once suggestive of a silver-scaled fish and a mechanical heart, Gehry's sculpture in titanium, limestone, and glass is the perfect habitat for the contemporary and postmodern artworks it contains. The smoothly rounded jumble of surfaces and cylindrical shapes recalls Bilbao's shipbuilding and steel-manufacturing past, whereas the transparent and reflective materials create a shimmering, futuristic luminosity. With the final section of the La Salve bridge over the Nervión folded into the structure, the Guggenheim is both a doorway to Bilbao and an urban forum: the atrium looks up into the center of town and across the river to the Old City and the green hillsides of Artxanda where livestock graze tranquilly. Gehry's intent to build something as moving as a Gothic cathedral in which "you can feel your soul rise up," and to make it as poetically playful and perfect as a fish—as per Schubert's ichthyological homage in his famous "Trout Quintet"—is patent: "I wanted it to be more than just a dumb building; I wanted it to have a plastic sense of movement!"

Covered with 30,000 sheets of titanium, the Guggenheim became Bilbao's main attraction overnight. Despite unexpected cleaning problems (Bilbao's industrial grime knows no equal), which was solved in 2002 using a customized procedure, the museum's luster endures. The enormous atrium, more than 150 feet high, is connected to the 19 galleries by a system of suspended metal walkways and glass elevators. Vertical windows reveal the undulating titanium flukes and contours of this beached whale. With most of its modern art drawn from New York's

Solomon R. Guggenheim Museum, the Bilbao Guggenheim is a magnet for visitors from all over the world. Inquisitive museumgoers will want to rent the Acoustiguide (€4), the battery-operated telephone-like apparatus that explains everything you always wanted to know about modern art, contemporary art, and the Guggenheim. Frank Gehry talks of his love of fish and how his creative process works, while the pieces in the collection are presented one by one (a Kokoschka painting includes a description of Alma Mahler's lethal romance with the painter).

The collection, described by Krens as "a daring history of the art of the 20th century," consists of more than 250 works, most from the New York Guggenheim and the rest acquired by the Basque government. The second and third floors reprise the original Guggenheim collection of abstract expressionist, cubist, surrealist, and geometrical works. Artists whose names are synonymous with the art of the 20th century (Kandinsky, Picasso, Ernst, Braque, Miró, Pollock, Calder, Malevich) and European artists of the '50s and '60s (Chillida, Tàpies, Iglesias, Clemente, and Kiefer) are joined by contemporary figures (Nauman, Muñoz, Schnabel, Badiola, Barceló, Basquiat). The ground floor is dedicated to large-format and installation work, some of which—like Richard Serra's *Serpent*—were created specifically for the spaces they occupy. Claes Oldenburg's *Knife Ship,* Robert Morris's walk-in *Labyrinth,* and pieces by Beuys, Boltansky, Long, Holzer, and others round out the heavyweight division in one of the largest galleries in the world.

On holidays and weekends long lines develop, though between the playful clarinetist making a well-deserved killing on the front steps and the general spell of the place (who can be irked in the shadow of Jeff Koons's flower-covered, 40-foot-high Westmoreland Terrier, *Puppy*?), no one seems too impatient. Advance tickets from Servicaixa ATM machines or, in the Basque Country, the BBK bank machines are the way to miss the line. Failing that (sometimes they run out), go around at closing time and buy tickets for the next few days. The museum has no parking of its own, but underground lots throughout the area provide alternatives; check the Web site for information. ⊠ *Abandoibarra Etorbidea 2, El Ensanche* ☎ *94/435–9080* ⊕ *www.guggenheim-bilbao. es* ☎ *€10.50, €12 for special exhibits; Bono Artean combined ticket with Museo de Bellas Artes €14 plus €2 additional on admittance to 2nd museum* ⊙ *Tues.–Sun. 11–8* Ⓜ *Moyúa.*

❷ **Museo Marítimo Ría de Bilbao** *(Maritime Museum of Bilbao).* This interesting nautical museum on the Left Bank of the Ría de Bilbao reconstructs the history of the Bilbao waterfront and shipbuilding industry beginning with medieval times. Temporary exhibits range from visits by extraordinary seacraft such as tall ships or traditional fishing vessels to thematic displays on 17th- and 18th-century clipper ships or the sinking of the *Titanic.* ⊠ *Muelle Ramón de la Sota, San Mamés* ☎ *902/131000* ⊕ *www.museomaritimobilbao.org* ☎ *€5; free Wed.* ⊙ *Tues.–Sun. 10–8* Ⓜ *San Mamés.*

❶ **Palacio de Euskalduna.** In homage to the Astilleros Euskalduna (Basque Country shipbuilders) that operated shipyards here beside the Euskalduna bridge into the late 20th century, this music venue and convention hall, in stark counterpoint to Frank Gehry's shimmering titanium fantasy just up the Nervión, resembles a rusting ship. Designed by architects Federico Soriano and Dolores Palacios, Euskalduna opened in 1999 and is Bilbao's main opera venue and home of the Bilbao Symphony Orchestra. The auditorium has a 2,200-person capacity, three smaller music halls, eight practice rooms, seven lecture halls and press conference spaces, as well as a restaurant, a cafeteria, and a shopping center. A 71-stop organ, Spain's largest, offers quite a different tune from the past pitched battles waged here between workers, Basque nationalists, management, and police as the shipyards laid off thousands in the mid-1980s. ⊠ *Av. Abandoibarra 4, El Ensanche* ☎ *94/403–5000* 📠 *94/403–5001* ⊕ *www. euskalduna.net* 🎫 *Tour €2* ⊙ *Office weekdays 9–2 and 4–7; box office Mon.–Sat. noon–2 and 5–8:30, Sun. noon–2; guided tours Sat. at noon or by appointment (fax Departamento Comercial)* Ⓜ *San Mamés.*

> ### BILBAO BLUE
>
> The Guggenheim office building near the Jeff Koons *Puppy* is startlingly, deeply, enormously blue. While working on the Guggenheim, Frank Gehry fell in love with this "Bilbao blue," so-called for the vivid blue sky seen on rare days over Bilbao when the Atlantic drizzle–the famous Basque siri-miri–permits. Curiously, as a result of either the Guggenheim's reflected light, less industrial smog, or climate change, Bilbao's blue skies supposedly have become less intense, leaving the Guggenheim offices and the Perro Chico restaurant, Gehry's favorite, among the few surviving outbursts of the city's emblematic color.

**❸ Parque de Doña Casilda de Iturrizar.** Bilbao's main park, this lush collection of exotic trees, ducks and geese, fountains, falling water, and great expanses of lawns usually dotted with lovers is a delight and a sanctuary from the hard-edged Ensanche, Bilbao's modern, post-1876 expansion. Doña Casilda de Iturrizar, a well-to-do 19th-century Bilbao matron, married a powerful banker and used his wealth to support various cultural and beneficent institutions in the city, including this grassy refuge. ⊠ *El Ensanche* Ⓜ *San Mamés.*

**⑪ Puente de la Ribera.** This little footbridge just downriver from the prow of the Mercado de la Ribera was traditionally known as the Puente del Perro Chico (now the name of an excellent restaurant at the far end of the bridge) for the coin once charged as a toll for crossing. The *real* (royal) or 25 *céntimo* piece, known as a *perro chico* (literally, little dog), was a fourth of a peseta, known as a *perra*, or female dog. Until Calatrava's Zubi-Zuri was built, this was the only pedestrian bridge of Bilbao's nine river crossings. The bridge is officially named the Puente-Pasarela Conde Mirasol for the street it leads into. ⊠ *Casco Viejo* Ⓜ *Casco Viejo.*

**❻ Puente de Zubi-Zuri.** Santiago Calatrava's signature span (the name means "white bridge" in Euskera) connects Campo Volantín on the Right Bank with the Ensanche on the Left. Just a few minutes east of the Guggenheim, the playful seagull-shape bridge swoops brightly over

## Abandoibarra: Bilbao's New Heart

The Abandoibarra project covers nearly a full square mile along the Nervión estuary. Until recently an area occupied by docks, warehouses, and shipyards, two-thirds of this new urban center are parks and open spaces. Javier López Chollet's 280,000-sq.-ft. Ribera Park borders the Parque de Doña Casilda between the Guggenheim and Palacio de Euskalduna. This green space joins the quais of La Naja, Ripa, and Uribitarte to connect with the Olabeaga park downriver, creating a riverside promenade over 3 km (2 mi) long.

The head architect for the project is the Connecticut-based César Pelli, designer of New York's World Financial Center and its Winter Garden fronting the Hudson River. Offices are also part of the project, as well as five apartment blocks and a residential building by Basque architect Luis Peña Ganchegui. Other buildings include the Sheraton Hotel by the Mexican architect Ricardo Legorreta; and American Robert Stern's shopping and leisure center, Zubiarte. Flanking the riverside thoroughfare named for Bilbao businessman and benefactor Ramón Rubial are the auditorium of the University of the Basque Country and the Deusto University library. Pedro Arrupe's footbridge, an exercise in rationalism with a simple geometrical form, connects Abandoibarra and Deusto University. The footbridge creates a complete urban promenade joining the Avenue of the Universities, the riverside walk, and the new streets of Abandoibarra, the culminating act of the revitalized, the 21st-century Bilbao.

the dark Nervión. The Plexiglas walkway suggests walking on water, though wear and tear has reduced the surface from transparent to a mere translucent. The airport just west of Bilbao at Loiu, also designed by Calatrava, resembles a massive, white Concorde plane and has been dubbed *La Paloma* (the dove), despite more closely resembling a snow goose poised for takeoff. Calatrava's third Vizcaya creation, the bridge at Ondarroa, completes this troika of gleaming white suspension bridges exploring the theme of flight. ⊠*El Ensanche* Ⓜ *Moyúa.*

🔟 **San Antón.** Both the church and bridge named for St. Anthony are emblematic symbols of Bilbao and appear on the municipal coat of arms. The original church was finished in 1433, though the structure underwent significant alterations up until the mid-17th century. The early bridge was swept away by an 1882 flood; its replacement, all but connected to the church, bears a pair of bas-relief wolves from the coat of arms of Don Diego López de Haro (from the Latin *lupus,* for wolf, as in López). ⊠*Calle de la Ribera s/n, Casco Viejo* Ⓜ *Casco Viejo.*

★ ⑧ **Teatro Arriaga.** A hundred years ago, this 1,500-seat theater was as exciting a source of Bilbao pride as the Guggenheim is today. Built between 1886 and 1890 when Bilbao's population was a mere 35,000, the Teatro Arriaga represented a gigantic per-capita cultural investment. Always a symbol of Bilbao's industrial might and cultural vibrancy, the original "Nuevo Teatro" (New Theater) de Bilbao was a lavish Belle Epoque, neo-baroque spectacular modeled after the Paris Opéra by architect

9

Joaquín Rucoba (1844–1909). The theater was renamed in 1902 for the Bilbao musician thought of as "the Spanish Mozart," Juan Crisóstomo de Arriaga (1806—26).

After a 1914 fire, the new version of the theater opened in 1919. Following years of splendor, the Teatro Arriaga (along with Bilbao's economy) gradually lost vigor; it closed down in 1978 for restoration work that was finally concluded in 1986. Now largely eclipsed by the splendid and more spacious Palacio de Euskalduna, the Arriaga stages opera, theater, concerts, and dance events from September through June. Walk around the building to see the stained glass on its rear facade and the exuberant caryatids holding up the arches facing the river. ⊠ *Plaza Arriaga 1, Casco Viejo* ☎ *94/416–3333* ⊕ *www. teatroarriaga.com* Ⓜ *Casco Viejo.*

### ARRIAGA, THE SPANISH MOZART

Juan Crisóstomo Arriaga (1806–26), for whom the Teatro Arriaga is named, is Bilbao's musical hero. Considered the Spanish Mozart for his fame as a child prodigy Arriaga was born in Bilbao's original Siete Calles neighborhood. First taught by his father and older brother, Arriaga composed symphonies by the age of 11. At the age of 16 he enrolled in the Conservatory of Music in Paris. Before his death of tuberculosis at 19, he was appointed the school's youngest-ever assistant professor. His string quartets, composed at the age of 18, are considered his finest works.

## EL CASCO VIEJO

Walled until the 19th century, Bilbao's Casco Viejo (Old Quarter, the city's oldest nucleus) is often synonymous with Siete Calles, so called for the original "seven streets" of proto-Bilbao in 1442. A finer distinction separates the Casco Viejo per se—the newer part of the old part of town around the 19th-century Plaza Nueva (New Square)—from the original 15th-century Siete Calles, the seven streets between the Santiago cathedral and the Mercado de la Ribera. Both parts of this warren of antiquity are filled with some of Bilbao's oldest and most charming architecture. It's all miraculously connected to modern Bilbao, and even the beach at Getxo, by Norman Foster's spotless "*fosterito,*" the streamlined subway stop across the square from the outstanding Museo Vasco.

### A GOOD WALK

Starting at the church of **San Nicolás de Bari** ⑫, walk through neoclassical 19th-century **Plaza Nueva** ⑬, with its rows of excellent cafés, restaurants, and tapas emporiums, into Calle Sombrería. A left turn takes you into Calle de la Cruz; there the **Museo Vasco** ⑭—devoted to Basque archaeology and history—occupies one side of **Plaza Miguel de Unamuno** ⑮, with its bust of the great Basque philosopher, professor, and novelist in the center. At the far side of the square, 313 stairs lead up to the **Basílica de Nuestra Señora de Begoña** ⑯, patron saint of Vizcaya (you could also use the *ascensor,* [aka] elevator, to reach it). Retrace your steps from the base of the stairway up to the basilica and pass the baroque-era church of **Santos Juanes** ⑰ on Calle de la Cruz; then continue to the **Portal de Zamudio** ⑱, more a tiny square than a street, from which a swing to the left leads into **Calle de la Somera** ⑲, the first, highest, and driest of the original seven streets. After a walk through Calle Somera past the Juan Crisóstomo Arriaga plaque at No. 12, cross to the church of San Antón and walk left to the narrow-gauge railroad station, the **Estación de Atxuri** ⑳ and Plaza de la Encarnación and the 16th-century Basque Gothic **Convento de la Encarnación** ㉑. From here, return downriver past the Puente de Sant Antón to Calle Tenderia, where a right turn leads to the early-15th-century Gothic **Catedral de Santiago** ㉒, the oldest church in the Casco Viejo. Near the cathedral, a few steps away on the corner of Calle de Perro and Calle Torres, is the **Palacio Yohn** ㉓ cultural center, with elements dating back to the 14th century. Directly across from the portal of the Palacio Yohn is a feast-day **paving stone** ㉔, marked with a star from which, as you face the Palacio Yohn and look up to the left, the Basilica de Nuestra Señora de Begoña is discernible towering in the distance. From here walk down Calle Bidebarrieta to the **Biblioteca de Bidebarrieta** ㉕, a public library, concert hall, and heir to Bilbao's liberal intellectual tradition.

TIMING  This browsing and grazing itinerary is at least a three-hour project and probably ought to take four or five, depending on stops. Add two hours for a careful visit to the Museo Vasco.

### WHAT TO SEE

OFF THE BEATEN PATH

**Ascensor de Begoña** *(Begoña Elevator)*. This popular Bilbao landmark is an elevator that connects the Casco Viejo with points overlooking the city. La Basilica de la Begoña is the classic pilgrimage and site of weddings and christenings. ⊠ *Entrance at Calle Esperanza 6, Casco Viejo* €0.35 Ⓜ *Casco Viejo.*

⑯ **Basílica de Nuestra Señora de Begoña.** Bilbao's most cherished religious sanctuary, dedicated to the patron saint of Vizcaya, can be reached by the 313 stairs from Plaza de Unamuno or by the gigantic elevator (the Ascensor de Begoña) looming over Calle Esperanza 6 behind the San Nicolás church. The church's Gothic nave was begun in 1519 on the site of an early hermitage where the Virgin Mary was alleged to have appeared long before. Finished in 1620, the basilica was completed with the economic support of the shipbuilders and merchants of Bilbao, many of whose businesses are commemorated on the inner walls of the church. The high ground the basilica occupies was strategically important during the Carlist Wars of 1836 and 1873, and as a result, La Begoña suffered significant damage that was not restored until the beginning of the 20th century. Comparable in importance (if not in geographical impact) to Barcelona's Virgen de Montserrat, the Basílica de la Begoña is where the Athletic de Bilbao soccer team makes its pilgrimage, some of the players often barefoot, in gratitude for triumphs. ⊠ *Calle Virgen de Begoña 38, Begoña* ☎ *94/412–7091* ⊕ *www.basilicadebegona.com* Free ☉ *Weekdays 9:30–1:30 and 4:30–8:30* Ⓜ *Casco Viejo.*

★ ㉕ **Biblioteca de Bidebarrieta.** This historic library and intellectual club was originally called "El Sitio" (the siege) in memory of Bilbao's successful resistance to the Carlist siege of 1876 (Carlists were supporters of Fernando VII's brother, Don Carlos, over his daughter Isabella II as rightful heir to the Spanish throne). Now a municipal library, the Bidebarrieta has a music auditorium that is one of Bilbao's most beautiful venues and a spot to check for the infrequent performances held there. The reading rooms are open to the public, a good place to read newspapers, make notes, or just enjoy the historical echoes of the place. ⊠*Calle Bidebarrieta 4, Casco Viejo* ☎*94/415–6930* ☉*Weekdays 8:30–8:30, Sat. 8:30–2* Ⓜ*Casco Viejo.*

㉙ **Calle de la Somera.** The first, highest, and driest of the early city's original seven streets—*Zazpikaleak*, in Euskera—Calle Somera would have been called High Street in early London. A mere three streets until 1375, the seven streets cut by *cantons* (narrow alleys) were in place by 1442. The Siete Calles nearly formed a peninsula, as the Arenal and Plaza Nueva parts of the Casco Viejo were under water. Arenal means "sandy area" and was originally a sandy shore where the river deposited sediment in the eddy formed by the point of land at the end of Calle Santa María. Ⓜ*Casco Viejo.*

㉒ **Catedral de Santiago** *(St. James's Cathedral).* Bilbao's earliest church was a pilgrimage stop on the coastal route to Santiago de Compostela. Work on the structure began in 1379, but fire delayed completion until the early 16th century. The florid Gothic style with Isabelline elements features a nave in the form of a Greek cross, with ribbed vaulting resting on cylindrical columns. The notable outdoor arcade, or *pórtico*, was used for public meetings of the early town's governing bodies. ⊠*Plaza de Santiago 1, Casco Viejo* ☎*94/415–3627* ▣*Free* ☉*Tues.– Sat. 10–1:30 and 4–7, Sun. 10:30–1:30* Ⓜ*Casco Viejo.*

㉑ **Convento de la Encarnación.** The Basque Gothic architecture of this early-16th-century convent, church, and museum gives way to Renaissance and baroque ornamentation high on the main facade. The **Museo Diocesano de Arte Sacro** (Diocesan Museum of Sacred Art) occupies a carefully restored 16th-century cloister. The inner patio alone, ancient and intimate, more than amortizes the visit. On display are religious silverwork, liturgical garments, sculptures, and paintings dating back to the 12th century. The convent is across from the Atxuri station just upstream from the Puente de San Antón. ⊠*Plaza de la Encarnación 9, Casco Viejo* ☎*94/432–0125* ▣*Free* ☉*Tues.–Sat. 10:30–1:30 and 4–7, Sun. 10:30–1* Ⓜ*Casco Viejo.*

㉐ **Estación de Atxuri.** Bilbao's narrow-gauge railroad station at Atxuri connects with Gernika, Mundaka, and Bermeo on the Basque coast, a spectacular ride through the Ría de Gernika that allows the best available views of the Urdaibai natural park (unless you're in a boat). The train to San Sebastián is another favorite excursion, chugging through villages such as Zumaya and Zarautz. You can even get off and walk for a few hours, catching a later train. Narrow-gauge railways were the standard in Vizcaya and in much of northern Spain, owing to steep grades and tight quarters, as well as economics. Today only a few remain. Check with **FEVE** ( ☞ *Ferrocarriles Españoles de Via Estrecha* 🕾*94/423–2266* ⊕*www.transcantabrico.feve.es*) for information about the luxury Cantabrican Express that runs from San Sebastián to Santiago de Compostela, with stops for wining, dining, and sightseeing. ⊠*Calle Atxuri s/n, Casco Viejo* 🕾*902/543210* Ⓜ*Casco Viejo.*

**OFF THE BEATEN PATH**

**Funicular de Artxanda.** The panorama from the hillsides of Artxanda is the most comprehensive view of Bilbao, and the various typical *asadors* (roasters) here serve delicious beef or fish cooked over coals. ⊠*Entrance on Plaza de Funicular s/n, Matiko* 🕾*94/445–4956* 🎫*€1* Ⓜ*Casco Viejo.*

★ ⓮ **Museo Vasco (Museo Arqueológico, Etnográfico e Histórico Vasco)** *(Basque Museum; Museum of Basque Archaeology, Ethnology, and History).* One of the stand-out, not-to-miss visits in Bilbao, this museum occupies an austerely elegant 16th-century convent. The collection centers on Basque ethnography, Bilbao history, and comprehensive displays from the lives of Basque shepherds, fishermen, and farmers. Highlights include *El Mikeldi* in the cloister, a pre-Christian iron-age stone animal representation that may be 4,000 years old; the room dedicated to Basque shepherds and the pastoral way of life; the "*Mar de los Vascos*" exhibit featuring whaling, fishing, and maritime activities; the second-floor prehistoric exhibit featuring a wooden harpoon, recovered in the Santimamiñe caves at Kortezubi, that dates from the 10th century BC; and the third-floor scale model of Vizcaya province with the *montes bocineros* (bugling mountains), showing the five peaks of Vizcaya used for calling the different *anteiglesias* (parishes) with bonfires or *txalaparta* (percussive sticks) to the general assemblies held in Gernika. ⊠*Calle Cruz 4, Casco Viejo* 🕾*94/415–5423* ⊕*www.euskal-museoa. org* 🎫*€3; free Thurs.* ⊙*Tues.–Sat. 11–5, Sun. 11–2* Ⓜ*Casco Viejo.*

㉓ **Palacio Yohn.** Now used for the Centro Cívico de la Bolsa, a municipal cultural center, the palace has medieval ceilings that are covered with graceful vaulting. This ancient building, oddly and erroneously known as "La Bolsa" (the stock exchange)—though no exchange of stock has ever taken place here—is thought to be built over a 14th-century structure. Immigrants from Central Europe moved here in the 18th century and apparently set up such a thriving commercial enterprise that it became known as "the exchange." The building takes its name from Leandro Yohn, one of the successful merchants. ⊠*Calle Pelota 10, Casco Viejo* 🕾*94/416–3199* ⊙*Oct.–May, Mon.–Sat. 9–1:30 and 4–9; June–Sept., Mon.–Sat. 9–1:30* Ⓜ*Casco Viejo.*

㉔ **Paving Stone.** Directly across from Palacio Yohn is a star-shape design on a paving stone, from which, looking up to the left, the Basílica de la Begoña is visible towering over the Casco Viejo. Every October 11 *txikiteros* (people handing out *txikis* ("little ones," shot glasses of wine) celebrate the feast day of the Virgin of la Begoña here, dispensing and dancing the honorary and athletic Aurresku. ⊠*Corner of Calle Pelota and Calle del Perro, Casco Viejo* Ⓜ*Casco Viejo.*

🄯 **Plaza Miguel de Unamuno.** Named for Bilbao's all-time greatest intellectual, figure of fame and fable throughout Spain and beyond, this plaza honors Miguel de Unamuno (1864–1936)—a philosopher, novelist, professor, and wit as well as a man of character and temperament. De Unamuno wrote some of Spain's most seminal works, including *Del sentimiento trágico de la vida en los hombres y los pueblos* (*The Tragic Sense of Life in Men and Nations*); his *Niebla* (*Mist*) has been generally accepted as the first existentialist novel, published in 1914 when Jean-Paul Sartre was but nine years old. Remembrances to Unamuno in the Casco Viejo include the philosopher's bust here, his birthplace at No. 7 Calle de la Cruz, and the nearby Filatelia Unamuno, a rare stamp emporium that is a favorite of collectors. Ⓜ *Casco Viejo.*

🄯 **Plaza Nueva.** This 64-arch neoclassical plaza seems to be typical of every Spanish city from San Sebastián to Salamanca to Seville. With its Sunday-morning market, its December 21 natural-produce Santo Tomás market, and its permanent tapas and restaurant offerings, Plaza Nueva is an easy place in which to spend a lot of time. It was finished in 1851 as part of an ambitious housing project designed to ease the pressure on limited mid-19th-century Bilbao space. Note the size of the houses' balconies: it was the measure—the bigger, the better—of the social clout of their inhabitants. The tiny windows near the top of the facades were servants' quarters. The building behind the powerful coat of arms at the head of the square was originally the Diputación, or provincial government office, but is now the **Academia de la Lengua Vasca** (Academy of the Basque Language). The coat of arms shows the tree of Gernika, symbolic of Basque autonomy, with the two wolves representing Don Diego López de Haro (López derives from *lupus,* meaning wolf). The bars and shops around the arcades include two versions of **Victor Montes** establishments, one for tapas at Plaza Nueva 8 and the other for more serious sit-down dining at Plaza Nueva 2. The **Café Bar Bilbao,** at Plaza Nueva 6, also known as Casa Pedro, has photos of early Bilbao, while the **Argoitia** at No. 15 across the square has a nice angle on the midday sun and a coat of arms inside with the *zatzpiakbat* ("seven-one" in Basque), referring to the cultural unity of the three French and four Spanish Basque provinces. Ⓜ *Casco Viejo.*

🄯 **Portal de Zamudio.** This short street (one house) or small plaza is significant in the Casco Viejo as the first and most important entry through the walls of 15th-century Siete Calles. The upper street, Calle Somera, is early Bilbao's first and most important thoroughfare; Zamudio was the name of an important early noble Bilbao family whose house was near this entryway. Ⓜ *Casco Viejo.*

🄯 **San Nicolás de Bari.** Honoring the patron saint of mariners, San Nicolás de Bari, the city's early waterfront church, was built over an earlier eponymous hermitage and opened in 1756. With a powerful facade over the Arenal, originally a sandy beach, San Nicolás was much abused by French and Carlist troops throughout the 19th century. Sculptures by Juan Pascual de Mena adorn the inside of the church. Look for the oval plaque to the left of the door marking the high-water mark of the flood of 1983. ⊠ *Plaza de San Nicolás 1, Casco Viejo* ☎ *94/416–3424* Ⓜ *Casco Viejo.*

⑰ **Santos Juanes.** Distinguished for accumulating the deepest water of any building in the Casco Viejo during the disastrous 1983 flood, as can be witnessed by the water mark more than 14 feet above the floor in the back of the church (to the left as you come in), this simple baroque church was the first Jesuit building in Bilbao, built in 1604. Originally the home of the Colegio de San Andrés de la Compañía de Jesús (St. Andrew's School of the Order of Jesuits), the original school is now divided between the Museo Vasco and the church dedicated to both St. Johns, the Evangelist and the Baptist. The church's most important relic is the *Relicario de la Vera Cruz* (Relic of the True Cross), a silver-plated cross containing what is widely believed to be the largest existing fragment of the cross used at Calvary to execute Jesus in AD 33. ⊠ *Calle de la Cruz 4, Casco Viejo* ☎ *94/415–3997* Ⓜ *Casco Viejo.*

## EL ENSANCHE

Bilbao's busy Ensanche (Widening) has a rhythm and timbre more redolent of Manhattan or London than of Paris or Barcelona. Once Bilbao *saltó el río* (jumped the river) from the Casco Viejo in 1876, the new city center became Plaza Moyúa—at the heart of the Ensanche—with the Gran Vía as the district's most important thoroughfare. The late-19th-century and early-20th-century architecture typical of this part of town is colossal, ornate, and formal, with only a few eruptions into Art Nouveau. Bilbao expressed its euphoria and wealth in the Ensanche as Barcelona did in its famous Art Nouveau neighborhood, the Eixample, though the distinct tastes and sensibilities of Basques and Catalans are nowhere more manifest than in these two wildly divergent turn-of-the-20th-century urban developments.

### A GOOD WALK

From the graceful railroad station **Estación de la Concordia** ㉖ (also known as Estación de Santander), as you overlook Teatro Arriaga from the Left Bank of the Nervión, it's just a two-minute walk roughly north to Plaza Circular, with its monument to Don Diego López de Haro and its *fosterito,* the transparent tube leading into **Metro Bilbao's Norman Foster subway station** ㉗. As you walk south on Hurtado de Amézaga, Calle Ayala is the first right, leading past the Iglesia del Sagrado Corazón to Alameda Urquijo. Take a left up Alameda Urquijo to Calle Bertendona and go left again to the Moderniste facade of the **Teatro Campos Elíseos** ㉘. Crossing back over Alameda Urquijo and Calle Gardoqui, cut past the municipal library to the opulent government seat at **Palacio Foral** ㉙. From there it's just another two blocks to Plaza Moyúa, the hub of the Ensanche, where the **Hotel Carlton** ㉚ and the Flemish Renaissance–style **Palacio de Chavarri** ㉛ face each other across the flower beds in the center of the circle. One block farther down Gran Vía are the colossal **Casas de Sota** ㉜—a 1919 block of apartments and offices—taking up an entire city block. At this point either cut south to Plaza de Indautxu for a look at the 1920s painted murals on the facade of the

**Casa Pintada** ㉝ or go directly north on Ercilla to Plaza Dejado, turn left on Calle de los Heros, and right on Cosme Echevarrieta, to reach Alameda de Mazarredo and the surprising midtown *caserío* (country house), the **Palacio de Ibaigane** ㉞, once home to one of Bilbao's richest and most prominent citizens. From here, consider a stop at the little café at No. 12 overlooking Santiago Calatrava's Zubi-Zuri footbridge. From there continue along Alameda de Mazarredo to the next street on the left, Calle Arbolantxa, leading into a pretty square with several inviting places, including the Kafe Antzokia. Back on Alameda de Mazarredo it's just another block to Plaza San Vicente and **Los Jardines de Albia** ㉟, one of the Ensanche's capital destinations and home of the landmark, neo-Mudejar **Café Iruña** ㊱.

TIMING   This is a three-hour tour, adding time for stops in cafés and shops.

**WHAT TO SEE**

㊱ **Café Iruña.** Famous for its decor and its boisterous and ebullient ambience, the Iruña is an essential Bilbao haunt on the Ensanche's most popular garden and square, Los Jardines de Albia. The neo-Mudejar dining room overlooking the square is the place to be (if they try to stuff you in the back dining room, resist or come back another time). The bar has two distinct sections: the elegant side near the dining room, where sculptor Lorenzo Quinn's bronze arm hoists a beer tankard at the center of the counter; and the older, more bare-bones Spanish side on the Calle Berástegui side, with its plain marble counters and *pinchos morunos de carne de cordero* (lamb brochettes) as the house specialty. This place was founded by a Navarran restaurateur (Iruña is Euskera for Pamplona) in 1903; the Moorish decor in the dining room has been understood as an echo of the town hall's Salón Árabe (Arabian Hall). Jumping from dawn until after midnight, the Iruña is Bilbao's most cosmopolitan café. ✉*Calle Berástegui 5, El Ensanche* ☎*94/423–7021* Ⓜ*Moyúa.*

㉝ **Casa Pintada.** Just off Plaza Indautxu, this unusual painted facade, formally known as **La Casa de los Aldeanos** (The House of the Villagers), is a 1929 construction designed by the architect Adolfo Gil. The painted images evoke an idealized rural Vizcayan village, a pastoral paradise in the midst of Bilbao's industrial and urban austerity. The house is not open to the public. ✉*Calle Aretxabaleta 6, El Ensanche* Ⓜ*Moyúa.*

㉜ **Casas de Sota.** This immense block of houses, offices, and apartments was built by Manuel María de Smith in 1919 and remains a good example of an early-20th-century bourgeois residence. The horizontal line of the red rooftops, arches, and galleries seems to reflect the Basque *caserío* (farmhouse) architecture translated to big-city splendor. ✉*Gran Vía 45, El Ensanche* Ⓜ*Moyúa.*

㉖ **Estación de la Concordia.** Designed by the engineer Valentín Gorbeña in 1893 and finished by architect Severino Achúcarro in 1898, this colorful railroad station looks across the Nervión River to the Paris Opéra–inspired Teatro Arriaga, responding with its own references to the colonnaded Parisian Louvre. The peacock-fan-shape, yellow-and-green-tiled entrance is spectacular, along with the immense stained-glass window over the access to the tracks in which facets of Vizcayan life and work are represented, from farmers and fishermen to factory workers and jai alai players. Meanwhile, the graceful arch of the hangar over the tracks is typical of traditional railroad terminals around Europe. ⊠*Calle Bailén 2, El Ensanche* ☎*94/423–2266* Ⓜ*Abando.*

**30** **Hotel Carlton.** Bilbao's grande-dame favorite has hosted top-tier celebrities over the last century, from Orson Welles and Ernest Hemingway to Ava Gardner, casting giant Gretchen Rennell, and music czar John Court, not to mention Francis Ford Coppola. Architect Manuel María de Smith based this project on the London hotel of the same name, although the stained glass in the oval reception area is a reduced version of the one in Nice's Hotel Negresco. The hotel's bar, the Grill, has a clubby English feel to it, with murals painted by client Martinez Ortiz in 1947. The murals, representing an equestrian scene and some 10 bourgeois figures, are remarkable for the detailed painting of every hand and each finger of the personae. ⊠*Plaza Federico Moyúa 2, El Ensanche* ☎*944/162200* Ⓜ*Moyúa.*

**35** **Los Jardines de Albia.** One of the two or three places all bilbainos will insist you see is this welcoming green space in the concrete and asphalt surfaces of this part of town. Overlooking the square is the lovely Basque Gothic **Iglesia de San Vicente Mártir,** its Renaissance facade facing its own Plaza San Vicente. The amply robed sculpture of the Virgin on the main facade, as the story goes, had to be sculpted a second time after the original version was deemed too scantily clad. The Jardines de Albia are centered on the bronze effigy of writer Antonio de Trueba by the famous Spanish sculptor Mariano Benlliure (1866–1947), creator of monuments to the greatest national figures of the epoch. ⊠*Calle Colón de Larreátegui s/n, El Ensanche* Ⓜ*Moyúa.*

**27** **Metro Bilbao (Norman Foster subway station).** The city's much-cherished subway system opened in 1995, and was designed by British architect Sir Norman Foster, winner of the 1999 Pritzker Architecture Prize and author of Barcelona's 1992 Collserola Communications tower, and, most recently, of the world's highest bridge, the Millau viaduct over the French Tarn valley that opened in December 2004. Bilbao's first metro has become a source of great pride for bilbainos. Only a necessity when Bilbao began to spread up and down the Nervión estuary, the Bilbao subway now connects Bolueta, upstream from the Casco Viejo, with Plentzia, a run of 30 km (19 mi). The metro is invariably spotless, graffiti is scarce, and most of its passengers are well dressed and ride in a respectful silence. A new line running down the Left Bank of the Nervión to Portugalete and Santurtzi is presently under construction.

Winner of the railway architecture Brunel Prize of 1996, the metro in general and the Sarriko station in particular were designated as the prizewinning elements. The Sarriko station, the largest of all of the 23 stops, is popularly known as *El Fosterazo* (the Big Foster); the others are *Fosteritos* (Little Fosters). The most spectacular are segmented glass tubes curving up from underground, such as those at Plaza Cir-

9

cular and Plaza Moyúa, widely thought to resemble transparent snails. ⊠*Plaza Circular, El Ensanche* Ⓜ*Abando.*

**NEED A BREAK?**

Founded in 1926, **Café La Granja** ( ⊠*Plaza Circular 3, El Ensanche* Ⓜ*Moyúa*), near the Puente del Arenal, is a Bilbao classic, offering excellent coffee, cold beer, *tortilla de patata* (potato omelet), and a good lunch menu.

❸ **Palacio de Chávarri.** Víctor Chávarri, a leading *prohombre* (captain of industry) of the last quarter of the 19th century, was a force in mining and every other area of Bilbao's economic life. (His descendants are still prominent socialites in Madrid.) The industrialist's Flemish Renaissance palace was intended to recall his student epoch in Liège, Belgium. Built by Belgian architect Paul Hankar in 1889, the ornate ocher structure is based on Hankar's Hotel Zegers-Regnard in Brussels. Every set of windows is unique. The building now holds apartments and offices. ⊠*Plaza de Federico Moyúa 5, El Ensanche* Ⓜ*Moyúa.*

❸ **Palacio de Ibaigane.** This graceful manor-house design is the only one of its kind left in Bilbao. It is an elegant and sweeping country house with classic *caserío* (farmhouse) details surrounded by the generally hard-edged Ensanche. Now the official seat of the Athletic de Bilbao soccer club, the house was originally the residence of the de la Sota family, whose most outstanding member, Ramón de la Sota, founded the company Euskalduna and became one of the most important shipbuilders in Europe. His company specialized in ship repair and opened shipyards in New York, London, Rotterdam, and Paris. Awarded the title "sir" by Great Britain for his services to the Allied cause in World War I, de la Sota went on to found the Euskalerria Basque rights organization, which later joined forces with the Basque Nationalist party. Because of his affiliation with Basque nationalism, Sir Ramón de la Sota's properties and businesses were seized by the Franco regime in 1939 and not returned to the family until 1973. ⊠*Alameda de Mazarredo 15, El Ensanche* Ⓜ*Moyúa.*

❸ **Palacio Foral.** Architect Luis Aladrén created this intensely decorated facade just two blocks from Plaza Moyúa for the seat of the Diputación (provincial government) in 1900. A manifestation of the bullish economic moment Bilbao was experiencing as the 20th century kicked off, the building was much criticized for its combination of overwrought aesthetic excess on the outside and minimally practical use of the interior space. The 19th-century Venetian motifs of its halls and salons, the chapel, and the important collection of paintings and sculptures are the best reasons to see the inside of the building. ⊠*Gran Vía 45, El Ensanche* 🎫*Free* ⊘ *Weekdays 9–2 and 4–8* Ⓜ*Moyúa.*

**OFF THE BEATEN PATH**

**Puente de Vizcaya.** Commonly called the **Puente Colgante** (Hanging Bridge), this has been one of Bilbao's most extraordinary sights ever since it was built in 1893. The bridge, a transporter hung from cables, ferries cars and passengers across the Nervión, uniting two distinct worlds: exclusive, bourgeois Las Arenas and Portugalete, a much older, working-class town. (Dolores Ibarruri, the famous Republican orator of the Spanish civil war, known as *La Pasionaria* for her ardor, was born here.) Portugalete is a 15-minute walk from Santurce, where the quay-side Hogar del Pescador serves simple fish specialties. *Besugo* (sea bream) is the traditional choice, but the grilled sardines are hard to surpass. To reach the bridge, take the subway to Areeta, or drive across the Puente de Deusto, turn left on Avenida Lehenda-kari Aguirre, and follow signs for Las Arenas; it's a 10- or 15-minute drive from downtown. ☎ *94/480–1012* ⊕ *www.puente-colgante.org* ⊠ *€0.30 to cross on foot, €1.10 by car; €4 for visit to observation deck* Ⓜ *Areeta.*

❷❽ **Teatro Campos Elíseos.** If you've come from Barcelona, this extraordinary facade built in 1901 by architects Alfredo Acebal and Jean Baptiste Darroquy may seem familiar. The wild Moderniste (Art Nouveau) excitement of the intensely ornate circular arch—nearly plateresque in its intricate decorative detail—is a marked contrast to the more sober Bilbao interpretation of the turn-of-the-20th-century Art Nouveau euphoria. Predictably, bilbainos don't think very highly of this—to the Basque eye—exaggerated ornamentation. The theater is called Campos Elíseos after Paris's Champs-Elysées (a brief spasm of Francophilia in a town of Anglophiles), as this area of town was a favorite for early-20th-century promenades. During most of the 20th century, Bilbao's theatrical life had two poles: the Casco Viejo's Teatro Arriaga and the Ensanche's Campos Elíseos. Known as *"la bombonera de Bertendona"* the candy box of Bertendona) for its intimate and vertical distribution of stage and boxes, the 742-seat theater, presently being restored, is scheduled to reopen in late 2008. ⊠ *Calle Bertendona 3, El Ensanche* Ⓜ *Moyúa.*

# WHERE TO EAT

Though top restaurants are expensive in Bilbao, some of what is undoubtedly Europe's finest cuisine is served here in settings that range from the traditional hewn beams and stone walls to sleekly contemporary international restaurants all the way up to the Guggenheim itself, where San Sebastián superstar Martín Berasategui runs a dining room as superb as its habitat.

| WHAT IT COSTS IN EUROS | | | | |
|---|---|---|---|---|
| ¢ | $ | $$ | $$$ | $$$$ |
| AT DINNER | €8 or less | €9–€11 | €12–€18 | €19–€25 | over €25 |

Prices are per person for a main course at dinner.

$$$$ ✕**Bermeo.** Named after and decorated in the style of the coastal fishing village to the north, this perennially top Bilbao restaurant housed in the Hotel Ercilla specializes in fresh market cuisine and traditional Basque interpretations of fish, shellfish, and seafood of all kinds. The *rodaballo* (turbot) in vinaigrette sauce is a good choice. ⊠ *Calle Ercilla 37, El Ensanche* ☎ *94/470–5700* ⚑ *Reservations essential* ▤ *AE, DC, MC, V* ☉ *Closed Aug 1–15. No lunch Sat. No dinner Sun.* Ⓜ *Moyúa.*

$$$$   ✕**Guria.** Born in the smallest village in Vizcaya, Arakaldo, Guria's
Fodor'sChoice   founder, the late Genaro Pildain, learned cooking from his mother and
★   talked more about his potato soup than about truffles and caviar. Don
Genaro's influence is still felt here in Guria's streamlined traditional
Basque cooking that dazzles with simplicity. Every ingredient and preparation is perfect. Pildain's *alubias "con sus sacramentos"* (fava beans,
chorizo, and blood sausage) are deconstructed to a puree. His *crema
de puerros y patatas* (cream of potato and leek soup) is as perfect as his
lobster salad with, in season, *perretxikos de Orduña* (small spring wild
mushrooms). ⊠*Gran Vía 66, El Ensanche* ☎94/441–5780 ⌂*Reservations essential* ▤*AE, DC, MC, V* ☉*No dinner Sun.* Ⓜ*Indautxu.*

$$$$   ✕**Zortziko.** An ultramodern kitchen is folded into a historic building in
this lovely place. Try the *langostinos con risotto de perretxikos* (prawns
with wild mushroom risotto) or the *suprema de pintada asada a la
salsa de trufas* (guinea hen in truffle sauce). Chef Daniel García, one of
the Basque Country's culinary stars, also offers a cooking exhibition
for groups of 10 or more at a special table where diners can watch
the chef in action, as well as another exclusive table surrounded by
historic vintages in the wine cellar. ⊠*Calle Alameda Mazarredo 17, El
Ensanche* ☎94/423–9743 ⌂*Reservations essential* ▤*AE, DC, MC,
V* ☉*Closed Sun., Mon., and late Aug.–mid-Sept.* Ⓜ*Moyúa.*

$$$–$$$$   ✕**Aizian.** Euskera for "in the wind," the Sheraton Bilbao restaurant
under the direction of chef José Miguel Olazabalaga has in record time
become one of the city's most respected dining establishments. Typical
bilbaino culinary classicism doesn't keep Mr. Olazabalaga from creat-
ing surprising reductions and contemporary interpretations of tradi-
tional dishes such as *la marmita de chipirón,* a stew of sautéed cuttlefish
with a topping of whipped potatoes covering the sauce of squid ink.
⊠*C. Lehendakari Leizaola 29, El Ensanche* ☎94/428–0035 ▤*AE,
DC, MC, V* ☉*Closed Sun. and Aug. 1–15* Ⓜ*San Mamés.*

$$$–$$$$   ✕**Arbola Gaña.** On the top floor of the Museo de Bellas Artes, this
Fodor'sChoice   elegant space has bay windows overlooking the lush Parque de Doña
★   Casilda. Chef Aitor Basabe's cuisine is modern and streamlined, offering
innovative versions of classic Basque dishes. The €38 *menú de degus-
tación* (taster's menu) is superb and affordable. ⊠*Plaza del Museo
2, El Ensanche* ☎94/442–4657 ⌂*Reservations essential* ▤*AE, DC,
MC, V* ☉*Closed Mon.* Ⓜ*Moyúa.*

★ $$$–$$$$   ✕**Etxanobe.** This luminous corner of the Euskalduna palace overlooks
the Nervión River, the hills of Artxanda, and Bilbao. Fernando Cana-
les creates sleek, homegrown contemporary cuisine on a par with
the Basque Country's finest. ⊠*Av. de Abandoibarra 4, El Ensanche*
☎94/442–1071 ▤*AE, DC, MC, V* ☉*Closed Sun., Aug. 1–20, and
holidays* Ⓜ*San Mamés.*

$$$–$$$$   ✕**Goizeko Kabi.** You can choose your own crab or crayfish at this excel-
lent and famous sanctuary for first-rate Basque cuisine. The dining
rooms are of brick and wood accented by plush Persian rugs and chairs
upholstered with tapestries. Chef Fernando Canales's creations include
*láminas de bacalao en ensalada con pimientos rojos asados* (sliced cod in
green salad with roasted red peppers) and *hojaldre de verdura a la plan-
cha con manito de cordero* (grilled vegetables in puff pastry with leg of

lamb). ⊠*Particular de Estraunza 4–6, El Ensanche* ☎*94/442–1129* ♨*Reservations essential* ▤*AE, DC, MC, V* ☽*Closed Sun. and July 31–Aug. 20* Ⓜ*Indautxu.*

★ $$$–$$$$  ✕**Gorrotxa.** Carmelo Gorrotxategui's fine eclectic menu mixes Basque, French, and Castilian cuisines. The man can do anything from *foie gras con uvas* (goose liver with grapes) to lobster Thermidor to *txuleta de buey* (beef chops). The *costillar,* roast rack of lamb with potatoes, is beyond satisfying. Enjoy it in English decor, complete with wood paneling. ⊠*Alameda Urquijo 30, El Ensanche* ☎*94/443–4937* ▤*AE, DC, MC, V* ☽*Closed Sun., Holy Week, 1 wk in July, and 1 wk in Aug.* Ⓜ*Indautxu.*

## MACHISMO AND MATRIARCHY

Basque men-only eating societies may seem just another example of misogyny. But ethnologists have long defined Basque society as a matriarchy wherein the authority of the *etxekoandre* (female house honcho) has been so absolute that men were forced out of the home to cook, play cards, or drink. The exiles formed drinking clubs. Food came later, and with the Basque passion for competition, cooking contests followed. Today, there are mixed and even all-women's eating clubs, to which men are rarely, if ever, invited.

$$$–$$$$  ✕**Guggenheim Bilbao.** Complementing the Guggenheim's visual feast with more sensorial elements, this spot overseen by Martín Berasategui is on everyone's short list of Bilbao restaurants. Try the *lomo de bacalao asado en aceite de ajo con txangurro a la donostiarra i pilpil* (cod flanks in garlic oil with crab San Sebastián–style and emulsified juices)—a postmodern culinary pun on Bilbao's traditional codfish addiction. A lobster salad with lettuce-heart shavings and tomatoes at a table overlooking the Nervión, the University of Deusto, and the heights of Artxanda qualifies as a perfect 21st-century Bilbao moment. ⊠*Av. Abandoibarra 2, El Ensanche* ☎*94/423–9333* ♨*Reservations essential* ▤*AE, DC, MC, V* ☽*Closed Mon. and late Dec.–early Jan. No dinner Sun. or Tues.* Ⓜ*Moyúa.*

$$$–$$$$  ✕**Jolastoki.** Begoña Beaskoetxea's graceful mansion, one of Bilbao's finest tables, is 20 minutes from downtown (and then a 7-minute walk) on the city's Norman Foster subway. At Jolastoki ("place to play" in Basque), wild salmon, from the Cares River; dark, red Bresse pigeon roasted in balsamic vinegar; *lubina al vapor* (steamed sea bass) as light as a soufflé; and encyclopedic salads are done to perfection. The red fruit dessert includes 11 varieties with sorbet in raspberry coulis. Afterward, digest with a walk through the fishing quarter or a swim at the beach. ⊠*Los Chopos 24, Getxo* ☎*94/491–2031* ♨*Reservations essential* ▤*AE, DC, MC, V* ☽*Closed Sun.* Ⓜ*Gobela, Neguri.*

$$$–$$$$  ✕**Public Lounge.** For designer cuisine in a designer setting, this new Guggenheim-inspired meteorite creates sleek, postmodern fare in an exciting environment. The VIP table serves diners on Versace crockery and Baccarat crystal, and the cooking is no less exquisite than the pots and pans. ⊠*Calle Henao 54, El Ensanche* ☎*94/405–2824* ▤*AE, DC, MC, V* Ⓜ*Moyúa.*

9

$$$
**✕Casa Rufo.** Charming and cozy, this series of nooks and crannies
Fodor'sChoice  tucked into a fine food, wine, olive-oil, cheese, and ham emporium
★  has become famous for its *txuleta de buey* (beef chops). Let the affable
owners size you up and bring on what you crave. The house wine is an
excellent *crianza* (two years in oak, one in bottle) from La Rioja, but
the wine list offers a good selection of wines from Ribera de Duero,
Somantano, and El Priorat as well. ⊠*Calle Hurtado de Amézaga 5, El
Ensanche* ☎*94/443–2172* ⚄*Reservations essential* ⊟*AE, DC, MC,
V* ⊘*Closed Sun.* Ⓜ*Moyúa.*

$$–$$$
**✕El Perro Chico.** The global glitterati who adopted post-Guggenheim
Fodor'sChoice  Bilbao favor this spot across the Puente de la Ribera footbridge below
★  the market. Frank Gehry discovered, on the walls here, the color "Bil-
bao blue"—the azure of the skies over (usually rainy) Bilbao—and
used it for the Guggenheim's office building. Chef Rafael García Rossi
and owner Santiago Diez Ponzoa run a happy ship. Noteworthy are
the *alcachofas con almejas* (artichokes with clams), the extraordinarily
light *bacalao con berenjena* (cod with eggplant), and the dark and fresh
*pato a la naranja* (duck à l'orange). ⊠*Calle Aretxaga 2, El Ensanche*
☎*94/415–0519* ⚄*Reservations essential* ⊟*AE, DC, MC, V* ⊘*Closed
Sun. No lunch Mon.* Ⓜ*Casco Viejo.*

$$–$$$
**✕La Gallina Ciega.** With some of Bilbao's finest *pintxos* (morsels impaled
on toothpicks) at the bar and a single table serving the chef's daily
whim, this modern, clean-lined tavern decorated in eclectic patterns of
wood, glass, and marble is one of Bilbao's favorite foodie haunts. The
table, as might be expected, is rarely empty and must be reserved well
in advance. ⊠*Máximo Aguirre 2, El Ensanche* ☎*94/442–3943* ⊟*AE,
DC, MC, V* Ⓜ*Moyúa.*

$$–$$$
**✕Matxinbenta.** Mixing Basque cooking with an international flair, this
cozy spot presents innovative seafood dishes and roasts. Best in show
goes to the *bacalao Matxinbenta con base vizcaina* (cod prepared on
a red-pepper base), and the wine list is comprehensive. The *delicia de
verduras con foie gras* (vegetables with goose liver) displays broccoli,
spinach, carrots, and zucchini with a cream of tomato sauce. The train
decor includes separate glass compartments allowing you to study fel-
low diners freely without eavesdropping at the same time. ⊠*Ledesma
26, El Ensanche* ☎*94/424–8495* ⊟*AE, DC, MC, V* ⊘*Closed Sun.*
Ⓜ*Moyúa.*

$$–$$$
**✕Yandiola.** On the Right Bank of the Nervión just up from the Santiago
Calatrava Zubi-Zuri bridge, this minimalist black-and-white eating
spot serves chic designer cuisine to match. The atmosphere is cool and
casual and the market cooking is creative but sound. ⊠*Paseo Campo
Volantín 15, El Arenal* ☎*94/413–4013* ⊟*AE, DC, MC, V* ⊘*Closed
Sun. and Easter wk* Ⓜ*Abando.*

$$
**✕Berton.** Dinner is served until 11:30 in this sleek, contemporary bistro
in the Casco Viejo. Fresh wood tables with a green-tint polyethylene
finish and exposed ventilation pipes give the dining room a designer
look, while the classic cuisine ranges from Iberian ham to smoked
salmon, foie gras, cod, beef, and lamb. ⊠*Jardines 11, Casco Viejo*
☎*94/416–7035* ⊟*AE, DC, MC, V* ⊘*No dinner Sun. and holidays*
Ⓜ*Casco Viejo.*

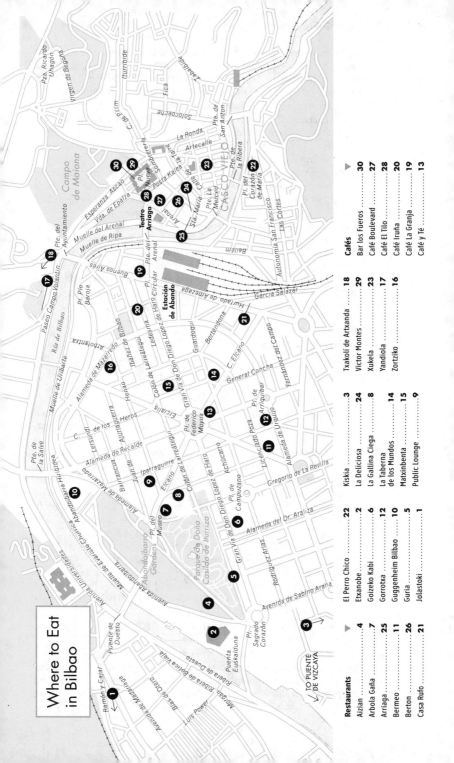

# Where to Eat in Bilbao

**Restaurants** ▶

| | |
|---|---|
| Aizian | **4** |
| Arbola Gaña | **7** |
| Arriaga | **25** |
| Bermeo | **11** |
| Berton | **26** |
| Casa Rufo | **21** |

| | |
|---|---|
| El Perro Chico | **22** |
| Etxanobe | **2** |
| Goizeko Kabi | **6** |
| Gorrotxa | **12** |
| Guggenheim Bilbao | **10** |
| Guria | **5** |
| Jolastoki | **1** |

| | |
|---|---|
| Kiskia | **3** |
| La Deliciosa | **24** |
| La Gallina Ciega | **8** |
| La Taberna de los Mundos | **14** |
| Matxinbenta | **15** |
| Public Lounge | **9** |

| | |
|---|---|
| Txakoli de Artxanda | **18** |
| Víctor Montes | **29** |
| Xukela | **23** |
| Yandiola | **17** |
| Zortziko | **16** |

**Cafés** ▶

| | |
|---|---|
| Bar los Fueros | **30** |
| Café Boulevard | **27** |
| Café El Tilo | **28** |
| Café Iruña | **20** |
| Café La Granja | **19** |
| Café y Té | **13** |

**$–$$**   ✕**Kiskia.** A modern take on the traditional cider house, this rambling
Fodor's Choice   tavern near the San Mamés soccer stadium serves the classical *sidrería*
★   menu of chorizo sausage cooked in cider, codfish omelet, *txuleta de buey* (beef chops), Idiazabal (Basque smoked cheese) with quince jelly and nuts, and as much cider as you can drink, all for €25. Actors, sculptors, writers, soccer stars, and Spain's who's who frequent this boisterous marvel. ⊠*Pérez Galdós 51, San Mamés* ☎94/441–3469 ▤*AE, DC, MC, V* ☉*No dinner Sun.–Tues.* Ⓜ*San Mamés.*

**$–$$**   ✕**La Deliciosa.** For carefully prepared food at friendly prices, this is one of the best values in the Casco Viejo. The *crema de puerros* (cream of leeks) is as good as any in town, and the *dorada al horno* (roast gilthead bream) is fresh from the nearby La Ribera market. ⊠*Jardines 1, Casco Viejo* ☎94/415–0944 ▤*AE, DC, MC, V* Ⓜ*Casco Viejo.*

**$–$$**   ✕**La Taberna de los Mundos.** Sandwich-maker Ander Calvo is famous throughout Spain, and his masterpiece is a slipper bread sandwich of melted goat cheese with garlic, wild mushrooms, organic tomatoes, and sweet red piquillo peppers on a bed of acorn-fed wild Iberian ham. Calvo's restaurants in Bilbao and Vitoria include creative interpretations of the sandwich along with photography, art exhibits, travel lectures, and a global interest reflected in his obsession with early maps and navigational techniques. ⊠*Calle Luchana 1, El Ensanche* ☎94/416–8181 ▤*AE, DC, MC, V* ☉*Closed Mon. mid-Sept.–mid-June* Ⓜ*Moyúa.*

**$–$$**   ✕**Txakolí de Artxanda.** The funicular from the end of Calle Múgica y Butrón up to the mountain of Artxanda deposits you next to an excellent spot for a roast of one kind or another after a hike around the heights. Whether ordering lamb, beef, or the traditional Basque *besugo* (sea bream), you can't go wrong at this picturesque spot with unbeatable panoramas over Bilbao. ⊠*Monte Artxanda, El Arenal* ☎94/445–5015 ▤*AE, DC, MC, V* ☉*Closed Mon. mid-Sept.–mid-June* Ⓜ*Abando.*

**$–$$**   ✕**Victor Montes.** A hot spot for the daily *tapeo* (tapas tour), this place is always crowded with congenial grazers. The well-stocked counter might offer anything from wild mushrooms to *txistorra* (spicy sausages), Idiazabal (Basque smoked cheese), or, for the adventurous, *huevas de merluza* (hake roe), all taken with splashes of Rioja, *txakolí* (a young, white brew made from tart green grapes), or cider. ⊠*Pl. Nueva 8, Casco Viejo* ☎94/415–7067 ⌲*Reservations essential* ▤*AE, DC, MC, V* ☉*Closed Sun. and Aug. 1–15* Ⓜ*Casco Viejo.*

**¢–$**   ✕**Arriaga.** The cider-house experience is a must in the Basque Country. Cider *al txotx* (poured straight out of the barrel), sausage stewed in apple cider, codfish omelets, *txuleton de buey* (beef steaks), and Idiazabal cheese with quince jelly are the classic fare. Reserving a table is a good idea, on weekends especially. ⊠*Santa Maria 13, Casco Viejo* ☎94/416–5670 ▤*AE, DC, MC, V* ☉*No dinner Sun.* Ⓜ*Casco Viejo.*

**★ ¢**   ✕**Xukela.** This tapas sanctuary will spoil you for all the rest: chef Santiago Ruíz Bombin loves making bits of food into delectable paintings and watching his clients inhale them. The combinations of green and red peppers, truffles, red and black caviar, anchovies, parsley, thyme, and other ingredients are deployed much as a painter dispenses pigments on a palette, with the important difference that in this art gallery you get to munch on the work. ✉ *Calle del Perro 2, Casco Viejo* ☎ *94/415–9772* ⊟ *AE, DC, MC, V* Ⓜ *Casco Viejo.*

## CAFÉS

Bilbao's many coffeehouses and bistros have long provided refuge from the North Atlantic climate and the steel mills (now abandoned) outside.

**Bar los Fueros.** As much a watering hole as a café, this is one of Bilbao's most authentic enclaves, perfect for an *aperitivo* or a nightcap. ✉ *Calle de los Fueros 6, Casco Viejo* ☎ *94/415–0614* Ⓜ *Casco Viejo.*

**Café Boulevard.** This is Bilbao's oldest café, dating back to 1871 and occupying a privileged position across from the Teatro Arriaga. Behind its colorful 1929 Art Deco facade, the Boulevard is known for its literary *tertulias* (semiformal intellectual get-togethers). ✉ *Calle Arenal 3, Casco Viejo* ☎ *94/415–3128* Ⓜ *Casco Viejo.*

**Café El Tilo.** Named for the linden tree typical of Bilbao, this may be the best of all the cafés, featuring original frescoes by Basque painter Juan de Aranoa (1901–73). ✉ *Calle Arenal 1, Casco Viejo* ☎ *94/415–0282* Ⓜ *Casco Viejo.*

**Café Iruña.** One of Bilbao's most beloved architectural gems combines neo-Mudéjar fantasy and retro-saloon reality. The enormous, turn-of-the-20th-century classic is a perfect place to dine, read, graze, tipple, or just people-watch. ✉ *Jardines de Albia, El Ensanche* ☎ *94/423–7021* Ⓜ *Moyúa.*

**Café La Granja.** First opened in 1926, this landmark serves up Bilbao panache as well as fine beers, coffees, and food, with the lunch menu a reasonably priced delight. ✉ *Plaza Circular 3, El Ensanche* ☎ *94/423–1813* Ⓜ *Moyúa.*

**Café y Té.** This Bilbao favorite has a pleasant marble counter and balances a rural-urban aesthetic. Along with coffee and tea, beers, wines, whiskeys and gins flow freely here, along with fine pintxos and sandwiches. ✉ *Plaza Federico Moyúa 1, El Ensanche* ☎ *94/416–0108* Ⓜ *Moyúa.*

9

# WHERE TO STAY

Post-Guggenheim Bilbao's fleet of new hotels has expanded and reflected (in the case of the Gran Hotel Domine, literally) the glitter and panache of Gehry's museum. Boutique hotels such as the Miró, design hotels such as the Gran Hotel Domine, and high-rise mammoths such as the Sheraton have made the classic Carlton begin to seem small and quaint in comparison. Despite new developments, the López de Haro remains the city's best lodging option, and many longtime Bilbao visitors prefer the memory-encrusted halls of the Carlton to the glass and steel labyrinths overlooking Abandoibarra and the Nervion estuary. Some of the hotels in the Casco Viejo are charming, while others are merely economical. Nocturnal reverberations in Casco Viejo, a festive part of town, can pose a serious sleeping problem for those in rooms over the street.

| WHAT IT COSTS IN EUROS | | | | |
|---|---|---|---|---|
| ¢ | $ | $$ | $$$ | $$$$ |
| FOR TWO PEOPLE | under €75 | €75–€100 | €101–€150 | €151–€190 | over €190 |

Prices are for a standard double room for two people, excluding service and tax.

**$$$$**
Fodor's Choice
★
**Gran Hotel Domine.** As much modern design festival as hotel, this Silken chain establishment directly across the street from the Guggenheim showcases the conceptual wit of Javier Mariscal, creator of Barcelona's 1992 Olympic mascot Cobi, and the structural know-how of Bilbao architect Iñaki Aurrekoetxea. With adjustable windowpanes reflecting Gehry's titanium leviathan and every lamp and piece of furniture reflecting Mariscal's playful whimsy, this is the brightest star in Bilbao's design firmament. Comprehensively equipped and comfortable, it's the next best thing to moving into the Guggenheim. **Pros:** at the very epicenter and, indeed, part of Bilbao's art and architecture excitement, the place to cross paths with Catherine Zeta-Jones or Antonio Banderas. **Cons:** hard on the wallet and a little full of its own glamour. ⊠ *Alameda de Mazarredo 61, El Ensanche, 48009* ☎ *94/425–3300* ⊕ *www.granhoteldominebilbao.com* ⊠ *131 rooms, 14 suites* ⚲ *In-room: Wi-Fi. In-hotel: restaurant, bar, gym, parking (fee)* ⊟ *AE, DC, MC, V* ⎯|⎯*EP* Ⓜ *Moyúa.*

**$$$$**
**Sheraton Bilbao Hotel.** This colossus erected in 2004 over what was once the nerve center of Bilbao's shipbuilding industry feels like a futuristic ocean liner. Designed by architect Ricardo Legorreta and inspired by the work of Basque sculptor Eduardo Chillida (1920–2002), the Sheraton is filled with contemporary art and a collection of Spanish ship models, many of which were constructed in Bilbao's historic shipyards. Rooms are high, wide, and handsome, with glass, steel, stone, and wood trimmings. Although massive in scope, the comforts and the views from upper floors are superb. Both the Chillida café and the restaurant, Aizian, are excellent. **Pro:** great views over the whole shebang if you can get a room facing the Guggenheim. **Con:** a high-rise colossus that might be more at home in Miami or Malibu. ⊠ *C. Lehendakari Leizaola 29, El Ensanche, 48001* ☎ *94/428–0000* ⊕ *www.sheraton-bilbao.com/esp* ⊠ *199 rooms, 12 suites* ⚲ *In-room: Wi-Fi. In-hotel: 2 restaurants, bar, gym, parking (fee)* ⊟ *AE, DC, MC, V* ⎯|⎯*EP* Ⓜ *San Mamés.*

★ **$$$–$$$$**
**Hotel Carlton.** Luminaries who have trod the halls of this elegant white elephant of a hotel include Orson Welles, Ava Gardner, Ernest Hemingway, Lauren Bacall, Federico García Lorca, Albert Einstein, and Alfonso XIII, grandfather of Spain's King Juan Carlos I. During the Spanish civil war it was the seat of the Republican Basque government; later it housed a number of Nationalist generals. The hotel exudes Old World grace and charm along with a sense of history. Squarely in the middle of the Ensanche, the Carlton is equidistant from the Casco Viejo and Abandoibarra area. **Pro:** historic, old-world surroundings that remind you that Bilbao has an illustrious past. **Con:** surrounded by plenty of concrete and urban frenzy. ⊠ *Plaza Federico Moyúa 2, El Ensanche, 48009* ☎ *94/416–2200* ⊕ *www. aranzazu-hoteles.com* ⊠ *148 rooms* ⚲ *In-room: Wi-Fi. In-hotel: restaurant, bar, parking (fee)* ⊟ *AE, DC, MC, V* ⎯|⎯*EP* Ⓜ *Moyúa.*

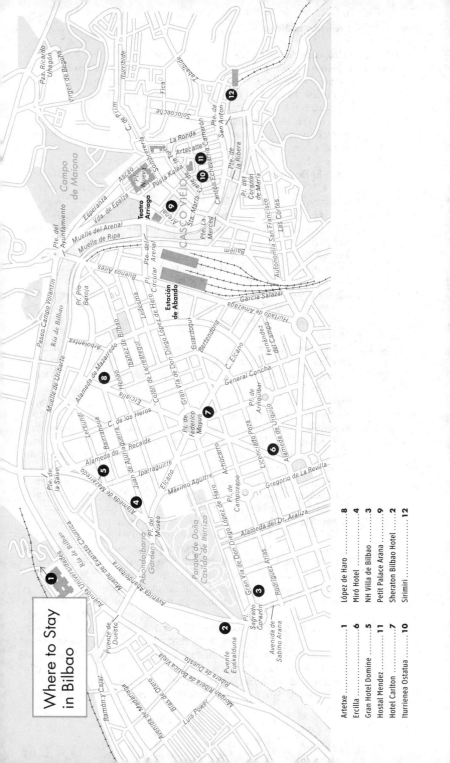

# Where to Stay in Bilbao

**$$$-$$$$**  ⚏ **López de Haro.** This luxury hotel, five minutes from the Guggenheim,
Fodor'sChoice  is becoming quite a scene now that the city is a bona fide nexus for con-
★  temporary art. A converted 19th-century building, López de Haro has
an English feel and all the comforts your heart desires. The excellent
restaurant, the Club Náutico, serves modern Basque dishes created by
Alberto Vélez—a handy alternative on one of Bilbao's many rainy eve-
nings. **Pros:** state-of-the-art comfort, service, and cuisine in a traditional
and aristocratic setting. **Cons:** a less than relaxing, slightly hushed and
stuffy scene. Not for the shorts and tank tops set. ⊠*Obispo Oru-
eta 2, El Ensanche, 48009* ☎*94/423–5500* ⊕*www.hotellopezdeharo.
com* ⇘*49 rooms, 4 suites* ⚏*In-room: Wi-Fi. In-hotel: restaurant, bar,
parking (fee)* ⊟*AE, DC, MC, V* ⦿*EP* Ⓜ*Moyúa.*

**$$-$$$**  ⚏ **Ercilla.** The taurine crowd fills this modern hotel during Bilbao's
Semana Grande in early August, partly because it's near the bullring
and partly because it has taken over from the Carlton as the place to
see and be seen. Impeccable rooms, amenities, and service underscore
its reputation. **Pro:** a Bilbao nerve center for journalists, politicians, and
businessmen. **Con:** This might not be the place to stay if you're look-
ing for a quiet getaway. ⊠*Calle Ercilla 37–39, El Ensanche, 48011*
☎*94/470–5700* ⊕*www.hotelercilla.es* ⇘*338 rooms* ⚏*In-room: Wi-
Fi. In-hotel: restaurant, bar, parking (fee)* ⊟*AE, DC, MC, V* ⦿*EP*
Ⓜ*Moyúa.*

**$$-$$$**  ⚏ **Miró Hotel.** Perfectly placed between the Guggenheim and Bilbao's
excellent Museo de Bellas Artes, this boutique hotel refurbished by Bar-
celona fashion designer Toni Miró competes with the reflecting facade
of Javier Mariscal's Domine just up the street. Comfortable and dar-
ingly innovative, it is one of the city's sleek new fleet of hotels inspired
by the world's most talked-about and architecturally revolutionary art
museum. Rooms are spacious, lavishly draped in fabrics and colors,
and ultra-high-tech contemporary. **Pro:** a design refuge that places you
in the eye of Bilbao's art and architecture hurricane. **Con:** not unpreten-
tious, a hint of preciosity pervades these ultra-chic halls. ⊠*Alameda
de Mazarredo 77, El Ensanche, 48001* ☎*94/661–1880* ⊕*www.miro-
hotelbilbao.com* ⇘*50 rooms* ⚏*In-room: Wi-Fi. In-hotel: restaurant,
bar, gym, spa, parking (fee)* ⊟*AE, DC, MC, V* ⦿*EP* Ⓜ*Moyúa.*

**$$-$$$**  ⚏ **NH Villa de Bilbao.** Although a bit big-city brisk (very bilbaino, not
unlike New York City), this businesslike place offers great extras—
morning newspapers at your door, great breakfasts, and modern rooms
that are comprehensively equipped. Nearby Doña Casilda Park becomes
part of your day as you set out for the Guggenheim, the Museo de Bel-
las Artes, or any other point in Bilbao (the farthest of which is a 45-
minute hike away). Five minutes from the Palacio de Euskalduna or the
taverns of Licenciado Poza, this is a fine location from which to tackle
Bilbao. **Pros:** terrific breakfasts and latest technology and comfort, a ver-
dant walk through the park to the Bellas Artes and Guggenheim muse-
ums. **Cons:** the disco next door can occasionally be heard pounding at
4 in the morning from certain rooms, a primarily business hotel that
seems to pride itself on no-nonsense, big-city manners. ⊠*Gran Vía 87,
El Ensanche, 48011* ☎*94/441–6000* ⊕*www.nh-hoteles.com* ⇘*139*

*rooms ⟨In-hotel: Wi-Fi, restaurant, bar, parking (fee) ☰AE, DC, MC, V ⍩◯⍩EP ⓜSan Mamés.*

**$–$$** 🏨**Petit Palace Arana.** Next to the Teatro Arriaga in the Casco Viejo this contemporary-antique design has a blended style: centenary limestone blocks, exposed brickwork, hand-hewn beams, and spiral wooden staircases are juxtaposed with clean new surfaces of glass and steel. The standard rooms and the showers are a tight fit, and the street below can be noisy on weekends, depending on your location. Fifteen executive rooms have exercise bikes and computers, while all rooms have hot tubs with hydro-massage and computer hookups. **Pro:** being next to the Casco Viejo and the Mercado de la Ribera places you in the heart of traditional Bilbao. **Con:** the night can be noisy on the Casco Viejo side of the building. Ask for a room overlooking the Teatro Arriaga and the Nervión, for the views and for less night racket. *⊠Bidebarrieta 2, Casco Viejo, 48005 ☎94/415–6411 ⊕www.hthotels.com ⇴64 rooms ⟨In-room: Wi-Fi. In-hotel: bar ☰AE, DC, MC, V ⍩◯⍩EP ⓜAbando.*

**¢–$** 🏨**Artetxe.** With rooms overlooking Bilbao from the heights of Artxanda, this Basque farmhouse with wood trimmings and eager young owners offers excellent value and quiet. It's surrounded by the green hills and meadows you see from the Guggenheim museum, so what you lose here in big-city ambience you gain in good air and peace. Local *asadores* (restaurants specializing in meat or fish cooked over coals) are good dining options. You'll need a car to connect easily with downtown Bilbao. **Pro:** a peaceful, grassy place from which to enjoy Bilbao and the Basque countryside. **Cons:** far from the center, the museums, and the action. *⊠C. de Berriz 112 (off Ctra. Enékuri–Artxanda, Km 7), Artxanda, 48015 ☎94/474–7780 ⊕www.hotelartetxe.com ⇴12 rooms ⟨In-hotel: parking (no fee) ☰AE, DC, MC, V ⍩◯⍩EP ⓜSarriko.*

**¢–$** 🏨**Iturrienea Ostatua.** Extraordinarily beautiful, this traditional Basque
★ town house in Bilbao's Old Quarter has charm to spare. With wooden ceiling beams, stone floors, and ethnographical and historical objects including a portable Spanish civil war combat confessional, there is plenty to learn and explore without leaving the hotel. The staff is eager to please. **Pros:** budget friendly and exquisite rustic decor. **Con:** there is, especially on Friday and Saturday nights in summer, nocturnal noise on the front side. Try for a room in the back or bring earplugs. *⊠Santa María Kalea 14, Casco Viejo, 48005 ☎94/416–1500 ⊕www.iturrieneaostatua.com ⇴21 rooms ⟨In-room: no a/c. In-hotel: no elevator ☰AE, DC, MC, V ⍩◯⍩EP ⓜCasco Viejo.*

**¢–$** 🏨**Sirimiri.** A small, attentively run hotel near the Atxuri station, this modest spot has modern rooms with views over some of Bilbao's oldest architecture. The buffet-style breakfast is excellent, and the owner and manager helpful with advice about Bilbao. **Pros:** handy to the Mercado de la Ribera, Casco Viejo, and the Atxuri train station. **Cons:** tight quarters and noisy on weekends. *⊠Plaza de la Encarnación, Casco Viejo, 48006 ☎94/433–0759 ⊕www.hotelsirimiri.com ⇴28 rooms ⟨In-hotel: restaurant, bar, gym, parking (fee) ☰AE, DC, MC, V ⍩◯⍩EP ⓜCasco Viejo.*

¢   ☆ **Hostal Mendez.** This may be the best value in town, with small but impeccable and well-appointed rooms, some of which (Nos. 1 and 2) overlook the facade of the Palacio Yohn (pretty views but noisy at night). A brace of handsome sculpted setters stands vigil at the bottom of lovely, creaky wooden stairs. Fourth-floor rooms are even less expensive in this century-old walk-up building. **Pros:** excellent value and location in the middle of the Casco Viejo. **Cons:** with no air-conditioning, summer on the street side with the windows can be very noisy. ⊠ *Santa María Kalea 13, Casco Viejo, 48005* ☎ *94/416–0364* ⊕ *www.pensionmendez.com* ➷ *12 rooms* ⚒ *In-room: no a/c* ☰ *AE, DC, MC, V* ⏽⃝ *EP* Ⓜ *Casco Viejo.*

# NIGHTLIFE & THE ARTS

Bilbao's nightlife comes in various stages and levels of intensity. For relaxed, bar-to-bar, tavern-to-tavern wining and dining on the run, the action begins in places such as the Casco Viejo's Siete Calles and, in the Ensanche, around Plaza de Indautxu and along Calle Licenciado Poza, where serious *poteo* (tippling), *txikiteo* (tippling), and *tapeo* (tippling and tapa grazing) continue late into most nights, especially Thursday– Sunday. Music bars and dance clubs provide plenty of late-night action, especially on weekends.

## THE ARTS

As a prosperous industrial city might be expected to, Bilbao has always had an intense artistic, musical, and theatrical life, even before the Guggenheim recast the Vizcayan capital as what some publicity denizen christened the "Athens of the Basque Country." The superb ABAO (Asociación Bilbaína de Amigos de la Opera) has a calendar of world-class opera events, and the Symphony Orchestra of Bilbao and the Symphony Orchestra of the Basque Country perform in the Palacio de Euskalduna and the Teatro Arriaga. The Teatro Arriaga puts on dance and theater performances as well as opera and concerts. In addition, Bilbao hosts a blues festival in June, a jazz festival in July, and a folk and habaneras festival in September.

### PERFORMANCE VENUES

**Asociación Bilbaína de Amigos de la Opera (ABAO).** This excellent and prestigious organization of opera buffs, with its resident Coro de Opera de Bilbao, stages eight operas annually, contracting leading opera companies and performers from around the world. Most performances are held in the elegant and spacious Palacio de Euskalduna. ☎ *94/435– 5100 for opera tickets* Ⓜ *San Mamés.*

**Café-Teatro Mistyk.** This classic theatrical and musical café offers a wide range of attractions from magicians to jazz musicians. Performances are held throughout the week at hours compatible with the realities of the working life (8:30–11) and without cover charge. ⊠ *Calle Ercilla 1, El Ensanche* ☎ *94/423–6342* Ⓜ *Moyúa.*

**Palacio de Euskalduna.** Having largely replaced the Arriaga as Bilbao's top venue for ballet, opera, and classical music, this sleek modern venue frequently hosts the Orquesta Sinfónica de Bilbao. ✉*Calle Abandoibarra 4, El Ensanche* ☎*94/330–8372* Ⓜ*Moyúa.*

**Teatro Arriaga.** Originally built at what was the heart of the shipbuilding and commercial district of Bilbao, this much-prized hall continues to stage ballet, theater, concerts, opera, and *zarzuela* (comic opera). ✉*Plaza Arriaga s/n, Casco Viejo* ☎*94/416–3244* Ⓜ*Casco Viejo.*

### ROCK, JAZZ & POP

**Bilbaína Jazz Club.** This versatile club offers jazz, blues, and ethnic fusion music along with dinner, drinks, and general hanging out. Thursday is the big night here. ✉*Calle Navarra s/n, El Ensanche* ☎*94/424–6573* Ⓜ*Moyúa.*

**Bilborock.** Theater, poetry readings, and top rock groups from Spain and abroad share time on the boards at this artistic hot spot just across the Nervión from Siete Calles and the Mercado de la Ribera. ✉*Muelle de la Merced 1, El Ensanche* ☎*94/415–1306* Ⓜ*Abando.*

**Kafe Antzokia.** Local and international groups perform in this popular multidisciplinary space alternating folk, rock, jazz, and pop nights. ✉*Calle San Vicente 2, El Ensanche* ☎*94/424–4625* Ⓜ*Moyúa.*

## NIGHTLIFE

After Athletic de Bilbao soccer victories in the San Mamés stadium, "*Poza arde*" ("Poza is burning"), as the saying goes, meaning that the bars and taverns along Ensanche's Calle Licenciado Poza are crackling with ecstatic soccer fans. Even after defeats, Poza smolders with mourners and Sunday-morning quarterbacks analyzing the defeat. Licenciado Poza's taverns, in fact, are never without clientele, and one wonders what this modest *Licenciado* (master or schoolteacher) would think if he knew his name had become synonymous with Bilbao's most bacchic pleasures.

**9**

Other top bar-hopping zones include Paseo del Arenal, Calle Ledesma, and Calle Elcano. Los Jardines de Albia, with the Café Iruña in the forefront, is also a hub for cafés, bars, and taverns. Dance clubs and *bares musicales,* music bars, defined as any bar with music loud enough to block normal conversation, are heavily concentrated in the Indautxu district around the intersection of the Alameda de Urquijo and the Alameda de San Mamés. Music bars are often the way station after dinner or tapas and before clubbing. The music bar's mission in the mating ritual is to give those looking for action some degree of inebriation and rhythmic predisposition before proceeding to the next stage, which is frenzied dancing. Discos and dance clubs don't get going until well after midnight.

### BARS

For straight-up cocktails, all hotel bars, especially the Hotel Carlton's, are hands-down leaders in this area.

**Bilbost.** This cocktail master serves a wide variety of expertly prepared alcoholic concoctions ranging from manhattans to mai tais. ⊠ *Calle Pedro Eguillor 2, El Ensanche* ☎*94/415–9172* Ⓜ*Moyúa.*

**Museo del Whisky.** Some 3,000 different kinds of whiskey and a piano bar downstairs make this an Anglophile favorite in foggy Bilbao. ⊠ *Alameda del Bulevard, El Ensanche* ☎*94/342–6478* Ⓜ*Moyúa.*

**Old Tavern.** Drinks of every kind and aperitifs with attitude make this a good spot for a predinner drink and a cozy place for late-night conversations. ⊠ *Calle Rodríguez Arias 3, El Ensanche* ☎*94/415–0744* Ⓜ*Moyúa.*

### DANCE CLUBS

**Caché Latino.** As the name of the place suggests, this is a steady winner for salsa and Latin rhythms. ⊠ *Calle Ripa 3, El Ensanche* ☎*94/423–3607* Ⓜ*Abando.*

**Cotón Club.** One of the hottest addresses in Bilbao, this happening spot keeps its clientele coming back to see the latest changes in decor. The live music features many of Spain's best groups. ⊠ *Alameda Gregorio de la Revilla 25, El Ensanche* ☎*94/410–4951* Ⓜ*Moyúa.*

**Harry's Romántico.** Down a flight of stairs through mirrored passageways, this intimate venue (capacity 58 people) is the only one of its kind in Bilbao. Ballroom dancers can twirl and swing out without bumping into a cast (or a crush) of thousands. ⊠ *Alameda de Recalde 45, El Ensanche* ☎*94/443–2566* Ⓜ*Moyúa.*

**Oboe.** A relatively quiet and elegant dance club with a small bar for conversation and a larger room for dancing, this nightspot offers musical selections ranging from disco to pop, funk, and dance classics. ⊠ *Ercilla 44, El Ensanche* ☎*94/441–5616* Ⓜ*Moyúa.*

**Rock Star.** Part of the Villa de Bilbao hotel, this '50s-style dance club lives up to its name. A huge portrait of Elvis welcomes the predominantly young crowd to nights of rock, house, hip-hop, and funk. ⊠ *Gran Via de Don Diego López de Haro 89, El Ensanche* ☎*94/441–1060* Ⓜ*Moyúa.*

### PUBS

"Pubs" in Spain, and especially Bilbao, are smokier, noisier places with louder music compared to "bars." Consider it a sort of halfway house between bars and discos. Pubs are for drinking serious *copas,* which are understood as either beer or mixed drinks such as *cubatas* (Cuba libres, or Coca-Cola and rum).

**Naschcafé.** For an original combination of copas, music, general partying, and art exhibits, this well-loved standby is worth seeking out. ⊠ *Simon Bolivar 11, El Ensanche* ☎*94/427–1876* Ⓜ*Moyúa.*

**Nashville.** A refuge for postgraduates, Nashville plays good recorded music in a wide range of styles and rhythms and at a decibel level you can converse over. The drinks spur on conversation, as does the relatively breathable air not solidified by smoke. ⊠ *Licenciado Poza 24, El Ensanche* ☎*94/427–8081* Ⓜ*Moyúa.*

**Twiggy.** This extraordinarily reserved club (for a Bilbao nightlife venue) offers no dancing, just a wide range of heavily amplified music and an imaginative decor to lounge in. ⊠ *Alameda de Urquijo 37, El Ensanche* ☎*94/410–3814* Ⓜ*Moyúa.*

# SPORTS & THE OUTDOORS

"Sports" in Bilbao means the Athletic de Bilbao soccer team, traditionally one of Spain's top *fútbol* powers during the city's heyday as an industrial power. While it has been 30 years or so since Bilbao has won a league title, "the lions" are often in the top half of the league standings and seem to take special pleasure in tormenting powerhouses Madrid and Barcelona. The local rivalry with San Sebastián's Real Sociedad is as bitter as baseball's Yankees–Red Sox feud. Athletic de Bilbao's headquarters on Alameda de Mazarredo occupy a lovely mansion, while **San Mamés Stadium** ( ✉ *Rafael Moreno Pichichi s/n, San Mamés* ☎ *94/441–3954* Ⓜ *San Mamés*) is the place to buy tickets to games and have a look through the Museo del Athletic de Bilbao. The stadium has always been known as *La Catedral* (the cathedral).

## BEACHES

Surfing, windsurfing, and general beach activities begin within 13 km (8 mi) of Bilbao. To the northwest are the five beaches of Getxo; Gorliz to the north (reachable via the Plentzia metro stop); and 37 km (23 mi) northeast of Bilboa, Mundaka and its famous left-breaking surfing wave. The Eusko train from Atxuri station runs through the Ría de Gernika's Urdaibai Reserva de la Biósfera on the way to Mundaka, a lovely natural wetlands and estuary.

## BULLFIGHTS

Bilbao's Semana Grande (Grand Week), in early August, is famous for scheduling Spain's largest bullfights of the season, an example of the Basque Country's tendency to favor contests of strength and character over art. Bullfights take place in the **Plaza de Toros Vista Alegre** ( ✉ *Plaza Vista Alegre s/n, San Mamés* ☎ *94/444–8698* Ⓜ *San Mamés* ⊕ *www. torosbilbao.com*).

## JAI ALAI

Basques are famous for *jai alai* and the different forms of *pelota* (ball) games ranging from handball to *pala* (paddle) to *cesta punta* (played with wicker basket-like gloves). In Bilbao inquire about pelota and jai alai events at **Club Deportivo** ( ☎ *94/441–3954*).

The best local *frontón* (pelota court), from which the finest players depart for Miami and other jai alai centers in the United States, is **Gernika Jai Alai** ( ✉ *Calle Carlos Gangoiti 14, Gernika* ☎ *94/625–6250*); games are held on Monday at 5 PM (Gernika is 33 km [20 mi] north of Bilbao). **Durango Ezkurdi Jai Alai** ( ✉ *Plaza Ezkurdi s/n, Durango* ☎ *94/625–6250 central jai alai information*) holds pelota and cesta punta matches all year on Monday at 5 PM in Durango, 20 minutes northeast of Bilbao. **Markina** ( ✉ *El Prado s/n, Markina* ☎ *94/625–6250*), 51 km (32 mi) north of Bilbao, is a pelota pilgrimage for enthusiasts.

# SHOPPING

The main stores for clothing are found around Plaza Moyúa in the Ensanche along streets such as Calle Iparraguirre and Calle Rodríguez Arias. The Casco Viejo has dozens of smaller shops, many of them handsomely restored early houses with gorgeous wooden beams and ancient stones, specializing in an endless variety of products from crafts to antiques. Wool items, foodstuffs, and wood carvings from around the Basque Country can be found throughout Bilbao. *Txapelas* (berets) are famous worldwide and make fine gifts. Best when waterproofed, they'll keep you remarkably warm in rain and mist.

The city is home to international fashion names from Coco Chanel to Zara to Toni Miró, Calvin Klein, and Adolfo Domínguez. The ubiquitous department store Corte Inglés is an easy one-stop shop, if a bit routine. Benetton and Marks & Spencer grace Bilbao's Gran Vía.

### ARTS & CRAFTS

**Basandere.** This diverse emporium just across from the Guggenheim sells quality artisanal products made from all around the Basque Country. ⊠ *Calle Iparraguirre 4, El Ensanche* ☎ *94/423–6386* Ⓜ *Moyúa.*

**Regalos Rui-Wamba.** Silver icons, enamel work, Basque crafts, and religious articles can be found here. ⊠ *Plaza Nueva 10, Casco Viejo* ☎ *94/415–4238* Ⓜ *Casco Viejo.*

**Tallerías San Antón.** This artisanal glass cutter produces a wide range of glasses and heraldic carvings. ⊠ *Zabalbide 7, El Ensanche* ☎ *94/416–8062* Ⓜ *Moyúa.*

### BOOKS & MUSIC

**Gordon.** Classical music and Basque folk music are the main specialties in this Ensanche music shop. ⊠ *Autonomía 33, El Ensanche* ☎ *94/444–3399* Ⓜ *Moyúa.*

**Urretxindorra.** An ample range of books in English, French, German, Spanish, and Euskera is available here, along with music and videos. ⊠ *Calle Iparraguirre 26, El Ensanche* ☎ *94/424–0228* Ⓜ *Moyúa.*

**Vellido.** This popular music store on Plaza Moyúa is a leading source of all kinds of recordings. ⊠ *Plaza Moyúa 4, El Ensanche* ☎ *94/415–7748* Ⓜ *Moyúa.*

### CLOTHING

**Derby.** A Bilbao men's fashion favorite for over a century, Derby outfits Bilbao's industrial elite. ⊠ *Alameda Urquijo 6, El Ensanche* ☎ *94/415–9277* Ⓜ *Moyúa.*

**La Palma.** With styles and makes for every taste, La Palma is a top Bilbao footwear specialist. ⊠ *Correo 3, El Ensanche* ☎ *94/415–3800* Ⓜ *Moyúa.*

**Man.** Styles for young men are the theme at Man, founded by the grandson of the original Derby founder. ⊠ *Ercilla 6, El Ensanche* ☎ *94/423–5529* Ⓜ *Moyúa.*

**Muselina.** This store sells handmade clothes for babies and children up to the age of eight. ⊠ *Calle Colón de Larreátegui 41, El Ensanche* ☎ *94/423–6985* Ⓜ *Moyúa.*

**Penny Black.** Stylish but classical clothes for young women, especially Max Mara Group trademarks, attract style-conscious *bilbainas* to this shop. ⊠*Gran Vía 24, El Ensanche* ☎94/479–5527 Ⓜ*Moyúa.*

**Revólver.** Revólver sells national and international clothing for both guys and gals. ⊠*Ledesma 18, El Ensanche* ☎94/423–9095 Ⓜ*Moyúa.*

**Sombreros Gorostiaga.** This is Bilbao's most famous outlet for the most classic of all Basque *txapelas* (*boinas* in Spanish, or berets), the Elósegui. ⊠*Calle Victor 9, Casco Viejo* ☎94/416–1276 Ⓜ*Casco Viejo.*

### FOOD & WINE

**Colmado Ibérico.** This ham specialist offers a fine selection of acorn-fed, free-range Iberian hams. ⊠*Alameda Urquijo 20, El Ensanche* ☎94/443–6001 Ⓜ*Moyúa.*

**D'Vinno.** With a taste for Spain's newer wines, this ample selection offers more than 180 different labels in still, sparkling, and fortified wines. ⊠*Ibañez de Bilbao 6, El Ensanche* ☎94/423–4882 Ⓜ*Moyúa.*

**El Rincón del Vino.** One of Bilbao's top wine stores, this well-stocked cellar carries a variety of labels from all over Spain and beyond. ⊠*General Concha 1, El Ensanche* ☎94/410–4791 Ⓜ*Moyúa.*

# BILBAO ESSENTIALS

*To research prices, get advice from other travelers, and book travel arrangements, visit www.fodors.com.*

### AIR TRAVEL

Bilbao's airport terminal is a snowy pterodactyl-like structure, designed by flying-bridge specialist Santiago Calatrava, 12 km (7 mi) northeast of the city in Loiu. Iberia has regular connections with Madrid, Barcelona, the United Kingdom, France, and Belgium. Iberia, Spanair, and Air Europa flights from Barcelona arrive, on average, eight times a day and take just under an hour. The bus from the airport to Bilbao leaves every 30 minutes, takes 15–20 minutes, and costs about €1. Taxis cost about €22 and get you to town in under 15 minutes.

**Airport Information** **Aeropuerto Internacional de Bilbao** (☎94/486–9663 ⊕*www.aena.es*).

### BUS TRAVEL

Viacarsa Buses (⊕*www.alsa.es*) connect Barcelona and Bilbao. Viacarsa's buses from Barcelona to Bilbao leave from Barcelona Nord station at 7 AM, 10:15 AM, 3:15 PM, 10:45 PM, and 11:30 PM and take from seven to eight hours, arriving at, respectively, 3:15 PM, 5:30 PM, 10:45 PM, 7 AM, and 6:45 AM. A one-way ticket costs €39.49; round-trip is €75.03.

Buses from Bilbao to Barcelona leave from the Termibus station (metro: San Mamés) at 7 AM, 10:30 AM, 3:15 PM, and 10:30 PM and take from seven to eight hours, arriving at, respectively, 2:15 PM, 5:45 PM, 10:45 PM, and 6:15 AM. A one-way ticket costs €39.49; round-trip is €75.03.

9

**Information** **Estación d'autobuses de Barcelona Nord** ( ✉ *Ali Bei 80, El Ensanche* ☏ *902/260606* ⊕ *www.barcelonanord.com* Ⓜ *Arc de Triomf*). **Termibus Bilbao** ( ✉ *Gurtubay 1, San Mamés* ☏ *94/439–5205* ⊕ *www.termibus.es* Ⓜ *San Mamés*).

## CAR RENTALS

Car rentals from national or cheaper local agencies are available in town. At the airport are Avis, Hertz, Budget, and the European agency Europcar. National companies work through the Spanish agency Atesa. All agencies have a wide range of models, but cars with automatic transmission are less common. Rates begin at €66 a day and €232 a week for an economy car with air-conditioning, manual transmission, and unlimited mileage. This does not include the tax on car rentals, which is 16%. Look for cheaper arrangements through ⊕ *www.spaincarrental.com.*

**Agencies** **Alquibilbo** ( ✉ *General Eguía 20, El Ensanche* ☏ *94/441–2012* ⊕ *www. alquibilbo.com*). **A-Rental** ( ✉ *Pérez Galdós 24, El Ensanche* ☏ *94/427–0781*). **Atesa** ( ✉ *Sabino Arana 9, El Ensanche* ☏ *94/442–3290* ⊕ *www.atesa.es*). **Europcar** ( ✉ *Estación del Abando, El Ensanche* ☏ *94/423–9390* ⊕ *www.europcar.es*). **Hertz** ( ✉ *Doctor Achocarro 10, El Ensanche* ☏ *94/415–3677* ⊕ *www.hertz.es*).

## CAR TRAVEL

Bilbao is a scenic drive from Barcelona that can be accomplished in five hours or less. The drive from Barcelona through Zaragoza and Logroño is 613 km (368 mi) on the AP7–A68 freeway. Traveling at normal Spanish freeway speeds (140 kph [87 mph]), this is under 4½ hours. Plan on averaging about half that speed when you drive on non-freeways. Between construction, cycling events, herds of sheep, slow trucks, and curves, it's difficult (and dangerous) to do much better.

## EMERGENCIES

SOS Deiak is what to call for any emergency requiring police, ambulance, rescue squad, or firemen.

**Contacts** **Ambulance** ( ☏ *94/441–0081*). **Police** ( ☏ *091 national police, 092 municipal police*). **SOS Deiak** ( ☏ *112*).

## TAXIS

In Bilbao, taxis are normally hailed on the street. A taxi across the center of the city from Palacio de Euskalduna to the Atxuri station will rarely exceed €10. A taxi stand is called a *parada de taxis*; taxis charge extra for airport drop-offs and pickups as well as for baggage, and tipping is entirely optional.

## TOURS

Bilbao's tourist office, Iniciativas Turísticas, conducts weekend guided tours in English and Spanish. The Casco Viejo tour starts at 10 AM at the tourist office on the ground floor of the Teatro Arriaga. The Ensanche and Abandoibarra tour begins at noon at the tourist office located to the left of the Guggenheim entrance. The tours last 90 minutes and cost €3.

Bilbao Paso a Paso arranges custom-designed visits and tours of Bilbao throughout the week. Stop Bilbao leads visits and tours of Bilbao and the province of Vizcaya.

**Contacts Bilbao Paso a Paso** ( ✉ *Calle Bidebarrieta 12* ☎ *94/415–3892* ⊕ *www.bilbaopasoapaso.com*). **Iniciativas Turísticas** ( ✉ *Plaza Ensanche 11* ☎ *94/479–5760* ⊕ *www.bilbao.net*). **Stop Bilbao** ( ✉ *Gran Via 80* ☎ *94/442–4689* ⊕ *www.stop.es*).

## TRAIN TRAVEL

Trains from Barcelona's Sants station to Bilbao leave twice daily at 12:30 PM (arriving at 9:42 PM) and at 10 PM (arriving at 7:53 AM). The day train costs €38.10, while the overnight train costs €50.10 (with a bunk bed €98.70. Call RENFE for information or reserve online (see phone number and Web site below).

Within and around Bilbao, there are four railroad options as well as the subway system. Cercanías RENFE (local trains) will take you up and down the Left Bank of the river, notably to Santurtzi with its excellent Hogar del Pescador sardine sanctuary. The regional train company FEVE runs a narrow-gauge train to Santander. Euskotram sends a narrow-gauge railway to San Sebastián from Atxuri station near the Casco Viejo as well as trains to Gernika, Mundaka, and Bermeo.

**Train Information Bilbao** ( ✉ *Estación del Abando, Calle Hurtado de Amézaga* ☎ *94/423–8623 or 94/423–8636*). **FEVE** ( ✉ *Estación de FEVE, next to Estación del Abando* ☎ *94/423–2266* ⊕ *www.feve.es*). **RENFE** ( ☎ *902/240202* ⊕ *www. renfe.es*).

## TRANSPORTATION WITHIN BILBAO

Getting around Bilbao is easily accomplished on foot, though the occasional subway from, say, San Mamés at the western edge of town to the Casco Viejo at the other edge can be useful and save time. The Euskotram, Bilbao's tramway, runs from the Basurto hospital downriver from (southwest of) San Mamés soccer stadium along a grassy track past the Guggenheim and along the river, to Atxuri station just upriver from the Casco Viejo.

The Creditrans ticket is good for tram, metro, and bus travel and is available in values of €5, €10, and €15, though the €5 ticket should suffice for the few subway hops you might need to get around town. Creditrans can be purchased at newspaper stands, bus stops, metro stations, and from some drivers. The ticket is passed through a machine getting on and off metros, tramways, or buses, and your Creditrans is charged according to the length of your trip. Transfers cost extra. A single in-town (Zone 1) ride costs about €1 and can be purchased from a driver; with a Creditrans transaction the cost is reduced to about €0.50.

Bilbobus provides bus service 6 AM–10:20 PM. Plaza Circular and Plaza Moyúa are the principal hubs for all lines. Once the metro and normal bus routes stop service, take a night bus, known as a *Gautxori* ("night bird" in Euskera). Six lines run radially between Plaza Circular and

Plaza Moyúa and the city limits 11:30 PM–2 AM weekdays and until 6 AM on Saturday.

Metro Bilbao is lineal, running down the Nervión estuary from above, or east of, the Casco Viejo, all the way to the mouth of the Nervión at Getxo, before continuing on to the beach town of Plentzia. There is no main hub, but the Moyúa station is the most central stop and lies in the middle of Bilbao's Ensanche, or modern (post-1860) part. The second subway line down the Left Bank to Santurtzi is under construction.

Contacts **Bilbobus** (☎ 94/448–4080). **Euskotram** (✉ Atxuri 6, Casco Viejo ☎ 902/543210). **Metro Bilbao** (✉ Atxuri 10, Casco Viejo ☎ 94/425–4000).

**VISITOR INFORMATION**
Tourist offices are found at Plaza Ensanche 11 and Avenida de Abandoibarra 2. There are two other offices, one in the airport at Loiu and the other, with no telephone, in the Teatro Arriaga at the edge of the Casco Viejo.

Municipal Tourist Offices **Bilbao Iniciativas Turísticas** (✉ Plaza Ensdanche 11, El Ensanche ☎ 94/479–5760 ⊕ www.bilbao.net ✉ Aeropuerto de Loiu ☎ 94/471–0310 ✉ Av. de Abandoibarra 2 ☎ 94/479–5760 ✉ Teatro Arriaga office, Plaza Arriaga 1, Casco Viejo ☎ No phone).

# Barcelona Essentials

PLANNING TOOLS, EXPERT INSIGHT,
GREAT CONTACTS

There are planners and there are those who, excuse the pun, fly by the seat of their pants. We happily place ourselves among the planners. Our writers and editors try to anticipate all the issues you may face before and during any journey, and then they do their research. This section is the product of their efforts. Use it to get excited about your trip to Barcelona, to inform your travel planning, or to guide you on the road should the seat of your pants start to feel threadbare.

# GETTING STARTED

We're really proud of our Web site: Fodors.com is a great place to begin any journey. Scan Travel Wire for suggested itineraries, travel deals, restaurant and hotel openings, and other up-to-the-minute info. Check out Booking to research prices and book plane tickets, hotel rooms, rental cars, and vacation packages. Head to Talk for on-the-ground pointers from travelers who frequent our message boards. You can also link to loads of other travel-related resources.

## ▌RESOURCES

### ONLINE TRAVEL TOOLS
The chapters in this book include many Web sites, including those for regional and local tourist offices. For information on Spain, try the country's tourism site ⊕*www.okspain.org*, ⊕*www.tourspain. es*, ⊕*www.cyberspain.com*, and ⊕*www. red2000.com/spain*. Barcelona Web sites include ⊕*www.bcn.es*, run by Barcelona's city hall, and ⊕*www.barcelonaturisme. com*, operated by the tourism office.

### ALL ABOUT BARCELONA
**Currency Conversion Google** (⊕www. google.com) does currency conversion. Just type in the amount you want to convert and an explanation of how you want it converted (e.g., "14 Swiss francs in dollars"), and then voilà. **Oanda.com** (⊕www.oanda.com) also allows you to print out a handy table with the current day's conversion rates. **XE.com** (⊕www.xe.com) is a good currency conversion Web site.

**Safety Transportation Security Administration** (TSA; ⊕www.tsa.gov)

**Time Zones Timeanddate.com** (⊕www. timeanddate.com/worldclock) can help you figure out the correct time anywhere.

**Weather Accuweather.com** (⊕www. accuweather.com) is an independent weather-forecasting service with good coverage of hur-

ricanes. **Weather.com** (⊕www.weather.com) is the Web site for the Weather Channel.

**Other Resources CIA World Factbook** (⊕www.odci.gov/cia/publications/factbook/index.html) has profiles of every country in the world. It's a good source if you need some quick facts and figures.

### VISITOR INFORMATION
The Tourist Office of Spain (and its Web site) provides valuable practical information about visiting the country. Turisme de Barcelona has two main locations, both open Monday–Saturday 9–9 and Sunday 10–2: Plaça de Catalunya, in the center of town; and Plaça Sant Jaume, in the Gothic Quarter. Other tourist information stands are at the port end of the Rambla (just beyond the Columbus monument) and at the main entrance of the Sagrada Família. There are smaller facilities at the Sants train station, open daily 8–8; the Palau de la Virreina, open Monday–Saturday 9–9 and Sunday 10–2; and the Palau de Congressos, open daily 10–8 during trade fairs and conventions only. For general information in English, dial ☎010 between 8 AM and 10 PM any day but Sunday.

El Prat Airport has an office with information on Catalonia and the rest of Spain, open Monday–Saturday 9:30–8 and Sunday 9:30–3. The tourist office in Palau Robert, open Monday–Saturday 10–7, specializes in provincial Catalonia. From June to mid-September, tourist-information aides patrol the Gothic Quarter and Ramblas area 9 AM–9 PM. They travel in pairs and are recognizable by their uniforms of red shirts, white trousers or skirts, and badges.

**Barcelona Tourist Offices Estació de Sants** (✉Pl. dels Països Catalans s/n, Eixample ☎93/285–3834). **Palau de Congressos** (✉Av. Reina María Cristina 2–16, Eixample). **Plaça de Catalunya** (✉Pl. de Catalunya 17 bis, Eixample, 08002 ☎93/285–3834 ⊕www. barcelonaturisme.com). **Plaça Sant Jaume** (✉C/Ciutat 2, Barri Gòtic ☎93/285–3834). **Servei d'Informació Cultural–Palau de la Virreina** (✉Rambla 99, Rambla ☎93/301–7775 ⊕www.bcn.cat/cultura).

**Regional Tourist Offices El Prat Airport** (✉Terminal B ☎93/478–0565). **Palau Robert** (✉Passeig de Gràcia 107, at Diagonal, Eixample ☎012 ⊕www.gencat.net/probert).

**Tourist Office of Spain U.S.–General** (✉666 5th Ave., 35th fl., New York, NY 10103 ☎212/265–8822 🖷212/265–8864 ⊕www. okspain.org). **Chicago** (✉845 N. Michigan Ave., Chicago, IL 60611 ☎312/642–1992 🖷312/642–9817). **Los Angeles** (✉8383 Wilshire Blvd., Suite 960, Beverly Hills, CA 90211 ☎213/658–7188 🖷213/658–1061). **Miami** (✉1221 Brickell Ave., Suite 1850, Miami, FL 33131 ☎305/358–1992 🖷305/358–8223). **Canada** (✉2 Bloor St. W, 34th fl., Toronto, Ontario M4W 3E2, Canada ☎416/961–3131 🖷416/961–1992). **United Kingdom** (✉22–23 Manchester Sq., London W1M 5AP, England ☎020/7486–8977 🖷020/7486–8034 ⊕www.tourspain.co.uk).

# THINGS TO CONSIDER

## GOVERNMENT ADVISORIES

As different countries have different world views, look at travel advisories from a range of governments to get more of a sense of what's going on out there. And be sure to parse the language carefully. For example, a warning to "avoid all travel" carries more weight than one urging you to "avoid nonessential travel," and both are much stronger than a plea to "exercise caution." A U.S. government travel warning is more permanent (though not necessarily more serious) than a so-called public announcement, which carries an expiration date.

■TIP➔ Consider registering online with the State Department (http://travelregistration.state.gov/ibrs), so the government will know to look for you should a crisis occur in the country you're visiting.

The U.S. Department of State's Web site has more than just travel warnings and advisories. The consular information sheets issued for every country have general safety tips, entry requirements (though be sure to verify these with the country's embassy), and other useful details.

**General Information & Warnings Australian Department of Foreign Affairs & Trade** (⊕www.smartraveller.gov.au). **Consular Affairs Bureau of Canada** (⊕www.voyage. gc.ca). **U.K. Foreign & Commonwealth Office** (⊕www.fco.gov.uk/travel). **U.S. Department of State** (⊕www.travel.state.gov).

## GEAR

Pack light. Although baggage carts are free and plentiful in most Spanish airports, they're rare in train and bus stations. Summer will be hot nearly everywhere; visits in winter, fall, and spring call for warm clothing and, in winter, sturdy walking shoes or boots. On the whole, Spanish people dress up more than Americans or the British. It makes sense to wear casual, comfortable clothing and shoes for sightseeing, but you'll want to dress up a bit in Barcelona and Bilbao, especially for fine restaurants and nightclubs.

Top-level walking shoes make all the difference for exploring Barcelona. In summer, sturdy sandals that you might even wear mountain hiking are the best solution for city trekking, staying cool, and blending in (Americans are often identified by their sneakers). On the beach, anything goes; it's common to see females of all ages wearing only bikini bottoms, and many of the more-remote beaches allow nude sunbathing. Regardless of your style, bring a cover-up to wear over your bathing suit when you leave the beach. Shorts are acceptable, though light skirts and summery dresses are the norm.

### SHIPPING LUGGAGE AHEAD

Imagine globe-trotting with only a carry-on in tow. Shipping your luggage in advance via an air-freight service is a great way to cut down on backaches, hassles, and stress—especially if your packing list includes strollers, car seats, etc. There are some things to be aware of, though.

First, research carry-on restrictions; if you absolutely need something that's isn't practical to ship and isn't allowed in carry-ons, this strategy isn't for you. Second, plan to send your bags several days in advance to U.S. destinations and as much as two weeks in advance to some international destinations. Third, plan to spend some money: it will cost least $100 to send a small piece of luggage, a golf bag, or a pair of skis to a domestic destination, much more to places overseas.

Some people use Federal Express to ship their bags, but this can cost even more than air-freight services. All these services insure your bag (for most, the limit is $1,000, but you should verify that amount); you can, however, purchase additional insurance for about $1 per $100 of value.

Contacts **Luggage Concierge** (☎800/288-9818 ⊕www.luggageconcierge.com). **Luggage Express** (☎866/744-7224 ⊕www.usxpluggageexpress.com). **Luggage Free** (☎800/361-6871 ⊕www.luggagefree.com). **Sports Express** (☎800/357-4174 ⊕www.sportsexpress.com) specializes in shipping golf clubs and other sports equipment. **Virtual Bellhop** (☎877/235-5467 ⊕www.virtualbellhop.com).

### PASSPORTS & VISAS

Visitors from the United States, Australia, Canada, New Zealand, and the United Kingdom need a valid passport to enter Spain. No visa is required for U.S. passport holders for a stay of up to three months; for stays exceeding three months, contact the Consulate of Spain nearest you. Australians require a visa for stays of over a month. You should obtain it from the Spanish Embassy before you leave.

### PASSPORTS

A passport verifies both your identity and nationality—a great reason to have one.

U.S. passports are valid for 10 years. You must apply in person if you're getting a passport for the first time; if your previous passport was lost, stolen, or damaged; or if your previous passport has expired and was issued more than 15 years ago or when you were under 16. All children under 18 must appear in person to apply for or renew a passport. Both parents must accompany any child under 14 (or send a notarized statement with their permission) and provide proof of their relationship to the child.

∎TIP➔ Before your trip, make two copies of your passport's data page (one for someone at home and another for you to carry separately). Or scan the page and e-mail it to someone at home and/or yourself.

There are 13 regional passport offices, as well as 7,000 passport acceptance facilities in post offices, public libraries, and other governmental offices. If you're renewing a passport, you can do so by mail. Forms are available at passport acceptance facilities and online.

The cost to apply for a new passport is $97 for adults, $82 for children under 16; renewals are $67. Allow six weeks for processing, both for first-time passports and renewals. For an expediting fee of $60 you can reduce this time to about two weeks. If your trip is less than two weeks away, you can get a passport even more rapidly by going to a passport office with the necessary documentation. Private expediters can get things done in as little as 48 hours, but charge hefty fees for their services.

## VISAS

A visa is essentially formal permission to enter a country. Visas allow countries to keep track of you and other visitors—and generate revenue (from application fees). You *always* need a visa to enter a foreign country; however, many countries routinely issue tourist visas on arrival, particularly to U.S. citizens. When your passport is stamped or scanned in the immigration line, you're actually being issued a visa. Sometimes you have to stand in a separate line and pay a small fee to get your stamp before going through immigration, but you can still do this at the airport on arrival.

Getting a visa isn't always that easy. Some countries require that you arrange for one in advance of your trip. There's usually—but not always—a fee involved, and said fee may be nominal ($10 or less) or substantial ($100 or more).

If you must apply for a visa in advance, you can usually do it in person or by mail. When you apply by mail, you send your passport to a designated consulate, where your passport will be examined and the visa issued. Expediters—usually the same ones who handle expedited passport applications—can do all the work of obtaining your visa for you; however, there's always an additional cost (often more than $50 per visa).

Most visas limit you to a single trip—basically during the actual dates of your planned vacation. Other visas allow you to visit as many times as you wish for a specific period of time. Remember that requirements change, sometimes at the drop of a hat, and the burden is on you to make sure that you have the appropriate visas. Otherwise, you'll be turned away at the airport or, worse, deported after you arrive in the country. No company or travel insurer gives refunds if your travel plans are disrupted because you didn't have the correct visa.

**U.S. Passport Information U.S. Department of State** (☎877/487-2778 ⊕www.travel.state.gov/passport).

**U.S. Passport & Visa Expediters A. Briggs Passport & Visa Expediters** (☎800/806-0581 or 202/338-0111 ⊕www.abriggs.com). **American Passport Express** (☎800/455-5166 or 800/841-6778 ⊕www.americanpassport.com). **Passport Express** (☎800/362-8196 ⊕www.passportexpress.com). **Travel Document Systems** (☎800/874-5100 or 202/638-3800 ⊕www.traveldocs.com). **Travel the World Visas** (☎866/886-8472 or 301/495-7700 ⊕www.world-visa.com).

| GENERAL REQUIREMENTS FOR SPAIN | |
|---|---|
| Passport | Must be valid for 6 months after date of arrival. |
| Visa | Visa not required for Americans |
| Driving | International driver's license recommended but not required. |

## TRIP INSURANCE

What kind of coverage do you honestly need? Do you even need trip insurance at all? Take a deep breath and read on.

We believe that comprehensive trip insurance is especially valuable if you're booking a very expensive or complicated trip (particularly to an isolated region) or if you're booking far in advance. Who knows what could happen six months down the road? But whether or not you get insurance has more to do with how comfortable you are assuming all that risk yourself.

Comprehensive travel policies typically cover trip-cancellation and interruption, letting you cancel or cut your trip short because of a personal emergency, illness, or, in some cases, acts of terrorism in your destination. Such policies also cover evacuation and medical care. Some also cover you for trip delays because of bad weather or mechanical problems as well as for lost or delayed baggage. Another

## Trip Insurance Resources

| INSURANCE COMPARISON SITES | | |
|---|---|---|
| Insure My Trip.com | 800/487–4722 | www.insuremytrip.com |
| Square Mouth.com | 800/240–0369 | www.quotetravelinsurance.com |
| COMPREHENSIVE TRAVEL INSURERS | | |
| Access America | 866/807–3982 | www.accessamerica.com |
| CSA Travel Protection | 800/873–9855 | www.csatravelprotection.com |
| HTH Worldwide | 610/254–8700 or 888/243–2358 | www.hthworldwide.com |
| Travelex Insurance | 888/457–4602 | www.travelex-insurance.com |
| Travel Guard International | 715/345–0505 or 800/826–4919 | www.travelguard.com |
| Travel Insured International | 800/243–3174 | www.travelinsured.com |
| MEDICAL-ONLY INSURERS | | |
| International Medical Group | 800/628–4664 | www.imglobal.com |
| International SOS | 215/942–8000 or 713/521–7611 | www.internationalsos.com |
| Wallach & Company | 800/237–6615 or 504/687–3166 | www.wallach.com |

type of coverage to look for is financial default—that is, when your trip is disrupted because a tour operator, airline, or cruise line goes out of business. Generally you must buy this when you book your trip or shortly thereafter, and it's only available to you if your operator isn't on a list of excluded companies.

If you're going abroad, consider buying medical-only coverage at the very least. Neither Medicare nor some private insurers cover medical expenses anywhere outside the United States (including time aboard a cruise ship, even if it leaves from a U.S. port). Medical-only policies typically reimburse you for medical care (excluding that related to pre-existing conditions) and hospitalization abroad, and provide for evacuation. You still have to pay the bills and await reimbursement from the insurer, though.

Expect comprehensive travel insurance policies to cost about 4–8% of the total price of your trip (it's more like 8%–12%

if you're over age 70). A medical-only policy may or may not be cheaper than a comprehensive policy. Always read the fine print of your policy to make sure that you are covered for the risks that are of most concern to you. Compare several policies to make sure you're getting the best price and range of coverage available.

# BOOKING YOUR TRIP

Unless your cousin is a travel agent, you're probably among the millions of people who make most of their travel arrangements online.

But have you ever wondered just what the differences are between an online travel agent (a Web site through which you make reservations instead of going directly to the airline, hotel, or car-rental company), a discounter (a firm that does a high volume of business with a hotel chain or airline and accordingly gets good prices), a wholesaler (one that makes cheap reservations in bulk and then resells them to people like you), and an aggregator (one that compares all the offerings so you don't have to)?

Is it truly better to book directly on an airline or hotel Web site? And when does a real live travel agent come in handy?

## ▌ONLINE

You really have to shop around. A travel wholesaler such as Hotels.com or Hotel-Club.net can be a source of good rates, as can discounters such as Hotwire or Priceline, particularly if you can bid for your hotel room or airfare. Indeed, such sites sometimes have deals that are unavailable elsewhere. They do, however, tend to work only with hotel chains (which makes them just plain useless for getting hotel reservations outside major cities) or big airlines (so that often leaves out upstarts like jetBlue and some foreign carriers like Air India).

Also, with discounters and wholesalers you must generally prepay, and everything is nonrefundable. And before you fork over the dough, be sure to check the terms and conditions, so you know what a given company will do for you if there's a problem and what you'll have to deal with on your own.

■TIP➔ To be absolutely sure everything was processed correctly, confirm reservations made through online travel agents, discounters, and wholesalers directly with your hotel before leaving home.

Booking engines like Expedia, Travelocity, and Orbitz are actually travel agents, albeit high-volume, online ones. And airline travel packagers like American Airlines Vacations and Virgin Vacations—well, they're travel agents, too. But they may still not work with all the world's hotels.

An aggregator site will search many sites and pull the best prices for airfares, hotels, and rental cars from them. Most aggregators compare the major travel-booking sites such as Expedia, Travelocity, and Orbitz; some also look at airline Web sites, though rarely the sites of smaller budget airlines. Some aggregators also compare other travel products, including complex packages—a good thing, as you can sometimes get the best overall deal by booking an air-and-hotel package.

## ▌WITH A TRAVEL AGENT

If you use an agent—brick-and-mortar or virtual—you'll pay a fee for the service. And know that the service you get from some online agents isn't comprehensive. For example Expedia and Travelocity don't search for prices on budget airlines like jetBlue, Southwest, or small foreign carriers. That said, some agents (online or not) *do* have access to fares that are difficult to find otherwise, and the savings can more than make up for any surcharge.

A knowledgeable brick-and-mortar travel agent can be a godsend if you're booking a cruise, a package trip that's not available to you directly, an air pass, or a complicated itinerary including several overseas flights. What's more, travel agents that specialize in a destination may

# Online Booking Resources

| AGGREGATORS | | |
|---|---|---|
| Kayak | www.kayak.com | also looks at cruises and vacation packages. |
| Mobissimo | www.mobissimo.com | |
| Qixo | www.qixo.com | also compares cruises, vacation packages, and even travel insurance. |
| Sidestep | www.sidestep.com | also compares vacation packages and lists travel deals. |
| Travelgrove | www.travelgrove.com | also compares cruises and packages. |
| **BOOKING ENGINES** | | |
| Cheap Tickets | www.cheaptickets.com | a discounter. |
| Expedia | www.expedia.com | a large online agency that charges a booking fee for airline tickets. |
| Hotwire | www.hotwire.com | a discounter. |
| lastminute.com | www.lastminute.com | specializes in last-minute travel; the main site is for the U.K., but it has a link to a U.S. site. |
| Luxury Link | www.luxurylink.com | has auctions (surprisingly good deals) as well as offers on the high-end side of travel. |
| Onetravel.com | www.onetravel.com | a discounter for hotels, car rentals, airfares, and packages. |
| Orbitz | www.orbitz.com | charges a booking fee for airline tickets, but gives a clear breakdown of fees and taxes before you book. |
| Priceline.com | www.priceline.com | a discounter that also allows bidding. |
| Travel.com | www.travel.com | allows you to compare its rates with those of other booking engines. |
| Travelocity | www.travelocity.com | charges a booking fee for airline tickets, but promises good problem resolution. |
| **ONLINE ACCOMMODATIONS** | | |
| Hotelbook.com | www.hotelbook.com | focuses on independent hotels worldwide. |
| Hotel Club | www.hotelclub.net | good for major cities worldwide. |
| Hotels.com | www.hotels.com | a big Expedia-owned wholesaler that offers rooms in hotels all over the world. |
| Quikbook | www.quikbook.com | offers "pay when you stay" reservations that let you settle your bill at check out, not when you book. |
| **OTHER RESOURCES** | | |
| Bidding For Travel | www.biddingfortravel.com | a good place to figure out what you can get and for how much before you start bidding on, say, Priceline. |

have exclusive access to certain deals and insider information on things such as charter flights. Agents who specialize in types of travelers (senior citizens, gays and lesbians, naturists) or types of trips (cruises, luxury travel, safaris) can also be invaluable.

■TIP→ **Remember that Expedia, Travelocity, and Orbitz are travel agents, not just booking engines. To resolve any problems with a reservation made through these companies, contact them first.**

A top-notch agent planning your trip to Russia will make sure you get the correct visa application and complete it on time; the one booking your cruise may get you a cabin upgrade or arrange to have bottle of champagne chilling in your cabin when you embark. And complain about the surcharges all you like, but when things don't work out the way you'd hoped, it's nice to have an agent to put things right.

**Agent Resources American Society of Travel Agents** (☎703/739–2782 ⊕www. travelsense.org).

**Barcelona Travel Agents American Express** (✉Rosselló 257, at Passeig de Gràcia, Eixample ☎93/217–0070). **Bestours** (✉Diputació 241, Eixample ☎93/487–8580). **Iberia** (✉Diputació 258, at Passeig de Gràcia, Eixample ☎93/401–3381 ✉Pl. de Espanya, Eixample ☎93/325–7358). **WagonsLits Cook** (✉Passeig de Gràcia 8, Eixample ☎93/317–5500).

# ■ ACCOMMODATIONS

Most hotels and other lodgings require you to give your credit-card details before they will confirm your reservation. If you don't feel comfortable e-mailing this information, ask if you can fax it (some places even prefer faxes). However you book, get confirmation in writing and have a copy of it handy when you check in.

Be sure you understand the hotel's cancellation policy. Some places allow you to cancel without any kind of penalty—

## 10 WAYS TO SAVE

**1.Join "frequent guest" programs.** You may get preferential treatment in room choice and/or upgrades.

**2.Call direct.** You can sometimes get a better price if you call a hotel's local toll-free number (if available) rather than a central reservations number.

**3.Check online.** Check hotel Web sites, as not all chains are on all travel sites.

**4.Look for specials.** Always inquire about packages and corporate rates.

**5.Look for price guarantees.** For overseas trips, look for guaranteed rates. With your rate locked in you won't pay more, even if the price goes up in the local currency.

**6.Look for weekend deals at business hotels.** High-end chains catering to business travelers are often busy only on weekdays; to fill rooms they often drop rates dramatically on weekends.

**7.Ask about taxes.** Check whether taxes are included in quoted rates. In some places taxes can add 20% or more to your bill.

**8.Read the fine print.** Watch for add-ons, including resort fees, energy surcharges, and "convenience" fees for such things as local phone service you won't use or a newspaper in a language you can't read.

**9.Know when to go.** If high season is December through April and you're trying to book, say, in late April, you might save money by changing your dates by a week or two. Ask when rates go down, though: if your dates straddle peak and nonpeak seasons, a property may still charge peak-season rates for the entire stay.

**10.Weigh your options (we can't say this enough).** Weigh transportation times and costs against the savings of staying in a hotel that's cheaper because it's out of the way.

## Online Booking Resources

| CONTACTS | | |
|---|---|---|
| At Home Abroad | 212/421–9165 | www.athomeabroadinc.com |
| Barclay International Group | 516/364–0064 or 800/845–6636 | www.barclayweb.com |
| Drawbridge to Europe | 541/482–7778 or 888/268–1148 | www.drawbridgetoeurope.com |
| Forgetaway | | www.forgetaway.weather.com |
| Home Away | 512/493–0382 | www.homeaway.com |
| Homes Away | 416/920–1873 or 800/374–6637 | www.homesaway.com |
| Hometours International | 865/690–8484 | thor.he.net/~hometour |
| Interhome | 954/791–8282 or 800/882–6864 | www.interhome.us |
| Suzanne B. Cohen & Associates | 207/622–0743 | www.villaeurope.com |
| Vacation Home Rentals Worldwide | 201/767–9393 or 800/633–3284 | www.vhrww.com |
| Villanet | 206/417–3444 or 800/964–1891 | www.rentavilla.com |
| Villas & Apartments Abroad | 212/213–6435 or 800/433–3020 | www.vaanyc.com |
| Villas International | 415/499–9490 or 800/221–2260 | www.villasintl.com |
| Villas of Distinction | 707/778–1800 or 800/289–0900 | www.villasofdistinction.com |
| Wimco | 800/449–1553 | www.wimco.com |

even if you prepaid to secure a discounted rate—if you cancel at least 24 hours in advance. Others require you to cancel a week in advance or penalize you the cost of one night. Small inns and bed-and-breakfasts are most likely to require you to cancel far in advance. Most hotels allow children under a certain age to stay in their parents' room at no extra charge, but others charge for them as extra adults; find out the cutoff age for discounts.

■ TIP→ Assume that hotels operate on the European Plan (EP, no meals) unless we specify that they use the Breakfast Plan (BP, with full breakfast), Continental Plan (CP, Continental breakfast), Full American Plan (FAP, all meals), Modified American Plan (MAP, breakfast and dinner) or are all-inclusive (AI, all meals and most activities).

**APARTMENT & HOUSE RENTALS**

See chapter 4 Where to Stay for information on apartment and house rental in Barcelona.

**HOME EXCHANGES**

With a direct home exchange you stay in someone else's home while they stay in yours. Some outfits also deal with vacation homes, so you're not actually staying in someone's full-time residence, just their vacant weekend place.

**Exchange Clubs Home Exchange.com** (☎800/877–8723 ⊕www.homeexchange. com); $59.95 for a 1-year online listing. **HomeLink International** (☎800/638–3841 ⊕www.homelink.org); $90 yearly for Web-only membership; $140 includes Web access and two catalogs. **Intervac U.S.** (☎800/756–4663 ⊕www.intervacus.com); $78.88 for Web-only membership; $126 includes Web access and a catalog.

## HOSTELS

Hostels offer bare-bones lodging at low, low prices—often in shared dorm rooms with shared baths—to people of all ages, though the primary market is young travelers, especially students. Most hostels serve breakfast; dinner and/or shared cooking facilities may also be available. In some hostels you aren't allowed to be in your room during the day, and there may be a curfew at night. Nevertheless, hostels provide a sense of community, with public rooms where travelers often gather to share stories. Many hostels are affiliated with Hostelling International (HI), an umbrella group of hostel associations with some 4,000 member properties in more than 60 countries. Other hostels are completely independent and may be nothing more than a really cheap hotel.

Membership in any HI association, open to travelers of all ages, allows you to stay in HI-affiliated hostels at member rates. One-year membership is about $28 for adults. Rates in dorm-style rooms run about $15–$25 per bed per night; private rooms are more, but are still generally well under $100 a night. Members have priority if the hostel is full; they're also eligible for discounts around the world, even on rail and bus travel in some countries.

See chapter 4 Where to Stay for information on hostels in Barcelona.

**Information Hostelling International—USA** (☎301/495–1240 ⊕www.hiusa.org).

## ▌ AIRLINE TICKETS

Most domestic airline tickets are electronic; international tickets may be either electronic or paper. With an e-ticket the only thing you receive is an e-mailed receipt citing your itinerary and reservation and ticket numbers.

The greatest advantage of an e-ticket is that if you lose your receipt, you can simply print out another copy or ask the airline to do it for you at check-in. You usually pay a surcharge (up to $50) to get a paper ticket, if you can get one at all.

The sole advantage of a paper ticket is that it may be easier to endorse over to another airline if your flight is canceled and the airline with which you booked can't accommodate you on another flight.

▌**TIP→** Discount air passes that let you travel economically in a country or region must often be purchased before you leave home. In some cases you can only get them through a travel agent.

If you are traveling from North America, consider flying a British or other European carrier, especially if you are traveling to Barcelona or Bilbao. Though you may have to change planes in London, Paris, Amsterdam, Zurich, or even Rome, savings can be significant.

The least expensive airfares to Barcelona are priced for round-trip travel and must usually be purchased in advance. Airlines

## 10 WAYS TO SAVE

**1. Nonrefundable is best.** If saving money is more important than flexibility, then nonrefundable tickets work. Just remember that you'll pay dearly (as much as $200) if you change your plans.

**2. Comparison shop.** Web sites and travel agents can have different arrangements with the airlines and offer different prices for exactly the same flights.

**3. Beware the listed prices.** Many airline Web sites—and most ads—show prices *without* taxes and surcharges. Don't buy until you know the full price.

**4. Stay loyal.** Stick with one or two frequent-flier programs. You'll get free trips faster and you'll accumulate more quickly the perks that make trips easier. On some airlines these include a special reservations number, early boarding, and upgrades.

**5. Watch those ticketing fees.** Surcharges are usually added when you buy your ticket anywhere but on an airline Web site (that includes by phone, and paper tickets regardless of how you book).

**6. Check often.** Start looking for cheap fares from three months out to about one month. Keep looking till you find a price you like.

**7. Don't work alone.** Some Web sites have tracking features that will e-mail you immediately when good deals are posted.

**8. Jump on the good deals.** Waiting even a few minutes might mean paying more.

**9. Be flexible.** Check on prices for departures at different times and to and from alternative airports.

**10. Weigh your options.** What you get can be as important as what you save. A cheaper flight might have a long layover, or it might land at a secondary airport, where your ground transportation costs might be higher.

generally allow you to change your return date for a fee; most low-fare tickets, however, are nonrefundable.

If you buy a round-trip transatlantic ticket on the Spanish airline Iberia, you might purchase an Iberiabono España pass, good for major discounts on domestic flights during your trip. The pass must be purchased outside Spain at the time you purchase your international ticket. All internal Spain flights must be booked in advance. On certain days of the week, Iberia also offers minifares (*minitarifas*), which can save you 40% on domestic flights. Tickets must be purchased at least two days in advance, and you must stay over at the destination Saturday night.

**Air Pass Info FlightPass,** (EuropebyAir, ☎888/387–2479 ⊕www.europebyair.com). **Iberiabono España** ( ☎800/772–4642 in the U.S., 0845/850–9000 in the U.K. ⊕www.iberia.com).

## ∎ RENTAL CARS

When you reserve a car, ask about cancellation penalties, taxes, drop-off charges (if you're planning to pick up the car in one city and leave it in another), and surcharges (for being under or over a certain age, for additional drivers, or for driving across country borders or beyond a specific distance from your point of rental). All these things can add substantially to your costs. Request car seats and extras such as GPS when you book.

Rates are sometimes—but not always—better if you book in advance or reserve through a rental agency's Web site. There are other reasons to book ahead, though: for popular destinations, during busy times of the year, or to ensure that you get certain types of cars (vans, SUVs, exotic sports cars).

∎TIP➔ **Make sure that a confirmed reservation guarantees you a car. Agencies sometimes overbook, particularly for busy weekends and holiday periods.**

Currently, one of the best ways to rent a car, whether you arrange it from home or during your travels, is through the company's Web site—the rates are the best and the arrangements the easiest. Generally, you'll get a better deal if you book a car before you leave home. Avis, Hertz, Budget, and the European agency Europcar all have agencies at the airports in Barcelona and Bilbao and in other cities where you can book *un cotxe de lloguer* (a rental car). In Castilian, it's *un coche de alquiler*. National companies work through the Spanish agency Atesa. Smaller, local companies offer lower rates. All agencies have a wide range of models, though Seats (Spanish-built Fiats), Renaults, Opels, and Fords are common. Cars with automatic transmission are less common, so specify your need for one in advance.

Vanguard rents motorcycles as well as cars. Rates in Barcelona begin at the equivalents of U.S. $55 a day and $240 a week for an economy car with air-conditioning, manual transmission, and unlimited mileage. This does not include the tax on car rentals, which is 16%.

Your own driver's license is valid in Spain, but you may want to get an International Driver's Permit (IDP) for extra assurance. Permits are available from the American or Canadian Automobile Association, or, in the United Kingdom, from the Automobile Association or Royal Automobile Club. Check the AAA Web site for more info as well as for IDPs ($15) themselves. If you are stopped you will be asked to present your license and passport (or photocopy). In Spain, anyone over 18 with a valid license can drive; however, some rental companies will not rent a car to drivers under 21.

The cost for a child's car seat is €2.50 a day; the cost per day for an additional driver is €2.

## CAR-RENTAL RESOURCES

### AUTOMOBILE ASSOCIATIONS

**American Automobile Association** (AAA ☎315/797–5000 ⊕www.aaa.com); most contact with the organization is through state and regional members. **National Automobile Club** ( ☎650/294–7000 ⊕www.thenac.com); membership is open to California residents only.

### LOCAL AGENCIES IN BARCELONA

**Atesa** ( ✉El Prat Airport, El Prat del Llobregat ☎93/298–3433 ✉Muntaner 45, Eixample ☎93/323–0266). **Vanguard** ( ✉Londres 31, Eixample ☎93/439–3880).

### MAJOR AGENCIES

**Avis** ( ✉Casanova 209, Eixample ☎93/209–9533 ✉Aragó 235, Eixample ☎93/487–8754). **Europcar** ( ✉Viladomat 214, Eixample ☎93/439–8403 ✉Estació de Sants, Eixample ☎93/491–4822). **Hertz** ( ✉Estació de Sants, Eixample ☎93/490–8662 ✉Tuset 10, Eixample ☎93/217–3248).

### WHOLESALERS

**Auto Europe** ( ☎888/223–5555 ⊕www.autoeurope.com). **Europe by Car** ( ☎212/581–3040 in New York, 800/223–1516 ⊕www.europebycar.com). **Eurovacations** ( ☎877/471–3876 ⊕www.eurovacations.com). **Kemwel** ( ☎877/820–0668 ⊕www.kemwel.com).

### CAR-RENTAL INSURANCE

Everyone who rents a car wonders whether the insurance that the rental companies offer is worth the expense. No one—including us—has a simple answer. It all depends on how much regular insurance you have, how comfortable you are with risk, and whether or not money is an issue.

If you own a car, your personal auto insurance may cover a rental to some degree, though not all policies protect you abroad; always read your policy's fine print. If you don't have auto insurance, then seriously consider buying the collision- or loss-damage waiver (CDW or LDW) from the car-rental company, which eliminates your liability for damage to the car.

Some credit cards offer CDW coverage, but it's usually supplemental to your own insurance and rarely covers SUVs, minivans, luxury models, and the like. If your coverage is secondary, you may still be liable for loss-of-use costs from the car-rental company. But no credit-card insurance is valid unless you use that card for *all* transactions, from reserving to paying the final bill. All companies exclude car rental in some countries, so be sure to find out about the destination to which you are traveling.

■ TIP ➡ **Diners Club offers primary CDW coverage on all rentals reserved and paid for with the card. This means that Diners Club's company—not your own car insurance—pays in case of an accident. It *doesn't* mean your car-insurance company won't raise your rates once it discovers you had an accident.**

Some rental agencies require you to purchase CDW coverage; many will even include it in quoted rates. All will strongly encourage you to buy CDW—possibly implying that it's required—so be sure to ask about such things before renting. In most cases it's cheaper to add a supplemental CDW plan to your comprehensive travel-insurance policy ( ➡ *Trip Insurance under Things to Consider in Getting Started*) than to purchase it from a rental company. That said, you don't want to pay for a supplement if you're required to buy insurance from the rental company.

■ TIP ➡ **You can decline the insurance from the rental company and purchase it through a third-party provider such as Travel Guard (www.travelguard.com)—$9 per day for $35,000 of coverage. That's sometimes just under half the price of the CDW offered by some car-rental companies.**

# ■ VACATION PACKAGES

Packages *are not* guided excursions. Packages combine airfare, accommodations, and perhaps a rental car or other extras (theater tickets, guided excursions, boat trips, reserved entry to popular museums, transit passes), but they let you do your own thing. During busy periods packages may be your only option, as flights and rooms may be sold out otherwise.

Packages will definitely save you time. They can also save you money, particularly in peak seasons, but—and this is a really big "but"—you should price each part of the package separately to be sure. And be aware that prices advertised on Web sites and in newspapers rarely include service charges or taxes, which can up your costs by hundreds of dollars.

■ TIP ➡ **Some packages and cruises are sold only through travel agents. Don't always assume that you can get the best deal by booking everything yourself.**

Each year consumers are stranded or lose their money when packagers—even large ones with excellent reputations—go out of business. How can you protect yourself?

First, always pay with a credit card; if you have a problem, your credit-card company may help you resolve it. Second, buy trip insurance that covers default. Third, choose a company that belongs to the United States Tour Operators Association, whose members must set aside funds to cover defaults. Finally, choose a company that also participates in the Tour Operator Program of the American Society of Travel Agents (ASTA), which will act as mediator in any disputes.

You can also check on the tour operator's reputation among travelers by posting an inquiry on one of the Fodors.com forums.

**Organizations American Society of Travel Agents** (ASTA ☎ 703/739–2782 or 800/965–2782 ⊕ www.astanet.com). **United States Tour Operators Association** (USTOA ☎ 212/599–6599 ⊕ www.ustoa.com).

■ TIP ➡ **Local tourism boards can provide information about lesser-known and small-niche operators that sell packages to only a few destinations.**

# ❚ GUIDED TOURS

Guided tours are a good option when you don't want to do it all yourself. You travel along with a group (sometimes large, sometimes small), stay in prebooked hotels, eat with your fellow travelers (the cost of meals sometimes included in the price of your tour, sometimes not), and follow a schedule.

But not all guided tours are an if-it's-Tuesday-this-must-be-Belgium experience. A knowledgeable guide can take you places that you might never discover on your own, and you may be pushed to see more than you would have otherwise. Tours aren't for everyone, but they can be just the thing for trips to places where making travel arrangements is difficult or time-consuming (particularly when you don't speak the language).

Whenever you book a guided tour, find out what's included and what isn't. A "land-only" tour includes all your travel (by bus, in most cases) in the destination, but not necessarily your flights to and from or even within it. Also, in most cases prices in tour brochures don't include fees and taxes. And remember that you'll be expected to tip your guide (in cash) at the end of the tour.

## SPECIAL-INTEREST TOURS

### ART

Contact **Urbancultours** ( ☎93/417–1191).

### CULINARY

Contacts **Aula Gastronómica del Mercat de la Boqueria** ( ✉La Rambla 91, Rambla ☎93/304–0272 ⊕www.barcelonaculinaria. com). **Spanish Journeys** ( ✉La Rambla 91, Rambla ☎93/304–0272 ⊕www. spanishjourneys.com).

# ❚ CRUISES

Barcelona is the cruise capital of Spain, with many Mediterranean cruises originating there. Costa Cruises, Royal Caribbean, Holland America Line, the Norwegian Cruise Line, and Princess Cruises are among the lines that call in at Spain. Popular ports of call are Gibraltar, Málaga, Alicante, and Palma de Mallorca.

Cruise Lines **Celebrity Cruises** ( ☎800/647–2251 ⊕www.celebrity.com). **Costa Cruises** ( ☎954/266–5600 or 800/462–6782 ⊕www.costacruise.com). **Crystal Cruises** ( ☎310/785–9300 or 800/446–6620 ⊕www. crystalcruises.com). **Cunard Line** ( ☎661/753–1000 or 800/728–6273 ⊕www.cunard.com). **Holland America Line** ( ☎206/281–3535 or 877/932–4259 ⊕www.hollandamerica. com). **Mediterranean Shipping Cruises** ( ☎212/764–4800 or 800/666–9333 ⊕www. msccruises.com). **Norwegian Cruise Line** ( ☎305/436–4000 or 800/327–7030 ⊕www. ncl.com). **Oceania Cruises** ( ☎305/514–2300 or 800/531–5658 ⊕www.oceaniacruises. com). **Princess Cruises** ( ☎661/753–0000 or 800/774–6237 ⊕www.princess.com). **Regent Seven Seas Cruises** ( ☎954/776–6123 or 800/477–7500 ⊕www.rssc.com). **Royal Caribbean International** ( ☎305/539–6000 or 800/327–6700 ⊕www.royalcaribbean.com). **Seabourn Cruise Line** ( ☎305/463–3000 or 800/929–9391 ⊕www.seabourn.com). **SeaDream Yacht Club** ( ☎305/631–6110 or 800/707–4911 ⊕www.seadreamyachtclub. com). **Silversea Cruises** ( ☎954/522–4477 or 800/722–9955 ⊕www.silversea.com). **Star Clippers** ( ☎305/442–0550 or 800/442–0551 ⊕www.starclippers.com). **Windstar Cruises** ( ☎206/281–3535 or 800/258–7245 ⊕www. windstarcruises.com).

# TRANSPORTATION

## ∎ NAVIGATING BARCELONA

Addresses in Barcelona may include the street name, building number, floor level, and apartment number. For example, Carrer Balmes 155, 3º, 1ª indicates that the apartment is on the *tercero* (third) floor, *primera* (first) door. In older buildings, the first floor is often called the *entresuelo*; one floor above it is *principal*, and above this, the first floor. The top floor of a building is the *ático* (attic). In more modern buildings, there is often no *entresuelo* or *principal*.

Abbreviations used in the book for street names are Av., for *avinguda* (*avenida* in Spanish), and Ctra., for *carreter* (*carretera* in Spanish). The letters *s/n* following an address mean *sin número* (without a street number). *Carrer* (*Calle* in Castilian Spanish) is often dropped entirely or not abbreviated at all. *Camí* (*Camino* in Spanish) is abbreviated to C. *Passeig* (*paseo* in Spanish) is usually written out in full, or sometimes abbreviated as P. Plaça/Plaza is usually not abbreviated (in this book it is abbreviated as Pl.).

All of Barcelona's Ciutat Vella (Old City) can be explored on foot. Your only transport needs will be to get you to Sarrià, Gràcia, Parc Güell, Gaudí's Sagrada Família, and the Auditori near Plaça de les Glòries. A quick trip on the underground metro system will normally get you wherever you need to go. The FGC train to Sarrià is very handy, slicing up the middle of the city with stops at Provença in the middle of the Eixample, Gràcia next to the Llibertat market, Muntaner not far from El Racó de Can Freixa or Silvestre (two hot restaurants), Sarrià village, and Reina Elisenda for the Pedralbes monastery. This train is surprisingly new, bright, air-conditioned, and un-subway-like. The regular metro is a little seedier but, on the whole, acceptable, useful, and safe. Buses

can be practical for certain runs, such as the No. 64 bus from Pedralbes out to the beach in Barceloneta (though the Barceloneta metro stop and a walk through Barceloneta itself may be preferable), or the No. 66 bus from Sarrià to Plaça Catalunya. Taxis are inexpensive, around €10 for a complete crosstown ride, rarely much more.

Modern Barcelona, above the Plaça de Catalunya, is built on a grid system. The Old Town, however, from the Plaça de Catalunya to the port, is a labyrinth of narrow streets, so you'll need a good street map and good shoes for the Barri Gòtic. You'll probably want to avoid driving in the city. *(For information about driving, see By Car.)* Maps showing bus and metro routes are available free from booths in the Plaça de Catalunya.

You pay a flat fare of €1 no matter how far you travel, but it's more economical to buy a Targeta T10 (valid for bus, metro, and FGC [Ferrocarril de la Generalitat de Catalunya] trains, Tramvía Blau [Blue Trolley], and the Montjuïc Funicular), which costs €6 for 10 rides. These tickets, purchased from the vending machines in subway stations, from newspaper stands, from La Caixa ATM machines, and from lottery ticket vendors, are punched for each ride, remain valid for unlimited transfers for an hour, and can be shared by any number of riders (up to 10, legally), one punch per rider.

**Public Transportation** **Transports Metropolitans de Barcelona (TMB)** (☎93/298–7000 for lost and found and general info ⊕www.bcn.es/guia/welcomea.htm).

## ∎ BY AIR

Transatlantic flying time to Barcelona is 7 hours from New York. As there are no direct flights from the western United States to Barcelona or Bilbao, an additional flight is required from Madrid, involving a connecting flight lasting 1 hour to Barcelona or 40 minutes to Bilbao. A nonstop flight from Chicago to Madrid is 8 hours. Nonstop flights from London to Barcelona are 2¼ hours. There are several combinations when flying from Los Angeles; one possibility is to fly from Los Angeles to New York (5½ hours), and then to Madrid (7 hours). There are also numerous combinations when flying from Sydney. One option is to fly from Sydney to Johannesburg (14 hours), and then to Madrid (10 hours).

Regular nonstop flights connect the eastern United States with Barcelona. Flying from other cities in North America usually involves a stop. Flights from the United Kingdom to a number of destinations in Spain are frequent and offered at competitive fares, particularly on low-cost carriers such as Ryanair or easyJet. Beware of low-cost flights to "Barcelona" that, in fact, land in Girona, a 45-minute taxi ride north of Barcelona; often the taxi costs more than the flight.

Flights to and from the major cities in Europe and Spain also fly into and out of Bilbao's Loiu airport. There are no direct flights to Barcelona or anywhere in Spain from Australia or New Zealand.

For air travel within the regions covered in this book there are numerous regular flights, but rates tend to be high, so consider alternative ways of getting around. Bilbao, Girona, Pamplona, and San Sebastián all have small airports, and flights do run from Barcelona to each of them. However, flights between those cities are less common because of the short distance, and, in most cases, train or car travel is more prevalent.

Iberia operates a shuttle, the *puente aereo,* between Barcelona and Madrid from around 7 AM to 11 PM; planes depart hourly, and more frequently in the morning and afternoon commuter hours. You don't need to reserve ahead; you can buy your tickets at the ticket counter in the airport upon arriving. Note that Terminal C in the Barcelona airport is used exclusively by the shuttle; in Madrid, the shuttle departs from Terminal 3.

Arriving two hours in advance is more than enough for Spanish security. Arriving fewer than 40 minutes in advance is no longer possible, for either domestic or international flights.

**Airlines & Airports** **Airline and Airport Links.com** ( ⊕ www.airlineandairportlinks.com) has links to many of the world's airlines and airports.

**Airline Security Issues** **Transportation Security Administration** ( ⊕ www.tsa.gov) has answers for almost every question.

### AIRPORTS

Most flights arriving in Spain from the United States and Canada pass through Madrid's Barajas (MAD), but the major gateway to Catalonia and other regions in this book is Spain's second-largest airport, Barcelona's spectacular glass, steel, and marble El Prat de Llobregat (BCN). This airport is served by numerous international carriers, but Catalonia also has two other airports that handle air traffic, including charter flights. One is Girona, 90 km (56 mi) north of Barcelona and convenient to the resort coast of the Costa Brava. Bus and train connections from Girona to Barcelona work well and cheaply, provided you have the time (with the 90-minute advance check-in in Girona and travel by bus, set off from Barcelona at least three hours before your flight). The other Catalonia airport is at Reus, 110 km (68 mi) south of Barcelona and a gateway to Tarragona and the coastal towns of the Costa Daurada. Flights to and from the major cities in Europe and Spain also fly into and out of Bilbao's Loiu (BIL) airport. For information about airports in Spain, try ⊕ *www.aena.es*

**Airport Information** Barcelona: **El Prat de Llobregat (BCN** ☎ 93/298–3838). Bilbao: **Aeropuerto Internacional de Bilbao (BIL**

## FLYING 101

**Minimize the time spent standing in line.** Buy an e-ticket, check in at an electronic kiosk, or—even better—check in on your airline's Web site before leaving home.

**Get to the gate.** If you aren't at the gate at least 10 minutes before your flight is scheduled to take off (sometimes earlier), you won't be allowed to board.

**Double-check your flight times.** Do this especially if you reserved far in advance. Schedules change, and alerts may not reach you.

**Don't go hungry.** Ask whether your airline offers anything to eat; even when it does, be prepared to pay.

**Get the seat you want.** Often, you can pick a seat when you buy your ticket on an airline Web site. But it's not guaranteed; the airline could change the plane after you book, so double-check. You can also select a seat if you check in electronically.

**Got kids? Get info.** Sometimes infants and toddlers fly free if they sit on a parent's lap, and older children fly for half price in their own seats.

**Check your scheduling.** Don't buy a ticket if there's less than an hour between connecting flights.

**Bring paper.** Even when using an e-ticket, always carry a hard copy of your receipt; you may need it to get your boarding pass, which most airports require to get past security.

**Complain at the airport.** If your baggage goes astray or your flight goes awry, complain before leaving the airport.

**Beware of overbooked flights.** If you're bumped from a flight *involuntarily*, the airline must give you some kind of compensation if an alternate flight can't be found within one hour.

✉Loiu ☎94/486–9663). Girona: **Aeroport de Girona** (GRO ☎972/186600). Madrid: **Barajas Aeropuerto de Madrid** (MAD ☎91/305–8343). Reus: **Aeropuerto de Reus** (REU ☎977/779800).

### GROUND TRANSPORTATION

Check first to see if your hotel in Barcelona provides airport-shuttle service; otherwise, you can high-tail it into town via train, bus, taxi, or rental car.

The Aerobus leaves the airport for Plaça de Catalunya every 15 minutes (6 AM–11 PM) on weekdays and every 30 minutes (6:30 AM–10:30 PM) on weekends. From Plaça de Catalunya, the bus leaves for the airport every 15 minutes (5:30 AM–10 PM) on weekdays and every 30 minutes (6:30 AM–10:30 PM) on weekends. The fare is €3.75.

Cab fare from the airport into town is €18–€25, depending on traffic, the part of town you're heading to, and the number of larger bags you're carrying (€1 is charged for each larger bag). If you're driving your own car, follow signs to the CENTRE CIUTAT and you'll enter the city along Gran Via. For the port area, follow signs for the Ronda Litoral. The journey to the center of town can take anywhere from 15 to 45 minutes depending on traffic. If you have to get to the airport during rush hour, Barcelona's Ronda del Mig (the middle ring road, aka Ronda General Mitre) is often the way to go, as the ring roads are jammed up.

The train's only drawback is that it's a 10- to 15-minute walk (with moving walkway) from your gate through the terminal and over the bridge. Trains leave the airport every 30 minutes between 6:12 AM and 10:13 PM, stopping at the Estació de Sants, then at the Plaça de Catalunya, later at the Arc de Triomf, and finally at Clot. Trains going to the airport begin at 6 AM from the Clot station, stopping at the Arc de Triomf at 6:05 AM, Plaça de Catalunya at 6:08 AM, and Sants at 6:13 AM. The trip takes 19 minutes. The fare is €2.50.

## TRANSFERS BETWEEN AIRPORTS

To get to Girona Airport from Barcelona Airport you have to first catch the RENFE train that leaves from the airport and then change at Barcelona Sants station. From Barcelona Sants station you need to catch the train headed toward Figueres and then get off at Girona, which is 2 stops before. If you are going to Girona Airport you will then have to catch a bus from Girona center or take a taxi to the airport. Allow 30 minutes after arrival in Girona to get to the airport.

The "Autocares Julia Bus" services leaves from outside Terminal B and Terminal C of Barcelona Airport and will take you to Girona or Figueres. Transport time to Girona is approximately 1.5 hours. Ticket price is approximately €16 for an adult single. Please call the telephone numbers below for further information.

For bookings, timetable and up-to-date pricing information, call (0034) 93 402 6900 or (0034) 902 400 0080.

Alternatively, call the Barcelona Airport tourist information line and ask for further information on Autocares Julia: Barcelona Airport Tourist information 9:00 AM-9:00 PM, call (0034) 93 478 4704.

**Contact** **Transports Metropolitans de Barcelona (TMB) Estació del Nord** (✉Numero 62, Zona Franca, Eixample ☎93/298-7000).

### FLIGHTS

American, Continental, Delta, and Iberia fly to Madrid and Barcelona; US Airways, Air Europa, and Spanair fly to Madrid. Within Spain, Iberia is the main domestic airline; two independent airlines, Air Europa and Spanair, fly a number of domestic routes at somewhat lower prices.

**Airline Contacts** **Air Europa** (☎888/238-7672 ⊕www.air-europa.com). **American Airlines** (☎800/433-7300 ⊕www.aa.com). **British Airways** (☎0845/773-3377 ⊕www.britishairways.com). **Continental Airlines** (☎800/523-3273 for U.S. and Mexico reservations, 800/231-0856 for international reservations ⊕www.continental.

com). **Delta Airlines** (☎800/221-1212 for U.S. reservations, 800/241-4141 for international reservations ⊕www.delta.com). **easyJet** (☎0870/600-0000 ⊕www.easyjet.com). **Iberia** (☎800/772-4642 ⊕www.iberia.com). **Northwest Airlines** (☎800/225-2525 ⊕www.nwa.com). **Ryanair** (☎44/0871/246-0000 ⊕www.ryanair.com). **Spanair** (☎888/545-5757 ⊕www.spanair.com). **United Airlines** (☎800/864-8331 for U.S. reservations, 800/538-2929 for international reservations ⊕www.united.com). **USAirways** (☎800/428-4322 for U.S. and Canada reservations, 800/622-1015 for international reservations ⊕www.usairways.com).

**Within Spain** **Air Europa** (☎902/401501 ⊕www.air-europa.com). **Iberia** (☎902/400500 ⊕www.iberia.com). **Spanair** (☎902/131415 ⊕www.spanair.com).

# ▌ BY BOAT

There are regular ferry services between the United Kingdom and northern Spain. Brittany Ferries sails from Portsmouth to Santander, and P&O European Ferries sails from Plymouth to Bilbao. Spain's major ferry line, Trasmediterránea links mainland Spain (including Barcelona) with the Balearics and the Canary Islands. Trasmediterránea's fast catamaran service takes half the time of the standard ferry, but catamarans are often canceled because they can only navigate in very calm waters.

You can pick up schedules and buy tickets at the ferry ticket office in the port, and also at most travel agencies. Credit cards are accepted, but traveler's checks are usually not.

**From the U.K.** **Brittany Ferries** (☎0752/221321 or 0990/360360 ⊕www.brittany-ferries.com). **P&O European Ferries** (☎44/1870520-2020 ⊕www.poferries.com).

**In Spain** **Trasmediterránea** (☎902/454645 ⊕www.trasmediterranea.es).

# ▌ BY BUS

*For information about bus travel within Barcelona, see By Bus in Transportation.* Barcelona's main bus station for intra-Spain routes is Estació del Nord, a few blocks east of the Arc de Triomf. Buses also depart from the Estació de Sants for long-distance and international routes, as well as from the depots of Barcelona's various private bus companies. Spain's major national long-haul company is Alsa-Enatcar. Grup Sarbus serves Catalonia and, with its subsidiary Sarfa, the Costa Brava. Rather than pound the pavement (or the telephone, usually futile because of overloaded lines) trying to sort out Barcelona's complex and confusing bus system, plan your bus travel through a local travel agent, who can quickly book you the best bus passage to your destination.

Within Spain, private companies provide bus services from knee-crunchingly basic to luxurious. Depending on your destination, you will be able to choose more direct routes on more comfortable buses for higher fares or more basic local buses that are cheaper. Fares are lower than the corresponding train fares, and service is more extensive: if you want to reach a town not served by train, you can be sure a bus will go there. See the Essentials section at the end of Chapters 8 and 9 for companies serving the rest of Catalonia and Vizcaya. Note that there are fewer services during the weekend and on holidays.

Most larger bus companies have buses with comfortable seats and adequate legroom; on longer journeys (two to three hours or more) a movie is shown on board, and earphones are provided. Except for smaller, regional buses that travel short hops, buses have a bathroom on board. Smoking is prohibited. Most long-haul buses stop at least once every two to three hours for a snack and bathroom break. Although buses are prey to road and traffic conditions, highways in Catalonia and the Basque Country, particularly along major routes, are well maintained. That may not be the case in more rural areas, where you could be in for a bumpy ride—which is sometimes made worse by older buses with poor shock absorbers.

You can get to Spain by bus from London, Paris, Rome, Frankfurt, Prague, and other major European cities. It is a long journey, but the buses are modern and inexpensive. Eurolines, the main carrier, connects many European cities with Barcelona.

Alsa-Enatcar, Spain's largest national bus company, has two luxury classes in addition to its regular line. The top of the line is Supra Clase, with roomy leather seats and on-board meals; in this class, you also have the option of *asientos individuales,* individual seats (with no other seat next to you) that line one side of the bus. The next class is the Eurobus, with comfy seats and plenty of legroom, but no *asientos individuales* or on-board meals. The Supra Clase and Eurobus cost up to one-third and one-fourth more, respectively, than the regular line.

If you plan on returning to your initial destination, you can always save by buying a round-trip ticket, instead of one-way. Also, some smaller, regional bus lines offer multi-trip bus passes, which are worthwhile if you plan on making multiple trips between two destinations. Generally, these tickets offer a savings of 20% per journey; you can only buy them in the bus station (not on the bus). The general rule for children is that if they occupy a seat, they pay.

In Barcelona you can pick up schedule and fare information at the Tourist Information offices in Plaça Catalunya, Plaça Sant Jaume, or at the Sants train station. A better and faster solution is to click onto ⊕*www.barcelonanord.com.*

At bus-station ticket counters, major credit cards (except for American Express) are universally accepted. You must pay in cash for tickets purchased on the bus. Travelers' checks are almost never accepted.

During peak travel times (Easter, August, and Christmas), it's always a good idea to make a reservation at least three to four days in advance.

City buses run daily 5:30 AM–11:30 PM. Route maps are displayed at bus stops. Note that those with a red band always stop at a central square—Catalunya, Universitat, or Urquinaona—and blue indicates a night bus. Barcelona's 30 night buses generally run until about 4:30 AM, though some stop as early as 3:30 AM and others continue until as late as 5:20 AM.

Bus Companies Alsa-Enatcar ( ☎ 902/422242 ⊕ www.alsa.es) Alsina-Graells ( ⊠ Estació d'Autobusos Barcelona-Nord, Carrer Alí Bei 80, Eixample ☎ 93/265-6592 ⊕ www.alsinagraells.es). Grup Sarbus ( ⊠ Estació d'Autobusos Barcelona-Nord, Carrer d' Alí Bei 80, Eixample ☎ 93/265-6508, 902/303222 bus ticket delivery to your place of lodging ⊕ www.sarfa. com). Julià ( ⊠ Ronda Universitat 5, Eixample ☎ 93/342-5180 ⊕ www.eurolines.es).

Bus Terminals Estació del Nord ( ⊠ Carrer d'Ali Bei 80, Eixample ☎ 93/265-6508). Estació de Sants ( ⊠ Carrer de Viriat, Eixample ☎ 93/490-0202).

From the U.K. Eurolines/National Express ( ☎ 0870/580-8080 ⊕ www. nationalexpress.com).

International Bus Companies Eurolines ( ⊠ Carrer Viriato, Eixample ☎ 93/490-4000 ⊠ Estació del Nord, Carrer d'Ali Bei 80, Eixample ☎ 93/232-1092 ⊠ Ronda Universitat 5, Eixample ☎ 93/342-5180 ⊕ www.eurolines. es). Linebus ( ⊠ Estació d'Autobusos Barcelona-Nord, Carrer d' Alí Bei 80, Eixample ☎ 93/265-0700).

# BY CABLE CAR & FUNICULAR

The Montjuïc Funicular is a cog railway that runs from the junction of Avinguda Paral.lel and Nou de la Rambla to the Miramar station on Montjuïc (Metro: Paral.lel). It operates weekends and holidays 11 AM–8 PM in winter, daily 11 AM–9:30 PM in summer; the fare is €1.75 or you can use one punch on a T10 card. A *telefèric* (cable car) then takes you up to Montjuïc Castle. In winter the telefèric runs weekends and holidays 11–2:45 and 4–7:30; in summer, daily 11:30–9. The fare is €3.

A Transbordador Aeri del Port (Harbor Cable Car) runs between Miramar and Montjuïc across the harbor to Torre de Jaume I, on Barcelona's *moll* (quay), and on to Torre de Sant Sebastià, at the end of Passeig Joan de Borbó in Barceloneta. You can board at either stage. The fare is €7 round-trip, and the car runs October–June, weekdays noon–5:45, weekends noon–6:15, and July–September, daily 11–9.

To reach the summit of Tibidabo, take the metro to Avinguda de Tibidabo, then the Tramvía Blau (€2 one-way) to Peu del Funicular, and finally the Tibidabo Funicular (€3 one-way) from there to the Tibidabo fairground. It runs every 30 minutes, 7:05 AM–9:35 PM ascending, 7:25 AM–9:55 PM descending.

# BY CAR

Major routes throughout Spain bear heavy traffic, especially in peak holiday periods, so be extremely cautious. Spain's roads are shared by a mixture of local drivers, Moroccan immigrants traveling between northern Europe and northern Africa, and non-Spanish travelers on vacation, some of whom are more accustomed to driving on the left-hand side of the road. Watch out, too, for heavy truck traffic on national routes. Expect many difficult parking conditions on the streets of major cities. Parking garages are common and affordable and provide added safety to your vehicle and possessions.

The country's main cities are well connected by a network of four-lane *autovías* (freeways). The letter N stands for a national route (*carretera nacional*), either four- or two-lane. An *Autopista* (AP) is a toll road. At the toll-booth plazas (the Spanish term is *peaje*; in Catalan, *peatge*), there are three systems to choose from— *Automàtic,* with machines for credit cards or coins; *Manual,* with an attendant; or *Telepago,* an automatic chip-driven system mostly used by native regulars.

### GETTING AROUND & OUT OF BARCELONA

Arriving in Barcelona by car from the north along the AP7 *autopista* (freeway) or from the west along the AP2 autopista, you will encounter signs for the *rondes* (ring roads) constructed for the 1992 Olympics. Ronda Litoral (beware, it's most prominently marked *aeroport,* which can be misleading) will take you into lower and central Barcelona along the waterfront, while Ronda de Dalt (the upper Ronda) takes you along the edge of upper Barcelona to Horta, the Bonanova, Sarrià, and Pedralbes. For the center of town, take the Ronda Litoral and look for Exit 21 (paral.lel–les rambles) or 22 (barceloneta–via laietana–hospital de mar). If you are arriving from the Pyrenees on the C1411/E9 through the Tunel del Cadí, the Tunels de Vallvidrera will place you on the upper Via Augusta next to Sarrià, Pedralbes, and La Bonanova. The Eixample and Ciutat Vella are 10–15 minutes farther if traffic is fluid.

Barcelona's main crosstown traffic arteries are the Diagonal (so called as it runs diagonally to the meridian or longitudinal line going through the city) and the midtown speedways, Carrer d'Aragó, and Gran Via de les Corts Catalanes, both cutting northeast–southwest through the heart of the city. Passeig de Gràcia, which becomes Gran de Gràcia above the Diagonal, runs all the way from Plaça de Catalunya up to Plaça Lesseps, but the main up-and-down streets, for motorists, are Balmes, Muntaner, Aribau, and Comtes d'Urgell. The general urban speed limit is 50 kph (30 mph).

Getting around Barcelona by car is generally more trouble than it's worth unless there is some compelling reason for doing so. Even then (maybe even especially), a taxi would be preferable. The *rondes* make entering and exiting the city easy, unless it's rush hour, when traffic comes to a halt. Between parking, navigating, drunk-driving patrols, and the general wear and tear of driving in the city, the subway, taxis, buses, and walking are your best bets in Barcelona.

Leaving Barcelona is not difficult. Follow signs for the *rondes,* do some advance mapping, consult with a concierge, and you're off. Follow signs for Girona and França for the Costa Brava, Girona, Figueres, and France. Follow Via Augusta and signs for Tunels de Vallvidrera or E9 and Manresa for the Tunel del Cadí and the Pyrenean Cerdanya valley. Follow the Diagonal west and then the freeway AP7 signs for Lleida, Zaragoza, Tarragona, and Valencia to leave the city headed west. Look for airport, Castelldefells, and Sitges signs for heading straight southwest down the coast for these beach points on the Costa Daurada. This C32 freeway to Sitges joins the AP7 to Tarragona and Valencia.

For travel outside Barcelona, the freeways to Girona, Figueres, Sitges, Tarragona, and Lleida are surprisingly fast. The distance to Girona, 97 km (58 mi), is a 45-minute shot. The French border is an hour away. Perpignan is, at 188 km (113 mi), an hour and 20 minutes.

### GASOLINE

Gas stations are plentiful and often open 24 hours, especially around Barcelona's *rondas* (ring roads). Most stations are self-service, though prices are the same as those at full-service stations. At the tank, punch in the amount of gas you want (in euros, not in liters), unhook the nozzle, pump the gas, and then pay. At night, however, you must pay before you fill up. Most pumps offer a choice of gas, including leaded, unleaded, and diesel, so be careful to pick the right one for your car. All cars in Spain use unleaded gas (*gasolina sin plomo*), which is available in two grades, 95 and 98 octane. Prices per liter vary little between stations: €1.12 for *sin plomo* (unleaded; 95 octane); and €1.17 for unleaded, 98 octane. Diesel fuel, known as *gas-oleo*, is €1.03 a liter and, what's more, gets you 50% farther per liter, so renting a car with a diesel engine will save you major fuel money. Credit cards are widely accepted. For a receipt, which you will always receive with a credit-card purchase, ask for a *recibo* in Spanish or, in Catalan, a *rebut*.

## PARKING

Barcelona's underground parking lots (posted PARKING and symbolized by a white P on a blue background) are generally more than adequate to allow you to safely and conveniently park near your in-city destination. Garage prices vary; expect close to €2.40 an hour and €25–€38 per 24-hour day. The Diagonal Mar in the Fòrum at the east end of Avinguda Diagonal offers eight-day underground parking for €40. Airport Parking runs from €1.50 up to two hours to €12 per day for more than four days (€15 up to four days).

Barcelona's street-parking system runs 9 AM–2 PM and 4 PM–8 PM (with on-call attendants) weekdays and all day Saturday. Park in the specially marked blue spaces (about €2.30 per hour), with tickets valid for one, two, or three hours (€3.90), but renewable every half hour for €0.65. The ticket must be displayed on the front dashboard. On the streets, do not park where the pavement edge is yellow or where there is a private entry (*gual* or *vado*). No-parking signs, "1–15" or "15–30," signify you can park on those dates in the month on the side of the street where indicated. Towing is common. Whenever you feel you have found a lucky free parking spot, be alert for triangular yellow stickers on the pavement that indicate a tow-away zone. If your car is towed in Barcelona, you will find one of these yellow stickers, with the address of the municipal car deposit where your vehicle now resides, on the pavement where you left your car. A taxi will know where to take you to get it back. Costs are presently €142, plus the fine for the parking infraction (fines range €30–€90), reduced by half if you pay the same day, and car storage by the hour (€1.85 per hour or €18.50 per day). To avoid risking this annoying and expensive catastrophe, park in a parking lot or garage. If your car is towed in Bilbao, contact the *ayuntamiento*, or town hall.

**Towing Contact Information Barcelona** (☎901/513151). **Bilbao Ayuntamiento (Town Hall)** (☎94/424–1700).

## ROAD CONDITIONS

You can reach all major cities and destinations by high-speed *autopistas*, two- and three-lane freeways where 140 kph (84 mph) is a normal cruising speed. Tolls are steep, sometimes as high as €20, but these freeways are spectacular touring tracks with terrific views of the countryside (billboards are prohibited), *and* they make the Iberian Peninsula into a very small piece of geography. Once you are off these major roads, all bets are off. Trucks can hold up long lines of traffic, and averaging 60 kph (36 mph) can be challenging. Still, the scenery, by and large remains superb.

Traffic jams (*atascos*) can be a problem in and around Barcelona, where the *rondas* (ring roads) slow to a standstill at peak hours. If possible, avoid the rush hours, which can last from 8 AM until 9:30 AM and 7 PM to 9 PM.

Long weekends, called *puentes* (literally, bridges), particularly on Friday, routinely provoke delays leaving Barcelona. Avoiding the *rondas* in favor of the Tunels de Vallvidrera (straight out Via Augusta) can save time if you're headed north. Most of Barcelona vacations during August, so if you're hitting the road at the beginning or end of this month, you'll likely encounter lots of traffic, particularly on the roads heading up or down the coast.

### ROADSIDE EMERGENCIES

The rental agencies Hertz and Avis have 24-hour breakdown service. If you belong to an auto club (AAA or CAA), you can get emergency assistance from their Catalan counterpart, the Reial Automovil Club de Catalunya (RACC), or the Spanish branch Real Automovil Club de España (RACE). There are emergency telephones on all autopistas, every 2 km (1 mi), with service stations generally found every 40 km (25 mi). Traveling with a European cell phone is essential for safety and convenience, keeping in mind that coverage in the mountains is erratic.

If your rented car breaks down, be especially wary of anyone who stops to help you on the road: highway robbery has been known to be all too literal here on occasion, as bands of thieves puncture tires and steal belongings (nearly always on toll and freeways, sometimes at knife or gun point) while pretending to offer assistance.

**Emergency Services** **Real Automovil Club de Catalunya** (RACC ⊠ Diagonal 687, Barcelona ☎ 93/495–5000, 902/106106 for emergency aid ⊕ www.racc.es). **Real Automovil Club de España** (RACE ⊠ Muntaner 81-bajo, Barcelona ☎ 93/451–1551, 902/300505 for emergency aid ⊕ www.race.com).

### RULES OF THE ROAD

In Spain, motorists drive on the right. Horns are banned in cities, but that doesn't seem to keep irate drivers from blasting away. Children under 10 may not ride in the front seat, and seat belts are compulsory. Speed limits are 50 kph (31 mph) in cities; 100 kph (62 mph) on N roads; 120 kph (74 mph) on the *autopistas* (toll highways) and *autovías* (freeways); and, unless otherwise signposted, 90 kph (56 mph) on other roads, such as *carreteras nacionales* (main roads) and *carreteras comarcales* (secondary roads). Despite the law of the land, routine cruising speed on Spanish freeways is 140 kph (84 mph) or more. If you drive at the official speed limit of 120 kph (72 mph), you seriously risk high-speed rear-ending, so beware of the left lane.

Right turns on red are not permitted. In the cities, people are more often stopped for petty rule-breaking such as crossing a solid line or doing a U-turn than for speeding. However, Spanish highway police are especially vigilant regarding speeding and illegal passing, generally interpreted as crossing the solid line; fines start at €100 and, in the case of foreign drivers, police are empowered to demand payment on the spot. Beware of unclear directions on road signs. Indications are often confusing or insufficient.

On freeway ramps, expect to come to a full stop at the red stop (not yield) triangle at the end of the on-ramp and wait for a break in the traffic; expect no merging to the left lane, especially from trucks, which, by law, must remain in the right lane. Remember that motorists ahead of you in a traffic circle or roundabout have the right of way.

Drunk-driving tests are becoming more prevalent. It is illegal to drive with alcohol levels that exceed 0.5% BAC (blood alcohol count) or 0.25 on a breath test; this is about three medium-size glasses of wine or three beers for a man of average height and weight, but it's best to be cautious. Fines vary from one region of Spain to another.

# ▌ BY METRO

In Barcelona, the underground metro, or subway, is the fastest, cheapest, and easiest way to get around. Lines 2, 3, and 5 run weekdays 5 AM–midnight. Lines 1 and 4 close at 11. On Friday, Saturday, and holiday evenings all trains run 24 hours. The FGC trains run 5 AM–12:30 AM on weekdays and all night on weekends and the eves of holidays. Sunday trains run on weekday schedules.

When switching from the metro line to the FGC (or vice-versa), merely insert the card through the slot and the turnstile will open without charging you for a second ride provided less than an hour has elapsed since you punched in initially. Maps showing bus and metro routes are available free from booths in the Plaça de Catalunya.

| TICKET/<br>PASS | PRICE |
|---|---|
| Single Fare | €1.30 |
| 10-Ride Pass | €7 |

# ▌ BY TAXI

In Barcelona, taxis are black and yellow and show a green rooftop light on the front right corner when available for hire. The meter currently starts at €1.85 (€1.95 at night) and rises in increments of €0.10 every 100 meters. These rates apply 6 AM–10 PM weekdays. At hours outside of these, the rates rise 20%. There are official supplements of €1 per bag for luggage.

Trips from a train station or to the airport entail a supplemental charge of €2.50, as do trips to or from the bullring or a football match. There are cabstands (*parades,* in Catalan) all over town, and you can also hail cabs on the street, though if you are too close to an official stand they may not stop. You can call for a cab 24 hours a day. Drivers do not expect a tip, though rounding up in their favor is the norm.

---

TAXI TRAVEL

■ The Rambla can be a tricky place to find a taxi at night, and the taxi stand at Plaça Catalunya at the top of the Rambla is often a lengthy queue. Solutions: Plaça Sant Jaume is a nocturnal taxi hub with frequent arrivals of taxis. Another tactic is to walk up Rambla Catalunya, where a taxi will generally materialize.

■ Trying to make it to an evening concert at L'Auditori is best achieved by subway, or, even better, by tramway from the Ciutadella-Vil.la Olímpica stop, as rush-hour traffic slows down normal surface travel.

■ To get to Camp Nou soccer stadium for a Barça game while avoiding snail-like taxi or sardinelike subway transport, take the tramway from Plaça Francesc Macià to

---

**Taxi Companies Barna Taxi** (☎93/357–7755). **Cooperativa Radio-Taxi Metropolitana Barcelona** (☎93/225–0000). **Radio Taxi** (☎93/303–3033). **Taxi Class Rent** (☎93/307–0707). **Teocar Mercedes** (☎93/308–8434).

# ▌ BY TRAIN

International overnight trains to Barcelona arrive from many European cities, including Paris, Grenoble, Geneva, Zurich, and Milan; the route from Paris takes 11½ hours. Almost all long-distance trains arrive at and depart from Estació de Sants, though many make a stop at Passeig de Gràcia that comes in handy for hotels in the Eixample, such as the Majestic or the Condes de Barcelona, or hotels in the Ciutat Vella, such as the Regencia Colon or the Neri. The Estació de França, near the port, handles only a few regional trains within Catalonia. Train service connects Barcelona with most other major cities in Spain; in addition a high-speed Euromed route connects Barcelona to Tarragona and Valencia.

Spain's intercity services (along with some of Barcelona's *rodalies,* or local train routes) are handled by the government-run railroad system—RENFE (Red Nacional de Ferrocarriles Españoles). The high-speed AVE trains connect Lleida and Madrid and are scheduled to Barcelona sometime during 2008. The fast TALGO and ALTARIA trains are efficient, though local trains remain slow and tedious. In addition to RENFE, the Catalan government's FGC (Ferrocarril de la Generalitat de Catalunya) also provides train service, notably to Barcelona's commuter suburbs of Sant Cugat, Terrassa, and Sabadell. Commuter trains and many long-distance trains forbid smoking, though some long-distance trains have smoking cars.

Information on the local/commuter lines (*rodalies* in Catalan, *cercanias* in Spanish) can be found at www.renfe.es/cercanias. Rodalies goes to, for example, Sitges from Barcelona, whereas you would take a regular RENFE train to, say, Tarragona. It's important to know whether you are traveling RENFE or rodalies, distinguished by a stylized C, so you don't end up in the wrong line.

Both Catalonia and the Basque Country offer scenic railroad excursions. Particularly eye-catching is the train journey south of Barcelona, toward Sitges and Tarragona and on to Valencia, with its views of the Costa Daurada's craggy coastline. The day train from Barcelona to Madrid runs through bougainvillea-choked towns before leaping out across Spain's central Meseta to Zaragoza and Madrid, arriving in under five hours. This train departs every two hours from 7:30 AM to 6:30 PM and costs €65.80 one way, €95 round-trip. The train from Barcelona's Plaça Catalunya north to Sant Pol de Mar and Blanes runs along the edge of the beach.

First-class train service in Spain, with the exception of the *coche-cama* (Pullman) overnight service, barely differs from second class or *turista*. First-class trains, on the other hand, such as the TALGO or the AVE, are wildly faster than second-class carriers such as the slow-poke Estrella overnight from Barcelona to Madrid. Legroom and general comforts are about the same (that is, mediocre). The AVE is the exception, however. Between Lleida and Madrid (for the moment), or between Madrid and Sevilla, these sleek bullets with their tinted windows are superlative moving observation platforms.

After buses, trains are the most economical way to travel. Within the RENFE pricing system, there are 20% discounts on long-distance tickets if you buy a round-trip ticket, and there are 20% discounts for students and senior citizens (though they usually have to carry cards issued by the local government, the Generalitat, so they are not intended for tourists).

If you're planning extensive train travel, look into rail passes. If Spain is your only destination, consider a Spain Flexipass. Prices begin at U.S. $197 for three days of second-class travel within a two-month period and $253 for first class. Other passes cover more days and longer periods. The 10-day pass costs $427 in second class, $529 in first class.

Spain is one of 17 European countries in which you can use Eurailpasses, which buy you unlimited first-class rail travel in all participating countries for the duration of the pass. If you plan to rack up the miles, get a standard pass; these are available for 15 days ($675), 21 days ($877), one month ($1,085), two months ($1,538), and 3 months ($1,898). Eurail passes are also available for 10 days of travel over two months ($799) or for 15 days over two months ($1,050). If your needs are more limited, look into a Europass, which costs less than a Eurailpass and buys you a limited number of travel days, in a limited number of countries (France, Germany, Italy, Spain, and Switzerland), during a specified time period.

In addition to standard Eurailpasses, Rail Europe sells the Eurail Youthpass (for those under age 26), the Eurail Saverpass (which gives a discount for two or more people traveling together), a Eurail Flexipass (which allows a certain number of travel days within a set period), the Euraildrive Pass (4 days of train travel and 2 days of Avis or Hertz car rental), and the Europass Drive (which combines 3 days travel by train and 2 by rental car). Whichever pass you choose, remember that you must buy your pass before you leave for Europe.

Many travelers assume that rail passes guarantee them seats on the trains they wish to ride. Not so: you need to reserve seats in advance even if you're using a rail pass. Seat reservations are required on some European trains, particularly high-speed trains, and are wise on any train that might be crowded. You'll also need a reservation if you want sleeping accommodations.

For schedules and fares, call RENFE. The easiest way for non–Spanish speakers to obtain schedule information is to go the RENFE Web site, which has an English-language version (www.renfe.es/ingles).

Train services to Barcelona from the United Kingdom are not as frequent, fast, or affordable as flights, and you have to change trains (and stations) in Paris. From Paris, it's worth paying extra for a TALGO express to avoid having to change trains again at the Spanish border. Journey time to Paris (from London via Eurostar through the Channel Tunnel) is around three hours; from Paris to Barcelona, it's an additional seven hours. Allow at least two hours in Paris for changing trains.

Although overnight trains have comfortable sleeper cars for two or four in coche-cama class, first-class fares that include a sleeping compartment are comparable to airfares.

An overnight train from Barcelona to Madrid takes eight hours. A tourist-class seat costs €38.30. A bunk in a compartment with three other people, called *clase turista damas-caballeros* (tourist class), separates travelers by gender and costs €49.20, but the windows do not open and the heat can be suffocating. The air shuttle (or a scheduled flight) between Madrid and Barcelona can, if all goes well, get you door to door in under three hours for only about €40 more than the overnight train costs, and certain off-hour flights are available for as low as €20.

For shorter, regional train trips, you can often buy your tickets directly from machines in the main train stations. For a one-way ticket, ask for, in Catalan, *anada* (in Spanish it's *ida*) ; or for a round-trip ticket, *anada i tornada*. In Castilian, it's *ida y vuelta*.

Most travel agencies can sell you train tickets (though not for same-day travel), which saves standing in long lines at the station *taquilla* (ticket office). In Barcelona, a handy secret is the Passeig de Gràcia ticket office, where there is rarely a line. Lines at Sants can be long, though, with a separate line (marked *salida inmediata*), where same-day tickets can be obtained more quickly.

Visa and MasterCard are universally accepted at train-station ticket counters.

During peak travel times (Easter, August, and Christmas), it's important to make a reservation weeks or even months in advance; on routes between major cities (Barcelona to Bilbao or Madrid, for example), it's a good idea to reserve well in advance, especially for overnight trips. You can reserve over the phone by calling RENFE, by Internet, or, for the cyber-challenged, by waiting at the station ticket counter, preferably in Barcelona's Passeig de Gràcia, where lines are shorter or nonexistent.

The easiest way to make reservations is to use the TIKNET service on the

RENFE Web site. TIKNET involves registering and providing your credit card information. When you make the reservation, you will be given a car and seat assignment and a *localizador* (translated as "localizer" on the English version of the site). Print out the reservations page or write down car number, seat number, and localizer. When traveling, go to your assigned seat on the train. When the conductor comes round, give him the localizer, and he will issue the ticket on the spot. You will need your passport and, in most cases, the credit card you used for the reservation. The AVE trains check you in at the gate to the platform, where you provide the localizer. You can review your pending reservations online at any time.

Caveats: The first time you use TIKNET, you must pick up the tickets at a RENFE station; you can go to a RENFE booth at the airport as you get off your plane. A 15% cancellation fee is charged if you cancel more than two hours after making the reservation. You cannot buy tickets online for certain regional lines or for commuter lines (*cercanias*). Station agents cannot alter TIKNET reservations: you must do this yourself online. If a train is booked, the TIKNET process doesn't reveal this until the final stage of the reservation attempt. Then it gives you a cryptic error message in a little box, though if you reserve a few days in advance, it's unlikely you'll encounter this problem except at Easter, Christmas, or the first week of August.

There is no line per se at the train station for advance tickets (and often for information); you take a number and wait until it is called. Ticket clerks at stations rarely speak English, so if you need help or advice in planning a more complex train journey, you may be better off going to a travel agency that displays the blue-and-yellow RENFE sign. A small commission (American Express Viajes charges €3.50) should be expected.

**General Information Estació de França** (⊠ Marquès de l'Argentera s/n, Born-Ribera). **Estació de Sants** (⊠ Pl. dels Països Catalans s/n, Eixample). **Estació de Passeig de Gràcia** (⊠ Passeig de Gràcia at corner of Carrer Aragó, Eixample). **Ferrocarrils de la Generalitat de Catalunya (FGC)** (☎ 93/205–1515 ⊕ www.fgc.es). **RENFE** (☎ 902/240202 ⊕ www.renfe.es).

**Information & Passes CIT Tours Corp.** (⊠ 342 Madison Ave., Suite 207, New York, NY 10173 ☎ 212/697–2100, 800/248–8687, 800/248–7245 in western U.S. ⊕ www.cit-tours.com). **DER Tours** ( Box 1606, Des Plaines, IL 60017 ☎ 800/782–2424 800/282–7474). **Rail Europe** (⊠ 226–230 Westchester Ave., White Plains, NY 10604 ☎ 914/682–5172 or 800/438–7245 ⊠ 2087 Dundas E, Suite 105, Mississauga, Ontario L4X 1M2, Canada ☎ 416/602–4195 ⊕ www.raileurope.com).

**From the U.K. Eurostar** (☎ 01233/617575 or 0870/518–6186 ⊕ www.eurostar.co.uk). **National Rail Enquiries** (☎ 0845/748–4950 ⊕ www.nationalrail.co.uk). **Rail Europe** (☎ 800/942–4866 or 800/274–8724, 0870/584–8848 credit-card bookings ⊕ www.raileurope.com).

**Channel Tunnel Car Transport Eurotunnel** (☎ 0870/535–3535 in the U.K., 070/223210 in Belgium, 03–21–00–61–00 in France ⊕ www.eurotunnel.com). **French Motorail/Rail Europe** (☎ 0870/241–5415 ⊕ www.raileurope.co.uk/frenchmotorail).

**Channel Tunnel Passenger Service Eurostar** (☎ 0870/518–6186 in the U.K. ⊕ www.eurostar.co.uk). **Rail Europe** (☎ 888/382–7245 in the U.S., 0870/584–8848 in the U.K. inquiries and credit-card bookings ⊕ www.raileurope.com).

# ON THE GROUND

## ▮ COMMUNICATIONS

### INTERNET

Barcelona's largest and most convenient cyber-resource is Conundrum/Cybermundo just off Plaça Catalunya. With 70 machines available, laptop hookups, and a bar and restaurant downstairs that screens British and American sports events, this spot is open daily 9 AM–1 AM. Another, smaller solution is the art gallery–cum–Internet café bcnet, surrounded by medieval stone and offering everything from e-mail checking to video conferences until 1 AM. Idea, which also has a bookstore, is a chill place for drafting e-mails.

An important piece of computer gear to pack is the adapter that translates flat-edged plugs or triple plugs to round dual ones. Most Internet cafés have no equipment to get your laptop online, but Wi-Fi technology is common throughout Barcelona. Phone jacks or dedicated computer hookups in hotel rooms allowing you to dial your server and get online are becoming obsolete.

**Computer Supplies & Services GeoMac** (☎606/308932 ✎geomac@terra.es). **Microrent** (✉Roselló 35, Eixample ☎93/363–3250 ⊕www.microrent.es ⓂSants Estació, Entença).

**Cybercafe Resources Cybercafes** (⊕www.cybercafes.com) lists more than 4,000 Internet cafés worldwide. **Bar Travel** (✉Boqueria 27, Barri Gòtic ☎93/410–8592). **bcnet** (✉Barra de Ferro 3, Born-Ribera ☎93/268–1507). **Cafe Internet Navego** (✉Provença 546, Eixample ☎93/436–8459). **Conundrum/Cybermundo** (✉Bergara 3, The Rambla ☎93/317–7142). **Idea** (✉Pl. Comercial 2, Born-Ribera ☎93/268–8787).

### PHONES

The good news is that you can now make a direct-dial telephone call from virtually any point on Earth. The bad news? You can't always do so cheaply. Calling from a hotel is almost always the most expensive option; hotels usually add huge surcharges to all calls, particularly international ones. In some countries you can phone from call centers or even the post office. Calling cards usually keep costs to a minimum, but only if you purchase them locally. And then there are mobile phones (⇨*below*), which are sometimes more prevalent—particularly in the developing world—than land lines; as expensive as mobile phone calls can be, they are still usually a much cheaper option than calling from your hotel.

The country code for Spain is 34. To phone home from Spain, 00 gets you an international line; country codes are 1 for the United States and Canada, 61 for Australia, 64 for New Zealand, and 44 for the United Kingdom.

### CALLING WITHIN SPAIN

Spain's telephone system is efficient, and direct dialing is the norm everywhere. Only cell phones conforming to the European GSM standard will work in Spain.

All Spanish area codes begin with a 9; for instance, Barcelona is 93 and Bilbao is 94. The 900 code indicates a toll-free number. Numbers starting with a 6 indicate a cellular phone; note that calls to cell phones are significantly more expensive.

For general information in Spain, dial 1–18–18. The operator for international information and assistance is at 1–18–25 (some operators speak English). Barcelona information of all kinds, including telephone information, is available by dialing 010, where many operators speak English.

Calls within Spain require dialing 8, 9, or 10 digits (beginning with a 2- or 3-digit regional code), even within the same area code.

Making a long-distance call within Spain simply requires dialing the 8, 9, or 10-

## CON OR CONCIERGE?

Good hotel concierges are invaluable—for arranging transportation, getting reservations at the hottest restaurant, and scoring tickets for a sold-out show or entrée to an exclusive nightclub. They're in the know and well connected. That said, sometimes you have to take their advice with a grain of salt.

It's not uncommon for restaurants to ply concierges with free food and drink in exchange for steering diners their way. Indeed, European concierges often receive referral *fees*. Hotel chains usually have guidelines about what their concierges can accept. The best concierges, however, are above reproach. This is particularly true of those who belong to the prestigious international society of Les Clefs d'Or.

What can you expect of a concierge? At a typical tourist-class hotel you can expect him or her to give you the basics: to show you something on a map, make a standard restaurant reservation (particularly if you don't speak the language), or help you book a tour or airport transportation. In Asia concierges perform the vital service of writing out the name or address of your destination for you to give to a cab driver.

Savvy concierges at the finest hotels and resorts, can arrange for just about any good or service imaginable—and do so quickly. You should compensate them appropriately. A $10 tip is enough to show appreciation for a table at a hot restaurant. But the reward should really be much greater for tickets to that U2 concert that's been sold out for months or for those last-minute sixth-row-center seats for *The Lion King*.

digit number including the provincial area code and number.

Between phone booths in the street (ask for a *cabina telefónica*) and public phones in bars and restaurants, telephone communication in Spain functions as well as anyplace in the world. Many phones have digital readout screens, so you can see your money ticking away. If using coins, you need at least €0.30 for a local call, €0.50 to call another province. Pick up the phone, wait for the dial tone, and only then insert coins before dialing. Rates are reduced on weekends and after 8 PM on weekdays.

### CALLING OUTSIDE SPAIN

International calls are easiest from public pay phones using a phone card. Calls from hotels can be expensive, as they generally add a surcharge. The best way to phone home is to use a public phone that accepts phone cards (available from tobacconists and most newsagents) or go to the local telephone office or *locutorio*, a phone center, of which there many in Barcelona, and several in Bilbao. The best thing about the locutorio is the quiet, private booth. If the call costs over €5, you can often pay with Visa or MasterCard.

To make an international call yourself, dial 00, then the country code, then the area code and number. Ask at a tourist office for a list of locutorios and Internet centers that include phone service.

Before you go, find out your long-distance company's access code in Spain.

**Access Codes AT&T** (☎900/990011). **MCI WorldPhone** (☎900/990014). **Sprint International Access** (☎900/990013).

### CALLING CARDS

Pay phones work with a variety of phone cards (*tarjeta telefónica*), which you can buy at any tobacco shop or newsagent for €8 or €15.

## MOBILE PHONES

If you have a multiband phone (some countries use different frequencies from what's used in the United States) and your service provider uses the world-standard GSM network (as do T-Mobile, Cingular, and Verizon), you can probably use your phone abroad. Roaming fees can be steep, however: 99¢ a minute is considered reasonable. And overseas you normally pay the toll charges for incoming calls. It's almost always cheaper to send a text message than to make a call, since text messages have a very low set fee (often less than 5¢).

If you just want to make local calls, consider buying a new SIM card (note that your provider may have to unlock your phone for you to use a different SIM card) and a prepaid service plan in the destination. You'll then have a local number and can make local calls at local rates. If your trip is extensive, you could also simply buy a new cell phone in your destination, as the initial cost will be offset over time.

■**TIP**➔**If you travel internationally frequently, save one of your old mobile phones or buy a cheap one on the Internet; ask your cell phone company to unlock it for you, and take it with you as a travel phone, buying a new SIM card with pay-as-you-go service in each destination.**

**Cell Phone Rentals Rentaphone Taxi** (☎93/280–2131). **Telecon Iberica** (☎93/228–9110). **Telenisa** (☎93/414–1966). **Walkie Talkie** (☎93/238–0360).

**Contacts Cellular Abroad** (☎800/287–5072 ⊕www.cellularabroad.com) rents and sells GMS phones and sells SIM cards that work in many countries. **Mobal** (☎888/888–9162 ⊕www.mobalrental.com) rents mobiles and sells GSM phones (starting at $49) that will operate in 140 countries. Per-call rates vary throughout the world. **Planet Fone** (☎888/988–4777 ⊕www.planetfone.com) rents cell phones, but the per-minute rates are expensive.

## ■ CUSTOMS & DUTIES

You're always allowed to bring goods of a certain value back home without having to pay any duty or import tax. But there's a limit on the amount of tobacco and liquor you can bring back duty-free, and some countries have separate limits for perfumes; for exact figures, check with your customs department. The values of so-called "duty-free" goods are included in these amounts. When you shop abroad, save all your receipts, as customs inspectors may ask to see them as well as the items you purchased. If the total value of your goods is more than the duty-free limit, you'll have to pay a tax (most often a flat percentage) on the value of everything beyond that limit.

From countries that are not part of the European Union, visitors age 18 and over are permitted to bring into Spain duty free up to 200 cigarettes or 50 cigars, up to 1 liter of alcohol over 22 proof, and up to 2 liters of wine. Dogs and cats are admitted as long as they have up-to-date vaccination records from their home country. Visitors to Spain may bring in up to $10,000 in cash without having to declare it. The Web site www.spain.info has helpful information in its "Practical info" section.

**Information in Spain Administración de Aduanas del Aeropuerto de Barcelona** (✉El Prat de Llobregat, Barcelona ☎93/379–6451 ≞93/379–5492)

**U.S. Information U.S. Customs and Border Protection** (⊕www.cbp.gov).

## ■ DAY TOURS & GUIDES

### ART TOURS

The Ruta del Modernisme (Moderniste Route), a self-guided tour, provides an excellent guidebook (available in English) that interprets 100 Moderniste sites from the Sagrada Família and the Palau de la Música Catalana to Art Nouveau building facades, lampposts, and paving

# LOCAL DO'S & TABOOS

## CUSTOMS OF THE COUNTRY

Both Catalans and Basques are very tolerant of foreign visitors, but it always helps to be mindful of being polite yourself. Be respectful when visiting churches: casual dress is all right, as long as it is not too gaudy, unkempt, or skimpy. Bare-chested men other than at the beach or swimming pool are considered offensive, as are public displays of drunkenness.

When lining up at a bakery or a pharmacy or at a stall in the Boqueria, where lines or queues are not uncommon, it is customary to check by asking for "la tanda" (your turn) by saying "l'ultim, si us plau" (the last person in line, please). Whoever is last in line identifies him or herself and you officially become the last person in the line until the next person comes in and asks who's last, to which you respond, "Soc jo," thus passing the *tanda,* or turn, on to the next customer. If you fail to speak up, the tanda may be passed on by you, though normally everyone in the line recognizes that, as a foreigner, you may not be up to speed on this Catalan idiosyncrasy. More and more, little machines with small numbered tickets are replacing this custom, so look around for the tanda machine if you see people holding little slips of paper in their hands.

On trains and subways, putting your feet, with or without shoes, on the empty seat in front of you will invariably convert the tolerant, peace-loving local passenger into a fire-breathing defender of tidiness, good manners, law and order, and Western civilization in general.

## GREETINGS

When addressing people you are not well acquainted with, especially in formal or service situations, as with taxi drivers or waiters, use *usted,* the formal "you," rather than the familiar *tu.* When meeting people for the first time, it is appropriate to shake hands. Women often exchange kisses on each cheek when meeting men or other women.

## DOING BUSINESS

Catalans joke about how the only consistently late businesspeople they know are the British (the subtext being that the Briton, thinking he is in laid-back, sleepy Spain, doesn't bother to show up on time). This image of Spain is dated, and was probably never true for Catalonia anyway, where worship of the almighty euro keeps them hard at work and on time. In general, Europeans—and this includes the Catalans and the Spanish—consider it crass to "cut to the chase." The reigning philosophy is that, first we get to know each other, and then we might do business together. So the eating and drinking, wining and dining part of the transaction, far from a waste of time, is the most important part of the business encounter; because if you flunk that part, the deal's not happening no matter what conditions are offered.

Generally, the host pays, so if you are visiting Barcelona, it might seem arrogant to usurp the bill the first time out. Spouses are welcome unless otherwise indicated. Dress ranges from formal to elegant casual.

## LANGUAGE

Try to learn a little of the local language. You need not strive for fluency; even just mastering a few basic words and terms is bound to make chatting with the locals more rewarding.

Though Spain exported its language to most of Central and South America, Spanish is not the principal language in all of Spain. In Catalonia, you'll hear Catalan, while the Basques speak Euskera. Franco, in an attempt to foment Spanish nationalism over regional separatism, outlawed all these local languages and dialects in 1939. After Franco's death in 1975, a renaissance of Catalan language and literature began in Catalonia, and similar movements have gathered momentum in other regions. Catalans are proud of their language, which is heard and used everywhere.

In Bilbao you will hear Euskera, the Basque language, and signs are in Spanish and Euskera, but Euskera is less prevalent than Spanish in the city.

Although Barcelona, for the most part, is bilingual, many natives—even the proud *catalanoparlants*—read their newspapers and novels in Castilian Spanish. Of the city's five newspapers, three are published in Spanish, two in Catalan; however, the Spanish papers publish some 2 million copies, while the Catalan ones publish only about 300,000. When it comes to speaking, however, Catalans prefer their native language—local radio and television stations may broadcast in both Catalan and Spanish. Road signs are uniformly in Catalan. Spanish is referred to as Castellano (Castilian Spanish).

Fortunately, both Catalans and Basques speak Spanish, which is fairly straightforward and relatively easy to pick up. If your Spanish breaks down, you should have no trouble finding people who speak English in major cities and coastal resorts, but you won't necessarily be able to count on the bus driver or the passerby on the street. Those who do speak English may speak the British variety, so don't be surprised if you're told to queue (line up) or take the lift (elevator) to the loo (toilet). Most guided tours offered at museums and historic sites in Barcelona are in Catalan; ask about the language that will be spoken before signing up. Both in Catalonia and the Basque Country, any effort at all to speak the local language will be ecstatically received and applauded as a sign that you know where you are and what culture you are visiting.

A phrase book and language-tape set can help get you started. *Fodor's Spanish for Travelers* (available at bookstores everywhere) is excellent.

Catalan and Spanish are the official languages in Catalunya and both are used at the Universitat Autonom de Barcelona. Many subjects are taught both in Spanish and Catalan. The "Servei d'Idiomes" of the UAB offers Spanish and Catalan classes including initial intensive courses and maintenance classes during the year. Erasmus students can follow intensive courses in Catalan, free of charge.

A number of private schools offer Spanish courses for foreigners. Don Quijote is one network with schools in several locations around Spain. The international network Inlingua has 30 schools in Spain. Some Spanish universities, including that of Barcelona, have Spanish study programs, but these are over longer periods, usually two months or more. The state-run Cervantes Institute, devoted to promoting the Spanish language, organizes courses at its centers worldwide and can provide information on courses in Spain.

Language Study Programs **Cervantes Institute** ( ✉ *122 E. 42nd St., Suite 807, New York, NY 10168* ☎ *212/689–4232* ⊕ *www. cervantes.es*). **Don Quijote** ( ✉ *Calle Placentinos 2, Salamanca 37998* ☎ *923/268860* ⊕ *www.donquijote.org*). **Inlingua International** ( ✉ *Belpstrasse 11, Berne CH-3007, Switzerland* ☎ *4131/388–7777, 902/190468 in Barcelona* 🖷 *93/301–4352 in Barcelona* ✐ *inlingua.barcelona@ilingua.com* ⊕ *www. inlingua.com*). **Universitat Autonoma de Barcelona. Facultat de Traducció i d'interpretació** (*UAB* ✉ *Edifici M, Suite 807, Bellaterra, Barcelona 08193* ☎ *93/581–1374* 🖷 *93/581–1037*).

stones. Tickets (books of coupons valid for a year) and manuals are sold at the Plaça Catalunya Tourist Office, Pavellons Güell, and Hospital de Sant Pau.

The Palau de la Música Catalana offers guided tours in English every hour on the hour from 10 to 3. Sagrada Família guided tours cost extra. Casa Milà offers one guided tour daily (6 PM weekdays, 11 AM weekends). The ticket price, €15, gets you 50% discounts at numerous sites around town, as well as free guided tours (in English at specified hours) at Pavellons Güell, Hospital de Sant Pau, and the Manzana de la Discòrdia (at 11,12,1, 2:30, and 5).

Contact **Centre del Modernisme, Centre d'Informació de Turisme de Barcelona** ( ⊠ Pl. Catalunya, 17, soterrani, The Rambla). **Centre del Modernisme, Hospital de la Santa Creu i Sant Pau** ( ⊠ C. Sant Antoni Maria Claret, 167, Eixample). **Centre del Modernisme, Pavellons Güell** ( ⊠ Av. de Pedralbes 7, Pedralbes ☎(+34) 902/076621 ✉cultura-impuqv@bcn.cat).

**Centre d'Informació de Turisme de Barcelona** ( ⊠ Pl. Catalunya 17, soterrani, Eixample ☎93/488-0139).

**BOAT TOURS**

Golondrina harbor boats make short trips from the Portal de la Pau, near the Columbus monument. The fare is €7 for a 90-minute ride out past the beaches, half that for a 30-minute harbor ride. Departures are spring and summer (Easter week–September), daily 11–7; fall and winter, weekends and holidays only, 11–5. It's closed mid-December–early January. There is also a longer excursion in a glass-bottomed catamaran (Trimar y Ómnibus) that parallels the coast up to the Platja del Bogatell east of Barcelona's Olympic Port. Depending on the weather, the catamarans (€9 per person) leave every hour on the half hour 11:30–5:30 (6:30 Easter week–September).

Fees & Schedules **Las Golondrinas and Trimar y Ómnibus** ( ⊠ Plaza Portal de la Pau 1, Rambla ☎93/442-3106 Ⓜ Drassanes).

**BUS TOURS**

The Bus Turístic (9:30–7:30 every 10 to 30 minutes, depending on the season), sponsored by the tourist office, runs on three circuits that pass all the important sights. One covers upper Barcelona; another tours lower Barcelona; and a third runs from the Olympic Port to the Fòrum at the eastern end of the Diagonal. A day's ticket, which you can buy on the bus, costs €16 (a two-day ticket is €20) and also covers the fare for the Tramvía Blau, funicular, and Montjuïc cable car across the port. You receive a booklet with discount vouchers for various attractions. Rides for Buses 1 and 2 start at Plaça de Catalunya; Bus 3 starts at the Olympic Port. Each bus stops a dozen times, allowing visitors to jump off and catch the next bus after visiting each monument. A live narrator explains the sites and monuments. Julià Tours and Pullmantur run day and half-day excursions outside the city. The most popular trips are those to Montserrat and the Costa Brava resorts, the latter including a cruise to the Medes Isles.

Contacts **Bus Turístic** ( ☎93/368-9700 ⊕www.barcelonaturisme.com). **Julià Tours** ( ⊠ Ronda Universitat 5, Eixample ☎93/317-6454). **Pullmantur** ( ⊠ Gran Via 645, Eixample ☎93/317-1297).

**HELICOPTER TOURS**

Baló Tours S.L. runs balloon and helicopter tours in and around Barcelona. Cat Helicopters circles Barcelona for €70 per person for 10 minutes, €210 for 30 minutes.

Fees & Schedules **Baló Tours S.L.** ( ⊠ Montecassino 2, Eixample, 08006 ☎93/414-4774 ☎93/200-0588 ⊕www.balotour.com). **Cat Helicopters** ( ☎93/224-0710 ⊕www.cathelicopters.com).

## PRIVATE GUIDES

Nicholas Law of Spain Step by Step can take you on brilliantly planned and guided treks all over Spain, including walks through Barcelona, the Costa Brava, or the Catalan Pyrenees. Dominique Blinder at Urbancultours gives superb tours of Gaudí's Sagrada Família, the medieval Jewish quarter, as well as other parts of town. Guides from the other organizations listed below are generally competent and encyclopedic, though the quality of language skills and general showmanship may vary wildly. For customized tours including access to some of Barcelona's leading chefs, architects, art historians, and artists, Heritage Tours will set it all up from New York.

Contacts **Associació Professional d'Informadors Turístics** (☎93/319–8416). **Barcelona Guide Bureau** (☎93/268–2422). **City Guides Barcelona** (☎93/412–0674). **Heritage Tours** (☎800/378–4555 or 212/206–8400 in the U.S. ⊕www.heritage toursonline.com). **Spain Step by Step** (☎93/217–9395). **Urbancultours** (☎No phone ⊕www.urbancultours.com).

## WALKING TOURS

Turisme de Barcelona offers weekend walking tours of the Gothic Quarter and Picasso's Barcelona in English (at 10 AM) for €8. The Picasso tour, a real bargain, includes the entry free for the Picasso Museum (€6). Tours depart from the Plaça de Catalunya tourist office. For private tours, Julià Tours and Pullmantur *(⇨ Bus Tours)* both lead walks around Barcelona. Tours leave from their offices, but you may be able to arrange a pickup at your hotel. Prices per person are €30 for half a day and €65 for a full day, including lunch.

For the best English-language walking tour of the medieval Jewish Quarter (or Gaudí's Sagrada Família), contact Dominique Blinder at Urbancultours *(⇨ Private Guides)*.

Contact **Turisme de Barcelona** (✉Pl. de Catalunya 17 bis, La Rambla 99, Eixample ☎807/117222 ⊕www.barcelonaturisme.com).

# ▌ELECTRICITY

The electrical current in Spain is 220 volts, 50 cycles alternating current (AC); wall outlets take continental-type plugs, with two round prongs. An adapter from flat to round prongs is a must for computers and hair dryers.

Consider making a small investment in a universal adapter, which has several types of plugs in one lightweight, compact unit. Most laptops and mobile phone chargers are dual voltage (i.e., they operate equally well on 110 and 220 volts), so require only an adapter. These days the same is true of small appliances such as hair dryers. Always check labels and manufacturer instructions to be sure. Don't use 110-volt outlets marked FOR SHAVERS ONLY for high-wattage appliances such as hair dryers.

Contacts **Steve Kropla's Help for World Traveler's** (⊕www.kropla.com) has information on electrical and telephone plugs around the world. **Walkabout Travel Gear** (⊕www. walkabouttravelgear.com) has a good coverage of electricity under "adapters."

# ▌EMERGENCIES

You can expect local residents to be helpful if you have an emergency. For assistance, dial the pan-European emergency phone number 112, which is operative in northern Spain, but not all parts of Spain. Otherwise, dial the emergency numbers below for national police, local police, fire department, or medical services. On the road, there are emergency phones at frequent regular intervals on freeways (*autovías*) and toll highways (*autopistas*). They are marked S.O.S.

If your documents are stolen, contact both the police and your consulate or embassy

*(⇨below).* If you lose a credit card, phone the issuer immediately *(⇨Money).*

To find out which pharmacies are open late at night or 24 hours on a given day, look on the door of any pharmacy or in any local newspaper under *"Farmacias de Guardia"* or dial 010.

In Barcelona, Tourist Attention, a service provided by the local police department, can help if you're the victim of a crime or need medical or psychological assistance. English interpreters are on hand.

**Foreign Embassies Australia** (✉Plaza Descubridor Diegos de Ordas 3, Madrid ☎91/441-9300). **Canada** (✉Calle Nuñez de Balboa 35, Madrid ☎91/423-3250). **New Zealand** (✉Plaza Lealtad 2, Madrid ☎91/523-0226). **United Kingdom** (✉Calle Fernando el Santo 16, Madrid ☎91/319-0200). **United States** (✉Calle Serrano 75, Madrid ☎91/587-2200).

**Australia Barcelona** (✉Gran Via Carlos III 98, Les Corts ☎93/490-9013 ⊕www.embaustralia.es).

**Canada Barcelona** (✉Elisenda de Pinós, Pedralbes ☎93/204-2701 ⊕www.canada-es.org).

**New Zealand Barcelona** (✉Trav. de Gràcia 64, Gràcia ☎93/209-0399).

**United Kingdom Barcelona** (✉Av. Diagonal 477, Eixample ☎93/366-6200 ⊕www.ukinspain.com).

**United States Barcelona** (✉Passeig Reina Elisenda 23, Pedralbes ☎93/280-2227 ⊕www.embusa.es).

**General Emergency Contacts in Barcelona Ambulance** (Creu Roja ☎93/300-2020). **Dental Emergencies** (☎607/332335) **Fire department** (☎080). **Medical assistance** (☎061). **Police** (☎091 or 092 Main police station ✉Via Laietana 43, Barri Gòtic ☎93/301-6666). **Tourist Attention** (✉Guardia Urbana, Ramblas 43, Rambla ☎93/290-3440).

**Hospital Hospital Clinic** (✉Villarroel 170, Eixample ☎93/454-6000 or 93/454-7000 ⓂLine 5 (blue line) to Hospital Clinic).

**Hotlines Alcoholics Anonymous** (☎93/317-7777). **Narcotics Anonymous** (☎650/659085).

**Pharmacies 24-Hour Pharmacies** (☎010 ⊕www.farmaciesdeguardia.com).

# ▮ HEALTH

## SPECIFIC ISSUES IN BARCELONA

If you require medical attention, ask for assistance from the hotel front desk or go to the nearest public Centro de Salud (day hospital). For serious cases, you will be referred to the regional hospital. Medical care is good in Spain, but nursing is perfunctory: here relatives are expected to look after patients' needs while in the hospital.

Sunburn and sunstroke are real risks in summer. On the hottest sunny days, even those who are not normally bothered by strong sun should cover themselves up; apply sunblock lotion; drink plenty of fluids; and limit sun time for the first few days. It is safe to drink tap water all over Catalonia, the Basque Country, and throughout Spain.

## OVER-THE-COUNTER REMEDIES

Over-the-counter remedies are available at pharmacies *(farmacias).* Some names will be familiar, such as aspirin *(aspirina),* while other medications are sold under different brand names. If you regularly take a nonprescription medicine, take a sample box or bottle with you; the Spanish pharmacist will be able to provide you with its local equivalent. If you have a problem with diarrhea, ask for *un antidiarreico,* which is the general term for antidiarrheal medicine. Fortasec is a well-known over-the-counter brand.

You can generally buy much more potent medicine over the counter than in the United States, such as antibiotics and strong painkillers. Pharmacists are qualified to help you decide what to take if you describe your particular ailment, so in some cases a visit to a doctor can be avoided by simply asking for a good pharmacist's advice. Gelocatil is a standard (and effective) over-the-counter paracetamol-based painkiller and anti-inflammatory.

# HOURS OF OPERATION

If a public holiday falls on a Tuesday or Thursday, many businesses also close on the nearest Monday or Friday for a long weekend, called a *puente* (bridge). If a major holiday falls on a Sunday, businesses sometimes close Monday.

Banks are generally open weekdays from 8:30 or 9 to 2 or 2:30. Most banks also open on Saturday, from 8:30 or 9 to 2. From October to May, savings banks are also open Thursday afternoons 4:30–8. In summer many banks close at 2 PM weekdays and are closed Saturday. Currency exchanges at airports and train stations stay open later. Traveler's checks can also be cashed at El Corte Inglés department stores until 10 PM (some branches close at 9 PM or 9:30 PM). Most government offices are open mornings only, 9–2. ⇨ *See Mail for post-office hours.*

In major towns and on main routes, gas stations are open 24 hours a day. On less traveled routes, gas stations are usually open 7 AM–11 PM. A closed gas station is required by law to post the address of and directions to the nearest gas station that is open.

Most museums are open 9:30–2 and 4–7 and are closed one day a week, usually Monday. Opening hours vary widely, and there are often (slightly) different opening hours in summer and winter, with shorter winter hours. Several well-known sights, such as Barcelona's Picasso Museum and Sagrada Família and Bilbao's Guggenheim, do not close for the midday hours. Many churches and historic houses in smaller villages are often kept closed; to gain entrance, you need to obtain the key (*la clau*), often kept by a caretaker (in an adjacent house), at the local town hall (*ayuntamiento* in Castilian, *ajuntament* in Catalan), or even at the corner bar.

Pharmacies open normal business hours (9–1:30 and 5–8), but there is always a duty pharmacy open at other times in each city neighborhood. The location of the duty pharmacy is usually posted on the front door of neighborhood pharmacies.

When planning a shopping trip, keep in mind that almost all shops in Spain close at midday for at least three hours, except for the department-store chain El Corte Inglés and large supermarkets. Stores are generally open from 9 or 10 to 1:30 and 5–8. Most shops are closed Sunday, and in a few places they're also closed Saturday afternoon. That said, larger shops in tourist areas may stay open Sunday in summer and during the Christmas holiday.

## HOLIDAYS

Barcelona's 16 annual holidays include January 1, January 6 (Three Kings' Day, or Epiphany), Good Friday, Easter Monday, May 1 (May Day), May 16 (Pentecoste), June 24 (Saint John's feast), August 15 (Assumption), September 11 (Catalonia's National Day), September 24 (Our Lady of Mercy), October 12 (Spain's National Day), November 1 (All Saints'), December 6 (Constitution), December 8 (Immaculate Conception), December 25, and December 26 (St. Stephen's Day). April 23 (St. George), although not an official holiday, is a major annual celebration combining lovers' day and international book day.

# MAIL

The postal system in Spain, called *Correos,* does work, but delivery times can vary widely. An airmail letter to the United States may take four days to reach its destination, or it may take two weeks. Mail to the United Kingdom may range from overnight delivery to four days. Delivery to other places worldwide is equally unpredictable. Sending letters by special delivery (*urgente*) will ensure speedier delivery. Post offices are usually open 8:30–2:30 on weekdays, and 10–2 on Saturday, though hours vary. Some main post offices, including Barcelona's, which is on Plaça Antonio López, are open all day, 8:30 AM–8:30 PM Monday–Saturday, and 9–2:30 on Sunday.

Airmail letters to Australia, New Zealand, the United States, and Canada cost €0.80 up to 20 grams. Letters to the United Kingdom and other EU countries cost €0.55 up to 20 grams. Postcard rates are identical. An *urgente* (urgent) sticker costs €1.50. Letters within Spain are €0.30. Postcards carry the same rates as letters. You can buy stamps at post offices and at licensed tobacco shops.

To have mail held at the Barcelona post office, have it addressed to *Lista de Correos* (the equivalent of Poste Restante), Oficina Central de Correus i Telecomunicacions, Plaça Antonio López 1, 08002. Provincial postal addresses should include the name of the province in parentheses, e.g., Figueres (Girona). For Barcelona, this is not necessary.

Main Branches **Oficina Carrer Aragó** ( ⊠ Aragó 282, Eixample ☎ 93/216-0453 Ⓜ Passeig de Gràcia). **Oficina Central de Correus i Telecomunicacions** ( ⊠ Pl. Antonio López 1, Barri Gòtic 08002 ☎ 902/197197 ⊕ www.correos.es Ⓜ Jaume I).

SHIPPING PACKAGES

When speed is essential or when you must send valuable items or documents, you can use a courier service (*mensajero*), although it is expensive to ship items from Spain abroad, especially for overnight service. The major international agencies, such as Federal Express and UPS, have representatives in Spain, and the biggest Spanish courier service, Seur, has similar services and fees. Couriers will pick up the package at your door and can deliver

it anywhere in the world, usually within one to three days. It's best to call the day before for a next-day morning pickup. You can also drop off the package at an office. If the package is picked up before noon, it will usually arrive in New York or London the following day before 5 PM; delivery often takes another day in Australia or New Zealand. Prices vary from €20 to €60 per delivery.

Most stores, including shippers of fragile items such as ceramics or *Lladró*, will, for a price, wrap and ship purchases home. These arrangements almost invariably work out well. Depending on whether you choose surface or airmail, items may take from a week to a month. Logically, the farther away you send items, the longer it takes to get there. Sending a small package to Australia by boat should take a month, though by air it could arrive in under a week.

Express Services **DHL** ( ☎ 902/122424 ⊕ www.dhl.com). **Federal Express** ( ☎ 900/100871 ⊕ www.fedex.com). **MRW** ( ☎ 900/300400 ⊕ www.mrw.gi). **Seur** ( ☎ 902/101010 ⊕ www.seur.es). **UPS** ( ☎ 900/102410 ⊕ www.ups.com).

# ▌MONEY

Barcelona has long been Spain's most expensive city, but prices are still lower than they are an hour north across the French border. Coffee in a bar generally costs €1.30 (standing) or €1.50 (seated). Beer in a bar: €1.20 standing, €1.30 seated. Small glass of wine in a bar: around €1.50. Soft drink: €1.60–€1.80 a bottle. Ham-and-cheese sandwich: €3–€4. Two-km (1-mi) taxi ride: €4.50, but the meter keeps ticking in traffic jams. Local bus or subway ride: €1.30. Movie ticket: €7.50. Foreign newspaper: €3.50.

Prices throughout this guide are given for adults. Substantially reduced fees are almost always available for children, students, and senior citizens.

■TIP➜ Banks never have every foreign currency on hand, and it may take as long as a week to order. If you're planning to exchange funds before leaving home, don't wait till the last minute.

### ATMS & BANKS

Your own bank will probably charge a fee for using ATMs abroad; the foreign bank you use may also charge a fee. Nevertheless, you'll usually get a better rate of exchange at an ATM than you will at a currency-exchange office or even when changing money in a bank. And extracting funds as you need them is a safer option than carrying around a large amount of cash.

Before leaving home, make sure your credit cards are programmed for ATM use in Spain. Bank or credit cards that are part of the Plus or Cirrus network will work in Spanish ATMs that are part of those networks. If you don't have one, request a PIN (Personal Identification Number) with the proper number of digits for Spain (four) before leaving home in order to access money from your credit card at a foreign ATM. Request your PIN at least two to three weeks before your trip; it may need to be mailed to you. Some ATM keypads in Spain are the reverse of those in the United States, with "9, 8, 7" on the first row rather than "1, 2, 3."

Letters and numbers are the same, though sometimes the letters are not printed on ATM keys; thus, it's handy to know the number equivalent of your letter code, and vice versa. If the magnetic strip on your credit card doesn't work in an ATM, you can go into most main banks and request a cash advance via a manual transaction. All decent-size towns have ATMs. Notify your credit card company that you're going abroad—sometimes the companies see exotic destinations on charges and suspend service for security reasons.

### CREDIT CARDS

Throughout this guide, the following abbreviations are used: **AE,** American Express; **DC,** Diners Club; **MC,** Master-Card; and **V,** Visa.

It's a good idea to inform your credit-card company before you travel, especially if you're going abroad and don't travel internationally very often. Otherwise, the credit-card company might put a hold on your card owing to unusual activity—not a good thing halfway through your trip. Record all your credit-card numbers—as well as the phone numbers to call if your cards are lost or stolen—in a safe place, so you're prepared should something go wrong. Both MasterCard and Visa have general numbers you can call (collect if you're abroad) if your card is lost, but you're better off calling the number of your issuing bank, since MasterCard and Visa usually just transfer you to your bank; your bank's number is usually printed on your card.

If you plan to use your credit card for cash advances, you'll need to apply for a PIN at least two weeks before your trip. Although it's usually cheaper (and safer) to use a credit card abroad for large purchases (so you can cancel payments or be reimbursed if there's a problem), note that some credit-card companies *and* the banks that issue them add substantial percentages to all foreign transactions, whether they're in a foreign currency or not. Check on these fees before leaving home, so there won't be any surprises when you get the bill.

■TIP➜ Before you charge something, ask the merchant whether or not he or she plans to do a dynamic currency conversion (DCC). In such a transaction the credit-card *processor* (shop, restaurant, or hotel, not Visa or MasterCard) converts the currency and charges you in dollars. In most cases you'll pay the merchant a 3% fee for this service in addition to any credit-card company and issuing-bank foreign-transaction surcharges.

Dynamic currency conversion programs are becoming increasingly widespread. Merchants who participate in them are supposed to ask whether you want to be charged in dollars or the local currency, but they don't always do so. And even if they do offer you a choice, they may well avoid mentioning the additional surcharges. The good news is that you *do* have a choice. And if this practice really gets your goat, you can avoid it entirely thanks to American Express; with its cards, DCC simply isn't an option.

Note that in Spain, many restaurants don't accept American Express.

Reporting Lost Cards **American Express** (☎800/528–4800 in the U.S., 336/393–1111 collect from abroad ⊕www.american express.com). **Diners Club** (☎800/234–6377 in the U.S., 303/799–1504 collect from abroad ⊕www.dinersclub.com). **MasterCard** (☎800/627–8372 in the U.S., 636/722–7111 collect from abroad ⊕www.mastercard.com). **Visa** (☎800/847–2911 in the U.S., 410/581–9994 collect from abroad ⊕www.visa.com). [pth2]Toll free numbers in Spain

**American Express** (☎900/941413). **Diners Club** (☎901/101011). **MasterCard** (☎900/974445). **Visa** (☎900/971231).

### CURRENCY & EXCHANGE

On January 1, 2002, the European monetary unit, the euro (€), went into circulation in Spain and the other countries that have adopted it (Austria, Belgium, Finland, France, Germany, Greece, Ireland, Italy, Luxembourg, the Netherlands, and Portugal). Euro notes come in denominations of 5, 10, 20, 50, 100, 200, and 500 euros; coins are worth 1 cent of a euro, 2 cents, 5 cents, 10 cents, 20 cents, 50 cents, 1 euro, and 2 euros. All coins have one side with the value of the euro on it; the other side has each country's own national symbol. There are seven banknotes, or bills, in denominations of 5, 10, 20, 50, 100, 200, and 500 euros. Banknotes are the same for all European Union countries. At press time exchange rates were U.S. $1.41, U.K. @0.69, Australian $1.58, Canadian $1.39, New Zealand $1.86, and 9.72 South African rands to the euro.

■TIP➜ Even if a currency-exchange booth has a sign promising no commission, rest assured that there's some kind of huge, hidden fee. (Oh…that's right. The sign didn't say no *fee*.). And as for rates, you're almost always better off getting foreign currency at an ATM or exchanging money at a bank.

### TRAVELER'S CHECKS

Avoid taking traveler's checks to Barcelona, because few vendors accept them.

## ▌ RESTROOMS

The easiest restroom option is to use the facilities at a bar or cafeteria; it is customary, though not required, to order a drink if you plan to do so. Hotel lobbies and public rooms also have excellent bathroom facilities. The cleanliness of the establishment is a good indication of the conditions of their toilets. Gas stations have restrooms, but you sometimes have to request the key to use them.

Find a Loo **The Bathroom Diaries** (⊕www. thebathroomdiaries.com) is flush with unsanitized info on restrooms the world over—each one located, reviewed, and rated.

## ▌ SAFETY

Petty crime is a perennial problem in Barcelona. Pickpocketing and thefts from cars are the moreusual offenses. Certain areas in Barcelona, the lower Raval and parts of Poble Nou, are best avoided. Be especially cautious in train and bus stations in general, and in Barcelona on the Rambla, where masses of people sometimes offer camouflage for petty thieves.

Men should carry their wallet in the front pocket. On the beach, in cafés and restaurants (particularly in the well-touristed areas), and in Internet centers, always keep your belongings on your lap or tied to your person in some way. (Don't leave purses hanging from the back of your chair.) Additionally, be cautious of any odd or unnecessary human contact, verbal or physical, whether it's a tap on the shoulder or someone spilling a drink at your table. Thieves often work in twos, so while one is attracting your attention, the other is swiping your wallet.

If you do encounter a problem with theft, go to the police to file your claim. Give them your hotel name and room number, as stolen purses or bags are often recovered after their contents are taken.

As they say in Spanish, ¡ojo! (literally, "eye!," meaning "watch out!") when you roam Barcelona's Rambla and nearby streets, an area that's the scene of scams directed at tourists. Avoid the raucous "find the hidden ball" games, usually played on makeshift cardboard tables and presided over by a con man. You'll choose correctly and "win" at the beginning, but the moment you start handing over betting money, it becomes impossible to guess the right shell, and you can say good-bye to your cash. The folks "cheering on" the player are all accomplices. Also watch out for a flock of *gitanes* (gypsies), usually women, who come at tourists in a swarm of supposed goodwill, urging you to buy their bright flowers. As you're picking flowers, they're picking your pocket. Or, after the tumultuous transaction, you'll find that you didn't receive the proper change.

The traditional Spanish custom of the *piropo* (a shouted "compliment" to women walking in the street) is fast disappearing, but women traveling on their own are still likely to encounter it on occasion. The piropo is harmless, if annoying, and simply ignoring the perpetrator is the best tactic.

The Basque independence movement is made up of a small but radical sector of the political spectrum. The underground organization known as ETA, or Euskadi Ta Askatasuna (Basque Homeland and Liberty), has killed more than 800 people in more than a quarter century of terrorist activity. Violence in the Basque Country has waxed and waned since 1990, though the problem is extremely unlikely to affect the traveler. Both Bilbao and San Sebastián are 100% safe; Basque terrorism is a nonissue for tourists.

# ▌TAXES

Value-added tax (similar to sales tax) is called IVA (for *Impuesto sobre el valor añadido*) in Spain. It is levied on services, such as hotels and restaurants, and on consumer products. When in doubt about whether tax is included, ask, "*Está incluido el IVA* ("ee-vah")?"

The IVA rate for hotels and restaurants is 7%. Menus will generally say at the bottom whether tax is included (*IVA incluido*) or not (*más 7% IVA*). While food and basic necessities are taxed at the lowest rate, most consumer goods are taxed at 16%. Non- EU citizens can request a Tax-Free Cheque on purchases of €90.15 and over in shops displaying the Tax-Free Shopping sticker. This Cheque must be stamped at the customs office to the right of the arrivals exit in Barcelona Airport's Terminal A. After this is done, present it to one of the Caixa or Banco de España offices in the airport. The bank issues a certified check or credits the amount to your credit card.

Global Refund is a Europe-wide service with 225,000 affiliated stores and more than 700 refund counters at major airports and border crossings. Its refund form, called a Tax-Free Cheque, is the most common across the European continent. The service issues refunds in the form of cash, check, or credit-card adjustment.

**V.A.T. Refunds** **Global Refund** (☎800/566–9828 ⊕www.globalrefund.com).

# ▌ TIME

Spain is on Central European Time, one hour ahead of Greenwich Mean Time, six hours ahead of Eastern Standard Time. In other words, when it is 3 PM in Barcelona, it is 2 PM in London, 9 AM in New York City, and 6 AM in Los Angeles. Spain, like the rest of the European Union, switches to daylight saving time on the last weekend in March and switches back on the last weekend in October.

# ▌ TIPPING

A certain gallantry keeps Spanish service workers from seeming to care about your small change, but waiters and other service people expect to be tipped, and you can be sure that your contribution will be appreciated. On the other hand, if you experience bad or surly service, don't feel obligated to leave a tip.

Restaurant checks always include service. The bill may not tell you that the service is included, but it is. An extra tip of 5% to 10% of the bill is icing on the cake. Leave tips in cash, even if paying by credit card. If you eat tapas or sandwiches at a bar—just round up the bill to the nearest euro. Tip cocktail servers €0.20 a drink, depending on the bar. In a fancy establishment, leave no more than a 10% tip even though service is included—likewise if you had a great time.

Taxi drivers expect no tip at all and are happy if you round up in their favor. A tip of 5% of the total fare is considered generous. Long rides or extra help with luggage may merit a tip but if you're short of change, you'll never hear a complaint. On the contrary, your taxi driver may round down in *your* favor.

Tip hotel porters €1 a bag, and the bearer of room service €1. A doorman who calls a taxi for you gets €1. If you stay in a hotel for more than two nights, tip the maid about €1 per night. A concierge should receive a tip for service, from €1 for basic help to €5 or more for special assistance such as getting reservations at a popular restaurant.

Tour guides should be tipped about €2, barbers €0.30, and women's hairdressers at least €2 for a wash and style. Restroom attendants are tipped €0.50 or whatever loose change is at hand.

# SPANISH VOCABULARY

## Words and Phrases

When touring from Barcelona to Bilbao, you can be faced with a daunting number of languages, from Barcelona's Catalan to Bilbao's pre–Indo-European Basque, or Euskera. Whereas an effort to use phrases in the most universal and widely known form of Spanish (Castilian), which you will find in the following vocabulary pages, will be appreciated, a word or two of Catalan or Euskera will immediately make you into a local hero and elicit an entirely different (and much warmer) response.

From Galicia in Spain's northwestern corner to Catalonia's Cap de Creus, the Iberian Peninsula's easternmost point, some 14 recognized languages and dialects are spoken: Gallego; Lengua Asturiana (Bable); Basque (Euskera); Pyrenean dialects such as Béarnais and Toy on the French side of the border; Aragonese dialects such as Belsetan, Chistavino, and Patués; Castilian Spanish; Occitanian, Gascon French, Aranés, and Catalan.

If you wish to make a start in the languages of Barcelona and Bilbao—Catalan and Euskera—here are some words and phrases to keep in mind. After the English meaning, the Catalan and Euskera equivalencies are given.

My name is . . . (Em dic . . . /Ni . . . naiz); Hello, how are you? (Hola! Com va això?/Kaixo, zer moduz?); I'm very well, and you? (Molt bé, i vostè?/Ni oso ondo, ta su?); Good morning (Bon dia/Egun on); Good afternoon (Bona tarda/Arratsalde on); Goodnight (Bona nit/Gabon); Welcome (Benvingut(s)/Ongi etorri); Hello (Hola!/Kaixó!); Bye (Adéu/Agur); See you later (A reveure/Gero arte); Thank you (Gràcies/Eskerrik asko); Don't mention it (De res/Es horregatik); Please (Si us plau/Mesedez); Excuse me (Perdó/Barkatu); Yes (Sí/Bai); No (No/Ez); What is this? (Que es això?/Zer da Hau?); How much is this? (Cuan val?/Zenbat da?); One red wine (Un vi negre/Beltza bat); Good morning, where is the tourist office? (Bon dia, on es l'oficina de Turisme?/Egun on, non dago turismo bulegoa?); Straight (Tot recte/Zuzen); To the left (A l'esquerre/Ezkerretara); To the right (A la dreta/Eskubitara); Bank (Banc/Banketxea); Bookshop (Llibreria/Liburudenda); Art Gallery (Sala d'Exposicions/Erakusgela); Bus stop (Parada d'autobus/Autobus geltokia); Train station (Estació de tren/Tren geltokia); Hospital (Hospital/Ospitalea); Hotel (Hôtel/Hotela).

| English | Spanish | Pronunciation |
| --- | --- | --- |

## Basics

| English | Spanish | Pronunciation |
| --- | --- | --- |
| Yes/no | Sí/no | see/no |
| Please | Por favor | pohr fah-**vohr** |
| May I? | ¿Me permite? | meh pehr-**mee**-teh |
| Thank you (very much) | (Muchas) gracias | (**moo**-chas) **grah**-see-as |
| You're welcome | De nada | deh **nah**-dah |
| Excuse me | Con permiso/perdón | con pehr-**mee**-so/ pehr-**dohn** |

| | | |
|---|---|---|
| Pardon me/ what did you say? | ¿Perdón?/Mande? | pehr-**dohn**/**mahn**-deh |
| Could you tell me . . . ? | ¿Podría decirme . . . ? | po-**dree**-ah deh-**seer**-meh |
| I'm sorry | Lo siento | lo see-**en**-to |
| Good morning! | ¡Buenos días! | **bway**-nohs **dee**-ahs |
| Good afternoon! | ¡Buenas tardes! | **bway**-nahs **tar**-dess |
| Good evening! | ¡Buenas noches! | **bway**-nahs **no**-chess |
| Goodbye! | ¡Adiós!/ ¡Hasta luego! | ah-dee-**ohss**/ **ah**-stah-**lwe**-go |
| Mr./Mrs. | Señor/Señora | sen-**yor**/sen-**yohr**-ah |
| Miss | Señorita | sen-yo-**ree**-tah |
| Pleased to meet you | Mucho gusto | **moo**-cho **goose**-to |
| How are you? | ¿Cómo está usted? | **ko**-mo es-**tah** oo-**sted** |
| Very well, thank you. | Muy bien, gracias. | **moo**-ee bee-**en**, **grah**-see-as |
| And you? | ¿Y usted? | ee oos-**ted** |
| Hello (on the phone) | Diga | **dee**-gah |

## Numbers

| | | |
|---|---|---|
| 1 | un, uno | oon, **oo**-no |
| 2 | dos | dohs |
| 3 | tres | tress |
| 4 | cuatro | **kwah**-tro |
| 5 | cinco | **sink**-oh |
| 6 | seis | saice |
| 7 | siete | see-**et**-eh |
| 8 | ocho | **o**-cho |
| 9 | nueve | new-**eh**-veh |
| 10 | diez | dee-**es** |
| 11 | once | **ohn**-seh |
| 12 | doce | **doh**-seh |
| 13 | trece | **treh**-seh |
| 14 | catorce | ka-**tohr**-seh |
| 15 | quince | **keen**-seh |
| 16 | dieciséis | dee-**es**-ee-**saice** |
| 17 | diecisiete | dee-**es**-ee-see-**et**-eh |
| 18 | dieciocho | dee-**es**-ee-**o**-cho |

| 19 | diecinueve | dee-**es**-ee-new-**ev**-eh |
|----|------------|---------------------------|
| 20 | veinte | **vain**-teh |
| 21 | veinte y uno/ veintiuno | **vain**-te-oo-noh |
| 30 | treinta | **train**-tah |
| 32 | treinta y dos | train-tay-**dohs** |
| 40 | cuarenta | kwah-**ren**-tah |
| 50 | cincuenta | seen-**kwen**-tah |
| 60 | sesenta | sess-**en**-tah |
| 70 | setenta | set-**en**-tah |
| 80 | ochenta | oh-**chen**-tah |
| 90 | noventa | no-**ven**-tah |
| 100 | cien | see-**en** |
| 200 | doscientos | doh-see-**en**-tohss |
| 500 | quinientos | keen-**yen**-tohss |
| 1,000 | mil | meel |
| 2,000 | dos mil | dohs meel |

## Days of the Week

| Sunday | domingo | doh-**meen**-goh |
|--------|---------|------------------|
| Monday | lunes | **loo**-ness |
| Tuesday | martes | **mahr**-tess |
| Wednesday | miércoles | me-**air**-koh-less |
| Thursday | jueves | hoo-**ev**-ess |
| Friday | viernes | vee-**air**-ness |
| Saturday | sábado | **sah**-bah-doh |

## Useful Phrases

| Do you speak English? | ¿Habla usted inglés? | **ah**-blah oos-**ted** in-**glehs** |
|-----------------------|----------------------|--------------------------------------|
| I don't speak Spanish | No hablo español | no **ah**-bloh es-pahn-**yol** |
| I don't understand (you) | No entiendo | no en-tee-**en**-doh |
| I understand (you) | Entiendo | en-tee-**en**-doh |
| I don't know | No sé | no seh |
| I am American/ British | Soy americano (americana)/ inglés(a) | soy ah-meh-ree-**kah**-no (ah-meh-ree-**kah**-nah)/in-**glehs**(ah) |
| My name is . . . | Me llamo . . . | meh **yah**-moh |

| | | |
|---|---|---|
| Yes, please/<br>No, thank you | Sí, por favor/<br>No, gracias | **see** pohr fah-**vor**/<br>no **grah**-see-ahs |
| Yesterday/today/<br>tomorrow | Ayer/hoy/mañana | ah-**yehr**/oy/mahn-<br>**yah**-nah |
| This morning/<br>afternoon | Esta mañana/tarde | es-tah mahn-**yah**-<br>nah/**tar**-deh |
| Tonight | Esta noche | es-tah **no**-cheh |
| This/Next week | Esta semana/<br>la semana que<br>entra | es-tah seh-**mah**-<br>nah/lah seh-**mah**-nah<br>keh **en**-trah |
| This/Next month | Este mes/el<br>próximo mes | es-teh mehs/el<br>**prok**-see-moh mehs |
| How? | ¿Cómo? | **koh**-mo |
| When? | ¿Cuándo? | **kwahn**-doh |
| What? | ¿Qué? | keh |
| What is this? | ¿Qué es esto? | keh es **es**-toh |
| Why? | ¿Por qué? | por **keh** |
| Who? | ¿Quién? | kee-**yen** |
| Where is . . . ? | ¿Dónde está . . . ? | **dohn**-deh es-tah |
| the train station? | la estación del tren? | la es-tah-see-**on** del **train** |
| the subway station? | la estación del<br>metro? | la es-ta-see-**on** del<br>**meh**-tro |
| the bus stop? | la parada<br>del autobus? | la pah-**rah**-dah<br>del oh-toh-**boos** |
| the bank? | el banco? | el **bahn**-koh |
| the hotel? | el hotel? | el oh-**tel** |
| the post office? | la oficina de<br>correos? | la oh-fee-**see**-nah<br>deh-koh-**reh**-os |
| the museum? | el museo? | el moo-**seh**-oh |
| the hospital? | el hospital? | el ohss-pee-**tal** |
| the bathroom? | el baño? | el **bahn**-yoh |
| Here/there | Aquí/allá | ah-**key**/ah-**yah** |
| Open/closed | Abierto/cerrado | ah-bee-**er**-toh/<br>ser-**ah**-doh |
| Left/right | Izquierda/derecha | iss-key-**er**-dah/<br>dare-**eh**-chah |
| Straight ahead | Todo recto | **toh**-doh-**rec**-toh |
| Is it near/far? | ¿Está cerca/lejos? | es-**tah sehr**-kah/<br>**leh**-hoss |
| I'd like . . . | Quisiera . . . | kee-see-**ehr**-ah |
| a room | una habitación | **oo**-nah ah-bee-tah-see-**on** |
| the key | la llave | lah **yah**-veh |
| a newspaper | un periódico | oon pehr-ee-oh-**dee**-koh |
| a stamp | un sello | **say**-oh |

| How much is this? | ¿Cuánto cuesta? | **kwahn**-toh **kwes**-tah |
|---|---|---|
| A little/a lot | Un poquito/ mucho | oon poh-**kee**-toh/ **moo**-choh |
| More/less | Más/menos | mahss/**men**-ohss |
| I am ill | Estoy enfermo(a) | es-**toy** en-**fehr**-moh(mah) |
| Please call a doctor | Por favor llame un médico | pohr fah-**vor ya**-meh oon **med**-ee-koh |
| Help! | ¡Ayuda! | ah-**yoo**-dah |

## On the Road

| Avenue | Avenida | ah-ven-**ee**-dah |
|---|---|---|
| Broad, tree-lined boulevard | Paseo | pah-**seh**-oh |
| Highway | Carretera | car-reh-**ter**-ah |
| Port; mountain pass | Puerto | poo-**ehr**-toh |
| Street | Calle | **cah**-yeh |
| Waterfront promenade | Paseo marítimo | pah-**seh**-oh mahr-**ee**-tee-moh |

## In Town

| Cathedral | Catedral | cah-teh-**dral** |
|---|---|---|
| Church | Iglesia | **tem**-plo/ee-**glehs**-see-ah |
| City hall, town hall | Ayuntamiento | ah-yoon-tah-me-**yen**-toh |
| Door, gate | Puerta | poo-**ehr**-tah |
| Main square | Plaza Mayor | plah-thah mah-**yohr** |
| Market | Mercado | mer-**kah**-doh |
| Neighborhood | Barrio | **bahr**-ree-o |
| Tavern, rustic restaurant | Mesón | meh-**sohn** |
| Traffic circle, roundabout | Glorieta | glor-ee-**eh**-tah |
| Wine cellar, wine bar, wine shop | Bodega | boh-**deh**-gah |

## Dining Out

| A bottle of . . . | Una botella de . . . | **oo**-nah bo-**teh**-yah deh |
|---|---|---|
| A glass of . . . | Un vaso de . . . | oon **vah**-so deh |
| Bill/check | La cuenta | lah **kwen**-tah |
| Breakfast | El desayuno | el deh-sah-**yoon**-oh |

| | | |
|---|---|---|
| Dinner | La cena | lah **seh**-nah |
| Menu of the day | Menú del día | meh-**noo** del **dee**-ah |
| Fork | El tenedor | ehl ten-eh-**dor** |
| Is the tip included? | ¿Está incluida la propina? | es-**tah** in-cloo-**ee**-dah lah pro-**pee**-nah |
| Knife | El cuchillo | el koo-**chee**-yo |
| Large portion of tapas | Ración | rah-see-**ohn** |
| Lunch | La comida | lah koh-**mee**-dah |
| Menu | La carta, el menú | lah **cart**-ah, el meh-**noo** |
| Napkin | La servilleta | lah sehr-vee-**yet**-ah |
| Please give me . . . | Por favor déme . . . | pohr fah-**vor deh**-meh |
| Spoon | Una cuchara | **oo**-nah koo-**chah**-rah |

# INDEX

## PHOTO CREDITS

# NOTES

# ABOUT OUR WRITER

George Semler fell in love with Europe on a boat train to Paris during the 1960s and says he hasn't yet recovered—and doesn't want to. "It was the flat fish knives, the capers, and the snowy tablecloths that did it, not to mention the all but edible green fields of Normandy rolling by outside. I knew I was home. Later, Spain and the Mediterranean seemed even more exciting than Paris: the light, the decibel level, the sharpness of everything. A normal Monday morning in Spain generally seems to me about as festive as New Year's Eve in the rest of the world."

Since the initial *coup de foudre*, Semler has been out of his native United States nearly constantly, traveling and working in France, Greece, Vietnam, China, Morocco, Cuba, and Spain—among other destinations—over the last three decades. After settling in Madrid in 1970 with his wife, Lucie Hayes, Semler worked as a movie extra, hockey player–coach, translator, and freelance journalist while completing master's and doctoral studies in Spanish language and literature (to go with a Yale B.A. in French) and writing articles for publications ranging from the *International Herald Tribune* to the *Los Angeles Times*, *Forbes* to *Sky* and *Saveur*. Along with magazine pieces on food, travel, art, and sport he has published books of his own—including *Barcelonawalks* and *Madridwalks* (Henry Holt)—and contributed to *Fodor's Morocco, Cuba, Spain, Andalusia,* and *France*.

Presently at work on a book about a seven-week, 432-km (270-mi) hike from the Atlantic to the Mediterranean along the crest of the Pyrenees, Semler, a Barcelona resident, is also writing a memoir about bringing up his polyglot family of four in Madrid, San Sebastián, and Barcelona through the final five years of the Franco regime, the democratic transition years, and into the booming contemporary Spain of the early 21st century.

# NOTES

Praise for

# 5 STEPS TO EXPERT

*"If you are serious about yourself and your life's work, this is the perfect guidebook! You hold in your hands the blueprint for how to achieve success—applicable in the classroom, the boardroom, or the locker room. Leave it to an expert to document what it takes to join him in the top 5 percent!"*

> —Bob Rathbun, Emmy award–winning play-by-play broadcaster for Fox Sports Net and professional speaker

*"Finally! A book that gives us the real formula to achieve success and enhance our expertise, and delivers that formula with the impact of a bullet train—hard driving, efficient, and on track. Now there are no more excuses for not being the person others look to as a model for success. The exercises in this book force you to be brutally honest with yourself and pinpoint exactly what you need to achieve your goals. If you want to become the expert others envy and emulate, this book is for you."*

> —Diane Bogino, Performance Strategies, Inc.; author, *Finding Your Bootstraps* and *There's Something Funny About Humor in Presentations*

"5 Steps to Expert *offers busy executives some food for thought and practical advice about how to develop capacity and expertise for the demands of modern business, and how to find an extra gear of mental performance. This book provides a nice framework for addressing a lot of the issues we are currently facing in executive education.*"

    —**Dr. Kevin Morris, Director of Executive Development, University of Auckland Business School, New Zealand**

# 5 STEPS TO EXPERT

# 5

# STEPS TO EXPERT

## How to Go from Business Novice to Elite Performer

PAUL G. SCHEMPP

Performance Matters Press

ISBN: 0-9846-8920-6
ISBN-13: 9780984689200

# CONTENTS

# EXPERTISE EXERCISES

# ABOUT THE AUTHOR

Paul G. Schempp, PhD, named the 2004 Distinguished Scholar by the International Center for Performance Excellence at West Virginia University, has dedicated his professional life to understanding what it takes to be an expert performer. As a professor at the University of Georgia, he has spent more than a decade conducting award-winning research into the characteristics and development of expertise. His research has made him a much-sought-after keynote speaker for professional meetings and corporate conferences, including the American Society for Training and Development, BASF Corp., the Buckhead Business Association, the Club Corporation of America, the National Association for Sport and Physical Activity, the National Institute of Education (Singapore), the Swedish Golf Federation, the Society for Human Resource Management, and the Swiss Soccer Federation.

Schempp, president of Performance Matters, Inc., has more than twenty-five years of experience in the fields of research, education, and professional development. The author of four books, he is an

internationally renowned speaker, scholar, and consultant. He has served as a Senior Fulbright Research Scholar at the University of Frankfurt (Germany) and as a visiting professor at the Nanyang Technical University (Singapore).

# PREFACE

They make it look so easy. Whether it's Alex Rodriguez playing baseball, Maya Angelou reciting poetry, Donald Trump closing a deal, Warren Buffett investing in a promising venture, or Bono on stage, their actions appear elegant and effortless. So natural are experts that it seems impossible that they ever struggled to achieve their signature greatness. These elite performers seem to exude a talent few others are privileged to possess. Or, so I thought.

Like most people, I always wanted to be good at what I did. The truth? I wasn't. But the realization that I wasn't very good at most things I tried never deterred me from the belief that I could be. I watched others who were good and thought, *I* could do that. But how? What was it they were doing that I was not? Therein began my journey to discover what it takes to be an expert.

For the record, I'm still on that journey and still far from completing it. There has been some progress, however. In fact, one writer has described me as an "expert on expertise."[1] While such remarks are flattering, much remains to be explored and discovered despite

nearly twenty years of studying experts and helping professional athletes and business professionals develop their expertise.

As a professor at a major research university, my investigation into expertise allows me the privilege of studying many successful and interesting people. By sharing with others what I've learned about becoming expert, I have been richly rewarded. Experts in many diverse fields have shown their kindness by describing to me what has helped them on their journey. The feedback I've received from speaking to professional, business, and sports organizations around the world has convinced me that many people are not only seeking to become more expert in what they do but also succeeding in their quest for excellence. From organizations such as the American Society for Training and Development, corporations such as BASF, and professional athletes such as European PGA star Niclas Fasth, I have discovered that understanding the steps to expert helps people become better at what they do. This book was written to help you on your journey. It is a journey we obviously share, or you wouldn't be reading these words. Let's get started.

I thought I'd be a great teacher. I had no doubt. I loved children, loved my subject, and—bottom line—it didn't look all that hard. I had a wake-up call, however, during my senior year in college while I was student teaching. I felt fortunate to be placed with John Hichwa at John Read Middle School in Redding, Connecticut. Almost immediately I realized that there was magic to his teaching. John had a way of touching lives as he taught children. I couldn't put my finger on it because he made teaching look easy, natural—as if it required no effort at all. John got extraordinary results, while my attempts resulted in a collection of confused looks on my students' faces and chaos in the classroom. Clearly, I was not ready to teach, so I decided to pursue graduate school to better study teachers and how they achieved

great things. There, I learned to be a researcher. I studied great teachers and then great coaches. Now I study experts of any kind.

By studying experts, I have discovered that becoming expert is not innate behavior. The more experts I interview in more and more fields, this becomes increasingly clear: Experts are not born; they are self-made—they earn it. They earn it by gaining experience, by acquiring knowledge, and by developing skills. Jeff Thull makes this point clearly in his book *Exceptional Selling* when he writes about expert sales professionals: "Contrary to the popular image of salespeople as 'born communicators,' most people, and that includes salespeople, are not naturally effective communicators."[2]

Experts develop in specific, predictable steps—five to be exact. No matter how great people become in their field, they all start as a beginner. Alex Rodriguez, Maya Angelou, Donald Trump, Warren Buffett, and Bono were all beginners at one time.

Because of my work on experts and the development of expertise, I was invited to serve as a performance consultant for the Swedish Golf Federation. I was challenged to discover through theory and research which expertise skills, if any, would produce results in a sport. Swedish golf is a bit of an unexpected phenomenon. Sweden is known more for snow and ice than lush, green golf courses. You would expect to find outstanding skiers and hockey players in Sweden, not golfers. But, with innovative coaches, open-minded athletes, and the support of a dedicated federation, much is possible. The record of success gained by Swedish golfers, both men and women, is rivaled by very few countries. By way of example, in the 2002 Open Golf Championship in Muirfield, Scotland, only the United States, with a significantly larger population and more conducive golf climate, had more players in the field than Sweden. And while it would be overly simplistic and a mistake to think that the principles of expertise

development alone accounted for this success, success followed when these principles were applied.

Sports is not the only domain that has sought out and applied the principles of developing expertise—that is, moving people along the journey from beginner to expert. Corporations and professional associations are increasing their search for additional information about how their leaders, employees, and members can become consistently outstanding performers. The point is this: If you are willing to learn what it takes to become expert and are willing to apply these principles in practice, you will elevate your level of expertise and success.

While experts represent only a small percentage of the top performers in a field, everyone can become *more* expert in what they do. And that brings us to this book, which was written to share what I and other researchers have discovered about becoming expert. In this book, you can read about the research and hear the stories of those who have committed themselves to the journey toward becoming expert. By knowing the keys and steps to developing expertise, you too can become more expert in your trade, business, or profession.

# THE JOURNEY TOWARD BECOMING EXPERT

Mr. Scheidler was a history teacher at Martinsville High School in Indiana. Like many good teachers, he often discussed topics ranging beyond his subject area in an effort to guide his students in directions that would help them lead happy, productive, and successful lives. One March afternoon, Mr. Scheidler challenged his class to write a paper defining success. He wanted to start those young minds thinking about the concept of success and whether it means just becoming rich or famous or just winning a ball game. A sophomore thought hard about the topic. He continued thinking about the topic for a long time after completing Mr. Scheidler's homework assignment. In fact, he reflected on that assignment for decades.

In struggling to find an answer to the question Mr. Scheidler posed, the student also recalled the advice his father had frequently given him when he was growing up on the family farm: Don't worry much about trying to be better than someone else. Sometime later, the young man wrote this about his father's lessons: "Dad always added the following. 'Always try to be the very best that *you* can be.

Learn from others, yes. But don't just try to be better than they are. You have no control over that. Instead try, and try very hard, to be the best that you can be. That you have control over. Maybe you'll be better than someone else and maybe you won't. That part of it will take care of itself.'"[1]

Years later, that young man became a high school teacher himself, and he also began coaching. The lessons learned through Mr. Scheidler's assignment and his father's teachings followed him and became principles he lived by. In 1934, while teaching English and coaching basketball at Central High School in South Bend, Indiana, John Wooden put to paper the single sentence he had reflected on for so long: "Success is a peace of mind, which is a direct result of self-satisfaction in knowing you made the effort to become the best you are capable of becoming."[2] Leaving behind the classroom, Coach Wooden pursued a career as a college basketball coach and went on to lead UCLA to ten NCAA championships, seven in a row—a feat that has never been equaled and many believe never will be.

John Wooden was not born an expert basketball coach. He *learned* to be successful—in sports and in life. The search for ways by which people's endeavors can be promoted and improved has produced a fertile body of knowledge. Despite a long, rich, and rewarding journey, the search is far from over. The hunt for excellence in human performance has led to the exploration of many new areas. The development of expertise is among them. We long to know what it takes to be the best.

Scholars and scientists have attempted to unravel the mysteries and complexities surrounding the development and actions of those sitting atop the pinnacle of human performance. Though only a few scholars are currently investigating the phenomenon of extraordinary performance, their work has been vigorous and varied. Today,

we know a great deal more about becoming expert than we did just twenty years ago. Because this knowledge has been collected from experts in fields ranging from waiters and taxi drivers to nurses, surgeons, and military generals, this body of knowledge offers a rich resource for virtually anyone undertaking nearly any endeavor.

Tracing the development of experts from a variety of fields has made it possible to identify the steps experts follow in climbing to the top. At each step, or level, of expertise, the common characteristics that indicate that level have also been identified—regardless of the business, profession, or trade—or any other human endeavor. Stanford Graduate School of Business professor Charles O'Reilly makes the point that there is little difference between achieving success in business or in sports. For example, in the initial rounds of a golf or tennis tournament, players of differing abilities all begin at the same place. But, as the tournament progresses, the weaker performers are inevitably eliminated and the stronger performers advance.

> If you think about performance in organizations as being a function of motivation times ability—how smart you are and how hard you work—what makes a difference at the top level is effort; ability has been equilibrated. If somebody does 500 backhands a day and somebody else does only 100, then in the long-term, the person who does the more backhands is more likely to win. In one of our studies, we found that effort and ability by themselves don't appear to explain much, but the combination really matters. In other words, people who work harder, who are smarter, are going to have greater success.[3]

While the principles of expertise development are applicable to most aspects of life, they apply best to performance-oriented activities. After all, experts are those who consistently outperform their peers. In contemporary culture, few fields demand greater results

from the performance of their personnel than business and industry. With issues of succession planning, workforce retention and development, and the continual pressure to achieve more with fewer resources facing every aspect of business today, developing the expertise of industry leaders, executives, and employees has never been more critical.

## The Road Map

This book provides a road map for anyone in business—new graduates, staff, first-time or experienced managers, leaders, or executives—who aspire to advance from their present level of competence to higher levels of skill, knowledge, and performance. Specific characteristics that distinguish each of the five levels of expertise are described. With this information, you can identify your (or others') present expertise level—an important prerequisite to understanding how you arrived where you are and what next steps toward outstanding performance you need to take.

This book, however, provides more than just understanding of those steps. It suggests effective ways of learning based on your present level of expertise and offers a series of progressive tasks and activities to guide you through each step toward becoming expert. Each chapter includes a description of the learning modalities and strategies that can most effectively move you to the next level of expertise. Case studies, stories, and practical examples illustrate how the characteristics within each step can move you forward in your quest to become more expert in your chosen field. Developmental exercises at the end of each chapter provide checklists and worksheets to help you plan effective strategies to increase your experience, knowledge, and skills—the three keys to expertise—to improve your professional

performance. These developmental exercises will help you transition smoothly to the next level.

Chapter 1 opens with the three keys to expertise. The level of expertise you ultimately achieve is primarily dependent not on any characteristic, trait, or quality you were born with or anything you may have been given, but rather on these three keys. Each key is under your control and instrumental in moving through the five steps to expert:

1. Beginner
2. Capable
3. Competent
4. Proficient
5. Expert

Each step, as described separately in chapters 2–6, includes a learning strategy to move you to the next step. Research that supports each step and behavioral attribute, particularly as it applies to business and the workplace, is included. Each chapter contains real-world business or sports examples of that step's behavioral characteristics and learning modalities. Chapter 7 offers suggestions that have proven useful in navigating the journey from business novice to elite performer.

## Climbing the Steps

You cannot go directly from step 1 to step 5—from beginner to expert. As your experience, knowledge, and skills increase, you move from one step to the next, developing new characteristics that will help you perform at the next step.

The earliest, and most often cited, work on the stages of expertise development was *What Computers Can't Do* by Hubert Dreyfus in 1972.[4] His model proposed five stages to becoming expert: (1) novice, (2) advanced beginner, (3) competent, (4) proficient, and (5) expert. Since that time, a steady stream of research has revealed a great deal more information about the steps required for becoming an expert.

The steps to becoming expert represent a developmental process. When people are identified as competent, it implies that the majority of characteristics they exhibit are within the competent step. They may still hold some beginner characteristics, while at the same time may have acquired a few proficient, or perhaps even expert, characteristics.

Personal development is an individual endeavor, and none of us develops in the same way, at the same time, or for the same reasons. You, however, determine where you stop in developing your expertise—if you stop at all. You can ascend the steps, remain on your present step, or even descend the steps. Being competent today does not guarantee that you will be competent tomorrow. If you do not keep abreast of important new information, keep your skill set well honed, or learn from your increasing experience, you may find yourself at a lower level of expertise as the standards of success rise ever higher.

Climbing the steps to becoming expert does not mean that some of the lower-level characteristics are no longer applicable. Experts can still learn by someone else's example just as they did when they were a beginner. Performers who are proficient still use strategic knowledge to help them make insightful decisions, just as they did when they were at the capable level of expertise. Therefore, see these steps to expert as a guide, not a prescription, for becoming more expert in what you do. Becoming expert, in short, means becoming the best you can be at what you do.

## An Invitation

I am inviting you to take a journey—a journey toward becoming expert. By the time you finish reading this book, you should understand why you do so many things well and why there are some things you do not do so well. More important, you should understand how to improve just about everything you do—particularly those things that mean the most to you and have the most impact on your professional performance. The ideas shared in this book can help anyone do just about anything better. Research has proven it. People have proven it. And this book will prove it to you.

Before beginning the journey, complete expertise exercise 1 to gauge your current level. Next, read chapter 1 about the three keys to expertise to understand how to increase your performance. Then you will be ready to undertake the journey, which begins with chapter 2, "Beginning as a Beginner." Even if you are not a beginner, I encourage you to start there to better understand where you have come from. It also will help you recognize when other people are at this step and how you might help them on their journey. Of course, if you are in fact a beginner, that is the place for you to start.

# RATING YOUR EXPERTISE

*Choose only the response that best answers each question.*

1. How many years have you been in your present position?
   - a. ☒ 0–1 year
   - b. ____ 2–4 years
   - c. ____ 5–9 years
   - d. ____ 10–14 years
   - e. ____ 15 or more years

2. Where do you learn most of the new information you use in your current position?
   - a. ☒ Experience
   - b. ____ Mentor
   - c. ____ Colleagues
   - d. ____ Conferences, seminars
   - e. ____ Reading

3. Which of the following most often guides your decision making?
   - a. ____ Rules and norms
   - b. ☒ The situation
   - c. ____ Long-term goals
   - d. ____ Results from a careful analysis of the problem
   - e. ____ Intuition

4. When assessing the outcomes of your professional actions, what percentage is normally due to your actions versus external or situational factors?
   - a. ____ 10 percent
   - b. ____ 25 percent
   - c. ____ 50 percent
   - d. ☒ 75 percent
   - e. ____ 90 percent

5. If 10 were all the knowledge a person could possibly have to do your job and 0 were no knowledge at all, where would you rate your current level of knowledge?
    a. ___ 8
    b. ___ 7
    c. ___ 6
    d. ___ 5
    e. ___ 4

6. When planning occurs in your workplace, you
    a. ___ Are seldom involved
    b. ___ Like to see how things were done previously
    c. ___ Always have a primary plan and a backup plan
    d. ___ Gather all the pertinent information before attempting a plan
    e. ___ Usually analyze the results of your actions after plan execution

7. In the past twelve months, how many books have you read that have helped you in some way in your current position?
    a. ___ None
    b. ___ 1
    c. ___ 2–3
    d. ___ 4–5
    e. ___ 6 or more

8. When something does not go as planned or fails in your workplace, recently you have found that the reason is
    a. ___ Outside forces (e.g., competition, customers)
    b. ___ Failure to clearly communicate goals, expectations, or procedures within your organization
    c. ___ Lack of collaborative planning
    d. ___ Your team's failure to adequately anticipate or analyze the problem
    e. ___ Your decisions or actions

*(cont'd)*

---

**EXPERTISE EXERCISE 1 CONT'D**

9. If your on-the-job performance over the the past twelve months were measured, where would that performance rank against that of other people in your organization or in a position similar to yours?

    a. ____ 25% or below

    b. ____ Top 25–50%

    c. ____ Top 50–75%

    d. ☒ Top 75–95%

    e. ____ I would be the top performer

10. In matters related to your business or profession, you find that you can remember

    a. ____ Most of what you were told is important for the job

    b. ____ Most of what is necessary to get the job done

    c. ____ Enough to do the job right

    d. ☒ The most important information for making a sound decision

    e. ____ Every detail that might have an influence on the final outcome

---

**SCORING YOUR EXPERTISE**

Tally your responses using the following scale:

    a = 1
    b = 2
    c = 3
    d = 4
    e = 5

Total points: 23

Circle your level of expertise based on your total points:

    5–10    Beginner
    11–20   Capable
    (21–35   Competent)
    36–45   Proficient
    46–50   Expert

**ONE**

# THE THREE KEYS TO EXPERTISE

If you are attracted to fad diets to lose weight, lottery tickets to gain wealth, and the latest fashion statement to make yourself attractive, put this book down. You cannot be born to expertise, nor buy it or borrow it. You have to work at it. No exceptions. And you cannot work at it for just one day, one week, one month, or even one year. You have to work at it for years—many years. But, if you love what you do, then a labor of love is a highly attractive proposition.

## Experts: Made, Not Born

No one is born an expert. Some people may be fortunate to be endowed with certain physical, mental, social, or emotional characteristics that help them pursue superior performances. Those characteristics alone, however, have never made anyone an expert. In fact, what some people have overcome in the pursuit of elite achievement is often as inspirational as it is remarkable.

## Bobby's Shoes

Bobby's sneakers told him that he was growing, but it wasn't that the sneakers would become tight. As Bobby tells his story,

> They bought them for me extra big. The foster mom I lived with showed me how to crinkle up tissues and push them tight into the front of the sneaker. She told me that as my feet grew, I would need less tissues and take some out. So sometimes I'd check to see if I was growing by pulling out the tissues from each sneaker, remove a few, crinkle the rest, and fill the toe back up. That's how I knew I was growing, as the sneaker space shrunk, I knew I was growing bigger. Only problem was that nothing else in my life grew. My school awards didn't grow, so I didn't think my mind grew much. My friends didn't grow, 'cause I never stayed anywhere long enough to see anyone. All I have to show are these sneakers. And I don't even like them. Whenever I look at them I think about how they are all scuffed up . . . just like me, just like I'm scuffed up. No shine on my shoes. No shine on me.[1]

When he became a young man, Bobby got a job in a fruit and vegetable store. Every week he saved a small portion of his paycheck. One day he had saved enough to make his first real purchase—a pair of shoes. But they were not just any shoes. He bought a shiny pair of cordovan-colored shoes that he polished every day. His shoes carried him to a job as an office boy at the Albany, New York, *Times Union* newspaper. As his experience, knowledge, and skills increased, he continued walking up the corporate staircase until he reached the top, where he would spend nearly two decades as CEO of the Hearst Newspaper Group and vice president of the Hearst Corporation. Was it some innate characteristic, a birthright, or an inherent talent that took Bobby Danzig from scruffy, oversized sneakers to the corner office of a corporate empire? Unlikely.

The idea that talent makes you successful is folly. Perhaps that's why more often than not we hear about the people who never reached their potential or the can't-miss kid who missed. This point was driven home to me by one of my students at Kent State University. In the summer of 1984, Thomas Jefferson, or T.J. to those who know him best, qualified for the U.S. Olympic Team. In doing so, he fulfilled his dream to compete for the country he loves in a sport he loves in an event he loves. When he returned to campus after qualifying for the Olympic Games, I shook his hand to congratulate him. He looked me in the eye and said, "I have raced many runners a lot more talented than me. But no one ever worked harder for it than me." A few weeks later, T.J. completed his race in Los Angeles and stepped on the podium to have the Olympic bronze medal placed around his neck for his efforts in the 200-meter run.

Because expertise is neither a birthright nor an innate characteristic, most people have an opportunity to gain a high level of expertise in their chosen profession or business. Legendary business consultant Peter Drucker realized this early in his career:

> I soon learned that there is no "effective personality." The effective executives I have seen differ widely in their temperaments and their abilities, in what they do and how they do it, in their personalities, their knowledge, their interests—in fact in almost everything that distinguishes human beings. All they have in common is the ability to get the right things done.... Effectiveness, in other words, is a habit, that is, a complex of practices. And practices can always be learned.[2]

## Using the Three Keys

If you have a passion for what you do, can identify, practice, and apply the important skills of your industry, are open to learning what others

can teach you, and gain applicable experience, you will become more expert at your job. An expert is someone who consistently outperforms his or her peers. Everyone today who might be considered an expert has done this, and so can you. The secrets of their consistent and superior performance are found in factors I call the three keys to expertise:

- Experience
- Knowledge
- Skills

It is instructive to learn how these keys might best be used to elevate your performance. If you acquire and then make use of extensive experience, knowledge, and skills, you will develop expertise in what you do. Others may rival your experience, knowledge, or skills, but few will consistently outperform you.


## Experience: A Great Teacher


There is no substitute for experience when it comes to developing expertise. It's when you are actually performing a task that your knowledge and skills unite to determine your level of performance. Experience offers opportunities for learning. Unfortunately, all too often people ignore the lessons offered by their experience and simply repeat the same ineffective patterns of performance. Consider your handwriting. No doubt you have been writing for years. Has the quality of your handwriting improved? Despite your extensive handwriting experience, do you consider yourself a handwriting expert? If you are like most people, despite years of experience your handwriting has not improved much, and perhaps it has even worsened. To develop your expertise, you must let experience work for you.

Thoughtfully analyzing your experiences to identify what you did well and what could be improved leads to the insights that improve performance. Perhaps reflecting on their limited practical experience, beginners find real-world practice to be their most important source of information for increasing expertise. For them, verbal or written information takes second place to trial and error in acquiring knowledge and skills.

The greater the diversity of experiences in your field—as expanded by different people, situations, and purposes—the greater is the benefit offered by those experiences. Different experiences give you opportunities to apply your knowledge and skills in new and untested ways. Some companies commonly place novice executives in various positions so that, as they climb the corporate ladder, they gain firsthand experience with various aspects of the company's operations.

Experience alone neither increases expertise nor improves performance. This point was clearly made in a study comparing high- and average-performing professional software designers.[3] The designers were all assigned a design task and asked to report the strategies they used in accomplishing the task. High performers' strategies included planning and collecting more feedback as they progressed. Further, they devoted greater attention to understanding the problem and to collaborative efforts with colleagues. Average performers spent more time analyzing the task requirements and verbalizing thoughts largely irrelevant to the problem. Despite the differences in performance quality, the designers did not differ in length of experience. In other words, the differences between the two performance groups can be explained by strategic knowledge and skills—but not by experience alone. According to Anders Ericsson,

> Improvement in performance of aspiring experts does not happen automatically or casually as a function of further experience.

Improvements are caused by changes in cognitive mechanisms mediating how the brain and nervous system control performance and in the degree of adaptation of physiological systems of the body. The principal challenge to attaining expert-level performance is to induce stable specific changes that allow the performance to be incrementally improved.[4]

> Deliberate, systematic, and continual change brings about the improvements leading to expert performance.

Experience is a critical, but clearly not a singular, key to developing expertise.

## The Power of Knowledge

It should be obvious that experts have extensive knowledge, but the importance of this characteristic demands that it be examined thoroughly. Experts invest significantly in learning all they can about their field. Attend a conference and you will surely see experts. Because of their extensive knowledge, experts may be least likely to acquire more information at the conference, but they got where they are, in part, because they attended seminars long before they became experts. The relationships they formed and nurtured at such meetings are one reason they are now experts. They have learned that no knowledge source is too insignificant to overlook.

When experts stop learning, they soon stop being leaders in their field. Florida State University football coach Bobby Bowden clearly recognized this fact when he said, "I have been coaching fifty-one years, and I feel like I know about 60 percent of what is out there, no, maybe 50 percent. There is so much more out there. When I stop learning and adjusting, nobody will have to tell me to retire. There

ain't much wiggle room at our level. When we stop adapting, we'll be losing and I'll want out."[5]

This point is as pertinent to industry as it is to sports. In discussing the surge of the Japanese to the top of the automobile market, Volkswagen's Carl Hahn said, "We have to realize their achievement, grapple with it, and change our attitudes. We have to go and learn, we Germans, we Europeans. We have been so accustomed to teaching engineering to the world that we've lost some of our receptiveness to learning."[6]

> When you stop learning, you cannot lead—those who continue to learn will soon pass you by.

There are several characteristics of experts' knowledge, common strategies used in accumulating knowledge, and a few benefits in possessing a large quantity of exploitable information. First, experts' knowledge is specific to their area of expertise. When you refer to an expert's knowledge, that knowledge is largely confined to a single field of specialty. Because you are an expert in sales does not mean you are an expert in manufacturing or management. As Paul Feltovich, Michael Prietula, and Anders Ericsson describe it, our modern "conception of expertise seems to favor the specialist and specialized skills, honed over many years of extensive training and deliberate practice. The notion of the 'expert generalist' is difficult to capture within the current explanatory systems of expertise."[7] Experts are not all-knowing individuals who can speak authoritatively on any subject, but rather they possess a great deal of knowledge pertaining to a single subject, field, or domain.

Second, experts are not necessarily any more intelligent than the average person. Experts have, as you will read in later chapters, developed skills and strategies so that they can acquire, retain, and

apply large quantities of information. These skills are a result of effective memory strategies and practice rather than innate intelligence.[8] You do not acquire wisdom from your innate intelligence, but rather from multiple and continual attempts to learn all you can about what you do. Studies in a variety of fields have found that even though experts gain large amounts of knowledge related to their domain, they never believe they know all there is to know about their particular area and thus continue their search for useful information.[9]

The increased experience and practice that elevates your expertise also improves your knowledge. Specifically, as you gain experience and skills, your knowledge is reorganized in ways that enable you to both retain and access information efficiently. Your knowledge becomes organized into larger, more meaningful units and thus makes it possible to remember more and use more of what you remember.[10]

The accumulated knowledge of experts provides them with more options and alternatives in planning and executing action. In a study of differences between experts and beginners, I found that more knowledgeable professionals were able to devise more alternatives in situations and construct a greater number of solutions to problems than were beginners.[11]

Experts enjoy talking almost endlessly about their subject, gathering others' views on pertinent topics, and having extensive libraries devoted to their field. They use extensive resources to build a large store of knowledge. Experience and peers have been most often identified as key sources of experts' knowledge, but books, workshops, certification programs, journals and magazines, experiences, and even clients have been identified as important knowledge sources.

One of the world's greatest entrepreneurs, Sam Walton, offers an excellent example of an expert who never stopped building his

knowledge. He often talked with his frontline employees because he believed that "the ones on the front lines—the ones who talk with the customer—are the ones who really know what's going on out there. You better find out what they know."[12] Sam read extensively. As computers came into their own, Sam read all he could about them. He became so enthralled with the potential of computers that he enrolled in an IBM school and later hired some of their experts to help him expand Wal-Mart into the largest retailer in the world.

While experience and knowledge are important keys to expertise, they are not sufficient for the superior performance that is the signature of experts. Experience and knowledge provide the critical foundation for decision making, but achieving outstanding performance takes more than thinking—it takes action. And the actions of experts are defined by their skills. In other words, it is experts' highly developed skill sets that permit them to act in ways leading to consistently superior performance.

## Developing Essential Skills

Children with learning disabilities are often believed to have limited chances for success, and those with severe disabilities are often dismissed as hopeless or useless before even reaching the starting line of gainful employment. Imagine leaving high school having failed mathematics repeatedly and having been stigmatized since childhood because of dyslexia. In short, by age sixteen you could neither read nor write with even a functional capacity. This was precisely the hand dealt to young Sir Richard Branson.[13] We often hear people speak of high performers as talented in some physical or intellectual way. Branson was neither. Given his disabilities, he would never be able to read adequately a simple contract or decipher the balance sheet of a

corporation. What Branson could do was develop the skills that would make him successful, and as unlikely as that seems, that is precisely what he did.

While he could never become skilled at reading papers, he did become skilled at reading people, situations, and opportunities. He could never calculate the size of a profit margin, but he did learn how to calculate the depth of an individual's character. Branson used his acquired skills to found multiple corporations, including Virgin Atlantic Airways. In the process, he became a billionaire several times over. He developed the skills necessary to make him an elite business performer.

### Experts' Specific Skills

The skills of an expert can be viewed as a specific set of tasks or profession-related activities that have been acquired, developed, and mastered by the expert and account for and are critical to the expert's superior performance. For example, expert chefs have superior knife-handling skills, expert salespersons have superior customer relations skills, and expert financial investors have superior strategic asset selection skills.

There is no shortage of resources for identifying skills to be practiced and perfected to have a positive effect on your performance. Often, your job description lists the key skills of your position. Mentors and colleagues can be useful in helping recognize the important skills of your business or industry. As you observe the outstanding performers in your workplace, what do you observe that accounts for their success? Finally, books such as *The 21 Irrefutable Laws of Leadership, Skills for New Managers, The Success Principles,* and *The Ultimate Competitive Advantage* have all helped people identify critical skills that propelled their performance.[14]

## Experts' General Skills

Several skills are common to all experts, regardless of their field.

**Each of an expert's general skills is equally important in achieving top performance.**

These skills serve experts in making decisions, planning and executing actions, and evaluating performance. First, experts can distinguish the important elements from the unimportant elements in events, actions, or situations and identify which are most critical to cultivating a satisfactory response or solution. Experts can do this because they see the deeper structures of a problem—the root causes—whereas those with less expertise see only the symptoms and surface issues. Branson's ability to read people and associate with those who could make things happen is an example of the skill of identifying the important from the unimportant as it applies to people's character.

Second, experts spend more time analyzing a problem by gathering relevant information, understanding problem constraints, developing solutions, and assessing the adequacy of the attempted solutions. They like to have all the facts to devise the best strategy for moving forward. Third, experts are skilled at generating the best solutions to a given problem, and they do this faster and more accurately than nonexperts.[15]

Fourth, experts are better able to plan and implement strategies in reaching goals. They not only know which strategies are more likely to work in a given situation, but they also are more likely to use strategies with a proven track record. Fifth, experts can accurately identify deficiencies in their knowledge and skills, and locate resources or design strategies for overcoming these limitations. As good as experts are

today, they strive to be better tomorrow. This might help explain how they became superior performers in the first place.

Every skill in an expert's repertoire, whether it is specific to his or her profession or general in nature, was learned. What those skills look like in action are described in chapter 6, "Excelling to Expert." How those skills are mastered is detailed in chapter 7, "Navigating the Journey."

## Beginning the Journey

Every journey has a starting point, that is, a beginning. The expertise exercise you completed earlier provided an estimate of your present location along that journey. On which step are you? Beginner? Capable? Competent? Proficient? Perhaps you are already an expert. Regardless of your current level of expertise, it is helpful to understand how you got where you are and, then, where you need to go from here. Therefore, I encourage you to begin with the next chapter, "Beginning as a Beginner," which details the first steps in developing expertise, so that you know the characteristic benchmarks in becoming an expert—both for yourself and for others you may help on their journey.

Simply knowing the steps to and characteristics of becoming an expert is, however, not enough. The principles of expertise need to be purposefully practiced and applied. To achieve anything takes more than just knowing how to do something—it takes action. You decide if, when, or where the journey ends. The further you progress, the more productive you become, the better you perform, and the deeper your passion grows for what you do. The time to move forward is now. You can start by completing expertise exercises 2–4.

## Summary

The three keys to expertise are

- Experience
- Knowledge
- Skills

## EXPERTISE KEY 1: YOUR EXPERIENCE

Think about your professional experiences and describe a situation that provided one of your greatest learning experiences. Where did it take place? Who was involved? What happened? What did you learn?

SPR firing

## EXPERTISE KEY 2: YOUR KNOWLEDGE

If you were designing a training program for the person who will eventually replace you, what would be the four most important training topics?

1. _Smartsheet_
2. _Newsletter_
3. _Adaptability / Reliability_
4. _Quick response & action_

## EXPERTISE KEY 3: YOUR SKILLS

Picture yourself walking alone along an empty beach and discovering an ornate glass bottle sticking out of the sand. You reach down, pull it up, and, while rubbing the sand off the bottle to better see the intricate design, you feel the bottle rumble and see smoke shooting out the top. When the smoke clears, a magnificent genie stands before you. In a deep, booming voice, he says, "I am a genie. I can make you do whatever you do better than anyone in the world. Tell me what you do." You reply: "I am a n _Admin_ [your occupation]." The genie then says, "I will make you the best at the three most important skills for a n _Admin_ [your occupation]. Just tell me what they are."

You tell him the three most important skills for your job are

1. _Accuracy & efficiency_
2. _Communication_
3. _Intuition_

**T W O**

# BEGINNING AS A BEGINNER

In any new endeavor you undertake—be it social, recreational, or occupational—you must begin as a beginner. You can't avoid it. But being a beginner is not a bad thing. To the contrary, it means you are starting on a grand adventure to attain new experiences, new knowledge, and new skills. Every journey—including the journey to expertise—begins with a single step.

Although everyone is a beginner at sometime or something, those who enter a business or profession seldom do so knowing nothing. To every new job, you bring preconceived notions of what people in that workplace do and how they do it. Your preconceptions may be based on previous experience, schooling, training, casual reading, or, perhaps, only on assumptions that may or may not be correct. You envision yourself in this job. You believe you have the requisite attitudes and qualities for the job and therefore will be successful. One drawback is that, because you lack experience, knowledge, and skills, you often don't know just how little you know. In fact, beginners often think they know a great deal. Overestimating

both your knowledge and skills can keep you at the beginner level until you realize what you need to know and how you need to do something. Then you begin to gain the knowledge and skills that move you beyond the beginner level.

Beginners can generally be considered those with less than three years of experience. But more experience alone does not make beginners smarter or more skilled. The sad reality is that some people perform at the beginner level for a lifetime.

## Teacher as Beginner

At one time I supervised student teachers in public schools. It was enjoyable because I got to see many bright, enthusiastic young teachers instructing bright, enthusiastic young students. During one visit, the mentor teacher told me he was having a problem with the student teacher. "She shows no respect for my experience," he said. In a meeting together after class, the mentor was quick to air his concerns. The student teacher interjected, "But there are more contemporary ways..." She was quickly cut off by the mentor's loud proclamation, "I've been teaching for twenty-five years!" The student teacher revealed more pluck than tact when she corrected him, "No. You taught one year and repeated it twenty-four times!" She had a valid point. While the mentor teacher was considered a nice person, few considered him a good teacher. He had learned little from his experience. We quickly transferred the young student teacher to another school. Interestingly, years later she was named her state's teacher of the year.

## Beginner Characteristics

Beyond their lack of experience, generally beginners share four common characteristics. Recognizing these characteristics can help you

assess your present level of expertise as a beginner and understand what to do to become more expert. It can also help human resource and training personnel, or potential mentors, determine how to help someone move beyond the beginner level. Beginners commonly

- Behave in ways that are rational, procedural, and inflexible
- Make decisions guided by rules and norms
- Do not feel responsible for the outcomes of their actions
- Lack comfortable, efficient routines for everyday tasks

## Behaving Rationally, Procedurally, and Inflexibly

As a beginner, with your limited experience, knowledge, and skills, you have few options when it comes to taking action. Limited knowledge and skills provide you with limited options when identifying problems, planning actions, or completing tasks. As a result, you must rely on rational thought rather than on instinct or practical knowledge. As a beginner, you often look for procedures to follow and patterns of behavior to emulate. Lacking a deep understanding as to *why* something may be done in a particular way, you will often simply accept *how* it is done by those who seem to be in the know. Your actions therefore tend to be rigid and step-by-step as you attempt to follow established procedures learned in training programs or by reading manuals.

To help beginners become productive quickly, training instructions often offer a progressive sequence of steps that translate easily into action. Computer maker Hewlett-Packard, for example, offers beginning salespeople a seven-step procedure for selling digital printers:[1]

1. Get in the door.
2. Identify their pain.

3. Use a leadership sales approach.

4. Talk the talk.

5. Ask the right question.

6. Develop your solution.

7. Present the solution.

Tips for implementing each step are also offered. This procedure serves as a recipe for sales success and saves beginning salespeople much time—time that would otherwise be spent on experiments with various techniques and models. The steps are rational and procedural and, because they are sequential, they are also relatively inflexible.

While supplying beginners with rational procedures for accomplishing the fundamental tasks of their profession is an important and useful goal of training programs—and beginners adapting to accepted behavioral practices in their job is smart, profitable politics—serious and detrimental consequences can result if conditions and circumstances are not carefully considered. There are times when following established procedures may not be the best course of action. Ray Alcorn makes this point in his article "Top 5 Mistakes of Beginning Commercial Real Estate Investors" when he identifies the number one mistake beginning investors make as ignoring local market conditions.[2] A beginner often believes that a great property equals a great investment, but as Alcorn notes, "A great property in a bad market can be a big loser. Analyzing the demographic trends of population growth, income, and employment in the local market will tell you where opportunity lies, or not. Those conditions will make or break your investment." In other words, following a rigid set of procedures for all properties in all markets can lead to disaster for beginning investors.

Every organization has tasks for which specific, inflexible procedures work well. For example, completing travel reimbursements, processing orders, and posting organizationwide announcements are conducted more efficiently when everyone follows the same process—regardless of experience, position in the organization, or level of expertise. However,

**As beginners, we cannot stay stuck in a rigid approach forever if we want to advance to the next step.**

Strictly following traditional procedures helps beginners fit in a new organization, but if they do not explore alternatives, they will remain relatively low-level performers.

## Making Decisions Guided by Rules and Norms

When you are a beginner, your decisions usually are tied to the rules and norms of an organization. Rules offer guides to decisions and actions, and norms are the stuff of corporate cultures and traditions. Thus, rules represent the explicit or stated principles on which to make decisions, whereas norms are the implicit or unspoken beliefs and values that shape how people think in a workplace.

To become competent in your new role and prove yourself worthy, as a beginner, you learn the rules and norms that govern behavior in the new workplace. Your conception of doing the job correctly includes decisions based on the workplace rules and traditions, particularly those centered on establishing order and managing the workplace environment. You see established, orderly practices as characteristic of competence.

**Rules and norms can provide the foundation for greater understanding and expertise.**

## Changing Focus

The story of Marvin Traub demonstrates how an individual can learn the rules and norms on which to base decisions in his industry. During his first week at Bloomingdale's, Marvin was called into chairman Jed Davidson's office. Marvin was instructed to analyze the cost of *Daily News* full-color ads and to calculate how much was being lost on Bloomingdale's dresses that were selling for $2.99. (This was in 1950!) Marvin was surprised to learn that Mr. Davidson thought the dresses were losing money, because these particular dresses sold very well. But Jed Davidson was asking, Did it make good business sense? So Marvin added up the wholesale costs of the dresses sold and deducted the cost of advertising. He was shocked by what he found: Bloomingdale's lost twenty-five to thirty-five cents on every dress it sold. The more dresses it sold, the more money it lost. The store gave up the full-page ads, and Marvin learned the first rule of retailing: Focus not on gross sales but on profit! Later, as chairman and CEO, Marvin Traub used that rule to lead Bloomingdale's to a position of celebrated prominence in American retailing.[3]

## Genius in a Little Rule

I found a personal example of a foundational rule one evening in Home Depot. A broken toilet had sent me off in search of a replacement part. I walked into the plumbing section with a broken something-or-other. It was only a small piece of a larger part of the entire apparatus.

A young associate greeted me with a smile and a welcome: "How can I help you?" I presented the piece to him. "What is it?" he asked. "I don't know. It came out of my toilet tank," I replied. "Oh, I think we can help you." He then examined several possibilities for a re-

placement, and when he thought he found one, he confirmed his decision with a colleague. Next, he carefully explained, step-by-step, how to replace the part and assured me that I had all the tools I needed. The entire process took about thirty minutes. The total cost of the part was less than four dollars. Home Depot made no money on my purchase. When I complimented the associate on his excellent customer service, he said that during training he was told that he should "treat every customer like a relative." As we parted, he said, "I would have done the same for any member of my family." There is genius in that simple little rule: *Treat every customer like a relative.* First, it gave that beginner sales professional a clear guide when making customer service decisions. Second, it provided superior service that ensured that I will return many times to a place that treats me like family.

## Failing to Take Responsibility for One's Actions

On Friday, August 26, 2005, National Hurricane Center director Max Mayfield reported to the press, "I just don't see any reason why this will not become a very, very powerful hurricane before it is all over."[4] Three days later Hurricane Katrina came out of the Gulf of Mexico and slammed onto shore near the Louisiana–Mississippi state line. A short time later, two major flood control levees were breached, submerging New Orleans. Twelve hours later, one of the most powerful hurricanes in U.S. history was finally downgraded to a tropical storm; but, in Katrina's wake lay death, devastation, and hundreds of thousands of people without food, water, or shelter.

Michael Brown joined the Federal Emergency Management Agency (FEMA) in 2001 as legal counsel. In 2003, he became director. Prior to joining FEMA, he had spent ten years as a commissioner

for the International Arabian Horse Association. With no training or experience in emergency management, Michael Brown was a beginner in a position—heading the federal government's emergency management agency—needing an expert.

As is characteristic of beginners, Brown did not feel responsible for the disaster unfolding in New Orleans. He refused to shoulder responsibility for FEMA's slow response to the disaster, and instead blamed Louisiana's leaders for failing to act quickly enough to the approaching hurricane. When informed by a FEMA employee in New Orleans that they were running out of food and water, and that people were dying due to a lack of proper medical facilities, Brown e-mailed back, "Thanks for the update. Anything specific I need to do or tweak?"[5]

As a beginner, you seldom feel you have personal control over conditions and events. That feeling can lead to a lack of a sense of responsibility for the consequences of your actions or inactions. When you fail, you often blame conditions, resources, or others for your failure. "I wasn't trained for this," "That's not my job," or "If we had the same resources as our competitors, we would have won that contract" are thoughts commonly expressed by beginners and others with limited expertise. As a beginner, if you blindly follow the rules, you cannot adequately analyze a problem or see possible solutions that may actually be within your knowledge base or skill set. If you've followed procedures and made decisions guided by the rules and tradition, you may feel you've done all that can reasonably be expected and become a passive participant in the process.

## Taking Responsibility

In a recent study, twenty-one ultraendurance triathletes were divided by finishing times into three groups: leaders of the pack, middle of the

pack, and back of the pack. The triathletes' decision making during their performance was analyzed, and the findings are startling. The leaders focused tightly on actions to improve their performance, whereas middle- and back-of-the-pack triathletes reported a greater number of passive thoughts. For example, middle-of-the-packers might passively observe that it was a warm day, whereas leaders would consider how the temperature might impact their performance and subsequently make adjustments in their pace, nutrition, equipment, and hydration. Furthermore, leaders were more proactive in their approach to performance situations than were middle- and back-of-the-pack triathletes. They saw their performance as a direct result of their actions and took proactive responsibility. The lower performers felt no such responsibility and consequently were proactive in neither decisions nor actions.[6]

As a beginner, you may feel a lack of control and responsibility. If so, you may not be inclined to put much effort toward improving your performance when you feel you have neither responsibility for nor control of the results. You may even dismiss poor performance as normal and acceptable and give up early and easily. This characteristic is a watershed mark in developing expertise. When you feel responsible for outcomes and adjust your actions to improve your performance, you begin moving to the next step toward becoming expert.

**Whereas beginners may give up on clients, products, or plans too quickly, superior performers are never willing to give up.**

The drive to succeed and reach their full potential propels great leaders, inventors, writers, and entrepreneurs to the pinnacle of their profession. Should you ever find yourself giving up on a business matter, realize that you are also giving up on yourself as a businessperson.

Refusing to give up and searching for ways to turn defeat to victory help move you past the beginner step.

## Lacking Comfortable, Efficient Routines

Beginners sometimes become mired in the mundane because they haven't established personal work routines. They don't have the ability to see the interconnection of events in a business. A beginning sales representative may, for example, get caught up in friendly communications with a potential customer while overlooking more important tasks such as closing a sale, taking an order, or scheduling a delivery.

It's hard for beginners to sense the overall objective or see the relationships between events. The bigger picture that includes what came before and what will likely happen later eludes you as you concentrate solely on the immediate challenge before you. Which challenges or tasks are unique and which will repeat over time are a mystery, so every task is approached as a new challenge every time.

> With increased experience and discussions with colleagues, beginners start to recognize consistencies in the everyday or mundane activities of the workday.

As consistent activities recur, you start to develop effective routines to minimize organizational and management functions so that you can maximize your focus on completing the most essential tasks effectively. These routines are based on increased experience, knowledge, and skills, as well as familiarity, in the workplace. Through trial and error you find not only what works but also what feels comfortable. Being provided with examples and alternatives for conducting the ac-

tivities of a business can help you select and cultivate those routines that increase both the quality and the quantity of your work.

## How Beginners Learn

It's possible to remain a beginner for a lifetime. To move to the next level of expertise, you need to gain experience, to increase knowledge, and to develop some useful skills. Beginners have three preferred ways of learning:

- From experience
- With guidance from rules and established procedures
- Through mentoring

### Experience: The Greatest Teacher

For beginners, few things beat trial and error (especially error) for learning. Despite anything you're told, you just have to go out and see for yourself how things are. Perhaps reflecting your limited practical experience, real-world practice is your most important source of information for increasing competence. For beginners acquiring knowledge and skills, verbal or written information almost always takes second place to trial and error.

Simply put, there is no substitute for experience. Beginners usually develop a repertoire of professional skills by combining observations of experienced colleagues, personal trial-and-error experiences, and recollections of early role models. The more experiences and the greater the diversity of those experiences, the faster beginners learn and the more they improve. However, while experience is a critical aspect of improving performance, experience alone does not increase expertise.

## Rules and Established Procedures: Important

For organizations, having a clear set of written rules and established procedures—all consistently applied—can prove enormously useful to beginners in steering their decisions and actions during their first years on the job.

If you were a new employee at Monster Cable Products, Inc., for example, on your first day you would be handed a single laminated sheet called Monster Mottos. These are the company's operating principles and procedures as spelled out by visionary founder and head monster Dr. Noel Lee. Here is a sampling of the headings and some of the entries under each:

- Monsterous Business Strategy (Sooner is better than later.)
- Monsterous Personal Skills (Do what you say you are going to do within the time you say you are going to do it.)
- Monsterous Judgment (Find out what you don't know, that is, the root cause: Don't just treat the symptom; cure the disease.)

## Mentoring: Invaluable

Among a journalist's first assignments was covering city council meetings. What did she know about the city council or its meetings? Nothing. So what did she do? She was smart enough to know if she just plowed her way ignorantly through the assignment, she could miss something and her report would be neither accurate nor newsworthy. Rather than quietly taking a seat at the back of the room like many beginners would, she "walked into the city council meeting and announced to everybody there, 'This is my first day on the job, and I don't know anything. Please help me.' And they did."[7]

It is uncharacteristic for beginners to ask for help. No one likes to admit ignorance. But the cub reporter asked those with experience

for help—and got it. She did not remain a beginner for long. In fact, that reporter went on to become one of the most successful individuals in broadcast history. No one would have known her on that first assignment; but today, Oprah Winfrey is one of the most familiar faces on television.

As a beginning reporter, Winfrey realized that the importance of guidance and demonstrations from experienced professionals cannot be overstated. If we can't learn by doing, we can learn by observing. On the other hand, learning by listening is not a high-impact learning strategy for beginners: People need to be shown how it is done, not told. A good mentor has a longer-lasting effect on a person than any training manual or lecture. So, beginners who have not "been there, done that" should find people who have and learn from their experiences.

## Going Beyond Beginner

You need to do more than just spend time on the job to become more skilled. You need to learn from your experiences and gain a great deal more knowledge to reduce mistakes and increase successes. Combining experience with activities such as reflective practice, journal writing, professional meetings, reading, and networking with colleagues can help beginners gain knowledge and insight. This purposeful and sustained effort to improve increases your level of expertise—nothing less. When you work deliberately to learn from experience, gain more knowledge, and improve your skills, you do not remain a beginner for long.

In the next chapter, the characteristics that signal the rise from beginner to capable performer are identified and described. Prepare to take that step by completing expertise exercises 5–7.

## Summary

Beginner performers

- Behave in ways that are rational, procedural, and inflexible
- Make decisions guided by rules and norms
- Do not feel responsible for the outcomes of their actions
- Lack comfortable, efficient routines for everday tasks

---

**EXPERTISE EXERCISE 5**

## IDENTIFYING RULES TO LIVE BY

Identify workplace or professional rules to live by that you might write for beginners in your workplace.

**Rules to live by at**

_____

(your organization)

1. _____

2. _____

3. _____

4. _____

5. _____

---

# LEARNING FROM EXPERIENCE

Identify a recent experience you will likely encounter again in the near future. What will you do differently in the future that you did not do in the past to improve your efficiency, effectiveness, or performance?

_____

_____

_____

_____

_____

_____

_____

_____

_____

_____

_____

_____

_____

_____

_____

_____

_____

_____

_____

# MEETING MENTORS

Identify someone or some people in your workplace you would consider approaching as a mentor. Identify the characteristics and skills they possess that you would most like to possess as well.

Person 1: _____

    Characteristics: _____

    _____

    _____

    Skills: _____

    _____

Person 2: _____

    Characteristics: _____

    _____

    _____

    Skills: _____

    _____

Person 3: _____

    Characteristics: _____

    _____

    _____

    Skills: _____

    _____

# THREE

# CONVERTING TO CAPABLE

With a few years' experience, increased knowledge, and the development of some basic skills, you begin making the conversion from beginner to capable. When you are capable, you get the job done. For beginners, getting the job done can be a hit-or-miss proposition: Sometimes they do and sometimes they don't. Someone who is capable is far more consistent and efficient in completing assigned tasks and handling responsibilities. Decisions are made a bit faster, refined skills lead to better outcomes, procedures are executed smoothly, and transitions from one task to another are made more quickly. These are all signs of a capable performer.

In his book *Good to Great,* Jim Collins defines the level-one (first level) executive as a "highly capable individual [who] makes productive contributions through talent, knowledge, skills, and good work habits."[1] People at the capable level of expertise generally

- Have functional skills and focus on task requirements

- See similarities across contexts

- Can make decisions in a timely manner

- Are responsive to situations
- Use strategic knowledge in decision making
- Learn best from experience but develop other resources as well

## Having Functional Skills and Focusing on Task Requirements

The management team at Cabela's, one of the largest retailers of outdoor equipment in the United States, faced a mountain of challenges as it prepared to open a 175,000-square-foot megastore in Wheeling, West Virginia, in August 2004. Finding people to fill the four hundred frontline positions was high among those challenges. The criteria for selecting those who would be on the sales floor were clearly articulated by manager Tony Gatti: "You give me somebody who's dedicated and has a love and a passion for the outdoors, and I can teach him what he needs to know about retail."[2] In other words, beginners could be taught the functional retail skills to make them capable salespeople if they possessed experience, knowledge, and skills in the core industry—the outdoors.

When you perform a task or job on the capable level, you get the job done with serviceable skills; that is, the level of skill is adequate for the requirements of the task, but not extraordinary. Cabela's is clearly not the only business that relies on functional skills from certain employees. Many positions in business require only functional skills. Assembly-line workers, for example, are required to repeat the same skill again and again and again with a degree of both speed and accuracy. Most employees in the fast-food industry are required to have functional skills. As long as the skills are executed so as to complete the required task within acceptable standards, the job done is con-

sidered satisfactory. Capable employees who execute functional skills do so with consistency, which is critical to quality control. Because those with functional skills command a lower wage than those with more developed skills, these individuals are critical to cost control.

On most assembly lines, seldom is one worker identified as more skilled than another. All that is required of these employees is a capable level of performance. Because skills cannot be differentiated, experience is normally the primary determiner of wage standards (that is, those with more experience receive a greater wage). Training for such a position often extends no further than ensuring that the employee can perform a task or tasks to the required standard. Functional skills are not solely the domain of the blue-collar worker. Many such skills are found in every profession or occupation—and at every level.

Unlike beginners, capable performers have some relevant experience. When you have some level of experience in a workplace, you move beyond simply following procedures when undertaking tasks, but you still maintain a tight focus on meeting the job requirements rather than focusing on the purpose or quality of your performance. An example of this level of focus was revealed in a research investigation of forty professional software designers.[3] Highly rated performers undertook their designs with a focus on planning and results, whereas capable performers focused on analyzing the task requirements and verbalizing task-irrelevant thoughts. Interestingly, highly and moderately rated performers did not differ with respect to length of experience.

**The skills of a capable performer are focused on adequately meeting the task or job requirements—nothing more, nothing less.**

## Seeing Similarities Across Contexts

Edwin Land, founder of Polaroid and holder of more than five hundred U.S. patents, understood well the importance of capable individuals seeing and connecting similarities across contexts. In telling a story about how color film was invented, he spotlighted the benefit of that ability. He wrote,

> When I started on the actual program of making the black-and-white film for our camera, I set down broad principles that would also apply to color. I invited Howard Rogers, who had worked with me for many years in the field of polarized light, to sit opposite me in the black-and-white laboratory and think about color. For several years he simply sat and, saying very little, assimilated the techniques we were using in black-and-white. Then one day he stood up and said, "I'm ready to start now." So we built him the color laboratory next to the black-and-white laboratory.[4]

Over time, recurring events in the workplace are recognized and remembered. When the unfamiliar becomes familiar, knowledge of situations, people, and activities expands and deepens, and you can envision similarities across contexts. Being able to identify these similarities, you can select an appropriate solution from those tested during prior experiences. Increased expertise emerges when you examine a new experience by searching for a solution or decision from previous experiences rather than relying strictly on established rules or prescribed procedures as you did when you were a beginner.

Insight into similarities across contexts was first revealed in a classic study in 1981 by University of Pittsburgh researchers Michelene Chi, Paul Feltovich, and Robert Glaser. Physicists were given a series of problems and then asked to sort the problems and analyze the nature of their groupings. The scientists with more expertise used principles of mechanics to categorize the problems, while those with less

expertise used literal factors stated in the problem description to categorize the problems. The research team concluded that those with more expertise "are able to 'see' the underlying similarities in a great number of problems, whereas the novices 'see' a variety of problems that they consider to be dissimilar because the surface features are different."[5]

**Capable individuals with more expertise classify problems based on principles; beginners see problems based on surface features.**

This study suggests that to fully understand the nature of a problem, you must identify principles and similarities the current problem shares with previous problems. While this ability becomes highly developed in elite performers, it begins to emerge as you leave the beginner level and enter the capable level of expertise.

Because you recognize similarities across situations, you can make applications from one situation to another. This was a principle Sam Walton embraced when he was first starting out as a retailer. With a yellow legal pad or a tape recorder, he marched into every competitor's store he could find. He was seeking information about pricing, displays, and how competitors' businesses were run. He brought back the lessons he learned to Wal-Mart and applied the lessons that fit with similar situations in his stores. According to Walton, "We're really not concerned with what competitors are doing wrong; we're concerned with what they are doing right."[6] Few discount retailers would argue whether Sam Walton got it right.

### Making Decisions in a Timely Manner

Time-pressured situations call especially for the application of expertise. An offshore oil rig can be a dangerous place to work. With

large amounts of heavy and sophisticated equipment attended to by a small army, and all perched precariously over an ever-changing sea miles from dry land or help, the decisions made on the oil rig have serious and immediate consequences. A single mistake can quickly translate to a catastrophic disaster.

Researchers studied the decision making of eighteen offshore oil rig managers from two operating companies. In simulated emergencies, they found all of the managers could identify the first critical decisions to be made, as well as the cues, goals, and expectations for handling the emergency. They were all well trained. The decision-making responses of the most experienced managers, however, showed something a bit different from the rest. The seasoned veterans had recognition-based principles in place for managing emergencies. In other words, they used carefully considered criteria to determine the significance of the events unfolding; and, then, after they recognized the critical factors, they initiated previously tested solutions to handle the situation. With their experience, they were able to see similarities across the events that potentially could lead to disaster. They not only saw the similarities; they also were prepared to respond in ways that prevented catastrophe.[7]

Time is a luxury you do not have in situations where an action must be taken *now!* Research also has shown that the classical decision-making model guided by a rational thought process is not always used by those with more expertise to make decisions.[8] In situations and environments where time is of the essence, experts often trade decision accuracy for decision speed. The rational decision-making process requiring rich resources and careful consideration of multiple options is not effective in urgent situations.

Capable individuals in time-pressured situations typically look for patterns in the situational cues. When you see the features of the events unfolding now as similar to those of events you previously ex-

perienced, you can make decisions based on the decisions made in those previous, similar situations. These recognition-primed decisions and actions do not require a great deal of time or thought to achieve acceptable results and have the added benefit of reducing your vulnerability to the stress imposed by time pressure.

## Being Responsive to Situations

He had put in close to seventy hours that week knocking on front doors in small villages and farms in northern Indiana trying to sell books. For his efforts, Aaron Meyers made about sixty cents an hour. Minimum wage at the time was $1.25. Something had to change. He was wearing the skin off his knuckles pounding on doors, but people were not listening to his sales pitch. He was following rules and procedures but not getting the results. So Aaron tried something different: He began asking questions. When a potential customer would respond with a reason for not buying a book, Aaron would say, "I understand." He would then ask a couple of questions: "Wouldn't we have loved to have books like these in our home when we were kids?" and "If your children asked you the difference between a verb and an adverb, wouldn't you like to have a book like this to show them the difference?" He got his customers to talk. Specifically, he got his customers to talk *themselves* into the sale. Rather than strictly following the rules for pitching his books, Aaron was responding to the situation and his customers. His sales quickly began to climb as he became a capable sales professional. But he didn't stop developing sales skills or learning more about situations and customers. As the International Division president of the Tom James Clothing Company, the world's largest retailer of custom clothing, Aaron Meyers continues to learn today so he can find more success tomorrow.

Where beginners rely on rules and procedures to guide virtually all their actions, capable individuals let situations, in part, guide their actions and decisions.

**You are capable when you realize that not every rule applies in every situation.**

Rules and procedures remain useful, but decisions and actions become more responsive to the nuances and subtleties of a situation. For example, if hiring managers strictly follow a rule that they can hire only people with an appropriate and accredited college degree, they may miss the opportunity to hire an individual of exceptional competence and knowledge of the field. Albert Einstein's academic degrees were revoked by the Nazis in the 1930s, and Bill Gates has yet to complete his Harvard undergraduate degree. Does that mean the rule of hiring only those with a college degree is inadequate? Not necessarily. But there may be situations in which the application of the rule is counterproductive to the goals of the organization or person.

## Breaking the Rules

Dr. Rita Levi-Montalcini graduated summa cum laude in 1936 from the University of Turin Medical School. Just three years later, she was forced out of her research position by a Fascist law forbidding Jews to work in academic or professional fields. With the threat of arrest and deportation by the Nazis, her family went into hiding. While the rules forbade her to conduct research, she was not to be deterred. She built a small research laboratory in her bedroom to continue her study of neurological development in chick embryos. Heavy Allied bombing soon forced her to move into the country. She built another laboratory and resumed her experiments. She scoured the countryside, where food was scarce, for fertilized eggs for her research. Frequent power outages shut off the incubator that was used to grow the em-

bryos, often destroying weeks of work. Levi-Montalcini broke the rules, endured, and prevailed. In 1986, she was awarded a Nobel Prize for her nerve growth research that now helps combat dementia, tumors, and muscular dystrophy.[9] Had she not responded, and broken the rules, the world today clearly would be a poorer place.

To develop this characteristic, people must understand what needs to be done to reach the ultimate outcome and work within the immediate demands of the workplace. Beginners are still learning the fundamentals of the business and may be unable to see clearly the final result of their actions. Capable individuals with some experience and knowledge of the workplace understand the situation in which they find themselves and then take a course of action that achieves the desired outcome.

### Using Strategic Knowledge in Decision Making

A ticket agent in Minneapolis, on a wintry February Friday, cemented my loyalty to her airline. As I checked in at the gate for my late afternoon flight to Atlanta, the ticket agent informed me that there was room on an earlier flight to my home city. With a snowstorm moving in, she offered to put me on at no charge to ensure that I made it home for the weekend. The airline's charge for changing a ticket was $100. Needless to say, when it comes to future flight reservations, I will look to that airline, whose capable professionals use strategic knowledge in the best interests of their customers and, ultimately, their company.

When you are capable, you have an advantage over beginners in the area of experience. As you accumulate experience, you begin cataloging recurring events and problems, which leads to seeing similarities across contexts. But your experience also provides you with knowledge of the consequences of your previous actions. When

a problem presents itself, you can recall similar, previously solved problems for help in understanding which actions will lead to which outcomes.

**Capable performers use strategic knowledge by taking action based on knowledge of the consequences of previous actions.**

According to researchers Ann Graham and Vincent Pizzo, in the business world "understanding the business battleground, be it product or service dimensions (e.g., costs, precision, value, quality) or environmental factors (e.g., competitive forces, regulations, socio-economic trends), is a logical starting point for deciding how to organize and manage knowledge assets."[10] Because you have faced similar challenges and gained an understanding of the business battleground, you can better understand the long-term consequences of your actions. For example, something you did in a given situation may have solved the immediate problem but had long-term negative consequences. You have also acted in ways that not only solved the immediate problem but also prevented future problems and had long-term positive consequences. When the ticket agent moved me to that earlier flight, she took care of her immediate responsibility of getting me on a plane to Atlanta. The long-term consequence of bending that rebooking rule was that not only did she avoid having to find me a seat on a flight the next day if my original flight were canceled due to the storm, but she also gained a loyal customer for her company. A beginner would have strictly followed the rules and made life difficult for both me and possibly the airline.

By using strategic knowledge, as a capable person you are in a position to solve multiple problems and handle several tasks simultaneously. When you use strategic knowledge, you select actions that provide multiple benefits or consequences in a given situation. Beginners may solve the immediate problem with little understanding

of the long-term consequences of their actions. In a study of sales professionals, for example, the more capable salespeople had a deeper knowledge of both their customers' traits and effective sales strategies. Thus, they developed more sophisticated sales scripts that accommodated a wider range of both traits and strategies than did the less capable sales professionals.[11]

As a capable performer, you may still be somewhat rule oriented, but now circumstances and context can guide you in how to apply the rules and in knowing when to ignore or flex the rules as the situation dictates. Flexibility in following rules was observed in a recent study of physicians' decisions when they prescribe drugs. The study found that physicians with more experience in drug therapy were more idiosyncratic in prescribing drugs than physicians with less experience. Although both groups followed the prescription guidelines for each drug, those with more experience were more strategic in prescribing drugs because they saw the therapy in more holistic terms and adapted prescriptions to the individual patient. Junior physicians were more formulaic and rule-bound in their approach. This study suggests that it may be as important to know when to depart from standard medical practice as it is to know the standards of medical practice. Capable physicians develop strategic knowledge to guide their medical decision making.[12]

Strategic knowledge is incubated in experience and fed knowledge that is pertinent to accomplishing specific tasks. It grows from trial and error, tapping into knowledge sources and recognizing similarities in events. Developing this knowledge requires that you

- Acquire experience
- Reflect on decisions and actions to learn all you can from each experience
- Experiment with viable alternatives to repetitive tasks associated with your job

- See a variety of sources for helpful information (reading, talking with colleagues, observing others in action, etc.)

The greater your ability to leverage strategic knowledge in making decisions and taking action, the greater the gains you make toward becoming expert.

### Developing Other Learning Resources

Experience taught you well when you were a beginner, and it continues as your teacher when you are a capable performer. However, experience alone won't teach you all you seek to know. Capable performers therefore begin looking to sources outside their immediate circle of daily activities for new information to solve old problems, increase performance efficiency, or discover an innovative practice.

**Capable performers find accomplished colleagues particularly valuable.**

A host of factors inhibit beginners from depending on colleagues as an information source, including an unwillingness to admit a lack of knowledge or skills, a belief that colleagues don't know any more than they do, and a self-directed orientation—rather than a team or goal orientation—to every problem. With gains in experience and increased knowledge of both the work and the workplace, you develop relationships with colleagues and feel comfortable asking for help or an opinion without the fear of being thought incompetent. You also realize that others in the workplace are both knowledgeable and willing to help.

From the *Journal of Applied Business Research* comes a study on the performance of middle managers.[13] Middle managers achieve varying levels of success based on strategies they use in undertaking

projects. The most successful managers—"leaders" in the study—integrate their skills and expertise with that of colleagues through both formal and informal interactions. In their work, they not only are willing to lend their knowledge and skills to others but are also comfortable asking their colleagues for support in areas where they may lack expertise.

The least successful managers—"laggards" in the study—had the necessary skills and knowledge for success but were unable to mobilize the necessary social support network to shore up limitations or weaknesses. The point is this: The differences between middle managers who lead and those who lag are not found in experience, knowledge, or skills, but rather in the ability to utilize help from capable colleagues.

Interestingly, as you gain expertise, the fear of being perceived as incompetent fades. Experts seldom shy away from asking for needed help—even if the person who may be able to help them is a rank beginner who just happens to know something the expert does not. A new employee, for example, may have extensive knowledge of Web design and navigation. Experts in business are not necessarily expert in using the Internet, but they will quickly make use of their new colleagues with such expertise. Comfort in asking for help first begins to reveal itself at the capable level.

In addition to continued experience and depending on colleagues, capable people become aware of areas of strengths and weaknesses in their professional practice. They are learning to leverage their strengths, but at this stage they also realize they must shore up their shortcomings. To that end capable individuals may seek out varied sources of knowledge that help them to overcome their deficiencies. Books, journals, training programs, observing others, and so forth are tapped from time to time as knowledge sources. You may not realize just how rich these resources are for new knowledge until

much later in your development. But, as a capable performer, you begin to make that discovery.

## Moving Toward Competence

In many businesses being capable is sufficient, and you may find neither personal nor professional motivation to develop further. If being good enough is just not good enough for you, however, then you are likely to become more expert. If you are motivated to stretch your experience, increase your knowledge, and gain greater skills in executing professional actions, you may find several learning strategies that are especially helpful in climbing to the competent level—your next step toward becoming expert.

As you continue to increase your experience, knowledge, and deliberate practice of professional skills, your capable characteristics soon give way to characteristics that accompany the next step toward expertise: competence. Expertise exercises 8–10 can help further your development.

## Summary

Capable performers

- Have functional skills and focus on task requirements
- See similarities across contexts
- Can make decisions in a timely manner
- Are responsive to situations
- Use strategic knowledge in decision making
- Learn best from experience but develop other resources as well

EXPERTISE EXERCISE 8

## RESPONDING TO SITUATIONS

There are times when a capable performer gains a better result by responding to a situation rather than strictly following established rules. Recall a situation in which you found the rules of your organization inadequate for achieving a superior outcome. Describe the situation, the rule, and what you did (or speculate on what you might have done) rather than strictly following that rule in order to achieve a better outcome.

_____

_____

_____

_____

_____

EXPERTISE EXERCISE 9

## DEVELOPING STRATEGIC KNOWLEDGE

Capable individuals develop strategic knowledge, allowing them to ignore or flex rules or policies in certain situations. Recall a recent workplace event where you used strategic knowledge instead of a rule or policy. Was the outcome more positive or less positive than if you had followed the rule or policy? Explain.

_____

_____

_____

_____

_____

## MAXIMIZING RESOURCES

Describe some accessible resources that will increase your workplace performance. This might include registering for a seminar or class, reading a relevant book (e.g., a biography, self-help book, or how-to manual), or bookmarking a Web site that you can visit regularly for fresh information about your current, or future, job responsibilities.

1. _____

2. _____

3. _____

4. _____

5. _____

**FOUR**

# CULTIVATING COMPETENCE

When increases in knowledge and skills are combined with experiences accumulated as a capable performer, competence is cultivated. Competent performers not only get the job done—they get it done well. They are good at what they do, and people recognize them for their experience, knowledge, and skills. Competent performers commonly

- Use goals and long-term plans to guide decisions and actions
- Distinguish important from unimportant factors when analyzing situations or events
- Plan contingently
- Have a sense of timing and momentum in making decisions and taking actions

The majority of people in any organization are usually competent. To do a job well on a consistent basis normally satisfies the boss, the clients, and other stakeholders. If the majority of people in an organization are not at least competent, the business is likely to

languish, if not outright fail. It is therefore in the best interest of any organization to ensure that its people are provided the opportunity, experience, and education to become better at what they do. It is also incumbent on an organization to hire those people who are committed to becoming at least competent in executing the duties and obligations of their position. The level of competence for people in that organization is not only a direct reflection of the organization but also of them as individuals.

**If you are not committed to becoming competent, or beyond, there is little chance you will succeed in your business.**

If that is the case, perhaps it's time to find another business you can take pride in and have passion for.

It would be easy to think that the point in bold type above is a hollow motivational pitch. Far from it. It is part of the formula for success—yours, as well as your organization's. This point is best exemplified by one of the most successful airlines in the skies today—Southwest Airlines—on its Web site:

### The Mission of Southwest Airlines
The mission of Southwest Airlines is dedication to the highest quality of Customer Service delivered with a sense of warmth, friendliness, individual pride, and Company Spirit.

### To Our Employees
We are committed to provide our Employees a stable work environment with equal opportunity for learning and personal growth. Creativity and innovation are encouraged for improving the effectiveness of Southwest Airlines. Above all, Employees will be provided the same concern, respect, and caring attitude within the organization that they are expected to share externally with every Southwest Customer.[1]

The Southwest mission statement clearly reflects the belief that the success of an organization is dependent on its people's competence, and the competence of its people is clearly dependent on the organization. Make no mistake: Southwest Airlines has been successful. Its net profit margins have been the highest in the airline industry. From 1990 to 1996, its stock price rose 300 percent.[2]

As you learn more about the tasks to be completed and gain experience in accomplishing them, you begin to develop skills that allow you to perform with efficiency and effectiveness. At this level of expertise, you have a firm grasp on the tasks that pattern your daily business life, feel relatively comfortable in your working environment, and, for the most part, make people happy with your performance. And why shouldn't they be? You are competent and can get the job done!

You're competent because you now possess certain characteristics that you didn't have when you were a beginner or a capable performer. These characteristics contribute to your ability to undertake tasks and responsibilities with greater and more consistent success. Realize that they are cues signaling your ascension from the lower levels of expertise. Developing these characteristics enabled you to elevate your level of expertise, and continuing to cultivate them will maintain your level of competence and perhaps elevate it higher.

## Using Goals and Long-Term Plans to Guide Decisions and Actions

Shortly after the D-day invasion of France in World War II, Winston Churchill, the British prime minister, disagreed with the other Allied leaders about next steps. President Roosevelt wanted a follow-up invasion on the southern coast of France, whereas Churchill believed a

stronger push in Italy was a better use of resources. After a long and heated discussion with Army General Alan Brooke, Churchill recognized that, in the bigger scheme of the war, it was better to have a strong bond with his allies than to win every point of disagreement. He therefore gave his consent to Roosevelt and informed General Brooke, "All right, if you insist on being damned fools, sooner than falling out with you, which would be fatal, we shall be damned fools with you, and we shall see that we perform the role of damned fools damned well!"[3]

Where beginners struggle to apply the rules and handle the immediate challenges, competent people long ago mastered the rules and are comfortable with the everyday challenges of their job. Rather than being absorbed by the immediate and mundane demands of the workplace, those who are competent work toward broader goals to ensure long-term success.

**The practices of competent professionals are guided more by purpose than by policies and procedures.**

In describing the elements of decision making by effective executives, Peter Drucker identified the first question the effective decision maker asks: "Is this a generic situation or an exception?"[4] Is the cause of the situation something that underlies many occurrences, or is the cause unique to this particular event? Only in seeing the bigger picture do executives know if the situation is caused by a long-term problem or a blip in the process. If the situation is long-term and part of the bigger picture, then the decision must be one in which a principle is engaged and applied. The principle should support the long-term health and welfare of the organization, because making a series of temporary decisions is akin to putting your finger in a crumbling dike.

Competent performers also have a greater ability to plan. They possess the knowledge and skills to anticipate events, to adjust for changes in those events, and to implement plans to guide decisions and actions. This level of thinking and acting is beyond the abilities of most beginners and capable performers because they lack the experience, knowledge, and skills of a competent performer.[5]

Competent performers gain several advantages when they focus more on long-term goals rather than on near-term tasks. First, with the strategic knowledge gained as a capable performer, the competent performer knows the likely consequences of potential reaction. Selecting actions to meet long-term goals thus becomes easier. Second, with a long-term goal in mind, the competent performer is able to prioritize which tasks and strategies are most crucial in meeting the goal. Third, knowing the long-term goal and the tasks and actions that most likely lead to achieving the goal, the competent performer is able to be more judicious in resource allocation: Resources such as time, attention, and supplies can be dedicated to those actions that have the highest likelihood of accomplishing the objective.[6]

In a study comparing the planning of expert and beginner basketball coaches, several striking distinctions were discovered.[7] Experts focused more attention on information cues about player skill levels, abilities, and personal traits than did the beginner coaches. Consequently, the experts were more deliberate planners, requiring 60 percent more time to plan than beginners. Experts focused more attention than beginners did on establishing objectives for practice sessions and then developing activities to achieve the objectives as well as strategies for evaluating the attainment of objectives. An analysis of the experts' goal structures indicated that they knew many more routines and alternatives than did the beginners. Also, due to their extensive knowledge, the experts were more confident that their plans would be successful.

To cultivate competence, you must continually revisit the purposes behind your actions. If your only purpose is to maintain the status quo, complete a task, or just get through the day, you are mired in a beginner's perspective. If, however, your purpose is to think several steps ahead so that your efforts amount to something cumulative, a characteristic of competence is evident. Competent people rely on long-term goals and plans to ensure that their efforts work toward the bigger picture of progress and success. Stephen Covey describes this characteristic as follows: "By keeping the end clearly in mind, you can make certain that whatever you do on any particular day does not violate the criteria you have defined as supremely important, and that each day of your life contributes in a meaningful way to the vision you have of your life as a whole."[8] In short, competent people have a clear purpose for doing what they do.

### Distinguishing the Important from the Unimportant

Marion O'Brien Donovan is hardly a household name. Few people today, however, are unaffected by a solution she saw in 1946. In the middle of the night, and for the second time that night, she was dealing with a crying baby. The problem she faced was as messy as it was common: a wet diaper, wet bedding, wet clothes—and a wet, uncomfortable, unhappy infant. She was desperate for a solution to this recurring and exhausting problem. Seeing the shower curtain in her bathroom sparked an idea. She tore the curtain down and carried it to her sewing machine, where she fashioned a custom-fitted, leakproof, reusable diaper cover for her baby. She called her invention the "boater." Her invention was so popular that she soon became a millionaire. As an inventor, she found new ways of using common household items to solve common household problems. Donovan saw the

same things in her household that everyone else saw in theirs. She just perceived them differently.[9]

At the competent level, you are able to sort the important from the unimportant. For example, in the same meeting a beginner may notice the dress, writing instruments, or accents of those seated across the table, whereas you, the competent professional, overlook factors that don't bear directly on the intended outcome of the meeting. Instead, you locate the prime decision maker across the table and observe the keen interest she takes in the numbers and the bottom line with seemingly little regard for hypothetical discussions or speculation. During the break, you discover that she attended a well-regarded college and majored in accounting. Your astute perception of several important details has now provided you with valuable insight into the type of information necessary to secure a future with this client, while the beginner is left hoping things went well and wondering where to find an outfit like the one the decision maker was wearing.

The advantages of being able to distinguish the important from the unimportant in a situation should be obvious. This skill enables you to focus on those things that most likely will lead to decisions and actions that will most effectively realize your intended goal. But how do you learn to separate the useful from the useless? The simple answer is that your substantive workplace experience and broad knowledge of the factors that influence workplace performance are key elements in developing this skill. Research, however, has given us two helpful insights into how those with higher levels of expertise can distinguish the important from the unimportant: utility and principles.

### Tennis Lessons

A study of tennis instructors with varying levels of expertise revealed no differences in the quantity of cues detected in the instructional

environment. Put another way, there was no difference in *how much* information the teachers gathered from their observations. There were, however, substantial differences in *what* they saw. Those with lower levels of expertise identified a range of environmental factors, from what participants wore to where cars were parked. Those with higher levels of expertise saw a different set of factors in the environment. Specifically, they identified principles related to the performance, and from that they were able to locate cues that could be used in helping the performer improve. In other words, they were able to distinguish between the important and the unimportant factors in the environment by recognizing principles accounting for performance and identifying utilitarian information that would prove useful in taking performance-improving action.[10] The difference between important and unimportant information for the more expert teachers was found in the way that information was used for taking effective action.

**In business, if you are competent, in addition to utility you will likely use performance-related principles to sift the important factors from the unimportant.**

### Programming Abstractly Versus Concretely

The ability of competent performers to focus on more pertinent information was made clear in a study by Yale University professor Beth Adelson. Adelson gave computer programmers a series of tasks that required them to use both abstract and concrete representations of the tasks. She found the thought processes of the more expert programmers were more abstract and contained more general information about what the program did, whereas the beginners' thought processes were more concrete and focused on specific information

about how the program functioned. She concluded that "experts have learned that, during comprehension of this type of program, paying attention to the abstract elements of the program is more important than paying attention to the low-level details."[11] By seeing the program as a set of abstract principles, competent programmers do not get bogged down in details but rather focus on the principles to find optimal solutions to problems.

Selectivity is another way to think about this critical attribute of competence. When you have developed the skill of selectivity, you have developed the ability to select those environmental factors that will alter events or can be exploited to manipulate events. You can distinguish the important features from the unimportant in your business landscape.

## Planning Contingently

Two key differences emerged in a study of more expert and less expert pilots.[12] First, the more expert pilots spent significantly more time planning and preparing for a flight than did beginners. Second, competent pilots devoted greater effort to gathering the necessary information to plan for the contingencies that would ensure a successful flight. Third, beginners described themselves as passive recipients of information, whereas experts emphasized their active role in seeking information.

Like pilots, those with less business expertise passively, and heavily, rely on procedures and preplanning when conducting business. In contrast, competent businesspeople add another dimension—called contingency, or if-then, planning—that makes them more responsive to unanticipated events or shifting conditions when conducting business.

**When planning for an upcoming meeting or program, competent businesspeople are able to plan for contingencies and changes through if-then planning.**

For example, a competent salesperson might think something like the following: *If* the client looks interested, *then* I'll spend more time explaining the product. *If* the client looks disinterested in the explanation, *then* I'll go immediately into the demonstration. Again, experience enables you to notice similarities across contexts and provides you with the knowledge to offer a variety of alternatives depending on the situation.

In its early years, the Wm. Wrigley Jr. Company of Chicago sold baking powder. To boost sales, the young owner of the company offered free chewing gum to anyone who bought his baking powder. At the time, chewing gum was an uncertain product in an unproven market. Much to Wrigley's surprise, his dealers began asking if they could order the chewing gum without the baking powder. If they want to buy chewing gum, then I will sell them chewing gum, thought the budding entrepreneur. Now, almost two hundred years later, Wrigley's Spearmint, Juicy Fruit, and Doublemint gums are still in demand.[13]

Contingency planning provides alternatives, and it also makes decision making more fluid. Rather than scripting a series of events and then attempting to follow the script (as a beginner would), competent performers are prepared to make "in-flight" changes to their plans. What fate would have befallen the Wrigley company if its founder had steadfastly believed, "We are a baking powder company"? When you are at the competent level, you realize that no situation ever goes exactly as anticipated, so you are prepared to make adjustments as situations demand and as opportunities arise.

Competent business professionals are goal oriented, which establishes their direction, and their contingency plans help them ne-

gotiate the bumps in the road they encounter, as well as seize unexpected opportunities when they arise. Knowledge of their business environment helps them recognize anomalies and opportunities, and their increasing skills enable them to respond in ways that make success likely. Contingency planning bridges knowledge and skills, and converts any business event into a dynamic opportunity for success.

## Using Timing and Momentum in Making Decisions and Taking Actions

With the increased experience, knowledge, and skills that raise you to the competent level of expertise, you discover that the order and rhythm of your actions often can make or break an important business event. Accompanying a deeper understanding of the business landscape is the realization that the events unfolding are linked sequentially. That is, they have a history, are influenced by the people and current circumstances, and will affect the events that follow. To influence those events, you must learn to time your decisions and actions to have maximum impact and achieve a successful result.

As a beginner, you could rely on established procedures to guide what you did, and how and when you did it. These procedures served as a checklist to make sure that you accomplished each important step and that the steps were taken in the appropriate order. However, outstanding results are not achieved by following recipes. If that were the case, to become a master chef would require only that you purchase and follow a master chef's recipe book. But, as many cookbooks as celebrity chef Emeril Lagasse may have sold, just reading his books and following his recipes will not make you Lagasse's equal in the kitchen. It takes more.

As noted in the introduction, each step provides a foundation for the next. The procedures and rules learned at the beginner step and

the functional skills and strategic decision making learned at the capable level give you the basis for understanding the timing and momentum in thought and action of the competent performer. But where do those timing and momentum skills come from?

**Timing and momentum skills come first by understanding your business environment—the people, the resources, and how things work.**

A study of exceptional sales professionals revealed that they do not engage the sales process in a linear or procedural fashion.[14] Rather, they move around the sales process in what appears to be an almost random manner, until the researchers looked closer. Salespeople meet clients on an almost infinite number of points along their clients' decision-making processes, and the salespeople are not privy to all the information clients use to make their decisions. Competent salespeople therefore use their ability to distinguish the important from the unimportant to collect information relevant to the sales situation as opportunities present themselves. The process is not random. Valuable information is processed, stored, and then brought to bear *when the time is right* to usher the sales episode to a successful outcome.

Knowing what you are good at and how that can be aligned with the forces that drive your industry is critical to understanding the timing and momentum of your decisions and actions. Consider Michael McCafferty on St. Patrick's Day, 1983. On that day he both filed bankruptcy and began a new business. He slept on a used mattress in a bare apartment, lived on credit card debt, and had no job, no money, and no car. But he did have the knowledge and skills to show fledgling businesses how to solve common and recurring problems with computers.

With no funds for advertising and no car to make sales calls, he needed to make some critical decisions that would attract clients—

and quickly! In his cashless wallet, he found an old clipping listing ten rules for entrepreneurs. He reworked the list into a poster and gave it the title "The 10 Commandments for Managing a Young, Growing Company." McCafferty put his name and phone number at the bottom and smooth-talked a printer into producing two hundred copies on credit.

Next, he enlisted Marianne, an attractive friend of a friend. McCafferty offered to pay her a percentage of the profits from every client she recruited. She delivered the posters to every business in a large industrial park and said only, "Computers? If you would like more information, call the number at the bottom of the poster." Then she walked away. When the phone began to ring, Michael asked the prospective clients what problems they had with their business and offered them computer-based solutions. Because he knew which decisions needed to be made and when, Michael McCafferty had twenty-five clients in a short time, Marianne had $2,000 in commissions, and a new business was born.[15]

It is often most difficult to know what to do and when to do it when few, or apparently no, options are available. In Michael's case there were few standard business models that would have led to success. But Michael knew which decisions to make and when to make them. Timing and momentum in decision making are key factors in becoming a competent businessperson. Unlike Michael, most business professionals operate in an organization. In this setting the timing and momentum aspects of decisions and actions affect other people. You can make a good decision, but if people in your organization are not ready for it, it will be the wrong one.

When your business environment includes a corporate structure, you need to understand not only the external environment in which your clients and customers live but also the internal environment of your organization—its people, resources, structure, and mission. You

must be able to read the situation to influence the outcome. Former General Electric CEO Jack Welch put it this way: "What determines your destiny is not the hand you're dealt; it's how you play the hand. And the best way to play your hand is to face reality—see the world the way it is—and act accordingly."[16]

Therefore, it is usually best for you to begin by understanding, first, how decisions and plans are made in your organization and, second, how actions are initiated and measured. Then you need to know how your decisions and actions affect your coworkers. You must understand this from your coworkers' perspective, not yours. Most people will climb on board if they believe your decisions and plans represent a value proposition for them. In other words, if they believe what you are planning on doing will have positive benefits for them, then they will be inclined to align themselves with you. This is as true for your coworkers as it is for your clients. In any situation, therefore, you will gain an advantage by understanding what the others in the room or situation are thinking and what they need. This information will serve you well in timing your decisions and undertaking actions.

The timing of a decision and subsequent actions are as important as the decision itself. All rely on the wisdom that comes from experience in making decisions, knowledge of the critical aspects of your business environment, and skills to undertake the actions subsequent to your decisions in the business world.

## Avoiding the Competence Trap

In a typical workplace, the great majority of people are satisfied with being competent. They get the job done and get it done in a timely and reasonably accurate manner. Businesses cannot run without competent people doing what businesses need done. Like a cog in a

finely made watch, competent performers can be relied on to do their part time and again. They are appreciated for their dependability, knowledge, and skills. Employers and colleagues become comfortable with those who are competent, and in return competent people become comfortable with consistently meeting the expectations of others. For many people, the majority perhaps, the journey toward becoming expert ends here. But after years of being competent, some people find they have a desire to do better. For personal and professional reasons, they aspire to perform at a higher level. They seek to gain new experiences, increase their knowledge, and hone their skills. They want to know more and do more, and do their job better than they have ever done it before. They search for the next set of challenges.

For those at the competent level, a few learning modalities appear particularly useful for advancing to the next level of expertise. You may find that you are now learning more from others and less from experience. In particular, interactions with both colleagues and competitors are especially instructive. As you are already fairly familiar with your colleagues' thinking, you look increasingly to your competitors for new ideas and innovations. You especially want to know what they are doing right. Additionally, the resources—seminars, training programs, Web sites, books—that you found helpful when you were capable serve you even better as you move to the next level of expertise. You are beginning to get a clearer picture of what you don't know, and these resources can pinpoint the information you seek.

Good coaching and mentoring can significantly accelerate learning, particularly by identifying the knowledge and skills that will elevate your performance and structuring metrics to help you evaluate your progress. Setting goals, devising practice activities, selecting appropriate evaluation standards, and offering constructive feedback

are all functions of a good coach. Many competent people find it best to have a coach from outside their immediate work environment. Coaches can bring informed perspectives and fresh information, and they have the skills to take you to the next step along the journey toward becoming expert: proficient. Good coaches will also offer you exercises to improve your overall performance. Complete expertise exercises 11–14 to better reinforce the concepts from this chapter and prepare you for receiving the information on your next step.

## Summary

Competent performers

- Use goals and long-term plans to guide decisions and actions
- Distinguish important from unimportant factors when analyzing situations or events
- Plan contingently
- Have a sense of timing and momentum in making decisions and taking actions

## GUIDING ACTIONS WITH GOALS
## AND LONG-TERM PLANS

The actions of competent individuals are guided more by goals and long-term plans than by immediate concerns or situations. Identify below some immediate, intermediate, and long-term goals and some long-term plans that may serve to guide your actions.

Within one week: _____

_____

_____

Within one month: _____

_____

_____

Within six months: _____

_____

_____

Within one year: _____

_____

_____

Within five years: _____

_____

_____

## DISTINGUISHING WHAT'S IMPORTANT IN YOUR BUSINESS WORLD

Recall a recent business experience involving other people. First, identify three important factors you observed in that experience and the information each provided that was useful for taking appropriate action. Next, describe what action you took (or could have taken) based on that information that led (or could have led) to a successful outcome.

Factor 1: _____

    Action: _____

    _____

    _____

Factor 2: _____

    Action: _____

    _____

    _____

Factor 3: _____

    Action: _____

    _____

    _____

## PLANNING YOUR OPTIONS

Contingency planning is a tool that competent people use to ensure that they have a healthy complement of options for any activity they intend to undertake. In this exercise make three contingent (if-then) plans: a plan you will complete today, a plan you will complete six months from now, and a plan you will complete in one year.

Today: _____

_____

_____

In six months: _____

_____

_____

In one year: _____

_____

_____

# DEVELOPING YOUR CRITICAL SKILLS

List, in descending order, three work-related skills that, if improved, will have the biggest impact on your performance in the next twelve months. For each skill, list two practice activities and a metric you can use to measure your progress in developing the skill.

Critical skill 1: _____

    Practice activity 1: _____

    Practice activity 2: _____

    Progress metric: _____

Critical skill 2: _____

    Practice activity 1: _____

    Practice activity 2: _____

    Progress metric: _____

Critical skill 3: _____

    Practice activity 1: _____

    Practice activity 2: _____

    Progress metric: _____

**FIVE**

# PRACTICING PROFICIENCY

Competent performers do their job well, but those who step up to the proficient level of expertise not only get the job done well, they achieve results that are clearly and consistently above the standard. Proficient people are in the top 25 percent of their field in terms of experience, knowledge, skills, and performance. Few people know more, can do more, or outperform those who are proficient. In fact, only experts consistently outperform the proficient.

In top organizations, a significant number of people are proficient performers. An organization cannot consistently outperform the competition without people whose level of accomplishment is unfailingly above average. Proficient performers work harder and longer than most other people, but what really sets them apart is that they also work smarter and more skillfully. Gaining expertise takes exceeding dedication. Proficient performers dedicate themselves to actively searching for opportunities to gain new knowledge and perspectives, continually practicing and refining requisite skills, and working to learn all they can from their experiences.

Although proficient performers share many of the characteristics of capable and competent performers, they have additional characteristics that contribute to higher performance levels. Proficient performers

- Have a strong sense of personal responsibility
- Have highly developed perceptual skills
- Use efficient routines to handle everyday tasks
- Analyze and solve problems with forward thinking
- Predict future events with a high degree of accuracy

## Having a Strong Sense of Personal Responsibility

In 1977, the U.S. steel industry struggled to compete with foreign companies that could produce and ship steel to America cheaper than American companies could produce it. Many executives in the industry begged for government protection from the imports, but not Ken Iverson, CEO at Nucor. Iverson saw the imports as a blessing and spoke out against protectionist government policies. He saw the problems facing American steel as first and foremost stemming from poor management and the fact that management had failed to keep pace with innovation. In Iverson's tenure at Nucor, the stock of the company outperformed the stock market five times over.[1]

If you were to ask me for one characteristic that would differentiate the good from the great in any field, it would be this: feeling responsible. Those who achieve great heights in business, sports, or any other human endeavor do so largely because they believe the outcome is firmly in their hands. They feel that their level of achievement is chiefly their responsibility. Those who achieve less can easily find myriad reasons for a lack of success that reside outside their sphere of influence.

When you feel responsible for your success or lack of it, you work hard to learn whatever is necessary to become successful. When you believe that what you achieve is beyond your control, you give up responsibility for the outcomes of your actions and are therefore less inclined to work to turn a lackluster performance into an outstanding one. Less expert professionals lose sleep worrying about what might happen to them. Proficient performers lose sleep devising ways to be better tomorrow than they were today. They believe their efforts are ultimately measured in results, not in following procedures or completing tasks. For the most part, *how* they accomplish something is secondary to *what* they accomplish.

**Proficient performers take control of their destiny by planning their course of action.**

Proficient performers hold themselves accountable for problems and deficiencies they encounter, believing that the solutions to these problems reside within their capabilities and responsibilities. When problems arise or an action does not achieve the anticipated result, they analyze the situation, seeking alternatives that might produce the desired result when a similar situation arises.

It is not only those at the elite level of an organization who can take control of their actions. Fred Shea does not have a corner office, keys to a corporate jet, or an administrative assistant. Fred is a postman. He delivers mail. His level of proficiency is so great, however, that he inspired Mark Sanborn, one of the people on Fred's daily route, to write the national best seller *The Fred Factor*. What was the first principle Mark learned from Fred? "Everyone makes a difference. . . . Nobody can prevent you from choosing to be exceptional."[2] You are responsible for the difference you make.

This is a critical component in developing expertise, because when you feel personally responsible, you work diligently to produce

a satisfactory—or even superior—outcome. When you believe you have no control over or responsibility for an event, you can more easily walk away from failure, and thus not make the effort to take with you the lessons it may hold for the future. If you don't feel responsible for your mistakes, then you don't do anything about them, and consequently you never improve. Proficient performers take responsibility for their shortcomings, inadequacies, and failures and therefore seize the opportunity to change for the better. The quality of their performance is clearly up to them. They wouldn't have it any other way.

One evening when I was attending a dinner with the editors of *Golf* magazine, the discussion turned to the greatest golf shots ever hit. Carol Mann, a U.S. Open champion and LPGA Hall of Fame member, was at the table, so I asked her, "What was the greatest shot you ever hit in a tournament?" Without hesitation, Carol replied, "My tee shot on 16 in the final round of my U.S. Open win. I pulled it a little left and it stopped just inches from going out of bounds." Jaws dropped. When champions recall their greatest shots, they normally describe shots that flew through two time zones or a putt that tracked across the Andes Mountains before falling over the lip of the last hole—not a shot that stopped just inches from going out of bounds.

In a subsequent e-mail Carol wrote, "I had dreamed about this shot the night before—in my dream the ball went out. That fear was with me all day, and I tried to make some birdies before I got [to 16] so that in case I actually did go out, I would have a cushion of a lead." I gave Carol's comments considerable thought and began to realize how critical her perspective was to her being a champion.

Often we think champions are made in the great shots or great business moves that they execute at critical moments; but champions are also made in the mistakes they minimize or avoid. They take full responsibility for their weaknesses and mistakes, and therefore

focus as much attention and energy on eliminating or diminishing them as they do on building and capitalizing on their strengths.

## Having Highly Developed Perceptual Skills

Had you been a student at Cornell University in the fall of 1946, you might have witnessed, or perhaps even joined in, a food fight in one of the dining halls. A young professor named Richard was there, and as objects streaked through the air, one spinning plate with the university insignia stamped along the edge piqued his curiosity. As the plate spun through the air, Richard noticed that the wobbling of the edge increased as the spinning of the plate decreased. Most of us would have been more concerned with avoiding those flying plates than with noticing their rate of spin and wobble. This moment was, however, an epiphany for this young professor. As a physicist, he wondered whether the same phenomenon occurred in the electrons of atoms. His thoughts and experiments following that food fight led years later to Professor Richard Feynman being awarded the Nobel Prize for his fundamental work in the field of quantum electrodynamics.[3]

With their considerable accumulated experience and knowledge, proficient performers, like the young professor Feynman, perceive subtleties in the environment that can have profound significance. Years of experience and extensive knowledge have honed their perceptions to the point where anomalies are readily detected. In the business world, having a keen sense of timing comes from an intimate understanding of how one's industry and organization work. With an inability to discern the important from the unimportant, people on the lower steps of expertise struggle to effectively identify, and thus respond to, the most critical situational factors.

Business is a dynamic process where many people with different responsibilities, backgrounds, skills, and interests are engaged in the

myriad activities of an industry. While understanding business ma-
neuverings is essential, being able to focus on the individuals and
events that have the greatest effect on the outcome is critical. Being
able to correctly interpret the significance of unfolding events in business enables proficient performers to recognize the winds of opportunity in a meeting, market, or industry and to adroitly change the
course of action in a direction leading to greater success.

While beginner, capable, and competent performers often see the
symptoms, proficient performers see past the symptoms to identify
the cause of errors or inferior performance. By identifying the cause,
you can provide the appropriate cure more easily.

**A multitude of symptoms can be cured by eliminating the
cause.**

In a study of the professional orientations of the top one hundred
golf instructors in America, many viewed themselves as "repair" people. One instructor stated this important skill this way: "Every mistake
or swing fault has a reason; when you fix a problem at its cause you
can really help someone progress."[4]

Accurate perceptions and insightful interpretations begin with
up-to-date awareness regarding the conditions around you. In other
words, *situational awareness* is an important precursor to performing
well. A study of general-aviation pilots shed some light on this topic.
The pilots who scored better on situational awareness tasks were not
necessarily those with the most flight hours. While all of the pilots
with more than one thousand flight hours had high situational awareness scores, the scores of the remaining pilots, in both the experienced
and beginner groups, were not predicted by flight hours. The researchers concluded that flight hours were not predictive of situational awareness. Rather, pilots with greater skill in aircraft handling,

cockpit task management, task prioritization, and communication coordination, along with greater psychomotor abilities, were more situationally aware.[5] This study suggests that developing skills to levels of automatic performance eases attention demands, enabling people to concentrate less on skill mechanics and more on the situational factors that shape optimum performance. An automatic performance occurs when a skill becomes so highly developed that it takes no conscience thought to perform it—it is automatic. In everyday life, skills such as sitting, standing, walking, and typing are often performed with more thought devoted to the outcome than to the execution of the skill. Automatic skill performance, also known as *automaticity,* is a critical and often-used quality of an expert (discussed in greater detail in chapter 6). It is common, however, for proficient performers to begin to display automaticity in some of their repeatedly used business skills.

Obtaining up-to-date and accurate information in business can prove a challenge for those at the top of the management hierarchy. Seldom do staff want to be the bearers of bad news, especially if they believe such news reflects on their performance. Often information that CEOs receive is polished to take off the negative edge or is kept from them entirely. A recent study found that this was one reason many CEOs held inaccurate perceptions of their organization. In a survey of 124 CEOs and 579 other senior executives around the world, 52 percent of the non-CEOs reported that their teams did poorly in critical areas such as innovative thinking, leading change, developing talent, and building company culture. Only 28 percent of the CEOs reported problems in these areas.[6] Therefore, it is imperative that corporate leaders have firsthand observations and information regarding key elements of their industry. This point was not lost on Sam Walton, who believed that "if we don't have customer satisfaction at the cash register, none of us have a job." He instituted a

company policy that required all corporate staff to spend one week each year working as a salesclerk in a Wal-Mart store.[7]

Having highly developed perceptual abilities is not solely the domain of businesspeople. Being able to identify and respond to those things that are both important and within one's control is key to superior performance across the board.

Ivan Lendl was still moving up the ladder to the top of the tennis world when he achieved his first major victory—the 1984 French Open. This event was especially noteworthy because it revealed qualities in his character that would carry him to the ultimate level of expertise. In the final match of that championship, he was down two sets to none to the year's leading player, John McEnroe. Despite the large deficit, the twenty-four-year-old Lendl fought back to win the last three sets and capture his first of eight major championships. It was a feat that is still talked about today.

Being curious, when given the opportunity I asked Lendl what was going through his mind at the time. He said candidly that he wasn't thinking about the score, the match, or even that it was a major championship. He focused completely on each shot before him. He played one stroke at a time, one point at a time. His complete attention was devoted to winning the present point and nothing else. "Before I knew it," he said, "I was ahead and the momentum had shifted. *But I just kept my focus on the next stroke, and let the rest take care of itself.*"

It was deceptively simple. I wanted to say, "That's it?" But I realized the level of focus he was talking about is far deeper than the casual attention most of us give to the tasks before us. During the clamor and turmoil of a major championship, Lendl kept his focus on the essential element of the game of tennis and the one thing he could most control—the shot before him. I've often thought about the lesson behind Ivan's comment:

Recognize the environmental elements most critical for your success and give them your complete attention and your best effort.

## Using Efficient Routines
## to Handle Everyday Tasks

Established routines help proficient performers minimize time devoted to everyday, mundane, repetitive tasks so they can better manage their time and focus on issues and challenges that require more thought and attention. Routines are common in everyday life, from the time we get out of bed and off to work until we return home and retire at night. Efficient routines form the bedrock of how we orchestrate daily tasks efficiently. Unfortunately, we also tend to develop unproductive routines—gossiping, surfing the Internet, watching television, and so forth. We often waste time simply because something has become routine.

Organizations tend to have routines for handling tasks such as ordering, shipping, invoicing, and processing goods and services when attempting to do business with other organizations. But a 2002 study of 494 firms in the *Journal of International Business Management* reveals that adoption of standardized business routines and an unwillingness to adapt marketing practices seem to be associated with less success when entering new markets.[8] Clearly, routines that improve efficiency in one place or at one time may not work in all situations. When routines detract from success, they need revision to be effective.

Proficient business professionals, however, avoid these empty routines by focusing on getting things done.[9] They have a large toolbox of strategies to accomplish important tasks, and they use these

strategies as a matter of routine. For example, when reading a newspaper, they may skim the pages for a solution to a pressing problem or for information that may provide an advantage. When picking up the newspaper, they may say, "So what might be in here today that I can use?"

## Analyzing and Solving Problems with Forward Thinking

Decisions are made in the real, not the theoretical, world. Although many theories exist to guide strategic planning and decision making, professionals often find themselves forced to make complex decisions in unexpected circumstances. A study of the decision making of eighteen primary-care physicians offers an intriguing insight into how proficient performers make decisions.

A researcher worked with each physician to develop a task diagram of the various steps in which the doctor acquired patient information and incorporated it into decision making. The proficient decision makers demonstrated greater flexibility and a more automatic flow in their processes, which freed them to take advantage of new systems and limited their searches and processes to those essential to the situation. Consequently, proficient doctors responded well to unplanned situations and opportunities. Interestingly, the proficient doctors generated an "attentional surplus." Their efficient information retrieval and the automatic nature of certain decisions meant that they required less attention than beginner decision makers, leaving them with additional time to attend to other tasks.[10]

As a proficient performer, when you start to solve a problem you try to better understand the problem by analyzing it qualitatively. You rely on your extensive knowledge to construct a mental representation of the problem, from which you can

- Infer relations to help define the situation
- Identify constraints
- Isolate factors causing the problem and evaluate them
- Justify possible solutions

By analyzing and representing problems in this manner, you rely more on underlying principles and metaphors than on using literal and practical categorizations.

In solving problems, proficient people tend to use forward reasoning, working forward from known facts to the unknown, in contrast with backward reasoning, working backward from a hypothesis or to the known facts.[11] Backward problem solving is characteristic of those who are not yet proficient. Due to knowledge and skill limitations, they have a restricted set of solutions available. Therefore, when a problem arises, less proficient problem solvers usually select a solution they think will work and then reason backward to justify their selection. An old adage applies here: When all you have is a hammer, every problem looks like a nail.

Proficient problem solvers have a greater range of both knowledge and skills, are driven to devise the best solution possible, and are willing to construct an innovative or unique solution, if necessary. As a result, they invest time in carefully collecting all the facts before making decisions.

**Proficient problem solvers realize that if they don't get the problem right, there is no hope of getting the solution right.**

Proficient problem solvers sometimes may be slower than beginners in the early stages, but overall, they still solve problems faster.[12] More important, the solutions derived by the proficient decision makers using forward reasoning tend not only to produce superior results

but also to be more permanent. That is, not only do the solutions lead to better outcomes but they will less likely need to be changed, revised, or replaced.

An interesting study of managerial problem solving in the Netherlands revealed several valuable insights.[13] Some 115 managers were asked to diagnose and solve business cases. Capable and competent managers actually identified more case facts than did proficient managers, primarily because the more expert managers identified only those facts relevant to solving the case. Less expert managers identified both relevant and irrelevant facts. Due to their focusing on only relevant facts and relying on experiential versus theoretical knowledge, the proficient managers solved the cases more accurately and in less time than the capable and competent managers.

One reason that solutions reached by proficient decision makers are both more permanent and more accurate stems from these decision makers' relying more on underlying principles that may be creating the problem than on the surface features of the problem.[14] For example, a beginner manager may see a customer service problem being caused by an employee's particular personality. A proficient manager not only recognizes the individual's uniqueness but also reviews environmental factors that may be causing the problem, and then considers the underlying principles of human interaction and motivation. Essentially this means that the more proficient manager gathers all relevant facts before constructing a solution and then steeps the solution in proven principles rather than immediate concerns. As may be obvious, extensive experience and knowledge are required to develop the skill of proficient decision making.

Herb Kelleher, former president of Southwest Airlines, offers a poignant, if not humorous, point regarding the importance of analyzing problems: "Say there is a problem with anything. I—or somebody—goes out and experiences the problem. Someone says the bin

doors don't work. I want to see them not work, to feel them. How can I talk to Boeing about it if I haven't actually had the experience of it malfunctioning? How can I call Boeing and say, 'There's something wrong with the bin doors.' They'd say, 'Oh really, what?' And I'd have to say, 'Well, I don't know. I just heard that they're not working.'"[15]

## Accurately Predicting Future Events

We don't really believe proficient or expert performers have a crystal ball, but it often appears as if they do. Because proficient performers are extraordinarily good at recognizing similarities across situations, they can predict, or at least anticipate, potential and likely outcomes of unfolding events with a high degree of accuracy and precision.

A study comparing teachers with little, average, and above-average expertise demonstrated this ability.[16] The researchers asked teachers to view a series of slides of classroom events and comment about what they were thinking. The proficient teachers provided rich commentaries on their observations and drew on their experiences to make judgments about what they saw. They made many assumptions about what they saw, attempted to interpret the meaning of the events, and then inferred relationships between the actions observed and the likely outcomes.

The ability to predict potential outcomes proves useful in selecting activities because only those activities and strategies with the greatest chance of success are selected. For example, consultants' ability to predict which strategies and resources will help their clients improve in the most economical and efficient manner is a major benefit of proficient thinking. Being able to reasonably predict the success of an action plan can save time because you don't need to restart or retry the plan. Being able to predict the level of success increases the likelihood of a quality outcome.

> Being able to anticipate and predict likely events is based
> on years of experience in, and extensive knowledge of, the
> specific environment.

Having seen similar situations again and again, you can become
skilled at anticipating the outcomes of your actions, responses, and
behaviors. To accurately predict outcomes, proficient performers review actions, experiment with new ideas, converse with colleagues,
and want passionately to find the solution that is in the best interest
of the organization.

Research from Australia offers some exciting insights into using
video-based perceptual training to improve anticipation skills and
decision making.[17] The study used three groups of elite softball
players: trained, placebo, and control. In a laboratory setting, the
trained group watched various game scenarios on videotape. At the
beginning of the session, the players were instructed to focus their attention on particular anticipatory cues and then were asked questions to stimulate cue awareness and anticipatory judgment. Twelve
ten-minute training sessions were conducted over four weeks. The
researchers discovered that the trained group developed anticipatory
and decision-making skills superior to those of the other groups.
More important, these skills were shown to transfer to the field environment and live game play.

Anticipatory skills can be learned, and the advantages they offer
are well worth the effort for proficient performers. Imagine the advantage you gain when you can accurately anticipate the future.

## Taking the Final Step

Few people can achieve the level of performance consistently reached
by proficient performers. Being proficient puts you in the top 25 per-

cent of practicing professionals in your business or industry. You are in honored company. You can easily be satisfied with being within this elite circle. There are, however, those for whom being one of the best is not the same as being the best they can be.

For those who measure their performance by what they believe to be their potential and best efforts rather than by the achievements or standards of others, there is never a moment in which they feel they have succeeded completely. If this describes you, then you have an internal urge to move forward and experience new challenges, to learn more about what you do, and to execute your actions to greater effect. You have a passion and a drive that are never satisfied. Moving to the next step, expert, is not usually a conscious choice. Rather, moving to this step is more an attempt to satisfy a need to know, a belief that you can be better, and the knowledge that the only real limits placed on you are those you place yourself.

While proficient performers assume significant responsibility for personal and professional progress, notice similarities across situations, use well-established routines for everyday tasks, have heightened perceptual capacities, and show a greater sophistication in analyzing problems and deriving solutions, they still remain largely analytic and deliberate in their decision making as well as routine in their actions. That is, they still demonstrate a logical progression in their decision making and rely on patterned practices to carry out their daily tasks. But these are not necessarily the ways of experts or the top professional performers.

Several types of learning may help propel proficient performers to the final step of expertise. First, your interactions with others, both in your field and out, help you gain new perspectives on old problems, discover innovative strategies that work, and provide fresh leads to more knowledge. Working with people in your field keeps you apprised of trends and changes. Working with people outside your field

can help you bring innovative ideas to bear on old problems. Having learned much from their own experiences, proficient performers look to sources outside themselves for fresh ideas and innovations for knowledge critical to planning and decision making.

Peers, clients, and resources such as conferences, books, and videotapes become important sources of information to increase knowledge, but proficient performers find these sources a great reservoir of new skills that can be applied to their business. By tapping sources completely outside your field or profession, you can witness and practice skills from many areas, which can provide new revelations for your industry or profession. Many in business, for example, find communication skills effective for motivating employees, presenting plans to supervisors or board members, and interacting with clients. Because increased skill in communication is likely to improve the performance of any business professional, outside sources offer potent learning sources for guidance, models, and instruction. As described in the next chapter, the best performers never stop learning. If you are ready to learn what it takes to reach the final step in becoming expert, complete expertise exercises 15–18 and then turn the page to go forward!

## Summary

Proficient performers
- Have a strong sense of personal responsibility
- Have highly developed perceptual skills
- Use efficient routines to handle everyday tasks
- Analyze and solve problems with forward thinking
- Predict future events with a high degree of accuracy

### EXPERTISE EXERCISE 15

## TAKING RESPONSIBILITY

Identify a recent experience where the outcome was not to your liking. How much of that outcome was under your control? What will you do differently if a similar situation arises?

_____

_____

_____

_____

_____

### EXPERTISE EXERCISE 16

## PERFORMING ROUTINE TASKS

Identify a task or a series of tasks you routinely perform in the course of your professional duties and describe them briefly.

The purpose or outcome of the task(s): _____

_____

How you regularly perform the task(s): _____

_____

How the task(s) can be performed more efficiently: _____

_____

_____

How much time you would gain each time you performed the task(s) more efficiently: _____

## MAKING DECISIONS THAT MAKE A DIFFERENCE

Identify a problem you are currently facing and complete the steps below.

Clearly define the problem: _____

_____

_____

Isolate the factors (not the symptoms) causing the problem: _____

_____

_____

_____

Identify the constraints in finding solutions: _____

_____

_____

_____

_____

Evaluate possible solutions in terms of time, cost, and the likelihood of permanently solving the problem: _____

_____

_____

_____

_____

## EXPERTISE EXERCISE 18

# HARNESSING OUTSIDE RESOURCES

List three fields that can serve as effective information resources for your industry (e.g., psychology, sociology, engineering). For each field identify one specific resource you might use to gain knowledge, skills, or innovative insights (e.g., a book, consultant, or seminar).

Field 1: _____

    Resource: _____

Field 2: _____

    Resource: _____

Field 3: _____

    Resource: _____

# EXCELLING TO EXPERT

Experts are individuals who consistently outperform their peers—no one does it better than an expert. A group of experts may have different experiences, embrace different knowledge, use different skills, but they all consistently produce superior results. To state the obvious, experts have more experience, knowledge, skills, and success in their field than almost anyone. They are the best at what they do, and their record of performance proves it. This does not mean that experts can necessarily outperform everyone every time in every circumstance; rather, on an overall, long-term basis, expert performers get more done in less time, in more places, and with superior results more often than less expert performers do.

Interestingly, few experts see themselves as expert. Most see themselves as works in progress, that is, as still needing greater knowledge and increased skills, and still able to learn a great deal more from their experiences. Perhaps this perspective explains how they became experts in the first place.

Experts are all too aware that if they don't continue to make the effort to learn from experience, gain more knowledge, and develop new skills, they will be quickly surpassed by those who do. Therefore, experts are among the greatest learners in their respective fields. First and foremost, they read. The written word remains the most prominent source of knowledge in advanced civilizations. A true expert does not overlook such important sources of information. Experts also have highly developed networks of relationships. But it was not who they know that got them to the top; it was listening to the people they know that got them there. Experts use networks as a source of new insights, information, and skills—not for self-promotion.

The skills of experts are their signatures. To watch experts at work is to watch those who perform with what appears to be ease but certainly defines fluidity, gracefulness, and precision. Their professional skill sets are as extensive as they are refined; and, in an effort to constantly improve their performance, experts work continuously to sharpen their skills. Experts are also creative innovators. If a solution to a problem does not exist, or the present solutions are lacking, experts will devise or discover new methods, techniques, processes, or positions to elevate their personal and professional performance. The level of performance experts achieve is linked directly to the characteristics that define their presence in the workplace. Experts

- Seek knowledge insatiably
- Have a superior memory
- Attend to the atypical
- Plan extensively and act intuitively
- Execute skills gracefully and automatically
- Meet inadequacies and failures with corrective action
- Are self-monitoring

## Seeking Knowledge Insatiably

While it is obvious that experts have extensive knowledge, the importance of this characteristic demands that it be examined thoroughly. Business professionals who make the final step and become experts have made, and continue to make, significant investments in learning all they can about their industry, the requisite skills for good performance, and every factor that may influence the final outcome of their efforts. People seek more knowledge for a long list of reasons, but for experts that list inevitably includes passion for what they do. Meeting experts, you find people who enjoy talking endlessly about their business, seek others' views on pertinent topics, and have extensive libraries devoted to subjects that affect their enterprise.

Experts use extensive resources to build large stores of knowledge. Experience and colleagues represent essential sources of knowledge, but books, journals, and magazines, as well as conferences, education programs, and clients are also important sources for experts' knowledge.[1] Legendary IBM leader Thomas J. Watson Sr. was a knowledge sponge and offered insight into an important skill required of those seeking to scale the summit of the business world:

> Listening is one of the best ways in the world to learn. Sometimes we don't take the time to listen to the other fellow. That sometimes applies to the man when he is a supervisor. His manager is trying to tell him something, but he doesn't listen, he doesn't have his mind open. Sometimes you reverse that. Sometimes the man up above does not take the time to listen to other men, the men below him. Then he often loses a whole lot of knowledge and misses one of the greatest opportunities to study. We must therefore listen to each other.[2]

As you move up executive levels, you move further away from where the action takes place. It is easy to lose touch with what is really going on in the organization. A study of more than two hundred thousand executives, managers, and business professionals found that the most successful executives use a leadership style that keeps the information pipeline open and the critical data flowing freely.[3] The open pipeline, in turn, feeds the evolving thinking style of the analytic, information-hungry senior executive focused on finding the right answer. This skill manifests in public when senior executives encourage employees to offer information. In private, they use that information to narrow down options and identify the best one.

Taking this one step further, Stephen Covey describes highly effective people as those who "seek first to understand, then be understood." Specifically, he explained that empathetic listeners are those who "get inside another person's frame of reference. You look out through it, you see the world the way they see the world, you understand their paradigm, you understand how they feel."[4] Empathetic listening is "so powerful because it gives you accurate data to work with. Instead of projecting your own autobiography and assuming thoughts, feelings, motives, and interpretation, you're dealing with reality inside another person's head and heart."[5] The depth and accuracy of that data is a valued source of knowledge for experts.

**People who aspire to be the best they can be at what they do are sponges, constantly absorbing fresh ideas and information.**

To stop learning is to never improve. Experts know that. Lower-level performers are generally satisfied with what they know and, sur-

prisingly, believe they pretty much know all they need to know.[6] This point was particularly well illustrated by Florida State University coach Bobby Bowden as quoted earlier: "When I stop learning and adjusting, nobody will have to tell me to retire."[7]

Expert performers' superior knowledge permits them to use the workplace environment to great effect. For example, they demonstrate greater flexibility in using equipment or technology for greater efficiency of operation than lower-level performers. Make no mistake, however; experts do not use the latest and greatest technology only because it is available or because everyone else is using it. Only if a new piece of equipment will help them complete tasks with greater efficiency and produce greater quality will they consider using it.[8]

Experts do not collect information simply as a matter of habit or interest. They can tap their extensive knowledge to envision many ways of using equipment, skills, strategies, facts, facilities, or objects for multiple purposes, whereas those with less expertise might perceive only a single purpose.

Never one to waste anything for which a good purpose could be found, Dr. Waldo Semon, a leading chemist for the B.F. Goodrich Company, was using a chunk of industrial by-product as a paperweight. One morning in 1926, as he sat behind his desk, he pondered the paperweight. He thought to himself that, if he could find a way to make the substance pliable, perhaps it could be shaped into something useful. He thought some more and soon worked out a way to make his paperweight supple enough to pass through an extruder, a machine that shapes manufactured products. What was at one time only Dr. Semon's paperweight is now known to the world as polyvinyl chloride, or PVC, and people continue to find virtually countless uses for it to this day.

Interestingly, when experts are faced with relevant topics with which they have little or no familiarity, they take measures to gain

understanding. They take pains to talk with people who are experts on the topic, read pertinent materials, and even work on developing their own mastery of required skills. When you recognize the importance of your personal understanding of a subject in bringing it to bear on your success, you are seeing the world of information like an expert.

## Having a Superior Memory

It would be an exercise in futility if the knowledge you fought so hard to collect and construct filtered out of your memory like sand through a sieve. How are experts able to retain the knowledge they've been able to accumulate? It's not that they are any more intelligent than the average person, necessarily. Rather than large intellectual powers and capacities, they have skills that help them remember what they learn.

Testing the now famous memorist Rajan Mahadevan in a laboratory proved that he can recall from memory a remarkable number of numerals and letters. In 1981, Rajan recalled 31,811 digits of $\pi$ without an error. In replicating this research, researchers have now come to the conclusion that what originally appeared to be Rajan's innate ability has less to do with his superior memory than his thousand hours of practice in memorizing the mathematical constant $\pi$.[9] Rajan learned encoding techniques that helped him memorize large sets of numbers or letters through practice. Memory therefore is more accurately defined as a skill that can be learned rather than a characteristic possessed from birth.

Mark Cuban, founder of MicroSolutions and owner of the professional basketball team the Dallas Mavericks, wrote the following in his blog on May 7, 2004:

It's crazy the things that you remember. . . . I remember reading the PC DOS manual (I really did), and being proud that I could figure out how to set up startup menus for my customers. I remember going to every single retail store in town, BusinessLand, NYNEX, ComputerLand, CompuShop . . . and introducing myself to every salesperson to try to get leads. I would call every single big computer company that did anything at all with small businesses, IBM, Wang, Dec, Xerox, Data General, DataPoint (remember them?), setting meetings, asking to come to their offices since I couldn't afford to take them to lunch. I didn't need a lot of customers, but my business grew and grew. Not too fast, but fast enough that by the time MicroSolutions had been in business about 2 years, I had 85k dollars in the bank.[10]

I would disagree with Mr. Cuban on only one point: It is not crazy the things you remember—it is critical. That Mark Cuban never forgot what brought him success in the computer industry means he remembers the lessons learned and earned in his experiences. He actually noted this crucial point in his blog on April 25, 2004: "It's always the little decisions that have the biggest impact."[11] Experts remember the factors that have the biggest impact because those are the important things to remember.

I discovered another example of an expert's memory while studying the analytical skills of Charlie Sorrell, the 1990 National PGA Teacher of the Year. As part of the study, I had videotaped three golfers. One was an expert player. I asked Charlie to watch the tapes and just tell me what he observed. When we reached the expert player, Charlie exclaimed, "I know her! She took a lesson from me about ten years ago." I had to ask, "How do you know?" He replied, "You see her follow-through? See how she holds the club up? She did that ten years ago. Except it doesn't quite look the same. I wonder if she has a back injury." The player was Kelly Hester, and I asked her if she ever had taken a lesson from Charlie. "Yeah," she replied, "But just one." Then

I asked, "Kelly, do you have back problems?" "Yeah," she replied, "I injured my back about six months ago."

As demonstrated by Rajan, Mark, and Charlie, the memory of an expert is a remarkable attribute. The research of Anders Ericsson and colleagues[12] demonstrates that

**Superior memory comes from the ability to encode information as it is stored.**

A more recent study not only supports this finding but also offers additional insights that may prove useful for people attempting to improve their memory. In a study of experts' recall memory, two things happened when they encountered new information.[13] First, the experts evaluated the quality of the information. During this process they considered the reliability of the source, the contribution of the information to their current knowledge, and the significance of the information in terms of practical application. As they had since they were at the competent level, these experts sorted the important information from the unimportant in what they observed.

Second, the experts made predictions based on what they thought would happen next. From there they speculated on how they could use this information and on what effect it would have in influencing the next series of events. In short, a key to the superior memory of an expert is found in two questions—the same two questions you can ask yourself the next time you encounter new information regarding your business:

- How good is this information?
- How can I use this information?

If experts are dependent on their memory, will their expertise decline with age-related memory loss? UCLA professor Alan Casel addressed this question. Participants in his research studied sentences

that contained numeric quantity, object, and location information (for example, 26 cherries in a bowl). They were later cued with the location and asked to recall the object and its quantity. In general, there were significant age differences for recall of quantity and recall of arbitrary information but negligible age differences for recall of related objects. Interestingly, a group of older retired accountants and bookkeepers showed exceptional memory for numerical information. The findings suggest that experts retain their superior memory for domain-specific information even as they age.[14]

## Attending to the Atypical

In 1976, a young economics professor from Chittagong University in Bangladesh lent $27 out of his own pocket to a group of poor craftsmen. To boost the impact of that small sum, Muhammad Yunus volunteered to serve as guarantor on a larger loan from a traditional bank. A strange thing happened that no one in the traditional bank anticipated: The borrowers made good on their loan. This experience kindled the idea for a village-based enterprise called the Grameen Project. The project (and later a bank) was founded on Yunus' conviction that poor people can be both reliable borrowers and avid entrepreneurs—a conviction that ran entirely contrary to the thinking of traditional banks.

But Yunus understood economics and the people of Bangladesh. Therein was the basis for his seeing what was not typical in the banking business. For example, he focused his lending on women because they are most likely to think of family needs. This was a radical step in a traditional Muslim society, but as of this writing, 96 percent of Grameen's borrowers are women. Traditional banks favor large loans to big companies. Grameen offers poor entrepreneurs the small loans

they need. Grameen's rate of default is the envy of many larger banks. So astounding were the success and changes that took place with this project that Muhammad Yunus and Grameen Bank were awarded the Nobel Prize in 2005 "for their efforts to create economic and social development from below."[15]

When observing the events of business, experts such as Muhammed Yunus attend to the *atypical* in a situation. When situations are assessed as typical or predictable, experts let events unfold without interference and monitor them with an almost casual attention. On the other hand,

**When a situation appears to be unusual, experts attempt to make sense of the anomalies, looking for opportunities or dangers and anticipating outcomes.**

Expert business performers closely monitor situations in the business environment. When something atypical occurs, it receives rapid and thorough attention, followed by action. In a classic example, if you were a pharmacist in Chicago in the early 1900s, you might have noticed that several of your competitors began installing a small fountain behind their counter to dispense soda water as a health aid to their customers. Some of the pharmacists would even add a little flavor such as lemon or cherry to improve the otherwise slightly bitter taste of the bubbly water. To Charles Walgreen, this was not a typical activity for a pharmacy, and in it he saw opportunity. When the shop adjacent to his pharmacy became available, he expanded. The expansion featured a large soda fountain with an extended counter for his customers so they could sit comfortably while enjoying their drinks. He also extended the menu by offering sodas with ice cream and ice cream sundaes. Later he added soups and sandwiches to the menu to attract more customers. In attending to the atypical, Charles Walgreen found opportunity.[16]

When things are working in a normal pattern, however, experts tend not to reflect on what is occurring, but rather only monitor the process until something seems out of the ordinary. This conserves energy and does not allow experts to get bogged down in the mundane aspects of the operation. The bigger picture, which is framed by their goals and intentions, remains clearly visible.

It is the everyday anomalies that offer the early signals of both crisis and opportunity. Sometimes they are one in the same. By attending to the atypical, experts are able to see and seize opportunity or avoid disasters long before others and thus gain a decided advantage. When attending to the atypical, experts draw on their extensive and highly organized knowledge to efficiently and economically sift the information to determine their next set of actions.

## Planning Extensively and Acting Intuitively

At the competent step in developing expertise, preparation for action became more sophisticated as you planned contingently. As a proficient performer, you devoted more time to analyzing a problem and using pertinent information to think forward toward a workable solution. Experts build on these skills by improving planning and preparation and thereby set themselves up for taking effective, situational actions through intuitive responses.

### Extensive Planning

Expert performers have a high regard for planning and being prepared. Despite years of experience, they still feel the need to devise detailed plans to ensure that they meet their desired objectives. One example is former University of North Carolina coach Dean Smith, college basketball's winningest coach. In his 1999 memoir, Coach

Smith explained his view on planning: "Practice was the foundation of everything we did. Our practices were tough, carefully planned, and meticulously organized. . . . Each day, players received a typed copy of our practice plan. They would come into the locker room, and while dressing they would leaf through the plan, which would give them a precise schedule of what we would be working on that day."[17]

Experts see planning as an integral and necessary part of their duties. Basketball coaching great John Wooden dedicated two hours every morning to planning the afternoon's practice. He made notes on index cards and carried them to practice.[18] As he adjusted the plan, he noted the changes on the cards. Later, the schedule and notes were transferred to a notebook for future reference.

### The depth of planning increases with one's expertise.[19]

When you are an expert, your planning includes extensive evaluation of available information. You weigh action strategies to determine which external factors are most likely to influence outcomes and which action strategies may prove most effective in navigating the situation to meet the goal or achieve the desired result, given the resources available and the factors likely to be encountered. In preparing for a situation, you carefully review potential strategies relied on in the past and, because you have familiarized yourself with the situation you are about to face, you conceive new actions, which may be better than those used previously. Experts mentally plan out consequences of sequences of actions so they know the cost and benefits of each potential action prior to engagement.[20]

When you are an expert, your planning includes familiarizing yourself thoroughly with many of the factors you will likely face. You organize the knowledge and resources that are most useful in nego-

tiating the events that are likely to occur and assemble a catalog of strategies you can bring to bear on the situation as events unfold. Experts are seldom, if ever, caught unprepared. Experts' planning does not, however, create scripts that they follow to the letter once the situation or event begins. For experts, plans play an important preparatory role, particularly in dynamic and uncertain environments, but they do not inflexibly establish the expert's sequence of actions.[21] The following section explains why.

## Intuitive Action

It was a firmly entrenched belief in the pharmaceutical industry that you could not acquire a Japanese company and be profitable. After all, business is done differently there, making it difficult for westerners to understand and navigate the marketplace. But Franz Humer, chairman and CEO of the Roche pharmaceutical firm in Basel, Switzerland, saw opportunity—but he also had something else.[22] Roche already had a seventy-five-year presence in Japan under its own brand name, which helped Humer recognize the tremendous size of the pharmaceutical market there. As part of a deal with Chugai Pharmaceutical Company, Roche would give up its brand and integrate its operations, management, and products into those of the Japanese company. During negotiations, Humer's intuition told him that he could trust his Japanese counterpart across the table. That trust was built on a relationship that had been developed over a five-year period of discussions that had broken off but later resumed. When it came to decision time, Humer went with his gut feeling and closed the deal, and today Chugai Pharmaceutical is one of the top three companies in the world's second-largest pharmaceutical market.

A major divide between expert and less expert is the use of intuition in decision making.

> Experts use intuition—shaped by years of experience and sharpened by extensive knowledge—to make many of their most important decisions.

Experts get a gut feeling and have the confidence to go with those feelings—even if those feelings run counter to accepted logic or convention. They know they cannot know everything possible about the situation or the players involved, but they have planned and prepared extensively and are highly attuned to the important events as they unfold. Something has to be the trigger that signals the green or red light, and most often that trigger is the expert's intuitive feeling.

Intuitive decision making is a dangerous practice for beginners, and perhaps for even capable or competent performers, but it is the modus operandi for experts. Years of reflective practice, experimentation, trying, failing, and succeeding are required to gain an expert's intuitive ability. The criterion that separates the expert from the less expert is not the amount of intuition used but rather the superior performances and solutions the process yields.

How do experts develop intuition? According to Humer, "It's a matter of becoming hyperaware of your environment and learning to sense the vibe in the room. Especially in a negotiation setting, I try to have my entire body, my entire mind, all my emotions switched on to 'receiving.' How are people reacting? How are they behaving? If you can enter this mode, you can be sensitive to small changes that other people wouldn't even notice."[23] The genesis of intuition resides in two factors:

- Extensive knowledge
- Extensive familiarity with the environment—that is, experience

The years of study, the assembly of knowledge, and the careful planning are all needed to incubate intuition.

As Humer indicated, it also takes an intimate knowledge of your surroundings. You must know well the players and the activities that make up the social dance of your business. Who will do what, where, when, how, and why? Combined, there is no way to know precisely all of that information. But years of experience in similar business settings percolate with accumulated knowledge to enable you, the expert, to gain a sense of what is likely to happen, where and when it will happen, how, and why—and that sense, that deep feeling in your gut, is intuition. Often, as was the case with Humer in Japan, that feeling can run counter to conventional wisdom.

To develop a deeper intuitive sense for business decisions, you must practice using your intuition when it comes to you—and with experience and knowledge it will develop more. Learn to listen to it and trust it. For many who are schooled in logical analysis, trusting it is the hard part. In the initial phases of practicing intuition, look for a relative low-risk decision and go with the gut feeling when it comes. Soon you will come to trust that feeling like an old friend, and you will find yourself making superior decisions—but with no way to explain them other than "I just had this feeling." Intuition, remember, is not a logical or analytic process; it is indispensable in the decision-making process of experts. Extensive planning and intuitive action are a powerful combination in an expert's arsenal.

## Executing Skills Gracefully and Automatically

Gracefully executed skills are a hallmark of experts. The actions of experts account for their outstanding results. Knowledge helps you decide what to do, and your experience helps you know when to do it, but it is *what* you do (that is, the skills you execute) that is directly linked to your performance. In the case of experts, nobody does it

better. Experts have a wealth of skills and can perform them nearly flawlessly at the right time in almost any circumstance.

The years of experience and repeated routines in an expert's workday are performed with seemingly little effort, but the results are consistently extraordinary. Expert executives, for example, are highly skilled at planning, executing, and evaluating successful meetings due, in part, to the automatic routines used in conducting the meeting. The meeting may open with a statement of purpose, identification of the modes of interaction, and a closing statement that includes a follow-up. The meeting thus comes off with the optimum results in the least amount of time, largely due to the skillful behavior of the person in charge.

Performing a skill without conscious thought gives the actions of an expert a fluid, graceful, relaxed—almost effortless—appearance. A high degree of automatic behavior, described as experts' *knowing in action*,[24] is characteristic of expert performance. This skilled, automatic behavior is best viewed in an expert's daily routines. These routines are the repetitive activities that seemingly occur with little planning, practice, or forethought.

**An expert's automatic behavior stems from the ability to discriminate information early and respond quickly with practiced routines.[25]**

For example, a manager may know an employee so well that he detects apprehension while in the midst of an explanation of a new procedure and without much thought offers the employee reassurance that mollifies the apprehension.

This automatic behavior can be a double-edged sword. On one hand, it allows for the relaxed, fluid, unconscious performance of a skill. On the other hand, once a skill becomes automatic, the tendency is to let it lie and never improve it. A case in point: Very few people

practice improving everyday communication skills, such as writing or speaking—skills that, if improved, would no doubt improve virtually any business transaction.

It is also important to remember that as you gain experience in business, your web of responsibilities, and the skills necessary to meet those responsibilities, change. Put another way, as the inevitable change in business occurs, new skills are needed. Consider the outstanding performers in an organization who receive a promotion to the C-suite. While the skills they possessed in their previous positions may have made them stars, those skills may not be the same skills they now need to achieve outstanding results. It is common, for example, for those who receive a managerial promotion to be weaned away from individual performance skills in favor of skills that promote team and group performance.[26] The skills that get you promoted are not necessarily the ones that will keep you performing at an expert level. Given the shifting demands and dynamic challenges of business and industry, the development of business skills is an ongoing quest. Those who don't see it that way often wake up one morning wondering how the world has passed them by.

Experts, in their continual quest for improved performance, do not accept their present level of skills simply because it is automatic or comfortable, or because it accounts for their current success. If it will improve their performance, they will improve those skills. Tiger Woods, arguably the greatest golfer in the history of the sport, regularly visits his teacher for lessons. Woods knows that if he wants to improve, he needs a deeper understanding of the skills that lead to that improvement. After that knowledge is acquired, it must be practiced to be ingrained. It is no different in business than in sport.

When we observe the easy, graceful flow of an expert's skill, we often come to the conclusion that the expert is a "natural." No. No

one is born an expert, and no one is born skillful. Everyone must learn every skill they possess. While some may learn faster or to a greater level of proficiency, everyone learns skills the same way, and there are few shortcuts. The graceful, fluid performance of an expert is the result, not of any innate quality, but of years of practice. You must work hard at it to be good at it.

## Meeting Inadequacies and Failures with Corrective Action

When asked, "What is Nomura's greatest weakness?" Yoshihisa Tabuchi, CEO of Nomura, the world's largest and most profitable financial institution, replied,

> We haven't had a failure. To me that is a weakness. I think Nomura needs a failure. Past success can be as much a trap as a guide. Markets today are very volatile; the world can change in a day. But some people at Nomura believe that the way we succeeded in the past is the way to succeed in the future. It's natural to want to believe that. But unless you tear yourself away from that kind of thinking, you cripple your ability to cope with change and, more importantly, to create change.[27]

It may seem odd that an industry leader points to the lack of failure as a weakness. But this is not news to experts. To experts, today's failure may hold the key to tomorrow's success. Often the difference between proficient and expert performers is how they handle failure. Those who fear failure are seldom those who excel. Those who learn from their failures are the better for having failed. Experts view failure as an opportunity to learn.[28] Success reveals what you do well. Failure shows you what you can do better. Experts like Mr. Tabuchi are focused on being better. Research supports the notion that the inevitable failures resulting from years of practice and experience

are essential to developing expert skill levels.[29] So how do experts make failure work for them? Two processes come into play here. First, experts rigorously analyze the causes of failure. Second, they take corrective action.

## Analyzing the Causes of Failure

Because experts see failure as both a natural by-product of attempting to extend current performance levels and an opportunity to learn, they thoroughly analyze the cause of their failures to learn all they can from these experiences. Experts recognize that, in analyzing failure, they can learn to identify and correct deficient practices, reset goals, understand their current limitations, overcome weaknesses, and see possibilities for future performance.[30]

> **The only way to gain advantage from a failure is through a careful, objective, and honest analysis of the causes.**

Without understanding the cause of a failure, correcting the problem or ultimately finding a successful solution is impossible.

A situation does not have to result in a debacle or an obvious flop to receive scrutiny from an expert. For the beginner, capable, or even competent performer, solving the problem meets the goal or expectation. To these professionals, if the problem is solved, it needs no further consideration or thought because it is time to move on to the next challenge or problem. The adequacy or permanency of the solution is not an issue because the problem is solved. Experts think differently.

Although a solution may solve a problem, it may not satisfy the expert who is constantly asking the question "Could I have done that better?" When you ask yourself that question, you are thinking like an expert. You may discover that there is nothing wrong with your solu-

tion, decision, or action, but you may also find there may have been a better way. In assessing the quality of their solutions, experts are not looking to judge whether they were right or wrong. Rather, they are looking for a better way. Nothing is wrong with walking as a means of transportation. However, the person who first climbed on a horse found a better way. Nothing was wrong with horses for transportation, but the first person to assemble an automobile found a better way, and so it goes throughout history. In short, experts are rigorous in analyzing the causes of failure or determining the adequacy of the solutions so they can figure out precisely how to achieve success. After they have the root causes and deficiencies in hand, they are ready for the next step: taking corrective action.

## Taking Corrective Action

At one time Pioneer Hi-Bred International's sales representatives used handheld terminals to manage their daily sales information. Because they used so many of them, Pioneer bought Norand, the company that made them. Within a few years, laptop computer technology made handheld terminals obsolete. Pioneer sold the terminal company at a significant loss.

Pioneer's practice was to divide a percent of the annual profits equally among employees. In the year of that unprofitable sale, profit-sharing checks were noticeably smaller, and the employees' Pioneer stock values dropped. Soon after, when Pioneer CEO Tom Urban met with the Pioneer employees, he faced a disgruntled group. One employee described Urban's visit this way:

> When he walked into the meeting room for his first visit after the sale of Norand, he acknowledged the group, removed his jacket, and neatly folded it across the back of the chair. He loosened his tie, undid his collar, and rolled up his sleeves. The next thing he said was the last thing I ever expected to hear a CEO say. He said, "I made a mistake buying Norand and I am sorry. I am sorry your

profit-sharing was lower because of the purchase, and I am sorry your stock was hurt by the purchase. I will continue to take risks, but I am a bit smarter now, and I will work harder for you." ... As I sat listening to him, I knew I could trust him, and that he deserved every bit of loyalty I could give to him and to Pioneer. I recall thinking that I would follow him into any battle.[31]

Tom Urban understood that a mistake had been made, and he assessed both the causes and consequences of that failure. He then took corrective action. In this particular case, Pioneer's employees had been hurt by his actions. Consequently, he took action by recognizing and apologizing for the mistake and by assuring them that their concerns were his concerns. Why did an employee say that Urban's words were "the last thing I ever expected to hear a CEO say"? Because few people will admit mistakes or subsequently take corrective action. Experts do, but perhaps that is one reason we see so few of them: *It takes uncommon courage.*

Failure and rejection. Everyone experiences them. Some succumb. Those who will become expert learn from them. Consider the following examples:[32]

- Lucille Ball was told to forget about acting by her first coach.

- Decca Records informed The Beatles that "groups of guitars are on their way out."

- Dr. Seuss had his first book rejected twenty-seven times before finding a publisher.

- Elvis Presley was told to go back to driving a truck after his first (and only) Grand Ole Opry performance.

- The city leaders of Burbank, California, rejected the idea of a theme park that was submitted by a cartoonist named Walt Disney.

- Michael Jordan was cut from his high school basketball team.

Like us all, each of these people faced failure, but they used it as an opportunity to learn. They learned how to get better and how to succeed. Experts analyze the causes of failure and then take corrective action.

## Self-Monitoring

More than one expert has told me, "Just because I know more than most people about this business doesn't mean I know everything there is to know." An interesting phenomenon occurs in almost every field or business. Beginners believe they know a great deal more about the business than do experts. If you ask beginners how much they know in relation to all there is to know about their business, they are likely to tell you about 70 to 80 percent.

**Experts are likely to tell you that they know only about 50 to 60 percent of all there is to know about their business.[33]**

Obviously it is the expert who knows more, so why the difference in perception?

In reality, when you reach the expert level, you are far better at understanding the limits of your knowledge and skills. You are also more self-critical of your work and love what you do to such a degree that you strive to be even better than you are now—regardless of any success or awards you may have enjoyed. Beginners, in contrast, don't know enough to know just how little they know.

Self-monitoring is the careful observation and tracking of your performance and outcomes.[34] More than mere reflection on your experiences, self-monitoring pushes you to move beyond evaluating your business experiences and engage in critical self-analysis.[35] That's not to say that to be expert you must turn negative and self-

deprecating. Rather, you learn to identify elements of your professional practice that merit increased attention and scrutiny.

Goal setting and behavior modification become linked to your ongoing critique of your business performance, and you regularly monitor your progress toward reaching targeted objectives. Self-monitoring serves a wholly intrapersonal and goal-directed process of behavior analysis, modification, and implementation.[36] You become the steward of your professional growth and improvement.

Self-monitoring is not a practice confined to business professionals. It has been traced to superior performances in acting, academic achievement, and sport.[37] Expert physicists, writers, athletes, teachers, and musicians have all used self-monitoring to continue to improve their performance.[38]

As a result of this practice, experts are more aware of errors made and are better at accurately predicting which problems will be most difficult during problem solving.[39] Also, they are superior at understanding why they fail to comprehend certain elements of a problem and are more aware of the appropriateness or adequacy of the solutions they promote. They objectively and honestly assess and identify their shortcomings and knowledge deficiencies with a high degree of precision, making them better able to accurately analyze the causes of their failures and take corrective actions.

Recently, I studied just how experts keep on learning and why it takes people with less expertise longer to understand something.[40] I found that experts in my study closely and extensively monitored the things they do well and the things they believe they can do better. That is, they were keenly aware of the knowledge and skills critical to a good performance and routinely and consciously evaluated the quality of the results they obtained. This self-monitoring led them to identify both goals and actions that led to improved performance. In other words, in reflecting on their experiences and evaluating

their performance, experts develop self-improvement plans and programs.

While beginning performers may simply be unaware of how little they know, expert businesspeople are keenly aware of what they still don't know. They also understand why they fail to comprehend certain elements of problems when things don't work as intended. Further, they are acutely aware of the appropriateness or inadequacies of the solutions they attempt and practices they employ.

The founder of Wal-Mart, Sam Walton, revealed signs of self-monitoring, and it showed in his ability to improve his company's performance. When he realized that Wal-Mart had serious purchasing and merchandizing problems in the formative years of the business, he and his store managers critiqued themselves. "When somebody made a bad mistake—whether it was myself or anybody else—we talked about it, admitted it, tried to figure out how to correct it, and then moved on to the next day's work."[41]

## Maintaining Expertise

The hallmark of expert business professionals is their consistent and superior performance. They do not necessarily reveal signs of being any more intelligent than anyone else, nor do they necessarily appear to be devoting more effort than others during their performance. (At times they even seem surprisingly relaxed.) But appearances can be deceiving. The skills of experts are extensive, complex, earned over years of experience and deliberate practice, and dependent on extensive knowledge of all facets that affect the outcomes of their performance.

With clear goals, sustained practice, and a thirst for learning and experience, you can move into the elite ranks of your business, trade, or profession. The level of expertise you achieve is yours to determine.

The next chapter, "Navigating the Journey," can help you go as far as you choose to go. But first, complete expertise exercises 19–21. They will help you sustain your journey toward becoming expert.

## Summary

Expert performers consistently achieve outstanding results because they

- Seek knowledge insatiably
- Have a superior memory
- Attend to the atypical
- Plan extensively and act intuitively
- Execute skills gracefully and automatically
- Meet inadequacies and failures with corrective action
- Are self-monitoring

# SELF-MONITORING

Briefly describe a recent important business experience or event and then answer the questions that follow.

_____

_____

_____

_____

_____

In considering your role in this experience or event, what did you do well?

_____

_____

What could you have done better?_____

_____

_____

How could you have done it better?_____

_____

_____

What can you do to be better prepared should a similar experience occur again?

_____

_____

_____

# NETWORKING

List the names of six people you know who possess extraordinary knowledge or skills that may help you perform your job with greater expertise. Then identify a method for communicating with each person to access his or her information. You may want to offer to reverse the process to help that person.

Name 1: _____

    Knowledge/skills: _____

    Communication method: _____

Name 2: _____

    Knowledge/skills: _____

    Communication method: _____

Name 3: _____

    Knowledge/skills: _____

    Communication method: _____

Name 4: _____

    Knowledge/skills: _____

    Communication method: _____

Name 5: _____

    Knowledge/skills: _____

    Communication method: _____

Name 6: _____

    Knowledge/skills: _____

    Communication method: _____

# DEVISING AN EXPERT ACTION PLAN

Select three of the seven expert characteristics summarized on page 123 that, if improved, could elevate your level of expertise. Devise a series of actions you will undertake to practice, develop, and improve each characteristic. Finally, identify a colleague with whom you can share your ideas and who will give you feedback.

Expert characteristic 1: _____

    Actions: _____

    _____

    _____

    Colleague: _____

Expert characteristic 2: _____

    Actions: _____

    _____

    _____

    Colleague: _____

Expert characteristic 3: _____

    Actions: _____

    _____

    _____

    Colleague: _____

# SEVEN

# NAVIGATING THE JOURNEY

Becoming expert is a journey. In many ways, it is like life itself. When does one stop being a child? When does one stop being a beginner? In some ways, never. There are traits we had as children that we still have today. There are characteristics we displayed on the first day in business that we still display today. This book describes the development of expertise as a series of steps: the first step a beginner, the last step an expert. As with any set of steps, however, we can go both up and down—or never move off the first step at all.

In chapter 1, "The Three Keys to Expertise," we examined three factors that determine how high you will climb on the steps of becoming expert:

- Experience
- Knowledge
- Skills

As you gain more experience, knowledge, and skills, your professional characteristics change in ways that improve your professional performance. When the majority of your characteristics are

associated with a particular level of expertise, we say that you have achieved that level, whether it be that of beginner, capable, competent, proficient, or expert. But if you fail to learn from new experiences or to stay abreast of the latest information in your industry, or if you stop developing essential skills, you begin to lose expertise. If a rookie shows up with superior skills or knowledge, you can be outperformed. As a result, knowing how to navigate the journey toward becoming expert is important, as it allows you to continue to move forward. I hope you will also find, as most people do, that as you gain expertise and enjoy more success in your business, you also enjoy the journey more.

## Becoming Experienced

Simply put, you cannot become an expert business professional without substantial experience in your industry. Little evidence supports the idea that a person with no experience in a field can consistently outperform an individual with extensive experience in that same field. To the contrary, research consistently reveals that it takes extensive experience—a minimum of ten years in most fields—to reach the level of expert.[1]

Experience can serve you in two ways: first, your business experiences offer a wealth of knowledge; second, it is in your experiences that you can most accurately assess your skills. Skills seldom improve with experience—that takes practice—but experience quickly informs you about the adequacy of the skills you presently possess and indicates which skills are needed for greater success.

### Practical Knowledge: Making Experience, Not Waiting for It

While formal or theoretical knowledge has a cherished and valuable place in business, the practical knowledge earned through experience

is more helpful in meeting the daily challenges and demands of work. Practical knowledge holds several advantages over theoretical knowledge in business. First, the source of practical knowledge is everyday experience. You can easily turn that knowledge around and apply it to recurring everyday problems. Second, it has significant personal meaning for you. Meaningful information is far easier to commit to memory and to recall for application to impending challenges than a set of facts or axioms isolated from experience.

Several strategies can help you use experience to move you along the journey toward becoming expert. Perhaps most obvious is to gain as many experiences as possible. But be smart. Seek only those experiences outside your normal course of responsibility that can supply you with useful, practical knowledge that you can use now or in the future to improve your performance. So first, you must know what areas of knowledge are most helpful to you. If you are in sales, for example, sitting in on a product design meeting may give you an insight that can eventually help you sell your products or services to clients. If you are managing a group of line workers, taking a turn on a shift may supply you with some much-needed information on the challenges your workers face. If you have limited experience in your organization, get to know people in departments outside yours. You may want to shadow others during their daily routines to gain more insight about your company's operations. Information from other parts of your organization may come to bear on decisions and actions in your department. Experiences with clients, suppliers, and other people outside your organization who play a significant role in your success also can prove valuable. Don't wait for experiences that happen *to* you, but rather make them happen *for* you.

Secondhand experience can also be highly instructive. Therefore, seek opportunities to listen to and discuss pertinent business experiences, decisions, and strategies with your peers—and even competi-

tors. Professional organizations offer a wealth of knowledge based on the experiences of others. These "communities of practice" have the explicit mission of professional education and development for members.[2] They promote the exchange and dissemination of new information and time-tested knowledge through meetings, publications, and online resources.

## Applied Skills

As a coach for several professional golfers, I've spent considerable time on the practice tee watching seasoned pros and promising newcomers. It is not unusual to see a promising prospect with impeccable technique impressively launching golf balls long and straight from the practice tee. There are no style points in golf, however, and you get little credit for how far you can hit the golf ball in practice. The bottom line in performance is outcome. During a performance, skills are called on to produce results. If these promising golfers cannot produce the golf shots that give them an outstanding score in a tournament, they will never move from prospect to proven professional.

It is the same in business. Executing your business skills produces results—good or bad. Environmental conditions such as equipment, business climate, and competition play a role in the results you achieve, but everyone faces pretty much the same conditions you face. The difference is largely the skills you bring to the table. People with better sales skills sell more. People with better managerial skills manage better. People with better production skills produce more efficiently. But it is only in the performance that the quality and appropriateness of those skills are tested.

Therefore, in your experiences identify the skills you need to be successful. Objectively and honestly assess your skills in terms of both their appropriateness in meeting your business performance demands and their level of quality during performance. If your per-

formance is not where you want it to be, check your skills. Refer to expertise exercise 14, "Developing Your Critical Skills," in chapter 4, and ensure that the skills you believe are important to a superior performance are the skills you are developing.

## Learning from Experience

Experience alone does not make people experts, regardless of their years in the field or reputation. Rather, the ability to learn from experience and correctly structure the knowledge gained from experience is what separates experts from routine performers.

A recent study of instructors and students at a U.S. Postal Service training center revealed some interesting insights into experience and expertise.[3] The researchers looked for two characteristics commonly associated with expertise: holistic perception and the use of abstract concepts. Initially, they found no evidence of either in the more experienced group. However, when they regrouped the participants based on performance, the higher performers showed evidence of both characteristics. This finding led to the conclusion that experience alone is not an indicator of expertise.

This was not a singular finding. Other research has shown that people thought to be experts do not necessarily or always outperform their peers—or even beginners. Experienced professionals were not able to outperform peers, and in some cases beginners, in areas such as computer programming, stock investments, and clinical psychology.[4]

## Becoming Knowledgeable

That experts know a great deal is no surprise. "Knowledge is power" is a cliché that has gotten as much mileage as any and a great deal more than most. The secret to understanding the knowledge you need

to increase your expertise is not simply to load your brain with as much information as it will hold. The amount is not what makes the difference.

More important than the amount of knowledge is the organization of that knowledge. That's right. Your expertise is more dependent on how you organize knowledge than how much knowledge you have. Here's why: When you organize knowledge in ways that make it more accessible, functional, and efficient, you are able to tap into your knowledge stores quickly, thoroughly, and effectively when the knowledge is most needed.[5] This is not to say that the amount of knowledge is unimportant, because experts know more about their business and the factors that influence it than anyone. But how much knowledge you have is not nearly as important as how much knowledge you *use* and to what effect.

So how can the organization of your knowledge be leveraged for greater effect? Part of the answer lies in your experience. As you gain experience, you begin to understand what information is most useful to you in your business decisions and actions. When you are capable, you begin to see similarities across contexts and start using strategic knowledge when making decisions. When you reach competence, you add the ability to distinguish the important from the unimportant, and you have a sense of timing and momentum in decision making and plan execution. Additionally, you are guided by the bigger picture of long-term plans and goals. All of these characteristics contribute to your ability to organize knowledge in useful ways.

Research reveals that, as expertise grows, the sources of knowledge begin to shift.[6] The extensive and specialized knowledge of experts is accumulated both through years of experience and from numerous sources.[7] In their book *Mavericks at Work, Fast Company* magazine editors William Taylor and Polly LaBarre make the follow-

ing point: "One of the defining responsibilities of a 21st-century [business] leader is to attract the best ideas from the most people, wherever those people might be."[8] In my study of experts, I have found that they rely on four key sources in becoming knowledgeable:

- Wisdom gained through experience
- Networking and human interaction
- Formal education
- The written word[9]

### Wisdom Gained Through Experience

As noted earlier, experience serves as a valued teacher and wonderful source of knowledge. I learned that experts, in fact, consider experience to be their most valued source of knowledge.[10] The process of trial and error that defines experience proves critical in identifying successful business practices. Additionally, the opportunity to grow and develop, discover new ideas, detect gaps and deficiencies in knowledge, and apply knowledge from other sources in a practical setting all contribute to the wisdom of an expert.[11]

Experienced individuals often reflect on previous experiences to evaluate their current knowledge and to target areas for improvement. Experience teaches us what we do well and what we need to improve, and offers insight into how we might become better. Experience is cumulative, so we strive to improve today over what we accomplished yesterday by making adjustments to yesterday's actions.

### Networking and Human Interaction

When information holds meaning, we call it knowledge. Information is given meaning not only by us but also by others. We value knowledge not just for its own sake or what it means to us, but also for what

it means to others. Therefore, it's not surprising that you can gain a great deal of knowledge from your interactions with others. Others may know something you'd like—or need—to know.

Thus, human interaction is an important source of knowledge. Your network of personal contacts is a potentially valuable stream of critical information you can use in professional pursuits. Collegial contacts, client interactions, competitor observations and discussions, and the interactive nature of conferences, seminars, and workshops are all significant resources experts use to build their professional networks of relationships.[12] It is the value of experience that explains the importance of peers as a knowledge source. Experience is a common denominator: The most important knowledge for experts is conceived and incubated in the practical actions and events of professional practice—their own or others'.

Experts also cite clients as a critically useful source of knowledge. By attentively listening, experts gain access to information that will allow them to better meet client needs and adapt to different styles and personalities. Similarly, observing and listening to competitors gives a different perspective to solving similar problems that experts face in the business world.

Professional conferences, workshops, seminars, and other such meetings offer a unique opportunity for human interaction and knowledge acquisition that cannot be found in other sources. In these meetings you can learn from those people who are successful in your industry. Professional meetings are fertile ground for new ideas and innovations that can propel your performance forward.

To gain maximum knowledge from your network of peers, clients, and competitors, interviewing is an essential skill. By asking questions, you can access knowledge from others, particularly clients and competitors. You will find that the more you interview other professionals, the more willing they will be to share information and the

more you can learn from them. As with all skills, the more you practice interviewing, the better you become. When people perceive you as sincere in your desire to learn from them, they are more willing to share what they know—even competitors.

## Formal Education

Few experts cite formal education such as college study and recognized certification programs as the reason for their success or even for supplying the basic knowledge from which they make their most important decisions. In fact, two leading technology entrepreneurs, Bill Gates and Steve Jobs, never completed a college degree. That is not to say that a college education is eschewed by all experts. To the contrary, the overwhelming majority of successful business professionals have completed one or more college degree programs.

Formal education can represent an important foundation and a continuing source of knowledge for your business decisions and actions. It can teach you how to research information and give you structure for which to organize discipline-based knowledge such as mathematics, science, language, history, and so on. Professionally oriented programs such as business management and accounting, rather than discipline-based programs such as economics and psychology, provide more than just foundational knowledge. They also supply entry-level occupational skills and perhaps even initial professional experience through internships.

Formal education is the foundational knowledge from which other knowledge can grow and develop. In terms of your development as an expert, think of your formal education as a good start. But don't be fooled into thinking that because you have a degree you will be successful. Even with a college degree, you still have much to learn, and the sooner you realize that, the sooner your real education can begin.

## The Written Word

Those who have a thirst to learn make it a habit to read. Books, professional journals, magazines, the Internet, and the popular press all offer knowledge in a written format. Experts tend to be voracious readers. It is not a stretch to believe that one of the dividing lines between being proficient and expert is reading.

Reading gives you access to ideas, information, people, and places that may otherwise be far beyond your reach. The thoughts of business, political, or military leaders from eras long past as well as descriptions of the decision making or action initiatives in major contemporary innovations are accessible through the written word. You will never be able to discuss science with Marie Curie or negotiation strategies with John Rockefeller or business growth with Sam Walton; however, you can read about those people and the decisions they made and actions they took.

Professional and industry journals and magazines are valuable knowledge sources, particularly for the latest information affecting your business. You would be hard pressed to find an investment expert who did not read the *Wall Street Journal* or *Investor's Business Daily* regularly. These publications offer insights into thoughts and events that may influence decisions you need to make or actions you need to take. Additionally, you may gain insights into what is working (or not) for others and find new options in your own practices. Without industry sources it is virtually impossible to stay up to date with trends that will affect your business and you.

Reading is a major predictor of knowledge.[13] The more reading you do, the more you will learn and know. The more you know, the more able you are to appreciate and respond to a situation. One dedicated reader is Starbucks CEO Howard Schultz. To retain the spiritual experience of a trip to the Holy Land, he read Leon Uris's *The*

*Haj.* Reading *Memoirs of a Geisha* followed his trip to Japan, and Schultz read four separate biographies of Franklin Roosevelt after visiting the Roosevelt Memorial in Washington, DC. He confesses to being a voracious reader on airplanes, packing several books to ensure that he doesn't run out.[14]

## Becoming Skillful

After an extensive review of decades of research, the leading authority on the development of expertise, Anders Ericsson, concluded that it takes at least ten years of deliberate practice to reach the skill level of an expert.[15] You must *purposely practice* and refine the requisite skills of a business or profession to improve your performance. The steady application of critical skills in the business environment hones the skill sets that build expert performance. New skills are seldom neat or tidy, or yield the results one hopes for, but you will never grow without attempting to master the skills you need to be successful. Without intentional attention to improvement, new skills seldom develop and old skills soon plateau. In Ericsson's words,

> The development of high levels of skill requires the acquisition of representations that allow efficient control and execution of performance, as well as mechanisms that support planning, reasoning, and evaluation that mediate further improvement and maintenance of high levels of performance. Deliberate practice activities must be tightly coordinated and focus sequentially on improving one specified aspect of performance at a time. Furthermore, the amount of deliberate practice needed to win at an international level is massive and intimidating.[16]

Mark Twain, as expert an orator as he was a writer, recognized the importance of preparation and practice. In his opinion, "that impromptu speech is most worth listening to which has been carefully

prepared in private and tried on a plaster case or an empty chair or any other appreciative object that will keep quiet until the speaker has got his matter and his delivery limbered up so that they will seem impromptu to an audience."[17] What many believed came naturally to Twain was actually the result of years of deliberate practice. And so it is with the skills of an expert—so graceful, fluid, effortless, and effective are the skills of an expert that they seem as natural as breathing. But they are not; they were learned. And here is how they were learned.

## Three Steps to Learning New Skills

We often believe that people more skillful than ourselves were either endowed with something we were not or they know something we don't. Of the two options, the second is more likely. Any skill that has been mastered by anyone was learned. Skills—all skills—are learned in three steps:

1. Gain a better understanding of how the skill is performed.
2. Practice with activities that specifically develop the skill and have a feedback component.
3. Develop automatic execution, or automaticity.

Let's take each step in turn.

First, you must have a clear understanding of the scope and sequence of the skill or concept to be learned. Put another way, you must clearly understand how this activity is done correctly. For example, if you are a sales professional who can benefit from being more skilled at cold-calling clients, you must first understand what constitutes a good cold call. *What* do you do first, second, third, and so forth, and *how* do you follow each of those procedures? This is where the knowledge sources discussed previously in this chapter become so critical. This is also where beginners start: with the accepted procedures of an activity. In large part beginners must follow procedures

because they have yet to sufficiently practice their skills to attain mastery. But at every level of expertise, it is wise to revisit the fundamental components of your skills to ensure that you are performing each to the best of your ability.

Second, you must devote extensive time to activities that are goal oriented and in conditions similar to those found in the actual performance. Because practice is so essential to developing skills at the expert level of performance, the following section is devoted to the keys to quality practice.

Third, you develop automatic skill execution, or automaticity, when you attain a certain level of understanding and practice in a particular skill. At this step you can execute the skill with little or no conscious thought. Writing, walking, keyboarding, and driving an automobile are examples of skills automatically executed by many adults. The advantage of automaticity is that, during performance, you can concentrate on the purpose or goal of the performance without having to focus attention on the mechanics of the technique. The disadvantage is that once you can perform a skill automatically and are no longer giving it conscious attention, it becomes more difficult to modify it—and thus more difficult to improve it. That is not to say it is impossible to improve, but rather that it will take a great deal of focused practice to do so because you have reached a plateau in your performance.

## Keys to Quality Practice

Here is a key you must not forget if you hope to become a better business professional:

> Identify the one skill that, if improved, will make the biggest difference in your business success in the next six to twelve months.

Why only one skill? If it will indeed make the biggest difference in your business performance, then no other skill can be more important, and therefore it deserves spending time developing this skill more. Focus on one skill until it's mastered and then, when you begin to get noticeable improvements in your performance, identify the next skill that will elevate your performance even more.

After you know which skill to improve, develop a practice strategy and a realistic schedule. Both the quality and quantity of practice matter. Just putting in hours of practice does not improve skills. Remember the earlier example of handwriting. Is it any better today than it was a year ago or five years ago? It may have even deteriorated. Repeating a skill with no effort or repeating activities to improve a skill does not lead to a better performance. Experience alone does not make you better at what you do.

Quality practice consists of methods and activities that lead directly to improvement in those skills that account for performance. If you set aside even a few minutes a week to practicing proper letter formation and use activities such as tracing over well-formed letters or words, your handwriting will improve. The same is true of any skill necessary for your business practice. If you practice your cold-calling technique with a colleague, or even a phantom client, several times before calling real clients, your cold-calling skills will improve. To be better tomorrow than you were yesterday requires intentional effort on your part today.

Activities that are practiced must be appropriate for your current business knowledge and skills. If the activities you select are ill-suited to you, no amount of practice time can possibly lead to improvement. Choose activities that are directly targeted at improving that key skill you identified earlier—the one that will have the biggest impact on your business performance. Practice activities that are well suited for a seasoned sales manager may not be appropriate

for a beginner, so choose wisely. The differences in experience, knowledge, and skills are too great for the practice activity to benefit each level of expertise.

For example, if your organization is launching a new product, it is better for the novice salesperson to practice new presentations for colleagues before showing them to clients. The beginner is more able to accept feedback from colleagues and make adjustments to the presentations accordingly. Practicing before clients would make beginners too nervous and possibly defensive—and they would be unable to learn from the experience. However, seasoned professionals who are attempting to improve client interview skills may want to practice a new technique on established clients prior to facing potential clients. Most clients don't mind giving feedback about what they like or don't like about particular sales approaches, and proficient professionals have the skill and confidence to listen and learn from clients' comments.

A study at a music academy in Berlin, Germany, provides insightful guidance for the focused practice of experienced professionals. The violinists kept a diary of the time they spent each week on different activities. All groups of the violinists spent about the same amount of time (more than fifty hours) on music-related activities. The best violinists, however, spent more time per week on activities that were specifically designed to improve performance—for example, a solitary practice to master specific goals determined by their music teachers during weekly lessons.[18]

In addition, by focusing on practicing skills that have the most impact on performance, your quality-practice activities require your full concentration. Fatigue or boredom turns practice time into wasted time. Frequent breaks during practice help keep you fresh and alert. Short but frequent practice sessions yield better and faster results than a few marathon practice sessions.

In September 2004, Niclas Fasth and I sat watching an international golf championship, the Ryder Cup. Niclas had been a member of the previous and victorious 2002 European Ryder Cup team. But this year, he watched as others played. Niclas had competed full time on the PGA tour in the United States and had not played well enough to retain his playing privileges. I saw several reasons why Niclas hadn't played well: two bouts of the flu that affected his play for weeks, the jet lag from trips to and from his home in England and the United States, and the distraction of the birth of his second child.

Niclas, however, is not given to excuses. He does not brood about bad breaks or poor luck, and he never feels sorry for himself. Rather, he sees his destiny as resting firmly in his own hands and therefore constantly plans the future rather than lament the past. He writes out clear, specific goals that will lead him to success, and he regularly reviews them. He then sets up a practice plan to develop the skills and knowledge needed to improve his performance and achieve his goals. He regularly reviews this plan and makes changes when progress is wanting.

How much does Niclas practice? At the World Cup Championships on Kiawah Island, Niclas could be seen silhouetted against a setting sun as he continued practice until darkness prevented him from seeing the ball. A few months later, while I was having morning coffee with friends during the Deutsche Bank golf tournament, my cell phone rang just before 6:00 a.m. The sun was not even up. "Who would call you at this hour?" someone asked. "Niclas Fasth." I answered the phone and heard "Paul. This is Niclas. We're on our way to the practice tee. Can you join us there?"

Watching the 2004 Ryder Cup, Niclas was thinking ahead to 2005. How did 2005 end, and what did Niclas achieve? He finished thirteenth on the European Order of Merit (only twelve players had a better year), and he won—not once—but twice. Every year in the past

three years, Niclas has won at least two tournaments on the European professional golf tour, placed second at the British Open Championship, placed fourth at the U.S. Open Championship directly behind Tiger Woods, and at the time of this writing is ranked twenty-first in the world. Why? He has clear goals, practices during uncommon hours, and has never lost faith in his ability to navigate his way to being the best he is capable of becoming—an expert. It is a formula that has served well those who reach the top of their field. It is a formula that will work for you, too.

## Setting Your Course

So where to from here? Check back to pages 8–10 and review your score on expertise exercise 1, "Rating Your Expertise." This will give you a good indication of your present level. Begin there. Review the "Characteristics of the 5 Steps to Expert" table on page 144, focusing on your current level of expertise. Do you see characteristics in that level you may need to strengthen? You would be ill-advised to move to the next step until the step you are currently on is firmly in place. So review the expertise exercises you did in the chapter that corresponds to your current step, and make sure you have the experience, knowledge, and skills to advance to the next step. But also ask for honest feedback from trusted colleagues, seek knowledge you believe will help you perform at your best, and finally, enjoy the journey. Some people get a nosebleed when they climb too high, but experts enjoy both the challenge and the view in reaching the peak. See you at the top.

## CHARACTERISTICS OF THE 5 STEPS TO EXPERT

### 1. Beginners

- Behave in ways that are rational, procedural, and inflexible
- Make decisions guided by rules and norms
- Do not feel responsible for the outcomes of their actions
- Lack comfortable, efficient routines for everyday tasks

### 2. Capable Performers

- Have functional skills and focus on task requirements
- See similarities across contexts
- Can make decisions in a timely manner
- Are responsive to situations
- Use strategic knowledge in decision making
- Learn best from experience but develop other resources as well

### 3. Competent Performers

- Use goals and long-term plans to guide decisions and actions
- Distinguish important from unimportant factors when analyzing situations or events
- Plan contingently
- Have a sense of timing and momentum in making decisions and taking actions

### 4. Proficient Performers

- Have a strong sense of personal responsibility
- Have highly developed perceptual skills
- Use efficient routines to handle everyday tasks
- Analyze and solve problems with forward thinking
- Predict future events with a high degree of accuracy

### 5. Experts

- Seek knowledge insatiably
- Have a superior memory
- Attend to the atypical
- Plan extensively and act intuitively
- Execute skills gracefully and automatically
- Meet inadequacies and failures with corrective action
- Are self-monitoring

# AFTERWORD

Research has conclusively shown that experts are made, not born. Expertise is not the manifestation of innate traits or qualities nor does it come from possessing certain personality characteristics, physical attributes, or intellectual powers. Rather, it is earned from years of experience in the workplace, the acquisition of extensive knowledge of all the factors that shape the ultimate outcome of one's performance, and the deliberate practice of essential skills. Not everyone can become *the* top performer in their field, but everyone can increase their expertise and thus become better at what they do—even experts. Five steps will take you from business novice to elite performer. In developing expertise, take each step in turn. There is no other way. In so doing, you will climb higher in your pursuit of expertise. In the words of Henry Wadsworth Longfellow,

> *The heights by great men reached and kept*
> *Were not attained by sudden flight,*
> *But they, while their companions slept,*
> *Were toiling upward in the night.*

# NOTES

### Preface
1. See Kristen Heflin, "An Expert on Expertise," *Education* (2005): 15.
2. Jeff Thull, *Exceptional Selling* (New York: Wiley, 2006), 11.

### Introduction
1. John Wooden and Steve Jamison, *My Personal Best: Life Lessons from an All-American Journey* (New York: McGraw-Hill, 2004), 86–87.
2. John Wooden, www.coachjohnwooden.com.
3. Charles O'Reilly, "Winning the Career Tournament," *Fast Company* (January 2004), www.fastcompany.com/articles/2004/01/oreilly/.
4. Hubert L. Dreyfus, *What Computers Can't Do: A Critique of Artificial Reason* (New York: Harper, 1972).

### Chapter 1
1. Bob Danzig, *Conversations with Bobby: From Foster Child to Corporate Executive* (Arlington, VA: CWLA Press, 2007), 29–30.
2. Peter Drucker, *The Effective Executive* (New York: Harper & Row, 1966), 22–23.
3. Sabine Sonnetag, "Expertise in Professional Software Design: A Process Study," *Journal of Applied Psychology* 83 (1998): 703–715.
4. K. Anders Ericsson et al., eds., *The Cambridge Handbook of Expertise and Expert Performance* (New York: Cambridge University Press, 2006), 698.

5. See Mark Smith, "Lesson from Sidelines Past: A Story of Bobby Bowden" (unpublished doctoral dissertation, University of Georgia, Athens, 2004), 64.

6. See Bernard Avishai, "A European Platform for Global Competition: An Interview with VW's Carl Hahn," *Harvard Business Review* (July–August 1991): 2–11.

7. Paul Feltovich, Michael Prietula, and K. Anders Ericsson, "Studies in Expertise from Psychological Perspectives," in *The Cambridge Handbook of Expertise and Expert Performance,* ed. Ericsson et al., 41–67.

8. Eleanor Maguire et al., "Routes to Remembering: The Brains Behind Superior Memory," *Nature Neuroscience* 6 (2003): 90–95.

9. Michelene Chi, Robert Glaser, and Marshall Farr, *The Nature of Expertise* (Hillsdale, NJ: Lawrence Erlbaum, 1988), 129.

10. William Chase, ed., *Visual Information Processing* (New York: Academic Press, 1973).

11. Paul Schempp et al., "Subject Expertise and Teachers' Knowledge," *Journal of Teaching in Physical Education* 17 (1998): 342–356.

12. See William O'Neil, *Business Leaders and Success* (New York: McGraw-Hill, 2004), 47.

13. Fons Trompenaars, *21 Leaders for the 21st Century: How Innovative Leaders Manage in the Digital Age* (New York: McGraw-Hill, 2001).

14. John Maxwell, *The 21 Irrefutable Laws of Leadership: Follow Them and People Will Follow You* (Nashville, TN: Thomas Nelson, 2007); Morey Stettner, *Skills for New Managers* (New York: McGraw-Hill, 2000); Jack Canfield and Janet Switzer, *The Success Principles: How to Get from Where You Are to Where You Want to Be* (New York: HarperCollins, 2006); Donald Mitchell et al., *The Ultimate Competitive Advantage: Secrets of Continuously Developing a More Profitable Business Model* (San Francisco: Berrett-Koehler, 2003).

15. Gary Klein, *Sources of Power: How People Make Decisions* (Cambridge, MA: MIT Press, 1998).

## Chapter 2

1. "Seven Steps to Sales Success," http://h30267.www3.hp.com/ecasts/oct05/selling_digital_7steps.html.

2. Ray Alcorn, "Top 5 Mistakes of Beginning Commercial Real Estate Investors" (2008), www.creonline.com/articles/art-318.html.

3. Marvin Traub, *Like No Other Store . . . : The Bloomingdale's Legend and the Revolution in American Marketing* (New York: Random House, 1993), 46.

4. See "Forecasters: Katrina to Aim for Mississippi and Louisiana," CNN.com (August 26, 2005), www.cnn.com/2005/weather/08/06/tropical.weather/index.html.

5. See "'Can I Quit Now?' FEMA Chief Wrote as Katrina Raged," CNN.com (November 4, 2005), www.cnn.com/2005/US/11/03/brown.fema.emails.

6. Joseph Baker, Jean Côté, and Janice Deakin, "Cognitive Characteristics of Expert, Middle of the Pack and Back of the Pack Ultra-Endurance Triathletes," *Psychology of Sport and Exercise* 6 (2005): 551–558.

7. O'Neil, *Business Leaders and Success*, 14.

**Chapter 3**

1. Jim Collins, *Good to Great: Why Some Companies Make the Leap . . . and Others Don't* (New York: HarperCollins, 2001), 20.

2. See Rodd Wagner and James K. Harter, *12: The Elements of Great Managing* (New York: Gallup Press, 2006), 111.

3. Sonnetag, "Expertise in Professional Software Design," 703–715.

4. See Julie Fenster, *In the Words of Great Business Leaders* (New York: Wiley, 2000), 121.

5. Michelene Chi, Paul Feltovich, and Robert Glaser, "Categorization and Representation of Physics Problems by Experts and Novices," *Cognitive Science* 5 (1981): 130.

6. See O'Neil, *Business Leaders and Success*, 47.

7. Rhona Flin, Georgina Slaven, and Keith Stewart, "Emergency Decision Making in the Offshore Oil and Gas Industry," *Human Factors* 38 (1996): 262–277.

8. Klein, *Sources of Power*.

9. Rita Levi-Montalcini, *In Praise of Imperfection: My Life and Work* (New York: Basic Books, 1989).

10. Ann B. Graham and Vincent G. Pizzo, "A Question of Balance: Case Studies in Strategic Knowledge Management," in *The Strategic Management of Intellectual Capital: Resources for the Knowledge-Based Economy*, ed. David Klein (Oxford, England: Butterworth-Heineman, 1997), 22.

11. Harish Sujan, Mita Sujan, and James R. Bettman, "Knowledge Structure Differences Between More Effective and Less Effective Salespeople," *Journal of Marketing Research* 25 (1988): 81–86.

12. Mark P. Higgins and Mary P. Tully, "Hospital Doctors and Their Schemas About Appropriate Prescribing," *Medical Education* 39 (2005): 184–193.

13. Timm Kainen, "Who Succeeds in the Murky Middle?" *Journal of Applied Business Research* 23, no. 4 (2007): 61–68.

**Chapter 4**

1. Southwest Airlines Web site, http://southwest.com/about_swa/mission.html.

2. See Kevin Frieberg and Jackie Frieberg, *Nuts! Southwest Airlines' Crazy Recipe for Business and Personal Success* (New York: Broadway Books, 1996).

3. See Jon Meacham, *Franklin and Winston: An Intimate Portrait of an Epic Friendship* (New York: Random House, 2004), 285.

4. Drucker, *The Effective Executive*, 123.

5. Mica Endsley, "Toward a Theory of Situation Awareness in Dynamic Systems," *Human Factors* 37 (1995): 32–64.

6. Janet Davidson and Robert Sternberg, *The Psychology of Problem Solving* (New York: Cambridge University Press, 2003).

7. D. Floyd Jones, Lynn Housner, and Alan Kornspan, "Interactive Decision Making and Behavior of Experienced and Inexperienced Basketball Coaches During Practice," *Journal of Teaching in Physical Education* 64 (1997): 454–468.

8. Stephen Covey, *The 7 Habits of Highly Effective People* (New York: Simon & Schuster, 1989), 98.

9. Leaders & Success, *Investor's Business Daily*, November 16, 2006, A3.

10. Sophie Woorons, "An Analysis of Expert and Novice Tennis Instructors' Perceptual Capacities" (doctoral dissertation, University of Georgia, Athens, 2001), 85.

11. Beth Adelson, "When Novices Surpass Experts: The Difficulty of a Task May Increase with Expertise," *Journal of Experimental Psychology* 10 (1984): 494.

12. Carolyn Prince and Eduardo Salas, "Situation Assessment for Routine Flight and Decision Making," *International Journal of Cognitive Ergonomics* 1 (1998): 315–324.

13. Fenster, *In the Words of Great Business Leaders*, 33.

14. Thull, *Exceptional Selling*, 59.

15. Robert Shook, *The Greatest Sales Stories Ever Told: From the World's Best Salespeople* (New York: McGraw-Hill, 1997).

16. See Noel Tichy and Ram Charan, "Speed, Simplicity, Self-Confidence: An Interview with Jack Welch," *Harvard Business Review* 28, no. 4 (1989): 113–114.

## Chapter 5

1. Collins, *Good to Great*, 34.

2. Mark Sanborn, *The Fred Factor* (New York: Doubleday, 2004), 8–9.

3. James Gleick, *Genius: The Life and Science of Richard Feynman* (New York: Vintage Books, 1992), 215.

4. See Bryan McCullick, Russell Cummings, and Paul Schempp, "The Professional Orientations of Expert Golf Instructors," *International Journal of Physical Education* 36 (1999): 22.

5. Mica Endsley and Chris Bolstad, "Individual Differences in Pilot Situational Awareness," *International Journal of Aviation Psychology* 4 (1994): 241–264.

6. Richard M. Rosen and Fred Adair, "CEOs Misperceive Top Teams' Performance," *Harvard Business Review* (September 2007): 30.

7. Fenster, *In the Words of Great Business Leaders*, 88.

8. Bent Peterson and Torbin Pederson, "Coping with Liability of Foreignness: Different Learning Engagements of Entrant Firms," *Journal of International Business Management* 8, no. 3 (2002): 339–350.

9. John R. Anderson, *The Architecture of Cognition* (Cambridge, MA: Harvard University Press, 1983).

10. Robert E. Christensen, Michael D. Fetters, and Lee A. Green, "Opening the Black Box: Cognitive Strategies in Family Practice," *Annals of Family Medicine* 3 (2005): 144–150.

11. Vimla Patel and Guy J. Groen, "The General and Specific Nature of Medical Expertise: A Critical Look," in *Toward a General Theory of Expertise: Prospects and Limits*, ed. K. Anders Ericsson and Jacqui Smith (New York: Cambridge University Press, 1991), 93–125.

12. Ericsson et al., eds., *Cambridge Handbook of Expertise and Expert Performance.*

13. Jos Arts, Wim Gijselaers, and Henny Boshuizen, "Understanding Managerial Problem-Solving," *Contemporary Educational Psychology* 31 (2006): 387–410.

14. Chi, Feltovich, and Glaser, "Categorization and Representation of Physics Problems by Experts and Novices," 121–152.

15. See Fenster, *In the Words of Great Business Leaders,* 322.

16. Kathy Carter et al., "Processing and Using Information About Students: A Study of Expert, Novice, and Postulant Teachers," *Teaching and Teacher Education* 3 (1987): 147–157.

17. Tim Gabbett et al., "Testing and Training Anticipation Skills in Softball Fielders," *International Journal of Sports Science and Coaching* 2 (2007): 15–24.

**Chapter 6**

1. Paul Schempp, "Where Experts Find Answers," *American Society for Training and Development Research-to-Practice Conference Proceedings* (Alexandria, VA: ASTD, 2006).

2. See Fenster, *In the Words of Great Business Leaders,* 16.

3. Brousseau, Kenneth, et al., "The Seasoned Executive's Decision-Making Style," *Harvard Business Review* 84, no. 2 (2006): 110–121.

4. Covey, *The 7 Habits of Highly Effective People,* 240.

5. Ibid., 241.

6. Schempp et al., "Subject Expertise and Teachers' Knowledge," 342–356.

7. See Smith, "Lessons from Sidelines Past," 232.

8. Collins, *Good to Great,* 154.

9. K. Anders Ericsson et al., "Uncovering the Structure of a Memorist's Superior 'Basic' Memory Capacity," *Cognitive Psychology* 49 (2004): 191–238.

10. Mark Cuban, "Success and Motivation, Part 3," May 7, 2004, www.blogmaverick.com.

11. Mark Cuban, "Success and Motivation, Almost Part 2," April 25, 2004, www.blogmaverick.com.

12. Ericsson et al., "Uncovering the Structure of a Memorist's Superior 'Basic' Memory Capacity."

13. Bryan McCullick et al., "An Analysis of the Working Memory of Expert Sport Instructors," *Journal of Teaching in Physical Education* 25 (2006): 149–165.

14. Alan Casel, "Does Expertise Reduce Age Differences in Recall Memory?" *Journals of Gerontology Series B: Psychological Sciences and Social Sciences* 62 (2007): 194–196.

15. Jeffrey Gangemi, "Nobel Winner Yunus: Microcredit Missionary," *Business-Week*, December 26, 2005.

16. O'Neil, *Business Leaders and Success*, 65.

17. Dean Smith, with John Kilgo and Sally Jenkins, *A Coach's Life* (New York: Random House, 1999).

18. Wooden and Jamison, *My Personal Best*.

19. Neil Charness, "Age and Skilled Problem Solving," *Journal of Experimental Psychology: General* 110 (1981): 21–38.

20. Ericsson et al., eds., *Cambridge Handbook of Expertise and Expert Performance*, 233.

21. Vimla Patel, David Evans, and Guy Groen, "Diagnostic Reasoning and Expertise," *Psychology of Learning and Motivation* 31 (1989): 137–252.

22. Franz Humer, "Intuition," *Harvard Business Review* 85, no. 1 (2007): 17–18.

23. Ibid., 18.

24. Benjamin Bloom, "Automaticity," *Educational Leadership* (February 1986): 70–77.

25. Ibid.

26. Linda Hill, "Becoming the BOSS," *Harvard Business Review* 85, no. 1 (2007): 48–56.

27. See Michael Schrage, "A Japanese Giant Rethinks Globalization: An Interview with Yoshibisa Tabuchi," in *Leaders on Leadership: Interviews with Top Executives*, ed. Warren Bennis, Harvard Business Review Book Series (Boston: Bennis, 1992), 115.

28. K. Anders Ericsson, "The Scientific Study of Expert Levels of Performance: General Implications for Optimal Learning and Creativity," *High Ability Studies* 9 (1998): 75–100.

29. Ericsson et al., eds., *Cambridge Handbook of Expertise and Expert Performance*, 45.

30. Ericsson, "The Scientific Study of Expert Levels of Performance."

31. See Jack Canfield and Mark Victor Hansen, *Chicken Soup for the Soul: Inspirational Stories, Powerful Principles, and Practical Techniques to Help You Make Your Dreams Come True* (Deerfield Beach, FL: HCI, 2003), 73.

32. Leaders & Success, *Investor's Business Daily*, November 10, 2006, A3.

33. Schempp et al., "Subject Expertise and Teachers' Knowledge."

34. Barry Zimmerman and Anastasia Kitsantas, "Self-Regulated Learning of a Motoric Skill: The Role of Goal Setting and Self-Monitoring," *Journal of Applied Sport Psychology* 8 (1996): 60–75.

35. Paul Karoly, "Mechanisms of Self-Regulation: A Systems View," *Annual Review of Psychology* 44 (1993): 23–52.
36. Ibid.
37. See William Y. Lan and Jake Morgan, "Videotaping as a Means of Self-Monitoring to Improve Theater Students' Performance," *Journal of Experimental Education* 71 (2003): 371–381; William Y. Lan, "The Effects of Self-Monitoring on Students' Course Performance, Use of Learning Strategies, Attitude, Self-Judgment Ability, and Knowledge Representation," *Journal of Experimental Education* 64 (1996): 101–115; Zimmerman and Kitsantas, "Self-Regulated Learning of a Motoric Skill."
38. Chi et al., "Categorization and Representation of Physics Problems by Experts and Novices."
39. Chi, Glaser, and Farr, *The Nature of Expertise*, xx.
40. Paul Schempp, "The Self-Monitoring of Expert Sport Instructors," *International Journal of Sport Science & Coaching* 1 (2006): 25–35.
41. See O'Neil, *Business Leaders and Success*, 48.

## Chapter 7

1. Ericsson, "The Scientific Study of Expert Levels of Performance."
2. Etienne Wenger and William M. Snyder, "Communities of Practice: The Organizational Frontier," *Harvard Business Review* (January–February 2000): 139–145.
3. John Bradley, Ravi Paul, and Elaine Seeman, "Analyzing the Structure of Expert Knowledge," *Information & Management* 43 (2006): 77–91.
4. Ericsson et al., eds., *Cambridge Handbook of Expertise and Expert Performance*, 398.
5. Jean Bedard and Michelene Chi, "Expertise," *Current Directions in Psychological Science* 1, no. 4 (1992): 135–139.
6. K. Anders Ericsson, "Deliberate Practice and the Acquisition of and Maintenance of Expert Performance in Medicine and Related Domains," *Academic Medicine* 10 (2004): S1–S12.
7. Daniel Gould et al., "Educational Needs of Elite US National Team, Pan American, and Olympic Coaches," *Journal of Teaching in Physical Education* 9 (1990): 332–344.
8. William Taylor and Polly LaBarre, *Mavericks at Work: Why the Most Original Minds in Business Win* (New York: HarperCollins, 2006), 73.
9. Schempp, "Where Experts Find Answers," 146.
10. Paul Schempp, "Learning on the Job: An Analysis of the Acquisition of a Teacher's Knowledge," *Journal of Research and Development in Education* 28 (1995): 237–244.
11. Schempp, "Where Experts Find Answers," 146.
12. Ibid., 146.

13. Keith E. Stanovich and Anne E. Cunningham, "Where Does Knowledge Come From? Specific Associations Between Print Exposure and Information Acquisition," *Journal of Educational Psychology* 85 (1993): 211–229.

14. O'Neil, *Business Leaders and Success,* 171.

15. Ericsson, "Deliberate Practice and the Acquisition of and Maintenance of Expert Performance in Medicine and Related Domains," S1–S12.

16. K. Anders Ericsson, "Recent Advances in Expertise Research: A Commentary on the Contributions to the Special Issue," *Applied Cognitive Psychology* 19 (2005): 238.

17. See Alex Ayers, ed., *The Wit and Wisdom of Mark Twain* (New York: Meridian, 1984), 219.

18. K. Anders Ericsson, Ralf Th. Krampe, and Clements Tesch-Römer, "The Role of Deliberate Practice in the Acquisition of Expert Performance," *Psychological Review* 100 (1993): 363–406.

# REFERENCES

Adelson, Beth. "When Novices Surpass Experts: The Difficulty of a Task May Increase with Expertise." *Journal of Experimental Psychology* 10 (1984): 494.

Anderson, John R. *The Architecture of Cognition.* Cambridge, MA: Harvard University Press, 1983.

Arts, Jos, Wim Gijselaers, and Henny Boshuizen. "Understanding Managerial Problem-Solving." *Contemporary Educational Psychology* 31 (2006): 387–410.

Avishai, Bernard. "A European Platform for Global Competition: An Interview with VW's Carl Hahn." *Harvard Business Review* (July–August 1991): 2–11.

Ayers, Alex, ed. *The Wit and Wisdom of Mark Twain.* New York: Meridian, 1984.

Baker, Joseph, Jean Côté, and Janice Deakin. "Cognitive Characteristics of Expert, Middle of the Pack and Back of the Pack Ultra-Endurance Triathletes." *Psychology of Sport and Exercise* 6 (2005): 551–558.

Bedard, Jean and Michelene Chi. "Expertise." *Current Directions in Psychological Science* 1, no. 4 (1992): 135–139.

Bloom, Benjamin. "Automaticity." *Educational Leadership* (February 1986): 70–77.

Bradley, John, Ravi Paul, and Elaine Seeman. "Analyzing the Structure of Expert Knowledge." *Information & Management* 43 (2006): 77–91.

Brousseau, Kenneth, Michael Driver, Gary Hourihan, and Rikard Larsen. "The Seasoned Executive's Decision-Making Style." *Harvard Business Review* 84 no. 2 (2006): 110–121.

Canfield, Jack, and Mark Victor Hansen. *Chicken Soup for the Soul: Inspirational Stories, Powerful Principles, and Practical Techniques to Help You Make Your Dreams Come True.* Deerfield Beach, FL: HCI, 2003.

Canfield, Jack, and Janet Switzer. *The Success Principles: How to Get from Where You Are to Where You Want to Be.* New York: HarperCollins, 2006.

Carter, Kathy, Donna Sabers, Katherine Cushing, Stefinee Pinnegar, and David Berliner. "Processing and Using Information About Students: A Study of Expert, Novice, and Postulant Teachers." *Teaching and Teacher Education* 3 (1987): 147–157.

Casel, Alan. "Does Expertise Reduce Age Differences in Recall Memory?" *Journals of Gerontology Series B: Psychological Sciences and Social Sciences* 62 (2007): 194–196.

Charness, Neil. "Age and Skilled Problem Solving." *Journal of Experimental Psychology: General* 110 (1981): 21–38.

Chase, William, ed. *Visual Information Processing.* New York: Academic Press, 1973.

Chi, Michelene, Paul Feltovich, and Robert Glaser. "Categorization and Representation of Physics Problems by Experts and Novices." *Cognitive Science* 5 (1981): 130.

Chi, Michelene, Robert Glaser, and Marshall Farr. *The Nature of Expertise.* Hillsdale, NJ: Lawrence Erlbaum, 1988.

Christensen, Robert E., Michael D. Fetters, and Lee A. Green. "Opening the Black Box: Cognitive Strategies in Family Practice." *Annals of Family Medicine* 3 (2005): 144–150.

Collins, Jim. *Good to Great: Why Some Companies Make the Leap . . . and Others Don't.* New York: HarperCollins, 2001.

Covey, Stephen. *The 7 Habits of Highly Effective People.* New York: Simon & Schuster, 1989.

Cuban, Mark. "Success and Motivation, Almost Part 2." April 25, 2004, www.blogmaverick.com.

Cuban, Mark. "Success and Motivation, Part 3." May 7, 2004, www.blogmaverick.com.

Danzig, Bob. *Conversations with Bobby: From Foster Child to Corporate Executive.* Arlington, VA: CWLA Press, 2007.

Davidson, Janet, and Robert Sternberg. *The Psychology of Problem Solving.* New York: Cambridge University Press, 2003.

Dreyfus, Hubert L. *What Computers Can't Do: A Critique of Artificial Reason.* New York: Harper & Row, 1972.

Drucker, Peter. *The Effective Executive.* New York: Harper & Row, 1966.

Endsley, Mica. "Toward a Theory of Situation Awareness in Dynamic Systems." *Human Factors* 37 (1995): 32–64.

Endsley, Mica, and Chris Bolstad. "Individual Differences in Pilot Situational Awareness." *International Journal of Aviation Psychology* 4 (1994): 241–264.

Ericsson, K. Anders. "The Scientific Study of Expert Levels of Performance: General Implications for Optimal Learning and Creativity." *High Ability Studies* 9 (1998): 75–100.

Ericsson, K. Anders. "Deliberate Practice and the Acquisition of and Maintenance of Expert Performance in Medicine and Related Domains." *Academic Medicine* 10 (2004): S1–S12.

Ericsson, K. Anders. "Recent Advances in Expertise Research: A Commentary on the Contributions to the Special Issue." *Applied Cognitive Psychology* 19 (2005): 238.

Ericsson, K. Anders, Neil Charness, Paul Feltovich, and Robert Hoffman, eds. *The Cambridge Handbook of Expertise and Expert Performance.* New York: Cambridge University Press, 2006.

Ericsson, K. Anders, Peter Delaney, George Weaver, and Rajan Mahadevan. "Uncovering the Structure of a Memorist's Superior 'Basic' Memory Capacity." *Cognitive Psychology* 49 (2004): 191–238.

Ericsson, K. Anders, Ralf Th. Krampe, and Clements Tesch-Römer. "The Role of Deliberate Practice in the Acquisition of Expert Performance." *Psychological Review* 100 (1993): 363–406.

Fenster, Julie. *In the Words of Great Business Leaders.* New York: Wiley, 2000.

Flin, Rhona, Georgina Slaven, and Keith Stewart. "Emergency Decision Making in the Offshore Oil and Gas Industry." *Human Factors* 38 (1996): 262–277.

Frieberg, Kevin, and Jackie Frieberg. *Nuts! Southwest Airlines' Crazy Recipe for Business and Personal Success.* New York: Broadway Books, 1996.

Gabbett, Tim, Martin Rubinoff, Lachian Thorbum, and Damian Farrow. "Testing and Training Anticipation Skills in Softball Fielders." *International Journal of Sports Science and Coaching* 2 (2007): 15–24.

Gangemi, Jeffrey. "Nobel Winner Yunus: Microcredit Missionary," *BusinessWeek,* December 26, 2005.

Gleick, James. *Genius: The Life and Science of Richard Feynman.* New York: Vintage Books, 1992.

Gould, Daniel, et al. "Educational Needs of Elite US National Team, Pan American, and Olympic Coaches," *Journal of Teaching in Physical Education* 9 (1990): 332–344.

Graham, Ann B., and Vincent G. Pizzo. "A Question of Balance: Case Studies in Strategic Knowledge Management." In *The Strategic Management of Intellectual Capital: Resources for the Knowledge-Based Economy.* Edited by David Klein. Oxford, England: Butterworth-Heineman, 1997.

Heflin, Kristen. "An Expert on Expertise." *Education* (2005): 15.

Higgins, Mark P., and Mary P. Tully. "Hospital Doctors and Their Schemas About Appropriate Prescribing." *Medical Education* 39 (2005): 184–193.

Hill, Linda. "Becoming the BOSS." *Harvard Business Review* 85, no. 1 (2007): 48–56.

Humer, Franz. "Intuition." *Harvard Business Review* 85, no. 1 (2007): 17–18.

Jones, D. Floyd, Lynn Housner, and Alan Kornspan. "Interactive Decision Making and Behavior of Experienced and Inexperienced Basketball Coaches During Practice." *Journal of Teaching in Physical Education* 64 (1997): 454–468.

Kainen, Timm. "Who Succeeds in the Murky Middle?" *Journal of Applied Business Research* 23, no. 4 (2007): 61–68.

Karoly, Paul. "Mechanisms of Self-Regulation: A Systems View." *Annual Review of Psychology* 44 (1993): 23–52.

Klein, Gary. *Sources of Power: How People Make Decisions.* Cambridge, MA: MIT Press, 1998.

Lan, William Y. "The Effects of Self-Monitoring on Students' Course Performance, Use of Learning Strategies, Attitude, Self-Judgment Ability, and Knowledge Representation." *Journal of Experimental Education* 64 (1996): 101–115.

Lan, William Y., and Jake Morgan. "Videotaping as a Means of Self-Monitoring to Improve Theater Students' Performance." *Journal of Experimental Education* 71 (2003): 371–381.

Levi-Montalcini, Rita. *In Praise of Imperfection: My Life and Work.* New York: Basic Books, 1989.

Maguire, Eleanor, Elizabeth Valentine, John Wilding, and Narinder Kapur. "Routes to Remembering: The Brains Behind Superior Memory." *Nature Neuroscience* 6 (2003): 90–95.

Maxwell, John. *The 21 Irrefutable Laws of Leadership: Follow Them and People Will Follow You.* Nashville, TN: Thomas Nelson, 2007.

McCullick, Bryan, Russell Cummings, and Paul Schempp. "The Professional Orientations of Expert Golf Instructors." *International Journal of Physical Education* 36 (1999): 15–24.

McCullick, Bryan, Paul Schempp, Tiffany Tsu, Jinhong Jung, Brad Vickers, and Greg Schuknecht. "An Analysis of the Working Memory of Expert Sport Instructors." *Journal of Teaching in Physical Education* 25 (2006): 149–165.

Meacham, Jon. *Franklin and Winston: An Intimate Portrait of an Epic Friendship.* New York: Random House, 2004.

Mitchell, Donald, Carol Coles, B. Thomas Golisano, and Robert Knutson. *The Ultimate Competitive Advantage: Secrets of Continuously Developing a More Profitable Business Model.* San Francisco: Berrett-Koehler, 2003.

O'Neil, William. *Business Leaders and Success.* New York: McGraw-Hill, 2004.

O'Reilly, Charles. "Winning the Career Tournament." *Fast Company* (January 2004), www.fastcompany.com/articles/2004/01/oreilly/.

Patel, Vimla, David Evans, and Guy Groen. "Diagnostic Reasoning and Expertise." *Psychology of Learning and Motivation* 31 (1989): 137–252.

Patel, Vimla, and Guy J. Groen. "The General and Specific Nature of Medical Expertise: A Critical Look." In *Toward a General Theory of Expertise: Prospects and Limits.* Edited by K. Anders Ericsson and Jacqui Smith, pp. 93–125. New York: Cambridge University Press, 1991.

Peterson, Bent, and Torbin Pederson. "Coping with Liability of Foreignness: Different Learning Engagements of Entrant Firms." *Journal of International Business Management* 8, no. 3 (2002): 339–350.

Prince, Carolyn, and Eduardo Salas. "Situation Assessment for Routine Flight and Decision Making." *International Journal of Cognitive Ergonomics* 1 (1998): 315–324.

Rosen, Richard M., and Fred Adair. "CEOs Misperceive Top Teams' Performance." *Harvard Business Review* 85, no. 9 (September 2007): 30.

Sanborn, Mark. *The Fred Factor.* New York: Doubleday, 2004.

Schempp, Paul. "Learning on the Job: An Analysis of the Acquisition of a Teacher's Knowledge." *Journal of Research and Development in Education* 28 (1995): 237–244.

Schempp, Paul. "Where Experts Find Answers." *American Society for Training and Development Research-to-Practice Conference Proceedings.* Alexandria, VA: ASTD, 2006, 143–152.

Schempp, Paul, Dean Manross, Steven Tan, and Matthew Fincher. "Subject Expertise and Teachers' Knowledge." *Journal of Teaching in Physical Education* 17 (1998): 342–356.

Schempp, Paul, Bryan McCullick, Chris Busch, Collin Webster, and Ilse Mason. "The Self-Monitoring of Expert Sport Instructors." *International Journal of Sport Science & Coaching* 1 (2006): 25–35.

Schrage, Michael. "A Japanese Giant Rethinks Globalization: An Interview with Yoshibisa Tabuchi." In *Leaders on Leadership: Interviews with Top Executives.* Edited by Warren Bennis, Harvard Business Review Book Series. Boston: Bennis, 1992.

Shook, Robert. *The Greatest Sales Stories Ever Told: From the World's Best Salespeople.* New York: McGraw-Hill, 1997.

Smith, Dean, with John Kilgo and Sally Jenkins. *A Coach's Life.* New York: Random House, 1999.

Smith, Mark. "Lesson from Sidelines Past: A Story of Bobby Bowden." Unpublished doctoral dissertation, University of Georgia, Athens, 2004.

Sonnetag, Sabine. "Expertise in Professional Software Design: A Process Study." *Journal of Applied Psychology* 83 (1998): 703–715.

Stanovich, Keith E., and Anne E. Cunningham. "Where Does Knowledge Come From? Specific Associations Between Print Exposure and Information Acquisition." *Journal of Educational Psychology* 85 (1993): 211–229.

Stettner, Morey. *Skills for New Managers.* New York: McGraw-Hill, 2000.

Sujan, Harish, Mita Sujan, and James R. Bettman. "Knowledge Structure Differences Between More Effective and Less Effective Salespeople." *Journal of Marketing Research* 25 (1988): 81–86.

Taylor, William, and Polly LaBarre. *Mavericks at Work: Why the Most Original Minds in Business Win.* New York: HarperCollins, 2006.

Thull, Jeff. *Exceptional Selling.* New York: Wiley, 2006.

Tichy, Noel, and Ram Charan. "Speed, Simplicity, Self-Confidence: An Interview with Jack Welch." *Harvard Business Review* 28, no. 4 (1989): 113–114.

Traub, Marvin. *Like No Other Store . . . : The Bloomingdale's Legend and the Revolution in American Marketing.* New York: Random House, 1993.

Trompenaars, Fons. *21 Leaders for the 21st Century: How Innovative Leaders Manage in the Digital Age.* New York: McGraw-Hill, 2001.

Wagner, Rodd, and James K. Harter. *12: The Elements of Great Managing.* New York: Gallup Press, 2006.

Wenger, Etienne, and William M. Snyder. "Communities of Practice: The Organizational Frontier." *Harvard Business Review* (January–February 2000): 139–145.

Wooden, John, and Steve Jamison. *My Personal Best: Life Lessons from an All-American Journey.* New York: McGraw-Hill, 2004.

Woorons, Sophie. "An Analysis of Expert and Novice Tennis Instructors' Perceptual Capacities." Doctoral dissertation, University of Georgia, Athens, 2001.

Zimmerman, Barry, and Anastasia Kitsantas. "Self-Regulated Learning of a Motoric Skill: The Role of Goal Setting and Self-Monitoring." *Journal of Applied Sport Psychology* 8 (1996): 60–75.

# INDEX

*For Linda Lannon*
*with affection—*
*and gratitude for holding up*
*her end of the bargain.*

# Nothing to Do

"What do you want to do today?" I asked my friend Hannie.

"I don't know. Nancy, what do you want to do?" asked Hannie.

"I don't know. What do you want to do, Karen?"

"I asked first!" I replied. "I don't *know* what to do."

Hannie and Nancy and I are best friends. We call ourselves the Three Musketeers.

It was a Saturday afternoon. A really bor-

ing Saturday afternoon. My friends and I were sitting on the back steps at my father's house. Usually, we can think of lots of things to do.

But not that day.

"Let's play Going Camping," said Nancy.

"Nah," replied Hannie. "We need too much stuff for that. Hey, let's build a tree house."

"A tree house!" I exclaimed. "But we would need wood and nails and a ladder and probably Daddy."

Hannie and Nancy looked disappointed. "Yeah," they agreed.

"I know!" I cried. "Let's go to the playground."

"What playground?" asked Nancy.

"The one at Stoneybrook Elementary. Where David Michael goes to school." (David Michael is my stepbrother. We are both seven, but we go to different schools. I go to Stoneybrook Academy. So do Hannie and Nancy. We are in Ms. Colman's second-grade class.)

"The playground is pretty far away," said Nancy.

"We'll ride bikes, then," I replied. "I know how to get there. Nancy, you can borrow David Michael's bike." (Hannie lives across the street from Daddy's house. But Nancy does not live in the neighborhood. She lives next door to my mommy's house. Her father had driven her here to play with us. So she did not have a bicycle.)

"Okay!" cried Nancy. "Let's find your daddy and ask if we can go."

My friends and I clattered inside. We did not find Daddy. We found Elizabeth. Elizabeth is my stepmother.

Guess what. Elizabeth said we could not go to the playground. "It's too far away. I cannot let you ride there by yourselves."

"Can't Kristy come with us?" I asked. Kristy is my stepsister. She is thirteen years old and she is a *baby-sitter*.

"Kristy's not home, honey," said Elizabeth. "Neither are Sam and Charlie. I'll be happy to drive you to the playground, though. I bet Andrew and Emily Michelle would like to come, too."

"That's okay." I scuffed my feet. "Come on, you guys," I said to Nancy and Hannie.

This was the problem. I did not want to go to the playground with a grown-up and my little brother and sister. I wanted us to go on our own.

Boo.

Nancy and Hannie understood the problem. They followed me back to the porch.

"Now what?" asked Nancy. "There's nothing to do."

"We could go roller-skating," suggested Hannie. "Oh, wait. No, we couldn't. My skates do not fit anymore."

"And I don't have any skates," said Nancy.

"You really should have a pair," Hannie told her.

"It doesn't matter anyway," I said. "I left my skates at Mommy's."

"You are always leaving things at your mother's house," said Hannie crossly.

Well, for heaven's sake. Hannie ought to know why that happens.

# Here, There, and Everywhere

I am forever leaving things behind, because I live at two houses.

Who am I? I am Karen Brewer. I have freckles and blonde hair and blue eyes. I wear glasses — all the time.

I bet you are wondering why I live at two houses — Mommy's house and Daddy's house. Well, this is because my mommy and daddy are divorced. They used to be married. They loved each other then. So they had Andrew and me. (Andrew is four, going on five.) After awhile, Mommy and

Daddy realized they loved Andrew and me very much — but they did not love each other anymore. So they got divorced.

My family had been living in Daddy's big house. (He grew up there.) After the divorce, Mommy moved to another house here in Stoneybrook, Connecticut. It is littler than Daddy's house. Andrew and I moved with her. But do you know what? After awhile, Mommy and Daddy both got married again! Mommy married a man named Seth. He is my stepfather. And Daddy married Elizabeth.

At the little house live Mommy, Seth, Emily Junior (my rat), Rocky and Midgie (Seth's cat and dog), and Andrew and I. But Andrew and I only live there *most* of the time. Every other weekend, and on some holidays and vacations, we live at the big house.

A lot of other people live at the big house. Besides Daddy, Elizabeth, Andrew, and me there are Elizabeth's four kids: Kristy; my big stepbrothers Sam and Charlie, who go to high school; and David Michael. Then there is Emily Michelle, who is my adopted two-and-a-half-year-old sister (she comes from a faraway country called Vietnam). And there is Nannie, Elizabeth's mother, who watches Emily while everyone else is at work or school. There are some pets, too. There's Boo-Boo, Daddy's fat old cat; Shannon, David Michael's puppy; and Crystal Light the Second and Goldfishie, who are goldfish. (Duh.) Isn't that a lot? The big house is crowded and noisy. I just love it. Except for one thing. A witch lives next door. Her name is Morbidda Destiny. The grown-ups do not believe she is a witch. They say she is just an old lady. And that her name is Mrs. Porter. But I know better.

Can you guess why I gave the nicknames Andrew Two-Two and Karen Two-Two to my brother and me? I call us two-twos because we have two of so many things. Andrew and I have two houses, two mommies, and two daddies. I have two bicycles, one at each house. Andrew has two tricycles. We have toys and books and clothes at each house. I have a big-house best friend (Hannie), and a little-house best friend (Nancy). I even have two stuffed cats. They look just alike. Moosie lives at the big house, Goosie lives at the little house.

(I got the name "two-two" from the title of a book Ms. Colman read to my class this year. It was called *Jacob Two-Two Meets the Hooded Fang*.)

But Andrew and I do not have two of *every*thing, which can be hard. For example, I used to have only one special blanket. Tickly. I liked to sleep with Tickly every night. But I was always forgetting and leaving Tickly at one house or the other. Finally I had to tear Tickly into two pieces. That way, I could have a piece at each house. (I hope I did not hurt Tickly.)

I also do not have two pairs of roller skates. I *love* to skate. But I cannot remember everything. And sometimes Hannie gets mad when I forget to bring my skates to the big house. Hannie does not understand that being a two-two is difficult. I like having two houses and two families. But I do not like missing things. I do not like missing Emily Junior when I am at the big house. (Oh, by the way, I named my rat after Emily Michelle.) I do not like missing Mommy when I am at the big house. And when I am at the *little* house, I do not like missing Crystal Light the Second and Daddy and Emily Michelle, and Kristy, my special big sister.

But when you are a two-two, that's life.

# The Great Idea

"I *still* want to go skating," said Hannie.

I stretched my legs out in front of me. The sunshine felt good on them. But the porch stairs were uncomfortable. I wanted to go skating, too.

"Well, we can't," said Nancy. "We don't have skates. So that is that."

"Maybe we could *get* skates," said Hannie.

"How?" asked Nancy.

"I don't know. Borrow them."

"From who?"

12

"I don't *know*. Quit asking so many questions."

"Oh, cut it out, you guys," I said. I do not like my friends to fight.

"But I want skates!" cried Hannie. "We really should have them. I need a pair that fits. Karen needs a second pair, and Nancy needs her first pair."

"Maybe we could earn money to *buy* skates," I suggested.

"Yeah!" cried Hannie and Nancy.

"But we'll need an awful lot of money to buy three pairs of skates," I added.

Hannie and Nancy and I sat with our chins in our hands.

We were thinking.

"We could sell wildflowers," said Nancy. "We could pick bunches of them and sell them in front of your house, Karen. We could set up a stand."

"We could sell lemonade," said Hannie. "And maybe other things to eat. Like popcorn. Or — or — "

"Or cotton candy!" I cried.

Hannie gave me a Look. "How are we going to sell cotton candy?" she asked. "You can't make it. You need a machine."

"I know that," I replied. "I was thinking we could have a carnival. It would be a great way to earn money. We could have games *and* we could sell stuff. Maybe we could have a rummage sale at the carnival."

"A carnival would be so much fun!" exclaimed Nancy.

"Lots of fun," said Hannie.

"Gigundo fun," I said.

"What else could we do at a carnival?" Hannie wondered.

"Tell fortunes," said Nancy.

"I know!" I cried. "We could give pony rides. We could hire a magician — "

"Karen," said Nancy.

"We could borrow a cotton-candy machine," I went on. "We could borrow some animals, too. We could have a petting zoo."

"Karen," said Hannie.

"We could get a clown."

Nancy could not stand it any longer. She

jumped up. "Hey, we want to *make* money!" she said. "We can't afford to hire a magician and a clown. That's ex*pen*sive. We'll be broke even *after* we give the carnival."

"Oh, yeah," I said.

"Maybe we should just stick to games," said Hannie.

"A ringtoss and a bottle-cap throw," said Nancy.

"*And* we could sell things. Refreshments and — "

"Crafts!" suggested Nancy. "We'll make stuff and sell it. I know how to make friendship bracelets." She paused. Then she said, "Boy, is this going to be fun."

"Boy, will it be a lot of work," I added.

"*Oh*, boy!" cried Hannie. "We'll all get roller skates!"

# Mommy's Surprise

Late Sunday afternoon, our big-house weekend was over. Mommy and Seth picked up Andrew and me. They drove us to the little house.

On the way, Mommy asked, "What did you do this weekend?"

"Played," said Andrew.

"Got bored," I answered.

"*You* got *bored?*" Seth repeated.

"Well, not for very long. See, Hannie and Nancy and I wanted to go to the playground at David Michael's school. But Elizabeth would not let us go alone. She said it was too far away. Unless we went with a big person."

"So did Kristy go with you?" asked Mommy.

"No. She was busy. We decided we wanted to roller-skate instead."

"Roller-skate? You didn't go skating," said Andrew.

"I know. Nancy does not have skates, and Hannie's are too small, and I had left mine at the little house. Since we did not have skates, we decided to buy them."

Seth turned around to look at me, even though he was driving. "You *bought* three pairs of skates? How?" he asked.

"Well, we didn't exactly get them yet. But we are going to earn money to buy them. We are going to put on a carnival."

"A carvinal?" said Andrew.

"Car-ni-val," I corrected him. "You know. You went to one once. It's a fair where you play games and win prizes and eat food and buy stuff. We are thinking of having a magician and pony rides and a cotton-candy machine."

Andrew's eyes grew very wide.

I thought Mommy and Seth might laugh, but they did not. Instead, Mommy said, "Karen, I have a surprise for you."

She did? "You do?" I cried. (It was not anywhere near my birthday.)

"Yes," said Mommy. "Seth and I went to a meeting yesterday."

Oh. A meeting. Meetings are GIGUNDO boring. But Mommy was smiling, so I said, "What kind of meeting?"

"A town meeting. Lots of people who live in Stoneybrook went to it. The mayor was there, too."

"And guess what everyone decided," said Seth.

"What?" asked Andrew and I.

"We decided," said Mommy, "to build a community playground. A playground for the people of Stoneybrook. We will raise money to buy the supplies to build it, and then we will build it ourselves."

"And your mother," Seth went on, "was given a very important job. She is going to be in charge of fund-raising. That means she will think of ways to earn money so we can build the playground."

"Yea for Mommy!" cried Andrew.

"Guess what else," said Mommy. "The playground is going to be built very close to the big house. You will be able to walk there with your friends."

"All *right!*" I shouted. I started to make up a song. *"At last we will have a playground. A place to play around."* Before I finished my song, though, Seth parked the car at the little house.

I ran inside. I telephoned Hannie. "Hi! It's me!" I said. "Yesterday Mommy and Seth went to a meeting and they decided to build a playground!"

Then I telephoned Nancy. "Hi! It's me! I'm back!" I cried. "We're going to build a playground. I mean, everyone in Stoneybrook is. It will be right near the big house. Oh, I cannot wait!"

# Helping Out

I just love school. I really do. I like the weekends, and I also like Mondays, Tuesdays, Wednesdays, Thursdays, and Fridays. Ms. Colman is a very, very nice teacher. She does not yell. (Often.) She always helps kids. She is fair. And she is fun.

Ms. Colman makes lots of Surprising Announcements. One day she said, "Okay, boys and girls. Today I am going to read a special story to you. It's a newspaper story. Then we will talk about it. The story is called 'Helping Out.' "

"Oh, dis*gust*," said Bobby Gianelli with a groan. Bobby is sort of a bully. And he does not like school.

"Bobby?" said Ms. Colman. "Don't you want to hear a computer story?"

"Oh. Sure!" Bobby likes computers a lot.

"All right, then. Settle down."

Ms. Colman began reading. The story was about a classroom of kids who worked together to raise money. And they raised enough money to buy a computer for their school.

When Ms. Colman finished reading, she put the newspaper on her desk. "What do you think of that story?" she asked.

"Is it *true*?" Natalie Springer wanted to know.

Well, for heaven's sake.

I like Natalie a lot but sometimes she is a drip. Newspaper articles are not fairy tales. They are stories about true things. She should know that.

Ms. Colman just said, "Yes, it's a true story." She did not get cross.

21

"Those kids earned a *lot* of money," said Ricky Torres. He did not remember to raise his hand. (By the way, Ricky and I are pretend married. He is my pretend husband. Ricky and Natalie and I sit in the front row of desks. This is because we wear glasses. Nancy and Hannie get to sit in the back row.)

"They did earn a lot of money," Ms. Colman agreed.

"But they're just kids," said Pamela Harding. (Pamela is my enemy.)

"Kids can do a lot," I said. (I remembered to raise my hand.)

"That's right, Karen," said Ms. Colman. "Kids can volunteer. There are many ways they can help people or their schools or their town."

Leslie Morris (who is a mean friend of Pamela's) raised her hand. "Are we volunteering when we go to Stoneybrook Manor to visit our adopted grandparents?"

"You certainly are," replied Ms. Colman. "The elderly people who live there look forward to your visits. You cheer them up. What are some other ways kids could volunteer and help out?"

"By starting a pet-sitting business?" suggested Hank Reubens.

"Well, pet-sitting is an important job," replied Ms. Colman. "And it is very helpful. But if you are *paid* to do something, then you are not volunteering. Volunteering means helping out for free."

"Like when my mom and dad fight fires?" asked Bobby. "That's not their job. They are not firefighters all the time. But sometimes when there's a fire, they rush to it and help put it out for free."

"*That's* volunteering," said Ms. Colman.

"I know how kids could volunteer," I said. "They could pick up litter. They could write letters to people who are in hospitals. Oh . . . and they could raise money like the kids in the article did. Raising money for something is volunteering. And I know what *we* could raise money for."

Ms. Colman had not asked us to talk

about real projects. Even so, I told my class about the playground for Stoneybrook. "My mother is in charge of raising money," I said proudly. "We could help out."

"Yeah!" exclaimed Hannie. "We could have a toy sale with our old toys."

"We could have a bake sale or a car wash," said Pamela.

"We could mow lawns," said Natalie. (I sighed. None of us is allowed to mow lawns. I think Natalie's brain is on another planet.)

But I did not say that. I was getting a Very Good Idea.

# "Fight, Fight!"

I waited until lunchtime before I told Nancy and Hannie my Very Good Idea. (I *had* to wait until lunchtime. We were busy all morning. And it is hard to pass a note from the front row all the way to the back row.)

Nancy and Hannie and I sat together in the cafeteria. We opened our cartons of milk. I said, "Guess what. I have a Very Good Idea."

"What is it?" asked Hannie. She usually likes my ideas.

"I was thinking that we should hold our carnival — and then give the money we earn to the playground fund. That way we could help out."

"What about our skates?" asked Hannie.

"We'll get them some other time," I replied. "What do you guys think?"

"I think," said Nancy, "that helping out with the playground would be nice."

"Me, too," I said. "Gigundo nice. Okay, great. We will give our carnival money to my mom for the playground."

"Hey!" cried Hannie. "*I* don't like that idea. I want skates."

"But we need a playground more," said Nancy.

"Besides, practically everyone in town is going to help build the playground." (I did not know if that was true, but I thought it might be.)

"I don't care. I *want skates!*" said Hannie.

"You *have* skates," I reminded her.

"They don't fit. Anyway, *you* said we

should have a carnival to earn money for skates. *You* said it, Karen."

"Well, I changed my mind."

"No fair. You can't do that."

"Why not?"

"I don't know. You just can't."

Nancy ate her lunch quietly. After awhile she said, "Let's go play hopscotch. I don't want to waste recess."

"Okay," I mumbled.

Hannie and Nancy and I cleaned up our table. We went outside. As we walked across the playground, Hannie began to sing very quietly: *"Oh, how I want skates, before it's too late. Oh, how I want skates. . . . It's Karen I hate."*

"Shut up!" I yelled, even though I am not supposed to say that.

*"It's Karen I hate,"* Hannie sang more loudly.

"Stop it!" I reached out to cover Hannie's mouth with my hand.

And guess what. Hannie *hit* me. She put

her own arm out and she punched my hand. Hard.

So I pulled her hair.

"Cut it out, you guys!" yelled Nancy.

But Hannie and I fell to the ground. We rolled around.

"Fight!" I heard someone yell. It was a boy. It might have been Bobby.

A few seconds later, every kid in Ms. Colman's class was standing around us. "Fight! Fight!" they chanted.

A hand grabbed my arm. Another hand grabbed Hannie's arm. Ricky and Nancy pulled us apart.

"Say you're sorry," Nancy told us.

"No way," answered Hannie.

"Well, then, come on," said Nancy. "Recess is over."

My classmates and I walked back to our room. I guess Hannie and I looked as if we had been fighting. Our hair was all mashed around. We were dirty. A hole had been ripped in my shirt.

Ms. Colman made us write "I'm sorry" letters to each other. We did. But we were not really sorry.

And by the time school was over, we were not speaking.

# Enemies

Nancy and Hannie and I were standing in front of Stoneybrook Academy. We were waiting for our moms to pick us up and drive us home.

Hannie stood about ten feet away from me. Nancy stood between us. She talked to us. We talked to her — but not to each other.

At last Mrs. Papadakis pulled up. Hannie got into the car with her mother. Mrs. Dawes was right behind her. Nancy and I got into *her* car. We buckled our seat belts.

At the end of the road, Mrs. Papadakis turned right. Mrs. Dawes turned left. I looked at Hannie through the window. *She* was looking at *me*.

I stuck my tongue out. She stuck hers out.

I pointed to my head and made the "you're crazy" sign. Hannie did the same thing.

"Jerk," I muttered as I turned around.

"Why don't you come over and play when we get home?" Nancy asked me.

"Okay," I replied. "Thanks."

Later that afternoon, Nancy and I were sitting on the floor in Nancy's bedroom. We were making a village out of cereal boxes and stuff.

"You know what I decided?" I said.

"No. What?"

"I decided that Hannie was right about one thing today."

"What was she right about?"

"She was right that the carnival was my idea. So I think I ought to go ahead and

32

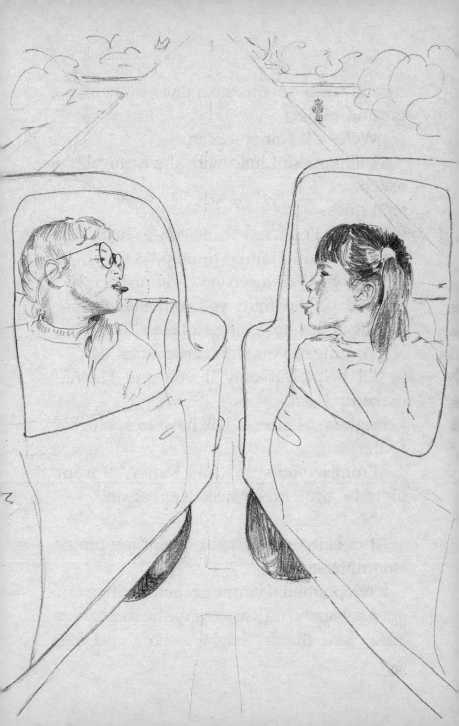

have it. And donate the money to the playground project."

"Well — " Nancy began.

"Will you still help with the carnival?" I asked.

"I guess — "

"Good. Because I want you to help. But I do not want Hannie to help."

"Uh-oh. Wait a second. I do not want to be part of the fight you and Hannie are having. I am not going to take sides."

"You mean you won't help after all?"

"I'll help. But only if you and Hannie make up," said Nancy.

I sighed. "I guess I will have to apologize to her."

"Promise you will," said Nancy. "I want us to be the Three Musketeers again."

After supper that night, I kept my promise to Nancy.

I telephoned Hannie. I had written an apology speech. (It was very different from my "I'm sorry" letter.) I planned to read it over the phone. "Dear Hannie," the letter began. "I am really, *really*, REALLY sorry about our fight. I am sorry I pulled your hair. I am sorry for anything I said that you did not like."

The letter went on. I had written quite a few sentences.

I felt nervous when I dialed Hannie's number. My heart was beating fast.

The phone began to ring.

Someone picked it up. "Hello?"

It was Hannie.

"Hi, Hannie," I said. "It's me, Karen. I'm — "

*CLUNK.*

Hannie hung up the phone on me!

I could not believe it. How rude. And just when I was about to apologize to her.

Hatey Hannie.

I tried to think of something rude I could do back. I could call her again and say, "Hannie, you are a monkey-head." I could bring her a mud brownie. (I did that once to Ricky when I was mad at *him*.)

But I knew I was not going to do those things.

Instead, I wandered into the living room. "Mommy?" I said.

# Potluck

Mommy was busy working. She was sitting at her desk. Papers were everywhere. Mommy was writing something.

"What are you doing?" I asked. Maybe she was already planning my birthday party — the one I would have next year.

"The fund-raising committee held a meeting today," Mommy replied. "We talked about ways to earn money to build the playground."

Mommy sounded very excited. So I tried to *look* excited. Even though I felt awful.

Hatey Hannie had been mean to me.

"What kinds of things are you going to do?" I asked.

"Well, we have lots of ideas. I'll tell you the best ones. Mrs. Reubens suggested holding a music festival. The players would perform for free, and the audience would pay to listen to them."

"Cool!" I exclaimed.

"And Mrs. Arnold suggested inviting an author to sign books at the Book Nook downtown. Lots of people would want to buy books then. Imagine having a book with the author's own signature in it! Later the store would donate money to the fund. Oh, and Mr. Pike said he thought a potluck supper would be fun."

"What's potluck?" I asked.

"That means that everybody brings something to the dinner. A casserole or a salad or a dessert. We set up tables at the community center or some place with a lot of space. Then people pay to come to an indoor picnic and try lots of different foods."

Wow. I could see that raising money was fun. But it was hard work, too. Probably, my carnival would be both fun and work. The work part would be worth it, though. Because I would be helping out. And in the end, Stoneybrook would have a beautiful new playground.

I hoped I could help with *every*thing. I wanted to cook something for the potluck supper. I wanted to listen to grown-up music at the festival. I wanted to meet an author who would sign a book for me.

And I wanted to plan my carnival. But who would help me? Nancy? Maybe. But not Hatey Hannie.

Boo.

# Games and Prizes

The next morning, I did not know what to do. I would see Hatey Hannie at school. What should I say to her? How should I act? What if Hatey Hannie never spoke to me again? I would feel very sad.

Mommy drove Nancy and me to school.

"Nancy?" I said. "What did I do wrong last night? I called Hannie to say 'I'm sorry,' and she hung up on me."

"That wasn't very nice," said Nancy.

"I had planned a whole speech, with lots

of 'I'm sorries' in it. Hannie did not even let me talk. I am calling her Hatey Hannie now."

"I don't think that will help," said Nancy.

We rode the rest of the way to school in silence.

Mommy dropped us off.

When we got out of the car, the first person I saw was . . . Hatey Hannie. I still did not know what to do. Maybe I had not been thoughtful when I said we should give our carnival money to the playground fund. After all, it had been Hannie's idea to earn money for skates. I know that I can be a little pushy. (I have been told this a number of times.) So I was ready to apologize to Hannie. But I did not think she would listen to me.

Hatey Hannie surprised me.

As soon as Nancy and I got out of the car, she ran to us.

"Karen?" she said.

"Yeah?"

"Can I say something to you?"

"Sure." (Hannie looked like she thought I would run away.)

"Well . . . well . . . I'm sorry."

I did not think I had heard Hannie right. "Excuse me?" I said.

"I'm sorry," Hannie repeated in a louder voice. "I'm sorry I hung up on you last night. And I'm sorry I didn't want to give money to the playground. I thought about what Ms. Colman said about helping out. I was being selfish. A playground for Stoneybrook is much more important than roller skates. And if you guys are going to help out, then I want to help out, too."

"You do?" I said.

"Yes," replied Hannie. (I decided never to call her Hatey Hannie again.)

"The Three Musketeers!" cried Nancy. Then she added, "Are you sure your fight is over?" She looked at Hannie and me.

"We're sure," said Hannie.

"Positive," I added. "Hey, we have a lot of work to do."

*  *  *

At recess that afternoon, Hannie and Nancy and I began planning our carnival. We sat under a tree, away from the rest of the kids.

"What do we do first?" asked Nancy.

"Mommy is making lists," I answered. "Maybe we should make lists, too. Hannie, did you bring your notebook?"

"Yup."

"Okay, take this down," I said. Then I paused. "Sorry. I did not mean to be bossy. Hannie, do you want to write the lists?"

"It's okay with me."

"Oh, good. Thank you. Now, let's see. First we should make a list of things to buy: prizes, lemonade mix, napkins — "

"And a list of games," said Nancy, "and a list of things we can borrow."

"Ooh," I said. I could see that we were going to be very busy.

# Announcing . . .
# Karen's Carnival!

"There," I said. "All done." I sat back and looked at my work.

Nancy and Hannie leaned over to look, too.

I had just finished our very first sign for the carnival. And I had worked hard on it. I had colored the letters red and outlined them in blue. I had glued sparkles around the edges of the sign. I had drawn a smiling clown.

But Hannie and Nancy did not say anything about my wonderful artwork.

They just stared. Finally Hannie exclaimed, "Your sign says:

ANNOUNCING . . .
KAREN'S CARNIVAL!"

"Yup," I replied.

"Well, why is it called *Karen's* Carnival? How did the carnival get to be *yours?*"

"Yeah," said Nancy. "How did that happen?"

"The carnival was my idea," I reminded my friends. "Besides, Karen's Carnival sounds better than Hannie's Carnival or Nancy's Carnival. I like the 'K' sounds together."

"I wanted to call it The Three Musketeers' Carnival," said Nancy.

"*I* wanted to call it Crazy Clown's Carnival," said Hannie.

"Who's Crazy Clown?" I asked.

Hannie shrugged. "I just liked the name."

I did not say anything.

Finally Hannie sighed. "Okay," she said. "We'll call it Karen's Carnival."

"Thank you," I replied.

After that we made lots more signs announcing my carnival. We wrote up a small flier, too. Mommy made copies of it at her office. By the end of the week, we had a big stack of posters. We had an even bigger stack of fliers.

On Friday night, Andrew and I went to the big house. I brought the posters and fliers with me. Everyone in the big house liked them very much. Charlie even said, "I'll drive you and Nancy and Hannie downtown tomorrow. I will go with you to the stores. Maybe you can put your posters in the store windows."

"Cool!" I said. "Thank you, Charlie."

The next day, Charlie kept his promise. He drove my friends and me into town in the Junk Bucket. (That is the name of his car.) He went with us from store to store. At each store, I said to the person at the cash register, "May we put a poster in your

window? It is for a carnival. We are going to give the money we earn to the Stoneybrook Playground Fund."

Some people said, "What a nice thing to do."

"It was my idea," I would tell them.

We ran out of posters before we ran out of stores to put them in. So Hannie and Nancy and Charlie and I climbed into the Junk Bucket. As we were riding back to the big house, I said, "What should we do with our fliers?"

"I could take some to the high school," said Charlie. "I could tack them to bulletin boards. Everyone would see them."

"Really?" cried Nancy. "That would be cool."

At home, Kristy said she would put up some fliers at the middle school.

David Michael said he would put up some at *his* school.

"Thank you, everyone!" I exclaimed. "Thank you for helping."

Hannie and Nancy and I gave a stack of

fliers to Charlie, to Kristy, and to David Michael. Some fliers were still left over.

"We can take them to *our* school," said Nancy. "We could put up one in the hallway, and one on each door, and one in the library, and one in the cafeteria — "

"And one in our classroom!" I exclaimed. "We want our friends to know what we're doing. We want them all to come to the carnival."

"Yeah!" cried Hannie and Nancy.

And I added, "Oh, boy! Karen's Carnival will be the most fun!"

# Dollars and Pennies

That afternoon, Nancy had to go home. While we waited for her father to pick her up, I thought of something.

"You know what, you guys?" I said.

"What?" asked Hannie. She was sitting on the ground. Nancy was sitting in front of her. Hannie was braiding Nancy's hair.

"So far, we have not spent any money on the carnival," I said. "We made the posters from stuff we found at our houses. And Mommy copied the fliers for us."

"That's good," said Hannie.

"I know. But soon we will have to buy some things. We will have to buy lemonade mix and game prizes and paper cups and lots of other stuff."

"Uh-oh," said Nancy. And then she added, "Ow, Hannie! Don't pull."

"Sorry," said Hannie.

"I think," I said, "that I remember Mommy saying that when you are fundraising, sometimes you have to *spend* money to *make* money. I did not understand what she meant then. Now I do. If we want to make money selling lemonade, we have to spend a *little* to buy the lemonade mix. Then when we sell the lemonade, we earn back what we spent, plus more."

"I get it," said Nancy.

"So," I went on, "we need money."

"I've got four dollars and fifty cents," said Hannie. "We can pay me back after the carnival."

"I've got four dollars and twenty-five cents," said Nancy.

"And I've got about five dollars. How much money is that?"

"Almost fourteen dollars!" exclaimed Nancy.

"That's not very much," I said. "Not when you think of everything we need to buy."

"What are we going to do?" Hannie wondered.

Mr. Dawes pulled into our driveway then. "Hey!" cried Nancy. "We could borrow money from our parents."

"Yeah!" I said. "Let's all ask our parents right now."

Nancy dashed to the car. Hannie dashed across the street. (She looked both ways first.) I dashed into my house.

"Daddy?" I called as I ran through the front door. "Daddy?"

"In the kitchen, Karen," he replied.

"Daddy, could I borrow some money?" I asked. I skidded into the kitchen and nearly fell down. "It's for stuff for the carnival. I could pay you back when the carnival is over. Mommy says you have to spend money to make money. Right now Nancy is asking her father for money, and Hannie is at *her* house asking for money. I think if you could — "

"Karen!" said Daddy.

"What?" I was out of breath.

"Is Mr. Dawes here?"

"He is parked in the driveway."

Daddy and I went outside. We saw Hannie and Mrs. Papadakis crossing the street. Daddy and Mr. Dawes and Mrs. Papadakis talked quietly together.

"What do you think they're saying?" Nancy whispered.

We did not have to wait long to find out.

"Girls?" said Daddy. "We have decided that we will each give you ten dollars for the carnival. And you do not have to pay us back."

"It will be our contribution to the playground," added Mr. Dawes.

"Yippee!" I cried.

And Hannie said, "I think *our* money should be a contribution, too."

"Yes," I agreed. I felt grown-up.

That night, Mommy and Seth promised us ten *more* dollars. All together we would have nearly fifty-four dollars to spend on the carnival.

# Cotton Candy!

Fifty-four dollars sounded like a fortune. Now that we had so much money, we decided to work on our "Things to Buy" list.

So on Sunday, Nancy and Hannie and I met in Hannie's room. After we kicked out her big brother, Linny, we got right to work. (Linny had been making bulldog faces at us. Hannie had to close the door so that we could not see him. Even so, we could hear him growling in the hallway.)

"Okay," I said. "I will write down the list." I sat at Hannie's desk. "Things to buy, things to buy," I murmured.

"Lots of prizes," said Nancy.

I wrote down: prizes.

"A wading pool," said Hannie.

"A *wading* pool?" I repeated.

"Yeah. For the duck pond. We need rubber ducks, too."

"We could borrow those things," suggested Nancy.

"Right," I agreed. "I better make another list." I wrote "Things to Borrow" across the top of a second piece of paper.

"I bet we could make some stuff, too," said Hannie. "Like the target for the dart-throw." (We planned to have a *safe* dart-throwing game. The darts would be Magic Markers. They would not stick to a dartboard. But we would be able to see where they had hit by the mark they left on the target.)

I wrote "Things to Make" across a third piece of paper.

"What kinds of refreshments are we going to sell?" asked Nancy. "Anything besides lemonade and popcorn? We will need to buy all the food stuff."

"We could sell cookies," I said. "The slice-and-bake kind. Kristy could help us with the oven." I thought for a moment. "I still don't see why we cannot sell cotton candy."

"Because we do not have a cotton-candy maker!" cried Nancy.

"Well, we can rent one. We have fifty-four dollars now," I pointed out.

"Do you know how much renting a cotton-candy machine would cost?" said Nancy.

"No. Do you?"

"Yes. I asked my father."

When Nancy told me what her father had said, I gasped. "You're kidding! That much? Then we probably cannot hire a clown or a magician, either."

"No," said Nancy and Hannie.

"Grrr," said Linny from the hallway.

# Mary R. Sanderson

One Saturday, I woke up feeling excited. It was a very special day. It was not a holiday. It was the day the famous author was coming to town. This author does not write long, hard books for big people. She writes funny books for kids. Her name is Mary R. Sanderson. I love her books! And now I was going to have a chance to meet her.

It was a little-house Saturday. As soon as I woke up, I scrambled out of bed. I ran into the hallway. I almost ran into Mommy.

"Mommy!" I cried. "It's Mary R. Sanderson Day!"

"Indoor voice, Karen," Mommy whispered. "We're the first ones up. Yes, it's a big day, isn't it? Not many people get to meet one of their favorite authors."

"What's an arthur?" (That was Andrew. He came out of his room, looking sleepy.)

"What's an — " I started to shout. Then I remembered to whisper. "What's an *author*? Andrew, don't you even know that? And anyway, it's *au*thor, not *ar*thur. An author is a person who writes books. An Arthur is just a guy."

"Oh," said Andrew.

"Mommy?" I asked as we went to the kitchen. "Do you think Mary R. Sanderson will write something in my autograph book, too?"

"Maybe," answered Mommy. "You can try."

"And I'm going to give her something special."

"You are?" Mommy looked a little nervous.

"Yes. Don't worry," I said. "I know Mary R. Sanderson will like it."

Later that morning, I was standing outside the Book Nook. I was waiting in a lo-o-o-o-ong line. Everyone seemed to want to meet the famous author. The line was so long that it ran from Mary R. Sanderson's table through the store, out the door, and down the sidewalk.

I knew a lot of people in the line. I was standing with Seth, Andrew, Nancy, Mr. and Mrs. Dawes, Hannie, Linny, and Mr. and Mrs. Papadakis. (Mommy was busy inside.) Ahead of me was a bunch of kids from Ms. Colman's class. Some of them had brought their autograph books, too. Behind me were Kristy, David Michael, and Daddy.

Everyone was talking, mostly about Mary R. Sanderson.

"Can you see her yet?" someone asked.

"Does she look the same as her picture?"

"Do you have her newest book?"

I did not have her newest book. But Mommy had said it would be on sale in the store. Seth was going to buy it for me. Then Mary R. Sanderson could sign it *and* my autograph book. And then I would give her my secret surprise.

The line moved along slowly. We reached the door. We walked through the front of the store. Seth picked up a copy of the new book. He handed it to me. And suddenly I saw . . . *her*.

"There she is!" I cried.

Hannie and Nancy and I leaned forward. Mary R. Sanderson did not look much different from other women we knew. In fact, she was young, like Ms. Colman. Even so, as I inched closer to the autographing table, I began to feel nervous.

At last it was my turn. I was looking right at the author.

Feeling very timid, I pushed my new book across the table to Mary R. Sanderson.

"Hi," she said. "What's your name?"

"Karen Brewer," I whispered. I remembered to add, "I really like your books."

Mary R. Sanderson smiled. She scribbled something in the front of my book and gave it back to me. "There you go," she said.

I took the book and I handed her an envelope. "This is for you. It's a letter."

"Thank you! I'll read it when I get home tonight."

"Could you sign my autograph book, too?" I whispered.

Mary R. Sanderson said she would be happy to. She was *so nice*.

Later, Nancy, Hannie, and I looked at what she had written in our books. My book said, "Happy Reading, Karen! From Mary R. Sanderson." In my autograph book was written, "Yours till the kitchen sinks!"

I was gigundo happy.

(I hoped Mary R. Sanderson liked my letter.)

# The Town Thermometer

One day Mommy drove Andrew and me downtown. She parked the car and we got out. Mommy said, "Come with me to Palmer Square. I want to show you something. A surprise was put up today."

"Oh, goody. A surprise!" cried Andrew.

We walked around a corner. In front of us was Palmer Square. It is kind of like a park. The ground is covered with grass, and green trees grow everywhere. Now a tall white sign stood right in the middle of the square. It looked like a thermometer.

At the bottom was a big fat zero. At the top was written "Hurray!"

I frowned. "It looks like a thermometer, Mommy," I said.

"Is Palmer Square sick?" asked Andrew. (When would he ever grow up?)

Mommy laughed. "It *is* a thermometer," she said. "But Palmer Square is not sick. The thermometer shows how much money we have earned for the playground. See the red line? It's about halfway to the top. That means we have earned almost half the money we need. Mary Sanderson helped us earn a lot. As we raise more money, we'll paint the line higher. When it reaches 'Hurray!' we will be ready to start the playground."

"Cool," I said.

"I don't get it," said Andrew.

In Ms. Colman's class, we were talking about the thermometer. Almost all the kids in my class had seen it.

"We have half the money," I announced.

66

"Duh!" said Bobby Gianelli.

"Shhh!" hissed Hannie. "Ms. Colman will be here any minute!"

"Duh," whispered Bobby.

"Well, when I am all done with my car wash," said Hank, "that thermometer will be a lot higher. I plan to make millions."

"Really?" asked Natalie.

(Oh, for heaven's sake.)

"Have you mowed any lawns yet?" I asked Natalie. (I could not help it.)

"No," she said. "But I weeded our garden. I earned fifty cents."

"*I* am going to have my bake sale on Saturday," spoke up Pamela. "My big sister and I have been baking forever. I hope you guys will come."

We said we would. We wanted to help the playground. Besides, we like cookies. Even cookies baked by Pamela.

"You know what?" said Leslie Morris. "I thought Hannie had a good idea. So me and Jannie and my brother are going to have a toy and jewelry sale. We are cleaning out our closets and our rec rooms."

"What kind of jewelry will you be selling?" asked Ricky, my husband.

"Oh, everything," said Jannie.

"Maybe I will buy you something, Karen," said Ricky. "It could be an anniversary present."

"Thanks!" I replied.

"I did not have much luck with my fundraising," said Bobby. "I put a sign up in our front yard. It said, THE FIX-IT GUY. I REPAIR TOYS. But nobody brought me any toys to fix. I even changed the sign. I made it say, I REPAIR TOYS *FREE*."

"How were you going to earn money fixing stuff for free?" I asked.

Bobby shrugged.

"Good morning, class," said Ms. Colman.

We ran for our seats.

# Dinosaur Erasers

"Are you guys ready?" I asked Nancy and Hannie.

School was over. Mommy was going to pick up the Three Musketeers. We had a big project to take care of downtown.

"I'm ready!" said Nancy.

"Me, too!" said Hannie.

We ran outside. (We are supposed to remember to walk.)

There was Mommy.

"Did you bring the money?" I cried. "Did you remember it?"

Mommy had been taking care of our fifty-four dollars for us. Now we needed it. We were going to go shopping for the carnival. We were going to buy the prizes.

Andrew shook his head. He looked very sad. "Mommy lost your money," he said.

"Mommy!" I cried.

"Mrs. Engle!" exclaimed Nancy and Hannie.

"I'm just kidding," said Andrew. "Mommy has your money."

"Andrew!" I yelled. But then I began to giggle.

Hannie and Nancy and I climbed into the car. We fastened our seat belts. Mommy drove us to a new store. It is gigundo wonderful. It only sells toys. The store is called Unicorn.

Inside Unicorn, Hannie and Nancy and I looked all around. My favorite part of the store is the shelf with the glass jars. Each jar is filled with little toys. There are lots of jars.

"Look! Teensy puzzles!" I cried.

"Little tiny troll dolls!" said Nancy.

"Dinosaur erasers!" said Hannie.

"Can I have one?" asked Andrew.

"You may choose *one* thing today," Mommy told him.

"Cool! Here are rubber spiders on strings!" I said.

Nancy held up a little yo-yo. "These would be good prizes."

"So would these," said Hannie. "Lookit. You drop this tablet in water and it turns into an animal. A foam animal, I mean."

"Can I have one?" asked Andrew.

"Hey, here are glow-in-the-dark dinosaurs!" I exclaimed.

"Can I have one?" asked Andrew.

My friends and I looked and looked. We wanted to buy everything. But we knew we could not. We had decided to buy just a certain number of prizes. We chose carefully. Even so, we spent an awful lot of our money.

"Do we have enough left over for lem-

onade and paper cups and stuff?" asked Nancy.

"I hope so," I answered.

We had to wait awhile for Andrew. He was still choosing his one toy. He took forever. At last he chose a dinosaur eraser. We had bought several of them. I was sure they would make good prizes.

On the way home, we passed the town thermometer.

"Ooh, look everyone!" I shouted. "The red line is higher!"

"Yea!" cried Nancy and Hannie.

But Mommy did not look very happy.

"What's wrong?" I asked her.

"We are not earning money as fast as we hoped we would."

"No playground?" whined Andrew.

"Oh, I think we'll be able to build the playground," Mommy replied. "But it might take longer than we thought."

"Don't worry," I said. "Karen's Carnival will save the day."

# The Carnival Begins

"IT'S CARNIVAL TIME!" I yelled.

"Karen, shh. You'll wake up the whole house," said Nannie.

"Sorry," I replied as I ran downstairs. "But today is the day of the carniva-a-al!"

Nancy and Hannie and I had worked gigundoly hard. We had made a booth for every game. (The booths were cardboard cartons.) We were going to set up a penny-pitch, a dart-throw, a ringtoss, a duck pond, a bottle-cap-throw, and a fortune-teller. We were also going to have the refreshment stand for lemonade and popcorn, but no cotton candy. (Boo.) We had collected enough junk for a teensy rummage sale, and Nancy was going to be selling all these friendship bracelets she had made.

"Oh, I can't wait, I can't wait, I can't wait!" I sang. "Look, Nannie. It is a perfect carnival day. All sunshine, no clouds."

"Maybe that's good luck," said Nannie.

"Oh, I *know* it is!"

Nancy came over to the big house early in the morning. Hannie came over just a few minutes later.

"Let's get to work!" I cried.

My friends and I moved the booths out of the garage. We set them up in two rows, with an aisle in-between. We had made a sign for each booth, so kids would know what the games were. Hannie and Nancy and I were going to stand behind the booths. We would yell out things like,

"Penny-pitch here!" or, "Play the ringtoss!" or, "Fabulous prizes!"

Then we dragged three tables into the yard. One was for refreshments, one was for the rummage sale, and one was for Nancy's friendship bracelets.

"Now," I said, "it's time to put up our sign and tie balloons to our mailbox. Nancy, you take care of the balloons. Hannie, you put up the sign."

"What are you going to do?" asked Hannie.

"Get the refreshments ready," I replied.

So Nancy tied a bunch of yellow and green balloons to our mailbox. We had blown up the balloons the night before. Hannie stuck the sign in our front lawn. The sign read: KAREN'S CARNIVAL HERE. And I brought a pitcher of lemonade and ten bags of popcorn to the refreshment stand. Nancy and I had made the popcorn at the little house. We had popped some every night all week until Seth said, "This house smells like a baseball stadium."

When Hannie and Nancy finished their jobs, they joined me in the backyard.

I was looking at our carnival. "Uh-oh," I said.

"What-oh?" replied Nancy.

"I just realized something. Nancy, you are going to be at your bracelet stand. Hannie, you wanted to sell refreshments. And I wanted to be the fortune-teller. If we do those things, who is going to run the games and the rummage sale?"

"Uh-oh," said Hannie and Nancy.

"It's nine-fifteen now. The carnival starts at ten. We better get help *fast!*"

We ran into the big house.

"HELP!" I yelled.

"Karen, what happened?" asked Daddy.

I told him our problem.

"I think we can take care of that," he said. "But from now on, don't yell 'help' unless there is a real emergency. Okay?"

"Okay," I replied.

Fifteen minutes later, Elizabeth was standing at the rummage table, and Kristy, Charlie, Sam, David Michael, and Linny Papadakis were at the game booths.

We were ready for our carnival.

# The Witch at the Carnival

"**S**tep right up! Getcher popcorn here!" cried Hannie.

"Bracelets for sale!" called Nancy. "No two alike. Buy one for your best friend!"

"Come and haff your fortune told," I said in a spooky voice. "Visit Madame Karen!"

It was eleven o'clock. Karen's Carnival had been open for an hour. *Nine* people were there. Besides Hannie and Nancy and me and my family, that is. Kids in the neighborhood were playing games. Mrs.

Papadakis was looking at the stuff on the rummage table.

"I want my fortune told, please," said Melody Korman. Melody is a friend of mine. She lives two houses away from Hannie.

"Okay. That'll be . . . I mean, all r-r-r-right. Zat vill be twenty-fife cents."

Melody held out a quarter. I added it to the two quarters I had already earned. Then I took Melody's hand in mine. I looked at her palm. "You vill liff for a very long time," I told her. "Vun day, you vill get a cat . . . no, a kitten. Oh, and you vill pr-r-robably make lots uff money."

"Thank you," said Melody.

"You are velcome."

At two-fifteen, our carnival was *gigundo* busy. Kids had come and gone. A lot of kids from Ms. Colman's class had arrived.

"Cool! A dart-throw!" exclaimed Bobby.

"What's the duck pond?" asked Jannie.

"Aw, that's a baby game," said Pamela. "All you do is pick up a duck, turn it over, and see what number is on the bottom. Then you match the number to a prize. Come on. I'll buy you a friendship bracelet." (Pamela is so bossy.)

Nobody wanted their fortune read. So I looked around the carnival. Ricky was buying a lemonade. Natalie had just won at the ringtoss.

"What prize do I get?" she asked.

David Michael handed her a dinosaur eraser. Then he dashed to my booth. "Karen!" he exclaimed. "I'm almost out of prizes! So are Linny and everyone. You didn't buy enough."

Oops. We were in trouble. But Charlie came to the rescue. I gave him some of the money we had earned. Then he roared downtown in the Junk Bucket to buy more prizes at Unicorn.

While Charlie was gone, the Awful Thing happened. I was minding my business when a croaky voice said, "Are you Madame Karen?"

I glanced up. In front of me stood . . .

Morbidda Destiny. The witch next door.

I gasped.

Morbidda held out her hand. A quarter was in it.

I grabbed the quarter and said very quickly, "You'll live a long time, and, um, you're going to get a dog. And good luck in life."

"Thank you," said the witch.

Morbidda walked to the ringtoss game. She was here to jinx our carnival. I just knew it. I watched her very carefully. But the witch did not do anything bad. She played some games. She bought a friendship bracelet from Nancy. She said hello to Daddy and Elizabeth. Then she went home.

"The coast is clear!" I called to Hannie and Nancy.

The witch had spent over two dollars at my carnival.

FORTUNE TELL

# Thirty-two Dollars and Forty Cents

My feet ached. My back ached. The Madame Karen turban was hurting my hair. I looked at my watch. Ten minutes to four!

The carnival was supposed to end at four o'clock. But kids were everywhere. They were playing games, eating popcorn, choosing prizes. And more kids were coming.

I took off my turban. I ran to Hannie. "It's almost four," I told her. "We have to stop the carnival. I'm tired."

"Me, too. But how do we stop a carnival? We cannot just tell everyone to go away."

Nancy joined us. "I ran out of bracelets!" she exclaimed.

"Good," I replied. "Then you can help us." I told Nancy that we had to close up.

"How are we going to do that?" she asked.

The Three Musketeers thought very hard. We each decided to do one thing.

Nancy took the balloons off the mailbox.

Hannie made a "closed" sign. She made it quickly. In fact, she made it so quickly that it read CARNVAL CLOZED. She carried it to the front yard. Then she pulled the KAREN'S CARNIVAL sign out of the ground. She stuck the new one in the hole.

While Hannie was doing that, I found Charlie. He was working at the penny-pitch. "Step right up!" he was saying.

"Charlie, stop that!" I whispered loudly. "The carnival is over. We want people to go home. Can I borrow your megaphone?"

Charlie said I could.

The megaphone was in the garage. A megaphone is shaped like a cone. If you hold the small end to your mouth and yell through it, your voice sounds *very* loud.

I stood in the middle of the carnival with the megaphone. "Attention, everybody!" I yelled. "Karen's Carnival is over! Please finish whatever you are doing. Thank you very much for coming. We appreciate your business. Over and out!"

Slowly, people began to leave. My family and Linny went inside. Finally Hannie and Nancy and I were alone in the backyard.

"What a mess," said Hannie.

"We better clean it up," added Nancy.

"But first," I said, "we have to see how much money we made. Come on."

My friends and I went to each booth and table. We collected the money we had earned. Then we dumped it in a pile on the empty bracelet table.

"Whoa," I whispered. "Would you look at that?"

Before us was a mountain of money — a *huge* pile of quarters and dimes and nickels and pennies, plus some bills.

"I bet it's a zillion dollars!" cried Hannie.

We separated the money into piles that equaled a dollar: four quarters or ten dimes or twenty nickels or a hundred pennies. Then we counted our dollars.

"Thirty-two," I said slowly. "Thirty-two? Is that all?"

"Here's forty cents," said Nancy. "We earned thirty-two dollars and forty cents."

"But we *spent* fifty-four dollars. We did not even earn that back."

I almost began to cry. What had happened to my wonderful carnival?

Kristy came outside then. I told her what was wrong.

"That's too bad," she said. "Maybe you didn't charge enough money to play games. The games only cost twenty-five cents. How much did the prizes cost?"

"Fifty cents," I answered. "Or a dollar. And I had to ask Charlie to buy more."

"The prizes should not have cost so much," said Kristy gently. "But you know what? I think everyone had fun today. And you can still give the thirty-two dollars and forty cents to the playground fund."

# Hurray!

"All finished," said Nancy glumly.

"Yeah. I guess so." I looked around the yard. It was neat and tidy. Hannie and Nancy and I had thrown the trash away. We had taken down the booths. We had put the tables back in the house.

"Thank you, girls!" called Elizabeth from the back door. "Why don't you come inside now? The yard looks fine."

"Okay," I replied.

Nancy and Hannie and I scuffled into the

big house. We poured our mountain of money on the kitchen table.

"You're rich!" exclaimed Andrew. "Can I have some?"

"We are not rich," I replied. "Besides, the money is for the playground. So you can't have any."

"But look at all that!"

"It is only thirty-two dollars," I said. "Now go away."

"Karen?" called Elizabeth. "Please tell Andrew you are sorry."

"Sorry," I said.

Andrew left. Elizabeth came into the kitchen. "Would you like me to take the money to the bank for you? I could write you a check. Then you could give your mom the check instead of a bag of coins."

"All right. Thank you, Elizabeth."

Elizabeth wrote a check. She handed it to me. Then Hannie and Nancy had to go home. The carnival was over.

\* \* \*

On Sunday afternoon, Mommy drove to the big house. Andrew and I were waiting for her. Our knapsacks were packed.

"Good-bye!" called Daddy and Elizabeth and Nannie and Kristy and Sam and Charlie and David Michael.

"Bye-bye!" called Emily.

Andrew hugged everybody.

I just said, " 'Bye."

In the car, I gave Mommy the check.

"Thank you!" she said. "How was your carnival?"

"Look at the check," I replied. "I thought our carnival was going to be great. But we only earned thirty-two dollars and forty cents. And we ran out of prizes and the witch came. I'm really sorry, Mommy. I know it's hardly any money at all. And we need lots and lots more for the playground."

Mommy did not say anything. She just smiled.

"Hey, this isn't the way to the little house!" cried Andrew a moment later.

"I know," Mommy answered. "I have a surprise for you." Mommy drove us downtown. She stopped at Palmer Square.

"Is this the surprise?" asked Andrew.

"That is." Mommy pointed. She pointed to the town thermometer.

I looked at it and gasped. The red line almost reached "Hurray!"

"We held the music festival on Friday night," Mommy explained. "It was a big success. Lots of people came. And we have not given the potluck supper yet. With the money from the carnival and from the supper we will have more than enough for the playground. Thank you, Karen. The money you and Nancy and Hannie earned has helped to put us over the top."

"You mean we can build the playground?" I cried.

"We can build the playground," said Mommy.

"HURRAY!" I yelled.

# Stoneybrook Playground

"The ants go marching one by one, hurrah! Hurrah!" I sang.

Hannie and Nancy joined in. "The ants go marching one by one, hurrah! Hurrah! The ants go mar-arching one by one, the little one stops to suck his thumb, and they all go marching DOWN beYOND the EARTH."

The day was warm and sunny. My friends and I were swinging on tires. I was wearing a sparkly ring. Ricky had bought it for me at Leslie's toy and jewelry sale.

Hannie and Nancy and I scuffed our

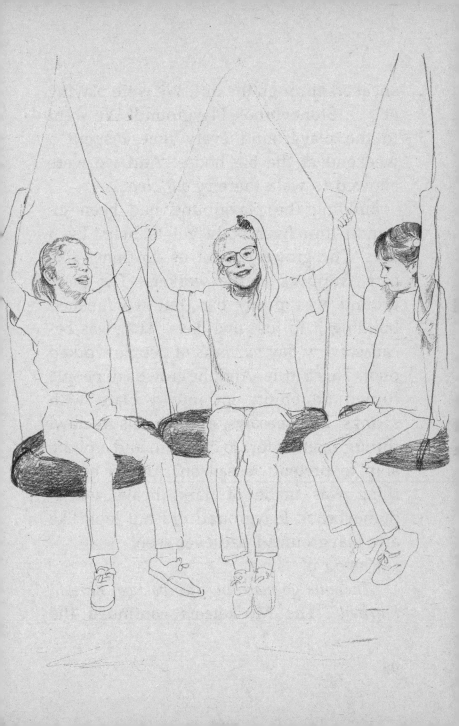

sneakers through the dirt. We were playing at . . . Stoneybrook Playground! We went to the playground every time I spent a weekend at the big house. And we were allowed to walk there *by ourselves*.

Building the playground had been gigundo fun. Everybody got to help. Even kids. The grown-ups let us do things like carry supplies to the workers. The playground was pretty big. But we finished building it in just five days. That was because every day *hundreds* of people worked on it. This is true. And the crowds of people turned an empty lot into a place with swings, and seesaws, and tunnels to crawl through, and a fort to climb in, and a pirate ship to pretend to sail on. Almost everything was made of dark, heavy wood. Stoneybrook Playground did not look like any playground I had ever seen.

I loved it.

*"The ants go marching two by two, hurrah! Hurrah!"* The Musketeers continued the

song. *"The ants go marching two by two, hurrah! Hurrah! The ants go mar-arching two by two, the little one stops to tie his shoe, and they all go marching DOWN beYOND the EARTH!"*

*Scuff, scuff* went our feet.

"Let's do something different," I said. "We have been singing and swinging for a long time. Let's pretend we are prisoners on the pirate ship."

"We did that yesterday," said Hannie. "Besides, some kids are already on the ship."

"Then let's play house in the fort. I could be the mommy who goes to work — "

"We played house yesterday, too," said Nancy.

"We could slide, but I don't want to wait in that line of kids." I emptied a pebble out of my sneaker.

Nancy looked at the blacktop. Kids were playing hopscotch and four-square there. "Let's play jacks!" she said. "Did anyone bring jacks?"

"No," answered Hannie and I.

"You know what would be so, so fun to do on the blacktop?" asked Hannie.

"What?" I said.

"Roller-skate. I sure wish I had skates that fit. I'd love to skate over there. Look at that girl. She can skate *back*ward."

"Well, my skates are at the little house," I said.

"And I still don't have any," added Nancy.

"Maybe we could raise some money to buy skates," said Hannie.

"We could hold another carnival," I suggested. "Only this time, we will rent a cotton-candy machine. And hire a magician. And a clown."

"Oh, Karen," groaned Hannie.

"Oh, Karen," groaned Nancy.

"It was just an idea," I said. I giggled. Then I began to sing again. *"The ants go marching three by three, hurrah! Hurrah! The ants go marching three by three, hurrah! Hurrah!*

*The ants go mar-arching three by three, the little one falls and skins his knee and they all go marching — "*

*"Down!"* sang Nancy.

*"BeYOND!"* sang Hannie.

*"The EARTH!"* I finished. I looked up. "Hey, the slide's free!" I cried. "Come on! I'll race you guys to it. Last one there's a rotten egg!"

My friends and I leaped off the tire swings. We ran across the playground.

The playground that we had helped to build.

## About the Author

ANN M. MARTIN lives in New York City and loves animals. Her cat, Mouse, knows how to take the phone off the hook.

Other books by Ann M. Martin that you might enjoy are *Stage Fright, Me and Katie (the Pest)*, and the books in *The Baby-sitters Club* series.

Ann likes ice cream, the beach, and *I Love Lucy*. And she has her own little sister, whose name is Jane.

# Little Sister

Don't miss #21

## KAREN'S NEW TEACHER

When the bell rang, the gray lady stood up. "Good Morning," she said. (She did not smile.) "My name is Mrs. Hoffman. I will be your teacher until Ms. Colman comes back. In my classroom, we do not talk unless we raise our hands." How silly. This was not Mrs. Hoffman's room. It belonged to Ms. Colman. "Also," Mrs. Hoffman went on, "you will be seated in alphabetical order. I will tell you where to sit. You may not change your seats after that."

Alphabetical order! Ms. Colman had never seated us that way.

But Mrs. Hoffman did.

# LITTLE APPLE™

# BABY-SITTERS™
## Little Sister

by Ann M. Martin,
author of The Baby-sitters Club ®

*More Titles...* ➡

## The Baby-sitters Little Sister titles continued...

------------------------------------------------

### Available wherever you buy books, or use this order form.

**Scholastic Inc., P.O. Box 7502, 2931 E. McCarty Street, Jefferson City, MO 65102**

Please send me the books I have checked above. I am enclosing $ _____
(please add $2.00 to cover shipping and handling). Send check or money order – no
cash or C.O.Ds please.

Name _____ Birthdate _____

Address _____

City _____ State/Zip _____

Please allow four to six weeks for delivery. Offer good in U.S.A. only. Sorry, mail orders are not
available to residents to Canada. Prices subject to change.

BLS1096